# Media Law

*Cases and Materials*

**Dr. Michael Jordan**
**Pepperdine University**

**Editing Assistant:**
**Scott Broadway**

**A supplemental text for media law and mass communication law courses**

KENDALL/HUNT PUBLISHING COMPANY
4050 Westmark Drive Dubuque, Iowa 52002

This edition was printed directly from camera-ready copy.



ISBN 0-7872-5174-7



Printed in the United States of America
10 9 8 7 6 5 4

# Media Law

*Cases and Materials**



***Cases have been substantially edited, and most footnotes eliminated**

# CONTENTS

## Part I: The First Amendment

## Part II: Libel and Privacy

## Part III: Free Press-Fair Trial



## Part IV: Protection of News Sources

## Part V: Broadcast-Cable-Internet



## Part VI: Advertising

## VII: Copyright



## VIII: Obscenity



## IX: National Security

# Part I: The First Amendment

NEAR
v.
STATE OF MINNESOTA ex rel. OLSON, Co. Atty.

283 U.S. 697

Decided June 1, 1931.

Mr. Justice BUTLER, Mr. Justice VAN DEVANTER, Mr. Justice McREYNOLDS, and Mr. Justice SUTHERLAND, dissenting.

Mr. Chief Justice HUGHES delivered the opinion of the Court.

Chapter 285 of the Session Laws of Minnesota for the year 1925 provides for the abatement, as a public nuisance, of a 'malicious, scandalous and defamatory newspaper, magazine or other periodical.' Section 1 of the act is as follows:

> 'Section 1. Any person who, as an individual, or as a member or employee of a firm, or association or organization, or as an officer, director, member or employee of a corporation, shall be engaged in the business of regularly or customarily producing, publishing or circulating, having in possession, selling or giving away.
> '(a) an obscene, lewd and lascivious newspaper, magazine, or other periodical, or
> '(b) a malicious, scandalous and defamatory newspaper, magazine or other periodical,
> -is guilty of a nuisance, and all persons guilty of such nuisance may be enjoined, as hereinafter provided.
> 'Participation in such business shall constitute a commission of such nuisance and render the participant liable and subject to the proceedings, orders and judgments provided for in this Act. Ownership, in whole or in part, directly or indirectly, of any such periodical, or of any stock of interest in any corporation or organization which owns the same in whole or in part, or which publishes the same, shall constitute such participation.
> 'In actions brought under (b) above, there shall be available the defense that the truth was published with good motives and for justifiable ends and in such actions the plaintiff shall not have the right to report (sic) to issues or editions or periodicals taking place more than three months before the commencement of the action.'

Section 2 provides that, whenever any such nuisance is committed or exists, the county attorney of any county where any such periodical is published or circulated, or, in case of his failure or refusal to proceed upon written request in good faith of a reputable citizen, the Attorney General, or, upon like failure or refusal of the latter, any citizen of the county, may maintain an action in the district court of the county in the name of the state to enjoin perpetually the persons committing or maintaining any such nuisance from further committing or maintaining it.

Upon such evidence as the court shall deem sufficient, a temporary injunction may be granted . . .

Under this statute, section 1, clause (b), the county attorney of Hennepin county brought this action to enjoin the publication of what was described as a 'malicious, scandalous and defamatory newspaper, magazine or other periodical,' known as The Saturday Press, published by the defendants in the city of Minneapolis. The complaint alleged that the defendants, on September 24, 1927, and on eight subsequent dates in October and November, 1927, published and circulated editions of that periodical which were 'largely devoted to malicious, scandalous and defamatory articles' concerning Charles G. Davis, Frank W. Brunskill, the Minneapolis Tribune, the Minneapolis Journal, Melvin C. Passolt, George E. Leach, the Jewish Race, the members of the grand jury of Hennepin county impaneled in November, 1927, and then holding office, and other persons, as more fully appeared in exhibits annexed to the complaint, consisting of copies of the articles described and constituting 327 pages of the record . . . .

Without attempting to summarize the contents of the voluminous exhibits attached to the complaint, we deem it sufficient to say that the articles charged, in substance, that a Jewish gangster was in control of gambling, bootlegging, and racketeering in Minneapolis, and that law enforcing officers and agencies were not energetically performing their duties. Most of the charges were directed against the chief of police; he was charged with gross neglect of duty, illicit relations with gangsters, and with participation in graft. The county attorney was charged with knowing the existing conditions and with failure to take adequate measures to remedy them. The mayor was accused of inefficiency and dereliction. One member of the grand jury was stated to be in sympathy with the gangsters. A special grand jury and a special prosecutor were demanded to deal with the situation in general, and, in particular, to investigate an attempt to assassinate one Guilford, one of the original defendants, who, it appears from the articles, was shot by gangsters after the first issue of the periodical had been published. There is no question but that the articles made serious accusations against the public officers named and others in connection with the prevalence of crimes and the failure to expose and punish them . . . .

The district court made findings of fact, which followed the allegations of the complaint and found in general terms that the editions in question were 'chiefly devoted to malicious, scandalous and defamatory articles' concerning the individuals named. The court further found that the defendants through these publications 'did engage in the business of regularly and customarily producing, publishing and circulating a malicious, scandalous and defamatory newspaper,' and that 'the said publication' 'under said name of The Saturday Press, or any other name, constitutes a public nuisance under the laws of the State.' Judgment was thereupon entered adjudging that 'the newspaper, magazine and periodical known as The Saturday Press,' as a public nuisance, 'be and is hereby abated.' The judgment perpetually enjoined the defendants 'from producing, editing, publishing, circulating, having in their possession, selling or giving away any publication whatsoever which is a malicious, scandalous or defamatory newspaper, as defined by law,' and also 'from further conducting said nuisance under the name and title of said The Saturday Press or any other name or title.'

The defendant Near appealed from this judgment to the Supreme Court of the State, again asserting his right under the Federal Constitution, and the judgment was affirmed upon the authority of the former decision . . . .

From the judgment as thus affirmed, the defendant Near appeals to this Court.
This statute, for the suppression as a public nuisance of a newspaper or periodical, is unusual, if not unique, and raises questions of grave importance transcending the local interests involved in the particular action. It is no longer open to doubt that the liberty of the press and of speech is within the liberty safeguarded by the due process clause of the Fourteenth Amendment from invasion by state action. It was found impossible to conclude that this essential personal liberty of the citizen was left unprotected by the general guaranty of fundamental rights of person and property. Gitlow v. New York, 268 U. S. 652, 666, 45 S. CT. 625, 69 L. Ed. 1138; Whitney v. California, 274 U. S. 357, 362, 373, 47 S. Ct. 641, 71 L. Ed. 1095; Fiske v. Kansas, 274 U. S. 380, 382, 47 S. Ct. 655, 71 L. Ed. 1108; Stromberg v. California, 283 U. S. 359, 51 S. Ct. 532, 75 L. Ed. 1117, decided May 18, 1931. In maintaining this guaranty, the authority of the state to enact laws to promote the health, safety, morals, and general welfare of its people is necessarily admitted. The limits of this sovereign power must always be determined with appropriate regard to the particular subject of its exercise .... Liberty of speech and of the press is also not an absolute right, and the state may punish its abuse. Whitney v. California, supra; Stromberg v. California, supra. Liberty, in each of its phases, has its history and connotation, and, in the present instance, the inquiry is as to the historic conception of the liberty of the press and whether the statute under review violates the essential attributes of that liberty . . . .

This suppression is accomplished by enjoining publication, and that restraint is the object and effect of the statute.

Fourth. The statute not only operates to suppress the offending newspaper or periodical, but to put the publisher under an effective censorship. When a newspaper or periodical is found to be 'malicious, scandalous and defamatory,' and is suppressed as such, resumption of publication is punishable as a contempt of court by fine or imprisonment. Thus, where a newspaper or periodical has been suppressed because of the circulation of charges against public officers of official misconduct, it would seem to be clear that the renewal of the publication of such charges would constitute a contempt, and that the judgment would lay a permanent restraint upon the publisher, to escape which he must satisfy the court as to the character of a new publication. Whether he would be permitted again to publish matter deemed to be derogatory to the same or other public officers would depend upon the court's ruling. In the present instance the judgment restrained the defendants from 'publishing, circulating, having in their possession, selling or giving away any publication whatsoever which is a malicious, scandalous or defamatory newspaper, as defined by law.' The law gives no definition except that covered by the words 'scandalous and defamatory,' and publications charging official misconduct are of the class. While the court, answering the objection that the judgment was too broad, saw no reason for construing it as restraining the defendants 'from operating a newspaper in harmony with the public welfare to which all must yield,' and said that the defendants had not indicated 'any desire to conduct their business in the usual and legitimate manner,' the manifest inference is that, at least with respect to a new publication directed against official misconduct, the defendant would be held, under penalty of punishment for contempt as provided in the statute, to a manner of publication which the court considered to be 'usual and legitimate' and consistent with the public welfare.

If we cut through mere details of procedure, the operation and effect of the statute in substance is that public authorities may bring the owner or publisher of a newspaper or periodical before a judge upon a charge of conducting a business of publishing scandalous and defamatory matter-in particular that the matter consists of charges against public officers of official dereliction-and, unless the owner or publisher is able and disposed to bring competent evidence to satisfy the judge that the charges are true and are published with good motives and for justifiable ends, his newspaper or periodical is suppressed and further publication is made punishable as a contempt. This is of the essence of censorship.

The question is whether a statute authorizing such proceedings in restraint of publication is consistent with the conception of the liberty of the press as historically conceived and guaranteed. In determining the extent of the constitutional protection, it has been generally, if not universally, considered that it is the chief purpose of the guaranty to prevent previous restraints upon publication. The struggle in England, directed against the legislative power of the licenser, resulted in renuciation of the censorship of the press. The liberty deemed to be established was thus described by Blackstone: 'The liberty of the press is indeed essential to the nature of a free state; but this consists in laying no previous restraints upon publications, and not in freedom from censure for criminal matter when published. Every freeman has an undoubted right to lay what sentiments he pleases before the public; to forbid this, is to destroy the freedom of the press; but if he publishes what is improper, mischievous or illegal, he must take the consequence of his own temerity.' 4 Bl. Com. 151, 152. See Story on the Constitution, ss 1884, 1889. The distinction was early pointed out between the extent of the freedom with respect to censorship under our constitutional system and that enjoyed in England. Here, as Madison said, 'the great and essential rights of the people are secured against legislative as well as against executive ambition. They are secured, not by laws paramount to prerogative, but by constitutions paramont to laws. This security of the freedom of the press requires that it should be exempt not only from previous restraint by the Executive, as in Great Britain, but from legislative restraint also.' Report on the Virginia Resolutions, Madison's Works, vol. IV, p. 543. This Court said, in Patterson v. Colorado, 205 U. S. 454, 462, 27 S. Ct. 556, 558, 51 L. Ed. 879, 10 Ann. Cas. 689: 'In the first place, the main purpose of such constitutional provisions is 'to prevent all such previous restraints upon publications as had been practiced by other governments,' and they do not prevent the subsequent punishment of such as may be deemed contrary to the public welfare. Commonwealth v. Blanding, 3 Pick. (Mass.) 304, 313, 314 (15 Am. Dec. 214);

Respublica v. Oswald, 1 Dall. 319, 325, 1 L. Ed. 155, 158. The preliminary freedom extends as well to the false as to the true; the subsequent punishment may extend as well to the true as to the false. This was the law of criminal libel apart from statute in most cases, if not in all. Commonwealth v. Blanding, ubi supra; 4 Bl. Com. 150.'

The criticism upon Blackstone's statement has not been because immunity from previous restraint upon publication has not been regarded as deserving of special emphasis, but chiefly because that immunity cannot be deemed to exhaust the conception of the liberty guaranteed by State and Federal Constitutions. The point of criticism has been 'that the mere exemption from restraints cannot be all that is secured by the constitutional provisions,' and that 'the liberty of the press might be rendered a mockery and a delusion, and the phrase itself a by-word, if, while every man was at liberty to publish what he pleased, the public authorities might nevertheless punish him for harmless publications.' 2 Cooley, Const. Lim. (8th Ed.) pp. 885. But it is recognized that punishment for the abuse of the liberty accorded to the press is essential to the protection of the public, and that the common-law rules that subject the libeler to responsibility for the public offense, as well as for the private injury, are not abolished by the protection extended in our Constitutions Id. pp. 883, 884. The law of criminal libel rests upon that secure foundation. There is also the conceded authority of courts to punish for contempt when publications directly tend to prevent the proper discharge of judicial functions. Patterson v. Colorado, supra; Toledo Newspaper Company v. United States, 247 U. S. 402, 419, 38 S. Ct. 560, 62 L. Ed. 1186. In the present case, we have no occasion to inquire as to the permissible scope of subsequent punishment. For whatever wrong the appellant has committed or may commit, by his publications, the state appropriately affords both public and private redress by its libel laws. As has been noted, the statute in question does not deal with punishments; it provides for no punishment, except in case of contempt for violation of the court's order, but for suppression and injunction-that is, for restraint upon publication.

The objection has also been made that the principle as to immunity from previous restraint is stated too broadly, if every such restraint is deemed to be prohibited. That is undoubtedly true; the protection even as to previous restraint is not absolutely unlimited. But the limitation has been recognized only in exceptional cases. 'When a nation is at war many things that might be said in time of peace are such a hindrance to its effort that their utterance will not be endured so long as men fight and that no Court could regard them as protected by any constitutional right.' Schenck v. United States, 249 U. S. 47, 52, 39 S. Ct. 247, 249, 63 L. Ed. 470. No one would question but that a government might prevent actual obstruction to its recruiting service or the publication of the sailing dates of transports or the number and location of troops. On similar grounds, the primary requirements of decency may be enforced against obscene publications. The security of the community life may be protected against incitements to acts of violence and the overthrow by force of orderly government. The constitutional guaranty of free speech does not 'protect a man from an injunction against uttering words that may have all the effect of force. Gompers v. Buck's Stove & Range Co., 221 U. S. 418, 139, 31 S. Ct. 492, 55 L. Ed. 797, 34 L. R. A. (N. S.) 874.' Schenck v. United States, supra. These limitations are not applicable here.

Nor are we now concerned with questions as to the extent of authority to prevent publications in order to protect private rights according to the principles governing the exercise of the jurisdiction of courts of equity.

The exceptional nature of its limitations places in a strong light the general conception that liberty of the press, historically considered and taken up by the Federal Constitution, has meant, principally although not exclusively, immunity from previous restraints or censorship. The conception of the liberty of the press in this country had broadened with the exigencies of the colonial period and with the efforts to secure freedom from oppressive administration. That liberty was especially cherished for the immunity it afforded from previous restraint of the publication of censure of public officers and charges of official misconduct. As was said by Chief Justice Parker, in Commonwealth v. Blanding, 3 Pick. (Mass.) 304, 313, 15 Am. Dec. 214, with respect to the Constitution of Massachusetts: 'Besides, it is well understood and received as a commentary on this provision for the liberty of the press, that it was intended to prevent all such previous restraints upon publications as had been practiced by other governments, and in early times here, to stifle the efforts of patriots towards enlightening their fellow subjects upon their rights and the duties of rulers. The liberty of the press was to be unrestrained, but he who used it was to be responsible in case of its abuse.' In the letter sent by the Continental Congress (October 26, 1774) to the Inhabitants of Quebec, referring to the 'five great rights' it was said: 'The last right we shall mention, regards the freedom of the press. The importance of this consists, besides the advancement of truth, science, morality, and arts in general, in its diffusion of liberal sentiments on the administration of Government, its ready communication of thoughts between subjects, and its consequential promotion of union among them, whereby oppressive officers are shamed or intimidated, into more honourable and just modes of conducting affairs.' Madison, who was the leading spirit in the preparation of the First Amendment of the Federal Constitution, thus described the practice and sentiment which led to the guaranties of liberty of the press in State Constitutions:

'In every State, probably, in the Union, the press has exerted a freedom in canvassing the merits and measures of public men of every description which has not been confined to the strict limits of the common law. On this footing the freedom of the press has stood; on this footing it yet stands. * * * Some degree of abuse is inseparable from the proper use of everything, and in no instance is this more true than in that of the press. It has accordingly been decided by the practice of the States, that it is better to leave a few of its noxious branches to their luxuriant growth, than, by pruning them away, to injure the vigour of those yielding the proper fruits. And can the wisdom of this policy be doubted by any who reflect that to the press alone, chequered as it is with abuses, the world is indebted for all the triumphs which have been gained by reason and humanity over error and oppression; who reflect that to the same beneficent source the United States owe much of the lights which conducted them to the ranks of a free and independent nation, and which have improved their political system into a shape so auspicious to their happiness? Had 'Sedition Acts,' forbidding every publication that might bring the constituted agents into contempt or disrepute, or that might excite the hatred of the people against the authors of unjust or pernicious measures, been uniformly enforced against the press, might not the United States have been languishing at this day under the infirmities of a sickly Confederation? Might they not, possibly, be miserable colonies, groaning under a foreign yoke?'

The fact that for approximately one hundred and fifty years there has been almost an entire absence of attempts to impose previous restraints upon publications relating to the malfeasance of public officers is significant of the deep-seated conviction that such restraints would violate constitutional right. Public officers, whose character and conduct remain open to debate and free discussion in the press, find their remedies for false accusations in actions under libel laws providing for redress and punishment, and not in proceedings to restrain the publication of newspapers and periodicals. The general principle that the constitutional guaranty of the liberty of the press gives immunity from previous restraints has been approved in many decisions under the provisions of state constitutions.

The importance of this immunity has not lessened. While reckless assaults upon public men, and efforts to bring obloquy upon those who are endeavoring faithfully to discharge official duties, exert a baleful influence and deserve the severest condemnation in public opinion, it cannot be said that this abuse is greater, and it is believed to be less, than that which characterized the period in which our institutions took shape. Meanwhile, the administration of government has become more complex, the opportunities for malfeasance and corruption have multiplied, crime has grown to most serious proportions, and the danger of its protection by unfaithful officials and of the impairment of the fundamental security of life and property by criminal alliances and official neglect, emphasizes the primary need of a vigilant and courageous press, expecially in great cities. The fact that the liberty of the press may be abused by miscreant purveyors of scandal does not make any the less necessary the immunity of the press from previous restraint in dealing with offical misconduct. Subsequent punishment for such abuses as may exist is the appropriate remedy, consistent with constitutional privilege . . . .

For these reasons we hold the statute, so far as it authorized the proceedings in this action under clause (b) of section 1, to be an infringement of the liberty of the press guaranteed by the Fourteenth Amendment. We should add that this decision rests upon the operation and effect of the statute, without regard to the question of the truth of the charges contained in the particular periodical. The fact that the public officers named in this case, and those associated with the charges of official dereliction, may be deemed to be impeccable, cannot affect the conclusion that the statute imposes an unconstitutional restraint upon publication.

Judgment reversed.

Excerpts from *Saturday Review*

Nov. 19, 1927 (From Near v. Minnesota)

FACTS NOT THEORIES (headline)

"'I am a bosom friend of Mr. Olson,' snorted a gentleman of Yiddish blood, 'and I want to protest against your article,' and blah, blah, blah, ad infinitum, ad nauseam.

I am not taking orders from men of Barnett faith, at least right now. There have been too many men in this city and especially those in official life, who HAVE been taking orders and suggestions from JEW GANGSTERS, therefore we HAVE Jew Gangsters, practically ruling Minneapolis.

It was buzzards of the Barnett stripe who shot down my buddy. It was Barnett gunmen who staged the assault on Samuel Shapiro. It is Jew thugs who have 'pulled' practically every robbery in this city. It was a member of the Barnett gang who shot down George Rubenstein (Ruby) while he stood in the shelter of Mose Barnett's ham-cavern on Hennepin avenue. It was at Mose Barnett's place of 'business' that the '13 dollar Jew' found a refuge while the police of New York were combing the country for him. It was a gang of Jew gunmen who boasted that for five hundred dollars they would kill any man in the city. It was Mose Barnett, a Jew, who boasted that he held the chief of police of Minneapolis in his hand -- had bought and paid for him.

It is Jewish men and women - pliant tools of the Jew gangster, Mose Barnett, who stand charged with having falsified the election records and returns in the third ward. And it is Mose Barnett himself, who, indicted for his part in the Shapiro assault, is a fugitive from justice today.

Practically every vendor of vile hooch, every owner of a moonshine still, every snake-faced gangster and exbryonic yegg in the Twin Cities is a JEW.

Having these examples before me, I feel that I am justified in my refusal to take orders from a Jew who boasts that he is a 'bosom fried' of Mr. Olson.

I find in the mail at least twice per week, letters from gentlemen of Jewish faith who advise me against 'launching an attack on the Jewish people.' These gentlemen have the cart before the horse. I am launching, nor is Mr. Guilford, no attack against any race, BUT: When I find men of a certain race banding themselves together for the purpose of preying upon Gentile or Jew; gunmen, KILLERS, roaming our streets shooting down men against whom they have no personal grudge (or happen to have); defying OUR laws; corrupting OUR officials; assaulting business men; beating up unarmed citizens; spreading a reign of terror through every walk of life, then I say to you in all sincerity, that I refuse to back up a single step from that 'issue' -- if they choose to make it so.

If the people of Jewish faith in Minneapolis wish to avoid criticism of these vermin whom I rightfully call 'Jews' they can easily do so BY THEMSELVES CLEANING HOUSE.

I'm not out to cleanse Israel of the filth that clings to Israel's skirts. I'm out to 'hew to the line, let the chips fly where they may.

I simply state a fact when I say that ninety per cent of the crimes committed against society in this city are committed by Jew gangsters.

It was a Jew who employed JEWS to shoot down Mr. Guilford. It was a Jew who employed a Jew to intimidate Mr. Shapiro and a Jew who employed JEWS to assault that gentleman when he refused to yield to their threats. It was a JEW who wheedled or employed Jews to manipulate the election records and returns in the Third ward in flagrant violation of law. It was a Jew who left two hundred dollars with another Jew to pay to our chief of police just before the last municipal election, and it is Jew, Jew, as long as one cares to comb over the records.

I am launching no attack against the Jewish people AS A RACE. I am merely calling attention to a FACT. And if the people of that race and faith wish to rid themselves of the odium and stigma THE RODENTS OF THEIR OWN RACE HAVE BROUGHT UPON THEM, they need only to step to the front and help the decent citizens of Minneapolis rid the city of these criminal Jews.

Paul SCHENCK and Dwight Saunders, Petitioners,
v.
PRO-CHOICE NETWORK OF WESTERN NEW YORK, et al.

117 S.Ct. 855

Supreme Court of the United States

Decided Feb. 19, 1997

Justice Scalia filed an opinion concurring in part and dissenting in part, in which Justices Kennedy and Thomas joined.

Justice Breyer filed an opinion concurring in part and dissenting in part.

(Some footnotes ommitted)

Chief Justice REHNQUIST delivered the opinion of the Court.

The question presented is whether an injunction that places restrictions on demonstrations outside abortion clinics violates the First Amendment. We uphold the provisions imposing "fixed bubble" or "fixed buffer zone" limitations, as hereinafter described, but hold that the provisions imposing "floating bubble" or "floating buffer zone" limitations violate the First Amendment.

I

Respondents include three doctors and four medical clinics (two of which are part of larger hospital complexes) in and around Rochester and Buffalo in upstate New York. These health care providers perform abortions and other medical services at their facilities. The eighth respondent is Pro-Choice Network of Western New York, a not-for-profit corporation dedicated to maintaining access to family planning and abortion services.

On September 24, 1990, respondents filed a complaint in the District Court for the Western District of New York against fifty individuals and three organizations--Operation Rescue, Project Rescue Western New York, and Project Life of Rochester. The complaint alleged that defendants had consistently engaged in illegal blockades and other illegal conduct at facilities in the Western District of New York where abortions were performed. (For convenience, we refer to these facilities as "clinics" throughout.) The complaint alleged one federal and six state causes of action: conspiracy to deprive women seeking abortions or other family planning services of the equal protection of the laws, in violation of Rev.Stat. § 1980, 42 U.S.C. § 1985(3); discrimination against and harassment of women seeking abortions and other family planning services, in violation of N.Y. Civ. Rights Law § 40-c (McKinney 1992) and N.Y. Exec. Law § 296 (McKinney 1993); trespass; tortious interference with business; tortious harassment; false imprisonment; and intentional infliction of emotional harm. The complaint alleged that a large blockade was planned for September 28, and requested that the court issue a temporary restraining order (TRO) to stop it. The complaint also sought a permanent injunction and damages.

Before the complaint was filed, the clinics were subjected to numerous large-scale blockades in which protesters would march, stand, kneel, sit, or lie in parking lot driveways and in doorways. This conduct blocked or hindered cars from entering clinic parking lots, and patients, doctors, nurses, and other clinic employees from entering the clinics.

In addition to these large-scale blockades, smaller groups of protesters consistently attempted to stop or disrupt clinic operations. Protesters trespassed onto clinic parking lots and even entered the clinics themselves. Those trespassers who remained outside the clinics crowded around cars or milled around doorways and driveway entrances in an effort to block or hinder access to the clinics. Protesters sometimes threw themselves on top of the hoods of cars or crowded around cars as they attempted to turn into parking lot driveways. Other protesters on clinic property handed literature and talked to people entering the clinics--especially those women they believed were arriving to have abortions--in an effort to persuade them that abortion was immoral. Sometimes protesters used more aggressive techniques, with varying levels of belligerence: getting very close to women entering the clinics and shouting in their faces; surrounding, crowding, and yelling at women entering the clinics; or jostling, grabbing, pushing, and shoving women as they attempted to enter the clinics. Male and female clinic volunteers who attempted to escort patients past protesters into the clinics were sometimes elbowed, grabbed, or spit on. Sometimes the escorts pushed back. Some protesters remained in the doorways after the patients had entered the clinics, blocking others from entering and exiting.

On the sidewalks outside the clinics, protesters called "sidewalk counselors" used similar methods. Counselors would walk alongside targeted women headed toward the clinics, handing them literature and talking to them in an attempt to persuade them not to get an abortion. Unfortunately, if the women continued toward the clinics and did not respond positively to the counselors, such peaceful efforts at persuasion often devolved into "in your face" yelling, and sometimes into pushing, shoving, and grabbing. Men who accompanied women attempting to enter the clinics often became upset by the aggressive sidewalk counseling and sometimes had to be restrained (not always successfully) from fighting with the counselors.

The District Court found that the local police had been "unable to respond effectively" to the protests, for a number of reasons: the protests were constant, overwhelming police resources; when the police arrived, the protesters simply dispersed and returned later; prosecution of arrested protesters was difficult because patients were often reluctant to cooperate for fear of making their identity public; and those who were convicted were not deterred from returning to engage in unlawful conduct. In addition, the court found that defendants harassed the police officers verbally and by mail, including the deputy police chief. Also harassed were people who testified against the protesters and "those who invoke[d] legal process against" the protesters. This, testified the deputy police chief, "made it more difficult for him to do his job." Pro-Choice Network of Western N.Y. v. Project Rescue Western N. Y., 799 F.Supp. 1417, 1426-1427 (W.D.N.Y.1992). See also id., at 1431 ("[T]here has been substantial uncontradicted evidence that defendants' activities are intended, and do in fact, prevent and hinder local police from protecting the right of women to choose to have an abortion").

On September 27, 1990, three days after respondents filed their complaint and one day before the scheduled large-scale blockade, the District Court issued a TRO. The parties stipulated that the TRO might remain in force until decision on respondents' motion for a preliminary injunction. In pertinent part, the TRO enjoined defendants from physically blockading the clinics, physically abusing or tortiously harassing anyone entering or leaving the clinics, and "demonstrating within 15 feet of any person" entering or leaving the clinics. As an exception to this 15-foot "buffer zone" around people, the TRO allowed two sidewalk counselors to have "a conversation of a nonthreatening nature" with individuals entering or leaving the clinic. If the individuals indicated that they did not want the counseling, however, the counselors had to "cease and desist" from counseling. 1

> (footnote)1. Although the TRO (and the preliminary injunction) states that the "cease and desist" provision is triggered whenever the individual "wants to not have counseling," the District Court has construed this provision to apply only if "the targeted person or group of persons indicates, either verbally or non-verbally, that they do not wish to be counseled." 799 F.Supp., at 1434. See also 67 F.3d 377, 391 (C.A.2 1995) (same).

At first, defendants complied with the TRO, holding a peaceful demonstration rather than the scheduled blockade. Subsequently, they stipulated that "physical blockades" could be enjoined, and they conducted no such blockades between the issuance of the TRO and the issuance of the preliminary injunction 17 months later. Defendants, however, continued to engage in protests that the District Court labeled "constructive blockades," as well as sidewalk counseling. Constructive blockades consisted of "demonstrating and picketing around the entrances of the clinics, and ... harassing patients and staff entering and leaving the clinics." Id., at 1424. This included many of the protest elements described above, including attempts to intimidate or impede cars from entering the parking lots, congregating in driveway entrances, and crowding around, yelling at, grabbing, pushing, and shoving people entering and leaving the clinics. The purpose of constructive blockades was the same as physical blockades: "to prevent or dissuade patients from entering the clinic." Ibid. Clinic volunteer escorts testified that the protests were much quieter, calmer, and smaller during the first month after the TRO issued, but that the protests returned to their prior intensity thereafter, including aggressive sidewalk counseling with occasional shoving and elbowing, trespassing into clinic buildings to continue counseling of patients, and blocking of doorways and driveways.

Alleging that Project Rescue and five individual defendants (including petitioner Schenck) breached the TRO on five separate occasions from late October 1990 through December 1990, respondents sought four contempt citations. A fifth contempt citation for a 1991 incident was sought against petitioner Schenck and another individual defendant. Throughout 1991 and into 1992, the District Court held 27 days of hearings in these contempt proceedings, and issued opinions concluding that five of the six incidents justified a finding of civil contempt.

In February 1992, after hearing 12 additional days of testimony, the District Court issued the injunction, parts of which are challenged here. The relevant provisions are set forth in the margin.3 Although the injunction largely tracked the TRO, there were significant changes. First, while the TRO banned "demonstrating ... within fifteen feet of any person" entering or leaving the clinics, the injunction more broadly banned "demonstrating within fifteen feet from either side or edge of, or in front of, doorways or doorway entrances, parking lot entrances, driveways and driveway entrances of such facilities" ("fixed buffer zones"), or "within fifteen feet of any person or vehicle seeking access to or leaving such facilities" ("floating buffer zones"). In addition, the injunction clarified the "cease and desist" provision, specifying that once sidewalk counselors who had entered the buffer zones were required to "cease and desist" their counseling, they had to retreat 15 feet from the people they had been counseling and had to remain outside the boundaries of the buffer zones.

(footnote)3. "Defendants, the officers, directors, agents, and representatives of defendants, and all other persons whomsoever, known or unknown, acting in their behalf or in concert with them, and receiving actual or constructive notice of this Order, are:

"1. Enjoined and restrained in any manner or by any means from:

"(a) trespassing on, sitting in, blocking, impeding, or obstructing access to, ingress into or egress from any facility, including, but not limited to, the parking lots, parking lot entrances, driveways, and driveway entrances, at which abortions are performed in the Western District of New York;

"(b) demonstrating within fifteen feet from either side or edge of, or in front of, doorways or doorway entrances, parking lot entrances, driveways and driveway entrances of such facilities, or within fifteen feet of any person or vehicle seeking access to or leaving such facilities, except that the form of demonstrating known as sidewalk counseling by no more than two persons as specified in paragraph (c) shall be allowed;

"(c) physically abusing, grabbing, touching, pushing, shoving, or crowding persons entering or leaving, working at or using any services at any facility at which abortions are performed; provided, however, that sidewalk counseling consisting of a conversation of a non-threatening nature by not more than two people with each person or group of persons they are seeking to counsel shall not be prohibited. Also provided that no one is required to accept or listen to sidewalk counseling, and that if anyone or any group of

> persons who is sought to be counseled wants to not have counseling, wants to leave, or walk away, they shall have the absolute right to do that, and in such event all persons seeking to counsel that person or group of persons shall cease and desist from such counseling, and shall thereafter be governed by the provisions of paragraph (b) pertaining to not demonstrating within fifteen feet of persons seeking access to or leaving a facility. In addition, it is further provided that this right to sidewalk counseling as defined herein shall not limit the right of the Police Department to maintain public order or such reasonably necessary rules and regulations as they decide are necessary at each particular demonstration site;
>
> "(d) using any mechanical loudspeaker or sound amplification device or making any excessively loud sound which injures, disturbs, or endangers the health or safety of any patient or employee of a health care facility at which abortions are performed, nor shall any person make such sounds which interfere with the rights of anyone not in violation of this Order;
>
> "(e) attempting, or inducing, directing, aiding, or abetting in any manner, others to take any of the actions described in paragraphs (a) through (d) above." 799 F.Supp., at 1440-1441 ....

.... In analyzing defendants' assertion that the injunction violated their First Amendment right to free speech, the court applied our standard "time, place, and manner analysis," asking whether the speech restrictions in the injunction (i) were content neutral, (ii) were narrowly tailored to serve a significant government interest, and (iii) left open ample alternative channels for communication of the information. Id., at 1432 (citing Frisby v. Schultz, 487 U.S. 474, 481, 108 S.Ct. 2495, 2500-2501, 101 L.Ed.2d 420 (1988)). The court held that the injunction was content neutral because "it merely restricts the volume, location, timing and harassing and intimidating nature of defendants' expressive speech." 799 F.Supp., at 1433. The court held that the injunction served three significant governmental interests-- public safety, ensuring that abortions are performed safely, and ensuring that a woman's constitutional rights to travel interstate and to choose to have an abortion were not sacrificed in the interest of defendants' First Amendment rights.

As to narrow tailoring, the court explained that the 15-foot buffer zones "around entrances and ... around people and vehicles seeking access ... are necessary to ensure that people and vehicles seeking access to the clinics will not be impeded, and will be able to determine readily where the entrances are located." Id., at 1434. The court added that the buffer zones would also provide the benefit of "prevent[ing] defendants from crowding patients and invading their personal space." Ibid. The court explained the "cease and desist" provision--allowing two sidewalk counselors inside the buffer zones but requiring them to "cease and desist" their counseling if the counselee asked to be left alone--as "an exception" to the buffer zones and as "an attempt to accommodate fully defendants' First Amendment rights." Ibid. The court held that this provision was "necessary in order to protect the right of people approaching and entering the facilities to be left alone." Id., at 1435. Finally, the court held that the injunction left open ample alternative channels for communication, because defendants could still "picket, carry signs, pray, sing or chant in full view of people going into the clinics." Id., at 1437 ....

Petitioners, two individual defendants, appealed to the Court of Appeals for the Second Circuit. While the case was on appeal, we decided Madsen v. Women's Health Center, Inc., 512 U.S. 753, 114 S.Ct. 2516, 129 L.Ed.2d 593 (1994), a case which also involved the effect of an injunction on the expressive activities of antiabortion protesters. (We discuss Madsen in greater depth in Part II-A, infra.) We held that "our standard time, place, and manner analysis is not sufficiently rigorous" when it comes to evaluating content-neutral injunctions that restrict speech. The test instead, we held, is "whether the challenged provisions of the injunction burden no more speech than necessary to serve a significant government interest." Id., at 765, 114 S.Ct., at 2525.

Applying Madsen, a panel of the Court of Appeals reversed the District Court in a split decision. 67 F.3d 359 (1994). The Court of Appeals then heard the case en banc, and affirmed the District Court by a divided vote. 67 F.3d 377 (1995). Each of two opinions garnered a majority of the court. Judge Oakes' lead opinion, joined by eight other judges, affirmed for reasons that closely track the reasoning of the District Court. Id., at 388-392. A concurring opinion by Judge Winter, joined by nine other judges, affirmed primarily on the ground that the protesters' expressive activities were not protected by the First Amendment at all, and because the District Court's injunction was a "reasonable response" to the protesters' conduct. Id., at 396, 398. We granted certiorari. 516 U.S. ----, 116 S.Ct. 1260, 134 L.Ed.2d 209 (1996).

## II

### A

Petitioners challenge three aspects of the injunction: (i) the floating 15- foot buffer zones around people and vehicles seeking access to the clinics; (ii) the fixed 15-foot buffer zones around the clinic doorways, driveways, and parking lot entrances; and (iii) the "cease and desist" provision that forces sidewalk counselors who are inside the buffer zones to retreat 15 feet from the person being counseled once the person indicates a desire not to be counseled. Because Madsen bears many similarities to this case and because many of the parties' arguments depend on the application of Madsen here, we review our determination in that case.

A Florida state court had issued a permanent injunction enjoining specified organizations and individuals from blocking or interfering with clinic access and from physically abusing people entering or leaving the clinic. Six months after the injunction issued, the court found that protesters still impeded access by demonstrating on the street and in the driveways, and that sidewalk counselors approached entering vehicles in an effort to hand literature to the occupants. In the face of this evidence, the court issued a broader injunction that enjoined the defendant protesters from " 'physically abusing, grabbing, intimidating, harassing, touching, pushing, shoving, crowding or assaulting' " anyone entering or leaving the clinic; from " 'congregating, picketing, patrolling, demonstrating or entering that portion of public right-of-way or private property within [36] feet of the property line of the Clinic' "; from approaching anyone " 'seeking the services of the Clinic' " who is within 300 feet of the clinic, unless the person " 'indicates a desire to communicate' "; and from making any noise or displaying any image which could be heard or seen inside the clinic. 512 U.S., at 759-760, 114 S.Ct., at 2522.

After determining that the injunction was not a prior restraint and was content neutral, id., at 762-764, 114 S.Ct., at 2522-2523, we held that the proper test for evaluating content-neutral injunctions under the First Amendment was "whether the challenged provisions of the injunction burden no more speech than necessary to serve a significant government interest," id., at 765, 114 S.Ct., at 2525. The Florida Supreme Court had concluded that the injunction was based on a number of governmental interests: protecting a woman's freedom to seek pregnancy-related services, ensuring public safety and order, promoting the free flow of traffic on streets and sidewalks, protecting property rights, and protecting the medical privacy of patients whose psychological and physical well-being were threatened as they were held "captive" by medical circumstance. Id., at 767-768, 114 S.Ct., at 2526. We held that the combination of these interests was "quite sufficient to justify an appropriately tailored injunction" to protect unimpeded access to the clinic by way of public streets and sidewalks. Id., at 768, 114 S.Ct., at 2526.

We held that some of the injunction's provisions burdened more speech than necessary to serve these interests, and that others did not. We upheld the 36- foot buffer zone as applied to the street, sidewalks, and driveways "as a way of ensuring access to the clinic." We explained that the trial court had few other options to protect access to the clinic: allowing protesters to remain on the sidewalks and in the clinic driveway was not a valid option because of their past conduct, and allowing them to stand in the street was obviously impractical. In addition, we stated that "some deference must be given to the state court's familiarity with the facts and the background of the dispute between the parties even under our heightened review." Id., at 769-770, 114 S.Ct., at 2527 (citing Milk Wagon Drivers v. Meadowmoor Dairies, Inc., 312 U.S. 287, 294, 61 S.Ct. 552, 555, 85 L.Ed. 836 (1941))

We struck down the 300-foot no-approach zone around the clinic, however, stating that it was difficult

> "to justify a prohibition on all uninvited approaches ... regardless of how peaceful the contact may be.... Absent evidence that the protesters' speech is independently proscribable (i.e., 'fighting words' or threats), or is so infused with violence as to be indistinguishable from a threat of physical harm, see Milk Wagon Drivers, 312 U.S., at 292-293 [61 S.Ct., at 554-555], this provision cannot stand. 'As a general matter, we have indicated that in public debate our own citizens must tolerate insulting, and even outrageous, speech in order to provide adequate breathing space to the freedoms protected by the First Amendment.' Boos v. Barry, 485 U.S. [312, 322, 108 S.Ct. 1157, 1164, 99 L.Ed.2d 333 (1988) ] (internal quotation marks omitted).

The 'consent' requirement alone invalidates this provision; it burdens more speech than is necessary to prevent intimidation and to ensure access to the clinic." 512 U.S., at 774, 114 S.Ct., at 2529.

We now apply Madsen to the challenged provisions of the injunction and ask whether they burden more speech than necessary to serve a significant governmental interest. 6

(footnote) 6. Petitioners argue that the injunction is an unlawful prior restraint and that the standard we set out in Madsen is therefore inapplicable. Because we rejected this argument in Madsen and because petitioners make no effort to distinguish Madsen on this ground, we reject it again. As in Madsen, alternative channels of communication were left open to the protesters, and "the injunction was issued not because of the content of [the protesters'] expression, ... but because of their prior unlawful conduct." Madsen, 512 U.S., at 764, n. 2, 114 S.Ct., at 2524, n. 2.

B

Petitioners first argue that there are no significant governmental interests that support the injunction. The argument goes as follows: of the seven causes of action in respondents' complaint, the only one left standing after the District Court's most recent opinion is respondents' trespass claim; a trespass cause of action can support an injunction banning trespass, but nothing else; thus, the injunction's provisions banning "demonstrating" within 15 feet of people, cars, and entrances are overbroad.

First, this argument is factually incorrect. The trespass claim is not the only one left standing at this point. In its opinion issuing the preliminary injunction, the District Court held that the conduct that satisfied the elements of a § 1985(3) claim under federal law also satisfied the elements of a § 40-c claim under state law. After our decision in Bray, the District Court dismissed respondents' § 1985(3) claim. Petitioners argue that in doing so, the District Court necessarily and implicitly dismissed the § 40-c claim as well, since the two claims were based on the same conduct. But our opinion in Bray did not attempt to construe any statute other than 42 U.S.C. § 1985(3). And the fact that certain conduct does not state a claim under § 1985(3) does not necessarily mean that the same conduct does not state a claim under a state law that uses the same or similar language as § 1985(3), since state courts may of course choose to construe their own law more broadly (or more narrowly) than its federal counterpart. In any event, the language of the two statutes is noticeably different. See n. 4, supra. Thus, the dismissal of the § 1985(3) claim in light of Bray did not also act as a dismissal of respondents' § 40-c claim. This is confirmed by the District Court's comment in its post-Bray opinion that "the preliminary injunction is grounded not only on the § 1985(3) claim, but two state-law claims as well." 828

F.Supp., at 1026, n. 4.

Although petitioners contend that the § 40-c cause of action is no longer valid simply because the § 1985(3) claim is no longer valid, an argument we reject, they do not contend that the District Court erred in concluding as an independent matter that respondents were likely to succeed on their § 40-c and trespass claims. See Brief for Petitioners 32. The injunction's terms are clearly crafted to remedy these violations.

An injunction tailored to respondents' claims for relief may nonetheless violate the First Amendment. In making their First Amendment challenge, petitioners focus solely on the interests asserted by respondents in their complaint. But in assessing a First Amendment challenge, a court looks not only at the private claims asserted in the complaint, but also inquires into the governmental interests that are protected by the injunction, which may include an interest in public safety and order. Madsen, 512 U.S., at 767- 768, 114 S.Ct., at 2525-2526; Milk Wagon Drivers, 312 U.S., at 294-295, 61 S.Ct., at 555-556. Both the injunction in Madsen and the injunction here are supported by this governmental interest. In Madsen, it was permissible to move protesters off the sidewalk and to the other side of the street in part because other options would block the free flow of traffic on the streets and sidewalks. 512 U.S., at 767-768, 114 S.Ct., at 2525-2526. Here, the District Court cited public safety as one of the interests justifying the injunction--certainly a reasonable conclusion, if only because of the dangerous situation created by the interaction between cars and protesters and because of the fights that threatened to (and sometimes did) develop. Even though the governmental interest in public safety is clearly a valid interest here, as it was in Madsen, plaintiffs in neither case pleaded a claim for "threat to public safety." Indeed, this would be a strange concept, since a plaintiff customarily alleges violations of private rights, while "public safety" expresses a public right enforced by the government through its criminal laws and otherwise. Thus, the fact that "threat to public safety" is not listed anywhere in respondents' complaint as a claim does not preclude a court from relying on the significant governmental interest in public safety in assessing petitioners' First Amendment argument.

Given the factual similarity between this case and Madsen, we conclude that the governmental interests underlying the injunction in Madsen--ensuring public safety and order, promoting the free flow of traffic on streets and sidewalks, protecting property rights, and protecting a woman's freedom to seek pregnancy-related services also underlie the injunction here, and in combination are certainly significant enough to justify an appropriately tailored injunction to secure unimpeded physical access to the clinics.

### C

We strike down the floating buffer zones around people entering and leaving the clinics because they burden more speech than is necessary to serve the relevant governmental interests. The floating buffer zones prevent defendants--except for two sidewalk counselors, while they are tolerated by the targeted individual--from communicating a message from a normal conversational distance or handing leaflets to people entering or leaving the clinics who are walking on the public sidewalks. This is a broad prohibition, both because of the type of speech that is restricted and the nature of the location. Leafletting and commenting on matters of public concern are classic forms of speech that lie at the heart of the First Amendment, and speech in public areas is at its most protected on public sidewalks, a prototypical example of a traditional public forum. See, e.g., Boos v. Barry, 485 U.S. 312, 322, 108 S.Ct. 1157, 1164, 99 L.Ed.2d 333 (1988); United States v. Grace, 461 U.S. 171, 180, 103 S.Ct. 1702, 1708- 1709, 75 L.Ed.2d 736 (1983). On the other hand, we have before us a record that shows physically abusive conduct, harassment of the police that hampered law enforcement, and the tendency of even peaceful conversations to devolve into aggressive and sometimes violent conduct. In some situations, a record of abusive conduct makes a prohibition on classic speech in limited parts of a public sidewalk permissible. See, e.g., Part II-D infra; Madsen, 512 U.S. at 769-770, 114 S.Ct., at 2526-2527. We need not decide whether the governmental interests involved would ever justify some sort of zone of separation between individuals entering the clinics and protesters, measured by the distance between the two. We hold here that because this broad prohibition on speech "floats," it cannot be sustained on this record.

Since the buffer zone floats, protesters on the public sidewalks who wish (i) to communicate their message to an incoming or outgoing patient or clinic employee and (ii) to remain as close as possible (while maintaining an acceptable conversational distance) to this individual, must move as the individual moves, maintaining 15 feet of separation. But this would be difficult to accomplish at, for instance, the GYN Womenservices clinic in Buffalo, one of the respondent clinics. The sidewalk outside the clinic is 17- feet wide. This means that protesters who wish to walk alongside an individual entering or leaving the clinic are pushed into the street, unless the individual walks a straight line on the outer edges of the sidewalk. Protesters could presumably walk 15 feet behind the individual, or 15 feet in front of the individual while walking backwards. But they are then faced with the problem of watching out for other individuals entering or leaving the clinic who are heading the opposite way from the individual they have targeted. With clinic escorts leaving the clinic to pick up incoming patients and entering the clinic to drop them off, it would be quite difficult for a protester who wishes to engage in peaceful expressive activities to know how to remain in compliance with the injunction.9 This lack of certainty leads to a substantial risk that much more speech will be burdened than the injunction by its terms prohibits. That is, attempts to stand 15 feet from someone entering or leaving a clinic and to communicate a message--certainly protected on the face of the injunction--will be hazardous if one wishes to remain in compliance with the injunction.10 Since there may well be other ways to both effect such separation and yet provide certainty (so that speech protected by the injunction's terms is not burdened), we conclude that the floating buffer zones burden more speech than necessary to serve the relevant governmental interests. Because we strike down the floating buffer zones, we do not address the constitutionality of the "cease and desist" provision that allows sidewalk counselors within those buffer zones.

(footnote)9. We suspect that these floating buffer zones would also be quite difficult for a District Court to enforce. Contempt proceedings would likely focus on whether protesters who thought they were keeping pace with the targeted individual from a distance of 15 feet actually strayed to within 14 or 13 feet of the individual for a certain period of time.

(footnote)10. Significantly, the District Judge himself expressed this same concern at the September 27 TRO hearing, stating his understanding that a "moving" buffer zone would be quite infeasible. Nevertheless, the terms of the TRO and the injunction provide exactly that, and the District Court never authoritatively put a limiting construction on the injunction. Justice BREYER in dissent places great stress on the District Court's statement at this September 27 hearing, and concludes that the District Court never understood the TRO, or even the injunction, to contain floating buffer zones. We believe Justice BREYER misreads the record.

First, despite the District Court's statements at the September 27 hearing, the court held petitioner and one other defendant in contempt for violating paragraph 1(a) of the TRO, because they came within 15 feet of an individual attempting to enter the clinic even though they were more than 15 feet from any doorway or driveway entrance to the clinic. See Pro- Choice Network of Western N.Y. v. Project Rescue Western N. Y., No. 90-CV-1004A (WDNY) Sept 28, 1992, pp. 7-8, 20-21 (doctor parked several hundred feet from clinic and then attempted to walk on sidewalk toward clinic; contemnors followed doctor the length of the sidewalk, yelling at him from a distance of only a few feet, up until the point where doctor was 10 to 20 feet from clinic driveway entrance; court held that this conduct violates the TRO's "proscription against demonstrating within fifteen feet of any person seeking access to a clinic"). Thus, we conclude that the District Court read the TRO the way an ordinary person would--to create a floating buffer zone.

Second, the District Court's opinion accompanying the issuance of the preliminary injunction shows that the court interpreted the injunction to contain floating buffer zones. The court described paragraph (b) of the injunction as "setting dual 'clear zones' of fifteen feet around entrances and fifteen feet around people and vehicles seeking access." 799 F.Supp., at 1434 (emphasis added). And the injunction by its terms bans "demonstrating" within 15 feet of clinic entrances "or within fifteen feet of any person or vehicle seeking access to [the clinic]" (emphasis added).

Finally, we note that no judge of the en banc Court of Appeals expressed doubt that the injunction included floating buffer zones, cf. 67 F.3d, at 389, n. 4 (discussing "how far from a clinic a floating buffer zone may reach," not, as Justice BREYER suggests, whether the injunction creates floating buffer zones at all), and that none of the parties before us has suggested that the injunction does not provide for such zones.

We likewise strike down the floating buffer zones around vehicles. Nothing in the record or the District Court's opinion contradicts the commonsense notion that a more limited injunction--which keeps protesters away from driveways and parking lot entrances (as the fixed buffer zones do) and off the streets, for instance--would be sufficient to ensure that drivers are not confused about how to enter the clinic and are able to gain access to its driveways and parking lots safely and easily. In contrast, the 15-foot floating buffer zones would restrict the speech of those who simply line the sidewalk or curb in an effort to chant, shout, or hold signs peacefully. We therefore conclude that the floating buffer zones around vehicles burden more speech than necessary to serve the relevant governmental interests.

D

We uphold the fixed buffer zones around the doorways, driveways, and driveway entrances. These buffer zones are necessary to ensure that people and vehicles trying to enter or exit the clinic property or clinic parking lots can do so. As in Madsen, the record shows that protesters purposefully or effectively blocked or hindered people from entering and exiting the clinic doorways, from driving up to and away from clinic entrances, and from driving in and out of clinic parking lots. Based on this conduct--both before and after the TRO issued--the District Court was entitled to conclude that the only way to ensure access was to move back the demonstrations away from the driveways and parking lot entrances. Similarly, sidewalk counselors--both before and after the TRO--followed and crowded people right up to the doorways of the clinics (and sometimes beyond) and then tended to stay in the doorways, shouting at the individuals who had managed to get inside. In addition, as the District Court found, defendants' harassment of the local police made it far from certain that the police would be able to quickly and effectively counteract protesters who blocked doorways or threatened the safety of entering patients and employees. Based on this conduct, the District Court was entitled to conclude that protesters who were allowed close to the entrances would continue right up to the entrance, and that the only way to ensure access was to move all protesters away from the doorways.11 Although one might quibble about whether 15 feet is too great or too small a distance if the goal is to ensure access, we defer to the District Court's reasonable assessment of the number of feet necessary to keep the entrances clear. See Madsen, 512 U.S., at 769-770, 114 S.Ct., at 2526-2527 ("[S]ome deference must be given to the state court's familiarity with the facts and the background of the dispute between the parties even under our heightened review").

(footnote)11. The fact that the injunction allows two sidewalk counselors into the fixed buffer zones--subject to the "cease and desist" provision--does not detract from this conclusion. It is clear from the District Court's opinion that its decision to allow two sidewalk counselors inside the buffer zones was an effort to bend over backwards to "accommodate" defendants' speech rights. See 799 F.Supp., at 1434. Because the District Court was entitled to conclude on this record that the only feasible way to shield individuals within the fixed buffer zone from unprotected conduct--especially with law enforcement efforts hampered by defendants' harassment of the police--would have been to keep the entire area clear of defendant protesters, the District Court's extra effort to enhance defendants' speech rights by allowing an exception to the fixed buffer zone should not redound to the detriment of respondents.

Petitioners claim that unchallenged provisions of the injunction are sufficient to ensure this access, pointing to the bans on trespassing, excessive noise, and "blocking, impeding or obstructing access to" the clinics. They claim that in light of these provisions, the only effect of a ban on "demonstrating" within the fixed buffer zone is "a ban on peaceful, nonobstructive demonstrations on public sidewalks or rights of way." Brief for Petitioners 47. This argument, however, ignores the record in this case. Based on defendants' past conduct, the District Court was entitled to conclude that some of the defendants who were allowed within 5 to 10 feet of clinic entrances would not merely engage in stationary, nonobstructive demonstrations but would continue to do what they had done before: aggressively follow and crowd individuals right up to the clinic door and then refuse to move, or purposefully mill around parking lot entrances in an effort to impede or block the progress of cars. And because defendants' harassment of police hampered the ability of the police to respond quickly to a problem, a prophylactic measure was even more appropriate. Cf. Burson v. Freeman, 504 U.S. 191, 206-207, 112 S.Ct. 1846, 1855-1856, 119 L.Ed.2d 5 (1992) (upholding 100-foot "no-campaign zone" around polling places: "Intimidation and interference laws fall short of serving a State's compelling interests because they 'deal with only the most blatant and specific attempts' to impede elections. Moreover, because law enforcement officers generally are barred [under state law] from the vicinity of the polls to avoid any appearance of coercion in the electoral process, many acts of interference would go undetected. These undetected or less than blatant acts may nonetheless drive the voter away before remedial action can be taken" (citations omitted)). The ban on "blocking, impeding, and obstructing access" was therefore insufficient by itself to solve the problem, and the fixed buffer zone was a necessary restriction on defendans' demonstrations.

Petitioners also argue that under Madsen, the fixed buffer zones are invalid because the District Court could not impose a "speech- restrictive" injunction (or TRO) without first trying a "non-speech- restrictive" injunction, as the trial court did in Madsen. But in Madsen we simply stated that the failure of an initial injunction "to accomplish its purpose may be taken into consideration" in determining the constitutionality of a later injunction. 512 U.S., at 770, 114 S.Ct., at 2527. The fact that the District Court's TRO included a "speech-restrictive" provision certainly does not mean that the subsequent injunction is automatically invalid. Since we can uphold the injunction under the Madsen standard without this "consideration" being present, petitioners' argument fails.

Finally, petitioners make several arguments that may be quickly refuted. They argue that, unlike Madsen, there is "no extraordinary record of pervasive lawlessness," Brief for Petitioners 45, and that the buffer zones are therefore unnecessary. As explained above, our review of the record convinces us that defendants' conduct was indeed extraordinary, and that based on this conduct the District Court was entitled to conclude that keeping defendants away from the entrances was necessary to ensure access. Petitioners also argue that the term "demonstrating" is vague. When the injunction is read as a whole, see Grayned v. City of Rockford, 408 U.S. 104, 110, 92 S.Ct. 2294, 2299-2300, 33 L.Ed.2d 222 (1972), we believe that people "of ordinary intelligence" (and certainly defendants, whose demonstrations led to this litigation in the first place) have been given "a reasonable opportunity to know what is prohibited," id., at 108, 92 S.Ct., at 2298-2299.

Petitioners also contend that the "cease and desist" provision which limits the exception for sidewalk counselors in connection with the fixed buffer zone is contrary to the First Amendment. We doubt that the District Court's reason for including that provision--"to protect the right of the people approaching and entering the facilities to be left alone"--accurately reflects our First Amendment jurisprudence in this area. Madsen sustained an injunction designed to secure physical access to the clinic, but not on the basis of any generalized right "to be left alone" on a public street or sidewalk. As we said in Madsen, quoting from Boos v. Barry, 485 U.S. at 322, 108 S.Ct., at 1164, " '[a]s a general matter, we have indicated that in public debate our own citizens must tolerate insulting, and even outrageous, speech in order to provide adequate breathing space to the freedoms protected by the First Amendment.' " 512 U.S., at 774, 114 S.Ct., at 2529. But as earlier noted, the entire exception for sidewalk counselors was an effort to enhance petitioners' speech rights, see n. 11, supra, and the "cease and desist" limitation must be assessed in that light.12

(footnote)12. Although petitioners argue that our disapproval of the 300-foot no approach zone in Madsen requires disapproval of the "cease and desist" provision, Madsen is easily distinguishable on this point, since the no- approach zone was eight times broader than the "buffer zone" deemed necessary to ensure access to the clinic in Madsen.

Justice SCALIA in dissent suggests that our failure to endorse the District Court's reason for including the "cease and desist" provision requires us to reverse the District Court's decision setting the injunction's terms. This suggestion is inconsistent with our precedents. See, e.g., Rutan v. Republican Party of Ill., 497 U.S. 62, 76, 110 S.Ct. 2729, 2737-2738, 111 L.Ed.2d 52 (1990) ("[A]lthough we affirm the Seventh Circuit's judgment ..., we do not adopt the Seventh Circuit's reasoning"); Smith v. Phillips, 455 U.S. 209, 215, n. 6, 102 S.Ct. 940, 945, n. 6, 71 L.Ed.2d 78 (1982) ("Respondent may, of course, defend the judgment below on any ground which the law and the record permit, provided the asserted ground would not expand the relief which has been granted"); SEC v. Chenery Corp., 318 U.S. 80, 88, 63 S.Ct. 454, 459, 87 L.Ed. 626 (1943) ("[W]e do not disturb the settled rule that, in reviewing the decision of a lower court, it must be affirmed if the result is correct 'although the lower court relied upon a wrong ground or gave a wrong reason' ") (quoting Helvering v. Gowran, 302 U.S. 238, 245, 58 S.Ct. 154, 158, 82 L.Ed. 224 (1937)); Langnes v. Green, 282 U.S. 531, 536-537, 51 S.Ct. 243, 245- 246, 75 L.Ed. 520 (1931) ("[T]he entire record is before this court with power to review the action of the court of appeals and direct such disposition of the case as that court might have done upon the writ of error sued out for the review of the [district] court"); Williams v. Norris, 12 Wheat. 117, 120, 6 L.Ed. 571 (1827) (Marshall, C.J.) ("If the judgment [of the lower court] should be correct, although the reasoning, by which the mind of the Judge was conducted to it, should be deemed unsound, that judgment would certainly be affirmed in [this] Court").

Petitioners and some of their amici attack the "cease and desist" provision accompanying the exception for sidewalk counselors as content based, because it allows a clinic patient to terminate a protester's right to speak based on, among other reasons, the patient's disagreement with the message being conveyed. But in Madsen we held that the injunction in that case was not content based, even though it was directed only at abortion protesters, because it was only abortion protesters who had done the acts which were being enjoined. Here, the District Court found that "[m]any of the 'sidewalk counselors' and other defendants ha[d] been arrested on more than one occasion for harassment, yet persist in harassing and intimidating patients, patient escorts and medical staff." 799 F.Supp., at 1425. These counselors remain free to espouse their message outside the 15-foot buffer zone, and the condition on their freedom to espouse it within the buffer zone is the result of their own previous harassment and intimidation of patients.

The judgment of the Court of Appeals is affirmed in part and reversed in part, and the case is remanded for further proceedings consistent with this opinion.

It is so ordered.

Justice SCALIA, with whom Justice KENNEDY and Justice THOMAS join, concurring in part and dissenting in part . . . .

. . . . The Court proceeds from there to make a much more significant point: An injunction on speech may be upheld even if not justified on the basis of the interests asserted by the plaintiff, as long as it serves "public safety." "[I]n assessing a First Amendment challenge, a court ... inquires into the governmental interests that are protected by the injunction, which may include an interest in public safety and order.... Here, the District Court cited public safety as one of the interests justifying the injunction.... [T]he fact that 'threat to public safety' is not listed anywhere in respondents' complaint as a claim does not preclude a court from relying on the significant governmental interest in public safety in assessing petitioners' First Amendment argument." Ante, at 866.

This is a wonderful expansion of judicial power. Rather than courts' being limited to according relief justified by the complaints brought before them, the Court today announces that a complaint gives them, in addition, ancillary power to decree what may be necessary to protect--not the plaintiff, but the public interest! Every private suit makes the district judge a sort of one-man Committee of Public Safety. There is no precedent for this novel and dangerous proposition. In Madsen, the Court says, "it was permissible to move protesters off the sidewalk and to the other side of the street in part because other options would block the free flow of traffic on the streets and sidewalks." Ante, at 866; see also Madsen, 512 U.S., at 769, 114 S.Ct., at 2526. But acknowledging, as we did in Madsen, that some remedial options are eliminated because they conflict with considerations of public safety is entirely different from asserting, as the Court does today, that public safety can provide part of the justification for the remedy. 3 The only other case cited by the Court is Milk Wagon Drivers v. Meadowmoor Dairies, Inc., 312 U.S. 287, 294-295, 61 S.Ct. 552, 555-556, 85 L.Ed. 836 (1941). Ante, at 866. But Meadowmoor upheld an injunction against a union's intimidation of storekeepers, not because "the public interest" demanded it, but because the storekeepers were customers of the plaintiff dairy, which it was the purpose and effect of the intimidation to harm. 312 U.S., at 294-295, 61 S.Ct., at 555-556.

(footnote)3. Madsen also refers to "public safety" as one of the government interests on which the state court relied in justifying the challengedinjunction, 512 U.S., at 768, 114 S.Ct., at 2526, but nothing in our decision approved or relied upon that feature of the state court's approach.

We have in our state and federal systems a specific entity charged with responsibility for initiating action to guard the public safety. It is called the Executive Branch. When the public safety is threatened, that branch is empowered, by invoking judicial action and by other means, to provide protection. But the Judicial Branch has hitherto been thought powerless to act except as invited by someone other than itself. That is one of the reasons it was thought to be "the least dangerous to the political rights of the [C]onstitution"--because it "can take no active resolution whatever" and "may truly be said to have neither FORCE nor WILL, but merely judgment." The Federalist No. 78, p. 396 (M. Beloff ed.1987). It is contrary to the most fundamental principles of separation of powers for the District Court to decree measures that would eliminate obstruction of traffic, in a lawsuit which has established nothing more than trespass. 4

(footnote)4. The Court approves reliance on "public safety" not "as an element which supported respondents' claim for an injunction," but only "as a basis for rejecting petitioners' challenge to the injunction on First Amendment grounds." Ante, at 866, n. 7. Such a distinction makes no sense. In the context before us here, whether there is "a basis for rejecting petitioners' challengeto the injunction on First Amendment grounds" depends entirely on whether the "element[s] which suppor[t] the respondents' claim for an injunction" are strong enough. The issues are one and the same.

Any injunction must be justified by the elements that support it. The involvement of First Amendment rights does not alter that rule, but merely increases the degree of justification required. Of course, illogical or not, by simply saying so, the Court can limit its novel "public safety" rationale to injunctions involving the freedom of speech. But I would hardly consider that a small and unimportant area for the newly created judicial Committees of Public Safety to control.

* * *

Today's opinion makes a destructive inroad upon First Amendment law in holding that the validity of an injunction against speech is to be determined by an appellate court on the basis of what the issuing court might reasonably have found as to necessity, rather than on the basis of what it in fact found. And it makes a destructive inroad upon the separation of powers in holding that an injunction may contain measures justified by the public interest apart from remediation of the legal wrong that is the subject of the complaint. Insofar as the first point is concerned, the Court might properly have upheld the fixed buffer zone without the cease-and-desist provision, since the District Court evidently did conclude (with proper factual support, in my view) that limiting the protesters to two was necessary to prevent repetition of the obstruction of access that had occurred in the past. But even that more limited injunction would be invalidated by the second point: the fact that no cause of action related to obstruction of access was properly found to support the injunction. Accordingly, I dissent from the Court's judgment upholding the fixed buffer zone, and would reverse the decision of the Court of Appeals in its entirety.

Justice BREYER, concurring in part and dissenting in part.

Words take on meaning from context. Considered in context, the preliminary injunction's language does not necessarily create the kind of "floating bubble" that leads the Court to find the injunction unconstitutionally broad. See Part II-C, supra. And until quite recently, no one thought that it did. The "floating bubble" controversy apparently arose during oral argument before the en banc Court of Appeals. The Court of Appeals then gave the District Judge, who has ongoing responsibility for administering the injunction, an initial opportunity to consider the petitioners' claim and, if necessary, to clarify or limit the relevant language. 67 F.3d 377, 389, n. 4 (C.A.2 1995) (en banc). The Court of Appeals' response, in my view, is both legally proper and sensible. I therefore would affirm its judgment.

The preliminary injunction's key languageprohibits demonstrating "within fifteen feet of any person or vehicle seeking access to or leaving such facilities." This languagefirst appeared in the temporary restraining order (TRO), where it defined the precise scope of the order's prohibition against blocking "ingress into or egress from" facilities. That portion of the TRO enjoined the defendants from

> "trespassing on, sitting in, blocking, impeding or obstructing access to, ingress into or egress from any facility at which abortions are performed in the Western District of New York, including demonstrating within 15 feet of any person seeking access to or leaving such facilities ...." App. 23 (emphasis added).

Before the District Court issued the TRO, Reverend Schenck asked whether this languagewould create a floating bubble. The District Court replied:

> "THE COURT: I don't think that was the intent.... [W]e're talking about ... free access.... It's not a moving 15 feet.
>
> "REV. SCHENCK: So in other words, you're speaking of the facility itself?

"THE COURT: I think that's what we were talking about.... We're talking fifteen feet from [e.g., a doorway] ... to go right out to where ever you're going.... [M]y gosh, you would never be able ... to deal with that if it was a moving length.

"It's fifteen feet from the entrance.... [Y]ou have to apply common sense ... and [an interpretation of the languagecreating a moving zone] would not in any way at all be a fair interpretation of what we're talking about.

"REV. SCHENCK: Well, I'm glad you pointed that out.... [T]here is, I think, a very high degree of ambiguity ... and no one ... said what we're talking about here is 15 feet from an entranceway.

"THE COURT: I think everyone is clear on that now." App. to Reply Brief for Petitioner A-2 to A-3 . . . .

. . . . Nor is there anything in the many District Court filings in respect to the preliminary injunction that suggests an intent to create a floating bubble of the sort contemplated by this Court. The diagrams that plaintiffs submitted to clarify the injunction's scope contain no reference to a floating zone. Rather, they are marked to indicate 15-foot fixed buffer zones from entrances to clinic property. See Appendix B, infra.

In fact, at oral argument before the appeals court panel, counsel for the petitioners confirmed that the injunction's bubble did not "float" in the way contemplated by this Court. At that time an appeals court judge asked counsel (for the demonstrators) whether the 15-foot zone would apply after "someone leaves the abortion clinic and goes to a grocery store," perhaps "three miles away," and counsel replied as follows:

"COUNSEL: I don't think that would [be] prohibit[ed] [by] the court's order. I think the court's order provides for a 15-foot setback or bubble zone around the clinic property....

"APPEALS COURT: Well, my question is to what extent can you ... 'leave' and still be subject to this injunction?

"COUNSEL: Maybe I just didn't see the full implications of the injunction, but I never considered that beyond the 15-foot bubble zone there would be this same restriction. Even I'm not arguing that the injunction goes that far. Maybe I just didn't see that but I didn't interpret it that way."

Not surprisingly, the appeals court's panel opinion did not mention floating bubbles. Nor did the parties mention the matter in subsequent District Court proceedings related to modifying or restoring the injunction--proceedings that took place after the Court of Appeals' panel decision invalidating the injunction, but before the Court of Appeals heard the case en banc and reversed. At the latter time, apparently for the first time, the parties agreed that the injunction's language produced a zone that moved in some way or another.

Given this posture, it is not surprising that the en banc Court of Appeals did not deny the existence of a floating bubble zone, but left the initial resolution of the floating bubble controversy to the District Court. The Court of Appeals addressed the parties' argument regarding what the court termed a "floating buffer"--an issue that had never been raised before--by holding that the "floating buffer" was permissible, 67 F.3d, at 389, on the assumption that the District Court would apply it in a constitutional manner, 67 F.3d, at 389, n. 4. Thus, the Court of Appeals did not definitively interpret the scope of the relevant language,but instead left it to the District Court to resolve in the first instance any linguistic ambiguity that might create a constitutional problem.

In my view, this action by the Court of Appeals was appropriate, and this Court should do the same . . . . Some bubbles that "float" in time or space would seem to raise no constitutional difficulty. For example, a 15-foot buffer zone that is "fixed" in place around a doorway but that is activated only when a clinic patient is present can be said to "float" in time or, to a small degree, in space. See Appendix B, infra, Diagram 1 (Point X). Another example of a possibly constitutional "floating" bubble would be one that protects a patient who alights from a vehicle at the curbside in front of the Buffalo GYN Womenservices clinic and must cross the two-foot stretch of sidewalk that is outside the 15-foot fixed buffer. See Appendix B, infra, Diagram 2 (Point Y). Other bubbles, such as a bubble that follows a clinic patient to a grocery store three miles away, apparently are of no interest to anyone in this case. A floating bubble that follows a patient who is walking along the sidewalk just in front of a clinic, but outside the 15-foot fixed zone, could raise a constitutional problem. See Appendix B, infra, Diagram 3 (Point Z). But the constitutional validity of that kind of bubble should depend upon the particular clinic and the particular circumstances to which the District Court would point in justification. The Court of Appeals wisely recognized that these matters should be left in the first instance to the consideration of the District Court.

In sum, ordinary principles of judicial administration would permit the District Court to deal with the petitioners' current objection. These principles counsel against this Court's now offering its own interpretation of the injunction--an interpretation that is not obvious from the language and that has never been considered by the District Court. I do not see how the Court's review of the key language, in the absence of special need and in violation of those principles, can make the lower courts' difficult, ongoing, circumstance-specific task any easier. To the contrary, district judges cannot assure in advance, without the benefit of argument by the parties, that the language of complex, fact-based injunctions is free of every ambiguity that later interpretation or misinterpretation finds possible. And I see no special need here for the Court to make an apparently general statement about the law of "floating bubbles," which later developments may show to have been unnecessary or unwise.

Hence, I would affirm the judgment of the Court of Appeals in its entirety.

John F. TINKER and Mary Beth Tinker, Minors, etc., et al., Petitioners,
v.
DES MOINES INDEPENDENT COMMUNITY SCHOOL DISTRICT et al.

393 U.S. 503

Supreme Court of the United States

Decided Feb. 24, 1969.

Mr. Justice Black and Mr. Justice Harlan dissented

Mr. Justice FORTAS delivered the opinion of the Court.

Petitioner John F. Tinker, 15 years old, and petitioner Christopher Eckhardt, 16 years old, attended high schools in Des Moines, Iowa. Petitioner Mary Beth Tinker, John's sister, was a 13-year-old student in junior high school.

In December 1965, a group of adults and students in Des Moines held a meeting at the Eckhardt home. The group determined to publicize their objections to the hostilities in Vietnam and their support for a truce by wearing black armbands during the holiday season and by fasting on December 16 and New Year's Eve. Petitioners and their parents had previously engaged in similar activities, and they decided to participate in the program.

The principals of the Des Moines schools became aware of the plan to wear armbands. On December 14, 1965, they met and adopted a policy that any student wearing an armband to school would be asked to remove it, and if he refused he would be suspended until he returned without the armband. Petitioners were aware of the regulation that the school authorities adopted.

On December 16, Mary Beth and Christopher wore black armbands to their schools. John Tinker wore his armband the next day. They were all sent home and suspended from school until they would come back without their armbands. They did not return to school until after the planned period for wearing armbands had expired--that is, until after New Year's Day.

This complaint was filed in the United States District Court by petitioners, through their fathers, under s 1983 of Title 42 of the United States Code. It prayed for an injunction restraining the respondent school officials and the respondent members of the board of directors of the school district from disciplining the petitioners, and it sought nominal damages. After an evidentiary hearing the District Court dismissed the complaint. It upheld the constitutionality of the school authorities' action on the ground that it was reasonable in order to prevent disturbance of school disipline. 258 F.Supp. 971 (1966). The court referred to but expressly declined to follow the Fifth Circuit's holding in a similar case that the wearing of symbols like the armbands cannot be prohibited unless it 'materially and substantially interfere(s) with the requirements of appropriate discipline in the operation of the school.' Burnside v. Byars, 363 F.2d 744, 749 (1966).

On appeal, the Court of Appeals for the Eighth Circuit considered the case en banc. The court was equally divided, and the District Court's decision was accordingly affirmed, without opinion, 383 F.2d 988 (1967). We granted certiorari. 390 U.S. 942, 88 S.Ct. 1050, 19 L.Ed.2d 1130 (1968).

I.

The District Court recognized that the wearing of an armband for the purpose of expressing certain views is the type of symbolic act that is within the Free Speech Clause of the First Amendment. See West Virginia State Board of Education v. Barnette, 319 U.S. 624, 63 S.Ct. 1178, 87 L.Ed. 1628 (1943); Stromberg v. California, 283 U.S. 359, 51 S.Ct. 532, 75 L.Ed. 1117 (1931). Cf. Thornhill v. Alabama, 310 U.S. 88, 60 S.Ct. 736, 84 L.Ed. 1093 (1940); Edwards v. South Carolina, 372 U.S. 229, 83 S.Ct. 680, 9 L.Ed.2d 697 (1963); Brown v. Louisiana, 383 U.S. 131, 86 S.Ct. 719, 15 L.Ed.2d 637 (1966). As we shall discuss, the wearing of armbands in the circumstances of this case was entirely divorced from actually or potentially disruptive conduct by those participating in it. It was closely akin to 'pure speech' which, we have repeatedly held, is entitled to comprehensive protection under the First Amendment. Cf. Cox v. Louisiana, 379 U.S. 536, 555, 85 S.Ct. 453, 464, 13 L.Ed.2d 471 (1965); Adderley v. Florida, 385 U.S. 39, 87 S.Ct. 242, 17 L.Ed.2d 149 (1966).

First Amendment rights, applied in light of the special characteristics of the school environment, are available to teachers and students. It can hardly be argued that either students or teachers shed their constitutional rights to freedom of speech or expression at the schoolhouse gate. This has been the unmistakable holding of this Court for almost 50 years. In Meyer v. Nebraska, 262 U.S. 390, 43 S.Ct. 625, 67 L.Ed. 1042 (1923), and Bartels v. Iowa, 262 U.S. 404, 43 S.Ct. 628, 67 L.Ed. 1047 (1923), this Court, in opinions by Mr. Justice McReynolds, held that the Due Process Clause of the Fourteenth Amendment prevents States from forbidding the teaching of a foreign language to young students. Statutes to this effect, the Court held, unconstitutionally interfere with the liberty of teacher, student, and parent . . . .

II.

The problem posed by the present case does not relate to regulation of the length of skirts or the type of clothing, to hair style, or deportment. Cf. Ferrell v. Dallas Independent School District, 392 F.2d 697 (C.A.5th Cir. 1968); Pugsley v. Sellmeyer, 158 Ark. 247, 250 S.W. 538, 30 A.L.R. 1212 (1923). It does not concern aggressive, disruptive action or even group demonstrations.

Our problem involves direct, primary First Amendment rights akin to 'pure speech.'

The school officials banned and sought to punish petitioners for a silent, passive expression of opinion, unaccompanied by any disorder or disturbance on the part of petitioners. There is here no evidence whatever of petitioners' interference, actual or nascent, with the schools' work or of collision with the rights of other students to be secure and to be let alone. Accordingly, this case does not concern speech or action that intrudes upon the work of the schools or the rights of other students.

Only a few of the 18,000 students in the school system wore the black armbands. Only five students were suspended for wearing them. There is no indication that the work of the schools or any class was disrupted. Outside the classrooms, a few students made hostile remarks to the children wearing armbands, but there were no threats or acts of violence on school premises.

The District Court concluded that the action of the school authorities was reasonable because it was based upon their fear of a disturbance from the wearing of the armbands. But, in our system, undifferentiated fear or apprehension of disturbance is not enough to overcome the right to freedom of expression. Any departure from absolute regimentation may cause trouble. Any variation from the majority's opinion may inspire fear. Any word spoken, in class, in the lunchroom, or on the campus, that deviates from the views of another person may start an argument or cause a disturbance. But our Constitution says we must take this risk, Terminiello v. Chicago, 337 U.S. 1, 69 S.Ct. 894, 93 L.Ed. 1131 (1949); and our history says that it is this sort of hazardous freedom--this kind of openness--that is the basis of our national strength and of the independence and vigor of Americans who grow up and live in this relatively permissive, often disputations, society.

In order for the State in the person of school officials to justify prohibition of a particular expression of opinion, it must be able to show that its action was caused by something more than a mere desire to avoid the discomfort and unpleasantness that always accompany an unpopular viewpoint. Certainly where there is no finding and no showing that engaging in the forbidden conduct would 'materially and substantially interfere with the requirements of appropriate discipline in the operation of the school,' the prohibition cannot be sustained. Burnside v. Byars, supra, 363 F.2d at 749.

In the present case, the District Court made no such finding, and our independent examination of the record fails to yield evidence that the school authorities had reason to anticipate that the wearing of the armbands would substantially interfere with the work of the school or impinge upon the rights of other students.

.... The principle of these cases is not confined to the supervised and ordained discussion which takes place in the classroom. The principal use to which the schools are dedicated is to accommodate students during prescribed hours for the purpose of certain types of activities.

Among those activities is personal intercommunication among the students. This is not only an inevitable part of the process of attending school; it is also an important part of the educational process. A student's rights, therefore, do not embrace merely the classroom hours. When he is in the cafeteria, or on the playing field, or on the campus during the authorized hours, he may express his opinions, even on controversial subjects like the conflict in Vietnam, if he does so without 'materially and substantially interfer(ing) with the requirements of appropriate discipline in the operation of the school' and without colliding with the rights of others. Burnside v. Byars, supra, 363 F.2d at 749. But conduct by the student, in class or out of it, which for any reason--whether it stems from time, place, or type of behavior--materially disrupts classwork or involves substantial disorder or invasion of the rights of others is, of course, not immunized by the constitutional guarantee of freedom of speech. Cf. Blackwell v. Issaquena County Board of Education, 363 F.2d 749 (C.A.5th Cir. 1966) . . . .

As we have discussed, the record does not demonstrate any facts which might reasonably have led school authorities to forecast substantial disruption of or material interference with school activities, and no disturbances or disorders on the school premises in fact occurred. These petitioners merely went about their ordained rounds in school. Their deviation consisted only in wearing on their sleeve a band of black cloth, not more than two inches wide. They wore it to exhibit their disapproval of the Vietnam hostilities and their advocacy of a truce, to make their views known, and, by their example, to influence others to adopt them. They neither interrupted school activities nor sought to intrude in the school affairs or the lives of others. They caused discussion outside of the classrooms, but no interference with work and no disorder. In the circumstances, our Constitution does not permit officials of the State to deny their form of expression.

We express no opinion as to the form of relief which should be granted, this being a matter for the lower courts to determine. We reverse and remand for further proceedings consistent with this opinion.

Reversed and remanded.

HAZELWOOD SCHOOL DISTRICT, et al., Petitioners
v.
Cathy KUHLMEIER et al.

484 U.S. 260

Supreme Court of the United States

Decided Jan. 13, 1988.

Justice Brennan, dissented and filed opinion, in which Justice Marshall and Justice Blackmun joined

Justice WHITE delivered the opinioin of the Court.

This case concerns the extent to which educators may exercise editorial control over the contents of a high school newspaper produced as part of the school's journalism curriculum.

I

Petitioners are the Hazelwood School District in St. Louis County, Missouri; various school officials; Robert Eugene Reynolds, the principal of Hazelwood East High School; and Howard Emerson, a teacher in the school district. Respondents are three former Hazelwood East students who were staff members of Spectrum, the school newspaper. They contend that school officials violated their First Amendment rights by deleting two pages of articles from the May 13, 1983, issue of Spectrum.

Spectrum was written and edited by the Journalism II class at Hazelwood East. The newspaper was published every three weeks or so during the 1982-1983 school year. More than 4,500 copies of the newspaper were distributed during that year to students, school personnel, and members of the community.

The Board of Education allocated funds from its annual budget for the printing of Spectrum. These funds were supplemented by proceeds from sales of the newspaper. The printing expenses during the 1982-1983 school year totaled $4,668.50; revenue from sales was $1,166.84. The other costs associated with the newspaper--such as supplies, textbooks, and a portion of the journalism teacher's salary--were borne entirely by the Board.

The Journalism II course was taught by Robert Stergos for most of the 1982- 1983 academic year. Stergos left Hazelwood East to take a job in private industry on April 29, 1983, when the May 13 edition of Spectrum was nearing completion, and petitioner Emerson took his place as newspaper adviser for the remaining weeks of the term.

The practice at Hazelwood East during the spring 1983 semester was for the journalism teacher to submit page proofs of each Spectrum issue to Principal Reynolds for his review prior to publication. On May 10, Emerson delivered the proofs of the May 13 edition to Reynolds, who objected to two of the articles scheduled to appear in that edition. One of the stories described three Hazelwood East students' experiences with pregnancy; the other discussed the impact of divorce on students at the school.

Reynolds was concerned that, although the pregnancy story used false names "to keep the identity of these girls a secret," the pregnant students still might be identifiable from the text. He also believed that the article's references to sexual activity and birth control were inappropriate for some of the younger students at the school. In addition, Reynolds was concerned that a student identified by name in the divorce story had complained that her father "wasn't spending enough time with my mom, my sister and I" prior to the divorce, "was always out of town on business or out late playing cards with the guys," and "always argued about everything" with her mother. App. to Pet. for Cert. 38. Reynolds believed that the student's parents should have been given an opportunity to respond to these remarks or to consent to their publication. He was unaware that Emerson had deleted the student's name from the final version of the article.

Reynolds believed that there was no time to make the necessary changes in the stories before the scheduled press run and that the newspaper would not appear before the end of the school year if printing were delayed to any significant extent. He concluded that his only options under the circumstances were to publish a four-page newspaper instead of the planned six-page newspaper, eliminating the two pages on which the offending stories appeared, or to publish no newspaper at all. Accordingly, he directed Emerson to withhold from publication the two pages containing the stories on pregnancy and divorce. He informed his superiors of the decision, and they concurred.

Respondents subsequently commenced this action in the United States District Court for the Eastern District of Missouri seeking a declaration that their First Amendment rights had been violated, injunctive relief, and monetary damages. After a bench trial, the District Court denied an injunction, holding that no First Amendment violation had occurred. 607 F.Supp. 1450 (1985).

The District Court concluded that school officials may impose restraints on students' speech in activities that are " 'an integral part of the school's educational function' "--including the publication of a school-sponsored newspaper by a journalism class--so long as their decision has " 'a substantial and reasonable basis.' " . . . .

The Court of Appeals for the Eighth Circuit reversed. 795 F.2d 1368 (1986). The court held at the outset that Spectrum was not only "a part of the school adopted curriculum," id., at 1373, but also a public forum, because the newspaper was "intended to be and operated as a conduit for student viewpoint." Id., at 1372. The court then concluded that Spectrum's status as a public forum precluded school officials from censoring its contents except when " 'necessary to avoid material and substantial interference with school work or discipline ... or the rights of others.' " Id., at 1374 (quoting Tinker v. Des Moines Independent Community School Dist., 393 U.S. 503, 511, 89 S.Ct. 733, 739, 21 L.Ed.2d 731 (1969)).

The Court of Appeals found "no evidence in the record that the principal could have reasonably forecast that the censored articles or any materials in the censored articles would have materially disrupted classwork or given rise to substantial disorder in the school."

We granted certiorari, 479 U.S. 1053, 107 S.Ct. 926, 93 L.Ed.2d 978 (1987), and we now reverse.

## II

Students in the public schools do not "shed their constitutional rights to freedom of speech or expression at the schoolhouse gate." Tinker, supra, 393 U.S., at 506, 89 S.Ct., at 736. They cannot be punished merely for expressing their personal views on the school premises--whether "in the cafeteria, or on the playing field, or on the campus during the authorized hours," 393 U.S., at 512-513, 89 S.Ct., at 739-740--unless school authorities have reason to believe that such expression will "substantially interfere with the work of the school or impinge upon the rights of other students." Id., at 509, 89 S.Ct., at 738.

We have nonetheless recognized that the First Amendment rights of students in the public schools "are not automatically coextensive with the rights of adults in other settings," Bethel School District No. 403 v. Fraser, 478 U.S. 675, 682, 106 S.Ct. 3159, 3164, 92 L.Ed.2d 549 (1986), and must be "applied in light of the special characteristics of the school environment." Tinker, supra, 393 U.S., at 506, 89 S.Ct., at 736; cf. New Jersey v. T.L.O., 469 U.S. 325, 341-343, 105 S.Ct. 733, 743-744, 83 L.Ed.2d 720 (1985). A school need not tolerate student speech that is inconsistent with its "basic educational mission," Fraser, supra, 478 U.S., at 685, 106 S.Ct., at 3165, even though the government could not censor similar speech outside the school. Accordingly, we held in Fraser that a student could be disciplined for having delivered a speech that was "sexually explicit" but not legally obscene at an official school assembly, because the school was entitled to "disassociate itself" from the speech in a manner that would demonstrate to others that such vulgarity is "wholly inconsistent with the 'fundamental values' of public school education." 478 U.S., at 685-686, 106 S.Ct., at 3165. We thus recognized that "[t]he determination of what manner of speech in the classroom or in school assembly is inappropriate properly rests with the school board," id., at 683, 106 S.Ct., at 3164, rather than with the federal courts. It is in this context that respondents' First Amendment claims must be considered.

### A

We deal first with the question whether Spectrum may appropriately be characterized as a forum for public expression. The public schools do not possess all of the attributes of streets, parks, and other traditional public forums that "time out of mind, have been used for purposes of assembly, communicating thoughts between citizens, and discussing public questions." Hague v. CIO, 307 U.S. 496, 515, 59 S.Ct. 954, 964, 83 L.Ed. 1423 (1939). Cf. Widmar v. Vincent, 454 U.S. 263, 267-268, n. 5, 102 S.Ct. 269, 273, n. 5, 70 L.Ed.2d 440 (1981). Hence, school facilities may be deemed to be public forums only if school authorities have "by policy or by practice" opened those facilities "for indiscriminate use by the general public," Perry Education Assn. v. Perry Local Educators' Assn., 460 U.S. 37, 47, 103 S.Ct. 948, 956, 74 L.Ed.2d 794 (1983), or by some segment of the public, such as student organizations. Id., at 46, n. 7, 103 S.Ct., at 955, n. 7 (citing Widmar v. Vincent ). If the facilities have instead been reserved for other intended purposes, "communicative or otherwise," then no public forum has been created, and school officials may impose reasonable restrictions on the speech of students, teachers, and other members of the school community. 460 U.S., at 46, n. 7, 103 S.Ct., at 955, n. 7. "The government does not create a public forum by inaction or by permitting limited discourse, but only by intentionally opening a nontraditional forum for public discourse." Cornelius v. NAACP Legal Defense & Educational Fund, Inc., 473 U.S. 788, 802, 105 S.Ct. 3439, 3449, 87 L.Ed.2d 567 (1985).

The policy of school officials toward Spectrum was reflected in Hazelwood School Board Policy 348.51 and the Hazelwood East Curriculum Guide. Board Policy 348.51 provided that "[s]chool sponsored publications are developed within the adopted curriculum and its educational implications in regular classroom activities." App. 22. The Hazelwood East Curriculum Guide described the Journalism II course as a "laboratory situation in which the students publish the school newspaper applying skills they have learned in Journalism I." Id., at 11. The lessons that were to be learned from the Journalism II course, according to the Curriculum Guide, included development of journalistic skills under deadline pressure, "the legal, moral, and ethical restrictions imposed upon journalists within the school community," and "responsibility and acceptance of criticism for articles of opinion." Ibid. Journalism II was taught by a faculty member during regular class hours. Students received grades and academic credit for their performance in the course.

School officials did not deviate in practice from their policy that production of Spectrum was to be part of the educational curriculum and a "regular classroom activit[y]." The District Court found that Robert Stergos, the journalism teacher during most of the 1982-1983 school year, "both had the authority to exercise and in fact exercised a great deal of control over Spectrum." 607 F.Supp., at 1453. For example, Stergos selected the editors of the newspaper, scheduled publication dates, decided the number of pages for each issue, assigned story ideas to class members, advised students on the development of their stories, reviewed the use of quotations, edited stories, selected and edited the letters to the editor, and dealt with the printing company. Many of these decisions were made without consultation with the Journalism II students. The District Court thus found it "clear that Mr. Stergos was the final authority with respect to almost every aspect of the production and publication of Spectrum, including its content." Ibid. Moreover, after each Spectrum issue had been finally approved by Stergos or his successor, the issue still had to be reviewed by Principal Reynolds prior to publication. Respondents' assertion that they had believed that they could publish "practically anything" in Spectrum was therefore dismissed by the District Court as simply "not credible." Id., at 1456. These factual findings are amply supported by the record, and were not rejected as clearly erroneous by the Court of Appeals.

The evidence relied upon by the Court of Appeals in finding Spectrum to be a public forum, see 795 F.2d, at 1372-1373, is equivocal at best. For example, Board Policy 348.51, which stated in part that "[s]chool sponsored student publications will not restrict free expression or diverse viewpoints within the rules of responsible journalism," also stated that such publications were "developed within the adopted curriculum and its educational implications." App. 22. One might reasonably infer from the full text of Policy 348.51 that school officials retained ultimate control over what constituted "responsible journalism" in a school-sponsored newspaper. Although the Statement of Policy published in the September 14, 1982, issue of Spectrum declared that "Spectrum, as a student-press publication, accepts all rights implied by the First Amendment," this statement, understood in the context of the paper's role in the school's curriculum, suggests at most that the administration will not interfere with the students' exercise of those First Amendment rights that attend the publication of a school-sponsored newspaper. It does not reflect an intent to expand those rights by converting a curricular newspaper into a public forum. Finally, that students were permitted to exercise some authority over the contents of Spectrum was fully consistent with the Curriculum Guide objective of teaching the Journalism II students "leadership responsibilities as issue and page editors." App. 11. A decision to teach leadership skills in the context of a classroom activity hardly implies a decision to relinquish school control over that activity. In sum, the evidence relied upon by the Court of Appeals fails to demonstrate the "clear intent to create a public forum." . . .

B

The question whether the First Amendment requires a school to tolerate particular student speech--the question that we addressed in Tinker--is different from the question whether the First Amendment requires a school affirmatively to promote particular student speech. The former question addresses educators' ability to silence a student's personal expression that happens to occur on the school premises. The latter question concerns educators' authority over school-sponsored publications, theatrical productions, and other expressive activities that students, parents, and members of the public might reasonably perceive to bear the imprimatur of the school. These activities may fairly be characterized as part of the school curriculum, whether or not they occur in a traditional classroom setting, so long as they are supervised by faculty members and designed to impart particular knowledge or skills to student participants and audiences.

Educators are entitled to exercise greater control over this second form of student expression to assure that participants learn whatever lessons the activity is designed to teach, that readers or listeners are not exposed to material that may be inappropriate for their level of maturity, and that the views of the individual speaker are not erroneously attributed to the school. Hence, a school may in its capacity as publisher of a school newspaper or producer of a school play "disassociate itself," Fraser, 478 U.S., at 685, 106 S.Ct., at 3165, not only from speech that would "substantially interfere with [its] work ... or impinge upon the rights of other students," Tinker, 393 U.S., at 509, 89 S.Ct., at 738, but also from speech that is, for example, ungrammatical, poorly written, inadequately researched, biased or prejudiced, vulgar or profane, or unsuitable for immature audiences. A school must be able to set high standards for the student speech that is disseminated under its auspices--standards that may be higher than those demanded by some newspaper publishers or theatrical producers in the "real" world--and may refuse to disseminate student speech that does not meet those standards. In addition, a school must be able to take into account the emotional maturity of the intended audience in determining whether to disseminate student speech on potentially sensitive topics, which might range from the existence of Santa Claus in an elementary school setting to the particulars of teenage sexual activity in a high school setting. A school must also retain the authority to refuse to sponsor student speech that might reasonably be perceived to advocate drug or alcohol use, irresponsible sex, or conduct otherwise inconsistent with "the shared values of a civilized social order," Fraser, supra, 478 U.S., at 683, 106 S.Ct., at 3164, or to associate the school with any position other than neutrality on matters of political controversy. Otherwise, the schools would be unduly constrained from fulfilling their role as "a principal instrument in awakening the child to cultural values, in preparing him for later professional training, and in helping him to adjust normally to his environment." Brown v. Board of Education, 347 U.S. 483, 493, 74 S.Ct. 686, 691, 98 L.Ed. 873 (1954).

Accordingly, we conclude that the standard articulated in Tinker for determining when a school may punish student expression need not also be the standard for determining when a school may refuse to lend its name and resources to the dissemination of student expression. Instead, we hold that educators do not offend the First Amendment by exercisingeditorial control over the style and content of student speech in school- sponsored expressive activities so long as their actions are reasonably related to legitimate pedagogical concerns . . . .

. . . . In sum, we cannot reject as unreasonable Principal Reynolds' conclusion that neither the pregnancy article nor the divorce article was suitable for publication in Spectrum. Reynolds could reasonably have concluded that the students who had written and edited these articles had not sufficiently mastered those portions of the Journalism II curriculum that pertained to the treatment of controversial issues and personal attacks, the need to protect the privacy of individuals whose most intimate concerns are to be revealed in the newspaper, and "the legal, moral, and ethical restrictions imposed upon journalists within [a] school community" that includes adolescent subjects and readers. Finally, we conclude that the principal's decision to delete two pages of Spectrum, rather than to delete only the offending articles or to require that they be modified, was reasonable under the circumstances as he understood them. Accordingly, no violation of First Amendment rights occurred.

The judgment of the Court of Appeals for the Eighth Circuit is therefore

Reversed.

Justice BRENNAN, with whom Justice MARSHALL and Justice BLACKMUN join, dissenting.

When the young men and women of Hazelwood East High School registered for Journalism II, they expected a civics lesson. Spectrum, the newspaper they were to publish, "was not just a class exercise in which students learned to prepare papers and hone writing skills, it was a ... forum established to give students an opportunity to express their views while gaining an appreciation of their rights and responsibilities under the First Amendment to the United States Constitution...." 795 F.2d 1368, 1373 (CA8 1986). "[A]t the beginning of each school year," id., at 1372, the student journalists published a Statement of Policy--tacitly approved each year by school authorities--announcing their expectation that "Spectrum, as a student-press publication, accepts all rights implied by the First Amendment.... Only speech that 'materially and substantially interferes with the requirements of appropriate discipline' can be found unacceptable and therefore prohibited." App. 26 (quoting Tinker v. Des Moines Independent Community School Dist., 393 U.S. 503, 513, 89 S.Ct. 733, 740, 21 L.Ed.2d 731 (1969)). The school board itself affirmatively guaranteed the students of Journalism II an atmosphere conducive to fostering such an appreciation and exercising the full panoply of rights associated with a free student press. "School sponsored student publications," it vowed, "will not restrict free expression or diverse viewpoints within the rules of responsible journalism." App. 22 (Board Policy 348.51).

This case arose when the Hazelwood East administration breached its own promise, dashing its students' expectations. The school principal, without prior consultation or explanation, excised six articles--comprising two full pages--of the May 13, 1983, issue of Spectrum. He did so not because any of the articles would "materially and substantially interfere with the requirements of appropriate discipline," but simply because he considered two of the six "inappropriate, personal, sensitive, and unsuitable" for student consumption. 795 F.2d, at 1371.

In my view the principal broke more than just a promise. He violated the First Amendment's prohibitions against censorship of any student expression that neither disrupts classwork nor invades the rights of others, and against any censorship that is not narrowly tailored to serve its purpose.

. . . . If mere incompatibility with the school's pedagogical message were a constitutionally sufficient justification for the suppression of student speech, school officials could censor each of the students or student organizations in the foregoing hypotheticals, converting our public schools into "enclaves of totalitarianism," id., at 511, 89 S.Ct., at 739, that "strangle the free mind at its source," West Virginia Board of Education v. Barnette, supra, 319 U.S., at 637, 63 S.Ct., at 1185. The First Amendment permits no such blanket censorship authority. While the "constitutional rights of students in public school are not automatically **575 coextensive with the rights of adults in other settings," Fraser, supra, 478 U.S., at 682, 106 S.Ct., at 3164, students in the public schools do not "shed their constitutional rights to freedom of speech or expression at the schoolhouse gate," Tinker, supra, 393 U.S., at 506, 89 S.Ct., at 736. Just as the public on the street corner must, in the interest of fostering "enlightened opinion," Cantwell v. Connecticut, 310 U.S. 296, 310, 60 S.Ct. 900, 906, 84 L.Ed. 1213 (1940), tolerate speech that "tempt[s] [the listener] to throw [the speaker] off the street," id., at 309, 60 S.Ct., at 906, public educators must accommodate some student expression even if it offends them or offers views or values that contradict those the school wishes to inculcate.

. . . . The Court's second excuse for deviating from precedent is the school's interest in shielding an impressionable high school audience from material whose substance is "unsuitable for immature audiences." Ante, at 570 (footnote omitted). Specifically, the majority decrees that we must afford educators authority to shield high school students from exposure to "potentially sensitive topics" (like "the particulars of teenage sexual activity") or unacceptable social viewpoints (like the advocacy of "irresponsible se[x] or conduct otherwise inconsistent with 'the shared values of a civilized social order' ") through school-sponsored student activities. Ante, at 570 (citation omitted).

Tinker teaches us that the state educator's undeniable, and undeniably vital, mandate to inculcate moral and political values is not a general warrant to act as "thought police" stifling discussion of all but state-approved topics and advocacy of all but the official position. See also Epperson v. Arkansas, 393 U.S. 97, 89 S.Ct. 266, 21 L.Ed.2d 228 (1968); Meyer v. Nebraska, 262 U.S. 390, 43 S.Ct. 625, 67 L.Ed. 1042 (1923). Otherwise educators could transform students into "closed-circuit recipients of only that which the State chooses to communicate," Tinker, 393 U.S., at 511, 89 S.Ct., at 739, and cast a perverse and impermissible "pall of orthodoxy over the classroom," Keyishian v. Board of Regents, 385 U.S. 589, 603, 87 S.Ct. 675, 683, 17 L.Ed.2d 629 (1967). Thus, the State cannot constitutionally prohibit its high school students from recounting in the locker room "the particulars of [their] teenage sexual activity," nor even from advocating "irresponsible se[x]" or other presumed abominations of "the shared values of a civilized social order." Even in its capacity as educator the State may not assume an Orwellian "guardianship of the public mind."

. . . . Official censorship of student speech on the ground that it addresses "potentially sensitive topics" is, for related reasons, equally impermissible. I would not begrudge an educator the authority to limit the substantive scope of a school-sponsored publication to a certain, objectively definable topic, such as literary criticism, school sports, or an overview of the school year. Unlike those determinate limitations, "potential topic sensitivity" is a vaporous nonstandard--like " 'public welfare, peace, safety, health, decency, good order, morals or convenience,' " Shuttlesworth v. Birmingham, 394 U.S. 147, 150, 89 S.Ct. 935, 938, 22 L.Ed.2d 162 (1969), or " 'general welfare of citizens,' " Staub v. Baxley, 355 U.S. 313, 322, 78 S.Ct. 277, 282, 2 L.Ed.2d 302 (1958)--that invites manipulation to achieve ends that cannot permissibly be achieved through blatant viewpoint discrimination and chills student speech to which school officials might not object. In part because of those dangers, this Court has consistently condemned any scheme allowing a state official boundless discretion in licensing speech from a particular forum. U.S., at 322-324, 78 S.Ct., at 282-283.

The case before us aptly illustrates how readily school officials (and courts) can camouflage viewpoint discrimination as the "mere" protection of students from sensitive topics. Among the grounds that the Court advances to uphold the principal's censorship of one of the articles was the potential sensitivity of "teenage sexual activity." Ante, at 570. Yet the District Court specifically found that the principal "did not, as a matter of principle, oppose discussion of said topi[c] in Spectrum." 607 F.Supp., at 1467. That much is also clear from the same principal's approval of the "squeal law" article on the same page, dealing forthrightly with "teenage sexuality," "the use of contraceptives by teenagers," and "teenage pregnancy," App. 4-5. If topic sensitivity were the true basis of the principal's decision, the two articles should have been equally objectionable. It is much more likely that the objectionable article was objectionable because of the viewpoint it expressed: It might have been read (as the majority apparently does) to advocate "irresponsible sex."

. . . . Finally, even if the majority were correct that the principal could constitutionally have censored the objectionable material, I would emphatically object to the brutal manner in which he did so. Where "[t]he separation of legitimate from illegitimate speech calls for more sensitive tools" Speiser v. Randall, 357 U.S. 513, 525, 78 S.Ct. 1332, 1342, 2 L.Ed.2d 1460 (1958); see Keyishian v. Board of Regents, supra, 385 U.S., at 602, 87 S.Ct., at 683, the principal used a paper shredder. He objected to some material in two articles, but excised six entire articles. He did not so much as inquire into obvious alternatives, such as precise deletions or additions (one of which had already been made), rearranging the layout, or delaying publication. Such unthinking contempt for individual rights is intolerable from any state official. It is particularly insidious from one to whom the public entrusts the task of inculcating in its youth an appreciation for the cherished democratic liberties that our Constitution guarantees.

## IV

The Court opens its analysis in this case by purporting to reaffirm Tinker 's time-tested proposition that public school students "do not 'shed their constitutional rights to freedom of speech or expression at the schoolhouse gate.' " Ante, at 567 (quoting Tinker, supra, 393 U.S., at 506, 89 S.Ct., at 736). That is an ironic introduction to an opinion that denudes high school students of much of the First Amendment protection that Tinker itself prescribed. Instead of "teach[ing] children to respect the diversity of ideas that is fundamental to the American system," Board of Education v. Pico, 457 U.S., at 880, 102 S.Ct., at 2814 (BLACKMUN, J., concurring in part and concurring in judgment), and "that our Constitution is a living reality, not parchment preserved under glass," Shanley v. Northeast Independent School Dist., Bexar Cty., Tex., 462 F.2d 960, 972 (CA5 1972), the Court today "teach[es] youth to discount important principles of our government as mere platitudes." West Virginia Board of Education v. Barnette, 319 U.S., at 637, 63 S.Ct., at 1185. The young men and women of Hazelwood East expected a civics lesson, but not the one the Court teaches them today.

I dissent.

LOVELL

v.

CITY OF GRIFFIN, GA.

303 U.S. 444

Decided March 28, 1938.

Mr. Chief Justice HUGHES delivered the opinion of the Court.

Appellant, Alma Lovell, was convicted in the recorder's court of the City of Griffin, Ga., of the violation of a city ordinance and was sentenced to imprisonment for fifty days in default of the payment of a fine of $50. The superior court of the county refused sanction of a petition for review; the Court of Appeals affirmed the judgment of the superior court, 55 Ga.App. 609, 191 S.E. 152; and the Supreme Court of the state denied an application for certiorari. The case comes here on appeal.

The ordinance in question is as follows:

'Section 1. That the practice of distributing, either by hand or otherwise, circulars, handbooks, advertising, or literature of any kind, whether said articles are being delivered free, or whether same are being sold, within the limits of the City of Griffin, without first obtaining written permission from the City Manager of the City of Griffin, such practice shall be deemed a nuisance, and punishable as an offense against the City of Griffin.

'Section 2. The Chief of Police of the City of Griffin and the police force of the City of Griffin are hereby required and directed to suppress the same and to abate any nuisance as is described in the first section of this ordinance.'

The violation, which is not denied, consisted of the distribution without the required permission of a pamphlet and magazine in the nature of religious tracts, setting forth the gospel of the 'Kingdom of Jehovah.' Appellant did not apply for a permit, as she regarded herself as sent 'by Jehovah to do His work' and that such an application would have been 'an act of disobedience to His commandment.'

Upon the trial, with permission of the court, appellant demurred to the charge and moved to dismiss it upon a number of grounds, among which was the contention that the ordinance violated the Fourteenth Amendment of the Constitution of the United States in abridging 'the freedom of the press' and prohibiting 'the free exercise of petitioner's religion.' This contention was thus expressed:

'Because said ordinance is contrary to and in violation of the first amendment to the Constitution of the United States, which reads:
"Congress shall make no law respecting an establishment of religion, or prohibiting the free exercise thereof, or abridging the freedom of speech or of the press; or the right of the people peaceably to assemble and to petition the government for a redress of grievances.'

'Said ordinance is also contrary to and in violation of the fourteenth amendment to the Constitution of the United States, which had the effect of making the said first amendment applicable to the States, and which reads:

"All persons born or naturalized in the United States, and subject to the jurisdiction thereof, are citizens of the United States, and of the State wherein they reside. No State shall make or enforce any law which shall abridge the privileges or immunities of citizens of the United States; nor shall any State deprive any person of life, liberty, or property without due process of law; nor deny to any person within its jurisdiction the equal protection of the laws.'

'Said ordinance absolutely prohibits the distribution of any literature of any kind within the limits of the City of Griffin without the permission of the City Manager and thus abridges the freedom of the press, contrary to the provisions of said quoted amendments.

'Said ordinance also prohibits the free exercise of petitioner's religion and the practice thereof by prohibiting the distribution of literature about petitioner's religion in violation of the terms of said quoted amendments.'

The Court of Appeals, overruling these objections, sustained the constitutional validity of the ordinance, saying: 'The said ordinance is not unconstitutional because it abridges the freedom of the press or prohibits the distribution of literature about petitioner's religion in violation of the Fourteenth Amendment to the Constitution of the United States.' . . . .

Freedom of speech and freedom of the press, which are protected by the First Amendment from infringement by Congress, are among the fundamental personal rights and liberties which are protected by the Fourteenth Amendment from invasion by state action. Gitlow v. New York, 268 U.S. 652, 666, 45 S.Ct. 625, 629, 69 L.Ed. 1138; Stromberg v. California, 283 U.S. 359, 368, 51 S.Ct. 532, 535, 75 L.Ed. 1117, 73 A.L.R. 1484; Near v. Minnesota, 283 U.S. 697, 707, 51 S.Ct. 625, 627, 75 L.Ed. 1357; Grosjean v. American Press Company, 297 U.S. 233, 244, 56 S.Ct. 444, 80 L.Ed. 660; De Jonge v. Oregon, 299 U.S. 353, 364, 57 S.Ct. 255, 259, 81 L.Ed. 278. See, also, Palko v. Connecticut, 302 U.S. 319, 58 S.Ct. 149, 82 L.Ed. 288, decided December 6, 1937. It is also well settled that municipal ordinances adopted under state authority constitute state action and are within the prohibition of the amendment. Raymond v. Chicago Union Traction Co., 207 U.S. 20, 28 S.Ct. 7, 52 L.Ed. 78, 12 Ann.Cas. 757; Home Telephone & Telegraph Co. v. Los Angeles, 227 U.S. 278, 33 S.Ct. 312, 57 L.Ed. 510; Cuyahoga River Power

Company v. Akron, 240 U.S. 462, 36 S.Ct. 402, 60 L.Ed. 743.

The ordinance in its broad sweep prohibits the distribution of 'circulars, handbooks, advertising, or literature of any kind.' It manifestly applies to pamphlets, magazines, and periodicals. The evidence against appellant was that she distributed a certain pamphlet and a magazine called the 'Golden Age.' Whether in actual administration the ordinance is applied, as apparently it could be, to newspapers does not appear. The city manager testified that 'every one applies to me for a license to distribute literature in this City. None of these people (including defendant) secured a permit from me to distribute literature in the City of Griffin.' The ordinance is not limited to 'literature' that is obscene or offensive to public morals or that advocates unlawful conduct. There is no suggestion that the pamphlet and magazine distributed in the instant case were of that character. The ordinance embraces 'literature' in the widest sense.

The ordinance is comprehensive with respect to the method of distribution. It covers every sort of circulation 'either by hand or otherwise.' There is thus no restriction in its application with respect to time or place. It is not limited to ways which might be regarded as inconsistent with the maintenance of public order, or as involving disorderly conduct, the molestation of the inhabitants, or the misuse or littering of the streets. The ordinance prohibits the distribution of literature of any kind at any time, at any place, and in any manner without a permit from the city manager.

We think that the ordinance is invalid on its face. Whatever the motive which induced its adoption, its character is such that it strikes at the very foundation of the freedom of the press by subjecting it to license and censorship. The struggle for the freedom of the press was primarily directed against the power of the licensor. It was against that power that John Milton directed his assault by his 'Appeal for the Liberty of Unlicensed Printing.' And the liberty of the press became initially a right to publish 'without a license what formerly could be published only with one.' While this freedom from previous restraint upon publication cannot be regarded as exhausting the guaranty of liberty, the prevention of that restraint was a leading purpose in the adoption of the constitutional provision. See Patterson v. Colorado, 205 U.S. 454, 462, 27 S.Ct. 556, 51 L.Ed. 879, 10 Ann.Cas. 689; Near v. Minnesota, 283 U.S. 697, 713--716, 51 S.Ct. 625, 630, 75 L.Ed. 1357; Grosjean v. American Press Company, 297 U.S. 233, 245, 246, 56 S.Ct. 444, 447, 80 L.Ed. 660. Legislation of the type of the ordinance in question would restore the system of license and censorship in its baldest form.

The liberty of the press is not confined to newspapers and periodicals. It necessarily embraces pamphlets and leaflets. These indeed have been historic weapons in the defense of liberty, as the pamphlets of Thomas Paine and others in our own history abundantly attest. The press in its connotation comprehends every sort of publication which affords a vehicle of information and opinion. What we have had recent occasion to say with respect to the vital importance of protecting this essential liberty from every sort of infringement need not be repeated. Near v. Minnesota, supra; Grosjean v. American Press Company, supra; De Jonge v. Oregon, supra.

The ordinance cannot be saved because it relates to distribution and not to publication. 'Liberty of circulating is as essential to that freedom as liberty of publishing; indeed, without the circulation, the publication would be of little value.' Ex parte Jackson, 96 U.S. 727, 733, 24 L.Ed. 877. The license tax in Grosjean v. American Press Company, supra, was held invalid because of its direct tendency to restrict circulation.

As the ordinance is void on its face, it was not necessary for appellant to seek a permit under it. She was entitled to contest its validity in answer to the charge against her. Smith v. Cahoon, 283 U.S. 553, 562, 51 S.Ct. 582, 585, 75 L.Ed. 1264.

The judgment is reversed and the cause is remanded for further proceedings not inconsistent with this opinion.

It is so ordered.

Reversed and remanded.

John J. Hurley and South Boston Allied War Veterans Council
Petitioners
v.
Irish-American Gay, Lesbian and Bisexual Group of Boston, etc., Et Al.

63 USLW 4625

Supreme Court of the United States

Decided June 19, 1995

JUSTICE SOUTER delivered the opinion of the Court.

The issue in this case is whether Massachusetts may require private citizens who organize a parade to include among the marchers a group imparting a message the organizers do not wish to convey. We hold that such a mandate violates the First Amendment.

I

March 17 is set aside for two celebrations in South Boston. As early as 1737, some people in Boston observed the feast of the apostle to Ireland, and since 1776 the day has marked the evacuation of royal troops and Loyalists from the city, prompted by the guns captured at Ticonderoga and set up on Dorchester Heights under General Washington's command. Washington himself reportedly drew on the earlier tradition in choosing "St. Patrick" as the response to "Boston," the password used in the colonial lines on evacuation day. See J. Crimmins, St. Patrick's Day: Its Celebration in New York and other American Places, 1737-1845, pp. 15, 19 (1902); see generally 1 H.S. Commager & R. Morris, The Spirit of 'Seventy Six 138-183 (1958); The American Book of Days 262-265 (J. Hatch ed., 3d ed. 1978). Although the General Court of Massachusetts did not officially designate March 17 as Evacuation Day until 1938, see Mass. Gen. Laws s6:12K (1992), the City Council of Boston had previously sponsored public celebrations of Evacuation Day, including notable commemorations on the centennial in 1876, and on the 125th anniversary in 1901, with its parade, salute, concert, and fireworks display. See Celebration of the Centennial Anniversary of the Evacuation of Boston by the British Army (G. Ellis ed. 1876); Irish-American Gay, Lesbian and Bisexual Group of Boston v. City of Boston et al., Civ. Action No. 92-1516 (Super. Ct., Mass., Dec. 15, 1993), reprinted in App. to Pet. for Cert. B1, B8-B9.

The tradition of formal sponsorship by the city came to an end in 1947, however, when Mayor James Michael Curley himself granted authority to organize and conduct the St. Patrick's Day-Evacuation Day Parade to the petitioner South Boston Allied War Veterans Council, an unincorporated association of individuals elected from various South Boston veterans groups. Every year since that time, the Council has applied for and received a permit for the parade, which at times has included as many as 20,000 marchers and drawn up to 1 million watchers. No other applicant has ever applied for that permit. Id., at B9. Through 1992, the city allowed the Council to use the city's official seal, and provided printing services as well as direct funding.

1992 was the year that a number of gay, lesbian, and bisexual descendants of the Irish immigrants joined together with other supporters to form the respondent organization, GLIB, to march in the parade as a way to express pride in their Irish heritage as openly gay, lesbian, and bisexual individuals, to demonstrate that there are such men and women among those so descended, and to express their solidarity with like individuals who sought to march in New York's St. Patrick's Day Parade. Id., at B3; App. 51. Although the Council denied GLIB's application to take part in the 1992 parade, GLIB obtained a state-court order to include its contingent, which marched "uneventfully" among that year's 10,000 participants and 750,000 spectators. App. to Pet. for Cert. B3, and n. 4.

In 1993, after the Council had again refused to admit GLIB to the upcoming parade, the organization and some of its members filed this suit against the Council, the individual petitioner John J. "Wacko" Hurley, and the City of Boston, alleging violations of the State and Federal Constitutions and of the state public accommodations law, which prohibits "any distinction, discrimination or restriction on account of . . . sexual orientation . . . relative to the admission of any person to, or treatment in any place of public accommodation, resort or amusement." Mass. Gen. Laws s272:98. After finding that "for at least the past 47 years, the Parade has traveled the same basic route along the public streets of South Boston, providing entertainment, amusement, and recreation to participants and spectators alike," App. to Pet. for Cert. B5-B6, the state trial court ruled that the parade fell within the statutory definition of a public accommodation, which includes "any place . . . which is open to and accepts or solicits the patronage of the general public and, without limiting the generality of this definition, whether or not it be . . . (6) a boardwalk or other public highway or . . . (8) a place of public amusement, recreation, sport, exercise or entertainment," Mass. Gen. Laws s272:92A. The court found that the Council had no written criteria and employed no particular procedures for admission, voted on new applications in batches, had occasionally admitted groups who simply showed up at the parade without having submitted an application, and did "not generally inquire into the specific messages or views of each applicant." App. to Pet. for Cert. B8- B9. The court consequently rejected the Council's contention that the parade was "private" (in the sense of being exclusive), holding instead that "the lack of genuine selectivity in choosing participants and sponsors demonstrates that the Parade is a public event."Id., at B6. It found the parade to be "eclectic," containing a wide variety of "patriotic, commercal, political, moral, artistic, religious, athletic, public service, trade union, and eleemosynary themes," as well as conflicting messages. Id., at B24. While noting that the Council had indeed excluded the Ku Klux Klan and ROAR (an antibusing group), id., at B7, it attributed little significance to these facts, concluding ultimately that "the only common theme among the participants and sponsors is their public involvement in the

Parade,"id., at B24.

The court rejected the Council's assertion that the exclusion of "groups with sexual themes merely formalized the fact that the Parade expresses traditional religious and social values,"id., at B3, and found the Council's "final position to be that GLIB would be excluded because of its values and its message, i.e., its members' sexual orientation,"id., at B4, n. 5, citing Tr. of Closing Arg. 43, 51-52 (Nov. 23, 1993). This position, in the court's view, was not only violative of the public accommodations law but "paradoxical" as well, since "a proper celebration of St. Patrick's and Evacuation Day requires diversity and inclusiveness." App. to Pet. for Cert. B24. The court rejected the notion that GLIB's admission would trample on the Council's First Amendment rights since the court understood that constitutional protection of any interest in expressive association would "require focus on a specific message, theme, or group" absent from the parade. Ibid. "Given the Council's lack of selectivity in choosing participants and failure to circumscribe the marchers' message," the court found it "impossible to discern any specific expressive purpose entitling the Parade to protection under the First Amendment."Id., at B25. It concluded that the parade is "not an exercise of the Council's constitutionally protected right of expressive association," but instead "an open recreational event that is subject to the public accommodations law."Id., at B27.

The court held that because the statute did not mandate inclusion of GLIB but only prohibited discrimination based on sexual orientation, any infringement on the Council's right to expressive association was only "incidental" and "no greater than necessary to accomplish the statute's legitimate purpose" of eradicating discrimination. Id., at B25, citing Roberts v. United States Jaycees, 468 U. S. 609, 628-629 (1984). Accordingly, it ruled that "GLIB is entitled to participate in the Parade on the same terms and conditions as other participants."Id., at B27.

The Supreme Judicial Court of Massachusetts affirmed. . . . .

Justice Nolan dissented. In his view, the Council "does not need a narrow or distinct theme or message in its parade for it to be protected under the First Amend ment."Id., at 256, 636 N. E. 2d, at 1303. First, he wrote, even if the parade had no message at all, GLIB's particular message could not be forced upon it. . . . . We granted certiorari to determine whether the requirement to admit a parade contingent expressing a message not of the private organizers' own choosing violates the First Amendment. 513 U. S. (1995). We hold that it does and reverse.

## III

### A

If there were no reason for a group of people to march from here to there except to reach a destination, they could make the trip without expressing any message beyond the fact of the march itself. Some people might call such a procession a parade, but it would not be much of one. Real "parades are public dramas of social relations, and in them performers define who can be a social actor and what subjects and ideas are available for communication and consideration." S. Davis, Parades and Power: Street Theatre in NineteenthCentury Philadelphia 6 (1986). Hence, we use the word "parade" to indicate marchers who are making some sort of collective point, not just to each other but to bystanders along the way. Indeed a parade's dependence on watchers is so extreme that nowadays, as with Bishop Berkeley's celebrated tree, "if a parade or demonstration receives no media coverage, it may as well not have happened."Id., at 171. Parades are thus a form of expression, not just motion, and the inherent expressiveness of marching to make a point explains our cases involving protest marches. In Gregory v. Chicago, 394 U. S. 111, 112 (1969), for example, petitioners had taken part in a procession to express their grievances to the city government, and we held that such a "march, if peaceful and orderly, falls well within the sphere of conduct protected by the First Amendment." Similarly, in Edwards v. South Carolina, 372 U. S. 229, 235 (1963), where petitioners had joined in a march of protest and pride, carrying placards and singing The Star Spangled Banner, we held that the activities "reflect an exercise of these basic constitutional rights in their most pristine and classic form." Accord, Shuttlesworth v. Birmingham, 394 U. S. 147, 152 (1969).

The protected expression that inheres in a parade is not limited to its banners and songs, however, for the Constitution looks beyond written or spoken words as mediums of expression. Noting that "symbolism is a primitive but effective way of communicating ideas,"West Virginia Bd. of Ed. v. Barnette, 319 U. S. 624, 632 (1943), our cases have recognized that the First Amendment shields such acts as saluting a flag (and refusing to do so), id., at 632, 642, wearing an arm band to protest a war, Tinker v. Des Moines Independent Community School Dist., 393 U. S. 503, 505-506 (1969), displaying a red flag, Stromberg v. California, 283 U. S. 359, 369 (1931), and even "marching, walking or parading" in uniforms displaying the swastika, National Socialist Party of America v. Skokie, 432 U. S. 43 (1977). As some of these examples show, a narrow, succinctly articulable message is not a condition of constitutional protection, which if confined to expressions conveying a "particularized message," cf. Spence v. Washington, 418 U. S. 405, 411 (1974) (per curiam), would never reach the unquestionably shielded painting of Jackson Pollock, music of Arnold Sch?nberg, or Jabberwocky verse of Lewis Carroll.

Not many marches, then, are beyond the realm of expressive parades, and the South Boston celebration is not one of them. Spectators line the streets; people march in costumes and uniforms, carrying flags and banners with all sorts of messages (e.g., "England get out of Ireland," "Say no to drugs"); marching bands and pipers play, floats are pulled along, and the whole show is broadcast over Boston television. See Record, Exh. 84 (video). To be sure, we agree with the state courts that in spite of excluding some applicants, the Council is rather lenient in admitting participants. But a private speaker does not forfeit constitutional protection simply by combining multifarious voices, or by failing to edit their themes to isolate an exact message as the exclusive subject matter of the speech. Nor, under our precedent, does First Amendment protection require a speaker to generate, as an original matter, each item featured in the communication. Cable operators, for example, are engaged in protected speech activities even when they only select programming originally produced by others. Turner Broadcasting System, Inc. v. FCC, 512 U. S. , (1994) (slip op., at 11) ("Cable programmers and cable operators engage in and transmit speech, and they are entitled to the protection of the speech and press provisions of the First Amendment"). For that matter, the presentation of an edited compilation of speech generated by other persons is a staple of most newspapers' opinion pages, which, of course, fall squarely within the core of First Amendment security, Miami Herald Publishing Co. v. Tornillo, 418 U. S. 241, 258 (1974), as does even the simple selection of a paid noncommercial advertisement for inclusion in a daily paper, see New York Times, 376 U. S., at 265-266. The selection of contingents to make a parade is entitled to similar protection.

Respondents' participation as a unit in the parade was equally expressive. GLIB was formed for the very purpose of marching in it, as the trial court found, in order to celebrate its members' identity as openly gay, lesbian, and bisexual descendants of the Irish immigrants, to show that there are such individuals in the community, and to support the like men and women who sought to march in the New York parade. App. to Pet. for Cert. B3. The organization distributed a fact sheet describing the members' intentions, App. A51, and the record otherwise corroborates the expressive nature of GLIB's participation, see Record, Exh. 84; App. A67 (photograph). In 1993, members of GLIB marched behind a shamrock-strewn banner with the simple inscription "Irish American Gay, Lesbian and Bisexual Group of Boston." GLIB understandably seeks to communicate its ideas as part of the existing parade, rather than staging one of its own.

B

The Massachusetts public accommodations law under which respondents brought suit has a venerable history. At common law, innkeepers, smiths, and others who "made profession of a public employment," were prohibited from refusing, without good reason, to serve a customer. . . . As one of the 19th century English judges put it, the rule was that "the innkeeper is not to select his guests; he has no right to say to one, you shall come into my inn, and to another you shall not, as every one coming and conducting himself in a proper manner has a right to be received; and for this purpose innkeepers are a sort of public servants." . . . .

After the Civil War, the Commonwealth of Massachusetts was the first State to codify this principle to ensure access to public accommodations regardless of race. . . . As with many public accommodations statutes across the Nation, the legislature continued to broaden the scope of legislation, to the point that the law today prohibits discrimination on the basis of "race, color, religious creed, national origin, sex, sexual orientation . . ., deafness, blindness or any physical or mental disability or ancestry" in "the admission of any person to, or treatment in any place of public accommodation, resort or amusement." . . . .

C

In the case before us, however, the Massachusetts law has been applied in a peculiar way. Its enforcement does not address any dispute about the participation of openly gay, lesbian, or bisexual individuals in various units admitted to the parade. The petitioners disclaim any intent to exclude homosexuals as such, and no individual member of GLIB claims to have been excluded from parading as a member of any group that the Council has approved to march. Instead, the disagreement goes to the admission of GLIB as its own parade unit carrying its own banner. See App. to Pet. for Cert. B26-B27, and n. 28. Since every participating unit affects the message conveyed by the private organizers, the state courts' application of the statute produced an order essentially requiring petitioners to alter the expressive content of their parade. Although the state courts spoke of the parade as a place of public accommodation, see, e.g., 418 Mass., at 247-248, 636 N. E. 2d, at 1297- 1298, once the expressive character of both the parade and the marching GLIB contingent is understood, it becomes apparent that the state courts' application of the statute had the effect of declaring the sponsors' speech itself to be the public accommodation. Under this approach any contingent of protected individuals with a message would have the right to participate in petitioners' speech, so that the communication produced by the private organizers would be shaped by all those protected by the law who wished to join in with some expressive demonstration of their own. But this use of the State's power violates the fundamental rule of protection under the First Amendment, that a speaker has the autonomy to choose the content of his own message. . . . .

Petitioners' claim to the benefit of this principle of autonomy to control one's own speech is as sound as the South Boston parade is expressive. Rather like a composer, the Council selects the expressive units of the parade from potential participants, and though the score may not produce a particularized message, each contingent's expression in the Council's eyes comports with what merits celebration on that day. Even if this view gives the Council credit for a more considered judgment than it actively made, the Council clearly decided to exclude a message it did not like from the communication it chose to make, and that is enough to invoke its right as a private speaker to shape its expression by speaking on one subject while remaining silent on another. The message it disfavored is not difficult to identify. Although GLIB's point (like the Council's) is not wholly articulate, a contingent marching behind the organization's banner would at least bear witness to the fact that some Irish are gay, lesbian, or bisexual, and the presence of the organized marchers would suggest their view that people of their sexual orientations have as much claim to unqualified social acceptance as heterosexuals and indeed as members of parade units organized around other identifying characteristics. The parade's organizers may not believe these facts about Irish sexuality to be so, or they may object to unqualified social acceptance of gays and lesbians or have some other reason for wishing to keep GLIB's message out of the parade. But whatever the reason, it boils down to the choice of a speaker not to propound a particular point of view, and that choice is presumed to lie beyond the government's power to control. . . . .

IV

Our holding today rests not on any particular view about the Council's message but on the Nation's commitment to protect freedom of speech. Disapproval of a private speaker's statement does not legitimize use of the Commonwealth's power to compel the speaker to alter the message by including one more acceptable to others. Accordingly, the judgment of the Supreme Judicial Court is reversed and the case remanded for proceedings not inconsistent with this opinion.

It is so ordered.

SIMON & SCHUSTER, INC., Petitioner

v.

MEMBERS OF THE NEW YORK STATE CRIME VICTIMS BOARD, et al.

502 U.S. 105

Supreme Court of the United States

Decided Dec. 10, 1991.

Justice Blackmun and Justice Kennedy issued opinions concurring in judgment.

Justice O'CONNOR delivered the opinion of the Court.

New York's "Son of Sam" law requires that an accused or convicted criminal's income from works describing his crime be deposited in an escrow account. These funds are then made available to the victims of the crime and the criminal's other creditors. We consider whether this statute is consistent with the First Amendment.

I

A

In the summer of 1977, New York was terrorized by a serial killer popularly known as the Son of Sam. The hunt for the Son of Sam received considerable publicity, and by the time David Berkowitz was identified as the killer and apprehended, the rights to his story were worth a substantial amount. Berkowitz's chance to profit from his notoriety while his victims and their families remained uncompensated did not escape the notice of New York's Legislature. The State quickly enacted the statute at issue, N.Y.Exec.Law § 632-a (McKinney 1982 and Supp.1991).

The statute was intended to "ensure that monies received by the criminal under such circumstances shall first be made available to recompense the victims of that crime for their loss and suffering." Assembly Bill Memorandum Re: A 9019, July 22, 1977, reprinted in Legislative Bill Jacket, 1977 N.Y.Laws, ch. 823. As the author of the statute explained: "It is abhorrent to one's sense of justice and decency that an individual ... can expect to receive large sums of money for his story once he is captured--while five people are dead, [and] other people were injured as a result of his conduct." Memorandum of Sen. Emanuel R. Gold, reprinted in New York State Legislative Annual, 1977, p. 267.

The Son of Sam law, as later amended, requires any entity contracting with an accused or convicted person for a depiction of the crime to submit a copy of the contract to respondent New York State Crime Victims Board (Board), and to turn over any income under that contract to the Board. This requirement applies to all such contracts in any medium of communication:

"Every person, firm, corporation, partnership, association or other legal entity contracting with any person or the representative or assignee of any person, accused or convicted of a crime in this state, with respect to the reenactment of such crime, by way of a movie, book, magazine article, tape recording, phonograph record, radio or television presentation, live entertainment of any kind, or from the expression of such accused or convicted person's thoughts, feelings, opinions or emotions regarding such crime, shall submit a copy of such contract to the board and pay over to the board any moneys which would otherwise, by terms of such contract, be owing to the person so accused or convicted or his representatives." N.Y.Exec.Law § 632- a(1) (McKinney 1982).

The Board is then required to deposit the payment in an escrow account "for the benefit of and payable to any victim ... provided that such victim, within five years of the date of the establishment of such escrow account, brings a civil action in a court of competent jurisdiction and recovers a money judgment for damages against such [accused or convicted] person or his representatives." Ibid. After five years, if no actions are pending, "the board shall immediately pay over any moneys in the escrow account to such person or his legal representatives." § 632-a(4). This 5-year period in which to bring a civil action against the convicted person begins to run when the escrow account is established, and supersedes any limitations period that expires earlier. § 632-a(7).

Subsection (8) grants priority to two classes of claims against the escrow account. First, upon a court order, the Board must release assets "for the exclusive purpose of retaining legal representation." § 632-a(8). In addition, the Board has the discretion, after giving notice to the victims of the crime, to "make payments from the escrow account to a representative of any person accused or convicted of a crime for the necessary expenses of the production of the moneys paid into the escrow account." Ibid. This provision permits payments to literary agents and other such representatives. Payments under subsection (8) may not exceed one-fifth of the amount collected in the account. Ibid.

Claims against the account are given the following priorities: (a) payments ordered by the Board under subsection (8); (b) subrogation claims of the State for payments made to victims of the crime; (c) civil judgments obtained by victims of the crime; and (d) claims of other creditors of the accused or convicted person, including state and local tax authorities. N.Y.Exec.Law § 632-a(11) (McKinney Supp.1991).

Subsection (10) broadly defines "person convicted of a crime" to include "any person convicted of a crime in this state either by entry of a plea of guilty or by conviction after trial and any person who has voluntarily and intelligently admitted the commission of a crime for which such person is not prosecuted." § 632-a(10)(b) (emphasis added). Thus a person who has never been accused or convicted of a crime in the ordinary sense, but who admits in a book or other work to having committed a crime, is within the statute's coverage.

As recently construed by the New York Court of Appeals, however, the statute does not apply to victimless crimes. Children of Bedford, Inc. v. Petromelis, 77 N.Y.2d 713, 726 ...

The Son of Sam law supplements pre-existing statutory schemes authorizing the Board to compensate crime victims for their losses, see N.Y.Exec.Law § 631 (McKinney 1982 and Supp.1991), permitting courts to order the proceeds of crime forfeited to the State, see N.Y.Civ.Prac.Law §§ 1310- 1352 (McKinney Supp.1991), providing for orders of restitution at sentencing, N.Y.Penal Law § 60.27 (McKinney 1987), and affording prejudgment attachment procedures to ensure that wrongdoers do not dissipate their assets, N.Y.Civ.Prac.Law §§ 6201-6226 (McKinney 1980 and Supp.1991). The escrow arrangement established by the Son of Sam law enhances these provisions only insofar as the accused or convicted person earns income within the scope of § 632-a(1).

Since its enactment in 1977, the Son of Sam law has been invoked only a handful of times. As might be expected, the individuals whose profits the Board has sought to escrow have all become well known for having committed highly publicized crimes. These include Jean Harris, the convicted killer of "Scarsdale Diet" Doctor Herman Tarnower; Mark David Chapman, the man convicted of assassinating John Lennon; and R. Foster Winans, the former Wall Street Journal columnist convicted of insider trading. Ironically, the statute was never applied to the Son of Sam himself; David Berkowitz was found incompetent to stand trial, and the statute at that time applied only to criminals who had actually been convicted. N.Y.Times, Feb. 20, 1991, p. B8, col. 4. According to the Board, Berkowitz voluntarily paid his share of the royalties from the book Son of Sam, published in 1981, to his victims or their estates. Brief for Respondents 8, n. 13.

This case began in 1986, when the Board first became aware of the contract between petitioner Simon & Schuster and admitted organized crime figure Henry Hill.

B

Looking back from the safety of the Federal Witness Protection Program, Henry Hill recalled: "At the age of twelve my ambition was to be a gangster. To be a wiseguy. To me being a wiseguy was better than being president of the United States." N. Pileggi, Wiseguy: Life in a Mafia Family 19 (1985) (hereinafter Wiseguy). Whatever one might think of Hill, at the very least it can be said that he realized his dreams. After a career spanning 25 years, Hill admitted engineering some of the most daring crimes of his day, including the 1978-1979 Boston College basketball point-shaving scandal, and the theft of $6 million from Lufthansa Airlines in 1978, the largest successful cash robbery in American history. Wiseguy 9. Most of Hill's crimes were more banausic: He committed extortion, he imported and distributed narcotics, and he organized numerous robberies.

Hill was arrested in 1980. In exchange for immunity from prosecution, he testified against many of his former colleagues. Since his arrest, he has lived under an assumed name in an unknown part of the country.

In August 1981, Hill entered into a contract with author Nicholas Pileggi for the production of a book about Hill's life. The following month, Hill and Pileggi signed a publishing agreement with Simon & Schuster, Inc. Under the agreement, Simon & Schuster agreed to make payments to both Hill and Pileggi. Over the next few years, according to Pileggi, he and Hill "talked at length virtually every single day, with not more than an occasional Sunday or holiday skipped. We spent more than three hundred hours together; my notes of conversations with Henry occupy more than six linear file feet." App. 27. Because producing the book required such a substantial investment of time and effort, Hill sought compensation. Ibid.
The result of Hill and Pileggi's collaboration was Wiseguy, which was published in January 1986. The book depicts, in colorful detail, the day-to- day existence of organized crime, primarily in Hill's first-person narrative. Throughout Wiseguy, Hill frankly admits to having participated in an astonishing variety of crimes. He discusses, among other things, his conviction of extortion and the prison sentence he served. . . .

From Henry Hill's perspective, however, the publicity generated by the book's success proved less desirable. The Crime Victims Board learned of Wiseguy in January 1986, soon after it was published.

C

On January 31, the Board notified Simon & Schuster: "It has come to our attention that you may have contracted with a person accused or convicted of a crime for the payment of monies to such person." App. 86. The Board ordered Simon & Schuster to furnish copies of any contracts it had entered into with Hill, to provide the dollar amounts and dates of all payments it had made to Hill, and to suspend all payments to Hill in the future. Simon & Schuster complied with this order. By that time, Simon & Schuster had paid Hill's literary agent $96,250 in advances and royalties on Hill's behalf, and was holding $27,958 for eventual payment to Hill.

The Board reviewed the book and the contract, and on May 21, 1987, issued a proposed determination and order. The Board determined that Wiseguy was covered by § 632-a of the Executive Law, that Simon & Schuster had violated the law by failing to turn over its contract with Hill to the Board and by making payments to Hill, and that all money owed to Hill under the contract had to be turned over to the Board to be held in escrow for the victims of Hill's crimes. The Board ordered Hill to turn over the payments he had already received, and ordered Simon & Schuster to turn over all money payable to Hill at the time or in the future.

Simon & Schuster brought suit in August 1987, under 42 U.S.C. § 1983, seeking a declaration that the Son of Sam law violates the First Amendment and an injunction barring the statute's enforcement. After the parties filed cross-motions for summary judgment, the District Court found the statute to be consistent with the First Amendment. 724 F.Supp. 170 (SDNY 1989). A divided Court of Appeals affirmed. Simon & Schuster, Inc. v. Fischetti, 916 F.2d 777 (CA2 1990).

Because the Federal Government and most of the States have enacted statutes with similar objectives, see 18 U.S.C. § 3681; Note, Simon & Schuster, Inc. v. Fischetti: Can New York's Son of Sam Law Survive First Amendment Challenge?, 66 Notre Dame L.Rev. 1075, n. 6 (1991) (listing state statutes), the issue is significant and likely to recur. We accordingly granted certiorari, 498 U.S. 1081, 111 S.Ct. 950, 112 L.Ed.2d 1039 (1991), and we now reverse.

II

A

A statute is presumptively inconsistent with the First Amendment if it imposes a financial burden on speakers because of the content of their speech. Leathers v. Medlock, 499 U.S. 439, 447, 111 S.Ct. 1438, 1443-1444, 113 L.Ed.2d 494 (1991). As we emphasized in invalidating a content-based magazine tax: "[O]fficial scrutiny of the content of publications as the basis for imposing a tax is entirely incompatible with the First Amendment's guarantee of freedom of the press." Arkansas Writers' Project, Inc. v. Ragland, 481 U.S. 221, 230, 107 S.Ct. 1722, 1728, 95 L.Ed.2d 209 (1987).

This is a notion so engrained in our First Amendment jurisprudence that last Term we found it so "obvious" as to not require explanation. Leathers, supra, 499 U.S., at 447, 111 S.Ct., at 1444. It is but one manifestation of a far broader principle: "Regulations which permit the Government to discriminate on the basis of the content of the message cannot be tolerated under the First Amendment." Regan v. Time, Inc., 468 U.S. 641, 648-649, 104 S.Ct. 3262, 3266-3267, 82 L.Ed.2d 487 (1984). See also Police Dept. of Chicago v. Mosley, 408 U.S. 92, 95, 92 S.Ct. 2286, 2289, 33 L.Ed.2d 212 (1972). In the context of financial regulation, it bears repeating, as we did in Leathers, that the government's ability to impose content-based burdens on speech raises the specter that the government may effectively drive certain ideas or viewpoints from the marketplace. 499 U.S., at 448-449, 111 S.Ct., at 1444-1445. The First Amendment presumptively places this sort of discrimination beyond the power of the government. As we reiterated in Leathers: " 'The constitutional right of free expression is ... intended to remove governmental restraints from the arena of public discussion, putting the decision as to what views shall be voiced largely into the hands of each of us ... in the belief that no other approach would comport with the premise of individual dignity and choice upon which our political system rests.' " Id., at 448-449, 111 S.Ct., at 1444-1445 (quoting Cohen v. California, 403 U.S. 15, 24, 91 S.Ct. 1780, 1787, 29 L.Ed.2d 284 (1971)).

The Son of Sam law is such a content-based statute. It singles out income derived from expressive activity for a burden the State places on no other income, and it is directed only at works with a specified content. Whether the First Amendment "speaker" is considered to be Henry Hill, whose income the statute places in escrow because of the story he has told, or Simon & Schuster, which can publish books about crime with the assistance of only those criminals willing to forgo remuneration for at least five years, the statute plainly imposes a financial disincentive only on speech of a particular content. . . . .

. . . . The Son of Sam law establishes a financial disincentive to create or publish works with a particular content. In order to justify such differential treatment, "the State must show that its regulation is necessary to serve a compelling state interest and is narrowly drawn to achieve that end." Arkansas Writers' Project, 481 U.S., at 231, 107 S.Ct., at 1728 . . . .

. . . . There can be little doubt, on the other hand, that the State has a compelling interest in ensuring that victims of crime are compensated by those who harm them. Every State has a body of tort law serving exactly this interest. The State's interest in preventing wrongdoers from dissipating their assets before victims can recover explains the existence of the State's statutory provisions for prejudgment remedies and orders of restitution.

. . . . The State likewise has an undisputed compelling interest in ensuring that criminals do not profit from their crimes. Like most if not all States, New York has long recognized the "fundamental equitable principle," Children of Bedford v. Petromelis, 77 N.Y.2d, at 727, 570 N.Y.S.2d, at 460, 573 N.E.2d, at 548, that "[n]o one shall be permitted to profit by his own fraud, or to take advantage of his own wrong, or to found any claim upon his own iniquity, or to acquire property by his own crime." . . . .

. . . . As a means of ensuring that victims are compensated from the proceeds of crime, the Son of Sam law is significantly overinclusive. As counsel for the Board conceded at oral argument, the statute applies to works on any subject, provided that they express the author's thoughts or recollections about his crime, however tangentially or incidentally. See Tr. of Oral Arg. 30, 38; see also App. 109. In addition, the statute's broad definition of "person convicted of a crime" enables the Board to escrow the income of any author who admits in his work to having committed a crime, whether or not the author was ever actually accused or convicted. § 632-a(10)(b).

These two provisions combine to encompass a potentially very large number of works. Had the Son of Sam law been in effect at the time and place of publication, it would have escrowed payment for such works as The Autobiography of Malcolm X, which describes crimes committed by the civil rights leader before he became a public figure; Civil Disobedience, in which Thoreau acknowledges his refusal to pay taxes and recalls his experience in jail; and even the Confessions of Saint Augustine, in which the author laments "my past foulness and the carnal corruptions of my soul," one instance of which involved the theft of pears from a neighboring vineyard. See A. Haley & Malcolm X, The Autobiography of Malcolm X 108-125 (1964); H. Thoreau, Civil Disobedience 18-22 (1849, reprinted 1969); The Confessions of Saint Augustine

31, 36-37 (Franklin Library ed. 1980). Amicus Association of American Publishers, Inc., has submitted a sobering bibliography listing hundreds of works by American prisoners and ex-prisoners, many of which contain descriptions of the crimes for which the authors were incarcerated, including works by such authors as Emma Goldman and Martin Luther King, Jr. A list of prominent figures whose autobiographies would be subject to the statute if written is not difficult to construct: The list could include Sir Walter Raleigh, who was convicted of treason after a dubiously conducted 1603 trial; Jesse Jackson, who was arrested in 1963 for trespass and resisting arrest after attempting to be served at a lunch counter in North Carolina; and Bertrand Russell, who was jailed for seven days at the age of 89 for participating in a sit-down protest against nuclear weapons. The argument that a statute like the Son of Sam law would prevent publication of all of these works is hyperbole-- some would have been written without compensation--but the Son of Sam law clearly reaches a wide range of literature that does not enable a criminal to profit from his crime while a victim remains uncompensated.

Should a prominent figure write his autobiography at the end of his career, and include in an early chapter a brief recollection of having stolen (in New York) a nearly worthless item as a youthful prank, the Board would control his entire income from the book for five years, and would make that income available to all of the author's creditors, despite the fact that the statute of limitations for this minor incident had long since run. That the Son of Sam law can produce such an outcome indicates that the statute is, to say the least, not narrowly tailored to achieve the State's objective of compensating crime victims from the profits of crime.

III

The Federal Government and many of the States have enacted statutes designed to serve purposes similar to that served by the Son of Sam law. Some of these statutes may be quite different from New York's, and we have no occasion to determine the constitutionality of these other laws. We conclude simply that in the Son of Sam law, New York has singled out speech on a particular subject for a financial burden that it places on no other speech and no other income. The State's interest in compensating victims from the fruits of crime is a compelling one, but the Son of Sam law is not narrowly tailored to advance that objective. As a result, the statute is inconsistent with the First Amendment.

The judgment of the Court of Appeals is accordingly

Reversed.

Justice THOMAS took no part in the consideration or decision of this case.

Paul Robert COHEN, Appellant,
v.
State of CALIFORNIA.

403 U.S. 15

Supreme Court of the United States

Decided June 7, 1971.

Mr. Justice Blackmun, dissented and filed an opinion in which Mr. Chief Justice Burger, and Mr. Justice Black joined and in which Mr. Justice White joined in part.

Mr. Justice HARLAN delivered the opinion of the Court.

This case may seem at first blush too inconsequential to find its way into our books, but the issue it presents is of no small constitutional significance.

Appellant Paul Robert Cohen was convicted in the Los Angeles Municipal Court of violating that part of California Penal Code s 415 which prohibits 'maliciously and willfully disturb(ing) the peace or quiet of any neighborhood or person * * * by * * * offensive conduct * * *.' 1 He was given 30 days' imprisonment. The facts upon which his conviction rests are detailed in the opinion of the Court of Appeal of California, Second Appellate District, as follows:

> (footnote)1. The statute provides in full:
> 'Every person who maliciously and willfully disturbs the peace or quiet of any neighborhood or person, by loud or unusual noise, or by tumultuous or offensive conduct, or threatening, traducing, quarreling, challenging to fight, or fighting, or who, on the public streets of any unincorporated town, or upon the public highways in such unincorporated town, run any horse race, either for a wager of for amusement, or fire any gun or pistol in such unincorporated town, or use any vulgar, profane, or indecent language within the presence or hearing of women or children, in a loud and boisterous manner, is guilty of a misdemeanor, and upon conviction by any Court of competent jurisdiction shall be punished by fine not exceedingtwo hundred dollars, or by imprisonment in the County Jail for not more than ninety days, or by both fine and imprisonment, or either, at the discretion of the Court.'

'On April 26, 1968, the defendant was observed in the Los Angeles County Courthouse in the corridor outside of division 20 of the municipal court wearing a jacket bearing the words 'Fuck the Draft' which were plainly visible. There were women and children present in the corridor. The defendant was arrested. The defendant testified that he wore the jacket knowing that the words were on the jacket as a means of informing the public of the depth of his feelings against the Vietnam War and the draft.

'The defendant did not engage in, nor threaten to engagein, nor did anyone as the result of his conduct in fact commit or threaten to commit any act of violence. The defendant did not make any loud or unusual noise, nor was there any evidence that he uttered any sound prior to his arrest.' 1 Cal.App.3d 94, 97--98, 81 Cal.Rptr. 503, 505 (1969).

In affirming the conviction the Court of Appeal held that 'offensive conduct' means 'behavior which has a tendency to provoke others to acts of violence or to in turn disturb the peace,' and that the State had proved this element because, on the facts of this case, '(i)t was certainly reasonably foreseeable that such conduct might cause others to rise up to commit a violent act against the person of the defendant or attempt to forceably remove his jacket.' 1 Cal.App.3d, at 99--100, 81 Cal.Rptr., at 506. The California Supreme Court declined review by a divided vote . . . .

I

In order to lay hands on the precise issue which this case involves, it is useful first to canvass various matters which this record does not present.

The conviction quite clearly rests upon the asserted offensiveness of the words Cohen used to convey his message to the public. The only 'conduct' which the State sought to punish is the fact of communication. Thus, we deal here with a conviction resting solely upon 'speech,' cf. Stromberg v. California, 283 U.S. 359, 51 S.Ct. 532, 75 L.Ed. 1117 (1931), not upon any separately identifiable conduct which allegedly was intended by Cohen to be perceived by others as expressive of particular views but which, on its face, does not necessarily convey any message and hence arguably could be regulated without effectively repressing Cohen's ability to express himself. Cf. United States v. O'Brien, 391 U.S. 367, 88 S.Ct. 1673, 20 L.Ed.2d 672 (1968). Further, the State certainly lacks power to punish Cohen for the underlying content of the message the inscription conveyed. At least so long as there is no showing of an intent to incite disobedience to or disruption of the draft, Cohen could not, consistently with the First and Fourteenth Amendments, be punished for asserting the evident position on the inutility or immorality of the draft his jacket reflected. Yates v. United States, 354 U.S. 298, 77 S.Ct. 1064, 1 L.Ed.2d 1356 (1957).

Appellant's conviction, then, rests squarely upon his exercise of the 'freedom of speech' protected from arbitrary governmental interference by the Constitution and can be justified, if at all, only as a valid regulation of the manner in which he exercised that freedom, not as a permissible prohibition on the substantive message it conveys. This does not end the inquiry, of course, for the First and Fourteenth Amendments have never been thought to give absolute protection to every individual to speak whenever or wherever he pleases or to use any form of address in any circumstances that he chooses. In this vein, too, however, we think it important to note that several issues typically associated with such problems are not presented here.

In the first place, Cohen was tried under a statute applicable throughout the entire State. Any attempt to support this conviction on the ground that the statute seeks to preserve an appropriately decorous atmosphere in the courthouse where Cohen was arrested must fail in the absence of any language in the statute that would have put appellant on notice that certain kinds of otherwise permissible speech or conduct would nevertheless, under California law, not be tolerated in certain places. See Edwards v. South Carolina, 372 U.S. 229, 236--237, 83 S.Ct. 680, 683--684, 9 L.Ed.2d 697, and n. 11 (1963). Cf. Adderley v. Florida, 385 U.S. 39, 87 S.Ct. 242, 17 L.Ed.2d 149 (1966). No fair reading of the phrase 'offensive conduct' can be said sufficiently to inform the ordinary person that distinctions between certain locations are thereby created. 3

(footnote)3. It is illuminatingto note what transpired when Cohen entered a courtroom in the building. He removed his jacket and stood with it folder over his arm. Meanwhile, a policeman sent the presiding judge a note suggestingthat Cohen be held in contempt of court. The judge declined to do so and Cohen was arrested by the officer only after he emerged from the courtroom. App. 18--19.

In the second place, as it comes to us, this case cannot be said to fall within those relatively few categories of instances where prior decisions have established the power of government to deal more comprehensively with certain forms of individual expression simply upon a showing that such a form was employed. This is not, for example, an obscenity case. Whatever else may be necessary to give rise to the States' broader power to prohibit obscene expression, such expression must be, in some significant way, erotic. Roth v. United States, 354 U.S. 476, 77 S.Ct. 1304, 1 L.Ed.2d 1498 (1957). It cannot plausibly be maintained that this vulgar allusion to the Selective Service System would conjure up such psychic stimulation in anyone likely to be confronted with Cohen's crudely defaced jacket.

This Court has also held that the States are free to ban the simple use, without a demonstration of additional justifying circumstances, of so-called 'fighting words,' those personally abusive epithets which, when addressed to the ordinary citizen, are, as a matter of common knowledge, inherently likely to provoke violent reaction. Chaplinsky v. New Hampshire, 315 U.S. 568, 62 S.Ct. 766, 86 L.Ed. 1031 (1942). While the four-letter word displayed by Cohen in relation to the draft is not uncommonly employed in a personally provocative fashion, in this instance it was clearly not 'directed to the person of the hearer.' Cantwell v. Connecticut, 310 U.S. 296, 309, 60 S.Ct. 900, 906, 84 L.Ed. 1213 (1940). No individual actually or likely to be present could reasonably have regarded the words on appellant's jacket as a direct personal insult. Nor do we have here an instance of the exercise of the State's police power to prevent a speaker from intentionally provoking a given group to hostile reaction. Cf. Feiner v. New York, 340 U.S. 315, 71 S.Ct. 303, 95 L.Ed. 295 (1951); Terminiello v. Chicago, 337 U.S. 1, 69 S.Ct. 894, 93 L.Ed. 1131 (1949). There is, as noted above, no showing that anyone who saw Cohen was in fact violently aroused or that appellant intended such a result.

Finally, in arguments before this Court much has been made of the claim that Cohen's distasteful mode of expression was thrust upon unwilling or unsuspecting viewers, and that the State might therefore legitimately act as it did in order to protect the sensitive from otherwise unavoidable exposure to appellant's crude form of protest. Of course, the mere presumed presence of unwitting listeners or viewers does not serve automatically to justify curtailing all speech capable of giving offense. See, e.g., Organization for a Better Austin v. Keefe, 402 U.S. 415, 91 S.Ct. 1575, 29 L.Ed.2d 1 (1971). While this Court has recognized that government may properly act in many situations to prohibit intrusion into the privacy of the home of unwelcome views and ideas which cannot be totally banned from the public dialogue, e.g., Rowan v. United States Post Office Dept., 397 U.S. 728, 90 S.Ct. 1484, 25 L.Ed.2d 736 (1970), we have at the same time consistently stressed that 'we are often 'captives' outside the sanctuary of the home and subject to objectionable speech.' Id., at 738, 90 S.Ct., at 1491. The ability of government, consonant with the Constitution, to shut off discourse solely to protect others from hearing it is, in other words, dependent upon a showing that substantial privacy interests are being invaded in an essentially intolerable manner. Any broader view of this authority would effectively empower a majority to silence dissidents simply as a matter of personal predilections.

In this regard, persons confronted with Cohen's jacket were in a quite different posture than, say, those subjected to the raucous emissions of sound trucks blaring outside their residences. Those in the Los Angeles courthouse could effectively avoid further bombardment of their sensibilities simply by averting their eyes. And, while it may be that one has a more substantial claim to a recognizable privacy interest when walking through a courthouse corridor than, for example, strolling through Central Park, surely it is nothing like the interest in being free from unwanted expression in the confines of one's own home. Cf. Keefe, supra. Given the subtlety and complexity of the factors involved, if Cohen's 'speech' was otherwise entitled to constitutional protection, we do not think the fact that some unwilling 'listeners' in a public building may have been briefly exposed to it can serve to justify this breach of the peace conviction where, as here, there was no evidence that persons powerless to avoid appellant's conduct did in fact object to it, and where that portion of the statute upon which Cohen's conviction rests evinces no concern, either on its face or as construed by the California courts, with the special plight of the captive auditor, but, instead, indiscriminately sweeps within its prohibitions all 'offensive conduct' that disturbs 'any neighborhood or person.' Cf. Edwards v. South Carolina, supra.

## II

Against this background, the issue flushed by this case stands out in bold relief. It is whether California can excise, as 'offensive conduct,' one particular scurrilous epithet from the public discourse, either upon the theory of the court below that its use is inherently likely to cause violent reaction or upon a more general assertion that the States, acting as guardians of public morality, may properly remove this offensive word from the public vocabulary.

The rationale of the California court is plainly untenable. At most it reflects an 'undifferentiated fear or apprehension of disturbance (which) is not enough to overcome the right to freedom of expression.' Tinker v. Des Moines Indep. Community School Dist., 393 U.S. 503, 508, 89 S.Ct. 733, 737, 21 L.Ed.2d 731 (1969). We have been shown no evidence that substantial numbers of citizens are standing ready to strike out physically at whoever may assault their sensibilities with execrations like that uttered by Cohen . . . .

Against this perception of the constitutional policies involved, we discern certain more particularized considerations that peculiarly call for reversal of this conviction. First, the principle contended for by the State seems inherently boundless. How is one to distinguish this from any other offensive word? Surely the State has no right to cleanse public debate to the point where it is grammatically palatable to the most squeamish among us. Yet no readily ascertainable general principle exists for stopping short of that result were we to affirm the judgment below. For, while the particular four-letter word being litigated here is perhaps more distasteful than most others of its genre, it is nevertheless often true that one man's vulgarity is another's lyric. Indeed, we think it is largely because governmental officials cannot make principled distinctions in this area that the Constitution leaves matters of taste and style so largely to the individual.

Additionally, we cannot overlook the fact, because it is well illustrated by the episode involved here, that much linguistic expression serves a dual communicative function: it conveys not only ideas capable of relatively precise, detached explication, but otherwise inexpressible emotions as well. In fact, words are often chosen as much for their emotive as their cognitive force. We cannot sanction the view that the Constitution, while solicitous of the cognitive content of individual speech has little or no regard for that emotive function which practically speaking, may often be the more important element of the overall message sought to be communicated. Indeed, as Mr. Justice Frankfurter has said, '(o)ne of the prerogatives of American citizenship is the right to criticize public men and measures--and that means not only informed and responsible criticism but the freedom to speak foolishly and without moderation.' Baumgartner v. United States...

Finally, and in the same vein, we cannot indulge the facile assumption that one can forbid particular words without also running a substantial risk of suppressing ideas in the process. Indeed, governments might soon seize upon the censorship of particular words as a convenient guise for banning the expression of unpopular views. We have been able, as noted above, to discern little social benefit that might result from running the risk of opening the door to such grave results.

It is, in sum, our judgment that, absent a more particularized and compelling reason for its actions, the State may not, consistently with the First and Fourteenth Amendments, make the simple public display here involved of this single four-letter expletive a criminal offense. Because that is the only arguably sustainable rationale for the conviction here at issue, the judgment below must be reversed.

Reversed.

Mr. Justice BLACKMUN, with whom THE CHIEF JUSTICE and Mr. Justice BLACK join.

I dissent . . . .

1. Cohen's absurd and immature antic, in my view, was mainly conduct and little speech . . . . The California Court of Appeal appears so to have described it, 1 Cal.App.3d 94, 100, 81 Cal.Rptr 503, 507, and I cannot characterize it otherwise. Further, the case appears to me to be well within the sphere of Chaplinsky v. New Hampshire, 315 U.S. 568, 62 S.Ct. 766, 86 L.Ed. 1031 (1942), where Mr. Justice Murphy, a known champion of First Amendment freedoms, wrote for a unanimous bench. As a consequence, this Court's agonizing over First Amendment values seem misplaced and unnecessary . . . .

The VILLAGE OF SKOKIE, Appellee,
v.
The NATIONAL SOCIALIST PARTY OF AMERICA et al., Appellants.

373 N.E.2d 21.

Supreme Court of Illinois.

Jan. 27, 1978.

Clark, J., dissented.

PER CURIAM:

Plaintiff, the village of Skokie, filed a complaint in the circuit court of Cook County seeking to enjoin defendants, the National Socialist Party of America (the American Nazi Party) and 10 individuals as "officers and members" of the party, from engaging in certain activities while conducting a demonstration within the village. The circuit court issued an order enjoining certain conduct during the planned demonstration. The appellate court modified the injunction order, and, as modified, defendants are enjoined from "(i) ntentionally displaying the swastika on or off their persons, in the course of a demonstration, march, or parade." (51 Ill.App.3d 279, 295, 9 Ill.Dec. 90, 100, 366 N.E.2d 347, 357.) We allowed defendants' petition for leave to appeal.

The pleadings and the facts adduced at the hearing are fully set forth in the appellate court opinion, and only those matters necessary to the discussion of the issues will be repeated here. The facts are not disputed.

It is alleged in plaintiff's complaint that the "uniform of the National Socialist Party of America consists of the storm trooper uniform of the German Nazi Party embellished with the Nazi swastika"; that the plaintiff village has a population of about 70,000 persons of which approximately 40,500 persons are of "Jewish religion or Jewish ancestry" and of this latter number 5,000 to 7,000 are survivors of German concentration camps; that the defendant organization is "dedicated to the incitation of racial and religious hatred directed principally against individuals of Jewish faith or ancestry and non- Caucasians"; and that its members "have patterned their conduct, their uniform, their slogan and their tactics along the pattern of the German Nazi Party * * *."

Defendants moved to dismiss the complaint. In an affidavit attached to defendants' motion to dismiss, defendant Frank Collin, who testified that he was "party leader," stated that on or about March 20, 1977, he sent officials of the plaintiff village a letter stating that the party members and supporters would hold a peaceable, public assembly in the village on May 1, 1977, to protest the Skokie Park District's requirement that the party procure $350,000 of insurance prior to the party's use of the Skokie public parks for public assemblies. The demonstration was to begin at 3 p. m., last 20 to 30 minutes, and consist of 30 to 50 demonstrators marching in single file, back and forth, in front of the village hall. The marchers were to wear uniforms which include a swastika emblem or armband. They were to carry a party banner containing a swastika emblem and signs containing such statements as "White Free Speech," "Free Speech for the White Man," and "Free Speech for White America." The demonstrators would not distribute handbills, make any derogatory statements directed to any ethnic or religious group, or obstruct traffic. They would cooperate with any reasonable police instructions or requests.

At the hearing on plaintiff's motion for an "emergency injunction" a resident of Skokie testified that he was a survivor of the Nazi holocaust. He further testified that the Jewish community in and around Skokie feels the purpose of the march in the "heart of the Jewish population" is to remind the two million survivors "that we are not through with you" and to show "that the Nazi threat is not over, it can happen again." Another resident of Skokie testified that as the result of defendants' announced intention to march in Skokie, 15 to 18 Jewish organizations, within the village and surrounding area, were called and a counterdemonstration of an estimated 12,000 to 15,000 people was scheduled for the same day. There was opinion evidence that defendants' planned demonstration in Skokie would result in violence.

The circuit court entered an order enjoining defendants from "marching, walking or parading in the uniform of the National Socialist Party of America; marching, walking or parading or otherwise displaying the swastika on or off their person; distributing pamphlets or displaying any materials which incite or promote hatred against persons of Jewish faith or ancestry or hatred against persons of any faith or ancestry, race or religion" within the village of Skokie. The appellate court, as earlier noted, modified the order so that defendants were enjoined only from intentional display of the swastika during the Skokie demonstration.

The appellate court opinion adequately discussed and properly decided those issues arising from the portions of the injunction order which enjoined defendants from marching, walking, or parading, from distributing pamphlets or displaying materials, and from wearing the uniform of the National Socialist Party of America. The only issue remaining before this court is whether the circuit court order enjoining defendants from displaying the swastika violates the first amendment rights of those defendants.

In defining the constitutional rights of the parties who come before this court, we are, of course, bound by the pronouncements of the United States Supreme Court in its interpretation of the

United States Constitution. (Ableman v. Booth (1859), 62 U.S. (21 How.) 506, 16 L.Ed. 169; Cooper v. Aaron (1958), 358 U.S. 1, 78 S.Ct. 1401, 3 L.Ed.2d 5.) The decisions of that court, particularly Cohen v. California (1971), 403 U.S. 15, 91 S.Ct. 1780, 29 L.Ed.2d 284, in our opinion compel us to permit the demonstration as proposed, including display of the swastika.

"It is firmly settled that under our Constitution the public expression of ideas may not be prohibited merely because the ideas are themselves offensive to some of their hearers" (Bachellar v. Maryland (1970), 397 U.S. 564, 567, 90 S.Ct. 1312, 1315, 25 L.Ed.2d 570, 574), and it is entirely clear that the wearing of distinctive clothing can be symbolic expression of a thought or philosophy. The symbolic expression of thought falls within the free speech clause of the first amendment (Tinker v. Des Moines Independent Community School District (1969), 393 U.S. 503, 89 S.Ct. 733, 21 L.Ed.2d 731), and the plaintiff village has the heavy burden of justifying the imposition of a prior restraint upon defendants' right to freedom of speech (Carroll v. President of Princess Anne County (1968), 393 U.S. 175...

The village of Skokie seeks to meet this burden by application of the "fighting words" doctrine first enunciated in Chaplinsky v. New Hampshire (1942), 315 U.S. 568, 62 S.Ct. 766, 86 L.Ed. 1031. That doctrine was designed to permit punishment of extremely hostile personal communication likely to cause immediate physical response, "no words being 'forbidden except such as have a direct tendency to cause acts of violence by the persons to whom, individually, the remark is addressed.' " (315 U.S. 568, 573, 62 S.Ct. 766, 770, 86 L.Ed. 1031, 1036.) In Cohen the Supreme Court restated the description of fighting words as "those personally abusive epithets which, when addressed to the ordinary citizen, are, as a matter of common knowledge, inherently likely to provoke violent reaction." (403 U.S. 15, 20, 91 S.Ct. 1780, 1785, 29 L.Ed.2d 284, 291.) Plaintiff urges, and the appellate court has held, that the exhibition of the Nazi symbol, the swastika, addresses to ordinary citizens a message which is tantamount to fighting words. Plaintiff further asks this court to extend Chaplinsky, which upheld a statute punishing the use of such words, and hold that the fighting-words doctrine permits a prior restraint on defendants' symbolic speech. In our judgment we are precluded from doing so.

In Cohen, defendant's conviction stemmed from wearing a jacket bearing the words "Fuck the Draft" in a Los Angeles County courthouse corridor. The Supreme Court for reasons we believe applicable here refused to find that the jacket inscription constituted fighting words . . . .

The display of the swastika, as offensive to the principles of a free nation as the memories it recalls may be, is symbolic political speech intended to convey to the public the beliefs of those who display it. It does not, in our opinion, fall within the definition of "fighting words," and that doctrine cannot be used here to overcome the heavy presumption against the constitutional validity of a prior restraint.

Nor can we find that the swastika, while not representing fighting words, is nevertheless so offensive and peace threatening to the public that its display can be enjoined. We do not doubt that the sight of this symbol is abhorrent to the Jewish citizens of Skokie, and that the survivors of the Nazi persecutions, tormented by their recollections, may have strong feelings regardingits display. Yet it is entirely clear that this factor does not justify enjoining defendants' speech . . . .

In summary, as we read the controlling Supreme Court opinions, use of the swastika is a symbolic form of free speech entitled to first amendment protections. Its display on uniforms or banners by those engaged in peaceful demonstrations cannot be totally precluded solely because that display may provoke a violent reaction by those who view it. Particularly is this true where, as here, there has been advance notice by the demonstrators of their plans so that they have become, as the complaint alleges, "common knowledge" and those to whom sight of the swastika banner or uniforms would be offense are forewarned and need not view them. A speaker who gives prior notice of his message has not compelled a confrontation with those who voluntarily listen.

As to those who happen to be in a position to be involuntarily confronted with the swastika, the following observations from Erznoznik v. City of Jacksonville (1975), 422 U.S. 205, 95 S.Ct. 2268, 45 L.Ed.2d 125, are appropriate:

"The plain, if at all times disquieting, truth is that in our pluralistic society, constantly proliferating new and ingenious forms of expression, 'we are inescapably captive audiences for many purposes.' Rowan v. Post Office Dept., (397 U.S. 728,) 736, 90 S.Ct. 1484, 25 L.Ed.2d 736. Much that we encounter offends our esthetic, if not our political and moral, sensibilities. Nevertheless, the Constitution does not permit government to decide which types of otherwise protected speech are sufficiently offensive to require protection for the unwilling listener or viewer. Rather, absent the narrow circumstances described above (home intrusion or captive audience), the burden normally falls upon the viewer to 'avoid further bombardment of (his) sensibilities simply by averting (his) eyes.' Cohen v. California (403 U.S. 15,) 21, 91 S.Ct. 1780, 29 L.Ed.2d 284." 422 U.S. 205, 210-11, 95 S.Ct. 2268, 2273, 45 L.Ed.2d 125, 131-32.

Thus by placing the burden upon the viewer to avoid further bombardment, the Supreme Court has permitted speakers to justify the initial intrusion into the citizen's sensibilities.

We accordingly, albeit reluctantly, conclude that the display of the swastika cannot be enjoined under the fighting-words exception to free speech, nor can anticipation of a hostile audience justify the prior restraint. Furthermore, Cohen and Erznoznik direct the citizens of Skokie that it is their burden to avoid the offensive symbol if they can do so without unreasonable inconvenience. Accordingly, we are constrained to reverse that part of the appellate court judgment enjoining the display of the swastika. That judgment is in all other respects affirmed.

Affirmed in part and reversed in part.

CLARK, Justice, dissenting.

R.A.V., Petitioner,
v.
CITY OF ST. PAUL, MINNESOTA.

505 U.S. 377

Supreme Court of the United States

Decided June 22, 1992.

Justice White filed an opinion concurring in the judgment in which Justice Blackmun and Justice O'Connor joined and in which Justice Stevens joined in part.

Justice Blackmun filed an opinion concurring in the judgment.

Justice Stevens filed an opinion concurring in the judgment in which Justice White and Justice Blackmun joined in part.

Some footnotes omitted.

Justice SCALIA delivered the opinion of the Court.

In the predawn hours of June 21, 1990, petitioner and several other teenagers allegedly assembled a crudely made cross by taping together broken chair legs. They then allegedly burned the cross inside the fenced yard of a black family that lived across the street from the house where petitioner was staying. Although this conduct could have been punished under any of a number of laws, one of the two provisions under which respondent city of St. Paul chose to charge petitioner (then a juvenile) was the St. Paul Bias-Motivated Crime Ordinance, St. Paul, Minn., Legis.Code § 292.02 (1990), which provides:

> "Whoever places on public or private property a symbol, object, appellation, characterization or graffiti, including, but not limited to, a burning cross or Nazi swastika, which one knows or has reasonable grounds to know arouses anger, alarm or resentment in others on the basis of race, color, creed, religion or gender commits disorderly conduct and shall be guilty of a misdemeanor."

Petitioner moved to dismiss this count on the ground that the St. Paul ordinance was substantially overbroad and impermissibly content based and therefore facially invalid under the First Amendment. The trial court granted this motion, but the Minnesota Supreme Court reversed. That court rejected petitioner's overbreadth claim because, as construed in prior Minnesota cases, see, e.g., In re Welfare of S.L.J., 263 N.W.2d 412 (Minn.1978), the modifying phrase "arouses anger, alarm or resentment in others" limited the reach of the ordinance to conduct that amounts to "fighting words," i.e., "conduct that itself inflicts injury or tends to incite immediate violence ...," In re Welfare of R.A.V., 464 N.W.2d 507, 510 (Minn.1991) (citing Chaplinsky v. New Hampshire, 315 U.S. 568, 572, 62 S.Ct. 766, 769, 86 L.Ed. 1031 (1942)), and therefore the ordinance reached only expression "that the first amendment does not protect," 464 N.W.2d, at 511. The court also concluded that the ordinance was not impermissibly content based because, in its view, "the ordinance is a narrowly tailored means toward accomplishing the compelling governmental interest in protecting the community against bias-motivated threats to public safety and order."

I

In construing the St. Paul ordinance, we are bound by the construction given to it by the Minnesota court . . . . Accordingly, we accept the Minnesota Supreme Court's authoritative statement that the ordinance reaches only those expressions that constitute "fighting words" within the meaning of Chaplinsky. 464 N.W.2d, at 510-511. Petitioner and his amici urge us to modify the scope of the Chaplinsky formulation, thereby invalidating the ordinance as "substantially overbroad," Broadrick v. Oklahoma, 413 U.S. 601, 610, 93 S.Ct. 2908, 2914-2915, 37 L.Ed.2d 830 (1973). We find it unnecessary to consider this issue. Assuming, arguendo, that all of the expression reached by the ordinance is proscribable under the "fighting words" doctrine, we nonetheless conclude that the ordinance is facially unconstitutional in that it prohibits otherwise permitted speech solely on the basis of the subjects the speech addresses . . . .

. . . The content-based discrimination reflected in the St. Paul ordinance comes within neither any of the specific exceptions to the First Amendment prohibition we discussed earlier nor a more general exception for content discrimination that does not threaten censorship of ideas. It assuredly does not fall within the exception for content discrimination based on the very reasons why the particular class of speech at issue (here, fighting words) is proscribable. As explained earlier, see supra, at 2545, the reason why fighting words are categorically excluded from the protection of the First Amendment is not that their content communicates any particular idea, but that their content embodies a particularly intolerable (and socially unnecessary) mode of expressing whatever idea the speaker wishes to convey. St. Paul has not singled out an especially offensive mode of expression--it has not, for example, selected for prohibition only those fighting words that communicate ideas in a threatening (as opposed to a merely obnoxious) manner. Rather, it has proscribed fighting words of whatever manner that communicate messages of racial, gender, or religious intolerance. Selectivity of this sort creates the possibility that the city is seeking to handicap the expression of particular ideas. That possibility would alone be enough to render the ordinance presumptively invalid, but St. Paul's comments and concessions in this case elevate the possibility to a certainty . . . .

Finally, St. Paul and its amici defend the conclusion of the Minnesota Supreme Court that, even if the ordinance regulates expression based on hostility towards its protected ideological content, this discrimination is nonetheless justified because it is narrowly tailored to serve compelling state interests. Specifically, they assert that the ordinance helps to ensure the basic human rights of members of groups that have historically been subjected to discrimination, including the right of such group members to live in peace where they wish. We do not doubt that these interests are compelling, and that the ordinance can be said to promote them. But the "danger of censorship" presented by a facially content-based statute, Leathers v. Medlock, 499 U.S., at 448, 111 S.Ct., at 1444, requires that that weapon be employed only where it is "necessary to serve the asserted [compelling] interest," Burson v. Freeman, 504 U.S. 191, 199, 112 S.Ct. 1846, 1852, 119 L.Ed.2d 5 (1992) (plurality opinion) (emphasis added); Perry Ed. Assn. v. Perry Local Educators' Assn., 460 U.S. 37, 45, 103 S.Ct. 948, 954-955, 74 L.Ed.2d 794 (1983). The existence of adequate content-neutral alternatives thus "undercut[s] significantly" any defense of such a statute, Boos v. Barry, supra, 485 U.S., at 329, 108 S.Ct., at 1168, casting considerable doubt on the government's protestations that "the asserted justification is in fact an accurate description of the purpose and effect of the law," Burson, supra, 504 U.S., at 213, 112 S.Ct., at 1859 (KENNEDY, J., concurring). See Boos, supra, 485 U.S., at 324-329, 108 S.Ct., at 1165-1168; cf. Minneapolis Star & Tribune Co. v. Minnesota Comm'r of Revenue, 460 U.S. 575, 586-587, 103 S.Ct. 1365, 1372-1373, 75 L.Ed.2d 295 (1983). The dispositive question in this case, therefore, is whether content discrimination is reasonably necessary to achieve St. Paul's compelling interests; it plainly is not. An ordinance not limited to the favored topics, for example, would have precisely the same beneficial effect. In fact the only interest distinctively served by the content limitation is that of displaying the city council's special hostility towards the particular biases thus singled out. That is precisely what the First Amendment forbids. The politicians of St. Paul are entitled to express that hostility--but not through the means of imposing unique limitations upon speakers who (however benightedly) disagree.

* * *

Let there be no mistake about our belief that burning a cross in someone's front yard is reprehensible. But St. Paul has sufficient means at its disposal to prevent such behavior without adding the First Amendment to the fire.

The judgment of the Minnesota Supreme Court is reversed, and the case is remanded for proceedings not inconsistent with this opinion.

It is so ordered.

Justice WHITE, with whom Justice BLACKMUN and Justice O'CONNOR join, and with whom Justice STEVENS joins except as to Part I-A, concurring in the judgment.

I agree with the majority that the judgment of the Minnesota Supreme Court should be reversed. However, our agreement ends there.

This case could easily be decided within the contours of established First Amendment law by holding, as petitioner argues, that the St. Paul ordinance is fatally overbroad because it criminalizes not only unprotected expression but expression protected by the First Amendment. See Part II, infra. Instead, "find[ing] it unnecessary" to consider the questions upon which we granted review, ante, at 2542, the Court holds the ordinance facially unconstitutional on a ground that was never presented to the Minnesota Supreme Court, a ground that has not been briefed by the parties before this Court, a ground that requires serious departures from the teaching of prior cases and is inconsistent with the plurality opinion in Burson v. Freeman, 504 U.S. 191, 112 S.Ct. 1846, 119 L.Ed.2d 5 (1992), which was joined by two of the five Justices in the majority in the present case.

This Court ordinarily is not so eager to abandon its precedents. Twice within the past month, the Court has declined to overturn longstanding but controversial decisions on questions of constitutional law. See Allied- Signal, Inc. v. Director, Division of Taxation, 504 U.S. 768, 112 S.Ct. 2251, 119 L.Ed.2d 533 (1992); Quill Corp. v. North Dakota, 504 U.S. 298, 112 S.Ct. 1904, 119 L.Ed.2d 91 (1992). In each case, we had the benefit of full briefing on the critical issue, so that the parties and amici had the opportunity to apprise us of the impact of a change in the law. And in each case, the Court declined to abandon its precedents, invoking the principle of stare decisis. Allied-Signal, Inc., supra, 504 U.S., at 783-786, 112 S.Ct., at 2261; Quill Corp., supra, 504 U.S., at 317-318, 112 S.Ct., at 1915-1916.

But in the present case, the majority casts aside long-established First Amendment doctrine without the benefit of briefing and adopts an untried theory. This is hardly a judicious way of proceeding, and the Court's reasoning in reaching its result is transparently wrong.

I

A

This Court's decisions have plainly stated that expression falling within certain limited categories so lacks the values the First Amendment was designed to protect that the Constitution affords no protection to that expression. Chaplinsky v. New Hampshire, 315 U.S. 568, 62 S.Ct. 766, 86 L.Ed. 1031 (1942), made the point in the clearest possible terms:

> "There are certain well-defined and narrowly limited classes of speech, the prevention and punishment of which have never been thought to raise any Constitutional problem.... It has been well observed that such utterances are no essential part of any exposition of ideas, and are of such slight social value as a step to truth that any benefit that may be derived from them is clearly outweighed by the social interest in order and morality." Id., at 571-572, 62 S.Ct., at 769.

See also Bose Corp. v. Consumers Union of United States, Inc., 466 U.S. 485, 504, 104 S.Ct. 1949, 1961, 80 L.Ed.2d 502 (1984) (citing Chaplinsky ).

Thus, as the majority concedes, see ante, at 2543, this Court has long held certain discrete categories of expression to be proscribable on the basis of their content. For instance, the Court has held that the individual who falsely shouts "fire" in a crowded theater may not claim the protection of the First Amendment. Schenck v. United States, 249 U.S. 47, 52, 39 S.Ct. 247, 249, 63 L.Ed. 470 (1919). The Court has concluded that neither child pornography nor obscenity is protected by the First Amendment. New York v. Ferber, 458 U.S. 747, 764, 102 S.Ct. 3348, 3358, 73 L.Ed.2d 1113 (1982); Miller v. California, 413 U.S. 15, 20, 93 S.Ct. 2607, 2612, 37 L.Ed.2d 419 (1973); Roth v. United States, 354 U.S. 476, 484-485, 77 S.Ct. 1304, 1308- 1309, 1 L.Ed.2d 1498 (1957). And the Court has observed that, "[l]eaving aside the special considerations when public officials [and public figures] are the target, a libelous publication is not protected by the Constitution." Ferber, supra, 458 U.S., at 763, 102 S.Ct., at 3358 (citations omitted).

All of these categories are content based. But the Court has held that the First Amendment does not apply to them because their expressive content is worthless or of de minimis value to society. Chaplinsky, supra, 315 U.S., at 571-572, 62 S.Ct., at 768-769. We have not departed from this principle, emphasizing repeatedly that, "within the confines of [these] given classification[s], the evil to be restricted so overwhelmingly outweighs the expressive interests, if any, at stake, that no process of case-by-case adjudication is required." Ferber, supra, 458 U.S., at 763-764, 102 S.Ct., at 3358-3359; Bigelow v. Virginia, 421 U.S. 809, 819, 95 S.Ct. 2222, 2231, 44 L.Ed.2d 600 (1975). This categorical approach has provided a principled and narrowly focused means for distinguishing between expression that the government may regulate freely and that which it may regulate on the basis of content only upon a showing of compelling need.

Today, however, the Court announces that earlier Courts did not mean their repeated statements that certain categories of expression are "not within the area of constitutionally protected speech." . . . The present Court submits that such clear statements "must be taken in context" and are not "literally true." . . .

To borrow a phrase: "Such a simplistic, all-or-nothing-at-all approach to First Amendment protection is at odds with common sense and with our jurisprudence as well." It is inconsistent to hold that the government may proscribe an entire category of speech because the content of that speech is evil, Ferber, supra, 458 U.S., at 763-764, 102 S.Ct., at 3358-3359; but that the government may not treat a subset of that category differently without violating the First Amendment; the content of the subset is by definition worthless and undeserving of constitutional protection.

The majority's observation that fighting words are "quite expressive indeed," ante, at 2544, is no answer. Fighting words are not a means of exchanging views, rallying supporters, or registering a protest; they are directed against individuals to provoke violence or to inflict injury. Chaplinsky, 315 U.S., at 572, 62 S.Ct., at 769. Therefore, a ban on all fighting words or on a subset of the fighting words category would restrict only the social evil of hate speech, without creating the danger of driving viewpoints from the marketplace. See ante, at 2545.

Therefore, the Court's insistence on inventing its brand of First Amendment underinclusiveness puzzles me.

B

In a second break with precedent, the Court refuses to sustain the ordinance even though it would survive under the strict scrutiny applicable to other protected expression. Assuming, arguendo, that the St. Paul ordinance is a content-based regulation of protected expression, it nevertheless would pass First Amendment review under settled law upon a showing that the regulation " 'is necessary to serve a compelling state interest and is narrowly drawn to achieve that end.' " Simon & Schuster, Inc. v. Members of N.Y. State Crime Victims Bd., 502 U.S. 105, 118, 112 S.Ct. 501, 509, 116 L.Ed.2d 476 (1991) (quoting Arkansas Writers' Project, Inc. v. Ragland, 481 U.S. 221, 231, 107 S.Ct. 1722, 1728, 95 L.Ed.2d 209 (1987)). St. Paul has urged that its ordinance, in the words of the majority, "helps to ensure the basic human rights of members of groups that have historically been subjected to discrimination...." Ante, at 2549. The Court expressly concedes that this interest is compelling and is promoted by the ordinance. Ibid. Nevertheless, the Court treats strict scrutiny analysis as irrelevant to the constitutionality of the legislation . . . .

III

Today, the Court has disregarded two established principles of First Amendment law without providing a coherent replacement theory. Its decision is an arid, doctrinaire interpretation, driven by the frequently irresistible impulse of judges to tinker with the First Amendment. The decision is mischievous at best and will surely confuse the lower courts. I join the judgment, but not the folly of the opinion.

Justice BLACKMUN, concurring in the judgment.

I regret what the Court has done in this case. The majority opinion signals one of two possibilities: It will serve as precedent for future cases, or it will not. Either result is disheartening.

In the first instance, by deciding that a State cannot regulate speech that causes great harm unless it also regulates speech that does not (setting law and logic on their heads), the Court seems to abandon the categorical approach, and inevitably to relax the level of scrutiny applicable to content-based laws. As Justice WHITE points out, this weakens the traditional protections of speech. If all expressive activity must be accorded the same protection, that protection will be scant. The simple reality is that the Court will never provide child pornography or cigarette advertising the level of protection customarily granted political speech. If we are forbidden to categorize, as the Court has done here, we shall reduce protection across the board. It is sad that in its effort to reach a satisfying result in this case, the Court is willing to weaken First Amendment protections . . . .

I see no First Amendment values that are compromised by a law that prohibits hoodlums from driving minorities out of their homes by burning crosses on their lawns, but I see great harm in preventing the people of Saint Paul from specifically punishing the race-based fighting words that so prejudice their community.

I concur in the judgment, however, because I agree with Justice WHITE that this particular ordinance reaches beyond fighting words to speech protected by the First Amendment.

TEXAS, Petitioner
v.
Gregory Lee JOHNSON.

491 U.S. 397

Supreme Court of the United States

Decided June 21, 1989.

Justice Kennedy concurred and filed an opinion.

Chief Justice Rehnquist dissented and filed an opinion in which Justice White and Justice O'Connor joined.

Justice Stevens dissented and filed an opinion.

Justice BRENNAN delivered the opinion of the Court.

After publicly burning an American flag as a means of political protest, Gregory Lee Johnson was convicted of desecrating a flag in violation of Texas law. This case presents the question whether his conviction is consistent with the First Amendment. We hold that it is not.

I

While the Republican National Convention was taking place in Dallas in 1984, respondent Johnson participated in a political demonstration dubbed the "Republican War Chest Tour." As explained in literature distributed by the demonstrators and in speeches made by them, the purpose of this event was to protest the policies of the Reagan administration and of certain Dallas- based corporations. The demonstrators marched through the Dallas streets, chanting political slogans and stopping at several corporate locations to stage "die-ins" intended to dramatize the consequences of nuclear war. On several occasions they spray-painted the walls of buildings and overturned potted plants, but Johnson himself took no part in such activities. He did, however, accept an American flag handed to him by a fellow protestor who had taken it from a flagpole outside one of the targeted buildings.

The demonstration ended in front of Dallas City Hall, where Johnson unfurled the American flag, doused it with kerosene, and set it on fire. While the flag burned, the protestors chanted: "America, the red, white, and blue, we spit on you." After the demonstrators dispersed, a witness to the flag burning collected the flag's remains and buried them in his backyard. No one was physically injured or threatened with injury, though several witnesses testified that they had been seriously offended by the flag burning.

Of the approximately 100 demonstrators, Johnson alone was charged with a crime. The only criminal offense with which he was charged was the desecration of a venerated object in violation of Tex.Penal Code Ann. § 42.09(a)(3) (1989). 1 After a trial, he was convicted, sentenced to one year in prison, and fined $2,000. The Court of Appeals for the Fifth District of Texas at Dallas affirmed Johnson's conviction, 706 S.W.2d 120 (1986), but the Texas Court of Criminal Appeals reversed, 755 S.W.2d 92 (1988), holding that the State could not, consistent with the First Amendment, punish Johnson for burning the flag in these circumstances.

(footnote)1. Texas Penal Code Ann. § 42.09 (1989) provides in full:

"§ 42.09. Desecration of Venerated Object

"(a) A person commits an offense if he intentionally or knowingly desecrates:

"(1) a public monument;

"(2) a place of worship or burial; or

"(3) a state or national flag.

"(b) For purposes of this section, 'desecrate' means deface, damage, or otherwise physically mistreat in a way that the actor knows will seriously offend one or more persons likely to observe or discover his action."(c) An offense under this section is a Class A misdemeanor. '

The Court of Criminal Appeals began by recognizing that Johnson's conduct was symbolic speech protected by the First Amendment: "Given the context of an organized demonstration, speeches, slogans, and the distribution of literature, anyone who observed appellant's act would have understood the message that appellant intended to convey. The act for which appellant was convicted was clearly 'speech' contemplated by the First Amendment." Id., at 95. To justify Johnson's conviction for engaging in symbolic speech, the State asserted two interests: preserving the flag as a symbol of national unity and preventing breaches of the peace. The Court of Criminal Appeals held that neither interest supported his conviction . . . .

. . . As to the State's goal of preventing breaches of the peace, the court concluded that the flag-desecration statute was not drawn narrowly enough to encompass only those flag burnings that were likely to result in a serious disturbance of the peace. And in fact, the court emphasized, the flag burning in this particular case did not threaten such a reaction. " 'Serious offense' occurred," the court admitted, "but there was no breach of peace nor does the record reflect that the situation was potentially explosive. One cannot equate 'serious offense' with incitement to breach the peace." Id., at 96. The court also stressed that another Texas statute, Tex.Penal Code Ann. § 42.01 (1989), prohibited breaches of the peace. Citing Boos v. Barry, 485 U.S. 312, 108 S.Ct. 1157, 99 L.Ed.2d 333 (1988), the court decided that § 42.01 demonstrated Texas' ability to prevent disturbances of the peace without punishing this flag desecration. 755 S.W.2d, at 96.

Because it reversed Johnson's conviction on the ground that § 42.09 was unconstitutional as applied to him, the state court did not address Johnson's argument that the statute was, on its face, unconstitutionally vague and overbroad. We granted certiorari, 488 U.S. 907, 109 S.Ct. 257, 102 L.Ed.2d 245 (1988), and now affirm.

II

Johnson was convicted of flag desecration for burning the flag rather than for uttering insulting words. This fact somewhat complicates our consideration of his conviction under the First Amendment. We must first determine whether Johnson's burning of the flag constituted expressive conduct, permitting him to invoke the First Amendment in challenginghis conviction. See, e.g., Spence v. Washington, 418 U.S. 405, 409-411, 94 S.Ct. 2727, 2729- 31, 41 L.Ed.2d 842 (1974). If his conduct was expressive, we next decide whether the State's regulation is related to the suppression of free expression. See, e.g., United States v. O'Brien, 391 U.S. 367, 377, 88 S.Ct. 1673, 1679, 20 L.Ed.2d 672 (1968); Spence, supra, at 414, n. 8, 94 S.Ct., at 2732, n. 8. If the State's regulation is not related to expression, then the less stringent standard we announced in United States v. O'Brien for regulations of noncommunicative conduct controls. See O'Brien, supra, at 377, 88 S.Ct., at 1679. If it is, then we are outside of O'Brien's test, and we must ask whether this interest justifies Johnson's conviction under a more demanding standard. See Spence, supra, at 411, 94 S.Ct., at 2730 . . . .

. . . Johnson burned an American flag as part--indeed, as the culmination--of a political demonstration that coincided with the convening of the Republican Party and its renomination of Ronald Reagan for President. The expressive, overtly political nature of this conduct was both intentional and overwhelmingly apparent. At his trial, Johnson explained his reasons for burning the flag as follows: "The American Flag was burned as Ronald Reagan was being renominated as President. And a more powerful statement of symbolic speech, whether you agree with it or not, couldn't have been made at that time. It's quite a just position [juxtaposition]. We had new patriotism and no patriotism." 5 Record 656. In these circumstances, Johnson's burning of the flag was conduct "sufficiently imbued with elements of communication," Spence, 418 U.S., at 409, 94 S.Ct., at 2730, to implicate the First Amendment.

III

A

Texas claims that its interest in preventing breaches of the peace justifies Johnson's conviction for flag desecration. However, no disturbance of the peace actually occurred or threatened to occur because of Johnson's burning of the flag. Although the State stresses the disruptive behavior of the protestors during their march toward City Hall, Brief for Petitioner 34-36, it admits that "no actual breach of the peace occurred at the time of the flagburningor in response to the flagburning." Id., at 34. The State's emphasis on the protestors' disorderly actions prior to arriving at City Hall is not only somewhat surprising given that no charges were brought on the basis of this conduct, but it also fails to show that a disturbance of the peace was a likely reaction to Johnson's conduct. The only evidence offered by the State at trial to show the reaction to Johnson's actions was the testimony of several persons who had been seriously offended by the flag burning. Id., at 6-7.

The State's position, therefore, amounts to a claim that an audience that takes serious offense at particular expression is necessarily likely to disturb the peace and that the expression may be prohibited on this basis. Our precedents do not countenance such a presumption. On the contrary, they recognize that a principal "function of free speech under our system of government is to invite dispute. It may indeed best serve its high purpose when it induces a condition of unrest, creates dissatisfaction with conditions as they are, or even stirs people to anger." . . . It would be odd indeed to conclude both that "if it is the speaker's opinion that gives offense, that consequence is a reason for according it constitutional protection," FCC v. Pacifica Foundation, 438 U.S. 726, 745, 98 S.Ct. 3026, 3038, 57 L.Ed.2d 1073 (1978) (opinion of STEVENS, J.), and that the government may ban the expression of certain disagreeable ideas on the unsupported presumption that their very disagreeableness will provoke violence.

Thus, we have not permitted the government to assume that every expression of a provocative idea will incite a riot, but have instead required careful consideration of the actual circumstances surrounding such expression, asking whether the expression "is directed to inciting or producing imminent lawless action and is likely to incite or produce such action" . . . . To accept Texas' arguments that it need only demonstrate "the potential for a breach of the peace," Brief for Petitioner 37, and that every flag burning necessarily possesses that potential, would be to eviscerate our holding in Brandenburg. This we decline to do.

Nor does Johnson's expressive conduct fall within that small class of "fighting words" that are "likely to provoke the average person to retaliation, and thereby cause a breach of the peace." Chaplinsky v. New Hampshire, 315 U.S. 568, 574, 62 S.Ct. 766, 770, 86 L.Ed. 1031 (1942). No reasonable onlooker would have regarded Johnson's generalized expression of dissatisfaction with the policies of the Federal Government as a direct personal insult or an invitation to exchange fisticuffs. See id., at 572-573, 62 S.Ct., at 769- 770; Cantwell v. Connecticut, 310 U.S. 296, 309, 60 S.Ct. 900, 905-06, 84 L.Ed. 1213 (1940); FCC v. Pacifica Foundation, supra, at 745, 98 S.Ct., at 3038 (opinion of STEVENS, J.).

We thus conclude that the State's interest in maintaining order is not implicated on these facts. The State need not worry that our holding will disable it from preserving the peace. We do not suggest that the First Amendment forbids a State to prevent "imminent lawless action." Brandenburg, supra, at 447, 89 S.Ct., at 1829. And, in fact, Texas already has a statute specifically prohibiting breaches of the peace, Tex.Penal Code Ann. § 42.01 (1989), which tends to confirm that Texas need not punish this flag desecration in order to keep the peace . . . .

B

The State also asserts an interest in preserving the flag as a symbol of nationhood and national unity . . . .

According to the principles announced in Boos, Johnson's political expression was restricted because of the content of the message he conveyed. We must therefore subject the State's asserted interest in preserving the special symbolic character of the flag to "the most exacting scrutiny." Boos v. Barry, supra, 485 U.S., at 321, 108 S.Ct., at 1164.

Texas argues that its interest in preserving the flag as a symbol of nationhood and national unity survives this close analysis. Quoting extensively from the writings of this Court chronicling the flag's historic and symbolic role in our society, the State emphasizes the " 'special place' " reserved for the flag in our Nation. Brief for Petitioner 22, quoting Smith v. Goguen, 415 U.S., at 601, 94 S.Ct., at 1261 (REHNQUIST, J., dissenting). The State's argument is not that it has an interest simply in maintaining the flag as a symbol of something, no matter what it symbolizes; indeed, if that were the State's position, it would be difficult to see how that interest is endangered by highly symbolic conduct such as Johnson's. Rather, the State's claim is that it has an interest in preserving the flag as a symbol of nationhood and national unity, a symbol with a determinate range of meanings. Brief for Petitioner 20-24. According to Texas, if one physically treats the flag in a way that would tend to cast doubt on either the idea that nationhood and national unity are the flag's referents or that national unity actually exists, the message conveyed thereby is a harmful one and therefore may be prohibited.

If there is a bedrock principle underlying the First Amendment, it is that the government may not prohibit the expression of an idea simply because society finds the idea itself offensive or disagreeable. . . . .

There is, moreover, no indication--either in the text of the Constitution or in our cases interpreting it--that a separate juridical category exists for the American flag alone. Indeed, we would not be surprised to learn that the persons who framed our Constitution and wrote the Amendment that we now construe were not known for their reverence for the Union Jack. The First Amendment does not guarantee that other concepts virtually sacred to our Nation as a whole--such as the principle that discrimination on the basis of race is odious and destructive--will go unquestioned in the marketplace of ideas. See Brandenburg v. Ohio, 395 U.S. 444, 89 S.Ct. 1827, 23 L.Ed.2d 430 (1969). We decline, therefore, to create for the flag an exception to the joust of principles protected by the First Amendment.

. . . We are tempted to say, in fact, that the flag's deservedly cherished place in our community will be strengthened, not weakened, by our holding today. Our decision is a reaffirmation of the principles of freedom and inclusiveness that the flag best reflects, and of the conviction that our toleration of criticism such as Johnson's is a sign and source of our strength. Indeed, one of the proudest images of our flag, the one immortalized in our own national anthem, is of the bombardment it survived at Fort McHenry. It is the Nation's resilience, not its rigidity, that Texas sees reflected in the flag--and it is that resilience that we reassert today . . . .

V

Johnson was convicted for engagingin expressive conduct. The State's interest in preventing breaches of the peace does not support his conviction because Johnson's conduct did not threaten to disturb the peace. Nor does the State's interest in preserving the flag as a symbol of nationhood and national unity justify his criminal conviction for engagingin political expression. The judgment of the Texas Court of Criminal Appeals is therefore

Affirmed.

Chief Justice REHNQUIST, with whom Justice WHITE and Justice O'CONNOR join, dissenting.

In holding this Texas statute unconstitutional, the Court ignores Justice Holmes' familiar aphorism that "a page of history is worth a volume of logic." New York Trust Co. v. Eisner, 256 U.S. 345, 349, 41 S.Ct. 506, 507, 65 L.Ed. 963 (1921). For more than 200 years, the American flag has occupied a unique position as the symbol of our Nation, a uniqueness that justifies a governmental prohibition against flag burning in the way respondent Johnson did here . . . .

. . . The American flag, then, throughout more than 200 years of our history, has come to be the visible symbol embodying our Nation. It does not represent the views of any particular political party, and it does not represent any particular political philosophy. The flag is not simply another "idea" or "point of view" competing for recognition in the marketplace of ideas. Millions and millions of Americans regard it with an almost mystical reverence regardless of what sort of social, political, or philosophical beliefs they may have. I cannot agree that the First Amendment invalidates the Act of Congress, and the laws of 48 of the 50 States, which make criminal the public burning of the flag . . . .

Justice STEVENS, dissenting.

As the Court analyzes this case, it presents the question whether the State of Texas, or indeed the Federal Government, has the power to prohibit the public desecration of the American flag. The question is unique. In my judgment rules that apply to a host of other symbols, such as state flags, armbands, or various privately promoted emblems of political or commercial identity, are not necessarily controlling. Even if flag burning could be considered just another species of symbolic speech under the logical application of the rules that the Court has developed in its interpretation of the First Amendment in other contexts, this case has an intangible dimension that makes those rules inapplicable.

A country's flag is a symbol of more than "nationhood and national unity." Ante, at 2541, 2542, 2544, and n. 9, 2546, 2548. It also signifies the ideas that characterize the society that has chosen that emblem as well as the special history that has animated the growth and power of those ideas. The fleurs-de-lis and the tricolor both symbolized "nationhood and national unity," but they had vastly different meanings. The message conveyed by some flags-- the swastika, for example--may survive long after it has outlived its usefulness as a symbol of regimented unity in a particular nation.

So it is with the American flag. It is more than a proud symbol of the courage, the determination, and the gifts of nature that transformed 13 fledgling Colonies into a world power. It is a symbol of freedom, of equal opportunity, of religious tolerance, and of good will for other peoples who share our aspirations. The symbol carries its message to dissidents both at home and abroad who may have no interest at all in our national unity or survival.

The value of the flag as a symbol cannot be measured. Even so, I have no doubt that the interest in preserving that value for the future is both significant and legitimate. Conceivably that value will be enhanced by the Court's conclusion that our national commitment to free expression is so strong that even the United States as ultimate guarantor of that freedom is without power to prohibit the desecration of its unique symbol. But I am unpersuaded. The creation of a federal right to post bulletin boards and graffiti on the Washington Monument might enlarge the market for free expression, but at a cost I would not pay . . . .

I respectfully dissent.

# Part II: Libel and Privacy

## The Five Elements of Libel

1. PUBLISHED: The libel was published
2. OF AND CONCERNING: Words were of and concerning plaintiff.
3. DEFAMATORY: Material is defamatory
4. FALSE: Material is false
5. FAULT: Defendant was at fault

## The Five Categories of Libel Plaintiffs

1. Public Officials
2. Pervasive Public Figures
3. Vortex Public Figures
4. Involuntary Public Figures
5. Private Individuals

Harry P. HORNBY, Jr., Individually and d/b/a The Uvalde Leader-News, Appellant,
v.
Curtis P. HUNTER, Appellee.

385 S.W.2d 473

Court of Civil Appeals of Texas, Corpus Christi.

Dec. 3, 1964.

NYE, Justice.

This is a libel suit on appeal from an order overruling a plea of privilege. The appellee Curtis H. Hunter instituted this suit against Harry P. Hornby, Jr., the appellant, individually and d/b/a The Uvalde Leader-News, for damages, alleging that he had been libelled by the publication of an article in the Uvalde Leader-News, a newspaper published bi-weekly by the appellant. Hunter is a resident of Nueces County, Texas, and the appellant is a resident of Uvalde County, Texas, at which place he publishes the Uvalde Leader-News. The suit was filed in Nueces County, Texas.

The news story which forms the basis of Hunter's suit was, according to the appellant, a report made to the newspaper by a deputy sheriff of Uvalde County. The article printed on the front page of the paper reads as follows:

'STOLEN CAR FOUND IN SABINAL

'Clarence Large, Deputy Sheriff of Uvalde County, reported that a stolen 1959 Cadillac was discovered on the Jack Griffin ranch, five miles northeast of Sabinal, Saturday, October 5.

'The car was stolen in Corpus Christi according to Laege. The lawman reported that he and Texas Ranger Levi Duncan were checking the area when they discovered the automobile. They radioed to their headquarters in Uvalde to see if the car had been stolen and received an answer from the Hondo Sheriff who was monitering the call. It appeared that the car had been stolen and that a warrant for C. H. 'Curly' Hunter of Corpus Christi had been issued in connection with the theft.

'Hunter and another man, Al Smith, had previously leased the pasture where the car was found. The seven room house on the lease was well stocked, according to Deputy Large, with food, ammunition, a radio and TV set.'

We hold that appellee Hunter has met this burden.

The trial court filed findings of fact and conclusions of law as follows: That Hunter is a resident of Nueces County, Texas, and was a resident of said County on October 13, 1963, the date the article appeared; that the appellant is a resident of Uvalde County, Texas, and is doing business as and is the owner of the Uvalde Leader-News which is a locally owned, independent newspaper in said County; that the newspaper has a circulation of around 3900 copies which extends into South Texas and into Nueces County; that the appellant published the article set forth above; that C. H. 'Curly' Hunter was identified as being the person, and the only person, to whom said article was referring; that the 1959 Cadillac automobile referred to in said article had been in the custody, control and possession of Hunter and his wife for about a year preceding the publication; that Hunter did not steal the automobile referred to in the article and that no complaint had been filed and no warrant issued for the arrest of C. H. 'Curly' Hunter for the theft of a 1959 Cadillac automobile in Corpus Christi, Texas. The court concluded that the article alleging and imputing the theft of the 1959 Cadillac automobile by Hunter is not true and that the article is defamatory and libelous per se.

The appellant raised six points upon which the appeal is based. The appellant complains that the trial court erred in concluding that the article in question was defamatory and libelous per se for the reason that there is no evidence to support the same, and that Hunter failed to prove that he suffered any damage by reason of such publication. The appellant admits that there was no indictment pending in Nueces County against C. H. 'Curly' Hunter for the theft of a Cadillac automobile. Appellant argues that the article does not state that Hunter stole said automobile but only relates to the fact that a warrant had been issued against Hunter of Nueces County. Appellant proved that there was pending an indictment against 'Curly' Hunter for receiving and concealing stolen property but it was developed in the testimony that the complaint did not involve an automobile. In view of our holding herein, the indictment concerning another criminal offense remote and unconnected with the publication before this Court would not be a defense to the libel published even though the offenses are of a similar character. Art. 5431, V. A.T.S.; Herald News Co. v. Wilkinson, 239 S.W 294 (Tex.Civ.App.1922, Dism. w.o.j.); 36 Tex.Jur.2d 340, § 54.

The article begins with the headline which states 'Stolen Car Found in Sabinal.' The article goes on to say that: 'It appeared that the car had been stolen and that a warrant for C. H. 'Curly' Hunter of Corpus Christi had been issued in connection with the theft.' It is not necessary that the publication of a charge of violating a criminal statute be made in a technical manner the same as might be required of an indictment. It is sufficient on reading the article that an ordinary person would draw a reasonable conclusion that the complaining party was charged with a violation of some criminal law.

. . . We hold that the subject article does impute to Hunter the commission of a crime for which punishment by imprisonment in jail or the penitentiary may be imposed and is, therefore, libelous per se.

. . . Appellant argues in another point that the appellee Hunter failed to prove that the printed matter complained of was ever read. Mrs. Harry P. Hornby, Jr., wife of the defendant, testified that the Uvalde Leader-News was published twice a week; that approximately 4100 copies are published and that they have a circulation of approximately 3900; she testified that several companies actually subscribed to their paper in Nueces County, Texas; that the paper printed on Sunday, October 13th, contained the article complained about and that it was circulated in South Texas and in Nueces County. We hold that a libel committed by a newspaper publication is accomplished when the publication goes into circulation. It is not necessary to prove that the article was read as that can be presumed. 53 C.J.S. Libel and Slander § 82, p. 133; Brian v. Harper, 144 La. 585, 80 So. 885.

Sarah WEINSTEIN

v.

Richard BULLICK and CBS, Inc. d/b/a WCAU-TV.

827 F.Supp. 1193

United States District Court,
E.D. Pennsylvania.

June 15, 1993.

GILES, District Judge.

Plaintiff brings claims against defendants for defamation, invasion of privacy, and intentional infliction of emotional distress. Jurisdiction is based upon diversity of citizenship and the case is governed by Pennsylvania law. Defendants have filed motions for summary judgment. For the reasons stated below, both motions are granted in part and denied in part.

## I. FACTUAL AND PROCEDURAL BACKGROUND

The complaint alleges that Sarah Weinstein ("Weinstein") was abducted in November 1991 from a street in the City of Philadelphia by an unknown assailant who thereafter sexually assaulted her. Following her release by her abductor, plaintiff complained to the Philadelphia Police Department, giving officers of the Sex Crimes Unit a detailed description of the assault in a recorded interview.

Richard Bullick ("Bullick") was commanding officer of the Sex Crimes Unit at the time of the above described events. In an on-camera interview with reporters from WCAU-TV, Bullick made statements which Weinstein alleges defamed her. She further alleges that Bullick knew that his statements were improper, erroneous, misleading, untrue and defamatory. WCAU-TV broadcasted Bullick's remarks throughout the Philadelphia area on its evening news program. Weinstein alleges that Bullick's statements were broadcast by WCAU in spite of the fact that WCAU knew or should have known that the information contained in the broadcast was erroneous, misleading, untrue, and defamatory.

Based upon the above-described allegations, Weinstein brought the instant action against Bullick and WCAU, claiming defamation, see Complaint Count I, invasion of privacy by casting her in a false light, see Count II, and intentional infliction of emotional distress, see Count III. Defendants have moved to dismiss the complaint, or in the alternative, for summary judgment. In an Order dated February 8, 1993, the court informed the parties that it would consider defendants' motions to be for summary judgment, and gave plaintiff time to file additional evidence in opposition to defendants' motions. See Fed.R.Civ.P. 12(b) (if matters outside the pleading are submitted with 12(b)(6) motion, the motion shall be treated as Rule 56 motion, and parties given reasonable opportunity to present pertinent material). Weinstein filed several additional evidentiary items, and we now consider the motions.

## II. STANDARD FOR SUMMARY JUDGMENT

Summary judgment is to be granted only "if the pleadings, depositions, answers to interrogatories, and admissions on file, together with the affidavits, if any, show that there is no genuine issue as to any material fact and that the moving party is entitled to judgment as a matter of law." Fed.R.Civ.P. 56(c). Where, as here, the non-moving party has the burden of proof at trial, the movant need not produce evidence negating the non-movant's case. Instead, the moving party need only demonstrate that there is a lack of any evidence to support the non-movant's claim. Celotex Corp. v. Catrett, 477 U.S. 317, 323-25, 106 S.Ct. 2548, 2552-54, 91 L.Ed.2d 265 (1986). Once the movant satisfies this initial burden, the non-movant cannot rest solely upon the allegations of her pleadings. Fed.R.Civ.P. 56(e). Instead, she must demonstrate that there is sufficient evidence for a jury to return a verdict in her favor. Anderson v. Liberty Lobby, Inc., 477 U.S. 242, 249, 106 S.Ct. 2505, 2510-11, 91 L.Ed.2d 202 (1986). The court must determine "whether the evidence presents a sufficient disagreement to require submission to a jury or whether it is so one-sided that one party must prevail as a matter of law." Id., 477 U.S. at 251-52, 106 S.Ct. at 2512. With these general considerations in mind, we will examine each count of the complaint . . . .

Defendants also assert that, even if the statements were defamatory, plaintiff cannot establish that they applied to her . . . .

With these general considerations in mind, we examine the content of the allegedly defamatory broadcast. It is undisputed that the following is the transcript of the November 7, 1991 broadcast in its entirety:

Jane Robelot: And tonight authorities are investigating a complicated case of abduction and rape that allegedly occurred last Friday. Channel 10 News reporter Andrew Glassman has learned that while the Philadelphia Sex Crimes Division is actively investigating the case, some say they have reservations.

Andrew Glassman: The Bryn Mawr student told police a man forced his way into her car outside a party at the University of Pennsylvania, pulled what appeared to be a gun, forced her to take off her clothes and have sex with him while he drove across the Walt Whitman Bridge, then stopped the car and raped her again. The woman had a plan: she told her attacker she'd bring him back here--to her dorm room at Bryn Mawr College. She said she'd get her instant teller card and get him cash. She was trying to lure him to a public place to get someone's attention--an officer or a security guard. But even after all that, she couldn't find anyone to help her out. Bryn Mawr Public Safety Chief Steven Heath was sorry his officers were not able to respond.
Steven Heath: There is a bright side of this whole tragic event is the fact that the victim really

used her head. There could have been a textbook response to such a concern. She most certainly used it.

Andrew Glassman: But this was the reaction today from Captain Richard Bullick, Sex Crimes Division of the Philadelphia Police. He is investigating this case.

Richard Bullick: She's saying a lot of things that went on in the car--she's driving--she's driving 80 miles an hour having sex with the guy--in a little Nissan. I couldn't do it, maybe she could. I don't know. And even if there was sex, that doesn't mean it was forcible sex. So it's all of these things we have to look into before we come to a conclusion. But, you know, I'm skeptical at the beginning of the investigation.

Andrew Glassman: You're skeptical at the beginning of this investigation? Or?

Richard Bullick: Both. As we are now, I'm a little skeptical about it. But until we get--

Andrew Glassman: Captain Bullick later phoned us to say he knew we were recording him but was uncomfortable with what he had said. He said he did not wish to appear insensitive to the alleged victim. This was his official statement on the case:

Richard Bullick: It's a very sensitive investigation as they all are. And we handle it just as we handle every other investigation that until it's proven to be factual or non-factual, we handle it as if it is factual.

Andrew Glassman: A source at Bryn Mawr College in contact with the alleged victim told us late tonight that she would be devastated if she heard that Philadelphia police did not believe her story. Officially the police department continues to seek this man in connection with the incident and Bullick says, he plans to interview the alleged victim again tomorrow. Andrew Glassman, Channel 10 News.

Transcript of November 7, 1991 Broadcast, attached as Exhibit "1" to Motion of Defendant CBS Inc. to Dismiss the Complaint, or, in the Alternative, for Summary Judgment ("Broadcast Tr.")....

Application of the Defamatory Statements to the Plaintiff: the "of and concerning" requirement: Defendants argue that Weinstein cannot establish the application of the allegedly defamatory statements to her, that is, the broadcast was not "of and concerning" her, and, therefore, her defamation claim fails as a matter of law. The court disagrees.

It is undisputed that plaintiff was not named in the allegedly defamatory broadcast. However, a defamed party need not be specifically named in a defamatory statement in order to recover, if she is pointed to by description or circumstances tending to identify her. Redco, 758 F.2d at 972; Cosgrove Studio & Camera Shop, Inc. v. Pane, 408 Pa. 314, 319, 182 A.2d 751, 753 (1962); Restatement (Second) of Torts § 564, Comment b. When the plaintiff is not named in the broadcast, the court must determine if a viewer could reasonably conclude that the broadcast referred to the plaintiff. If the court decides in the affirmative, the jury must determine if the recipient actually concluded that the defamatory matter referred to the plaintiff. Farrell v. Triangle Publications, Inc., 399 Pa. 102, 109-110, 159 A.2d 734, 739 (1960).

The broadcast contains numerous details that would help a viewer identify the subject of the allegedly defamatory statements. The subject of the broadcast is identified as a female Bryn

Mawr student who was the reported victim of a rape on a certain day. Some of the unusual details of the abduction leading to the rape are given. The victim is said to live in a dorm at Bryn Mawr College, to drive a Nissan, and to have attended a party at the University of Pennsylvania shortly before her abduction. See Broadcast Tr. All of these things are the types of "description of or reference to" the plaintiff that could lead those who saw the broadcast to "reasonably understand the plaintiff to be the person intended." Restatement (Second) of Torts § 564, Comment b.

The possibility that plaintiff would be identified by a viewer as the subject of the broadcast is heightened when we consider evidence submitted by defendants that Bryn Mawr is a small school, with approximately 1,200 undergraduate students and 550 graduate students. Motion of Defendant CBS Inc. to Dismiss the Complaint, or, in the Alternative, for Summary Judgment, Exhibit 2 at 8. The defendants' own submission also indicates that "Bryn Mawr's size allows its students and faculty to work closely together and to know each other well." Id. at 3. In this type of environment, it would not be surprising if some people could identify plaintiff from the information supplied in the broadcast.

Of course, we are not free to base our decision on speculation that someone might have identified plaintiff as the subject of the broadcast. Because the applicability of the defamatory matter to Weinstein depends upon extrinsic circumstances, rather than upon her being identified by name, the evidence must be able to support a conclusion that some person who saw the broadcast was familiar with the circumstances and reasonably believed that the broadcast referred to plaintiff. Restatement (Second) of Torts § 564, Comment b. The court is satisfied that the evidence submitted by the parties does support such a conclusion.

Weinstein has submitted affidavits from two Bryn Mawr students stating that "news of Sarah Weinstein's rape spread quickly across the campus." Affidavits of Bonnie Shinkle and Judy Kellem, attached as Exhibits A & B to Plaintiff's Memorandum in Support of Additional Evidence. The affiants further declare that when the broadcast was "aired lots of people on campus were talking about it." Id. Read in the light most favorable to the plaintiff, these affidavits indicate that many Bryn Mawr students, faculty and staff knew that a rape had allegedly occurred, could identify plaintiff as the alleged victim of the rape, and could reasonably have identified her as the subject of the broadcast.

Even if we were to ignore those portions of the affidavits which are arguably based upon hearsay, the affidavits show that the affiants had personal knowledge that could have led them to conclude reasonably that the broadcast was of and concerning plaintiff. The affidavits state that shortly after the alleged abduction and rape Weinstein told affiants about her ordeal. Shinkle Aff., Kellem Aff., supra. As a result, each of these Bryn Mawr students has sworn that "[e]ven though her name was never mentioned, I knew that the broadcast was about [plaintiff]." Id. Because the information given in the broadcast was sufficient to make the affiants' association of the broadcast with plaintiff a reasonable one, plaintiff's evidence is sufficient to withstand defendants' motions for summary judgment as to the "of and concerning" requirement.

NEIMAN-MARCUS et al.
v.
LAIT et al.

United States District Court S. D. New York.

13 F.R.D. 311

Dec. 15, 1952.

IRVING R. KAUFMAN, District Judge.

The defendants have moved to dismiss the amended complaint in this action (1) as to those plaintiffs described as salesmen and saleswomen for failure to state a claim upon which relief can be granted, and (2) in its entirety for failure to comply with the Federal Rules of Civil Procedure, 28 U.S.C.A., or in the alternative to require plaintiffs to serve an amended complaint in which the claim of each plaintiff shall be separately stated.

The defendants are authors of a book entitled 'U.S.A. Confidential'. The plaintiffs are the Neiman-Marcus Company, a Texas corporation operating a department store at Dallas, Texas, and three groups of its employees. They allege that the following matter libelled and defamed them:

'Pages 39-40:

'The telephone had come into its own. Whores are 'call girls,' 'party girls' or 'company girls.' Instead of your visiting them, they come to see you.

'This resulted in a complete change in the economic set-up of the oldest profession. Since houses are not needed, neither are large investments. Without houses immovably located, pay-offs to bluecoats on the beat have become almost extinct and so, for that matter, have raids. Only the lowest streetwalkers are collared. Meanwhile, the price is up; the old 50-cent house girl is insulted with $10 for a quick visit to your hotel room. The younger, fresher and smarter talent asks $100 and frequently gets it.

* * *

'Some people call them call girls and others refer to them as party girls; because you call them when you want a party.

'Page 196:

'He [Stanley Marcus, president of plaintiff Neiman-Marcus Company] may not know that some Neiman models are call girls--the top babes in town. The guy who escorts one feels in the same league with the playboys who took out Ziegfeld's glorified. Price, a hundred bucks a night.

'The salesgirls are good, too--pretty, and often much cheaper--twenty bucks on the average. They're more fun, too, not as snooty as the models. We got this confidential, from a Dallas wolf.

'Neiman-Marcus also contributes to the improvement of the local breed when it imports New York models to make a flash at style shows. These girls are the cream of the crop. Oil millionaires toss around thousand-dollar bills for a chance to take them out.

'Neiman's was a women's specialty shop until the old biddies who patronized it decided their husbands should get class, too. So Neiman's put in a men's store. Well, you should see what happened. You wonder how all the faggots got to the wild and wooly. You thought those with talent ended up in New York and Hollywood and the plodders got government jobs in Washington. Then you learn the nucleus of the Dallas fairy colony is composed of many Neiman dress and millinery designers, imported from New York and Paris, who sent for their boy friends when the men's store expanded. Now most of the sales staff are fairies, too.

'Page 208:

'Houston is faced with a serious homosexual problem. It is not as evident as Dallas', because there are no expensive imported faggots in town like those in the Neiman-Marcus set.'

The original complaint, filed in this action on April 14, 1952, was dismissed, with leave to amend, insofar as it related to the individual plaintiffs, pursuant to the opinion of the Hon. Thomas J. Murphy, dated August 19, 1952, 107 F.Supp. 96. The dismissal was based on the failure of the individual plaintiffs to specify that they were members of the libelled groups at the time the cause of action is alleged to have arisen, and also that they failed to disclose the numerical size of the groups at such time.

The individual plaintiffs have cured these defects in the amended complaint and they now state that they were employed by the Neiman-Marcus Company at the time the alleged libel was published and that the groups of individual plaintiffs are composed as follows:

(1) Nine individual models who constitute the entire group of models at the time of the publication [Amended Complaint, pars. 3, 12];

(2) Fifteen salesmen of a total of twenty-five suing on their own behalf and on behalf of the others pursuant to Rule 23(a)(3) of the Federal Rules of Civil Procedure [Amended Complaint, pars. 4, 8];

(3) Thirty saleswomen of a total of 382 suing on their own behalf and on behalf of the others pursuant to Rule 23(a)(3), supra. [Amended Complaint, pars. 5, 9].

The first part of defendants' motion is to dismiss the amended complaint as to the salesmen and saleswomen for failure to state a cause of action for libel since, it is alleged, no ascertainable person is identified by the words complained of . . . .

This Court is of the opinion that the motion to dismiss the salesmen's and saleswomen's causes of action must be denied at this stage of the proceedings, if such plaintiffs have a cause of action in any state of the United States in which it is alleged the defendants' book was distributed to the public.

An examination of the case and text law of libel reveals that the following propositions are rather widely accepted:

(1) Where the group or class libelled is large, none can sue even though the language used is inclusive.
(2) Where the group or class libelled is small, and each and every member of the group or class is referred to, then any individual member can sue.

Conflict arises when the publication complained of libels some or less than all of a designated small group. Some courts say no cause of action exists in any individual of the group. Latimer v. Chicago Daily News, Inc., 1947, 330 Ill.App. 295, 71 N.E.2d 553; Kassowitz v. Sentinel Co., 1938, 226 Wis. 468, 277 N.W. 177. Other courts in other states would apparently allow such an action. Montgomery Ward & Co. v. Skinner, 1946, 200 Miss. 44, 25 So.2d 572; cf. Hardy v. Williamson, 1891, 86 Ga. 551, 12 S.E. 874; Kenworthy v. Journal Co., 1906, 117 Mo.App. 327, 93 S.W. 882.

While no choice of law is made at this time, it appears from the complaint that Texas or New York law will be of greatest importance at the trial because of the many contacts with these states; not of small significance is the fact that the individual plaintiffs' community and place of livelihood is in Texas (Amended Complaint, par. 20).

The courts of Texas do not seem to have spoken on the 'some' allegation of libel. A reading of the New York cases indicates a trend towards submitting to the jury the question as to whether the 'charge against several individuals, under some general description or general name * * * has the personal application averred by the plaintiff.' Gross v. Cantor, 1936, 270 N.Y. 93, 96, 200 N.E. 592, 593; Kirkman v. Westchester Newspapers, 1st Dept., 1941, 261 App.Div. 181, 24 N.Y.S.2d 860, reversed 1942, 287 N.Y. 373, 39 N.E.2d 919.

The Court of Appeals for this Circuit has referred to the Restatement of Torts for the 'general law'. Mattox v. News Syndicate Co., supra, 176 F.2d at page 901. If we do so in this instance, we find that Illustration 2 of § 564, Comment (c) reads as follows:

> 'A newspaper publishes the statement that some member of B's household has committed murder. In the absence of any circumstances indicating that some particular member of B's household was referred to, the newspaper has defamed each member of B's household.'

Thus the Restatement of Torts would authorize suit by each member of a small group where the defamatory publication refers to but a portion of the group. This result seems to find support in logic and justice, as well as the case law mentioned above. See Riesman, Group Libel, 42 Col.

Law Review 727, 768 (1942). An imputation of gross immorality to some of a small group casts suspicion upon all, where no attempt is made to exclude the innocent.

Applying the above principles to the case at bar, it is the opinion of this Court that the plaintiff salesmen, of whom it is alleged that 'most * * * are fairies' have a cause of action in New York and most likely other states; where the courts have specifically held to the contrary, a fortiori no cause exists. Defendants' motion to dismiss as to the salesmen for failure to state a claim upon which relief can be granted is denied.

The plaintiff saleswomen are in a different category. The alleged defamatory statement in defendants' book speaks of the saleswomen generally. While it does not use the word 'all' or similar terminology, yet it stands unqualified. However, the group of saleswomen is extremely large, consisting of 382 members at the time of publication. No specific individual is named in the alleged libellous statement. I am not cited to a single case which would support a cause of action by an individual member of any group of such magnitude. The courts have allowed suit where the group consisted of four coroners [Weston v. Commercial Advertiser Ass'n, supra], twelve doctors composing the residential staff of a hospital [Bornmann v. Star Co., supra], a posse [Chapa v. Abernethy, supra] twelve radio editors [Gross v. Cantor, supra], and in similar cases involving small groups.

But where the group or class disparaged is a large one, absent circumstances pointing to a particular plaintiff as the person defamed, no individual member of the group or class has a cause of action . . . .

Accordingly it is the opinion of this Court that as a matter of law the individual saleswomen do not state a claim for libel upon which relief can be granted and the motion to dismiss their cause of action is granted.

George POWERS
v.
DURGIN-SNOW PUBLISHING CO., Inc.
George POWERS
v.
Clifford N. OLESEN.

144 A.2d 294

Supreme Judicial Court of Maine.

Aug. 7, 1958.

WILLIAMSON, Chief Justice.

These two actions of libel arise from the publication of an article written by defendant Olesen in the weekly newspaper owned and published by defendant Durgin-Snow Publishing Co., Inc. The cases are before us on exceptions in each instance to the overruling of defendant's demurrer and present identical issues. For convenience we will refer only to the case against the publisher.

The declaration reads in part:

'* * * the defendant * * * with intent to injure, degrade and disgrace the Plaintiff and bring him into hatred, contempt, ridicule and distrust and to deprive him of the benefit of public confidence, and subject him to the scoffs and sneers of society, did maliciously, willfully, recklessly and falsely write, compose, print, publish, circulate and sell in said Westbrook American the following false, scandalous and defamatory article appearing on Page Six (6) thereof under the heading: 'Milling Around' by Sunny Olesen:

'George Powers, Coating Department, is a fellow who believes in looking ahead. He's also a classic example of typical Yankee thrift. Take his idea on caskets now--George says, "Why spend a lot of money for a casket when, for $15 or $20 you can build one, yourself. After all, your family can always use the money you've saved in that one item, alone."

'Suiting the action to the word, George is now busily sawing and hammering away on his own tailored-to-fit coffin. And, as a sort of package deal, he's making plans to dig the space for it next.

'From all outward appearances, this thrifty, if slightly ghoulish gent can take his time on his project, because. * * *

'He turned (approximately) 35 on his last birthday.' (Innuendoes omitted)

'And the Plaintiff avers that by writing, printing, publishing, circulating and selling the papers containing the above false, malicious, defamatory and scandalous article as aforesaid, the defendant has greatly injured the Plaintiff in his good name and reputation, has deprived him of

PLAINTIFF Statement

public confidence, and exposed him and his family to public hatred, contempt and ridicule, and the Plaintiff has suffered great pain and distress of body and mind, has been shunned by many of his former acquaintances, and in his general reputation has been otherwise greatly injured and prejudiced . . . .'

The rules governing the remaining issues on the demurrer are stated in Brown v. Guy Gannett Publishing Co., 147 Me. 3, 4, 82 A.2d 797, 798:

'By its demurrer the defendant has admitted the truth of each and every one of the foregoing allegations.

* * *

'It is not necessary in order for printed words to be libelous that they naturally tend to expose the plaintiff to public hatred and contempt and ridicule, and deprive him of the benefit of public confidence and social intercourse. It is sufficient if they naturally tend to bring about any one of the foregoing consequences. The governing principle of law is stated in the alternative or disjunctive, not in the conjunctive.'

In our view the article naturally tended to expose the plaintiff to laughter tinged with contempt, or in other words to ridicule. 'Ridicule' has been defined as follows: 'The act or practice of exciting laughter at a person or thing by means of jesting words, caricature, mocking, etc.; remarks, etc. intended to show one in an amusing or absurd light; slightly contemptuous banter; as, an object of ridicule; to suffer from ridicule; cutting ridicule.' Webster's New International Dictionary, 2d Ed., Unabridged.

The reader is given the impression that the plaintiff is at best an odd or unusual character acting in a manner far removed from the ordinary standards of the day. The man who builds his own coffin and is planning to dig his own grave is described as a 'thrifty, if slightly ghoulish gent.' The reader may well laugh with the writer at the victim with a laughter mixed with contempt.

The defendant does not escape liability on the ground the article was written in jest, if such was the fact. The joke that goes too far and causes harm, not laughter, is within our common experience . . . .

Of course not every jest is a libel. We must not be too sensitive. In the words of Judge Learned Hand, in Burton v. Crowell Pub. Co., 2 Cir., 82 F.2d 154, 155, 'A man must not be too thin-skinned or a self-important prig.' We cannot, however, say that the article 'could in no respect be regarded as an attack upon the reputation' of the plaintiff. Triggs v. Sun Printing & Publishing Ass'n, supra.

We hold, the article, if believed, has a natural tendency to expose the plaintiff to ridicule that is more than trivial. It thus is libelous per se and no allegation of special damages is necessary to sustain the action. Tillson v. Robbins, supra. The declaration is sufficient. The attack by demurrer fails.

AIDS COUNSELING AND TESTING CENTERS

v.

GROUP W TELEVISION, INCORPORATED; Stuart Caplan, Defendants-Appellees.

903 F.2d 1000

United States Court of Appeals,
Fourth Circuit.
Decided May 22, 1990.
As Amended June 13, 1990.

Before SPROUSE and CHAPMAN, Circuit Judges, and HOFFMAN, Senior United States District Judge for the Eastern District of Virginia, sitting by designation.

CHAPMAN, Circuit Judge:

This appeal arises out of a suit for defamation and false-light invasion of privacy. In this court, the appellants-plaintiffs contest a number of the district court's rulings that led the court to hold that it had jurisdiction over the matter and to dismiss most of the claims in the complaint. We hold that the appellants have failed to demonstrate that the district court erred in any respect and we therefore affirm the judgment.

I.

Plaintiff AIDS Counseling & Testing Centers (ACT) was an unincorporated business venture organized in Maryland for the purpose of providing AIDS testing to the public as a profit-making enterprise. The individual plaintiffs, ACT's investors, attempted to advertise their business as a faster, easier alternative to the free AIDS testing provided by public agencies in Maryland. The investors touted their business as providing complete confidentiality, as returning test results faster than the public agencies, and as giving customers a written copy of their test results rather than the oral report provided at many other testing centers. One aspect of ACT's operation that proved particularly controversial was its practice of offering an ID card documenting that the bearer had tested negative for AIDS infection.

In order to bring its services to the attention of prospective clients, ACT undertook an aggressive publicity campaign. It distributed over 10,000 flyers in and around Baltimore. It sent information to dating services around the area and actively sought references from these services. It placed advertisements in supermarkets and in several of the local commercial and campus newspapers and it sent press releases to various of the broadcast media in the Baltimore area.

In a turn of events reminiscent of the tale of King Midas, the appellants succeeded in generating far more publicity for their enterprise than they wished. Their publicity activities drew substantial public attention to the operation of the business, but, unfortunately for ACT and its investors, much of the more widespread publicity was not of the positive tenor that they had hoped to generate. The present action arose out of news stories that the Baltimore television station, WJZ-TV, broadcast on October 29 and November 4, 1987. These broadcasts featured Denise Koch, a reporter for WJZ-TV, and were critical of several aspects of ACT's operation. In the first broadcast the reporter made a number of statements that were incorrect. She reported that ACT had closed its office in Cockeysville, Maryland, and was moving its operation to Baltimore. In fact, the Cockeysville office remained open and ACT was merely opening a second office in Baltimore. Ms. Koch also incorrectly stated that ACT would sell ID cards certifying the test results of those individuals who tested negative for AIDS infection. ACT's practice was to "give" ID cards to those with negative test results, once they had paid ACT's fifty-dollar fee for a test that was available free of charge at public health agencies throughout the state. Finally, the story incorrectly stated that ACT's move into Baltimore had led state officials to "take a hard look" at the firm. The investigations had actually been prompted by consumer complaints filed against ACT with the state Attorney General.

These misstatements were not, however, the aspects of the broadcasts that appear to have been the most harmful to ACT. In both the October 29 and the November 4 stories, Ms. Koch stated that ACT was under investigation by both the State Department of Health and the Maryland Attorney General's Office. She stated that ACT appeared to be operating as a blood collection center without the license that state regulations required. Both broadcasts also reported that many members of the public health community strongly opposed the use of ID cards showing AIDS test results. Ms. Koch explained that the opposition to the cards arose because any test for AIDS represented only a snapshot in time. The cards were meaningless from the moment they were issued because they showed only that the subject had not developed antibodies to the virus before submitting to the test. In the story that aired on November 4, Ms. Koch also interviewed Stuart Caplan, a member of the Baltimore County AIDS Task Force. Mr. Caplan also expressed the concern that ACT's cards could create the erroneous belief that an individual was free of the AIDS virus. Neither of the broadcasts mentioned by name or contained any other information about ACT's investors.

ACT and its investors alleged claims against two defendants: Stuart Caplan and Group W Television. Before the subject broadcasts, Caplan had written several letters to different state agencies severely criticizing ACT's operation of a testing center as a profit-making venture. In addition to denouncing ACT's operation on the November 4 broadcast, Caplan had also spoken with and written to an employee of WJZ-TV before the October 29 broadcast. The purpose of these communications appears to have been to create negative publicity for ACT . . . .

Grant of Summary Judgment to Group W:

In granting summary judgment to Group W on the claims brought by ACT, the district court ruled that the inaccuracies in Group W's story of October 29 were immaterial and therefore not defamatory. Group W incorrectly stated that ACT had closed its Cockeysville office, that it "sold" ID cards, and that the state's investigation of ACT was prompted by the opening of its Baltimore office. Applying the test articulated in Gomba v. McLaughlin, 180 Colo. 232, 504 P.2d 337, 338-39 (1972) (en banc), the district court held that these statements, although false, did not cause the story to produce a different effect on the audience than would have been produced had the truth of the matter been spoken. Since they were immaterial, the false statements were not defamatory.

This was certainly a proper application of the law of defamation. If the gist or "sting" of a statement is substantially true, "minor inaccuracies will not give rise to a defamation claim." Liberty Lobby, Inc. v. Rees, 852 F.2d 595, 601 (D.C.Cir.1988), cert. denied, 489 U.S. 1010, 109 S.Ct. 1118, 103 L.Ed.2d 181 (1989). Here, the district court correctly found that Group W's false statements did not occur in connection with any portion of the broadcast that tended to injure ACT's reputation. There can be little doubt that, had Group W reported that ACT charged nothing for its ID cards and that the Cockeysville office remained open, the story would have affected ACT's reputation in the community in substantially the same manner. The damaging portions of the broadcast were those disclosing that ACT was under investigation by state authorities and those discussing the existence of official concern about the use of ID cards showing test results. These statements were true and true statements, no matter how damaging to the plaintiff, may never provide the foundation for a defamation claim.

Anthony S. JONES, Appellee,
v.
PALMER COMMUNICATIONS, INCORPORATED
440 N.W.2d 884

Supreme Court of Iowa.

May 17, 1989.

Rehearing Denied June 8, 1989.

ANDREASEN, Justice.

Anthony S. Jones filed a lawsuit alleging libel and false light invasion of privacy stemming from a news telecast concerning his termination from employment as a Des Moines firefighter. The trial court denied a motion for summary judgment filed by the media defendants: Palmer Communications, Inc., Steve Oswalt and Scott Pope (hereinafter referred to as Palmer). We granted Palmer's application for interlocutory appeal. This appeal does not involve claims filed by Jones against the nonmedia defendants, Des Moines Fire Chief Robert V. Armstrong and the City of Des Moines.

In this appeal we have the difficult task of defining the conflicting interests between the constitutional protection afforded the free press and the protection of individuals from defamation. In reaching a decision we must reconcile the general law of defamation with the freedoms guaranteed by the first amendment of the United States Constitution and article I, section 7 of the Iowa Constitution . . . .

Summary of the Record:

A summary of this record provides the following information. Jones was hired by the City of Des Moines as a fire fighter on December 17, 1984, under the provisions of a consent decree issued by the United States District Court concerningthe hiring of minorities. This decree was the result of a widely- publicized, class-action lawsuit allegingthat discriminatory practices had prevented qualified minority applicants from obtaining employment with the Des Moines Fire Department. Jones was dismissed on July 9, 1986, for failure to pass a written Emergency Medical Technician (EMT) examination. Jones failed the EMT test on six different occasions and had received tutoring in an effort to pass the examination. At the time of Jones' discharge, all newly-hired fire fighters in Des Moines were required to become EMT qualified.

News reporters employed by Palmer Communications, Inc., learned that a black fire fighter had been dismissed by the Des Moines Fire Department. In light of the recent federal action for discrimination, the reporters felt that Jones' dismissal was newsworthy. In researching this story, an interview was conducted with Des Moines Fire Chief Robert V. Armstrong.

During the interview, Armstrong stated that Jones had a reading problem which led to his inability to pass the EMT examination. Armstrong said that Jones was tested for reading comprehension at Drake University and was found to read at a third-grade level. Armstrong went on to say that Jones had received special tutoring at Des Moines Area Community College (DMACC) at taxpayer expense. On August 6, 1986, the news story concerning Jones' termination was broadcast at 6:00 p.m. on a local television station owned by Palmer Communications, Inc. Prior to the broadcast, news reporter Steve Oswalt contacted Jones' lawyer, who declined to respond. The media defendants allege that Oswalt made unsuccessful attempts to contact Jones personally. Jones disputes this allegation. At this time, the record does not include a tape or transcript of the broadcast in question.

Complete Defenses:

A. Substantial Truth.

In Iowa, we recognize substantial truth as an absolute defense in a defamation action. See Behr, 414 N.W.2d at 342. The libel defendant need not establish the literal truth of every detail of the broadcast so long as the "gist" or "sting" of the broadcast in question is substantially true. Id. The "gist" or "sting" of the broadcast is "the heart of the matter in question--the hurtfulness of the utterance." Id. We determine the "gist" or "sting" by "look[ing] at the highlight of the [broadcast], the pertinent angle of it, and not to the items of secondary importance which are inoffensive details, immaterial to the truth of the defamatory statement." Id. at 342.

If the underlying facts as to the gist or sting of the defamatory charge are undisputed, the court may determine substantial truth as a matter of law. Id. The test for summary judgment is whether the plaintiff would have been exposed to any more public disgrace had the publication been free of error. Id.

In considering the content of any television broadcast, it is important to see the actual broadcast. A written summary is insufficient to provide the full impact of the telecast. In this case, we do not have the benefit of viewing the challenged statements in the context of the broadcast. We do know, however, that the broadcast incorrectly implied that Jones' training was entirely subsidized by taxpayers and that he read at a third-grade level when he actually read at a level comparable with the lower one-third of junior college students. We cannot say, as a matter of law, that these statements were of secondary importance to the broadcast concerning the dismissal of Jones. We are also unable to conclude that these statements did not, by themselves, cause damage to Jones' reputation. We therefore reject Palmer's defense of substantial truth.

The NEW YORK TIMES COMPANY, Petitioner,
v.
L. B. SULLIVAN.
Ralph D. ABERNATHY et al., Petitioners,
v.
L. B. SULLIVAN.

376 U.S. 254

Supreme Court of the United States

Decided March 9, 1964.

Mr. Justice BRENNAN delivered the opinion of the Court.

We are required in this case to determine for the first time the extent to which the constitutional protections for speech and press limit a State's power to award damages in a libel action brought by a public official against critics of his official conduct.

Respondent L. B. Sullivan is one of the three elected Commissioners of the City of Montgomery, Alabama. He testified that he was 'Commissioner of Public Affairs and the duties are supervision of the Police Department, Fire Department, Department of Cemetery and Department of Scales.' He brought this civil libel action against the four individual petitioners, who are Negroes and Alabama clergymen, and against petitioner the New York Times Company, a New York corporation which publishes the New York Times, a daily newspaper. A jury in the Circuit Court of Montgomery County awarded him damages of $500,000, the full amount claimed, against all the petitioners, and the Supreme Court of Alabama affirmed. 273 Ala. 656, 144 So.2d 25.

Respondent's complaint alleged that he had been libeled by statements in a full-page advertisement that was carried in the New York Times on March 29, 1960. Entitled 'Heed Their Rising Voices,' the advertisement began by stating that 'As the whole world knows by now, thousands of Southern Negro students are engaged in widespread non-violent demonstrations in positive affirmation of the right to live in human dignity as guaranteed by the U.S. Constitution and the Bill of Rights.' It went on to charge that 'in their efforts to uphold these guarantees, they are being met by an unprecedented wave of terror by those who would deny and negate that document which the whole world looks upon as setting the pattern for modern freedom. * * *' Succeedingparagraphs purported to illustrate the 'wave of terror' by describing certain alleged events. The text concluded with an appeal for funds for three purposes: support of the student movement, 'the struggle for the right-to- vote,' and the legal defense of Dr. Martin Luther King, Jr., leader of the movement, against a perjury indictment then pending in Montgomery.

The text appeared over the names of 64 persons, many widely known for their activities in public affairs, religion, trade unions, and the performing arts. Below these names, and under a line reading 'We in the south who are struggling daily for dignity and freedom warmly endorse this appeal,' appeared the names of the four individual petitioners and of 16 other persons, all but two of whom were identified as clergymen in various Southern cities. The advertisement was signed at the bottom of the page by the 'Committee to Defend Martin Luther King and the Struggle for Freedom in the South,' and the officers of the Committee were listed.

Of the 10 paragraphs of text in the advertisement, the third and a portion of the sixth were the basis of respondent's claim of libel. They read as follows:

Third paragraph:

'In Montgomery, Alabama, after students sang 'My Country, 'Tis of Thee' on the State Capitol steps, their leaders were expelled from school, and truckloads of police armed with shotguns and tear-gas ringed the Alabama State College Campus. When the entire student body protested to state authorities by refusing to re-register, their dining hall was padlocked in an attempt to starve them into submission.'

Sixth paragraph:

'Again and again the Southern violators have answered Dr. King's peaceful protests with intimidation and violence. They have bombed his home almost killing his wife and child. They have assaulted his person. They have arrested him seven times--for 'speeding,' 'loitering' and similar 'offenses.' And now they have charged him with 'perjury'--a felony under which they could imprison him for ten years. * * *'

Although neither of these statements mentions respondent by name, he contended that the word 'police' in the third paragraph referred to him as the Montgomery Commissioner who supervised the Police Department, so that he was being accused of 'ringing' the campus with police. He further claimed that the paragraph would be read as imputing to the police, and hence to him, the padlocking of the dining hall in order to starve the students into submission. As to the sixth paragraph, he contended that since arrests are ordinarily made by the police, the statement 'They have arrested (Dr. King) seven times' would be read as referring to him; he further contended that the 'They' who did the arresting would be equated with the 'They' who committed the other described acts and with the 'Southern violators.' Thus, he argued, the paragraph would be read as accusing the Montgomery police, and hence him, of answering Dr. King's protests with 'intimidation and violence,' bombing his home, assaulting his person, and charging him with perjury. Respondent and six other Montgomery residents testified that they read some or all of the statements as referring to him in his capacity as Commissioner.

It is uncontroverted that some of the statements contained in the two paragraphs were not accurate descriptions of events which occurred in Montgomery. Although Negro students staged a demonstration on the State Capital steps, they sang the National Anthem and not 'My Country, 'Tis of Thee.' Although nine students were expelled by the State Board of Education, this was not for leading the demonstration at the Capitol, but for demanding service at a lunch counter in the Montgomery County Courthouse on another day. Not the entire student body, but most of it, had protested the expulsion, not by refusing to register, but by boycotting classes on a single day; virtually all the students did register for the ensuing semester. The campus dining hall was not padlocked on any occasion, and the only students who may have been barred from eating there were the few who had neither signed a preregistration application nor requested temporary meal tickets. Although the police were deployed near the campus in large numbers on three occasions, they did not at any time 'ring' the campus, and they were not called to the campus in connection with the demonstration on the State Capitol steps, as the third paragraph implied. Dr. King had not been arrested seven times, but only four; and although he claimed to have been assaulted some years earlier in connection with his arrest for loitering outside a courtroom, one of the officers who made the arrest denied that there was such an assault.

On the premise that the charges in the sixth paragraph could be read as referring to him, respondent was allowed to prove that he had not participated in the events described. Although Dr. King's home had in fact been bombed twice when his wife and child were there, both of these occasions antedated respondent's tenure as Commissioner, and the police were not only not implicated in the bombings, but had made every effort to apprehend those who were. Three of Dr. King's four arrests took place before respondent became Commissioner. Although Dr. King had in fact been indicted (he was subsequently acquitted) on two counts of perjury, each of which carried a possible five-year sentence, respondent had nothing to do with procuring the indictment.

Respondent made no effort to prove that he suffered actual pecuniary loss as a result of the alleged libel. One of his witnesses, a former employer, testified that if he had believed the statements, he doubted whether he 'would want to be associated with anybody who would be a party to such things that are stated in that ad,' and that he would not re-employ respondent if he believed 'that he allowed the Police Department to do the things that the paper say he did.' But neither this witness nor any of the others testified that he had actually believed the statements in their supposed reference to respondent.

The cost of the advertisement was approximately $4800, and it was published by the Times upon an order from a New York advertising agency acting for the signatory Committee. The agency submitted the advertisement with a letter from A. Philip Randolph, Chairman of the Committee, certifying that the persons whose names appeared on the advertisement had given their permission. Mr. Randolph was known to the Times' Advertising Acceptability Department as a responsible person, and in accepting the letter as sufficient proof of authorization it followed its established practice. There was testimony that the copy of the advertisement which accompanied the letter listed only the 64 names appearing under the text, and that the statement, 'We in the south * * * warmly endorse this appeal,' and the list of names thereunder, which included those of the individual petitioners, were subsequently added when the first proof of the advertisement was received. Each of the individual petitioners testified that he had not authorized the use of his name, and that he had been unaware of its use until receipt of respondent's demand for a retraction. The manager of the Advertising Acceptability Department testified that he had approved the advertisement for publication because he knew nothing to cause him to believe that anything in it was false, and because it bore the endorsement of 'a number of people who are well known and whose reputation' he 'had no reason to question.' Neither he nor anyone else at the Times made an effort to confirm the accuracy of the advertisement, either by checking it against recent Times news stories relating to some of the described events or by any other means . . . .

Because of the importance of the constitutional issues involved, we granted the separate petitions for certiorari of the individual petitioners and of the Times. 371 U.S. 946, 83 S.Ct. 510, 9 L.Ed.2d 496. We reverse the judgment. We hold that the rule of law applied by the Alabama courts is constitutionally deficient for failure to provide the safeguards for freedom of speech and of the press that are required by the First and Fourteenth Amendments in a libel action brought by a public official against critics of his official conduct. We further hold that under the proper safeguards the evidence presented in this case is constitutionally insufficient to support the judgment for respondent.

II.

Under Alabama law as applied in this case, a publication is 'libelous per se' if the words 'tend to injure a person * * * in his reputation' or to 'bring (him) into public contempt'; the trial court stated that the standard was met if the words are such as to 'injure him in his public office, or impute misconduct to him in his office, or want of official integrity, or want of fidelity to a public trust * * *.' The jury must find that the words were published 'of and concerning' the plaintiff, but where the plaintiff is a public official his place in the governmental hierarchy is sufficient evidence to support a finding that his reputation has been affected by statements that reflect upon the agency of which he is in charge. Once 'libel per se' has been established, the defendant has no defense as to stated facts unless he can persuade the jury that they were true in all their particulars. Alabama Ride Co. v. Vance, 235 Ala. 263, 178 So. 438 (1938); Johnson Publishing Co. v. Davis, 271 Ala. 474, 494--495, 124 So.2d 441, 457--458 (1960). His privilege of 'fair comment' for expressions of opinion depends on the truth of the facts upon which the comment is based. Parsons v. Age-Herald Publishing Co., 181 Ala. 439, 450, 61 So. 345, 350 (1913). Unless he can discharge the burden of proving truth, general damages are presumed, and may be awarded without proof of pecuniary injury. A showing of actual malice is apparently a prerequisite to recovery of punitive damages, and the defendant may in any event forestall a punitive award by a retraction meeting the statutory requirements. Good motives and belief in truth do not negate an inference of malice, but are relevant only in mitigation of punitive damages if the jury chooses to accord them weight. Johnson Publishing Co. v. Davis, supra, 271 Ala., at 495, 124 So.2d, at 458.

The question before us is whether this rule of liability, as applied to an action brought by a public official against critics of his official conduct, abridges the freedom of speech and of the press that is guaranteed by the First and Fourteenth Amendments.

Respondent relies heavily, as did the Alabama courts, on statements of this Court to the effect that the Constitution does not protect libelous publications. Those statements do not foreclose our inquiry here. None of the cases sustained the use of libel laws to impose sanctions upon expression critical of the official conduct of public officials. The dictum in Pennekamp v. Florida, 328 U.S. 331, 348--349, 66 S.Ct. 1029, 1038, 90 L.Ed. 1295, that 'when the statements amount to defamation, a judge has such remedy in damages for libel as do other public servants,' implied no view as to what remedy might constitutionally be afforded to public officials. In Beauharnais v. Illinois, 343 U.S. 250, 72 S.Ct. 725, 96 L.Ed. 919, the Court sustained an Illinois criminal libel statute as applied to a publication held to be both defamatory of a racial group and 'liable to cause violence and disorder.' But the Court was careful to note that it 'retains and exercises authority to nullify action which encroaches on freedom of utterance under the guise of punishing libel'; for 'public men, are, as it were, public property,' and 'discussion cannot be denied and the right, as well as the duty, of criticism must not be stifled.' Id., at 263--264, 72 S.Ct. at 734, 96 L.Ed. 919 and n. 18. In the only previous case that did present the question of constitutional limitations upon the power to award damages for libel of a public official, the Court was equally divided and the question was not decided. Schenectady Union Pub. Co. v. Sweeney, 316 U.S. 642, 62 S.Ct. 1031, 86 L.Ed. 1727. In deciding the question now, we are compelled by neither precedent nor policy to give any more weight to the epithet 'libel' than we have to other 'mere labels' of state law. N.A.A.C.P. v. Button, 371 U.S. 415, 429, 83 S.Ct. 328, 9 L.Ed.2d 405. Like insurrection, contempt, advocacy of unlawful acts, breach of the peace, obscenity, solicitation of legal business, and the various other formulae for the repression of expression that have been challenged in this Court, libel can claim no talismanic immunity from constitutional limitations. It must be measured by standards that satisfy the First Amendment.

The general proposition that freedom of expression upon public questions is secured by the First Amendment has long been settled by our decisions. The constitutional safeguard, we have said, 'was fashioned to assure unfettered interchange of ideas for the bringing about of political and social changes desired by the people.' Roth v. United States, 354 U.S. 476, 484, 77 S.Ct. 1304, 1308, 1 L.Ed.2d 1498. 'The maintenance of the opportunity for free political discussion to the end that government may be responsive to the will of the people and that changes may be obtained by lawful means, an opportunity essential to the security of the Republic, is a fundamental principle of our constitutional system.' Stromberg v. California, 283 U.S. 359, 369, 51 S.Ct. 532, 536, 75 L.Ed. 1117. '(I)t is a prized American privilege to speak one's mind, although not always with perfect good taste, on all public institutions,' Bridges v. California, 314 U.S. 252, 270, 62 S.Ct. 190, 197, 86 L.Ed. 192, and this opportunity is to be afforded for 'vigorous advocacy' no less than 'abstract discussion.' N.A.A.C.P. v. Button, 371 U.S. 415, 429, 83 S.Ct. 328, 9 L.Ed.2d 405. The First Amendment, said Judge Learned Hand, 'presupposes that right conclusions are more likely to be gathered out of a multitude of tongues, than through any kind of authoritative selection. To many this is, and always will be, folly; but we have staked upon it our all.' United States v. Associated Press, 52 F.Supp. 362, 372 (D.C.S.D.N.Y.1943). Mr. Justice Brandeis, in his concurring opinion in Whitney v. California, 274 U.S. 357, 375--376, 47 S.Ct. 641, 648, 71 L.Ed. 1095, gave the principle its classic formulation:

'Those who won our independence believed * * * that public discussion is a political duty; and that this should be a fundamental principle of the American government. They recognized the risks to which all human institutions are subject. But they knew that order cannot be secured merely through fear of punishment for its infraction; that it is hazardous to discourage thought, hope and imagination; that fear breeds repression; that repression breeds hate; that hate menaces stable government; that the path of safety lies in the opportunity to discuss freely supposed grievances and proposed remedies; and that the fitting remedy for evil counsels is good ones. Believing in the power of reason as applied through public discussion, they eschewed silence coerced by law--the argument of force in its worst form. Recognizing the occasional tyrannies of governing majorities, they amended the Constitution so that free speech and assembly should be guaranteed.'

Thus we consider this case against the background of a profound national commitment to the principle that debate on public issues should be uninhibited, robust, and wide-open, and that it may well include vehement, caustic, and sometimes unpleasantly sharp attacks on government and public officials. See Terminiello v. Chicago, 337 U.S. 1, 4, 69 S.Ct. 894, 93 L.Ed. 1131; De Jonge v. Oregon, 299 U.S. 353, 365, 57 S.Ct. 255, 81 L.Ed. 278. The present advertisement, as an expression of grievance and protest on one of the major public issues of our time, would seem clearly to qualify for the constitutional protection. The question is whether it forfeits that protection by the falsity of some of its factual statements and by its alleged defamation of respondent.

Authoritative interpretations of the First Amendment guarantees have consistently refused to recognize an exception for any test of truth--whether administered by judges, juries, or administrative officials--and especially one that puts the burden of proving truth on the speaker. Cf. Speiser v. Randall, 357 U.S. 513, 525--526, 78 S.Ct. 1332, 2 L.Ed.2d 1460. The constitutional protection does not turn upon 'the truth, popularity, or social utility of the ideas and beliefs which are offered.' N.A.A.C.P. v. Button, 371 U.S. 415, 445, 83 S.Ct. 328, 344, 9 L.Ed.2d 405. As Madison said, 'Some degree of abuse is inseparable from the proper use of every thing; and in no instance is this more true than in that of the press.' 4 Elliot's Debates on the Federal Constitution (1876), p. 571. In Cantwell v. Connecticut, 310 U.S. 296, 310, 60 S.Ct. 900, 906, 84 L.Ed. 1213, the Court declared:

'In the realm of religious faith, and in that of political belief, sharp differences arise. In both fields the tenets of one man may seem the rankest error to his neighbor. To persuade others to his own point of view, the pleader, as we know, at times, resorts to exaggeration,to vilification of men who have been, or are, prominent in church or state, and even to false statement. But the people of this nation have ordained in the light of history, that, in spite of the probability of excesses and abuses, these liberties are, in the long view, essential to enlightened opinion and right conduct on the part of the citizens of a democracy.'

That erroneous statement is inevitable in free debate, and that it must be protected if the freedoms of expression are to have the 'breathing space' that they 'need * * * to survive,' N.A.A.C.P. v. Button, 371 U.S. 415, 433, 83 S.Ct. 328, 338, 9 L.Ed.2d 405, was also recognized by the Court of Appeals for the District of Columbia Circuit in Sweeney v. Patterson, 76

U.S.App.D.C. 23, 24, 128 F.2d 457, 458 (1942), cert. denied, 317 U.S. 678, 63 S.Ct. 160, 87 L.Ed. 544. Judge Edgerton spoke for a unanimous court which affirmed the dismissal of a Congressman's libel suit based upon a newspaper article charging him with anti-Semitism in opposing a judicial appointment. He said:

> 'Cases which impose liability for erroneous reports of the political conduct of officials reflect the obsolete doctrine that the governed must not criticize their governors. * * * The interest of the public here outweighs the interest of appellant or any other individual. The protection of the public requires not merely discussion, but information. Political conduct and views which some respectable people approve, and others condemn, are constantly imputed to Congressmen. Errors of fact, particularly in regard to a man's mental states and processes, are inevitable. * * * Whatever is added to the field of libel is taken from the field of free debate.'

Injury to official reputation error affords no more warrant for repressing speech that would otherwise be free than does factual error. Where judicial officers are involved, this Court has held that concern for the dignity and reputation of the courts does not justify the punishment as criminal contempt of criticism of the judge or his decision. Bridges v. California, 314 U.S. 252, 62 S.Ct. 190, 86 L.Ed. 192. This is true even though the utterance contains 'half-truths' and 'misinformation.' Pennekamp v. Florida, 328 U.S. 331, 342, 343, n. 5, 345, 66 S.Ct. 1029, 90 L.Ed. 1295. Such repression can be justified, if at all, only by a clear and present danger of the obstruction of justice. See also Craig v. Harney, 331 U.S. 367, 67 S.Ct. 1249, 91 L.Ed. 1546; Wood v. Georgia, 370 U.S. 375, 82 S.Ct. 1364, 8 L.Ed.2d 569. If judges are to be treated as 'men of fortitude, able to thrive in a hardy climate,' Craig v. Harney, supra, 331 U.S., at 376, 67 S.Ct., at 1255, 91 L.Ed. 1546, surely the same must be true of other government officials, such as elected city commissioners. [FN14] Criticism of their official conduct does not lose its constitutional protection merely because it is effective criticism and hence diminishes their official reputations.

FN14. The climate in which public officials operate, especially during a political campaign, has been described by one commentator in the following terms: 'Charges of gross incompetence, disregard of the public interest, communist sympathies, and the like usually have filled the air; and hints of bribery, embezzlement, and other criminal conduct are not infrequent.' Noel, Defamation of Public Officers and Candidates, 49 Col.L.Rev. 875 (1949).
For a similar description written 60 years earlier, see Chase, Criticism of Public Officers and Candidates for Office, 23 Am.L.Rev. 346 (1889).

If neither factual error nor defamatory content suffices to remove the constitutional shield from criticism of official conduct, the combination of the two elements is no less inadequate. This is the lesson to be drawn from the great controversy over the Sedition Act of 1798, 1 Stat. 596, which first crystallized a national awareness of the central meaning of the First Amendment. See Levy, Legacy of Suppression (1960), at 258 et seq.; Smith, Freedom's Fetters (1956), at 426, 431 and passim. That statute made it a crime, punishable by a $5,000 fine and five years in prison, 'if any person shall write, print, utter or publish * * * any false, scandalous and malicious writing or writings against the government of the United States, or either house of the Congress * * *, or the

President * * *, with intent to defame * * * or to bring them, or either of them, into contempt or disrepute; or to excite against them, or either or any of them, the hatred of the good people of the United States.' The Act allowed the defendant the defense of truth, and provided that the jury were to be judges both of the law and the facts. Despite these qualifications, the Act was vigorously condemned as unconstitutional in an attack joined in by Jefferson and Madison. In the famous Virginia Resolutions of 1798, the General Assembly of Virginia resolved that it

> 'doth particularly protest against the palpable and alarminginfractions of the Constitution, in the two late cases of the 'Alien and Sedition Acts,' passed at the last session of Congress * * *. (The Sedition Act) exercises * * * a power not delegated by the Constitution, but, on the contrary, expressly and positively forbidden by one of the amendments thereto-- a power which more than any other, ought to produce universal alarm, because it is levelled against the right of freely examining public characters and measures, and of free communication among the people thereon, which has ever been justly deemed the only effectual guardian of every other right.' 4 Elliot's Debates, supra, pp. 553--554.

Madison prepared the Report in support of the protest. His premise was that the Constitution created a form of government under which 'The people, not the government, possess the absolute sovereignty.' The structure of the government dispersed power in reflection of the people's distrust of concentrated power, and of power itself at all levels. This form of government was 'altogether different' from the British form, under which the Crown was sovereign and the people were subjects. 'Is it not natural and necessary, under such different circumstances,' he asked, 'that a different degree of freedom in the use of the press should be contemplated?' Id., pp. 569--570. Earlier, in a debate in the House of Representatives, Madison had said: 'If we advert to the nature of Republican Government, we shall find that the censorial power is in the people over the Government, and not in the Government over the people.' 4 Annals of Congress, p. 934 (1794). Of the exercise of that power by the press, his Report said: 'In every state, probably, in the Union, the press has exerted a freedom in canvassing the merits and measures of public men, of every description, which has not been confined to the strict limits of the common law. On this footing the freedom of the press has stood; on this foundation it yet stands * * *.' 4 Elliot's Debates, supra, p. 570. The right of free public discussion of the stewardship of public officials was thus, in Madison's view, a fundamental principle of the American form of government.

Although the Sedition Act was never tested in this Court, the attack upon its validity has carried the day in the court of history. Fines levied in its prosecution were repaid by Act of Congress on the ground that it was unconstitutional. See, e.g., Act of July 4, 1840, c. 45, 6 Stat. 802, accompanied by H.R.Rep.No. 86, 26th Cong., 1st Sess. (1840). Calhoun, reporting to the Senate on February 4, 1836, assumed that its invalidity was a matter 'which no one now doubts.' Report with Senate bill No. 122, 24th Cong., 1st Sess., p. 3. Jefferson, as President, pardoned those who had been convicted and sentenced under the Act and remitted their fines, stating: 'I discharged every person under punishment or prosecution under the sedition law, because I considered, and now consider, that law to be a nullity, as absolute and as palpable as if Congress had ordered us to fall down and worship a golden image.' Letter to Mrs. Adams, July 22, 1804, 4 Jefferson's Works (Washington ed.), pp. 555, 556.

What a State may not constitutionally bring about by means of a criminal statute is likewise beyond the reach of its civil law of libel. The fear of damage awards under a rule such as that invoked by the Alabama courts here may be markedly more inhibiting than the fear of prosecution under a criminal statute. See City of Chicago v. Tribune Co., 307 Ill. 595, 607, 139 N.E. 86, 90 (1923). Alabama, for example, has a criminal libel law which subjects to prosecution 'any person who speaks, writes, or prints of and concerning another any accusation falsely and maliciously importing the commission by such person of a felony, or any other indictable offense involving moral turpitude,' and which allows as punishment upon conviction a fine not exceeding $500 and a prison sentence of six months. Alabama Code, Tit. 14, s 350. Presumably a person charged with violation of this statute enjoys ordinary criminal-law safeguards such as the requirements of an indictment and of proof beyond a reasonable doubt. These safeguards are not available to the defendant in a civil action. The judgment awarded in this case--without the need for any proof of actual pecuniary loss--was one thousand times greater than the maximum fine provided by the Alabama criminal statute, and one hundred times greater than that provided by the Sedition Act . . . .

The constitutional guarantees require, we think, a federal rule that prohibits a public official from recovering damages for a defamatory falsehood relating to his official conduct unless he proves that the statement was made with 'actual malice'--that is, with knowledge that it was false or with reckless disregard of whether it was false or not. An oft-cited statement of a like rule, which has been adopted by a number of state courts, is found in the Kansas case of Coleman v. MacLennan, 78 Kan. 711, 98 P. 281 (1908). The State Attorney General, a candidate for re-election and a member of the commission charged with the management and control of the state school fund, sued a newspaper publisher for alleged libel in an article purporting to state facts relating to his official conduct in connection with a school-fund transaction. The defendant pleaded privilege and the trial judge, over the plaintiff's objection, instructed the jury that

> 'where an article is published and circulated among voters for the sole purpose of giving what the defendant believes to be truthful information concerning a candidate for public office and for the purpose of enabling such voters to cast their ballot more intelligently, and the whole thing is done in good faith and without malice, the article is privileged, although the principal matters contained in the article may be untrue in fact and derogatory to the character of the plaintiff; and in such a case the burden is on the plaintiff to show actual malice in the publication of the article.'

In answer to a special question, the jury found that the plaintiff had not proved actual malice, and a general verdict was returned for the defendant. On appeal the Supreme Court of Kansas, in an opinion by Justice Burch, reasoned as follows (78 Kan., at 724, 98 P., at 286):

> '(I)t is of the utmost consequence that the people should discuss the character and qualifications of candidates for their suffrages. The importance to the state and to society of such discussions is so vast, and the advantages derived are so great that they more than counterbalance the inconvenience of private persons whose conduct may be involved, and occasional injury to the reputations of individuals must yield to the public welfare, although at times such injury may be great. The public benefit from publicity is so great and the chance of

injury to private character so small that such discussion must be privileged.'

The court thus sustained the trial court's instruction as a correct statement of the law, saying:

> 'In such a case the occasion gives rise to a privilege qualified to this extent. Any one claiming to be defamed by the communication must show actual malice, or go remediless. This privilege extends to a great variety of subjects and includes matters of public concern, public men, and candidates for office.' 78 Kan., at 723, 98 P., at 285.

Such a privilege for criticism of official conduct is appropriately analogous to the protection accorded a public official when he is sued for libel by a private citizen. In Barr v. Matteo, 360 U.S. 564, 575, 79 S.Ct. 1335, 1341, 3 L.Ed.2d 1434, this Court held the utterance of a federal official to be absolutely privileged if made 'within the outer perimeter' of his duties. The States accord the same immunity to statements of their highest officers, although some differentiate their lesser officials and qualify the privilege they enjoy. But all hold that all officials are protected unless actual malice can be proved. The reason for the official privilege is said to be that the threat of damage suits would otherwise 'inhibit the fearless, vigorous, and effective administration of policies of government' and 'dampen the ardor of all but the most resolute, or the most irresponsible, in the unflinching discharge of their duties.' Barr v. Matteo, supra, 360 U.S., at 571, 79 S.Ct., at 1339, 3 L.Ed.2d 1434. Analogous considerations support the privilege for the citizen-critic of government. It is as much his duty to criticize as it is the official's duty to administer. See Whitney v. California, 274 U.S. 357, 375, 47 S.Ct. 641, 648, 71 L.Ed. 1095 (concurring opinion of Mr. Justice Brandeis), quoted supra, pp. 720, 721. As Madison said, see supra, p. 723, 'the censorial power is in the people over the Government, and not in the Government over the people.' It would give public servants an unjustified preference over the public they serve, if critics of official conduct did not have a fair equivalent of the immunity granted to the officials themselves.

We conclude that such a privilege is required by the First and Fourteenth Amendments.

## III.

[21][22][23] We hold today that the Constitution delimits a State's power to award damages for libel in actions brought by public officials against critics of their official conduct. Since this is such an action, the rule requiring proof of actual malice is applicable.

Since respondent may seek a new trial, we deem that considerations of effective judicial administration require us to review the evidence in the present record to determine whether it could constitutionally support a judgment for respondent. This Court's duty is not limited to the elaboration of constitutional principles; we must also in proper cases review the evidence to make certain that those principles have been constitutionally applied. This is such a case, particularly since the question is one of alleged trespass across 'the line between speech unconditionally guaranteed and speech which may legitimately be regulated.'

Applying these standards, we consider that the proof presented to show actual malice lacks the convincing clarity which the constitutional standard demands, and hence that it would not constitutionally sustain the judgment for respondent under the proper rule of law. The case of the individual petitioners requires little discussion. Even assuming that they could constitutionally be found to have authorized the use of their names on the advertisement, there was no evidence whatever that they were aware of any erroneous statements or were in any way reckless in that regard. The judgment against them is thus without constitutional support.

As to the Times, we similarly conclude that the facts do not support a finding of actual malice. The statement by the Times' Secretary that, apart from the padlocking allegation, he thought the advertisement was 'substantially correct,' affords no constitutional warrant for the Alabama Supreme Court's conclusion that it was a 'cavalier ignoring of the falsity of the advertisement (from which), the jury could not have but been impressed with the bad faith of The Times, and its maliciousness inferable therefrom.' The statement does not indicate malice at the time of the publication; even if the advertisement was not 'substantially correct'--although respondent's own proofs tend to show that it was--that opinion was at least a reasonable one, and there was no evidence to impeach the witness' good faith in holding it. The Times' failure to retract upon respondent's demand, although it later retracted upon the demand of Governor Patterson, is likewise not adequate evidence of malice for constitutional purposes . . . .

Finally, there is evidence that the Times published the advertisement without checking its accuracy against the news stories in the Times' own files. The mere presence of the stories in the files does not, of course, establish that the Times 'knew' the advertisement was false . . . .

We also think the evidence was constitutionally defective in another respect: it was incapable of supporting the jury's finding that the allegedly libelous statements were made 'of and concerning' respondent. Respondent relies on the words of the advertisement and the testimony of six witnesses to establish a connection between it and himself. Thus, in his brief to this Court, he states:

> 'The reference to respondent as police commissioner is clear from the ad. In addition, the jury heard the testimony of a newspaper editor * * *; a real estate and insurance man * * *; the sales manager of a men's clothing store * * *; a food equipment man * * *; a service station operator * * *; and the operator of a truck line for whom respondent had formerly worked * * *. Each of these witnesses stated that he associated the statements with respondent * * *.' (Citations to record omitted.)

There was no reference to respondent in the advertisement, either by name or official position. A number of the allegedly libelous statements--the charges that the dining hall was padlocked and that Dr. King's home was bombed, his person assaulted, and a perjury prosecution instituted against him--did not even concern the police; despite the ingenuity of the arguments which would attach this significance to the word 'They,' it is plain that these statements could not reasonably be read as accusing respondent of personal involvement in the acts in question. The statements upon which respondent principally relies as referring to him are the two allegations that did concern the police or police functions: that 'truckloads of police * * * ringed the Alabama State College Campus' after the demonstration on the State Capitol steps, and that Dr. King had been 'arrested * * * seven times.' These statements were false only in that the police had been 'deployed near' the campus but had not actually 'ringed' it and had not gone there in connection with the State Capitol demonstration, and in that Dr. King had been arrested only four times. The ruling that these discrepancies between what was true and what was asserted were sufficient to injure respondent's reputation may itself raise constitutional problems, but we need not consider them here. Although the statements may be taken as referring to the police, they did not on their face make even an oblique reference to respondent as an individual . . . .

The judgment of the Supreme Court of Alabama is reversed and the case is remanded to that court for further proceedings not inconsistent with this opinion.

Reversed and remanded.

Mr. Justice BLACK, with whom Mr. Justice DOUGLAS joins (concurring).

I concur in reversing this half-million-dollar judgment against the New York Times Company and the four individual defendants. In reversing the Court holds that 'the Constitution delimits a State's power to award damages for libel in actions brought by public officials against critics of their official conduct.' Ante, p. 727. I base my vote to reverse on the belief that the First and Fourteenth Amendments not merely 'delimit' a State's power to award damages to 'public officials against critics of their official conduct' but completely prohibit a State from exercising such a power. The Court goes on to hold that a State can subject such critics to damages if 'actual malice' can be proved against them. 'Malice,' even as defined by the Court, is an elusive, abstract concept, hard to prove and hard to disprove. The requirement that malice be proved provides at best an evanescent protection for the right critically to discuss public affairs and certainly does not measure up to the sturdy safeguard embodied in the First Amendment. Unlike the Court, therefore, I vote to reverse exclusively on the ground that the Times and the individual defendants had an absolute, unconditional constitutional right to publish in the Times advertisement their criticisms of the Montgomery agencies and officials. I do not base my vote to reverse on any failure to prove that these individual defendants signed the advertisement or that their criticism of the Police Department was aimed at the plaintiff Sullivan, who was then the Montgomery City Commissioner having supervision of the City's police; for present purposes I assume these things were proved. Nor is my reason for reversal the size of the half-million-dollar judgment, large as it is. If Alabama has constitutional power to use its civil libel law to impose damages on the press for criticizing the way public officials perform or fail to perform their duties, I know of no provision in the Federal Constitution which either expressly or impliedly bars the State from fixing the amount of damages.

The half-million-dollar verdict does give dramatic proof, however, that state libel laws threaten the very existence of an American press virile enough to publish unpopular views on public affairs and bold enough to criticize the conduct of public officials. The factual background of this case emphasizes the imminence and enormity of that threat. One of the acute and highly emotional issues in this country arises out of efforts of many people, even including some public officials, to continue state-commanded segregation of races in the public schools and other public places, despite our several holdings that such a state practice is forbidden by the Fourteenth Amendment. Montgomery is one of the localities in which widespread hostility to desegregation has been manifested . . . . There is no reason to believe that there are not more such huge verdicts lurking just around the corner for the Times or any other newspaper or broadcaster which might dare to criticize public officials. In fact, briefs before us show that in Alabama there are now pending eleven libel suits by local and state officials against the Times seeking $5,600,000, and five such suits against the Columbia Broadcasting System seeking $1,700,000. Moreover, this technique for harassing and punishing a free press--now that it has been shown to be possible--is by no means limited to cases with racial overtones; it can be used in other fields where public feelings may make local as well as out-of-state news-papers easy prey for libel verdict seekers.

In my opinion the Federal Constitution has dealt with this deadly danger to the press in the only way possible without leaving the free press open to destruction--by granting the press an absolute immunity for criticism of the way public officials do their public duty.

Elmer GERTZ, Petitioner,
v.
ROBERT WELCH, INC.

418 U.S. 323

Supreme Court of the United States

Decided June 25, 1974.

Mr. Justice POWELL delivered the opinion of the Court.

This Court has struggled for nearly a decade to define the proper accommodation between the law of defamation and the freedoms of speech and press protected by the First Amendment. With this decision we return to that effort. We granted certiorari to reconsider the extent of a publisher's constitutional privilege against liability for defamation of a private citizen. 410 U.S. 925, 93 S.Ct. 1355, 35 L.Ed.2d 585 (1973).

## I

In 1968 a Chicago policeman named Nuccio shot and killed a youth named Nelson. The state authorities prosecuted Nuccio for the homicide and ultimately obtained a conviction for murder in the second degree. The Nelson family retained petitioner Elmer Gertz, a reputable attorney, to represent them in civil litigation against Nuccio.

Respondent publishes American Opinion, a monthly outlet for the views of the John Birch Society. Early in the 1960's the magazine began to warn of a nationwide conspiracy to discredit local law enforcement agencies and create in their stead a national police force capable of supporting a Communist dictatorship. As part of the continuing effort to alert the public to this assumed danger, the managing editor of American Opinion commissioned an article on the murder trial of Officer Nuccio. For this purpose he engaged a regular contributor to the magazine. In March 1969 respondent published the resulting article under the title 'FRAME-UP: Richard Nuccio And The War On Police.' The article purports to demonstrate that the testimony against Nuccio at his criminal trial was false and that his prosecution was part of the Communist campaign against the police.

In his capacity as counsel for the Nelson family in the civil litigation, petitioner attended the coroner's inquest into the boy's death and initiated actions for damages, but he neither discussed Officer Nuccio with the press nor played any part in the criminal proceeding. Notwithstanding petitioner's remote connection with the prosecution of Nuccio, respondent's magazine portrayed him as an architect of the 'frame-up.' According to the article, the police file on petitioner took 'a big, Irish cop to lift.' The article stated that petitioner had been an official of the 'Marxist League for Industrial Democracy, originally known as the Intercollegiate Socialist Society, which has advocated the violent seizure of our government.' It labeled Gertz a 'Leninist' and a 'Communist-fronter.' It also stated that Gertz had been an officer of the National Lawyers Guild, described as a Communist organization that 'probably did more than any other outfit to plan the Communist attack on the Chicago police during the 1968 Democratic Convention.'

These statements contained serious inaccuracies. The implication that petitioner had a criminal record was false. Petitioner had been a member and officer of the National Lawyers Guild some 15 years earlier, but there was no evidence that he or that organization had taken any part in planning the 1968 demonstrations in Chicago. There was also no basis for the charge that petitioner was a 'leninist' or a 'Communist-fronter.' And he had never been a member of the 'Marxist League for Industrial Democracy' or the 'Intercollegiate Socialist Society.'

The managingeditor of American Opinion made no effort to verify or substantiate the charges against petitioner. Instead, he appended an editorial introduction stating that the author had 'conducted extensive research into the Richard Nuccio Case.' And he included in the article a photograph of petitioner and wrote the caption that appeared under it: 'Elmer Gertz of Red Guild harasses Nuccio.' mespondent placed the issue of American Opinion containing the article on sale at newsstands throughout the country and distributed reprints of the article on the streets of Chicago.

Petitioner filed a diversity action for libel in the United States District Court for the Northern District of Illinois. He claimed that the falsehoods published by respondent injured his reputation as a lawyer and a citizen. Before filing an answer, respondent moved to dismiss the complaint for failure to state a claim upon which relief could be granted, apparently on the ground that petitioner failed to allege special damages. But the court ruled that statements contained in the article constituted libel per se under Illinois law and that consequently petitioner need not plead special damages. 306 F.Supp. 310 (1969).

After answering the complaint, respondent filed a pretrial motion for summary judgment, claiming a constitutional privilege against liability for defamation. It asserted that petitioner was a public official or a public figure and that the article concerned an issue of public interest and concern. For these reasons, respondent argued, it was entitled to invoke the privilege enunciated in New York Times Co. v. Sullivan, 376 U.S. 254, 84 S.Ct. 710, 11 L.Ed.2d 686 (1964). Under this rule respondent would escape liability unless petitioner could prove publication of defamatory falsehood 'with 'actual malice'--that is, with knowledge that it was false or with reckless disregard of whether it was false or not.' Id., at 279--280, 84 S.Ct., at 726. Respondent claimed that petitioner could not make such a showing and submitted a supporting affidavit by the magazine's managing editor. The editor denied any knowledge of the falsity of the statements concerning petitioner and stated that he had relied on the author's reputation and on his prior experience with the accuracy and authenticity of the author's contributions to American Opinion.

The District Court denied respondent's motion for summary judgment in a memorandum opinion of September 16, 1970. The court did not dispute respondent's claim to the protection of the New York Times standard. Rather, it concluded that petitioner might overcome the constitutional privilege by making a factual showing sufficient to prove publication of defamatory falsehood in reckless disregard of the truth. During the course of the trial, however, it became clear that the trial court had not acceped all of respondent's asserted grounds for applying the New York Times rule to this case. It thought that respondent's claim to the protection of the constitutional privilege depended on the contention that petitioner was either a public official under the New York Times decision or a public figure under Curtis Publishing Co. v. Butts, 388 U.S. 130, 87 S.Ct. 1975, 18 L.Ed.2d 1094 (1967), apparently discounting the argument that a privilege would arise from the presence of a public issue. After all the evidence had been presented but before submission of the case to the jury, the court ruled in effect that petitioner was neither a public official nor a public figure. It added that, if he were, the resulting application of the New York Times standard would require a directed verdict for respondent. Because some statements in the article constituted libel per se under Illinois law, the court submitted the case to the jury under instructions that withdrew from its consideration all issues save the measure of damages. The jury awarded $50,000 to petitioner.

Following the jury verdict and on further reflection, the District Court concluded that the New York Times standard should govern this case even though petitioner was not a public official or public figure. It accepted respondent's contention that that privilege protected discussion of any public issue without regard to the status of a person defamed therein. Accordingly, the court entered judgment for respondent notwithstanding the jury's verdict. This conclusion anticipated the reasoning of a plurality of this Court in Rosenbloom v. Metromedia, Inc., 403 U.S. 29, 91 S.Ct. 1811, 29 L.Ed.2d 296 (1971).

Petitioner appealed to contest the applicability of the New York Times standard to this case. Although the Court of Appeals for the Seventh Circuit doubted the correctness of the District Court's determination that petitioner was not a public figure, it did not overturn that finding. It agreed with the District Court that respondent could assert the constitutional privilege because the article concerned a matter of public interest, citing this Court's intervening decision in Rosenbloom v. Metromedia, Inc., supra. The Court of Appeals read Rosenbloom to require application of the New York Times standard to any publication or broadcast about an issue of significant public interest, without regard to the position, fame, or anonymity of the person defamed, and it concluded that respondent's statements concerned such an issue. After reviewing the record, the Court of Appeals endorsed the District Court's conclusion that petitioner had failed to show by clear and convincing evidence that respondent had acted with 'actual malice' as defined by New York Times. There was no evidence that the managing editor of American Opinion knew of the falsity of the accusations made in the article. In fact, he knew nothing about petitioner except what he learned from the article. The court correctly noted that mere proof of failure to investigate, without more, cannot establish reckless disregard for the truth. Rather, the publisher must act with a "high degree of awareness of . . . probable falsity." St. Amant v.

Thompson, 390 U.S. 727, 731, 88 S.Ct. 1323, 1325, 20 L.Ed.2d 262 (1968); accord, Beckley Newspapers Corp. v. Hanks, 389 U.S. 81, 84--85, 88 S.Ct. 197, 199--200, 19 L.Ed.2d 248 (1967); Garrison v. Louisiana, 379 U.S. 64, 75--76, 85 S.Ct. 209, 212, 216--217, 13 L.Ed.2d 125 (1964). The evidence in this case did not reveal that respondent had cause for such an awareness. The Court of Appeals therefore affirmed, 471 F.2d 801 (1972). For the reasons stated below, we reverse.

II

The principal issue in this case is whether a newspaper or broadcaster that publishes defamatory falsehoods about an individual who is neither a public official nor a public figure may claim a constitutional provilege against liability for the injury inflicted by those statements. The Court considered this question on the rather different set of facts presented in Rosenbloom v. Metromedia, Inc., 403 U.S. 29, 91 S.Ct. 1811, 29 L.Ed.2d 296 (1971). Rosenbloom, a distributor of nudist magazines, was arrested for selling allegedly obscene material while making a delivery to a retail dealer. The police obtained a warrant and seized his entire inventory of 3,000 books and magazines. He sought and obtained an injunction prohibiting further police interference with his business. He then sued a locl radio station for failing to note in two of its newscasts that the 3,000 items seized were only 'reportedly' or 'allegedly' obscene and for broadcasting references to 'the smut literature racket' and to 'girlie-book peddlers' in its coverage of the court proceeding for injunctive relief. He obtained a judgment against the radio station, but the Court of Appeals for the Third Circuit held the New York Times privilege applicable to the broadcast and reversed. 415 F.2d 892 (1969).

This Court affirmed the decision below, but no majority could agree on a controlling rationale. The eight Justices who participated in Rosenbloom announced their views in five separate opinions, none of which commanded more than three votes. The several statements not only reveal disagreement about the appropriate result in that case, they also reflect divergent traditions of thought about the general problem of reconciling the law of defamation with the First Amendment. One approach has been to extend the New York Times test to an expanding variety of situations. Another has been to vary the level of constitutional privilege for defamatory falsehood with the status of the person defamed. And a third view would grant to the press and broadcast media absolute immunity from liability for defamation. To place our holding in the proper context, we preface our discussion of this case with a review of the several Rosenbloom opinions and their antecedents.

In affirming the trial court's judgment in the instant case, the Court of Appeals relied on Mr. Justice Brennan's conclusion for the Rosenbloom plurality that 'all discussion and communication involving matters of public or general concern,' 403 U.S., at 44, 91 S.Ct., at 1820, warrant the protection from liability for defamation accorded by the rule originally enunciated in New York Times Co. v. Sullivan, 376 U.S. 254, 84 S.Ct. 710, 11 L.Ed.2d 686 (1964). There this Court defined a constitutional privilege intended to free criticism of public officials from the restraints imposed by the common law of defamation. The Times ran a political advertisement endorsing civil rights demonstrations by black students in Alabama and impliedly condemning the performance of local law-enforcement officials. A police commissioner established in state court that certain misstatements in the advertisement referred to him and that they constituted libel per se under Alabama law. This showing left the Times with the single defense of truth, for under Alabama law neither good faith nor reasonable care would protect the newspaper from liability. This Court concluded that a 'rule compelling the critic of official conduct to guarantee the truth of all his factual assertions' would deter protected speech, id., at 279, 84 S.Ct., at 725, and announced the constitutional privilege designed to counter that effect:

> 'The constitutional guarantees require, we think, a federal rule that prohibits a public official from recovering damages for a defamatory falsehood relating to his official conduct unless he proves that the statement was made with 'actual malice'--that is, with knowledge that it was false or with reckless disregard of whether it was false or not.' Id., at 279--280, 84 S.Ct. at 726.

Three years after New York Times, a majority of the Court agreed to extend the constitutional privilege to defamatory criticism of 'public figures.' This extension was announced in Curtis Publishing Co. v. Butts and its companion, Associated Press v. Walker, 388 U.S. 130, 162, 87 S.Ct. 1975, 1995, 18 L.Ed.2d 1094 (1967). The first case involved the Saturday Evening Post's charge that Coach Wally Butts of the University of Georgia had conspired with Coach 'Bear' Bryant of the University of Alabama to fix a football game between their respective schools. Walker involved an erroneous Associated Press account of former Major General Edwin Walker's participation in a University of Mississippi campus riot. Because Butts was paid by a private alumni association and Walker had resigned from the Army, neither could be classified as a 'public official' under New York Times. Although Mr. Justice Harlan announced the result in both cases, a majority of the Court agreed with Mr. Chief Justice Warren's conclusion that the New York Times test should apply to criticism of 'public figures' as well as 'public officials.' The Court extended the constitutional privilege announced in that case to protect defamatory criticism of nonpublic persons who 'are nevertheless intimately involved in the resolution of important public questions or, by reason of their fame, shape events in areas of concern to society at large.' Id., at 164, 87 S.Ct., at 1996 (Warren, C.J., concurring in result) . . . .

III

We begin with the common ground. Under the First Amendment there is no such thing as a false idea. However pernicious an opinion may seem, we depend for its correction not on the conscience of judges and juries but on the competition of other ideas. But there is no constitutional value in false statements of fact. Neither the intentional lie nor the careless error materially advances society's interest in 'uninhibited, robust, and wide-open' debate on public issues. New York Times Co. v. Sullivan, 376 U.S., at 270, 84 S.Ct., at 721. They belong to that category of utterances which 'are no essential part of any exposition of ideas, and are of such slight social value as a step to truth that any benefit that may be derived from them is clearly outweighed by the social interest in order and morality.' Chaplinsky v. New Hampshire, 315 U.S. 568, 572, 62 S.Ct. 766, 769, 86 L.Ed. 1031 (1942).

Although the erroneous statement of fact is not worthy of constitutional protection, it is nevertheless inevitable in free debate. As James Madison pointed out in the Report on the Virginia Resolutions of 1798: 'Some degree of abuse is inseparable from the proper use of every thing; and in no instance is this more true than in that of the press.' 4 J. Elliot, Debates on the Federal Constitution of 1787, p. 571 (1876). And punishment of error runs the risk of inducing a cautious and restrictive exercise of the constitutionally guaranteed freedoms of speech and press. Our decisions recognize that a rule of strict liability that compels a publisher or broadcaster to guarantee the accuracy of his factual assertions may lead to intolerable self-censorship. Allowing the media to avoid liability only by proving the truth of all injurious statements does not accord adequate protection to First Amendment liberties. As the Court stated in New York Times Co. v. Sullivan, supra, 376 U.S., at 279, 84 S.Ct., at 725: 'Allowance of the defense of truth, with the burden of proving it on the defendant, does not mean that only false speech will be deterred.' The First Amendment requires that we protect some falsehood in order to protect speech that matters.

The need to avoid self-censorship by the news media is, however, not the only societal value at issue. If it were, this Court would have embraced long ago the view that publishers and broadcasters enjoy an unconditional and indefeasible immunity from liability for defamation. See New York Times Co. v. Sullivan, supra, at 293, 84 S.Ct., at 733 (Black, J., concurring); Garrison v. Louisiana, 379 U.S., at 80, 85 S.Ct., at 218 (1964) (Douglas, J., concurring); Curtis Publishing Co. v. Butts, 388 U.S., at 170, 87 S.Ct., at 1999 (opinion of Black, J.). Such a rule would, indeed, obviate the fear that the prospect of civil liability for injurious falsehood might dissuade a timorous press from the effective exercise of First Amendment freedoms. Yet absolute protection for the communications media requires a total sacrifice of the competing value served by the law of defamation.

The legitimate state interest underlying the law of libel is the compensation of individuals for the harm inflicted on them by defamatory falsehood. We would not lightly require the State to abandon this purpose, for, as Mr. Justice Stewart has reminded us, the individual's right to the protection of his own good name

> 'reflects no more than our basic concept of the essential dignity and worth of every human being--a concept at the root of any decent system of ordered liberty. The protection of private personality, like the protection of life itself, is left primarily to the individual States under the Ninth and Tenth Amendments. But this does not mean that the right is entitled to any less recognition by this Court as a basic of our constitutional system.' Rosenblatt v. Baer, 383 U.S. 75, 92, 86 S.Ct. 669, 679, 15 L.Ed.2d 597 (1966) (concurring opinion).

Some tension necessarily exists between the need for a vigorous and uninhibited press and the legitimate interest in redressing wrongful injury. As Mr. Justice Harlan stated, 'some antithesis between freedom of speech and press and libel actions persists, for libel remains premised on the content of speech and limits the freedom of the publisher to express certain sentiments, at least without guaranteeing legal proof of their substantial accuracy.' Curtis Publishing Co. v. Butts, supra, 388 U.S., at 152, 87 S.Ct., at 1990. In our continuing effort to define the proper accommodation between these competing concerns, we have been especially anxious to assure to the freedoms of speech and press that 'breathing space' essential to their fruitful exercise. NAACP v. Button, 371 U.S. 415, 433, 83 S.Ct. 328, 338, 9 L.Ed.2d 405 (1963). To that end this Court has extended a measure of strategic protection to defamatory falsehood.

The New York Times standard defines the level of constitutional protection appropriate to the context of defamation of a public person. Those who, by reason of the notoriety of their achievements or the vigor and success with which they seek the public's attention, are properly classed as public figures and those who hold governmental office may recover for injury to reputation only on clear and convincing proof that the defamatory falsehood was made with knowledge of its falsity or with reckless disregard for the truth. This standard administers an extremely powerful antidote to the inducement to media self-censorship of the common-law rule of strict liability for libel and slander. And it exacts a correspondingly high price from the victims of defamatory falsehood. Plainly many deserving plaintiffs, including some intentionally subjected to injury, will be unable to surmount the barrier of the New York Times test. Despite this substantial abridgment of the state law right to compensation for wrongful hurt to one's reputation, the Court has concluded that the protection of the New York Times privilege should be available to publishers and broadcasters of defamatory falsehood concerning public officials and public figures. New York Times Co. v. Sullivan, supra; Curtis Publishing Co. v. Butts, supra. We think that these decisions are correct, but we do not find their holdings justified solely by reference to the interest of the press and broadcast media in immunity from liability. Rather, we believe that the New York Times rule states an accommodation between this concern and the limited state interest present in the context of libel actions brought by public persons. For the reasons stated below, we conclude that the state interest in compensating injury to the reputation of private individuals requires that a different rule should obtain with respect to them.

Theoretically, of course, the balance between the needs of the press and the individual's claim to compensation for wrongful injury might be struck on a case-by-case basis. As Mr. Justice Harlan hypothesized, 'it might seem, purely as an abstract matter, that the most utilitarian approach would be to scrutinize carefully every jury verdict in every libel case, in order to ascertain whether the final judgment leaves fully protected whatever First Amendment values transcend the legitimate state interest in protecting the particular plaintiff who prevailed.' Rosenbloom v. Metromedia, Inc., 403 U.S., at 63, 91 S.Ct., at 1829 (footnote omitted). But this approach would lead to unpredictable results and uncertain expectations, and it could render our duty to supervise the lower courts unmanageable. Because an ad hoc resolution of the competing interests at stake in each particular case is not feasible, we must lay down broad rules of general application. Such rules necessarily treat alike various cases involving differences as well as similarities. Thus it is often true that not all of the considerations which justify adoption of a given rule will obtain in each particular case decided under its authority.

With that caveat we have no difficulty in distinguishing among defamation plaintiffs. The first remedy of any victime of defamation is self-help--using available opportunities to contradict the lie or correct the error and thereby to minimize its adverse impact on reputation. Public officials and public figures usually enjoy significantly greater access to the channels of effective communication and hence have a more realistic opportunity to counteract false statements then private individuals normally enjoy. Private individuals are therefore more vulnerable to injury, and the state interest in protecting them is correstpondingly greater.

More important than the likelihood that private individuals will lack effective opportunities for rebuttal, there is a compelling normative consideration underlying the distinction between public and private defamation plaintiffs. An individual who decides to seek governmental office must accept certain necessary consequences of that involvement in public affairs. He runs the risk of closer public scrutiny than might otherwise be the case. And society's interest in the officers of government is not strictly limited to the formal discharge of official duties. As the Court pointed out in Garrison v. Louisiana, 379 U.S., at 77, 85 S.Ct., at 217, the public's interest extends to 'anything which might touch on an official's fitness for office. . . . Few personal attributes are more germane to fitness for office than dishonesty, malfeasance, or improper motivation, even though these characteristics may also affect the official's private character.'

Those classed as public figures stand in a similar position. Hypothetically, it may be possible for someone to become a public figure through no purposeful action of his own, but the instances of truly involuntary public figures must be exceedingly rare. For the most part those who attain this status have assumed roles of especial prominence in the affairs of society. Some occupy positions of such persuasive power and influence that they are deemed public figures for all purposes. More commonly, those classed as public figures have thrust themselves to the forefront of particular public controversies in order to influence the resolution of the issues involved. In either event, they invite attention and comment.

Even if the foregoing generalities do not obtain in every instance, the communications media are entitled to act on the assumption that public officials and public figures have voluntarily exposed themselves to increased risk of injury from defamatory falsehood concerning them. No such assumption is justified with respect to a rpivate individual. He has not accepted public office or assumed an 'influential role in ordering society.' Curtis Publishing Co. v. Butts, 388 U.S., at 164, 87 S.Ct., at 1996 (Warren, C.J., concurring in result). He has relinquished no part of his interest in the protection of his own good name, and consequently he has a more compelling call on the courts for redress of injury inflicted by defamatory falsehood. Thus, private individuals are not only more vulnerable to injury than public officials and public figures; they are also more deserving of recovery . . . .

We hold that, so long as they do not impose liability without fault, the States may define for themselves the appropriate standard of liability for a publisher or broadcaster of defamatory falsehood injurious to a private individual. This approach provides a more equitable boundary between the competing concerns involved here. It recognizes the strength of the legitimate state interest in compensating private individuals for wrongful injury to reputation, yet shields the press and broadcast media from the rigors of strict liability for defamation . . . .

V

Notwithstanding our refusal to extend the New York Times privilege to defamation of private individuals, respondent contends that we should affirm the judgment below on the ground that petitioner is either a public official or a public figure. There is little basis for the former assertion. Several years prior to the present incident, petitioner had served briefly on housing committees appointed by the mayor of Chicago, but at the time of publication he had never held any remunerative governmental position. Respondent admits this but argues that petitioner's appearance at the coroner's inquest rendered him a 'de facto public official.' Our cases recognized no such concept. Respondent's suggestion would sweep all lawyers under the New York Times rule as officers of the court and distort the plain meaning of the 'public official' category beyond all recognition. We decline to follow it.

Respondent's characterization of petitioner as a public figure raises a different question. That designation may rest on either of two alternative bases. In some instances an individual may achieve such pervasive fame or notoriety that he becomes a public figure for all purposes and in all contexts. More commonly, an individual voluntarily injects himself or is drawn into a particular public controversy and thereby becomes a public figure for a limited range of issues. In either case such persons assume special prominence in the resolution of public questions.

Petitioner has long been active in community and professional affairs. He has served as an officer of local civic groups and of various professional organizations, and he has published several books and articles on legal subjects. Although petitioner was consequently well known in some circles, he had achieved no general fame or notoriety in the community. None of the prospective jurors called at the trial had ever heard of petitioner prior to this litigation, and respondent offered no proof that this response was atypical of the local population. We would not lightly assume that a citizen's participation in community and professional affairs rendered him a public figure for all purposes. Absent clear evidence of general fame or notoriety in the community, and pervasive involvement in the affairs of society, an individual should not be deemed a public personality for all aspects of his life. It is preferable to reduce the public-figure question to a more meaningful context by looking to the nature and extent of an individual's participation in the particular controversy giving rise to the defamation.

In this context it is plain that petitioner was not a public figure. He played a minimal role at the coroner's inquest, and his participation related solely to his representation of a private client. He took no part in the criminal prosecution of Officer Nuccio. Moreover, he never discussed either the criminal or civil litigation with the press and was never quoted as having done so. He plainly did not thrust himself into the vortex of this public issue, nor did he engage the public's attention in an attempt to influence its outcome. We are persauded that the trial court did not err in refusing to characterize petitioner as a public figure for the purpose of this litigation.

We therefore conclude that the New York Times standard is inapplicable to this case and that the trial court erred in entering judgment for respondent. Because the jury was allowed to impose liability without fault and was permitted to presume damages without proof of injury, a new trial is necessary. We reverse and remand for further proceedings in accord with this opinion.

It is ordered.

Reversed and remanded.

Mr. Chief Justice BURGER, dissenting.

The doctrines of the law of defamation have had a gradual evolution primarily in the state courts. In New York Times Co. v. Sullivan, 376 U.S. 254, 84 S.Ct. 710, 11 L.Ed.2d 686 (1964), and its progeny this Court entered this field.

Agreement or disagreement with the law as it has evolved to this time does not alter the fact that it has been orderly development with a consistent basic rationale. In today's opinion the Court abandons the traditional thread so far as the ordinary private citizen is concerned and introduces the concept that the media will be liable for negligencein publishing defamatory statements with respect to such persons. Although I agreewith much of what Mr. Justice WHITE states, I do not read the Court's new doctrinal approach in quite the way he does. I am frank to say I do not know the parameters of a 'negligence'doctrine as applied to the news media. Conceivably this new doctrine could inhibit some editors, as the dissents of Mr. Justice DOUGLAS and Mr. Justice BRENNAN suggest. But I would prefer to allow this area of law to continue to evolve as it has up to now with respect to private citizens rather than embark on a new doctrinal theory which has no jurisprudential ancestry . . . .

Mr. Justice DOUGLAS, dissenting.

The Court describes this case as a return to the struggle of 'defin(ing) the proper accommodation between the law of defamation and the freedoms of speech and press protected by the First Amendment.' It is indeed a struggle, once described by Mr. Justice Black as 'the same quagmire' in which the Court 'is now helplessly struggling in the field of obscenity.' Curtis Publishing Co. v. Butts, 388 U.S. 130, 171, 87 S.Ct. 1975, 2000, 18 L.Ed.2d 1094 (concurring opinion). I would suggest that the struggle is a quite hopeless one, for, in light of the command of the First Amendment, no 'accommodation' of its freedoms can be 'proper' except those made by the Framers themselves.

Unlike the right of privacy which, by the terms of the Fourth Amendment, must be accommodated with reasonable searches and seizures and warrants issued by magistrates, the rights of free speech and of a free press were protected by the Framers in verbiage whose prescription seems clear. I have stated before my view that the First Amendment would bar Congress from passing any libel law. This was the view held by Thomas Jefferson and it is one Congress has never challengedthrough enactment of a civil libel statute. The sole congressional attempt at this variety of First Amendment muzzle was in the Sedition Act of 1798--a criminal libel act never tested in this Court and one which expired by its terms three years after enactment. As President, Thomas Jefferson pardoned those who were convicted under the Act, and fines levied in its prosecution were repaid by Act of Congress. The general consensus was that the Act constituted a regrettable legislative exercise plainly in violation of the First Amendment.

With the First Amendment made applicable to the States through the Fourteenth, I do not see how States have any more ability to 'accommodate' freedoms of speech or of the press than does Congress. This is true whether the form of the accommodation is civil or criminal since '(w)hat a State may not constitutionally bring about by means of a criminal statute is likewise beyond the reach of its civil law of libel.' New York Times Co. v. Sullivan, 376 U.S. 254, 277, 84 S.Ct. 710, 724, 11 L.Ed.2d 686. Like Congress, States are without power 'to use a civil libel law or any other law to impose damages for merely discussing public affairs.' Id., at 295, 84 S.Ct., at 734 (Black, J., concurring) . . . .

There can be no doubt that a State impinges upon free and open discussion when it sanctions the imposition of damages for such discussion through its civil libel laws. Discussion of public affairs is often marked by highly charged emotions, and jurymen, not unlike us all, are subject to those emotions. It is indeed this very type of speech which is the reason for the First Amendment since speech which arouses little emotion is little in need of protection . . . .

Since in my view the First and Fourteenth Amendments prohibit the imposition of damages upon respondent for this discussion of public affairs, I would affirm the judgment below.

Mr. Justice BRENNAN, dissenting.

. . . I adhere to my view expressed in Rosenbloom v. Metromedia, Inc., supra, that we strike the proper accommodation between avoidance of media self-censorship and protection of individual reputations only when we require States to apply the New York, Times Co. v. Sullivan, 376 U.S. 254, 84 S.Ct. 710, 11 L.Ed.2d 686 (1964), knowing-or-reckless-falsity standard in civil libel actions concerning media reports of the involvement of private individuals in events of public or general interest . . . .

Mr. Justice WHITE, dissenting.

For some 200 years--from the very founding of the Nation--the law of defamation and right of the ordinary citizen to recover for false publication injurious to his reputation have been almost exclusively the business of state courts and legislatures. Under typical state defamation law, the defamed private citizen had to prove only a false publication that would subject him to hatred, contempt, or ridicule. Given such publication, general damage to reputation was presumed, while punitive damages required proof of additional facts. The law governing the defamation of private citizens remained untouched by the First Amendment because until relatively recently, the consistent view of the Court was that libelous words constitute a class of speech wholly unprotected by the First Amendment, subject only to limited exceptions carved out since 1964.

But now, using that Amendment as the chosen instrument, the Court, in a few printed pages, has federalized major aspects of libel law by declaring unconstitutional in important respects the prevailing defamation law in all or most of the 50 States. That result is accomplished by requiring the plaintiff in each and every defamation action to prove not only the defendant's culpability beyond his act of publishing defamatory material but also actual damage to reputation resulting from the publication. Moreover, punitive damages may not be recovered by showing malice in the traditional sense of ill will; knowing falsehood or reckless disregard of the truth will not be required.

I assume these sweeping changes will be popular with the press, but this is not the road to salvation for a court of law. As I see it, there are wholly insufficient grounds for scuttling the libel laws of the States in such wholesale fashion, to say nothing of deprecating the reputation interest of ordinary citizens and rendering them powerless to protect themselves . . . .

J. Gordon EDWARDS,
v.
NATIONAL AUDUBON SOCIETY, INC.,
and
The New York Times Company

556 F.2d 113.

United States Court of Appeals,
Second Circuit.

Decided May 25, 1977.

Before KAUFMAN, Chief Judge, CLARK, Associate Justice and JAMESON, District Judge.

IRVING R. KAUFMAN, Chief Judge:

In a society which takes seriously the principle that government rests upon the consent of the governed, freedom of the press must be the most cherished tenet. It is elementary that a democracy cannot long survive unless the people are provided the information needed to form judgments on issues that affect their ability to intelligently govern themselves. As we said in James v Board of Education, 461 F.2d 566, 572, "To preserve the 'marketplace of ideas' so essential to our system of democracy, we must be willing to assume the risk of argument and lawful disagreement." In the thirteen years since New York Times v. Sullivan, 376 U.S. 254, 84 S.Ct. 710, 11 L.Ed.2d 686 (1964), the federal courts have steadfastly sought to afford broad protection to expression by the media, without unduly sacrificing the individual's right to be free of unjust damage to his reputation. See, e. g., Gertz v. Robert Welch, Inc., 418 U.S. 323 . . . . This important case requires us to return again to this task.

We are invited today to affirm a libel judgment against the New York Times for accurately reporting dramatic statements of the National Audubon Society attacking the good faith of prominent scientists supporting continued use of the insecticide DDT. There can be little doubt that the Times reasonably considered these accusations of a leading environmentalist organization to be newsworthy. We are further requested to affirm judgments against Roland Clement, a Vice-President of the Society, despite the absence of any evidence in the record that he endorsed or made the single statement that could be found to have been libelous under the Constitution. We are convinced that the First Amendment requires us to decline these invitations. Accordingly we will reverse and order the complaint dismissed.

I.

A brief summary of the facts is indispensable to understanding the difficult legal issues presented by this appeal.

The DDT debate. The publication fifteen years ago of Rachel Carson's Silent Spring set off a furious controversy that, even today, continues to rage around the insecticide DDT. Naturalists and environmentalist groups like the National Audubon Society have vigorously opposed DDT because, in their view, use of the chemical endangers bird life. Proponents of the pesticide deny this charge and forcefully urge that, without DDT, millions of human beings will die of insect-carried diseases and starvation caused by the destruction of crops by insect pests.

As might be expected when such fundamental questions of value enter the debate, at times the DDT controversy has exceeded the limits of temperance and good manners. Naturalists have insinuated that many proponents of DDT are unduly influenced by the selfish interests of the pesticide industry. On the other hand, such an outstanding advocate of DDT as appellee Dr. J. Gordon Edwards, has characterized a ban on export of the insecticide, supported by the Audubon Society, as "deliberately genocidal." Accusations of scientific bad faith have unfortunately become almost commonplace on both sides.

Arbib's "Foreword" to American Birds. The scientists who advocate continued use of DDT respond to charges that the chemical destroys bird life by citing the annual Audubon Society Christmas Bird Count, which shows a steady increase in bird sightings despite the growing employment of pesticides in the last thirty years. The Audubon Society believes this is an invalid use of its statistics because there are many more bird counters now and because bird watchers have grown more skilful in recent years with better access to observation areas. This dispute over the interpretation of the Society's statistics lies at the heart of the controversy over DDT's threat to bird life.

By 1972 the DDT controversy was raging at peak intensity, and the Audubon Society was acutely alarmed at what it considered the persistent misuse of its Bird Count data. Accordingly, Robert S. Arbib, Jr., a highly respected amateur ornithologist and editor of the Society's publication American Birds, determined to preface his report of the 1971 Christmas Count with a warning against distortion of the results. His foreword to the April, 1972, issue of American Birds, contained the following comment on the Count's significance:

> We are well aware that segments of the pesticide industry and certain paid "scientist-spokesmen" are citing Christmas Bird Count totals (and other data in AMERICAN BIRDS) as proving that the bird life of North America is thriving, and that many species are actually increasing despite the widespread and condemned use of DDT and other non-degradable hydrocarbon pesticides.
>
> This, quite obviously, is false and misleading, a distortion of the facts for the most self-serving of reasons. The truth is that many species high on the food chain, such as most bird-eating

> raptors and fisheaters, are suffering serious declines in numbers as a direct result of pesticide contamination; there is now abundant evidence to prove this. In addition, with the constant diminution of natural habitat, especially salt- and freshwater marshes, it is self-evident that species frequenting these habitats are less common than formerly.
>
> The apparent increases in numbers of species and individuals on the Christmas Bird Counts have, in most cases, nothing to do with real population dynamics. They are the result of ever-increasing numbers of birders in the field, better access to the Count areas, better knowledge of where to find the birds within each area, and increasing sophistication in identification.
>
> With increased local coverage by the press of Christmas Bird Count activities, it is important that Count spokesmen reiterate the simple and truthful fact that what we are seeing is result of not more birds, but more birders. Any time you hear a "scientist" say the opposite, you are in the presence of someone who is being paid to lie, or is parroting something he knows little about.

Despite the potentially explosive character of the allegation that scientists supporting DDT were paid liars, Arbib does not appear to have had any factual basis for the charge. Indeed, he testified that his comment was never intended to portray anyone in particular as a venal prevaricator; rather, it merely expressed his belief that many supporters of DDT use were spokesmen for the pesticide industry.

The New York Times Article. Arbib's general accusations came to the attention of New York Times nature reporter John Devlin in late July, 1972. Devlin immediately realized that the Audubon Society's charges were a newsworthy development in the already acrimonious DDT debate, and he accordingly telephoned Arbib to obtain the names of those the Society considered "paid liars". Arbib was initially reluctant to identify any individuals as the people referred to in his article. But, as a result of Devlin's persistent urging that many eminent persons associated with the pesticide industry might be hurt unnecessarily by the Society's indiscriminate attack, Arbib eventually promised to furnish the names of specific individuals whom he felt were justly subject to the Society's charges.

Arbib, of course, did not know of anyone in particular whom he could with assurance call a "paid liar". He turned, therefore, to Roland Clement, the Audubon Society's Staff Biologist and Vice-President, who more than any other official of the naturalist organization had embroiled himself in the DDT controversy and had knowledge of its participants. Arbib testified that Clement strongly emphasized he could not call anyone specifically a paid liar. He could, however, identify those who had most persistently misused Bird Count data, despite the Society's efforts to point out their error. Clement told Arbib he had just completed an article for an environmentalist journal which listed the scientists whose distortion of the Audubon statistics seemed most egregious, and, in Arbib's words,

> he believed it would be all right to give the names to Mr. Devlin as long as we qualified this by saying 'We don't have any knowledge of anyone being paid liars, and all we want to say is that they have been consistent misinterpretors of the information in American Birds.'

When Devlin telephoned again for the names, Arbib was prepared with Clement's article. But, Devlin and Arbib sharply disagreed at trial regarding the ensuing conversation. Arbib insisted that he conveyed, in essence, Clement's warning that the scientists discussed in Clement's article were not necessarily "paid liars". Devlin flatly denied that Arbib so cautioned him. He testified that Arbib made it clear that the scientists whose names were furnished to the Times were the persons referred to in Arbib's "Foreword" to American Birds. The list included the names of the appellees Dr. J. Gordon Edwards, Professor of Entomology at San Jose State College in California, Dr. Thomas M. Jukes, Professor of Medical Physics and Lecturer in Nutrition at the University of California, Berkeley, and Dr. Robert H. White-Stevens, Professor of Biology at The Rutgers University in New Jersey as well as Nobel Laureate Norman Borlaug and Dr. Donald Spencer, a lecturer of the National Agricultural Chemical Association. All of the accused were eminent scientists, though none were ornithologists.

Upon receiving these names from Arbib, Devlin attempted to secure comments from each of the five accused. He succeeded in reaching three: Dr. White- Stevens, Dr. Jukes, and Dr. Spencer. All of these scientists categorically denied the charges, and Dr. Spencer even referred to them as "almost libelous". Dr. White-Stevens and Dr. Jukes, in addition, sent Devlin voluminous supporting materials setting forth their side of the DDT debate. None of this material, however, responded directly to the Audubon Society's criticism of the use of Bird Count data by these scholars; it dealt almost entirely with the general merits of the pesticide controversy.

Having thus in good faith elicited both sides of the story to the best of his ability, Devlin wrote the article which is the sole ground for the libel judgment against the Times and the principal basis for the judgment against Clement. Devlin's story was published in the Times on August 14, 1972.

Pesticide Spokesmen Accused Of 'Lying' on Higher Bird Count Pes
By JOHN DEVLIN

"Segments of the pesticide industry and certain 'scientist-spokesmen,' " are accused in the current issue of American Birds of "lying" by saying that bird life in America is thriving despite the use of DDT.

The publication is sponsored by the National Audubon Society in collaboration with the United States Fish and Wildlife Service. The delayed current issue is devoted principally to results of the 72d Christmas Bird Count.

The accusation against the pesticide industry and some of its spokesmen is contained in the foreword by Robert S. Arbib Jr., editor.

He wrote that the reason the Christmas Bird Count showed more birds, as cited by the pesticide industry spokesmen, was not that there were more birds these days but simply "more birders" who go out on the annual counts and thus increase the size of the totals reported.

Accused Men Named

The persons under attack were not identified in the publication.

However, Mr. Arbib said in an interview that they included Robert H. White- Stevens, formerly with American Cyanamid Company, and now in the Bureau of Conservation and Environmental Science, Rutgers University; Thomas H. Jukes, a biochemist at the University of California; Norman E. Borlaug, Nobel Prize winner; Dr. J. Gordon Edwards, a lecturer and professor of entomology at San Jose State College; and Dr. Donald A. Spencer, a retired ecologist and lecturer of the National Agricultural Chemical Association who's now a private consultant and a member of the National Audubon Society.

Not all of the men could be reached for comment but those who could ridiculed the accusations as "emotional," "hysterical," and unfounded, and Dr. Spencer said they were "almost libelous."

"We are well aware," Mr. Arbib wrote, "that segments of the pesticide industry and certain paid 'scientist-spokesmen' are citing Christmas Bird Count totals and other data in American Birds as proving that the bird life of North America is thriving, and that many species are actually increasing despite the widespread and condemned use of DDT and other non-degradable hydro-carbon pesticides.

'Serious Declines' Found

"This, quite obviously, is false and misleading, a distortion of the facts for the most self-serving reasons. The truth is that many species high on the food chain, such as most bird-eating raptors and fisheaters, are suffering serious declines in numbers as a direct result of pesticide contamination; there is now abundant evidence to prove this."

He said that with the increased coverage of Christmas Bird Counts by the press, it was important for Christmas Count spokesmen to "reiterate what we are seeing is not more birds but more birders.

"Anytime you hear a 'scientist' say the opposite," he continued, "you are in the presence of someone who is being paid to lie, or is parroting something he knows little about."

The Clement letter. Roland Clement was astonished to read in the Times that the Audubon Society had called its critics "paid liars." In an internal memorandum circulated the following day, Clement wrote:

> Arbib was probably incautious in giving Devlin the names involved, something he got from me. Devlin probably asked whom do you consider liars, and Arbib was trapped into listing people I have never called liars, though they may be.

Nonetheless, Clement apparently decided that the unfortunate situation could best be turned to advantage by playing down the accusation against the appellees, Spencer, and Borlaug while reiterating and clarifying the Society's position on the merits of the Bird Count controversy. Accordingly, Clement sent the following letter to the Times over Arbib's signature.

> Jack Devlin's punchy piece on the Audubon Christmas Bird Count summary . . . unfortunately leaves out the most important qualifications we attach to these counts.
>
> It is not simply that more birds are reported because there are more birders, but that we have more birders who are also better birders . . ..
>
> Nor do we like to call people liars, but those who have most consistently misused our data Robert H. White-Stevens . . ., Thomas H. Jukes . . ., Donald A. Spencer . . ., J. Gordon Edwards . . ., and more recently Nobel laureate Norman E. Borlaug certainly have had time to

learn from our patient explanations of their misinterpretations of our data over the several years of the DDT controversy.

Judge Metzner ruled this letter libelous per se, though it eschewed all the suggestions of venality that had appeared in the American Birds Foreword and Times article, and though it fully explained the basis for Clement's view that the scientists were in bad faith. The letter was never published by the Times.

Litigation. The appellees filed their complaints against the Times and the National Audubon Society in April, 1973; subsequently Arbib and Clement were added as defendants. After nearly three years of discovery, Judge Metzner denied the defendants' motion for summary judgment, on the sole ground that there was a disputed issue of fact: whether Arbib actually told Devlin that those whose names were being furnished to the Times were not the "paid liars" referred to in American Birds. Despite his finding that the appellees were "public figures", Judge Metzner was of the view a jury might find actual malice on the part of one or another defendant, depending upon its resolution of this question of fact, even in the face of New York Times v. Sullivan, supra.

The district judge further simplified the issues by ruling that both the New York Times article of August 14, 1972, and Clement's rebuttal letter of the same day were defamatory per se because they impugned the professional integrity of the appellees. In addition, the jury was instructed that the Times could be found guilty of actual malice if Devlin had serious doubts about the truth of the statement that the appellees were paid liars, even if he did not have any doubt that he was reporting Arbib's allegations faithfully. The jury returned a verdict against both the Times and Clement, but exonerated Arbib. It awarded $20,000 damages to Dr. Jukes and Dr. White-Stevens, respectively, and $21,000 to Dr. Edwards.

The Times and Clement moved for judgment n. o. v. Judge Metzner interpreted the surprising verdict against both appellants as reflecting the jury's belief that, although Devlin had accurately reported the information received from Arbib, he had been "reckless" in failing to investigate further after the responses from White-Stevens, Jukes, and Spencer placed him on notice of the defamatory potential of his proposed article. The evidence, in his view, was sufficient to support this finding, and accordingly Judge Metzner denied the Times ' motion. The basis for Clement's liability was the jury's implicit finding that Clement gave Arbib the appellants' names knowing the purpose for which they would be used. Judge Metzner regarded the evidence sufficient to support this conclusion.

II.

Implicit in the jury's verdict against Clement is the finding, which we must accept, that the Times accurately reported the five scientists whose names were furnished by Arbib were the "paid liars" referred to in the American Birds Foreword. We believe that a libel judgment against the Times, in the face of this finding of fact, is constitutionally impermissible.

At stake in this case is a fundamental principle. Succinctly stated, when a responsible, prominent organization like the National Audubon Society makes serious charges against a public figure, the First Amendment protects the accurate and disinterested reporting of those charges, regardless of the reporter's private views regarding their validity. See Time, Inc. v. Pape, 401 U.S. 279, 91 S.Ct. 633, 28 L.Ed.2d 45 (1971); Medina v. Time, Inc., 439 F.2d 1129 (1st Cir. 1971). What is newsworthy about such accusations is that they were made. We do not believe that the press may be required under the First Amendment to suppress newsworthy statements merely because it has serious doubts regardingtheir truth. Nor must the press take up cudgels against dubious charges in order to publish them without fear of liability for defamation. Cf. Miami Herald Publishing Co. v. Tornillo, 418 U.S. 241, 94 S.Ct. 2831, 41 L.Ed.2d 730 (1974). The public interest in being fully informed about controversies that often rage around sensitive issues demands that the press be afforded the freedom to report such charges without assuming responsibility for them.

The contours of the press's right of neutral reportage are, of course, defined by the principle that gives life to it. Literal accuracy is not a prerequisite: if we are to enjoy the blessings of a robust and unintimidated press, we must provide immunity from defamation suits where the journalist believes, reasonably and in good faith, that his report accurately conveys the charges made. Time, Inc. v. Pape, supra. It is equally clear, however, that a publisher who in fact espouses or concurs in the charges made by others, or who deliberately distorts these statements to launch a personal attack of his own on a public figure, cannot rely on a privilege of neutral reportage. In such instances he assumes responsibility for the underlying accusations. See Goldwater v. Ginzburg, 414 F.2d 324 (2d Cir. 1969), cert. denied, 396 U.S. 1049, 90 S.Ct. 701, 24 L.Ed.2d 695 (1970).

It is clear here, that Devlin reported Audubon's charges fairly and accurately. He did not in any way espouse the Society's accusations: indeed, Devlin published the maligned scientists' outraged reactions in the same article that contained the Society's attack. The Times article, in short, was the exemplar of fair and dispassionate reporting of an unfortunate but newsworthy contretemps. Accordingly, we hold that it was privileged under the First Amendment.

V.

We do not underestimate the pain and distress which the publication of the Audubon Society's thoughtless charges has caused the appellees. And we are fully aware that, in Professor Emerson's words,

> A member of a civilized society should have some measure of protection against unwarranted attack upon his honor, his dignity and his standing in the community.

Our holding today does not in any way condone the mischievous and unwarranted assault on the good name of the appellees, who appear from their writings to have entered the lists in favor of DDT in good faith and from humanitarian motives that ought to be beyond reproach.

Nevertheless, we believe that the interest of a public figure in the purity of his reputation cannot be allowed to obstruct that vital pulse of ideas and intelligence on which an informed and self-governing people depend. It is unfortunate that the exercise of liberties so precious as freedom of speech and of the press may sometimes do harm that the state is powerless to recompense: but this is the price that must be paid for the blessings of a democratic way of life.

We believe that the New York Times cannot, consistently with the First Amendment, be afflicted with a libel judgment for the accurate reporting of newsworthy accusations made by a responsible and well-noted organization like the National Audubon Society. And, we are convinced that Roland Clement cannot be found liable for a defamatory statement which, as far as this record reveals, he never made. Accordingly, we reverse the judgments against the Times and Clement and dismiss the appellees' complaint.

Michael MILKOVICH,
v.
LORAIN JOURNAL CO. et al.

497 U.S. 1

Supreme Court of the United States

Decided June 21, 1990.

Chief Justice REHNQUIST delivered the opinion of the Court.

Respondent J. Theodore Diadiun authored an article in an Ohio newspaper implying that petitioner Michael Milkovich, a local high school wrestling coach, lied under oath in a judicial proceeding about an incident involving petitioner and his team which occurred at a wrestling match. Petitioner sued Diadiun and the newspaper for libel, and the Ohio Court of Appeals affirmed a lower court entry of summary judgment against petitioner. This judgment was based in part on the grounds that the article constituted an "opinion" protected from the reach of state defamation law by the First Amendment to the United States Constitution. We hold that the First Amendment does not prohibit the application of Ohio's libel laws to the alleged defamations contained in the article.

This lawsuit is before us for the third time in an odyssey of litigation spanning nearly 15 years. Petitioner Milkovich, now retired, was the wrestling coach at Maple Heights High School in Maple Heights, Ohio. In 1974, his team was involved in an altercation at a home wrestling match with a team from Mentor High School. Several people were injured. In response to the incident, the Ohio High School Athletic Association (OHSAA) held a hearing at which Milkovich and H. Don Scott, the Superintendent of Maple Heights Public Schools, testified. Following the hearing, OHSAA placed the Maple Heights team on probation for a year and declared the team ineligible for the 1975 state tournament. OHSAA also censured Milkovich for his actions during the altercation. Thereafter, several parents and wrestlers sued OHSAA in the Court of Common Pleas of Franklin County, Ohio, seeking a restraining order against OHSAA's ruling on the grounds that they had been denied due process in the OHSAA proceeding. Both Milkovich and Scott testified in that proceeding. The court overturned OHSAA's probation and ineligibility orders on due process grounds.

The day after the court rendered its decision, respondent Diadiun's column appeared in the News-Herald, a newspaper which circulates in Lake County, Ohio, and is owned by respondent Lorain Journal Co. The column bore the heading "Maple beat the law with the 'big lie,' " beneath which appeared Diadiun's photograph and the words "TD Says." The carryover page headline announced "... Diadiun says Maple told a lie." The column contained the following passages:

" '... [A] lesson was learned (or relearned) yesterday by the student body of Maple Heights High School, and by anyone who attended the Maple-Mentor wrestling meet of last Feb. 8.

" 'A lesson which, sadly, in view of the events of the past year, is well they learned early.

" 'It is simply this: If you get in a jam, lie your way out.

" 'If you're successful enough, and powerful enough, and can sound sincere enough, you stand an excellent chance of making the lie stand up, regardless of what really happened.

" 'The teachers responsible were mainly head Maple wrestling coach, Mike Milkovich, and former superintendent of schools H. Donald Scott.

. . . . .

" 'Anyone who attended the meet, whether he be from Maple Heights, Mentor, or impartial observer, knows in his heart that Milkovich and Scott lied at the hearing after each having given his solemn oath to tell the truth.

" 'But they got away with it.

" 'Is that the kind of lesson we want our young people learning from their high school administrators and coaches?

" 'I think not.' " Milkovich v. News-Herald, 46 Ohio App.3d 20, 21, 545 N.E.2d 1320, 1321-1322 (1989).

Petitioner commenced a defamation action against respondents in the Court of Common Pleas of Lake County, Ohio, allegingthat the headline of Diadiun's article and the nine passages quoted above "accused plaintiff of committing the crime of perjury, an indictable offense in the State of Ohio, and damaged plaintiff directly in his life-time occupation of coach and teacher, and constituted libel per se." App. 12. The action proceeded to trial, and the court granted a directed verdict to respondents on the ground that the evidence failed to establish the article was published with "actual malice" as required by New York Times Co. v. Sullivan, 376 U.S. 254, 84 S.Ct. 710, 11 L.Ed.2d 686 (1964). See App. 21-22. The Ohio Court of Appeals for the Eleventh Appellate District reversed and remanded, holding that there was sufficient evidence of actual malice to go to the jury. See Milkovich v. Lorain Journal, 65 Ohio App.2d 143, 416 N.E.2d 662 (1979). The Ohio Supreme Court dismissed the ensuing appeal for want of a substantial constitutional question, and this Court denied certiorari. 449 U.S. 966, 101 S.Ct. 380, 66 L.Ed.2d 232 (1980).

On remand, relying in part on our decision in Gertz v. Robert Welch, Inc., 418 U.S. 323, 94 S.Ct. 2997, 41 L.Ed.2d 789 (1974), the trial court granted summary judgment to respondents on the grounds that the article was an opinion protected from a libel action by "constitutional law," App. 55, and alternatively, as a public figure, petitioner had failed to make out a prima facie case of actual malice. Id., at 55-59. The Ohio Court of Appeals affirmed both determinations. Id., at 62-70. On appeal, the Supreme Court of Ohio reversed and remanded. The court first decided that petitioner was neither a public figure nor a public official under the relevant decisions of this Court. See Milkovich v. News-Herald, 15 Ohio St.3d 292, 294-299, 473 N.E.2d 1191, 1193-1196 (1984). The court then found that "the statements in issue are factual assertions as a matter of law, and are not constitutionally protected as the opinions of the writer.... The plain import of the author's assertions is that Milkovich, inter alia, committed the crime of perjury in a court of law." Id., at 298-299, 473 N.E.2d, at 1196-1197. This Court again denied certiorari. 474 U.S. 953, 106 S.Ct. 322, 88 L.Ed.2d 305 (1985).

Meanwhile, Superintendent Scott had been pursuing a separate defamation action through the Ohio courts. Two years after its Milkovich decision, in considering Scott's appeal, the Ohio Supreme Court reversed its position on Diadiun's article, concluding that the column was "constitutionally protected opinion." Scott v. News-Herald, 25 Ohio St.3d 243, 254, 496 N.E.2d 699, 709 (1986). Consequently, the court upheld a lower court's grant of summary judgment against Scott.

The Scott court decided that the proper analysis for determining whether utterances are fact or opinion was set forth in the decision of the United States Court of Appeals for the District of Columbia Circuit in Ollman v. Evans, 242 U.S.App.D.C. 301, 750 F.2d 970 (1984), cert. denied, 471 U.S. 1127, 105 S.Ct. 2662, 86 L.Ed.2d 278 (1985). See Scott, 25 Ohio St.3d, at 250, 496 N.E.2d, at 706. Under that analysis, four factors are considered to ascertain whether, under the "totality of circumstances," a statement is fact or opinion. These factors are: (1) "the specific language used"; (2) "whether the statement is verifiable"; (3) "the general context of the statement"; and (4) "the broader context in which the statement appeared." Ibid. The court found that application of the first two factors to the column militated in favor of deeming the challenged passages actionable assertions of fact. Id., at 250-252, 496 N.E.2d, at 706-707. That potential outcome was trumped, however, by the court's consideration of the third and fourth factors. With respect to the third factor, the general context, the court explained that "the large caption 'TD Says' ... would indicate to even the most gullible reader that the article was, in fact, opinion." Id., at 252, 496 N.E.2d, at 707. As for the fourth factor, the "broader context," the court reasoned that because the article appeared on a sports page--"a traditional haven for cajoling, invective, and hyperbole"--the article would probably be construed as opinion. Id., at 253-254, 496 N.E.2d, at 708.

Subsequently, considering itself bound by the Ohio Supreme Court's decision in Scott, the Ohio Court of Appeals in the instant proceedings affirmed a trial court's grant of summary judgment in favor of respondents, concluding that "it has been decided, as a matter of law, that the article in question was constitutionally protected opinion." 46 Ohio App.3d, at 23, 545 N.E.2d, at 1324. The Supreme Court of Ohio dismissed petitioner's ensuing appeal for want of a substantial constitutional question. App. 119. We granted certiorari, 493 U.S. 1055, 110 S.Ct. 863, 107 L.Ed.2d 947 (1990), to consider the important questions raised by the Ohio courts' recognition of a constitutionally required "opinion" exception to the application of its defamation laws. We now reverse.

Respondents would have us recognize, in addition to the established safeguards discussed above, still another First-Amendment-based protection for defamatory statements which are categorized as "opinion" as opposed to "fact." For this proposition they rely principally on the following dictum from our opinion in Gertz:

> "Under the First Amendment there is no such thing as a false idea. However pernicious an opinion may seem, we depend for its correction not on the conscience of judges and juries but on the competition of other ideas. But there is no constitutional value in false statements of fact." 418 U.S., at 339-340, 94 S.Ct., at 3007 (footnote omitted).

Judge Friendly appropriately observed that this passage "has become the opening salvo in all arguments for protection from defamation actions on the ground of opinion, even though the case did not remotely concern the question." Cianci v. New Times Publishing Co., 639 F.2d 54, 61 (CA2 1980). Read in context, though, the fair meaning of the passage is to equate the word "opinion" in the second sentence with the word "idea" in the first sentence. Under this view, the language was merely a reiteration of Justice Holmes' classic "marketplace of ideas" concept. See Abrams v. United States, 250 U.S. 616, 630, 40 S.Ct. 17, 22, 63 L.Ed. 1173 (1919) (dissenting opinion) ("[T]he ultimate good desired is better reached by free trade in ideas--... the best test of truth is the power of the thought to get itself accepted in the competition of the market").

Thus, we do not think this passage from Gertz was intended to create a wholesale defamation exemption for anything that might be labeled "opinion." See Cianci, supra, at 62, n. 10 (The "marketplace of ideas" origin of this passage "points strongly to the view that the 'opinions' held to be constitutionally protected were the sort of thing that could be corrected by discussion"). Not only would such an interpretation be contrary to the tenor and context of the passage, but it would also ignore the fact that expressions of "opinion" may often imply an assertion of objective fact.

If a speaker says, "In my opinion John Jones is a liar," he implies a knowledge of facts which lead to the conclusion that Jones told an untruth. Even if the speaker states the facts upon which he bases his opinion, if those facts are either incorrect or incomplete, or if his assessment of them is erroneous, the statement may still imply a false assertion of fact. Simply couching such statements in terms of opinion does not dispel these implications; and the statement, "In my opinion Jones is a liar," can cause as much damage to reputation as the statement, "Jones is a liar." As Judge Friendly aptly stated: "[It] would be destructive of the law of libel if a writer could escape liability for accusations of [defamatory conduct] simply by using, explicitly or implicitly, the words 'I think.' " See Cianci, supra, at 64. It is worthy of note that at common law, even the privilege of fair comment did not extend to "a false statement of fact, whether it was expressly stated or implied from an expression of opinion." Restatement (Second) of Torts, § 566, Comment a (1977).

Apart from their reliance on the Gertz dictum, respondents do not really contend that a statement such as, "In my opinion John Jones is a liar," should be protected by a separate privilege for "opinion" under the First Amendment. But they do contend that in every defamation case the First Amendment mandates an inquiry into whether a statement is "opinion" or "fact," and that only the latter statements may be actionable. They propose that a number of factors developed by the lower courts (in what we hold was a mistaken reliance on the Gertz dictum) be considered in deciding which is which. But we think the " 'breathing space' " which " '[f]reedoms of expression require in order to survive,' " Hepps, 475 U.S., at 772, 106 S.Ct., at 1561 (quoting New York Times, supra, 376 U.S., at 272, 84 S.Ct., at 721), is adequately secured by existing constitutional doctrine without the creation of an artificial dichotomy between "opinion" and fact.

Foremost, we think Hepps stands for the proposition that a statement on matters of public concern must be provable as false before there can be liability under state defamation law, at least in situations, like the present, where a media defendant is involved. Thus, unlike the statement, "In my opinion Mayor Jones is a liar," the statement, "In my opinion Mayor Jones shows his abysmal ignorance by accepting the teachings of Marx and Lenin," would not be actionable. Hepps ensures that a statement of opinion relating to matters of public concern which does not contain a provably false factual connotation will receive full constitutional protection.

Next, the Bresler-Letter Carriers-Falwell line of cases provides protection for statements that cannot "reasonably [be] interpreted as stating actual facts" about an individual. Falwell, 485 U.S., at 50, 108 S.Ct., at 879. This provides assurance that public debate will not suffer for lack of "imaginative expression" or the "rhetorical hyperbole" which has traditionally added much to the discourse of our Nation. See id., at 53-55, 108 S.Ct., at 880-882.

The New York Times-Butts-Gertz culpability requirements further ensure that debate on public issues remains "uninhibited, robust, and wide-open." New York Times, 376 U.S., at 270, 84 S.Ct., at 720. Thus, where a statement of "opinion" on a matter of public concern reasonably implies false and defamatory facts regarding public figures or officials, those individuals must show that such statements were made with knowledge of their false implications or with reckless disregard of their truth. Similarly, where such a statement involves a private figure on a matter of public concern, a plaintiff must show that the false connotations were made with some level of fault as required by Gertz. Finally, the enhanced appellate review required by Bose Corp. provides assurance that the foregoing determinations will be made in a manner so as not to "constitute a forbidden intrusion of the field of free expression." Bose Corp., 466 U.S., at 499, 104 S.Ct., at 1959 (quotation omitted).

We are not persuaded that, in addition to these protections, an additional separate constitutional privilege for "opinion" is required to ensure the freedom of expression guaranteed by the First Amendment. The dispositive question in the present case then becomes whether a reasonable factfinder could conclude that the statements in the Diadiun column imply an assertion that petitioner Milkovich perjured himself in a judicial proceeding. We think this question must be answered in the affirmative. As the Ohio Supreme Court itself observed: "[T]he clear impact in some nine sentences and a caption is that [Milkovich] 'lied at the hearing after ... having given his solemn oath to tell the truth.' " Scott, 25 Ohio St.3d, at 251, 496 N.E.2d, at 707. This is not the sort of loose, figurative, or hyperbolic language which would negate the impression that the writer was seriously maintaining that petitioner committed the crime of perjury. Nor does the general tenor of the article negate this impression.

We also think the connotation that petitioner committed perjury is sufficiently factual to be susceptible of being proved true or false. A determination whether petitioner lied in this instance can be made on a core of objective evidence by comparing, inter alia, petitioner's testimony before the OHSAA board with his subsequent testimony before the trial court. As the Scott court noted regarding the plaintiff in that case: "[W]hether or not H. Don Scott did indeed perjure himself is certainly verifiable by a perjury action with evidence adduced from the transcripts and witnesses present at the hearing. Unlike a subjective assertion the averred defamatory language is an articulation of an objectively verifiable event." Id., at 252, 496 N.E.2d, at 707. So too with petitioner Milkovich.

The numerous decisions discussed above establishing First Amendment protection for defendants in defamation actions surely demonstrate the Court's recognition of the Amendment's vital guarantee of free and uninhibited discussion of public issues. But there is also another side to the equation; we have regularly acknowledged the "important social values which underlie the law of defamation," and recognized that "[s]ociety has a pervasive and strong interest in preventing and redressing attacks upon reputation." Rosenblatt v. Baer, 383 U.S. 75, 86, 86 S.Ct. 669, 676, 15 L.Ed.2d 597 (1966). Justice Stewart in that case put it with his customary clarity:

> "The right of a man to the protection of his own reputation from unjustified invasion and wrongful hurt reflects no more than our basic concept of the essential dignity and worth of every human being--a concept at the root of any decent system of ordered liberty.
>
> * * *
>
> "The destruction that defamatory falsehood can bring is, to be sure, often beyond the capacity of the law to redeem. Yet, imperfect though it is, an action for damages is the only hope for vindication or redress the law gives to a man whose reputation has been falsely dishonored." Id., at 92-93, 86 S.Ct., at 679-680 (concurring opinion).

We believe our decision in the present case holds the balance true. The judgment of the Ohio Court of Appeals is reversed, and the case is remanded for further proceedings not inconsistent with this opinion.

Reversed.

Justice BRENNAN, with whom Justice MARSHALL joins, dissenting.

With all of the above, I am essentially in agreement. I part company with the Court at the point where it applies these general rules to the statements at issue in this case because I find that the challenged statements cannot reasonably be interpreted as either stating or implying defamatory facts about petitioner. Under the rule articulated in the majority opinion, therefore, the statements are due "full constitutional protection." I respectfully dissent.

LARRY L. MOYER,
v.
AMADOR VALLEY JOINT UNION HIGH SCHOOL DISTRICT

225 Cal.App.3d 720

Court of Appeal, First District, Division 1, California.

Nov. 27, 1990.

RACANELLI, P. J.

Plaintiff Larry L. Moyer, a teacher by profession, filed a 12-count complaint seeking damages on theories of defamation and infliction of emotional distress arising from the publication of a story in a high school student newspaper. Plaintiff now appeals from an order dismissing his complaint following the sustaining of general demurrers without leave to amend. The appeal is presented against the following factual and procedural background.

On March 11, 1988, an article appeared in In Flight, a student publication of Foothill High School, reporting that a smoke bomb had gone off in plaintiff's classroom. The headline stated: 'Students terrorize Moyer.' The article quoted the bomb-throwing student who merely 'wanted to play a joke' as well as 'The Shadow,' the student who supplied the smoke bomb because 'Mr. Moyer is a babbler, and babblers are annoying to me .... [¶] Also he pissed me off, he is the worst teacher at FHS.'

The complaint named as party defendants the school district, school principal, student newspaper adviser, the students who made and reported the comments, including another student who reported plaintiff's filing of a governmental tort (libel) claim and republished the 'babbler' and 'worst teacher' remarks. The opposing arguments below centered on whether the challenged remarks constituted nonactionable expressions of opinion or arguably triable factual issues.

While sustaining the general demurrers, the trial court denied the school district's motion for costs, including attorney fees, under the authority of Code of Civil Procedure section 1038. The district has filed a separate appeal from that order which we have consolidated herein.

Discussion

I. Defamation

Prior to the filing of briefs herein, the courts perceived a fundamental distinction between statements of fact and statements of opinion. Statements of opinion were held to be protected by the First Amendment and thus not actionable . . . . This prevailing rule was grounded primarily on dictum contained in Gertz v. Robert Welch, Inc. (1974) 418 U.S. 323, 339-340 [41 L.Ed.2d 789, 805, 94 S.Ct. 2997]: 'Under the First Amendment there is no such thing as a false idea. However pernicious an opinion may seem, we depend for its correction not on the conscience of judges and juries but on the competition of other ideas. But there is no constitutional value in false statements of fact.'

On June 21, 1990, while this appeal was pending, our highest court filed its opinion in Milkovich v. Lorain Journal Co. (1990) 497 U.S. ___ [111 L.Ed.2d 1, 110 S.Ct. 2695], in which it reexamined the law of defamation within the context of the First Amendment and rejected what it called 'the creation of an artificial dichotomy between 'opinion' and fact.' (Id. at p. ___ [111 L.Ed.2d at p. 18].) (1a) The court explained that the languagein Gertz had been interpreted too broadly and was not intended to create 'a wholesale defamation exemption for anything that might be labeled 'opinion.' ' (Id. at p. ___ [111 L.Ed.2d at p. 17]) Instead, the court made clear that a false assertion of fact could be libelous even though couched in terms of opinion.

Although the Milkovich court held that there is no separate First Amendment privilege for statements of opinion, the court recognized that existing constitutional doctrine remained operative to protect free expression of ideas. That is, statements that cannot be 'reasonably interpreted as stating actual facts' are still entitled to constitutional protection . . . .

Before Milkovich, the California courts had employed a 'totality of the circumstances' test to differentiate between fact and opinion: 'First, the languageof the statement is examined. For words to be defamatory, they must be understood in a defamatory sense .... [¶] Next, the context in which the statement was made must be considered. ... [¶] This contextual analysis demands that the courts look at the nature and full content of the communication and to the knowledge and understanding of the audience to whom the publication was directed.' (Baker v. Los Angeles Herald Examiner, supra, 42 Cal.3d at pp. 260-261.) The crucial determination whether the statement was fact or opinion was held to be a question of law for the court . . . .

Milkovich did not substantially change these principles; it underscored that in cases such as this, raising First Amendment issues, a reviewing court must make an independent examination of the whole record in order to ensure that there is no infringement of free expression . . . The dispositive question for the court is whether a reasonable fact finder could conclude that the published statements imply a provably false factual assertion. The answer to that question is determined by applying the 'totality of circumstances' test-a review of the meaning of the language in context and its susceptibility to being proved true or false . . . .

Turning to the relevant circumstances herein, plaintiff essentially asserts the publication contained three factual statements: (1) the headline, 'Students terrorize Moyer'; (2) 'Mr. Moyer is a babbler ....'; and (3) 'he is the worst teacher at FHS.' Thus, the narrow issue before this court is whether these statements can reasonably be understood to state actual facts about plaintiff. In determining that issue, we consider the nature and meaning of the language used, including the verifiability of the statements, and the context in which the statements appeared. Viewed through that analytical prism, we are impelled to conclude that the statements are not actionable.

As to the third or 'worst teacher' statement, there is no factual assertion capable of being proved true or false. Clearly, the statement is an expression of subjective judgment by the speaker. The full text of the sentence confirms that the statement was simply an expression of anger or disgust on the student- speaker's part. The statement contains no verifiable facts and is clearly protected under the First Amendment . . . .

Nor does the second or 'babbler' statement fall within the legal framework of actionable speech. A commonly accepted definition of 'babbler' is one who utters meaningless or unintelligible sounds, who talks foolishly or incessantly. (See Webster's New Collegiate Dict. (1977) p. 81.) Obviously, the readers of the article would have understood that the word was not used literally but as a form of exaggerated expression conveying the student- speaker's disapproval of plaintiff's teaching or speaking style. The statement could not reasonably have been understood to be stating actual facts about plaintiff . . . .

Finally, as to the first statement, we agree with plaintiff that by its nature a headline over a news story arguably implies a factual assertion. But even if the descriptive term 'terrorize' is an exaggeration of the actual event, it nonetheless falls within the protectible category of rhetorical hyperbole-a word used in a loose, figurative sense. Moreover, the article read in full context accurately reported that one student supplied another student with a smoke bomb that was set off during plaintiff's class.

In summary, we conclude that the statements are not actionable, that no fact finder could reasonably interpret the statements as stating actual facts about plaintiff, and, consequently, that the demurrers were properly sustained.

Ronald E. GALELLA, Plaintiff-Appellant,
v.
Jacqueline ONASSIS, Defendant-Appellee, John Walsh et al., Defendants, and
United States of America, Intervenor-Appellee.

487 F.2d 986

United States Court of Appeals,
Second Circuit.

Decided Sept. 13, 1973.
Rehearing and Rehearing En Banc Denied Nov. 13, 1973.

Before SMITH, HAYS and TIMBERS, Circuit Judges.

J. JOSEPH SMITH, Circuit Judge:

Donald Galella, a free-lance photographer, appeals from a summary judgment dismissing his complaint against three Secret Service agents for false arrest, malicious prosecution and interference with trade (S.D.N.Y., Edward C. McLean, Judge), the dismissal after trial of his identical complaint against Jacqueline Onassis and the grant of injunctive relief to defendant Onassis on her counterclaim and to the intervenor, the United States, on its intervening complaint and a third judgment retaxing transcript costs to plaintiff (S.D.N.Y., Irving Ben Cooper, Judge), 353 F.Supp. 196 (1972). In addition to numerous alleged procedural errors, Galella raises the First Amendment as an absolute shield against liability to any sanctions. The judgments dismissing the complaints are affirmed; the grant of injunctive relief is affirmed as herein modified. Taxation of costs against the plaintiff is affirmed in part, reversed in part.

Galella is a free-lance photographer specializing in the making and sale of photographs of well-known persons. Defendant Onassis is the widow of the late President, John F. Kennedy, mother of the two Kennedy children, John and Caroline, and is the wife of Aristotle Onassis, widely known shipping figure and reputed multimillionaire. John Walsh, James Kalafatis and John Connelly are U. S. Secret Service agents assigned to the duty of protecting the Kennedy children under 18 U.S.C. § 3056, which provides for protection of the children of deceased presidents up to the age of 16.

Galella fancies himself as a "paparazzo" (literally a kind of annoying insect, perhaps roughly equivalent to the English "gadfly.") Paparazzi make themselves as visible to the public and obnoxious to their photographic subjects as possible to aid in the advertisement and wide sale of their works.

Some examples of Galella's conduct brought out at trial are illustrative. Galella took pictures of John Kennedy riding his bicycle in Central Park across the way from his home. He jumped out into the boy's path, causing the agents concern for John's safety. The agents' reaction and interrogation of Galella led to Galella's arrest and his action against the agents; Galella on other occasions interrupted Caroline at tennis, and invaded the children's private schools. At one time he came uncomfortably close in a power boat to Mrs. Onassis swimming. He often jumped and postured around while taking pictures of her party notably at a theater opening but also on numerous other occasions. He followed a practice of bribing apartment house, restaurant and nightclub doormen as well as romancing a family servant to keep him advised of the movements of the family.

After detention and arrest following complaint by the Secret Service agents protecting Mrs. Onassis' son and his acquittal in the state court, Galella filed suit in state court against the agents and Mrs. Onassis. Galella claimed that under orders from Mrs. Onassis, the three agents had falsely arrested and maliciously prosecuted him, and that this incident in addition to several others described in the complaint constituted an unlawful interference with his trade.

Mrs. Onassis answered denying any role in the arrest or any part in the claimed interference with his attempts to photograph her, and counterclaimed for damages and injunctive relief, chargingthat Galella had invaded her privacy, assaulted and battered her, intentionally inflicted emotional distress and engaged in a campaign of harassment.

The action was removed under 28 U.S.C. § 1442(a) to the United States District Court. On a motion for summary judgment, Galella's claim against the Secret Service agents was dismissed, the court finding that the agents were acting within the scope of their authority and thus were immune from prosecution. At the same time, the government intervened requesting injunctive relief from the activities of Galella which obstructed the Secret Service's ability to protect Mrs. Onassis' children. Galella's motion to remand the case to state court, just prior to trial, was denied.

Certain incidents of photographic coverage by Galella, subsequent to an agreement among the parties for Galella not to so engage, resulted in the issuance of a temporary restraining order to prevent further harassment of Mrs. Onassis and the children. Galella was enjoined from "harassing, alarming, startling, tormenting, touching the person of the defendant . . . or her children . . . and from blocking their movements in the public places and thoroughfares, invading their immediate zone of privacy by means of physical movements, gestures or with photographic equipment and from performing any act reasonably calculated to place the lives and safety of the defendant . . . and her children in jeopardy." Within two months, Galella was charged with violation of the temporary restraining order; a new order was signed which required that the photographer keep 100 yards from the Onassis apartment and 50 yards from the person of the defendant and her children. Surveillance was also prohibited.

Upon notice of consolidation of the preliminary injunction hearing and trial for permanent injunction, plaintiff moved for a jury trial-nine months after answer was served, and to remand to state court. The first motion was denied as untimely, the second on grounds of judicial economy. Just prior to trial Galella deposed Mrs. Onassis. Under protective order of this court, the defendant was allowed to testify at the office of the U. S. Attorney and outside the presence of Galella.

After a six-week trial the court dismissed Galella's claim and granted relief to both the defendant and the intervenor. Galella was enjoined from (1) keeping the defendant and her children under surveillance or following any of them; (2) approaching within 100 yards of the home of defendant or her children, or within 100 yards of either child's school or within 75 yards of either child or 50 yards of defendant; (3) using the name, portrait or picture of defendant or her children for advertising; (4) attempting to communicate with defendant or her children except through her attorney.

We conclude that grant of summary judgment and dismissal of Galella's claim against the Secret Service agents was proper . . . .

Discrediting all of Galella's testimony the court found the photographer guilty of harassment, intentional infliction of emotional distress, assault and battery, commercial exploitation of defendant's personality, and invasion of privacy. Fully crediting defendant's testimony, the court found no liability on Galella's claim. Evidence offered by the defense showed that Galella had on occasion intentionally physically touched Mrs. Onassis and her daughter, caused fear of physical contact in his frenzied attempts to get their pictures, followed defendant and her children too closely in an automobile, endangered the safety of the children while they were swimming, water skiing and horseback riding. Galella cannot successfully challenge the court's finding of tortious conduct.

Finding that Galella had "insinuated himself into the very fabric of Mrs. Onassis' life . . ." the court framed its relief in part on the need to prevent further invasion of the defendant's privacy. Whether or not this accords with present New York law, there is no doubt that it is sustainable under New York's proscription of harassment. [FN12]

FN12. See n. 11, supra.
Although the New York courts have not yet recognized a common law right of privacy, if we were required to reach the question, we would be inclined to agree with the court below that when again faced with the issue the Court of Appeals may well modify or distinguish its 1902 holding in Roberson v. Rochester Folding-Box Co., 171 N.Y. 538, 64 N.E. 442 (1902), that "The so-called right of privacy has not as yet found an abiding place in our jurisprudence." There is substantive support today for the proposition that privacy is a "basic right" entitled to legal protection, Time v. Hill, 385 U.S. 374, 415, 87 S.Ct. 534, 17 L.Ed.2d 456 (1967) . . . .

Injunctive relief is appropriate. Galella has stated his intention to continue his coverage of defendant so long as she is newsworthy, and his continued harassment even while the temporary restraining orders were in effect indicate that no voluntary change in his technique can be expected. New York courts have found similar conduct sufficient to support a claim for injunctive relief. Flamm v. Van Nierop, 56 Misc.2d 1059, 291 N.Y.S.2d 189 (1968).

The injunction, however, is broader than is required to protect the defendant. Relief must be tailored to protect Mrs. Onassis from the "paparazzo" attack which distinguishes Galella's behavior from that of other photographers; it should not unnecessarily infringe on reasonable effors to "cover" defendant. Therefore, we modify the court's order to prohibit only (1) any approach within twenty-five (25) feet of defendant or any touching of the person of the defendant Jacqueline Onassis; (2) any blocking of her movement in public places and thoroughfares; (3) any act foreseeably or reasonably calculated to place the life and safety of defendant in jeopardy; and (4) any conduct which would reasonably be foreseen to harass, alarm or frighten the defendant.

Any further restriction on Galella's taking and selling pictures of defendant for news coverage is, however, improper and unwarranted by the evidence.

FLORIDA PUBLISHING COMPANY,

v.

FLETCHER.

340 So.2d 914

Supreme Court of Florida.

Oct. 7, 1976.

Sundberg, J., dissented and filed an opinion.

ROBERTS, Justice.

This cause is before us on petition for writ of certiorari to review the decision of the District Court of Appeal, First District, in Fletcher v. Florida Publishing Co., reported at 319 So.2d 100 (Fla.App. 1, 1975), which directly conflicts with Jacova v. Southern Radio and Television Co., 83 So.2d 34 (Fla.1955), thereby vesting jurisdiction in this Court pursuant to Article V, Section 3(b)(3), Florida Constitution.

The facts supported by the record are succinctly stated in the summary final judgment of the trial judge who determined that there was no real dispute as to the material facts. Respondent, Mrs. Fletcher, left Jacksonville for New York on September 15, 1972, to visit a friend. She left in Jacksonville her three young daughters, including seventeen-year-old Cindy. A 'baby sitter' was to spend the nights with the children, but there was no one with them in the home during the daytime except a young man who had a room in the house and whom Mrs. Fletcher described as Cindy's 'boy friend.' On the afternoon of September 15, 1972, while Cindy was alone in the house, a fire of undetermined origin did large damage to the home, and Cindy died.

The fire and police departments were called by a neighbor who discovered the fire, but too late to save the child. A large group of firemen, news media representatives, and onlookers gathered at the scene and on Mrs. Fletcher's property.

When the Fire Marshal and Police Sergeant Short entered the house to make their official investigation, they invited the news media to accompany them, as they deposed was their standard practice. The media representatives entered through the open door; there was no objection to their entry; they entered quietly and peaceably; they did no damage to the property; and their entry was for the purpose of their news coverage of this fire and death.

The Fire Marshal desired a clear picture of the 'silhouette' left on the floor after the removal of Cindy's body. He and Sergeant Short in their depositions explained that the picture was important for their respective investigations to show that the body was already on the floor Before the heat of the fire did any damage in the room. The Fire Marshal took one polaroid picture of the silhouette, but it was not too clear, he had no further film, and he requested photographer Cranford to take the 'silhouette' picture which was made a part of the official investigation file of both the Fire and Police.

This picture was not only a part of the investigation but News Photographer Cranford turned it and his other pictures over to the defendant newspaper. It and several other pictures appeared in the news story of The Florida Times- Union on September 16, 1972.

Respondent first learned of the facts surrounding the death of her daughter by reading the newspaper story and viewing the published photographs.

Respondent filed an amended complaint against petitioner alleging(1) trespass and invasion of privacy, (2) invasion of privacy, (3) wrong intentional infliction of emotional distress--seeking punitive damages.

. . . Relative to the granting of summary judgment for Petitioner as to Count I, the trial judge cogently explicated:

> 'As to Count I, the question raised by the motion for summary judgment is one of law as there is no genuine issue of material fact. The question raised is whether the trespass alleged in Count I of the complaint was consented to by the doctrine of common custom and usage.
> 'The law is well settled in Florida and elsewhere that there is no unlawful trespass when peaceable entry is made, without objection, under common custom and usage . . . .

On appeal, the District Court of Appeal reversed as to the granting of summary judgment on Count I, stating:

> 'We do not here hold that a trespass or 'intrusion' did in fact occur sub judice: We simply find that such is alleged in Count I of the amended complaint and that the proofs before the learned trial judge are insufficient to resolve the point by summary judgment.'

Although recognizing that consent is an absolute defense to an action for trespass and that the defense of custom and usage is but another way of expressing consent by implication--that is consent may be implied from custom, usage or conduct--the District Court commented that the emergency of the fire was over and that there was no contention that petitioner's employees entered the premises to render assistance, explained that respondent did not either impliedly or expressly invite petitioner's employees into her home, and concluded that the proofs before the court were not sufficient to show that there was no genuine issue of material fact as to whether implied consent by custom and usage authorized entry into the premises without invitation by appellant.

. . . The District Court erred in reversing summary judgment for petitioners as to Count I. The trial court properly determined from the record before it that there was no genuine issue of material fact insofar as the entry into respondent's home by petitioner's employees became lawful and non-actionable pursuant to the doctrine of common custom, usage, and practice and since it had been shown that it was common usage, custom and practice for news media to enter private premises and homes Under the circumstances present here.

Judge McCord in his dissenting opinion could not agree with the majority that the news photographer who entered the burned out home was a trespasser or that the photograph published by petitioner and the news story resulting from the entry were an actionable invasion of privacy. We agree with and approve the following well-reasoned explication by Judge McCord in his dissenting opinion:

> 'The only photographs taken and published were of fire damage--none were of deceased or injured persons. There, is no contention that the particular photograph complained of (the silhouette picture) and the news story were in any way false or inaccurate. There could, therefore, be no recovery under the 'false-light' doctrine of invasion of privacy. See Cantrell v. Forest City Publishing Company, 419 U.S. 245, 95 S.Ct. 465, 42 L.Ed.2d 419 (1974). Thus, there could be no recovery from the publication if the same photograph had come from a source other than from the news photographer's entry upon the premises. Any recovery in this case must necessarily be based upon trespass, and, therefore, the only question is whether or not there was a trespass by the news photographer. The majority opinion discusses the implied consent doctrine under which a person, who does not have express consent from the owner or possessor of premises, may legally enter under circumstances which infer or imply consent (common usage, custom and practice). It is my view that the entry in this case was by implied consent.
>
> 'It is not questioned that this tragic fire and death were being investigated by the fire department and the sheriff's office and that arson was suspected. The fire was a disaster of great public interest and it is clear that the photographer and other members of the news media entered the burned home at the invitation of the investigating officers. (Numerous members of the general public also went through the burned house.) Many affidavits of news editors throughout Florida and the nation and affidavits of Florida law enforcement officials were filed in support of appellee's motion for summary judgment. These affidavits were to the general effect that it has been a long-standing custom and practice throughout the country for representatives of the news media to enter upon private property where disaster of great public interest has occurred--entering in a peaceful manner, without causing any physical damage, and at the invitation of the officers who are investigating the calamity. The affidavits of law enforcement officers indicate that the presence of the news media at such investigations is often helpful to the investigations in developing leads, etc.
>
> 'The affidavits as to custom and practice do not delineate between various kinds of property where a tragedy occurs. They apply to any such place. If an entry is or is not a trespass, its character would not change depending upon whether or not the place of the tragedy is a burned

out home (as here), an office or other building or place. An analysis of the cases on implied consent by custom and usage, indicates that they do not rest upon the previous nonobjection to entry by the particular owner of the property in question but rest upon custom and practice generally. Implied consent would, of course, vanish if one were informed not to enter at that time by the owner or possessor or by their direction. But here there was not only no objection to the entry, but There was an invitation to enter by the officers investigating the fire. The question of implied consent to news media personnel to enter premises in a circumstance such as this appears to be one of first impression not only in this jurisdiction but elsewhere. This, in itself, tends to indicate that the practice has been accepted by the general public since it is a widespread practice of long-standing. Due to such widespread and long-standing custom, reason and logic support the application of implied consent to enter the premises in the case before us. It, therefore, was not a trespass, and I would affirm the trial court.' (emphasis supplied)

Accordingly, that portion of the decision of the District Court of Appeal, First District, reversing summary judgment for petitioner as to Count I is quashed, and the cause is remanded for further proceedings consistent herewith.

It is so ordered.

GREEN VALLEY SCHOOL, INC.,
v.
COWLES FLORIDA BROADCASTING, INC.

327 So.2d 810.

District Court of Appeal of Florida, First District.

Feb. 18, 1976.

RAWLS, Acting Chief Judge.

On February 10, 1973, at 6:00 p.m., appellees Todd and Rozier, employees of appellee Cowles Florida Broadcasting, Inc., published the following narration on WESH-TV, Channel 2 (television station owned by appellee Cowles):

'FRED BREWSTER (newscaster): The President of a controversial private school in West Volusia County was arrested last night along with three staff members as a platoon of law enforcement officers raided the facility. The President was charged with 'False Imprisonment' and the staffers held on narcotics charges. Channel 2's Dean Todd was there and files this report:

'DEAN TODD: No less than 50 law enforcement officers from all departments in Volusia County except DeLand and the Sheriff's Office gathered last night in DeLand under the leadership of Chief Investigator Jack Lynady of the State Attorney's Office. They were about to swoop down on the controversial Green Valley School in Orange City after over two years of investigation they planned to arrest Ronald Nowicki, Headmaster and President. Charge: 'False Imprisonment'

'The Law Department sprang after a Phys. Ed. Instructor, identified only as a Mr. Kelley, told police it was common practice to lock up the students for days, even weeks at a time. But there was even more. There were allegations of rempant sexual conduct between students themselves and between staff members and female students.

'Nowicki was rousted out of his bed at his small, untidy apartment in a building known as the Monastery. With him was a young, female staff member--he told investigators they were on night duty together.

'About 65 students live on the campus and while Nowicki was being advised of his rights the other officers began securing the other buildings in military fashion. According to officers, some of the male and female students were living in the same dormitories. Most of the rooms were in apparently permanent shambles. The rooms were filthy, even those of most of the staff members were in complete disarray.

'It wasn't long before officers began turning up drugs by the armload. Many were vitamins, many were prescription drugs which have not been identified by the searchers.

'Something else was turned up during the searches: These are electric shock collars. They are made for dog training, but here, according to some of the students, they are used on them, occasionally. Also turned up were a set of shackles and handcuffs used to bind the children. Apparently such implements were expected to be found by the raiders.

'This is 15 year old Mitchell Spalding of San Diego, California, on the right; 14 year old Marc Corren of Miami Beach. The State of California pays $16,000.00 a year for Spalding to stay here. The filth is astounding. Spalding and Corren both told Channel 2 News they had electric cattle prods used on them by staff members and that it was common.

'DEAN TODD: Did they use a cattle prod on you?

'MITCHELL SPALDING: Um, yea, they used it once on me.

'DEAN TODD: For what?

'MITCHELL SPALDING: For nothing. I was asleep and they came up drunk and

'DEAN TODD: Who did?

'MARC CORREN: Me.

'MITCHELL SPALDING: Ah . . .

'MARC CORREN: Staff, staff members man.

'MITCHELL SPALDING: Ah, it was Mike Hannigan and I, I was asleep at the time and so I don't know who else did it. But they come up with this bull shocker, ya see, ya know, they really bull shocked me but I hadn't done anything.

'MARC CORREN: I mean that is enough to drive a cow sick man, it could even hurt you, you can feel pain for the next four days.

'DEAN TODD: This is the block house, inside it is bare. Students are reportedly locked inside for days. Eighteen year old Sue Borman of Levitt Town, Pennsylvania, told us that she had been locked in there once, for a week.

'Simultaneously, a Marina, owned by the Green Valley School also was raided. Some six of the students were found when law enforcement officers came upon the area West of DeLand, a short distance South of the Hontoon Marina. The main object of the search was an old boat, a World War II mine-sweeper converted into a diving rig called the 'FEARLESS' and reportedly housed students in certain detention cells. But the 'FEARLESS' apparently has not left its birth (sic) for two years. It has, aboard it, a decompression chamber. It is supposed to be used primarily by divers stuck with the bends or nitrogen narcosis.

'Informed sources told us that students had been locked in here, as punishment. A brig, located in the bow of the ship, was filthy and rat infested, students reportedly were housed in here, human excrement was also found in this area.

'Back at the school, officers continued to find more pills, some in the room of an instructor. A collection of color slides which graphically detailed several nude women was found in the therapy room as well as a host of electric instruments.

'The searches continued until dawn. Investigator, Lynady summed up the arrest that had been made then:

'JACK LYNADY: A man was arrested for 'False Imprisonment', another man was arrested for possession of, ah, marijuana, and ah drug paraphernalia, two girls were arrested for ah . . .

'DEAN TODD: It may be sometime before the full implications of last nights raid are known.
'The Federal Government reportedly pays the School about $600,000.00 a year, various states and private individuals pay 'exorbitant' amounts to house delinquent children and some with medical problems here.
'The apparent owner, George von Hilshmier, was in Canada. He apparently runs one or two other similar schools; one located in New York.
'Accompanying the officers last night were Internal Revenue Agents who confiscated the School's financial records.
'Some of the children reacted to the raid with fear, some with surprise or amusement. They may have a lot to tell later.
'This investigation, which began two years ago, may be just begining.
'Dean Todd, Channel 2 News, Orange City.
'FRED BREWSTER: State Attorney, Steven Boyles, said the School could be closed as a public nuisance. Boyles told Channel 2 Green Valley is chartered by the Circuit Court under a State Statute on private schools, and that a ruling as to the application of the law as it relates to the Green Valley School might be obtained from the Attorney General.
'Further charges may be filed pending the outcome of the lab tests of the various drugs taken last night.'

As a result of the foregoing, Green Valley filed its complaint sounding in libel and slander and malicious trespass. Extensive discovery was had together with numerous hearing, resulting in a large pasteboard box of records numbering some 22 volumes and more than 3,000 pages. The trial court entered summary judgment in favor of appellees; hence this appeal.

Two points are posed for our consideration, viz: 1) The record shows substantial issues of material fact, and 2) The trial court erred in denying appellant's Motion and Application for Disqualification.

Additional facts are material. Prior to the above mentioned raid, Jack Lynady, Chief Investigator for the state attorney's office of the Seventh Judicial Circuit, Procured a search warrant commanding:

'. . . ALL AND SINGULAR THE SHERIFF AND/OR DEPUTY SHERIFFS OF VOLUSIA COUNTY, FLORIDA, OR INVESTIGATORS FOR THE STATE ATTORNEY'S OFFICE, SEVENTH JUDICIAL CIRCUIT, STATE OF FLORIDA (to search):
'. . . Those lands described in deed of record in Official Records Book 1196, page 629 of the Public Records of Volusia County, Florida, believed to be the property owned by Green Valley School, Inc., is being used as a means to commit the felony offenses of false imprisonment, child abuse, and lewd and lascivious behavior. . . .'

The warrant further authorized the search to be conducted either in the daytime or nighttime. Lynady arranged a raiding party of some fifty policemen from several municipalities within Volusia County and employees of the state attorney, who were designated 'special investigators' by the state attorney. Lynady also invited appellees Rozier and Todd and other news media personnel to participate in the midnight raid. The party was briefed by Lynady during the evening of February 9, 1973, and at approximately 11:30 p.m. the search party, accompanied by Rozier and Todd (and other news media personnel), arrived upon the premises of Green Valley. Excerpts from various affidavits and depositions regarding the raid reveal the following:

Edward Brenner--Teacher and Counsellor

'4. At about midnight or sometime thereafter, I was awakened by several beefy, ununiformed men who claimed that they were policemen and who ordered me to remain just outside my room. These individuals refused to produce identification, displayed no badges, and would not produce a warrant. I asked them by what authority they were there and they refused to tell me anything more than 'this is a raid, and we are going to get the goods on you.'

'6. These obese persons began abusing the children in my care with verbal threats and by telling them to 'tell everything you know and it will go easy on you kid'. They asked each child many leading questions. Two of the children, both of whom were obviously highly agitated, and both were known to me to be highly disturbed children began to answer questions about abuse and illegalities in a positive manner. They were then stopped by the cigar smoking fat man questioning them who shouted to others to 'call the TV camera, get Todd over here'.

'7. A white station wagon clearly marked as belonging to Channel Two then arrived and another plump man and a TV camera man with several other individuals got out. They then filmed Mitchel Spaulding, a boy then just a few months out of a mental hospital and now again in a state mental hospital, who was to my eyes and who appears to me on the TV program filmed by Channel Two, to be highly disturbed and agitated. They also filmed Michael Corren, a boy with a long delinquent history who also was very obviously under great mental strain.

'8. The cigar smoking person who claimed he was a policeman took the lead in telling the boys what to say. In no way did the transaction resemble a questioning. The boys were told what to say and parrotted it. This was obvious to the plump person from Channel Two who seemed to be the announcer and who subsequently has been identified to me on the TV program as Dean Todd. It was also obvious to the individual accompanying him.

'Any dirt, filth, pictures, or other disarray and mess was caused primarily by the first group of overweight cigar smoking men who called themselves police. These men pointedly and particularly arranged furniture, sheets, trash, and vitamin pills in groups for the TV camera men. This was done in the full view of the second group of men, including Dean Todd, the Plump man who seemed to be the leader of the group emerging from the white station wagon.'

Susan Borman--Student

'7. I love Green Valley School and I saw the television program on WESH-TV and it was just one lie after another. It was especially a lie when it said I said I had been locked up for weeks in the Bomb Shelter. I did not say it, I only Kept telling them to leave me alone and that I did not want to get into trouble. . . . I was afraid of what they would do to me especially after they (sic) way they tore up my room. I did not know what my rights were and they just came into my room like burglars and scared me to death and then told me I could go to jail after they tore my room all apart and made it a terrible mess. Every where you could see them tearing up rooms like animals.'

Faye Brown--Staff Member of Green Valley

'4. At 1:45 a.m. a group of roughly dressed men entered the Medical Center and announced that they were searching the entire building and campus.

'7. The WESH-TV Channel Two Team appeared at the Medical Center shortly after the men arrived and were told by one of them, 'We aren't ready for you yet, come back later.' They entered the building without knocking and were not invited to come in.'

Wendy Clark--Teacher

'2. I was awake when a group of men, who refused to identify themselves to me, swarmed into the Quads and made all the children leave their rooms and stand in front of them. They would not identify themselves to me, they showed me no warrant or any other piece of paper. They were dressed more or less like hunters and their mood and actions were like that of a group of college boys at a 'panty raid.' The only indication that they were policemen, was that they told me I would be arrested if I moved from in front of my room.

'3. I found the experience terrifying and so did the children in my charge. Several of the girls were jerred (sic) at and their inadequate clothing pointed at repeatedly by the strangers and especially the men from the station wagon from WESH-TV. . . . Their behavior was like that of nasty boys while crashing a girl's picnic when the adults are away.'

Harry Detweiler--Public School Teacher from Ashland, Oregon--Volunteer in order to learn about successful methods of working with very disruptive children.

'2. Sometime after midnight on February 9th (February 10), 1973, I was awakened by a great deal of racket in the Administration Building where I occupied the single bedroom upstairs. By the time I came down the stairs there were more than twenty people in the building.

'3. The men had obviously gotten in by breaking a door and one of the men had cut himself pretty badly. No one would give me a warrant or any identification although they asked for my identification.

'4. There are several thousand slides in one of the three treatment rooms upstairs. The men were going through the slides with a great air of comedy. The majority of the slides have to do with innocuous subjects and are used to treat phobias by the psychiatrists or their aides here. A few of the trays deal with nude human figures and these were greeted with great enthusiasm by the men, and especially those whom it was easy to identify as newsmen and the men from WESH-TV Channel Two.

'6. WESH-TV and the still photographers spent a great deal of film on a large plastic bag full of comfrey tea (an old fashioned herbal tea). It was clearly labeled and to the eye does not look anything like parsley, oregano or the marijuana identification kits they give out to school teachers. The newsmen were totally uninterested in my statements that it was unfair to take pictures of herb tea and call it drugs. In the WESH-TV program I saw that the bag of tea was shown while Dean Todd talked about 'armloads of drugs."

Carole Rice--Student at Green Valley for several years

'3. My girlfriend, Cathy Hynds, had been in bed dressed in a man's tee shirt. It was barely long enough to cover her legs. The police would not let her get dressed.

'4. The station wagon came over and the camera man took pictures of my room. The room looked awful, but I always have a clean room and it was only because the cops had torn it up.
'5. While the man who is called Dean Todd on the TV was standing by my room, he kept pointing at Cathy Hynds and laughing and joking and being awful. I was so mad that I cried. Poor Cathy was humiliated. When I saw that fat face again at a press conference I was so mad I had to leave. He acted like a bully that night. All of those men were joking and laughing and making nasty remarks. They must think we are stupid because one would be sticky sweet and say he was helping us and another would be nasty and say 'tell us where your drugs are,' 'do you take them in your arm,' 'where's your needles?' They kept it up for hours.
'7. I saw the TV broadcast that Dean Todd did and he is just a liar. He helped those cops mess up things, and he only took pictures after the cops called him over with some special goodie they had made up. He was ugly and obscene to the girls and made Cathy especially humiliated.' . . . .

To uphold appellees' assertion that their entry upon appellant's property at the time, manner, and circumstances as reflected by this record was as a Matter of law sanctioned by 'the request of and with the consent of the State Attorney' and within the 'common usage and custom in Florida' could well bring to the citizenry of this state the hobnail boots of a nazi stormtrooper equipped with glaring lights invading a couple's bedroom at midnight with the wife hovering in her nightgown in an attempt to shield herself from the scanning TV camera. In this jurisdiction, a law enforcement officer is not As a matter of law endowed with the right or authority to invite people of his choosing to invade private property and participate in a midnight raid of the premises . . . .

Reversed and remanded with directions.

LE MISTRAL, INC.,
v.
COLUMBIA BROADCASTING SYSTEM.

61 A.D.2d 491

Supreme Court, Appellate Division, First Department.

March 2, 1978.

LUPIANO, Justice:

Defendant Columbia Broadcasting System in its capacity as owner and operator of Television Channel 2 in New York, on July 6, 1972, directed defendant Lucille Rich, its employee, and a camera crew to visit a number of restaurants which had been cited for health code violations by the Health Services Administration of New York City. Plaintiff restaurant was on the list. The camera crew and Ms. Rich entered the restaurant at approximately 2:00 p. m. with the camera working ("rolling"), which necessitated the utilization of bright lights for filming purposes. After entering the premises in this fashion, Ms. Rich and the camera crew were commanded to leave by plaintiff's president. It appears that these CBS employees were on the premises for a period of time during which the camera continued to roll. Plaintiff, insofar as its action for trespass is concerned, was awarded compensatory and punitive damages by a jury. The trial court on defendant CBS's motion upheld the jury verdict in finding that the conduct of this defendant constituted a trespass, but set aside the damage awards.

Initially, we are confronted with defendant CBS's claim that despite the tort committed, defendant is insulated from any damage award by virtue of the First Amendment to the United States Constitution. Clearly, the First Amendment is not a shibboleth before which all other rights must succumb. This Court "recognizes that the exercise of the right of free speech and free press demands and even mandates the observance of the co-equal duty not to abuse such right, but to utilize it with right reason and dignity. Vain lip service to 'duties' in a vacuous reality wherein 'rights' exist, sovereign and independent of any balancing moral or social factor creates a semantical mockery of the very foundation of our laws and legal system" (Bavarian Motor v. Manchester, 61 Misc.2d 309, 311, 305 N.Y.S.2d 593, 596). In Dietemann v. Time, Inc., 449 F.2d 245, 249 (9th Cir. 1971), it was observed that "(t)he First Amendment has never been construed to accord newsmen immunity from torts or crimes committed during the course of news-gathering. The First Amendment is not a license to trespass . . . ." Similarly, the Second Circuit Court of Appeals in Galella v. Onassis, 487 F.2d 986, 995- 996, stated:

> "Crimes and torts committed in news gathering are not protected. See Branzburg v. Hayes, 408 U.S. 665, 92 S.Ct. 2646, 33 L.Ed.2d 626 (1972); Rosenbloom v. Metromedia, 403 U.S. 29, 91 S.Ct. 1811, 29 L.Ed.2d 296 (1971); Dietemann v. Time, Inc., 449 F.2d 245, 249-250 (9th Cir. 1971). See Restatement of Torts 2d s 652(f), comment K (Tent. Draft No. 13, 1967). There is no threat to a free press in requiring its agents to act within the law."

Scrutiny of the record demonstrates an adequate basis to justify the compensatory damage award rendered by the jury and, accordingly, such award must stand. Regarding punitive damages, it is well recognized that such damages "are penal in their nature and are different, both in nature and purpose, from compensatory damages. Such damages are allowed in addition to compensatory damages, and are awarded upon public consideration as a punishment of the defendant for the wrong in the particular case, and for the protection of the public against similar acts, to deter the defendant from a repetition of the wrongful act, and to serve as a warning to others" (14 N.Y.Jur., Damages s 176). "As a general rule, exemplary damages are recoverable in all actions ex delicto based upon tortious acts which involve ingredients of malice, fraud, oppression, insult, wanton or reckless disregard of the plaintiff's rights, or other circumstances of aggravation, as a punishment of the defendant and admonition to others . . .. Punitive damages have been allowed in actions for trespass . . .." (14 N.Y.Jur., supra s 180). The award of punitive damages under circumstances warranting the allowance of same rests in the discretion of the jury, or in the court where the case is tried without a jury. The basis for an award of exemplary damages depends upon a showing that the wrong is aggravated by evil or a wrongful motive or that there was wilful and intentional misdoing, or a reckless indifference equivalent thereto.

The trial court in setting aside the jury award of punitive damages, did so because of its exclusion of certain testimony by defense witness Dessartz relevant to defendant CBS's motive and purpose in entering the plaintiff's premises unannounced "with cameras rolling." The court noted: "As punitive damage involves malice, evidence of motivation and purpose are admissible, at least in mitigation of damages." As recovery of punitive damages depends upon the defendant acting with evil or wrongful motive or with a wilful and intentional misdoing, or with a reckless indifference equivalent thereto, "(a) ll . . . circumstances immediately connected with the transaction tending to exhibit or explain the motive of the defendant are admissible" (14 N.Y.Jur., supra s 189). Defendant CBS was entitled to demonstrate and explain its motive and the curtailment of this right by the trial court mandates re-trial of the punitive damage issue.

Accordingly, the order of the Supreme Court, New York County, entered January 19, 1977 which vacated the jury's award of $1,200 in compensatory damages and $250,000 in punitive damages and directed a new trial on the issue of damages, should be modified, on the law, to the extent of reinstating the jury's award of compensatory damages, severing the claim to punitive damages and remanding the matter for a trial on the issue of punitive damages, and as so modified, should be affirmed, without costs and without disbursements.

Order, Supreme Court, New York County, entered on January 19, 1977, modified, on the law, to the extent of reinstating the jury's award of compensatory damages, severing the claim to punitive damages and remanding the matter for a trial on the issue of punitive damages and, as so modified, affirmed, without costs and without disbursements.

DIETEMANN,
v.
TIME, INC.

449 F.2d 245

United States Court of Appeals,
Ninth Circuit.

Aug. 23, 1971.

James M. Carter, Circuit Judge, concurred and dissented and filed opinion.

Before CARTER and HUFSTEDLER, Circuit Judges, and VON DER HEYDT, District Judge.

HUFSTEDLER, Circuit Judge:

This is an appeal from a judgment for plaintiff in an action for invasion of privacy. Jurisdiction was grounded in diversity. The parties agreed that California law governed. After a court trial plaintiff was awarded $1000 general damages. On appeal we are asked to consider significant questions involving the relationship between personal privacy and the freedom of the press.

The district court's decision is reported in Dietemann v. Time, Inc., 284 F.Supp. 925 (1968). The facts, as narrated by the district court, are these:

"Plaintiff, a disabled veteran with little education, was engaged in the practice of healing with clay, minerals, and herbs-as practiced, simple quackery.

"Defendant, Time, Incorporated, a New York corporation, publishes Life Magazine. Its November 1, 1963 edition carried an article entitled 'Crackdown on Quackery.' The article depicted plaintiff as a quack and included two pictures of him. One picture was taken at plaintiff's home on September 20, 1963, previous to his arrest on a charge of practicing medicine without a license, and the other taken at the time of his arrest.

"Life Magazine entered into an arrangement with the District Attorney's Office of Los Angeles County whereby Life's employees would visit plaintiff and obtain facts and pictures concerning his activities. Two employees of Life, Mrs. Jackie Metcalf and Mr. William Ray, went to plaintiff's home on September 20, 1963. When they arrived at a locked gate, they rang a bell and plaintiff came out of his house and was told by Mrs. Metcalf and Ray that they had been sent there by a friend, a Mr. Johnson. The use of Johnson's name was a ruse to gain entrance. Plaintiff admitted them and all three went into the house and into plaintiff's den.

"The plaintiff had some equipment which could at best be described as gadgets, not equipment which had anything to do with the practice of medicine. Plaintiff, while examiningMrs. Metcalf, was photographed by Ray with a hidden camera without the consent of plaintiff. One of the pictures taken by him appeared in Life Magazine showing plaintiff with his hand on the upper portion of Mrs. Metcalf's breast while he was looking at some gadgets and holding what appeared to be a wand in his right hand. Mrs. Metcalf had told plaintiff that she had a lump in her breast. Plaintiff concluded that she had eaten some rancid butter 11 years, 9 months, and 7 days prior to that time. Other persons were seated in the room during this time.

"The conversation between Mrs. Metcalf and plaintiff was transmitted by radio transmitter hidden in Mrs. Metcalf's purse to a tape recorder in a parked automobile occupied by Joseph Bride, Life employee, John Miner of the District Attorney's Office, and Grant Leake, an investigator of the State Department of Public Health. While the recorded conversation was not quoted in the article in Life, it was mentioned that Life correspondent Bride was making notes of what was being received via the radio transmitter, and such information was at least referred to in the article.

"The foregoing events were photographed and recorded by an arrangement among Miner of the District Attorney's Office, Leake of the State Department of Pubic Health, and Bride, a representative of Life. It had been agreed that Life would obtain pictures and information for use as evidence, and later could be used by Life for publication.

"Prior to the occurrences of September 20, 1963, on two occasions the officials had obtained recordings of conversations in plaintiff's home; however, no pictures had been secured. Life employees had not participated in obtaining the recordings on these occasions.

"On October 15, 1963, plaintiff was arrested at his home on a charge of practicing medicine without a license in violation of Section 26280, California Health and Safety Code. At the time of his arrest, many pictures were made by Life of plaintiff at his home. Plaintiff testified that he did not agree to pose for the pictures but allowed pictures because he thought the officers could require it. Also present were newspaper men who had also been invited by the officials to be present at the time of arrest.

"Defendant contends that plaintiff posed for pictures at the time of his arrest and thus permission was given to take those pictures. As hereinafter pointed out, it is unnecessary to decide whether or not permission was given to take pictures at the time of his arrest.

"Plaintiff, although a journeyman plumber, claims to be a scientist. Plaintiff had no listings and his home had no sign of any kind. He did not advertise, nor did he have a telephone. He made no charges when he attempted to diagnose or to prescribe herbs and minerals. He did accept contributions.

"Life's article concerning plaintiff was not published until after plaintiff was arrested but before his plea on June 1, 1964 of nolo contendere for violations of Section 2141 of the California Business and Professions Code and Section 26280 of the California Health and Safety Code (misdemeanors).

"* * *

"Defendant's claim that the plaintiff's house was open to the public is not sustained by the evidence. The plaintiff was administering his so-called treatments to people who visited him. He was not a medical man of any type. He did not advertise. He did not have a phone. He did have a lock on his gate. To obtain entrance it was necessary to ring a bell. He conducted his activities in a building which was his home. The employees of defendant gained entrance by a subterfuge."

The district court concluded: "The publication in Life Magazine on November 1, 1963 of plaintiff's picture taken without his consent in his home on September 20, 1963 was an invasion of his privacy under California law for which he is entitled to damages. The acts of defendant also constituted an invasion of plaintiff's right of privacy guaranteed by the Constitution of the United States which would entitle him to relief under Section 1983, Title 42, United States Code." The court awarded $1,000 general damages "for injury to [Dietemann's] feelings and peace of mind. Time appeals from that decision.

The appeal presents three ultimate issues: (1) Under California law, is a cause of action for invasion of privacy established upon proof that defendant's employees, by subterfuge, gained entrance to the office portion of plaintiff's home wherein they photographed him and electronically recorded and transmitted to third persons his conversation without his consent as a result of which he suffered emotional distress? (2) Does the First Amendment insulate defendant from liability for invasion of privacy because defendant's employees did those acts for the purpose of gathering material for a magazine story and a story was thereafter published utilizing some of the material thus gathered? (3) Were the defendant's employees acting as special agents of the police and, if so, did their acts violate the First, Fourth, and Fourteenth Amendments of the Federal Constitution, thereby subjecting defendant to liability under the Civil Rights Act (42 U.S.C. § 1983)? Because we hold that plaintiff proved a cause of action under California law and that the First Amendment does not insulate the defendant from liability, we do not reach the third issue.

Were it necessary to reach the Civil Rights Act questions, we would be obliged to explore the relationship between the defendant's employees and the police for the purpose of ascertaining the existence of the "color of law" element of the Act. Because we do not reach the issue, we can and do accept the defendant's disclaimer that its employees were acting for or on behalf of the police.

In jurisdictions other than California in which a common law tort for invasion of privacy is recognized, it has been consistently held that surreptitious electronic recording of a plaintiff's conversation causing him emotional distress is actionable. Despite some variations in the description and the labels applied to the tort, there is agreement that publication is not a necessary element of the tort, that the existence of a technical trespass is immaterial, and that proof of special damages is not required. . . . .

Although the issue has not been squarely decided in California, we have little difficulty in concluding that clandestine photography of the plaintiff in his den and the recordation and transmission of his conversation without his consent resulting in his emotional distress warrants recovery for invasion of privacy in California. California began developing a common law privacy tort in 1931 with the decision of Melvin v. Reid, 112 Cal.App. 285, 297 P. 91. Since then, the California Supreme Court has decided a number of privacy cases in some of which there are indications that California would recognize the plaintiff's claim . . . .

Plaintiff's den was a sphere from which he could reasonably expect to exclude eavesdropping newsmen. He invited two of defendant's employees to the den. One who invites another to his home or office takes a risk that the visitor may not be what he seems, and that the visitor may repeat all he hears and observes when he leaves. But he does not and should not be required to take the risk that what is heard and seen will be transmitted by photograph or recording, or in our modern world, in full living color and hi-fi to the public at large or to any segment of it that the visitor may select. A different rule could have a most pernicious effect upon the dignity of man and it would surely lead to guarded conversations and conduct where candor is most valued, e.g., in the case of doctors and lawyers.

The defendant claims that the First Amendment immunizes it from liability for invading plaintiff's den with a hidden camera and its concealed electronic instruments because its employees were gathering news and its instrumentalities "are indispensable tools of investigative reporting." We agree that newsgathering is an integral part of news dissemination. We strongly disagree, however, that the hidden mechanical contrivances are "indispensable tools" of newsgathering Investigative reporting is an ancient art; its successful practice long antecedes the invention of miniature cameras and electronic devices. The First Amendment has never been construed to accord newsmen immunity from torts or crimes committed during the course of newsgathering. The First Amendment is not a license to trespass, to steal, or to intrude by electronic means into the precincts of another's home or office. [FN2] It does not become such a license simply because the person subjected to the intrusion is reasonably suspected of committing a crime.

Defendant relies upon the line of cases commencing with New York Times Co. v. Sullivan (1964) 376 U.S. 254, 84 S.Ct. 710, 11 L.Ed.2d 686 and extending through Rosenbloom v. Metromedia, Inc. (1971) 403 U.S. 29, 91 S.Ct. 1811, 29 L.Ed.2d 296 (1971) to sustain its contentions that (1) publication of news, however tortiously gathered, insulates defendant from liability for the antecedent tort, and (2) even of it is not thus shielded from liability, those cases prevent consideration of publication as an element in computing damages.

As we previously observed, publication is not an essential element of plaintiff's cause of action. Moreover, it is not the foundation for the invocation of a privilege. Privilege concepts developed in defamation cases and to some extent in privacy actions in which publication is an essential component are not relevant in determining liability for intrusive conduct antedating publication. (Cf. Nimmer, "The Right to Speak From Time to Time: First Amendment Theory Applied to Libel and Misapplied to Privacy" (1968) 56 Calif.L.Rev. 935, 957.) Nothing in New York Times or its progeny suggests anything to the contrary. Indeed, the Court strongly indicates that there is no First Amendment interest in protecting news media from calculated misdeeds. (E. g., Time, Inc. v. Hill, supra, 385 U.S. at 389-390 and 384 n. 9.)

No interest protected by the First Amendment is adversely affected by permitting damages for intrusion to be enhanced by the fact of later publication of the information that the publisher improperly acquired. Assessing damages for the additional emotional distress suffered by a plaintiff when the wrongfully acquired data are purveyed to the multitude chills intrusive acts. It does not chill freedom of expression guaranteed by the First Amendment. A rule forbidding the use of publication as an ingredient of damages would deny to the injured plaintiff recovery for real harm done to him without any countervailing benefit to the legitimate interest of the public in being informed. The same rule would encourage conduct by news media that grossly offends ordinary men.

The judgment is affirmed.

CASSIDY,

v.

AMERICAN BROADCASTING COMPANIES, INC.

377 N.E.2d 126

Appellate Court of Illinois, First District, First Division.

May 15, 1978.

GOLDBERG, Presiding Justice:

Arlyn Cassidy (plaintiff) filed a two count complaint seeking actual and punitive damages, as well as injunctive relief, from American Broadcasting Companies, Jay Levine, Don Ernst, Myron Renfrow and William Purdy (defendants). Count I alleged eavesdropping in violation of section 14-2 of the Illinois Criminal Code (Ill.Rev.Stat.1975, ch. 38, par. 14-2). Count II alleged invasion of plaintiff's right to privacy. Upon consideration of memoranda of law filed by the parties, discovery depositions and an affidavit by plaintiff, the court granted defendants' motion for summary judgment.

Plaintiff appeals. He contends defendants' actions constitute eavesdropping as defined in the Illinois Criminal Code; the complaint states a cause of action for invasion of privacy and any issue of consent is at best a disputed factual question. Defendants contend plaintiff has no cause of action for either eavesdropping or invasion of privacy and that, in view of the depositions and affidavit, plaintiff clearly consented to the filming complained of.

A review of the factual elements in the record is essential. In his deposition plaintiff stated that on November 6, 1975, he and several other Chicago police officers, acting as undercover agents were assigned to investigate a massage parlor on the near northside of Chicago. During the preceding two days, this establishment had been the site of arrests premised upon solicitation and obscenities. The vice-control division of the police department provided plaintiff with $60 to cover the initial undercover investigatory activities. Plaintiff stated he paid $30 admission fee to see "de-luxe" lingerie modelling. He was taken to a small room by one of the models. (Room No. 1). Upon entering the room he noticed "camera lights" on each side of the bed. He remarked to the model that the lights made the room quite warm. Plaintiff stated he then reclined on the bed and watched the model change her lingerie several times. He made several suggestive remarks and physical advances to her. He arrested the model for solicitation after she established "sufficient" physical contact with him. Three of the other undercover agents joined plaintiff and asked if anyone was in the room adjacent to the room in which plaintiff observed the model. (Room No. 2). The door to Room No. 2 opened, someone cried out "Channel 7 News" and the camera crew exited filming the scene before them.

Plaintiff further stated that after he and the model were in the room for some 10 minutes, the model told him "they were taking movies." Plaintiff stated he did not believe the model's statement but waved his hands and pretended he was being filmed. During the deposition plaintiff was asked, "Were you planning to do anything that you would not want the public to see, hear or record?" He responded, "No."

Depositions were also taken of defendants Jay Levine, Don Ernst and Myron Renfrow; all admittedly part of the camera crew. Levine, the reporter, stated he and the other members of the crew reported to the massage parlor in response to a call from the manager of the parlor. He complained his establishment was the subject of police harassment. The film crew was taken to Room No. 2 where they installed a camera behind a two-way mirror which provided visual access to Room No. 1. Levine explained that as the film crew was only preparing a visual recording it was not necessary to place a microphone in Room No. 1, which was used by plaintiff and the model. No such instrument was ever placed in that room. However, as ABC company policy required "room presence", i. e. background sound, to facilitate the subsequent mixingand editing of sound and silent film clips, the crew placed a microphone in Room No. 2. All of the recording equipment was within Room No. 2. When Levine later viewed the film taken of the events in Room No. 1, he was unable to hear any distinguishable conversation. The microphone in Room No. 2 transmitted only a mixture of incomprehensible sounds.

All members of the film crew remained in Room No. 2 throughout the interaction between plaintiff and the model and filmed this event. Levine also testified that as plaintiff entered Room No. 1, plaintiff said, "What is this? Are we on camera? Are we on TV?" Levine explained that these remarks were made before the camera had been started for the filming.

Don Ernst, the sound technician, stated in his deposition that he was wearing earphones and had a portable amplifier around his neck. He placed a microphone on a shelf in Room No. 2 to record "room presence." He explained that it would have been possible to disconnect the amplifier and microphone from the camera and record only a visual sequence, but because of ABC policy requiring "room presence", he utilized the microphone. He noted that becauseof the street noises emanating through a window facing Wells Street in Room No. 2, as well as the whirring of the camera equipment and other miscellaneous noises, he was unable to hear any conversation occurring in Room No. 1. He stated the sounds he heard were "garbled," "distorted," and "almost unintelligible." Ernst recalled plaintiff stating as he entered Room No. 1, "What are we on, TV?" and the model responding, "Sure, we're making movies."

Myron Renfrow, the lighting technician, also recalled the plaintiff stating, "What are we on, TV?" and the model responding, "Yes, we're making a movie." Renfrow stated this was the only conversation he heard. When the filming started, street noises and camera equipment drowned out the balance of the discussion ensuing in Room No. 1.

In the affidavit accompanying his memorandum in opposition to defendants' motion for summary judgment, plaintiff commented on the remarks made by himself and the model when they entered the room. The plaintiff stated:

> " * * * such conversation * * * was made in the line of my duty and performance as a Police Officer which at the time thereof, I believed possibly referred to a film being taken by (the model) and her coconspirators for sale to me as a putative customer which film would serve as evidence which was the subject of my investigation."

I.
Eavesdropping

Plaintiff contends that the actions of the film crew in both filming and employing recording equipment constitute eavesdropping within the meaning of section 14-2 of the Illinois Criminal Code, (Ill.Rev.Stat.1975, ch. 38, par. 14-2), which provides:

> "A person commits eavesdropping when he:
>
> (a) Uses an eavesdropping device to hear or record all or any part of any conversation unless he does so with the consent of any one party to such conversation and at the request of a State's Attorney; or
>
> (b) Uses or divulges, except in a criminal proceeding, any information which he knows or reasonably should know was obtained through the use of an eavesdropping device."

An "eavesdropping device" is defined as "any device capable of being used to hear or record oral conversation * * *." Ill.Rev.Stat.1975, ch. 38, par. 14- 1(a).

It has frequently been held that summary judgment should be granted "if the pleadings, depositions and admissions on file, together with the supporting affidavits, if any, show that there is no genuine issue as to any material fact and that the moving party is entitled to judgment as a matter of law." (Heidelberger v. Jewel Companies, Inc. (1974), 57 Ill.2d 87, 92, 312 N.E.2d 601, 604.) In the case before us the facts are not disputed. The issue therefore is whether the summary judgment appealed from was proper as a matter of law.

In our opinion, there are two principles of law which adequately support the result reached by the trial judge and which require its affirmance with reference to the dismissal of Count I . . . .

Examining the situation from a completely different point of view, and assuming for ease in exposition that an eavesdropping instrument had, in fact, been used, the issue arises as to whether plaintiff here intended his statements to be of a private nature. It appears strongly from the record that, when plaintiff entered Room No. 1 with the model, he questioned her regarding the lights. Plaintiff specifically asked the model if they were "on TV." The model responded, "Sure, we're making movies." It seems logical that if plaintiff intended that his conduct with the model was to be entirely private, he would then immediately have desisted from proceeding any further. However, as plaintiff stated in his affidavit, his conduct was performed in the line of his duty as an officer and if the model possibly wished to sell him a completed film, that would serve as evidence in plaintiff's investigation.

The issue posed by these facts is not exactly a matter of consent. It is rather a problem of determining whether plaintiff intended that his conduct was to be of a private nature. In People v. Klingenberg (1975), 34 Ill.App.3d 705, 339 N.E.2d 456, the defendant was arrested for driving while intoxicated. He was requested to perform certain physical acts intended to determine the extent of his coordination and an audio-visual recording was made of the process. Upon defendant's motion, the trial court suppressed the recording on the theory that it was made in violation of the eavesdropping statute above cited. This court reversed and held that there was no violation of the eavesdropping statute. The court pointed out that defendant's statements were intended to be heard by the police officers. In the case before us, although no verbal statements are involved, it seems clear that defendant intended his conduct and acts with the model to be filmed by whomever was operating the camera. The defendant in Klingenberg and the plaintiff in the case before us had no expectation of privacy. Citing various authorities, including Giannopoulos, this court held (Klingenberg, 34 Ill.App.3d 705, 708, 339 N.E.2d 456, 459):

> "Under such circumstances, we cannot conclude that the defendant intended his statements to be of a private nature, and we hold that where there is no interception of communication intended by the declarant to be private, there is no eavesdropping."

It follows that upon application of either or both of the principles above set forth, the decision of the trial court regarding Count I in the case before us was correct and summary judgment in favor of defendants on said count is affirmed . . . .

We agree with the argument advanced by defendants that the conduct of a policeman on duty is legitimately and necessarily an area upon which public interest may and should be focused. In the situation before us, we need not consider any theory of express consent. That defense was not pleaded by defendant and the issue is not before us. It may be urged with good reason that plaintiff gave consent by implication when he was advised that the incident was being filmed and still proceeded with his investigation. However, this evidence is not an essential part of the case. In our opinion, the very status of the policeman as a public official, as above pointed out, is tantamount to an implied consent to informing the general public by all legitimate means regarding his activities in discharge of his public duties. There is no allegation in any of the pleadings charging defendants or any of them with actual malice or with any wilful attempt to impede police work. The motives of the defendants are not impugned by the record before us. The judgment order appealed from is accordingly affirmed.

Judgment affirmed.

McGLOON and STAMOS, JJ., concur.

COX BROADCASTING CORP.,
v.
COHN.

420 U.S. 469

Supreme Court of the United States

Decided March 3, 1975.

Mr. Justice WHITE delivered the opinion of the Court.

The issue before us in this case is whether, consistently with the First and Fourteenth Amendments, a State may extend a cause of action for damages for invasion of privacy caused by the publication of the name of a deceased rape victim which was publicly revealed in connection with the prosecution of the crime.

I

In August 1971, appellee's 17-year-old daughter was the victim of a rape and did not survive the incident. Six youths were soon indicted for murder and rape. Although there was substantial press coverage of the crime and of subsequent developments, the identity of the victim was not disclosed pending trial, perhaps because of Ga.Code Ann. s 26--9901 (1972), [FN1] which makes it a misdemeanor to publish or broadcast the name or identity of a rape victim. In April 1972, some eight months later, the six defendants appeared in court. Five pleaded guilty to rape or attempted rape, the charge of murder having been dropped. The guilty pleas were accepted by the court, and the trial of the defendant pleading not guilty was set for a later date.

> FN1. 'It shall be unlawful for any news media or any other person to print and publish, broadcast, televise, or disseminate through any other medium of public dissemination or cause to be printed and published, broadcast, televised, or disseminated in any newspaper, magazine, periodical or other publication published in this State or through any radio or television broadcast originating in the State the name or identity or any female who may have been raped or upon whom an assault with intent to commit rape may have been made. Any person or corporation violating the provisions of this section shall, upon conviction, be punished as for a misdemeanor.'
> Three other States have similar statutes. See Fla.Stat.Ann. ss 794.03, 794.04 (1965 and Supp.1974--1975); S.C.Code Ann. s 16--81 (1962); Wis.Stat.Ann. s 942.02 (1958). The Wisconsin Supreme Court upheld the constitutionality of a predecessor of s 942.02 in State v. Evjue, 253 Wis. 146, 33 N.W.2d 305 (1948). The South Carolina statute was

involved in Nappier v. Jefferson Standard Life Insurance Co., 322 F.2d 502, 505 (CA4 1963), but no constitutional challengeto the statute was made. In Hunter v. Washington Post, 102 Daily Washington L.Rptr. 1561 (1974), the District of Columbia Superior Court denied the defendant's motion for judgment on the pleadings based upon constitutional grounds in an action brought for invasion of privacy resulting from the defendant's publication identifying the plaintiff as a rape victim and givingher name, age, and address.

In the course of the proceedings that day, appellant Wasell, [FN2] a reporter covering the incident for his employer, learned the name of the victim from an examination of the indictments which were made available for his inspection in the courtroom. [FN3] That the name of the victim appears in the indictments and that the indictments were public records available for inspection are not disputed. [FN4] Later that day, Wassell broadcast over the facilities of station WSB--TV, a television station owned by appellant Cox Broadcasting Corp., a news report concerning the court proceedings. The report named the victim of the crime and was repeated the following day. [FN5]

FN2. Wassell was employed at the time in question as a news staff reporter for WSB--TV and had been so employed for the prior nine years. His function was to investigate newsworthy stories and make televised news reports. He was assigned the coverage of the trial of the young men accused of the rape and murder of Cynthia Cohn on the morning of April 10, 1972, the day it began, and had not been involved with the story previously. He was present during the entire hearing that day except for the first 30 minutes. App. 16--17.

FN3. Wassell has described the way in which he obtained the information reported in the broadcast as follows:

'The information on which I prepared the said report was obtained from several sources. First, by personally attending and taking notes of the said trial and the subsequent transfer of four of the six defendants to the Fulton County Jail, I obtained personal knowledge of the events that transpired during the trial of this action and the said transfer of the defendants. Such personal observations and notes were the primary and almost exclusive source of the information upon which the said news report was based. Secondly, during a recess of the said trial, I approached the clerk of the court, who was sitting directly in front of the bench, and requested to see a copy of the indictments. In open court, I was handed the indictments, both the murder and the rape indictments, and was allowed to examine fully this document. As is shown by the said indictments . . . the name of the said Cynthia Cohn appears in clear type. Moreover, no attempt was made by the clerk or anyone else to withhold the name and identity of the victim from me or from anyone else and the said indictments apparently were available for public inspection upon request.' Id., at 17--18.

FN4. The indictments are in pertinent part as follows:

'THE GRAND JURORS selected, chosen and sworn for the County of Fulton . . . in the name and behalf of the citizens of Georgia, charge and accuse (the defendants) with the offense of:--'RAPE' for that said accused, in the County of Fulton and State of Georgia, on the 18th day of August, 1971 did have carnal knowledge of the person of Cynthia Leslie Cohn, a female, forcibly and against her will . . ..' Id., at 22--23. 'THE GRAND JURORS selected, chosen and sworn for the County of Fulton . . . in the name and behalf of the citizens of Georgia, charge and accuse (the defendants) with the offense of:-- 'MURDER' for that said accused, in the County of Fulton and State or Georgia, on the 18th day of August, 1971 did while in the commission of the offense of Rape, a felony, upon the person of Cynthia Leslie Cohn, a female human being, cause her death by causing her to suffocate. ...' Id., at 24-- 25.

FN5. The relevant portion of the transcript of the televised report reads as follows:

'Six youths went on trial today for the murder-rape of a teenaged girl. 'The six Sandy Springs High School boys were charged with murder and rape in the death of seventeen year old Cynthia Cohn following a drinking party last August 18th. The tragic death of the high school girl shocked the entire Sandy Springs community. Today the six boys had their day in court.' App. 19--20.

In May 1972, appellee brought an action for money damages against appellants, relying on s 26--9901 and claiming that his right to privacy had been invaded by the television broadcasts giving the name of his deceased daughter. Appellants admitted the broadcasts but claimed that they were privileged under both state law and the First and Fourteenth Amendments. The trial court, rejecting appellants' constitutional claims and holding that the Georgia statute gave a civil remedy to those injured by its violation, granted summary judgment to appellee as to liability, with the determination of damages to await trial by jury.

On appeal, the Georgia Supreme Court, in its initial opinion, held that the trial court had erred in construing s 26--9901 to extend a civil cause of action for invasion of privacy and thus found it unnecessary to consider the constitutionality of the statute. 231 Ga. 60, 200 S.E.2d 127 (1973). The court went on to rule, however, that the complaint stated a cause of action 'for the invasion of the appellee's right of privacy, or for the tort of public disclosure'--a 'common law tort exist(ing) in this jurisdiction without the help of the statute that the trial judge in this case relied on.' Id., at 62, 200 S.E.2d, at 130. Although the privacy invaded was not that of the deceased victim, the father was held to have stated a claim for invasion of his own privacy by reason of the publication of his daughter's name. The court explained, however, that liability did not follow as a matter of law and that summary judgment was improper; whether the public disclosure of the name actually invaded appellee's 'zone of privacy,' and if so, to what extent, were issues to be determined by the trier of fact. Also, 'in formulating such an issue for determination by the fact-finder, it is reasonable to require the appellee to prove that the appellants invaded his privacy with wilful or negligent disregard for the fact that reasonable men would find the invasion highly offensive.' Id., at 64, 200 S.E.2d, at 131. The Georgia Supreme Court did agree with the trial court, however, that the First and Fourteenth Amendments did not, as a matter of law, require judgment for appellants. The court concurred with the statement in Briscoe v. Reader's Digest Assn., Inc., 4 Cal.3d 529, 541, 93 Cal.Rptr. 866, 874, 483 P.2d 34, 42 (1971), that 'the rights guaranteed by the First Amendment do not require total abrogation of the right to privacy. The goals sought by each may be achieved with a minimum of intrusion upon the other.'

Upon motion for rehearing the Georgia court countered the argument that the victim's name was a matter of public interest and could be published with impunity by relying on s 26--9901 as an authoritative declaration of state policy that the name of a rape victim was not a matter of public concern. This time the court felt compelled to determine the constitutionality of the statute and sustained it as a 'legitimate limitation on the right of freedom of expression contained in the First Amendment.' The court could discern 'no public interest or general concern about the identity of the victim of such a crime as will make the right to disclose the identity of the victim rise to the level of First Amendment protection.' 231 Ga., at 68, 200 S.E.2d, at 134.

We postponed decision as to our jurisdiction over this appeal to the hearing on the merits. 415 U.S. 912, 94 S.Ct. 1406, 39 L.Ed.2d 466 (1974). We conclude that the Court has jurisdiction, and reverse the judgment of the Georgia Supreme Court . . . .

III

Georgia stoutly defends both s 26--9901 and the State's common-law privacy action challenged here. Its claims are not without force, for powerful arguments can be made, and have been made, that however it may be ultimately defined, there is a zone of privacy surrounding every individual, a zone within which the State may protect him from intrusion by the press, with all its attendant publicity. Indeed, the central thesis of the root article by Warren and Brandeis, The Right to Privacy, 4 Harv.L.Rev. 193, 196 (1890), was that the press was overstepping its prerogatives by publishing essentially private information and that there should be a remedy for the alleged abuses. [FN16]

> FN16. 'Of the desirability--indeed of the necessity--of some such protection (of the right of privacy), there can, it is believed, be no doubt. The press is overstepping in every direction the obvious bounds of propriety and of decency. Gossip is no longer the resource of the idle and of the vicious, but has become a trade, which is pursued with industry as well as effrontery. To satisfy a prurient taste the details of sexual relations are spread broadcast in the columns of the daily papers. To occupy the indolent, column upon column is filled with idle gossip, which can only be procured by intrusion upon the domestic circle. The intensity and complexity of life, attendant upon advancing civilization, have rendered necessary some retreat from the world, and man, under the refining influence of culture, has become more sensitive to publicity, so that solitude and privacy have become more essential to the individual; but modern enterprise and

invention have, through invasions upon his privacy, subjected him to mental pain and distress, far greater than could be inflicted by mere bodily injury. Nor is the harm wrought by such invasions confined to the suffering of those who may be made the subjects of journalistic or other enterprise. In this, as in other branches of commerce, the supply creates the demand. Each crop of unseemly gossip, thus harvested, becomes the seed of more, and, in direct proportion to its circulation, results in a lowering of social standards and of morality. Even gossip apparently harmless, when widely and persistently circulated, is potent for evil. It both belittles and perverts. It belittles by inverting the relative importance of things, thus dwarfing the thoughts and aspirations of a people. When personal gossip attains the dignity of print, and crowds the space available for matters of real interest to the community, what wonder that the ignorant and thoughtless mistake its relative importance. Easy of comprehension, appealing to that weak side of human nature which is never wholly cast down by the misfortunes and frailties of our neighbors, no one can be surprised that it usurps the place of interest in brains capable of other things. Triviality destroys at once robustness of thought and delicacy of feeling. No enthusiasm can flourish, no generous impulse can survive under its blighting influence.'

More compellingly, the century has experienced a strong tide running in favor of the so-called right of privacy. In 1967, we noted that '(i)t has been said that a 'right of privacy' has been recognized at common law in 30 States plus the District of Columbia and by statute in four States.' Time, Inc. v. Hill, 385 U.S. 374, 383 n. 7, 87 S.Ct. 534, 539, 17 L.Ed.2d 456. We there cited the 1964 edition of Prosser's Law of Torts. The 1971 edition of that same source states that '(i)n one form or another, the right of privacy is by this time recognized and accepted in all but a very few jurisdictions.' W. Prosser, Law of Torts 804 (4th ed.) (footnote omitted). Nor is it irrelevant here that the right of privacy is no recent arrival in the jurisprudence of Georgia, which has embraced the right in some form since 1905 when the Georgia Supreme Court decided the leading case of Pavesich v. New England Life Ins. Co., 122 Ga. 190, 50 S.E. 68.

These are impressive credentials for a right of privacy, but we should recognize that we do not have at issue here an action for the invasion of privacy involving the appropriation of one's name or photograph, a physical or other tangible intrusion into a private area, or a publication of otherwise private information that is also false although perhaps not defamatory. The version of the privacy tort now before us--termed in Georgia 'the tort of public disclosure,' 231 Ga., at 60, 200 S.E.2d, at 130--is that in which the plaintiff claims the right to be free from unwanted publicity about his private affairs, which, although wholly true, would be offensive to a person of ordinary sensibilities. Because the gravamen of the claimed injury is the publication of information, whether true or not, the dissemination of which is embarrassing or otherwise painful to an individual, it is here that claims of privacy most directly confront the constitutional freedoms of speech and press. The face-off is apparent, and the appellants urge upon us the broad holding that the press may not be made criminally or civilly liable for publishing information that is neither false nor misleading but absolutely accurate, however damagingit may be to reputation or individual sensibilities . . . .

Those precedents, as well as other considerations, counsel similar caution here. In this sphere of collision between claims of privacy and those of the free press, the interests on both sides are plainly rooted in the traditions and significant concerns of our society. Rather than address the broader question whether truthful publications may ever be subjected to civil or criminal liability consistently with the First and Fourteenth Amendments, or to put it another way, whether the State may ever define and protect an area of privacy free from unwanted publicity in the press, it is appropriate to focus on the narrower interface between press and privacy that this case presents, namely, whether the State may impose sanctions on the accurate publication of the name of a rape victim obtained from public records--more specifically, from judicial records which are maintained in connection with a public prosecution and which themselves are open to public inspection. We are convinced that the State may not do so.

In the first place, in a society in which each individual has but limited time and resources with which to observe at first hand the operations of his government, he relies necessarily upon the press to bring to him in convenient form the facts of those operations. Great responsibility is accordingly placed upon the news media to report fully and accurately the proceedings of government, and official records and documents open to the public are the basic data of governmental operations. Without the information provided by the press most of us and many of our representatives would be unable to vote intelligently or to register opinions on the administration of government generally. With respect to judicial proceedings in particular, the function of the press serves to guarantee the fairness of trials and to bring to bear the beneficial effects of public scrutiny upon the administration of justice. See Sheppard v. Maxwell, 384 U.S. 333, 350, 86 S.Ct. 1507, 1515, 16 L.Ed.2d 600 (1966).

Appellee has claimed in this litigation that the efforts of the press have infringed his right to privacy by broadcasting to the world the fact that his daughter was a rape victim. The commission of crime, prosecutions resulting from it, and judicial proceedings arising from the prosecutions, however, are without question events of legitimate concern to the public and consequently fall within the responsibility of the press to report the operations of government.

The special protected nature of accurate reports of judicial proceedings has repeatedly been recognized. This Court, in an opinion written by Mr. Justice Douglas, has said:

> 'A trial is a public event. What transpires in the court room is public property. If a transcript of the court proceedings had been published, we suppose none would claim that the judge could punish the publisher for contempt. And we can see no difference though the conduct of the attorneys, of the jury, or even of the judge himself, may have reflected on the court. Those who see and hear what transpired can report it with impunity. There is no special perquisite of the judiciary which enables it, as distinguished from other institutions of democratic government, to suppress, edit, or censor events which transpire in proceedings before it.' Craig v. Harney, 331 U.S. 367, 374, 67 S.Ct. 1249, 1254, 91 L.Ed. 1546 (1947) (emphasis added) . . . .

The developing law surrounding the tort of invasion of privacy recognizes a privilege in the press to report the events of judicial proceedings. The Warren and Brandeis article, supra, noted that the proposed new right would be limited in the same manner as actions for libel and slander where such a publication was a privileged communication: 'the right to privacy is not invaded by any publication made in a court of justice . . . and (at least in many jurisdictions) reports of any such proceedings would in some measure be accorded a like privilege.'

The Restatement of Torts, s 867, embraced an action for privacy. Tentative Draft No. 13 of the Second Restatement of Torts, ss 652A--652E, divides the privacy tort into four branches; and with respect to the wrong of giving unwanted publicity about private life, the commentary to s 652D states: 'There is no liability when the defendant merely gives further publicity to information about the plaintiff which is already public. Thus there is no liability for giving publicity to facts about the plaintiff's life which are matters of public record . . . .' The same is true of the separate tort of physically or otherwise intruding upon the seclusion or private affairs of another. Section 652B, Comment c, provides that 'there is no liability for the examination of a public record concerning the plaintiff, or of documents which the plaintiff is required to keep and make available for public inspection.' According to this draft, ascertaining and publishing the contents of public records are simply not within the reach of these kinds of privacy actions.

Thus even the prevailing law of invasion of privacy generally recognizes that the interests in privacy face when the information involved already appears on the public record. The conclusion is compelling when viewed in terms of the First and Fourteenth Amendments and in light of the public interest in a vigorous press. The Georgia cause of action for invasion of privacy through public disclosure of the name of a rape victim imposes sanctions on pure expression---the content of a publication--and not conduct or a combination of speech and nonspeech elements that might otherwise be open to regulation or prohibition. See United States v. O'Brien, 391 U.S. 367, 376--377, 88 S.Ct. 1673, 1678--1679, 20 L.Ed.2d 672 (1968). The publication of truthful information available on the public record contains none of the indicia of those limited categories of expression, such as 'fighting' words, which 'are no essential part of any exposition of ideas, and are of such slight social value as a step to truth that any benefit that may be derived from them is clearly outweighed by the social interest in order and morality.' Chaplinsky v. New Hampshire, 315 U.S. 568, 572, 62 S.Ct. 766, 769, 86 L.Ed. 1031 (1942) (footnote omitted).

By placing the information in the public domain on official court records, the State must be presumed to have concluded that the public interest was thereby being served. Public records by their very nature are of interest to those concerned with the administration of government, and a public benefit is performed by the reporting of the true contents of the records by the media. The freedom of the press to publish that information appears to us to be of critical importance to our type of government in which the citizenry is the final judge of the proper conduct of public business. In preserving that form of government the First and Fourteenth Amendments command nothing less than that the States may not impose sanctions on the publication of truthful information contained in official court records open to public inspection.

We are reluctant to embark on a course that would make public records generally available to the media but forbid their publication if offensive to the sensibilities of the supposed reasonable man.

Such a rule would make it very difficult for the media to inform citizens about the public business and yet stay within the law. The rule would invite timidity and self- censorship and very likely lead to the suppression of many items that would otherwise be published and that should be made available to the public. At the very least, the First and Fourteenth Amendments will not allow exposing the press to liability for truthfully publishing information released to the public in official court records. If there are privacy interests to be protected in judicial proceedings, the States must respond by means which avoid public documentation or other exposure of private information. Their political institutions must weigh the interests in privacy with the interests of the public to know and of the press to publish. Once true information is disclosed in public court documents open to public inspection, the press cannot be sanctioned for publishing it. In this instance as in others reliance must rest upon the judgment of those who decide what to publish or broadcast. See Miami Herald Publishing Co. v. Tornillo, 418 U.S., at 258, 94 S.Ct., at 2840.

Appellant Wassell based his televised report upon notes taken during the court proceedings and obtained the name of the victim from the indictments handed to him at his request during a recess in the hearing. Appellee has not contended that the name was obtained in an improper fashion or that it was not on an official court document open to public inspection. Under these circumstances, ***497** the protection of freedom of the press provided by the First and Fourteenth Amendments bars the State of Georgia from making appellants' broadcast the basis of civil liability.

Reversed.

Mr. Chief Justice BURGER concurs in the judgment.

Mr. Justice POWELL, concurring.

Mr. Justice DOUGLAS, concurring in the judgment.

Mr. Justice REHNQUIST, dissenting.

THE FLORIDA STAR, Appellant
v.
B.J.F.

491 U.S. 524

Supreme Court of the United States

Decided June 21, 1989.

Justice Scalia filed opinion concurring in part and concurring in the judgment.

Justice White filed dissenting opinion in which Chief Justice Rehnquist and Justice O'Connor joined.

Justice MARSHALL delivered the opinion of the Court.

Florida Stat. § 794.03 (1987) makes it unlawful to "print, publish, or broadcast ... in any instrument of mass communication" the name of the victim of a sexual offense. [FN1] Pursuant to this statute, appellant The Florida Star was found civilly liable for publishing the name of a rape victim which it had obtained from a publicly released police report. The issue presented here is whether this result comports with the First Amendment. We hold that it does not.

FN1. The statute provides in its entirety:

"Unlawful to publish or broadcast information identifying sexual offense victim.--No person shall print, publish, or broadcast, or cause or allow to be printed, published, or broadcast, in any instrument of mass communication the name, address, or other identifying fact or information of the victim of any sexual offense within this chapter. An offense under this section shall constitute a misdemeanor of the second degree, punishable as provided in § 775.082, § 775.083, or § 775.084." Fla.Stat. § 794.03 (1987).

I

The Florida Star is a weekly newspaper which serves the community of Jacksonville, Florida, and which has an average circulation of approximately 18,000 copies. A regular feature of the newspaper is its "Police Reports" section. That section, typically two to three pages in length, contains brief articles describing local criminal incidents under police investigation.

On October 20, 1983, appellee B.J.F. [FN2] reported to the Duval County, Florida, Sheriff's Department (Department) that she had been robbed and sexually assaulted by an unknown assailant. The Department prepared a report on the incident which identified B.J.F. by her full name. The Department then placed the report in its pressroom. The Department does not

restrict access either to the pressroom or to the reports made available therein.
FN2. In filing this lawsuit, appellee used her full name in the caption of the case. On appeal, the Florida District Court of Appeal sua sponte revised the caption, stating that it would refer to the appellee by her initials, "in order to preserve [her] privacy interests." 499 So.2d 883, 883, n. (1986). Respecting those interests, we, too, refer to appellee by her initials, both in the caption and in our discussion.

A Florida Star reporter-trainee sent to the pressroom copied the police report verbatim, including B.J.F.'s full name, on a blank duplicate of the Department's forms. A Florida Star reporter then prepared a one-paragraph article about the crime, derived entirely from the trainee's copy of the police report. The article included B.J.F.'s full name. It appeared in the "Robberies" subsection of the "Police Reports" section on October 29, 1983, one of 54 police blotter stories in that day's edition. The article read:
"[B.J.F.] reported on Thursday, October 20, she was crossing Brentwood Park, which is in the 500 block of Golfair Boulevard, enroute to her bus stop, when an unknown black man ran up behind the lady and placed a knife to her neck and told her not to yell. The suspect then undressed the lady and had sexual intercourse with her before fleeing the scene with her 60 cents, Timex watch and gold necklace. Patrol efforts have been suspended concerning this incident because of a lack of evidence."
In printing B.J.F.'s full name, The Florida Star violated its internal policy of not publishing the names of sexual offense victims.

On September 26, 1984, B.J.F. filed suit in the Circuit Court of Duval County against the Department and The Florida Star, alleging that these parties negligently violated § 794.03. See n. 1, supra. Before trial, the Department settled with B.J.F. for $2,500. The Florida Star moved to dismiss, claiming, inter alia, that imposing civil sanctions on the newspaper pursuant to § 794.03 violated the First Amendment. The trial judge rejected the motion. App. 4.

At the ensuing daylong trial, B.J.F. testified that she had suffered emotional distress from the publication of her name. She stated that she had heard about the article from fellow workers and acquaintances; that her mother had received several threatening phone calls from a man who stated that he would rape B.J.F. again; and that these events had forced B.J.F. to change her phone number and residence, to seek police protection, and to obtain mental health counseling. In defense, The Florida Star put forth evidence indicating that the newspaper had learned B.J.F.'s name from the incident report released by the Department, and that the newspaper's violation of its internal rule against publishing the names of sexual offense victims was inadvertent.

At the close of B.J.F.'s case, and again at the close of its defense, The Florida Star moved for a directed verdict. On both occasions, the trial judge denied these motions. He ruled from the bench that § 794.03 was constitutional because it reflected a proper balance between the First Amendment and privacy rights, as it applied only to a narrow set of "rather sensitive ... criminal offenses." App. 18-19 (rejecting first motion); see id., at 32-33 (rejecting second motion). At the close of the newspaper's defense, the judge granted B.J.F.'s motion for a directed verdict on the issue of negligence, finding the newspaper per se negligent based upon its violation of § 794.03. Id., at 33. This ruling left the jury to consider only the questions of causation and damages. The judge instructed the jury that it could award B.J.F. punitive damages if it found that the newspaper had "acted with reckless indifference to the rights of others." Id., at 35. The jury awarded B.J.F. $75,000 in compensatory damages and $25,000 in punitive damages. Against the actual damages award, the judge set off B.J.F.'s settlement with the Department.

The First District Court of Appeal affirmed in a three- paragraph per curiam opinion. 499 So.2d 883 (1986). In the paragraph devoted to The Florida Star's First Amendment claim, the court stated that the directed verdict for B.J.F. had been properly entered because, under § 794.03, a rape victim's name is "of a private nature and not to be published as a matter of law." Id., at 884, citing Doe v. Sarasota- Bradenton Florida Television Co., 436 So.2d 328, 330 (Fla.App.1983) (footnote omitted). The Supreme Court of Florida denied discretionary review.

The Florida Star appealed to this Court. We noted probable jurisdiction, 488 U.S. 887, 109 S.Ct. 216, 102 L.Ed.2d 208 (1988), and now reverse.

## II

The tension between the right which the First Amendment accords to a free press, on the one hand, and the protections which various statutes and common- law doctrines accord to personal privacy against the publication of truthful information, on the other, is a subject we have addressed several times in recent years. Our decisions in cases involving government attempts to sanction the accurate dissemination of information as invasive of privacy, have not, however, exhaustively considered this conflict. On the contrary, although our decisions have without exception upheld the press' right to publish, we have emphasized each time that we were resolving this conflict only as it arose in a discrete factual context.

The parties to this case frame their contentions in light of a trilogy of cases which have presented, in different contexts, the conflict between truthful reporting and state-protected privacy interests. In Cox Broadcasting Corp. v. Cohn, 420 U.S. 469, 95 S.Ct. 1029, 43 L.Ed.2d 328 (1975), we found unconstitutional a civil damages award entered against a television station for broadcasting the name of a rape-murder victim which the station had obtained from courthouse records. In Oklahoma Publishing Co. v. Oklahoma County District Court, 430 U.S. 308, 97 S.Ct. 1045, 51 L.Ed.2d 355 (1977), we found unconstitutional a state court's pretrial order enjoining the media from publishing the name or photograph of an 11-year-old boy in connection with a juvenile proceeding involving that child which reporters had attended. Finally, in Smith v. Daily Mail Publishing Co., 443 U.S. 97, 99 S.Ct. 2667, 61 L.Ed.2d 399 (1979), we found unconstitutional the indictment of two newspapers for violating a state statute forbidding newspapers to publish, without written approval of the juvenile court, the name of any youth charged as a juvenile offender. The papers had learned about a shooting by monitoring a police band radio frequency and had obtained the name of the alleged juvenile assailant from witnesses, the police, and a local prosecutor.

Appellant takes the position that this case is indistinguishable from Cox Broadcasting. Brief for Appellant 8. Alternatively, it urges that our decisions in the above trilogy, and in other cases in which we have held that the right of the press to publish truth overcame asserted interests other than personal privacy, can be distilled to yield a broader First Amendment principle that the press may never be punished, civilly or criminally, for publishing the truth. Id., at 19. Appellee counters that the privacy trilogy is inapposite, because in each case the private information already appeared on a "public record," Brief for Appellee 12, 24, 25, and because the privacy interests at stake were far less profound than in the present case. See, e.g., id., at 34. In the alternative, appellee urges that Cox Broadcasting be overruled and replaced with a categorical rule that publication of the name of a rape victim never enjoys constitutional protection. Tr. of Oral Arg. 44.

We conclude that imposing damages on appellant for publishing B.J.F.'s name violates the First Amendment, although not for either of the reasons appellant urges. Despite the strong resemblance this case bears to Cox Broadcasting, that case cannot fairly be read as controlling here. The name of the rape victim in that case was obtained from courthouse records that were open to public inspection, a fact which Justice WHITE's opinion for the Court repeatedly noted. 420 U.S., at 492, 95 S.Ct., at 1044-45 (noting "special protected nature of accurate reports of judicial proceedings") (emphasis added); see also id., at 493, 496, 95 S.Ct., at 1045, 1046-47. Significantly, one of the reasons we gave in Cox Broadcasting for invalidating the challenged damages award was the important role the press plays in subjecting trials to public scrutiny and thereby helping guarantee their fairness. Id., at 492-493, 95 S.Ct., at 1044-1045. That role is not directly compromised where, as here, the information in question comes from a police report prepared and disseminated at a time at which not only had no adversarial criminal proceedings begun, but no suspect had been identified.

Nor need we accept appellant's invitation to hold broadly that truthful publication may never be punished consistent with the First Amendment. Our cases have carefully eschewed reaching this ultimate question, mindful that the future may bring scenarios which prudence counsels our not resolving anticipatorily. See, e.g., Near v. Minnesota ex rel. Olson, 283 U.S. 697, 716, 51 S.Ct. 625, 75 L.Ed. 1357 (1931) (hypothesizing "publication of the sailing dates of transports or the number and location of troops"); see also Garrison v. Louisiana, 379 U.S. 64, 72, n. 8, 74, 85 S.Ct. 209, 215, n. 8, 216, 13 L.Ed.2d 125 (1964) (endorsing absolute defense of truth "where discussion of public affairs is concerned," but leaving unsettled the constitutional implications of truthfulness "in the discrete area of purely private libels"); Landmark Communications, Inc. v. Virginia, 435 U.S. 829, 838, 98 S.Ct. 1535, 1541, 56 L.Ed.2d 1 (1978); Time, Inc. v. Hill, 385 U.S. 374, 383, n. 7, 87 S.Ct. 534, 539-40, n. 7, 17 L.Ed.2d 456 (1967). Indeed, in Cox Broadcasting, we pointedly refused to answer even the less sweeping question "whether truthful publications may ever be subjected to civil or criminal liability" for invading "an area of privacy" defined by the State. 420 U.S., at 491, 95 S.Ct., at 1044. Respecting the fact that press freedom and privacy rights are both "plainly rooted in the traditions and significant concerns of our society," we instead focused on the less sweeping issue "whether the State may impose sanctions on the accurate publication of the name of a rape victim obtained from public records--more specifically, from judicial records which are maintained in connection with a public prosecution and which themselves are open to public inspection." Ibid. We continue to believe that the sensitivity and significance of the interests presented in clashes between First Amendment and privacy rights counsel relying on limited principles that sweep no more broadly than the appropriate context of the instant case.

In our view, this case is appropriately analyzed with reference to such a limited First Amendment principle. It is the one, in fact, which we articulated in Daily Mail in our synthesis of prior cases involving attempts to punish truthful publication: "[I]f a newspaper lawfully obtains truthful information about a matter of public significance then state officials may not constitutionally punish publication of the information, absent a need to further a state interest of the highest order." 443 U.S., at 103, 99 S.Ct., at 2671. According the press the ample protection provided by that principle is supported by at least three separate considerations, in addition to, of course, the overarching " 'public interest, secured by the Constitution, in the dissemination of truth.' " Cox Broadcasting, supra, 420 U.S., at 491, 95 S.Ct., at 1044, quoting Garrison, supra, 379 U.S., at 73, 85 S.Ct., at 215 (footnote omitted). The cases on which the Daily Mail synthesis relied demonstrate these considerations.

First, because the Daily Mail formulation only protects the publication of information which a newspaper has "lawfully obtain[ed]," 443 U.S., at 103, 99 S.Ct., at 2671, the government retains ample means of safeguarding significant interests upon which publication may impinge, including protecting a rape victim's anonymity. To the extent sensitive information rests in private hands, the government may under some circumstances forbid its nonconsensual acquisition, thereby bringing outside of the Daily Mail principle the publication of any information so acquired. To the extent sensitive information is in the government's custody, it has even greater power to forestall or mitigate the injury caused by its release. The government may classify certain information, establish and enforce procedures ensuring its redacted release, and extend a damages remedy against the government or its officials where the government's mishandling of sensitive information leads to its dissemination. Where information is entrusted to the government, a less drastic means than punishing truthful publication almost always exists for guarding against the dissemination of private facts. See, e.g., Landmark Communications, supra, 435 U.S., at 845, 98 S.Ct., at 1545 ("[M]uch of the risk [from disclosure of sensitive information regarding judicial disciplinary proceedings] can be eliminated through careful internal procedures to protect the confidentiality of Commission proceedings"); Oklahoma Publishing, 430 U.S., at 311, 97 S.Ct., at 1046-47 (noting trial judge's failure to avail himself of the opportunity, provided by a state statute, to close juvenile hearing to the public, including members of the press, who later broadcast juvenile defendant's name); Cox Broadcasting, supra, 420 U.S., at 496, 95 S.Ct., at 1047 ("If there are privacy interests to be protected in judicial proceedings, the States must respond by means which avoid public documentation or other exposure of private information").

A second consideration undergirding the Daily Mail principle is the fact that punishing the press for its dissemination of information which is already publicly available is relatively unlikely to advance the interests in the service of which the State seeks to act. It is not, of course, always the case that information lawfully acquired by the press is known, or accessible, to others. But where the government has made certain information publicly available, it is highly anomalous to sanction persons other than the source of its release. We noted this anomaly in Cox Broadcasting: "By placing the information in the public domain on official court records, the State must be presumed to have concluded that the public interest was thereby being served." 420 U.S., at 495, 95 S.Ct., at 1046. The Daily Mail formulation reflects the fact that it is a limited set of cases indeed where, despite the accessibility of the public to certain information, a meaningful public interest is served by restricting its further release by other entities, like the press. As Daily Mail observed in its summary of Oklahoma Publishing, "once the truthful information was 'publicly revealed' or 'in the public domain' the court could not constitutionally restrain its dissemination." 443 U.S., at 103, 99 S.Ct., at 2671.

A third and final consideration is the "timidity and self-censorship" which may result from allowing the media to be punished for publishing certain truthful information. Cox Broadcasting, supra, 420 U.S., at 496, 95 S.Ct., at 1046-47. Cox Broadcasting noted this concern with overdeterrence in the context of information made public through official court records, but the fear of excessive media self-suppression is applicable as well to other information released, without qualification, by the government. A contrary rule, depriving protection to those who rely on the government's implied representations of the lawfulness of dissemination, would force upon the media the onerous obligation of sifting through government press releases, reports, and pronouncements to prune out material arguably unlawful for publication. This situation could inhere even where the newspaper's sole object was to reproduce, with no substantial change, the government's rendition of the event in question.

Applied to the instant case, the Daily Mail principle clearly commands reversal. The first inquiry is whether the newspaper "lawfully obtain[ed] truthful information about a matter of public significance." 443 U.S., at 103, 99 S.Ct., at 2671. It is undisputed that the news article describing the assault on B.J.F. was accurate. In addition, appellant lawfully obtained B.J.F.'s name. Appellee's argument to the contrary is based on the fact that under Florida law, police reports which reveal the identity of the victim of a sexual offense are not among the matters of "public record" which the public, by law, is entitled to inspect. Brief for Appellee 17-18, citing Fla.Stat. § 119.07(3)(h) (1983). But the fact that state officials are not required to disclose such reports does not make it unlawful for a newspaper to receive them when furnished by the government. Nor does the fact that the Department apparently failed to fulfill its obligation under § 794.03 not to "cause or allow to be ... published" the name of a sexual offense victim make the newspaper's ensuing receipt of this information unlawful. Even assuming the Constitution permitted a State to proscribe receipt of information, Florida has not taken this step. It is, clear, furthermore, that the news article concerned "a matter of public significance," 443 U.S., at 103, 99 S.Ct., at 2671, in the sense in which the Daily Mail synthesis of prior cases used that term. That is, the article generally, as opposed to the specific identity contained within it, involved a matter of paramount public import: the commission, and investigation, of a violent crime which had been reported to authorities. See Cox Broadcasting, supra (article identifying victim of rape-murder); Oklahoma Publishing Co. v. Oklahoma County District Court, 430 U.S. 308, 97 S.Ct. 1045, 51 L.Ed.2d 355 (1977) (article identifying juvenile alleged to have committed murder); Daily Mail, supra (same); cf. Landmark Communications, Inc. v. Virginia, 435 U.S. 829, 98 S.Ct. 1535, 56 L.Ed.2d 1 (1978) (article identifying judges whose conduct was being investigated).

The second inquiry is whether imposing liability on appellant pursuant to § 794.03 serves "a need to further a state interest of the highest order." Daily Mail, 443 U.S., at 103, 99 S.Ct., at 2671. Appellee argues that a rule punishing publication furthers three closely related interests: the privacy of victims of sexual offenses; the physical safety of such victims, who may be targeted for retaliation if their names become known to their assailants; and the goal of encouraging victims of such crimes to report these offenses without fear of exposure. Brief for Appellee 29-30.

At a time in which we are daily reminded of the tragic reality of rape, it is undeniable that these are highly significant interests, a fact underscored by the Florida Legislature's explicit attempt to protect these interests by enacting a criminal statute prohibiting much dissemination of victim identities. We accordingly do not rule out the possibility that, in a proper case, imposing civil sanctions for publication of the name of a rape victim might be so overwhelmingly necessary to advance these interests as to satisfy the Daily Mail standard. For three independent reasons, however, imposing liability for publication under the circumstances of this case is too precipitous a means of advancing these interests to convince us that there is a "need" within the meaning of the Daily Mail formulation for Florida to take this extreme step. Cf. Landmark Communications, supra (invalidating penalty on publication despite State's expressed interest in nondissemination, reflected in statute prohibiting unauthorized divulging of names of judges under investigation).

First is the manner in which appellant obtained the identifying information in question. As we have noted, where the government itself provides information to the media, it is most appropriate to assume that the government had, but failed to utilize, far more limited means of guarding against dissemination than the extreme step of punishing truthful speech. That assumption is richly borne out in this case. B.J.F.'s identity would never have come to light were it not for the erroneous, if inadvertent, inclusion by the Department of her full name in an incident report made available in a pressroom open to the public. Florida's policy against disclosure of rape victims' identities, reflected in § 794.03, was undercut by the Department's failure to abide by this policy. Where, as here, the government has failed to police itself in disseminating information, it is clear under Cox Broadcasting, Oklahoma Publishing, and Landmark Communications that the imposition of damages against the press for its subsequent publication can hardly be said to be a narrowly tailored means of safeguarding anonymity. See supra, at 2609. Once the government has placed such information in the public domain, "reliance must rest upon the judgment of those who decide what to publish or broadcast," Cox Broadcasting, 420 U.S., at 496, 95 S.Ct., at 1047, and hopes for restitution must rest upon the willingness of the government to compensate victims for their loss of privacy and to protect them from the other consequences of its mishandling of the information which these victims provided in confidence.

That appellant gained access to the information in question through a government news release makes it especially likely that, if liability were to be imposed, self-censorship would result. Reliance on a news release is a paradigmatically "routine newspaper reporting techniqu[e]." Daily Mail, supra, at 103, 99 S.Ct., at 2671. The government's issuance of such a release, without qualification, can only convey to recipients that the government considered dissemination lawful, and indeed expected the recipients to disseminate the information further. Had appellant merely reproduced the news release prepared and released by the Department, imposing civil damages would surely violate the First Amendment. The fact that appellant converted the police report into a news story by adding the linguistic connecting tissue necessary to transform the report's facts into full sentences cannot change this result.

A second problem with Florida's imposition of liability for publication is the broad sweep of the negligenceper se standard applied under the civil cause of action implied from § 794.03. Unlike claims based on the common law tort of invasion of privacy, see Restatement (Second) of Torts § 652D (1977), civil actions based on § 794.03 require no case-by-case findings that the disclosure of a fact about a person's private life was one that a reasonable person would find highly offensive. On the contrary, under the per se theory of negligenceadopted by the courts below, liability follows automatically from publication. This is so regardless of whether the identity of the victim is already known throughout the community; whether the victim has voluntarily called public attention to the offense; or whether the identity of the victim has otherwise become a reasonable subject of public concern--because, perhaps, questions have arisen whether the victim fabricated an assault by a particular person. Nor is there a scienter requirement of any kind under § 794.03, engendering the perverse result that truthful publications challenged pursuant to this cause of action are less protected by the First Amendment than even the least protected defamatory falsehoods: those involving purely private figures, where liability is evaluated under a standard, usually applied by a jury, of ordinary negligence. See Gertz v. Robert Welch, Inc., 418 U.S. 323, 94 S.Ct. 2997, 41 L.Ed.2d 789 (1974). We have previously noted the impermissibility of categorical prohibitions upon media access where important First Amendment interests are at stake. See Globe Newspaper Co. v. Superior Court of Norfolk County, 457 U.S. 596, 608, 102 S.Ct. 2613, 2620-21, 73 L.Ed.2d 248 (1982) (invalidating state statute providing for the categorical exclusion of the public from trials of sexual offenses involving juvenile victims). More individualized adjudication is no less indispensable where the State, seeking to safeguard the anonymity of crime victims, sets its face against publication of their names.

Third, and finally, the facial underinclusiveness of § 794.03 raises serious doubts about whether Florida is, in fact, serving, with this statute, the significant interests which appellee invokes in support of affirmance. Section 794.03 prohibits the publication of identifying information only if this information appears in an "instrument of mass communication," a term the statute does not define. Section 794.03 does not prohibit the spread by other means of the identities of victims of sexual offenses. An individual who maliciously spreads word of the identity of a rape victim is thus not covered, despite the fact that the communication of such information to persons who live near, or work with, the victim may have consequences as devastating as the exposure of her name to large numbers of strangers. See Tr. of Oral Arg. 49-50 (appellee acknowledges that § 794.03 would not apply to "the backyard gossip who tells 50 people that don't have to know").

When a State attempts the extraordinary measure of punishing truthful publication in the name of privacy, it must demonstrate its commitment to advancing this interest by applying its prohibition evenhandedly, to the smalltime disseminator as well as the media giant. Where important First Amendment interests are at stake, the mass scope of disclosure is not an acceptable surrogate for injury. A ban on disclosures effected by "instrument [s] of mass communication" simply cannot be defended on the ground that partial prohibitions may effect partial relief. See Daily Mail, 443 U.S., at 104- 105, 99 S.Ct., at 2671-2672 (statute is insufficiently tailored to interest in protecting anonymity where it restricted only newspapers, not the electronic media or other forms of publication, from identifying juvenile defendants); id., at 110, 99 S.Ct., at 2674-75 (REHNQUIST, J., concurring in judgment) (same); cf. Arkansas Writers' Project, Inc. v. Ragland, 481 U.S. 221, 229, 107 S.Ct. 1722, 1727-1728, 95 L.Ed.2d 209 (1987); Minneapolis Star & Tribune Co. v. Minnesota Comm'r of Revenue, 460 U.S. 575, 585, 103 S.Ct. 1365, 1371-72, 75 L.Ed.2d 295 (1983). Without more careful and inclusive precautions against alternative forms of dissemination, we cannot conclude that Florida's selective ban on publication by the mass media satisfactorily accomplishes its stated purpose.

III

Our holding today is limited. We do not hold that truthful publication is automatically constitutionally protected, or that there is no zone of personal privacy within which the State may protect the individual from intrusion by the press, or even that a State may never punish publication of the name of a victim of a sexual offense. We hold only that where a newspaper publishes truthful information which it has lawfully obtained, punishment may lawfully be imposed, if at all, only when narrowly tailored to a state interest of the highest order, and that no such interest is satisfactorily served by imposing liability under § 794.03 to appellant under the facts of this case. The decision below is therefore

Reversed.

Justice WHITE, with whom THE CHIEF JUSTICE and Justice O'CONNOR join, dissenting.

"Short of homicide, [rape] is the 'ultimate violation of self.' " Coker v. Georgia, 433 U.S. 584, 597, 97 S.Ct. 2861, 2869, 53 L.Ed.2d 982 (1977) (opinion of WHITE, J.). For B.J.F., however, the violation she suffered at a rapist's knifepoint marked only the beginning of her ordeal. A week later, while her assailant was still at large, an account of this assault--identifying by name B.J.F. as the victim--was published by The Florida Star. As a result, B.J.F. received harassing phone calls, required mental health counseling, was forced to move from ***543** her home, and was even threatened with being raped again. Yet today, the Court holds that a jury award of $75,000 to compensate B.J.F. for the harm she suffered due to the Star's negligenceis at odds with the First Amendment. I do not accept this result . . . .

III

At issue in this case is whether there is any information about people, which--though true--may not be published in the press. By holding that only "a state interest of the highest order" permits the State to penalize the publication of truthful information, and by holding that protecting a rape victim's right to privacy is not among those state interests of the highest order, the Court accepts appellant's invitation, see Tr. of Oral Arg. 10-11, to obliterate one of the most noteworthy legal inventions of the 20th century: the tort of the publication of private facts. W. Prosser, J. Wade, & V. Schwartz, Torts 951-952 (8th ed. 1988). Even if the Court's opinion does not say as much today, such obliteration will follow inevitably from the Court's conclusion here. If the First Amendment prohibits wholly private persons (such as B.J.F.) from recovering for the publication of the fact that she was raped, I doubt that there remain any "private facts" which persons may assume will not be published in the newspapers or broadcast on television.

. . . Of course, the right to privacy is not absolute. Even the article widely relied upon in cases vindicating privacy rights, Warren & Brandeis, The Right to Privacy, 4 Harv.L.Rev. 193 (1890), recognized that this right inevitably conflicts with the public's right to know about matters of general concern--and that sometimes, the latter must trump the former. Id., at 214-215. Resolving this conflict is a difficult matter, and I fault the Court not for attempting to strike an appropriate balance between the two, but rather, fault it for according too little weight to B.J.F.'s side of equation, and too much on the other.

I would strike the balance rather differently. Writing for the Ninth Circuit, Judge Merrill put this view eloquently:

"Does the spirit of the Bill of Rights require that individuals be free to pry into the unnewsworthy private affairs of their fellowmen? In our view it does not. In our view, fairly defined areas of privacy must have the protection of law if the quality of life is to continue to be reasonably acceptable. The public's right to know is, then, subject to reasonable limitations so far as concerns the private facts of its individual members." Virgil v. Time, Inc., 527 F.2d 1122,

1128 (1975), cert. denied, 425 U.S. 998, 96 S.Ct. 2215, 48 L.Ed.2d 823 (1976).

Ironically, this Court, too, had occasion to consider this same balance just a few weeks ago, in United States Department of Justice v. Reporters Committee for Freedom of Press, 489 U.S. 749, 109 S.Ct. 1468, 103 L.Ed.2d 774 (1989). There, we were faced with a press request, under the Freedom of Information Act, for a "rap sheet" on a person accused of bribing a Congressman-- presumably, a person whose privacy rights would be far less than B.J.F.'s. Yet this Court rejected the media's request for disclosure of the "rap sheet," saying:

"The privacy interest in maintaining the practical obscurity of rap-sheet information will always be high. When the subject of such a rap sheet is a private citizen and when the information is in the Government's control as a compilation, rather than as a record of 'what the government is up to,' the privacy interest ... is ... at its apex while the ... public interest in disclosure is at its nadir." Id., at 780, 109 S.Ct., at 1485.

The Court went on to conclude that disclosure of rap sheets "categorical[ly]" constitutes an "unwarranted" invasion of privacy. Ibid. The same surely must be true--indeed, much more so--for the disclosure of a rape victim's name.

I do not suggest that the Court's decision today is a radical departure from a previously charted course. The Court's ruling has been foreshadowed. In Time, Inc. v. Hill, 385 U.S. 374, 383-384, n. 7, 87 S.Ct. 534, 539-540, n. 7, 17 L.Ed.2d 456 (1967), we observed that--after a brief period early in this century where Brandeis' view was ascendant--the trend in "modern" jurisprudence has been to eclipse an individual's right to maintain private any truthful information that the press wished to publish. More recently, in Cox Broadcasting, 420 U.S. at 491, 95 S.Ct., at 1044, we acknowledged the possibility that the First Amendment may prevent a State from ever subjecting the publication of truthful but private information to civil liability. Today, we hit the bottom of the slippery slope.

I would find a place to draw the line higher on the hillside: a spot high enough to protect B.J.F.'s desire for privacy and peace-of-mind in the wake of a horrible personal tragedy. There is no public interest in publishing the names, addresses, and phone numbers of persons who are the victims of crime-- and no public interest in immunizing the press from liability in the rare cases where a State's efforts to protect a victim's privacy have failed. Consequently, I respectfully dissent.

HOWARD,

v.

DES MOINES REGISTER.

283 N.W.2d 289

Supreme Court of Iowa.

Sept. 19, 1979.

Considered en banc.

McCORMICK, Justice.

The trial court entered summary judgment for defendant Des Moines Register and Tribune Company and its reporter Margaret Engel in this action for invasion of privacy. The action was brought by plaintiff Robbin Howard in an effort to obtain redress from these defendants and defendant Dr. Roy C. Sloan for a disclosure in a 1976 newspaper story that she had been involuntarily sterilized while a resident of the Jasper County Home in 1971. This appeal does not involve the claim against Dr. Sloan. The controlling questions are whether recovery from the newspaper and its reporter is precluded either because the information was already public or because the trier of fact would be unable to find it was not newsworthy. We affirm the trial court.

In Bremmer v. Journal-Tribune Publishing Co., 247 Iowa 817, 76 N.W.2d 762 (1956), this court held that a common-law action for invasion of privacy may be maintained in Iowa. We have adopted the principles of the tort delineated in Restatement (Second) of Torts s 652 (1977). See Winegard v. Larsen, 260 N.W.2d 816, 822 (Iowa 1977).

Plaintiff based this action on the theory that defendants invaded her privacy by giving unreasonable publicity to her private life. This theory of invasion of privacy is defined in Restatement section 652D:

> One who gives publicity to a matter concerning the private life of another is subject to liability to the other for invasion of his privacy, if the matter publicized is of a kind that
> (a) would be highly offensive to a reasonable person, and
> (b) is not of legitimate concern to the public.

In moving for summary judgment, defendants relied on several grounds. The trial court rejected public record and waiver of privacy grounds but sustained the motion on the newsworthiness ground. As they are entitled to do, defendants seek affirmance on grounds rejected by the trial court as well as on the ground which was accepted. See State ex rel. Miller v. National Farmers Organization, 287 N.W.2d 905, 906 (Iowa 1979); In re Estate of Poulos, 229 N.W.2d 721, 724-25 (Iowa 1975). In deciding the appeal, we find it necessary to consider only the public record and newsworthiness grounds.

We first summarize the summary judgment record, which includes pleadings, depositions and affidavits.

In her petition, plaintiff alleged she was formerly known as Robin Woody; in 1970, while a minor, she was confined in the Jasper County Home; she was at that time sterilized against her wishes; after her release from the home she led a quiet and respectable life and made friends and acquaintances who were not aware of her surgery; defendant Roy C. Sloan told defendant Margaret Engel about the 1970 sterilization in late 1975 or early 1976; on February 15, 1976, defendant Des Moines Register and Tribune Company published an article in the Des Moines Sunday Register written by Engel which revealed the 1970 sterilization; and this article subjected her to public contempt, ridicule and "inquisitive notice," humiliated her and caused her mental pain and anguish. In separate divisions she asked actual damages of $500,000 and punitive damages of $500,000 from each defendant.

A copy of the newspaper article accompanied the petition. Under a headline which read "Scalding deaths at Jasper Home revealed," and over Margaret Engel's byline, the article was as follows:

NEWTON, IA. The Jasper County Home, under fire from the state Health Department for poor care and lax administration, has a history marred by deaths from scalding baths, sterilizations of women who are not mentally disabled, and shipments of prescription drugs that apparently were illegal.

The administrator of the home for 22 years, Riva Ripper, quit in the wake of a Jan. 30 notice from the Health Department that the home's custodial and nursing licenses will be revoked. The revocation notices accused the home of a long list of health, safety and management violations.

The home's nursing director, Ruth Broderson, also resigned. Ripper's husband, Clarence, who ran the adjoining county farm, died of a heart attack Feb. 1.

Health officials say the home has had continual problems over the years. In checking county records, The Register has learned that two of the home's residents died as a result of scalding baths.

A grand jury investigation was held in 1969 in the death of Sheryl Anthony, 18, who died that May of thermal burns. No indictments were returned and the grand jury's minutes remain secret.

On Sept. 9, 1974, there was a second death from burns at the home.

Richard Shivers, 63, died 13 days after suffering from second and third-degree burns on his back. His aunt, Kathryn Gustafson of Newton, says Shivers told her before he died that he was bathing himself and mistakenly turned on the wrong faucet.

Shivers, who was classed as a chronic schizophrenic, probably got "over nervous and slipped in the tub and could not get out," she said, adding she does not believe anyone was negligent.
Dr. John Ferguson, who visits weekly at the home, said Shivers was able to bathe himself and that he was "momentarily left" by an aide when the accident occurred.

The state Health Department did not know of the deaths until recently, despite a rule requiring nursing homes to submit reports on such accidents. Jonn Wild, director of the department's licensing section, said few reports ever have been filed by the Jasper home.

The Register also learned that an 18-year-old woman sterilized in 1970 was not retarded or mentally disabled, but an "impulsive, hair-triggered young girl," in the words of Dr. Roy C. Sloan, the home's psychiatrist.

He said the decision to sterilize the resident, Robin Woody, was made by her parents and himself. He does not recall whether Woody agreed to the operation, but a woman who was a nurse at the home at the time said "she didn't want it at all" . . . .

In their answer, the newspaper and Engel admitted publication of the article but denied the material invasion of privacy allegations. They also asserted affirmative defenses on constitutional, newsworthiness, public record and waiver grounds . . . .

In January 1976 the state health department revoked the nursing and custodial licenses of the home because of its alleged failure to correct the deficiencies listed in its report of June 1, 1975. The original list of sixty- seven alleged violations had grown to one hundred twenty. The violations included a charge of physical, mental, and verbal abuse of patients . . . .

Various other news reports followed, including the story which is involved in this case. On February 3 a story appeared in which a threat against one of the county supervisors was reported. On February 4 a story written by defendant Engel reported a delay in a hearing scheduled by the board of supervisors to discuss revocation of the licenses. A supervisor was quoted as describing the former employees who complained about the home as "rabble-rousers that caused the problem."

The board of supervisors held several emergency meetings to respond to problems at the home. These meetings received extensive media coverage. Community feelings were aroused; rumors and accusations abounded. Considerable controversy existed about the merits of the department of health action.

On February 8 defendant newspaper carried a story written by Engel reporting the resignations of the administrator and head nurse of the home. Then on February 15 the story which is the subject of the present lawsuit appeared. The story commenced on page 1, but most of it, including the portion in which plaintiff's sterilization was discussed, was continued to page 8A.

Prior to writing the February 15 article, Engel spent two weeks investigating the problems at the home. During the course of her investigation she interviewed Opal Snyder, who showed Engel the documents she had given to the Governor, including her statement and that of Collene Blakely, both of which identified plaintiff as a sterilization victim. She also interviewed Blakely, Dr. Sloan, and the administrator of the home, all of whom confirmed the sterilization. She verified the term of plaintiff's residency and date of surgery through the county auditor's records. She discussed this and other matters with thirty-eight persons who had knowledge of relevant events. Although she attempted to locate plaintiff, she could not find her through records or other means. She was unable to document the sterilizations of the other women as completely as she could plaintiff's.

After the motion for summary judgment was submitted on this record, the trial court sustained the motion on the ground it could not be found that the disclosure of plaintiff's sterilization was not newsworthy. Plaintiff appealed . . . .

This brings us to the determination of whether the trial court erred in sustaining the motion for summary judgment in this case.

I. The public record ground. The public record defense arises from two limitations upon a cause of action for invasion of privacy under Restatement of Torts (Second) s 652D.

One is that the publicity must concern the private, as distinguished from the public, life of the individual. As noted in Comment b to Restatement section 652D, "There is no liability when the defendant merely gives further publicity to information about the plaintiff that is already public." See Warren & Brandeis, The Right to Privacy, 4 Harv.L.Rev. 193, 214 (1890). We recognized and applied this limitation in Winegard v. Larsen, 260 N.W.2d 816, 823 (Iowa 1977).

The other limitation is that the individual must prove the matter publicized is of a kind that "is not of legitimate concern to the public." Liability for disclosing public information is foreclosed on this basis because matters of public record are, as a matter of law, of legitimate concern to the public.

. . . The auditor's records were required to be kept by statute, See s 230.26, The Code 1966, and would have been deemed public records even before chapter 68A was enacted. Linder v. Eckard, 261 Iowa at 220, 152 N.W.2d at 836. They are well within the definition of public records in chapter 68A. See Osmundson, 248 N.W.2d at 501.

The Snyder and Blakely documents which were filed in the Governor's office also clearly come within the definition of public records in section 68A.1. Upon his acceptance of custody, the documents were in the lawful possession of his office and hence became documents "of or belonging to" the state. Furthermore, the documents are not exempted from disclosure by a specific statutory provision as section 68A.2 requires. No injunction was secured under section 68A.8, and no exemption under a section outside chapter 68A appears available. Section 68A.7(2), which exempts "hospital records" and "medical records" of a "patient or former patient, including outpatient," does not apply because the documents here were neither compiled for diagnostic or treatment purposes by hospital or medical personnel nor maintained as records of a hospital or physician. They are not hospital or medical records within the meaning of the statute. See Attorney General's Opinion 75-7-2, Reprinted in (1975-76) Iowa Att'y Gen. Biennial Rep. 160-62 (holding that auditor's records relating to alcoholic treatment are not within the exemption).

We think this case comes within the limitations on the tort imposed in Restatement s 652D and applied in Winegard. Because the documents were public, the information which they contained was in the public domain. Osmundson, 248 N.W.2d at 503.

The fact of plaintiff's sterilization was thus a public as opposed to a private fact and a matter of legitimate public concern. Therefore the disclosure is not actionable. See Winegard, 260 N.W.2d at 823; Metter v. Los Angeles Examiner, 35 Cal.App.2d 304, 95 P.2d 491 (1939); Meetze v. Associated Press, 230 S.C. 330, 95 S.E.2d 606 (1956).

This ground is sufficient to support the summary judgment.

II. The newsworthiness ground. The second ground which we consider is defendants' contention that the trier of fact would be precluded from finding that the disclosure was not of legitimate concern to the public because not newsworthy. Under the elements of the tort defined in Restatement section 652D, it is necessary for the plaintiff to prove the lack of newsworthiness of the disclosure as well as its invasiveness. Newsworthiness is thus not an issue of privilege which must be urged defensively but an element which must be negated by the plaintiff in meeting her burden of proof . . . .

Because we have adopted the Restatement definition of the invasion of privacy tort, it is reasonable to refer to the Restatement explanation of its elements. "News" is discussed in Comment g to section 652D as follows:

> Included within the scope of legitimate public concern are matters of the kind customarily regarded as "news." To a considerable extent, in accordance with the mores of the community, the publishers and broadcasters have themselves defined the term, as a glance at any morning paper will confirm. Authorized publicity includes publications concerning homicide and other crimes, arrests, police raids, suicides, marriages and divorces, accidents, fires, catastrophes of nature, a death from the use of narcotics, a rare disease, the birth of a child to a twelve-year-old

> girl, the reappearance of one supposed to have been murdered years ago, a report to the police concerning the escape of a wild animal and many other similar matters of genuine, even if more or less deplorable, popular appeal.

Insofar as relevant, "private facts" are explained in Comment h as follows:

> Permissible publicity to information concerning either voluntary or involuntary public figures is not limited to the particular events that arouse the interest of the public. That interest, once aroused by the event, may legitimately extend, to some reasonable degree, to further information concerning the individual and to facts about him, which are not public and which, in the case of one who had not become a public figure, would be regarded as an invasion of his purely private life. Thus the life history of one accused of murder, together with such heretofore private facts as may throw some light upon what kind of person he is, his possible guilt or innocence, or his reasons for committing the crime, are a matter of legitimate public interest. . . . On the same basis the home life and daily habits of a motion picture actress may be of legitimate and reasonable interest to the public that sees her on the screen.
>
> The extent of the authority to make public private facts is not, however, unlimited. There may be some intimate details of her life, such as sexual relations, which even the actress is entitled to keep to herself. In determining what is a matter of legitimate public interest, account must be taken of the customs and conventions of the community; and in the last analysis what is proper becomes a matter of the community mores. The line is to be drawn when the publicity ceases to be the giving of information to which the public is entitled, and becomes a morbid and sensational prying into private lives for its own sake, with which a reasonable member of the public, with decent standards, would say that he had no concern. The limitations, in other words, are those of common decency, having due regard to the freedom of the press and its reasonable leeway to choose what it will tell the public, but also due regard to the feelings of the individual and the harm that will be done to him by the exposure. Some reasonable proportion is also to be maintained between the event or activity that makes the individual a public figure and the private facts to which publicity is given. Revelations that may properly be made concerning a murderer or the President of the United States would not be privileged if they were to be made concerning one who is merely injured in an automobile accident.

Passage of time is a relevant factor, with other facts, in determining whether the publicity involves a matter of legitimate public concern. Restatement s 652D, Comment k . . . .

We must decide under the present record whether a reasonable person applying the community standard could find the disclosure of which plaintiff complains was a morbid and sensational prying into her life for its own sake.

The article is an example of investigative journalism. Its obvious purpose was to bring the problems of the Jasper County Home to public attention. In chronicling alleged abused in the home, defendants portrayed a pattern of incidents which cumulatively established more reason for public concern about management of the home than would any one incident viewed in isolation. This journalistic technique is basic and legitimate . . . .

In determining whether the disclosure had news value, it is helpful to consider the relationship between the invasive disclosure and the newsworthy subject(s) of the article; the contribution of the disclosed facts to the subject matter of the article whether it adds credibility, contributes further information not otherwise communicable, contributes to reader perception and understanding, or augments readership by drawing attention to the story; and the constitutional value of the contribution of the disclosure, including its necessity in achieving its purposes. Bezanson, Public Disclosures as News: Injunctive Relief and Newsworthiness in Privacy Actions Involving the Press, 64 Iowa L.Rev. 1061, 1098 (1979). This analysis requires an inquiry into the relevance, impact and value of the disclosure. Id. at 1099.

Here the disclosure of plaintiff's involuntary sterilization was closely related to the subject matter of the news story. It documented the article's theme of maladministration and patient abuses at the Jasper County Home. The home had been under the same administration for twenty-two years. Public controversy concerning alleged deficiencies in administration had existed for seven years. The incidents of involuntary sterilization were central to this ongoing dispute. Plaintiff's experience in 1971 was plainly relevant with other past events in evaluating the home's administration.

In the sense of serving an appropriate news function, the disclosure contributed constructively to the impact of the article. It offered a personalized frame of reference to which the reader could relate, fostering perception and understanding. Moreover, it lent specificity and credibility to the report.

In this way the disclosure served as an effective means of accomplishing the intended news function. It had positive communicative value in attracting the reader's attention to the article's subject matter and in supporting expression of the underlying theme.

Examined in the light of the first amendment, we do not believe the disclosure could reasonably be held to be devoid of news value. See Bezanson, Supra at 1099-104 . . . .

We hold that the trial court was right in sustaining defendants' motion for summary judgment on this ground.

AFFIRMED.

LARSON, Justice (dissenting).

I join the dissent of Justice McGiverin as to Division II of the plurality opinion. I dissent separately as to Division I.

Under the reasoning of Division I, the information found in the offices of the governor and the Jasper County auditor are "public records" under our freedom of information act and therefore proper subjects of publication. I believe that even if section 68A.2, The Code, would otherwise be available to permit publication of these items of "public" information, they are medical records within the exception to the disclosure act. It is probably true that they are not "medical records" in the traditional sense; and it may be conceded as the plurality contends that they were "neither compiled by a hospital or medical personnel nor maintained as records of a hospital or physician." However, the statute does not impose any such restrictions, and I believe it would be inconsistent with the spirit and context of the act for us to impose them. If the items of information here are "records" under the act as contended by the plurality, it is only necessary to determine whether they are Medical records for purposes of the exception. They are "medical" records if they pertain to "condition, diagnosis, care or treatment." s 68A.7(2), The Code. These records here did pertain to medical treatment of the plaintiff. She was sterilized by surgical procedure.

The underpinning of this statutory exception is, I believe, a recognition of the deeply personal and sensitive nature of medical information. This exception should be interpreted to effect this strong policy consideration. Dean Wigmore, while criticizing the analogous doctor-patient privilege, recognized some justification for the privilege in sex-related medical evidence. 8 J. Wigmore, Evidence in Trials at Common Law s 2380(a), at 830 (McNaughton rev. ed. 1961). Justice Blackmun, in advocating a broad scope of the medical file exception to the federal disclosure act, also recognized the strong policy considerations attending dissemination of medical information, saying:

> It is almost inconceivable to me that the Court is willing today to attach the qualification phrase to medical files and thereby open to the public what has been recognized as almost the essence of ultimate privacy. The law's long established physician-patient privilege establishes this. Anyone who has had even minimal contact with the practice of medicine surely cannot agree with this extension by judicial construction . . . .

Department of the Air Force v. Rose, 425 U.S. 352, 387-88, 96 S.Ct. 1592, 1611, 48 L.Ed.2d 11, 36 (1976) (dissenting opinion).

I believe the publication here could reasonably have been found by a factfinder to improperly invade plaintiff's privacy, and that chapter 68A does not place the underlying information into the public domain so as to emasculate the right to pursue that claim without a trial. I would reverse and remand for trial on the merits.

LeGRAND, J., joins in this dissent.

# TIME,
v.
HILL.

385 U.S. 374

Supreme Court of the United States

Decided Jan. 9, 1967.

Mr. Justice BRENNAN delivered the opinion of the Court.

The question in this case is whether appellant, publisher of Life Magazine, was denied constitutional protections of speech and press by the application by the New York courts of ss 50--51 of the New York Civil Rights Law, McKinney's Consol. Laws, c. 6 [FN1] to award appellee damages on allegations that Life falsely reported that a new play portrayed an experience suffered by appellee and his family.

FN1. The complete text of the New York Civil Rights Law ss 50--51 is as follows:
's 50. Right of privacy
'A person, firm or corporation that uses for advertising purposes, or for the purposes of trade, the name, portrait or picture of any living person without having first obtained the written consent of such person, or if a minor of his or her parent or guardian, is guilty of a misdemeanor.'
's 51. Action for injunction and for damages
'Any person whose name, portrait or picture is used within this state for advertising purposes or for the purposes of trade without the written consent first obtained as above provided may maintain an equitable action in the supreme court of this state against the person, firm or corporation so using his name, portrait or picture, to prevent and restrain the use thereof; and may also sue and recover damages for any injuries sustained by reason of such use and if the defendant shall have knowingly used such person's name, portrait or picture in such manner as is forbidden or declared to be unlawful by the last section, the jury, in its discretion, may award exemplary damages. But nothing contained in this act shall be so construed as to prevent any person, firm or corporation, practicing the profession of photography, from exhibiting in or about his or its establishment specimens of the work of such establishment, unless the same in continued by such person, firm or corporation after written notice objecting thereto has been given by the person portrayed; and nothing contained in this act shall be so construed as to prevent any person, firm or corporation from using the name, portrait or picture of any manufacturer or dealer in connection with the goods, wares and

merchandise manufactured, produced or dealt in by him which he has sold or disposed of with such name, portrait or picture used in connection therewith; or from using the name, portrait or picture of any author, composer or artist in connection with his literary, musical or artistic productions which he has sold or disposed of with such name, portrait or picture used in connection therewith.'

The article appeared in Life in February 1955. It was entitled 'True Crime Inspires Tense Play,' with the subtitle, 'The ordeal of a family trapped by convicts gives Broadway a new thriller, 'The Desperate Hours." The text of the article reads as follows:

'Three years ago Americans all over the country read about the desperate ordeal of the James Hill family, who were held prisoners in thier home outside Philadelphia by three escaped convicts. Later they read about it in Joseph Hayes's novel, The Desperate Hours, inspired by the family's experience. Now they can see the story re-enacted in Hayes's Broadway play based on the book, and next year will see it in his movie, which has been filmed but is being held up until the play has a chance to pay off.

'The play, directed by Robert Montgomery and expertly acted, is a heart- stopping account of how a family rose to heroism in a crisis. LIFE photographed the play during its Philadelphia tryout, transported some of the actors to the actual house where the Hills were besieged. On the next page scenes from the play are re-enacted on the site of the crime.'

The pictures on the ensuing two pages included an enactment of the son being 'roughed up' by one of the convicts, entitled 'brutish convict,' a picture of the daughter biting the hand of a convict to make him drop a gun, entitled 'daring daughter,' and one of the father throwing his gun through the door after a 'brave try' to save his family is foiled.

The James Hill referred to in the article is the appellee. He and his wife and five children involuntarily became the subjects of a front-page news story after being held hostage by three escaped convicts in their suburban, Whitemarsh, Pennsylvania, home for 19 hours on September 11--12, 1952. The family was released unharmed. In an interview with newsmen after the convicts departed, appellee stressed that the convicts had treated the family courteously, had not molested them, and had not been at all violent. The convicts were thereafter apprehended in a widely publicized encounter with the police which resulted in the killing of two of the convicts. Shortly thereafter the family moved to Connecticut. The appellee discouraged all efforts to keep them in the public spotlight through magazine articles or appearances on television.

In the spring of 1953, Joseph Hayes' novel, The Desperate Hours, was published. The story depicted the experience of a family of four held hostage by three escaped convicts in the family's suburban home. But, unlike Hill's experience, the family of the story suffer violence at the hands of the convicts; the father and son are beaten and the daughter subjected to a verbal sexual insult.

The book was made into a play, also entitled The Desperate Hours, and it is Life's article about the play which is the subject of appellee's action. The complaint sought damages under ss 50--51 on allegations that the Life article was intended, to, and did, give the impression that the play mirrored the Hill family's experience, which, to the knowledge of defendant '* * * was false and untrue.' Appellant's defense was that the article was 'a subject of legitimate news interest,' 'a subject of general interest and of value and concern to the public' at the time of publication, and that it was 'published in good faith without any malice whatsoever * * *.' A motion to dismiss the complaint for substantially these reasons was made at the close of the case and was denied by the trial judge on the ground that the proofs presented a jury question as to the truth of the article.

The jury awarded appellee $50,000 compensatory and $25,000 punitive damages. On appeal the Appellate Division of the Supreme Court ordered a new trial as to damages but sustained the jury verdict of liability. The court said as to liability:

> 'Although the play was fictionalized, Life's article portrayed it as a reenactment of the Hills' experience. It is an inescapable conclusion that this was done to advertise and attract further attention to the play, and to increase present and future magazine circulation as well. It is evident that the article cannot be characterized as a mere dissemination of news, nor even an effort to supply legitimate newsworthy information in which the public had, or might have a proper interest.' 18 A.D.2d 485, 489, 240 N.Y.S.2d 286, 290.

At the new trial on damages, a jury was waived and the court awarded $30,000 compensatory damages without punitive damages.

The New York Court of Appeals affirmed the Appellate Division 'on the majority and concurring opinions at the Appellate Division,' two judges dissenting. 15 N.Y.2d 986, 260 N.Y.S.2d 7, 207 N.E.2d 604. We noted probable jurisdiction of the appeal to consider the important constitutional questions of freedom of speech and press involved. 382 U.S. 936, 86 S.Ct. 392, 15 L.Ed.2d 348. After argument last Term, the case was restored to the docket for reargument, 384 U.S. 995, 86 S.Ct. 1911, 16 L.Ed.2d 1012. We reverse and remand the case to the Court of Appeals for further proceedings not inconsistent with this opinion . . . .

As the instant case went to the jury, appellee, too, was regarded to be a newsworthy person 'substantially without a right to privacy' insofar as his hostage experience was involved, but to be entitled to his action insofar as that experience was 'fictionalized' and 'exploited for the defendants' commercial benefit.' 'Fictionalization,' the Spahn opinion states, 'is the heart of the cases in point.' 18 N.Y.2d, at 328, 274 N.Y.S.2d, at 879, 221 N.E.2d, at 545.

The opinion goes on to say that the 'establishment of minor errors in an otherwise accurate' report does not prove 'fictionalization.' Material and substantial falsification is the test. However, it is not clear whether proof of knowledge of the falsity or that the article was prepared with reckless disregard for the truth is also required. In New York Times Co. v. Sullivan, 376 U.S. 254, 84 S.Ct. 710, 11 L.Ed.2d 686, we held that the Constitution delimits a State's power to award damages for libel in actions brought by public officials against critics of their official conduct. Factual error, content defamatory of official reputation, or both, are insufficient for an award of damages for false statements unless actual malice--knowledge that the statements are false or in reckless disregard of the truth--is alleged and proved. The Spahn opinion reveals that the defendant in that case relied on New York Times as the basis of an argument that application of the statute to the publication of a substantially fictitious biography would run afoul of the constitutional guarantees. The Court of Appeals held that New York Times had no application. The court, after distinguishing the cases on the ground that Spahn did not deal with public officials or official conduct, then says, 'The free speech which is encouraged and essential to the operation of a healthy government is something quite different from an individual's attempt to enjoin the publication of a fictitious biography of him. No public interest is served by protecting the dissemination of the latter. We perceive no constitutional infirmities in this respect.' 18 N.Y.2d at 329, 274 N.Y.S.2d, at 880, 221 N.E.2d, at 546.

If this is meant to imply that proof of knowing or reckless falsity is not essential to a constitutional application of the statute in these cases, we disagree with the Court of Appeals. We hold that the constitutional protections for speech and press preclude the application of the New York statute to redress false reports of matters of public interest in the absence of proof that the defendant published the report with knowledge of its falsity or in reckless disregard of the truth.

The guarantees for speech and press are not the preserve of political expression or comment upon public affairs, essential as those are to healthy government. One need only pick up any newspaper or magazine to comprehend the vast range of published matter which exposes persons to public view, both private citizens and public officials. Exposure of the self to others in varying degrees is a concomitant of life in a civilized community. The risk of this exposure is an essential incident of life in a society which places a primary value on freedom of speech and of press. 'Freedom of discussion, if it would fulfill its historic function in this nation, must embrace all issues about which information is needed or appropriate to enable the members of society to cope with the exigenciesof their period.' Thornhill v. State of Alabama, 310 U.S. 88, 102, 60 S.Ct. 736, 744, 84 L.Ed. 1093. 'No suggestion can be found in the Constitution that the freedom there guaranteed for speech and the press bears an inverse ratio to the timeliness and importance of the ideas seeking expression.' Bridges v. State of California, 314 U.S. 252, 269, 62 S.Ct. 190, 196, 86 L.Ed. 192. We have no doubt that the subject of the Life article, the opening of a new play linked to an actual incident, is a matter of public interest. 'The line between the informing and the entertaining is too elusive for the protection of * * * (freedom of the press).' Winters v. People of State of New York, 333 U.S. 507, 510, 68 S.Ct. 665, 667, 92 L.Ed. 840. Erroneous statement is no less inevitable in such a case than in the case of comment upon public affairs, and in both, if innocent or merely negligent, '* * * it must be protected if the freedoms of expression are to have the 'breathing space' that they 'need * * * to survive' * * *.' New York Times Co. v. Sullivan, supra, 376 U.S., at 271--272, 84 S.Ct., at 721, 11 L.Ed.2d 686. As James Madison said, 'Some degree of abuse is inseparable from the proper use of every thing, and in no instance is this more true than in that of the press.' 4 Elliot's Debates on the Federal Constitution 571 (1876 ed.). We create a grave risk of serious impairment of the indispensable service of a free press in a free society if we saddle the press with the impossible burden of verifying to a certainty the facts associated in news articles with a person's name, picture or portrait, particularly as related to nondefamatory matter. Even negligencewould be a most elusive standard, especially when the content of the speech itself affords no warning of prospective harm to another through falsity. A negligencetest would place on the press the intolerable burden of guessing how a jury might assess the reasonableness of steps taken by it to verify the accuracy of every reference to a name, picture or portrait.

In this context, sanctions against either innocent or negligent misstatement would present a grave hazard of discouraging the press from exercisingthe constitutional guarantees. Those guarantees are not for the benefit of the press so much as for the benefit of all of us. A broadly defined freedom of the press assures the maintenance of our political system and an open society. Fear of large verdicts in damage suits for innocent or merely negligent misstatement, even fear of the expense involved in their defense, must inevitably cause publishers to 'steer * * * wider of the unlawful zone,' New York Times Co. v. Sullivan, 376 U.S., at 279, 84 S.Ct., at 725, 11 L.Ed.2d 686; see also Speiser v. Randall, 357 U.S. 513, 526, 78 S.Ct. 1332, 1342, 2 L.Ed.2d 1460; Smith v. People of State of California, 361 U.S. 147, 153--154, 80 S.Ct. 215, 218--219, 4 L.Ed.2d 205; and thus 'create the danger that the legitimate utterance will be penalized.' Speiser v. Randall, supra, 357 U.S., at 526, 78 S.Ct., at 1342.

But the constitutional guarantees can tolerate sanctions against calculated falsehood without significant impairment of their essential function. We held in New York Times that calculated falsehood enjoyed no immunity in the case of alleged defamation of a public official concerning his official conduct. Similarly, calculated falsehood should enjoy no immunity in the situation here presented us. What we said in Garrison v. State of Louisiana, supra, 379 U.S., at 75, 85 S.Ct., at 216, 13 L.Ed.2d 125, is equally applicable:

> 'The use of calculated falsehood * * * would put a different cast on the constitutional question. Although honest utterance, even if inaccurate, may further the fruitful exercise of the right of free speech, it does not follow that the lie, knowingly and deliberately published * * * should enjoy a like immunity. * * * For the use of the known lie as a tool is at once at odds with the premises of democratic government and with the orderly manner in which economic, social, or political change is to be effected. Calculated falsehood falls into that class of utterances which 'are no essential part of any exposition of ideas, and are of such slight social value as a step to truth that any benefit that may be derived from them is clearly outweighed by the social interest in order and morality. * * *' Chaplinsky v. State of New Hampshire, 315 U.S. 568, 572, 62 S.Ct. 766, 769, 86 L.Ed. 1031. Hence the knowingly false statement and the false statement made with reckless disregard of the truth, do not enjoy constitutional protection' . . .

II.

Turning to the facts of the present case, the proofs reasonably would support either a jury finding of innocent or merely negligent misstatement by Life, or a finding that Life portrayed the play as a reenactment of the Hill family's experience reckless of the truth or with actual knowledge that the portrayal was false. The relevant testimony is as follows:

Joseph Hayes, author of the book, also wrote the play. The story theme was inspired by the desire to write about 'true crime' and for years before writing the book, he collected newspaper clippings of stories of hostage incidents. His story was not shaped by any single incident, but by several, including incidents which occurred in California, New York, and Detroit. He said that he did not consciously portray any member of the Hill family, or the Hill family's experience, although admitting that 'in a very direct way' the Hill experience 'triggered' the writing of the book and the play.

The Life article was prepared at the direction and under the supervision of its entertainment editor, Prideaux. He learned of the production of the play from a news story. The play's director, Robert Montgomery, later suggested to him that its interesting stage setting would make the play a worthwhile subject for an article in Life. At about the same time, Prideaux ran into a friend of author Hayes, a free-lance photographer, who told Prideaux in casual conversation that the play had a 'substantial connection with a true-life incident of a family being held by escaped convicts near Philadelphia.' As the play was trying out in Philadelphia, Prideaux decided to contact the author. Hayes confirmed that an incident somewhat similar to the play had occurred in Philadelphia, and agreed with Prideaux to find out whether the former Hill residence would be available for the shooting of pictures for a Life article. Prideaux then met with Hayes in Philadelphia where he saw the play and drove with Hayes to the former Hill residence to test its suitability for a picture story. Neither then nor thereafter did Prideaux question Hayes about the extent to which the play was based on the Hill incident. 'A specific question of that nature was never asked, but a discussion of the play itself, what the play was about, in the light of my own knowledge of what the true incident was about, confirmed in my mind beyond any doubt that there was a relationship, and Mr. Hayes' presence at this whole negotiation was tacit proof of that.'

Prideaux sent photographers to the Hill residence for location photographs of scenes of the play enacted in the home, and proceeded to construct the text of the article. In his 'story file' were several news clippings about the Hill incident which revealed its nonviolent character, and a New York Times article by Hayes in which he stated that the play 'was based on various news stories,' mentioning incidents in New York, California, Detroit and Philadelphia.

Prideaux's first draft made no mention of the Hill name except for the caption of one of the photographs. The text related that a true story of a suburban Philadelphia family had 'sparked off' Hayes to write the novel, that the play was a 'somewhat fictionalized' account of the family's heroism in time of crisis. Prideaux's research assistant, whose task it was to check the draft for accuracy, put a question mark over the words 'somewhat fictionalized.' Prideaux testified that the question mark 'must have been' brought to his attention, although he did not recollect having seen it. The draft was also brought before the copy editor, who, in the presence of Prideaux, made several changes in emphasis and substance. The first sentence was changed to focus on the Hill incident, using the family's name; the novel was said to have been 'inspired' by that incident, and the play was referred to as a 're-enactment.' The words 'somewhat fictionalized' were deleted.

Prideaux labeled as 'emphatically untrue' defense counsel's suggestion during redirect examination that from the beginning he knew that the play had no relationship to the Hill incident apart from being a hostage incident. Prideaux admitted that he knew the play was 'between a little bit and moderately factionalized,' but stated that he thought beyond doubt that the important quality, the 'heart and soul' of the play, was the Hill incident.

The jury might reasonably conclude from this evidence--particularly that the New York Times article was in the story file, that the copy editor deleted 'somewhat fictionalized' after the research assistant questioned its accuracy, and that Prideaux admitted that he knew the play was 'between a little bit and moderately fictionalized'--that Life knew the falsity of, or was reckless of the truth in, stating in the article that 'the story reenacted' the Hill family's experience. On the other hand, the jury might reasonably predicate a finding of innocent or only negligent misstatement on the testimony that a statement was made to Prideaux by the free-lance photographer that linked the play to an incident in Philadelphia, that the author Hayes cooperated in arranging for the availability of the former Hill home, and that Prideaux thought beyond doubt that the 'heart and soul' of the play was the Hill incident.

IV.

The appellant argues that the statute should be declared unconstitutional on its face if construed by the New York courts to impose liability without proof of knowing or reckless falsity. Such a declaration would not be warranted even if it were entirely clear that this had previously been the view of the New York courts. The New York Court of Appeals, as the Spahn opinion demonstrates, has been assiduous in construing the statute to avoid invasion of the constitutional protections of speech and press. We, therefore, confidently except that the New York courts will apply the statute consistently with the constitutional command. Any possible difference with us as to the thrust of the constitutional command is narrowly limited in this case to the failure of the trial judge to instruct the jury that a verdict of liability could be predicated only on a finding of knowing or reckless falsity in the publication of the Life article.

The judgment of the Court of Appeals is set aside and the case is remanded for further proceedings not inconsistent with this opinion.

It is so ordered.

# Part III: Free Press-Fair Trial

Samuel H. SHEPPARD, Petitioner,
v.
E. L. MAXWELL, Warden.

384 U.S. 333

Supreme Court of the United States

Decided June 6, 1966.

Mr. Justice CLARK delivered the opinion of the Court.

This federal habeas corpus application involves the question whether Sheppard was deprived of a fair trial in his state conviction for the second-degree murder of his wife because of the trial judge's failure to protect Sheppard sufficiently from the massive, pervasive and prejudicial publicity that attended his prosecution. The United States District Court held that he was not afforded a fair trial and granted the writ subject to the State's right to put Sheppard to trial again, 231 F.Supp. 37 (D.C.S.D.Ohio 1964). The Court of Appeals for the Sixth Circuit reversed by a divided vote, 346 F.2d 707 (1965). We granted certiorari, 382 U.S. 916, 86 S.Ct. 289, 15 L.Ed.2d 231 (1965). We have concluded that Sheppard did not receive a fair trial consistent with the Due Process Clause of the Fourteenth Amendment and, therefore, reverse the judgment.

I.

Marilyn Sheppard, petitioner's pregnant wife, was bludgeoned to death in the upstairs bedroom of their lakeshore home in Bay Village, Ohio, a suburb of Cleveland. On the day of the tragedy, July 4, 1954, Sheppard pieced together for several local officials the following story: He and his wife had entertained neighborhood friends, the Aherns, on the previous evening at their home. After dinner they watched television in the living room. Sheppard became drowsy and dozed off to sleep on a couch. Later, Marilyn partially awoke him saying that she was going to bed. The next thing he remembered was hearing his wife cry out in the early morning hours. He hurried upstairs and in the dim light from the hall saw a 'form' standing next to his wife's bed. As he struggled with the 'form' he was struck on the back of the neck and rendered unconscious. On regaining his senses he found himself on the floor next to his wife's bed. He rose, looked at her, took her pulse and 'felt that she was gone.' He then went to his son's room and found him unmolested. Hearing a noise he hurried downstairs. He saw a 'form' running out the door and pursued it to the lake shore. He grappled with it on the beach and again lost consciousness. Upon his recovery he was lying face down with the lower portion of his body in the water. He returned to his home, checked the pulse on his wife's neck, and 'determined or thought that she was gone.' He then went downstairs and called a neighbor, Mayor Houk of Bay Village. The Mayor and his wife came over at once, found Sheppard slumped in an easy chair downstairs and asked, 'What happened?' Sheppard replied: 'I don't know but somebody ought to try to do something for Marilyn.' Mrs. Houk immediately went up to the bedroom. The Mayor told Sheppard, 'Get hold of yourself. Can you tell me what happened?' Sheppard then related the above-outlined events. After Mrs. Houk discovered the body, the Mayor called the local police, Dr. Richard Sheppard, petitioner's brother, and the Ahems. The local police were the first to arrive. They in turn notified the Coroner and Cleveland police. Richard Sheppard then arrived, determined that Marilyn was dead, examined his brother's injuries, and removed him to the nearby clinic operated by the Sheppard family. When the Coroner, the Cleveland police and other officials arrived, the house and surrounding area were thoroughly searched, the rooms of the house were photographed, and many persons, including the Houks and the Ahems, were interrogated. The Sheppard home and premises were taken into 'protective custody' and remained so until after the trial . . . .

That night at 10 o'clock Sheppard was arrested at his father's home on a charge of murder. He was taken to the Bay VillageCity Hall where hundreds of people, newscasters, photographers and reporters were awaiting his arrival. He was immediately arraigned--havingbeen denied a temporary delay to secure the presence of counsel--and bound over to the grand jury.

The publicity then grew in intensity until his indictment on August 17. Typical of the coverage during this period is a front-page interview entitled: 'DR. SAM: 'I Wish There Was Something I Could Get Off My Chest--but There Isn't." Unfavorable publicity included items such as a cartoon of the body of a sphinx with Sheppard's head and the legend below: "I Will Do Everything In My Power to Help Solve This Terrible Murder.'--Dr. Sam Sheppard.' Headlines announced, inter alia, that: 'Doctor Evidence is Ready for Jury,' 'Corrigan Tactics Stall Quizzing.' 'Sheppard 'Gay Set' Is Revealed By Houk,' 'Blood Is Found In Garage,' 'New Murder Evidence Is Found, Police Claim,' 'Dr. Sam Faces Quiz At Jail On Marilyn's Fear Of Him.' On August 18, an article appeared under the headline 'Dr. Sam Writes His Own Story.' And reproduced across the entire front page was a portion of the typed statement signed by Sheppard: 'I am not guilty of the murder of my wife, Marilyn. How could I, who have been trained to help people and devoted my life to saving life, commit such a terrible and revolting crime?' We do not detail the coverage further. There are five volumes filled with similar clippings from each of the three Cleveland newspapers covering the period from the murder until Sheppard's conviction in December 1954 . . . .

While we cannot say that Sheppard was denied due process by the judge's refusal to take precautions against the influence of pretrial publicity alone, the court's later rulings must be considered against the setting in which the trial was held. In light of this background, we believe that the arrangements made by the judge with the news media caused Sheppard to be deprived of that 'judicial serenity and calm to which (he) was entitled.' Estes v. State of Texas, supra, 381

U.S., at 536, 85 S.Ct., at 1629. The fact is that bedlam reigned at the courthouse during the trial and newsmen took over practically the entire courtroom, hounding most of the participants in the trial, especially Sheppard. At a temporary table within a few feet of the jury box and counsel table sat some 20 reporters staring at Sheppard and taking notes. The erection of a press table for reporters inside the bar is unprecedented. The bar of the court is reserved for counsel, providing them a safe place in which to keep papers and exhibits, and to confer privately with client and co-counsel. It is designed to protect the witness and the jury from any distractions, intrusions or influences, and to permit bench discussions of the judge's rulings away from the hearing of the public and the jury. Having assigned almost all of the available seats in the courtroom to the news media the judge lost his ability to supervise that environment. The movement of the reporters in and out of the courtroom caused frequent confusion and disruption of the trial. And the record reveals constant commotion within the bar. Moreover, the judge gave the throng of newsmen gathered in the corridors of the courthouse absolute free rein. Participants in the trial, including the jury, were forced to run a gantlet of reporters and photographers each time they entered or left the courtroom. The total lack of consideration for the privacy of the jury was demonstrated by the assignment to a broadcasting station of space next to the jury room on the floor above the courtroom, as well as the fact that jurors were allowed to make telephone calls during their five-day deliberation.

VI.

There can be no question about the nature of the publicity which surrounded Sheppard's trial. We agree, as did the Court of Appeals, with the findings in Judge Bell's opinion for the Ohio Supreme Court:

> 'Murder and mystery, society, sex and suspense were combined in this case in such a manner as to intrigue and captivate the public fancy to a degree perhaps unparalleled in recent annals. Throughout the preindictment investigation, the subsequent legal skirmishes and the nine-week trial, circulation-conscious editors catered to the insatiable interest of the American public in the bizarre. * * * In this atmosphere of a 'Roman holiday' for the news media, Sam Sheppard stood trial for his life.' 165 Ohio St., at 294, 135 N.E.2d, at 342.

Indeed, every court that has considered this case, save the court that tried it, has deplored the manner in which the news media inflamed and prejudiced the public.

Much of the material printed or broadcast during the trial was never heard from the witness stand, such as the charges that Sheppard had purposely impeded the murder investigation and must be guilty since he had hired a prominent criminal lawyer; that Sheppard was a perjurer; that he had sexual relations with numerous women; that his slain wife had characterized him as a 'Jekyll-Hyde'; that he was 'a bare-faced liar' because of his testimony as to police treatment; and finally, that a woman convict claimed Sheppard to be the father of her illegitimate child. As the trial progressed, the newspapers summarized and interpreted the evidence, devoting particular attention to the material that incriminated Sheppard, and often drew unwarranted inferences from testimony. At one point, a front-page picture of Mrs. Sheppard's blood- stained pillow was published after being 'doctored' to show more clearly an alleged imprint of a surgical instrument.

Nor is there doubt that this deluge of publicity reached at least some of the jury. On the only occasion that the jury was queried, two jurors admitted in open court to hearing the highly inflammatory charge that a prison inmate claimed Sheppard as the father of her illegitimate child. Despite the extent and nature of the publicity to which the jury was exposed during trial, the judge refused defense counsel's other requests that the jurors be asked whether they had read or heard specific prejudicial comment about the case, including the incidents we have previously summarized. In these circumstances, we can assume that some of this material reached members of the jury. See Commonwealth v. Crehan, 345 Mass. 609, 188 N.E.2d 923 (1963).

VII.

The court's fundamental error is compounded by the holding that it lacked power to control the publicity about the trial. From the very inception of the proceedings the judge announced that neither he nor anyone else could restrict prejudicial news accounts. And he reiterated this view on numerous occasions. Since he viewed the news media as his target, the judge never considered other means that are often utilized to reduce the appearance of prejudicial material and to protect the jury from outside influence. We conclude that these procedures would have been sufficient to guarantee Sheppard a fair trial and so do not consider what sanctions might be available against a recalcitrant press nor the charges of bias now made against the state trial judge.

The carnival atmosphere at trial could easily have been avoided since the courtroom and courthouse premises are subject to the control of the court. As we stressed in Estes, the presence of the press at judicial proceedings must be limited when it is apparent that the accused might otherwise be prejudiced or disadvantaged. Bearing in mind the massive pretrial publicity, the judge should have adopted stricter rules governing the use of the courtroom by newsmen, as Sheppard's counsel requested. The number of reporters in the courtroom itself could have been limited at the first sign that their presence would disrupt the trial. They certainly should not have been placed inside the bar. Furthermore, the judge should have more closely regulated the conduct of newsmen in the courtroom. For instance, the judge belatedly asked them not to handle and photograph trial exhibits lying on the counsel table during recesses.

Secondly, the court should have insulated the witnesses. All of the newspapers and radio stations apparently interviewed prospective witnesses at will, and in many instances disclosed their testimony. A typical example was the publication of numerous statements by Susan Hayes, before her appearance in court, regarding her love affair with Sheppard. Although the witnesses were barred from the courtroom during the trial the full verbatim testimony was available to them in the press. This completely nullified the judge's imposition of the rule. See Estes v. State of Texas, supra, 381 U.S., at 547, 85 S.Ct., at 1635.

Thirdly, the court should have made some effort to control the release of leads, information, and gossip to the press by police officers, witnesses, and the counsel for both sides. Much of the information thus disclosed was inaccurate, leading to groundless rumors and confusion. That the judge was aware of his responsibility in this respect may be seen from his warning to Steve

Sheppard, the accused's brother, who had apparently made public statements in an attempt to discredit testimony for the prosecution. The judge made this statement in the presence of the jury:

'Now, the Court wants to say a word. That he was told--he has not read anything about it at all--but he was informed that Dr. Steve Sheppard, who has been granted the privilege of remaining in the court room during the trial, has been trying the case in the newspapers and making rather uncomplimentary comments about the testimony of the witnesses for the State.
'Let it be now understood that if Dr. Steve Sheppard wishes to use the newspapers to try his case while we are trying it here, he will be barred from remaining in the court room during the progress of the trial if he is to be a witness in the case.
'The Court appreciates he cannot deny Steve Sheppard the right of free speech, but he can deny him the * * * privilege of being in the courtroom, if he wants to avail himself of that method during the progress of the trial.'
Defense counsel immediately brought to the court's attention the tremendous amount of publicity in the Cleveland press that 'misrepresented entirely the testimony' in the case. Under such circumstances, the judge should have at least warned the newspapers to check the accuracy of their accounts. And it is obvious that the judge should have further sought to alleviate this problem by imposing control over the statements made to the news media by counsel, witnesses, and especially the Coroner and police officers. The prosecution repeatedly made evidence available to the news media which was never offered in the trial. Much of the 'evidence' disseminated in this fashion was clearly inadmissible. The exclusion of such evidence in court is rendered meaningless when news media make it available to the public. For example, the publicity about Sheppard's refusal to take a lie detector test came directly from police officers and the Coroner. The story that Sheppard had been called a 'Jekyll-Hyde' personality by his wife was attributed to a prosecution witness. No such testimony was given. The further report that there was 'a 'bombshell witness' on tap' who would testify as to Sheppard's 'fiery temper' could only have emanated from the prosecution. Moreover, the newspapers described in detail clues that had been found by the police, but not put into the record.

The fact that many of the prejudicial news items can be traced to the prosecution, as well as the defense, aggravates the judge's failure to take any action. See Stroble v. State of California, 343 U.S. 181, 201, 72 S.Ct. 599, 609, 96 L.Ed. 872 (1952) (Frankfurter, J., dissenting). Effective control of these sources--concededly within the court's power--might well have prevented the divulgence of inaccurate information, rumors, and accusations that made up much of the inflammatory publicity, at least after Sheppard's indictment.

More specifically, the trial court might well have proscribed extrajudicial statements by any lawyer, party, witness, or court official which divulged prejudicial matters, such as the refusal of Sheppard to submit to interrogation or take any lie detector tests; any statement made by Sheppard to officials; the identity of prospective witnesses or their probable testimony; any belief in guilt or innocence; or like statements concerning the merits of the case. See State v.

Van Duyne, 43 N.J., 369, 389, 204 A.2d 841, 852 (1964), in which the court interpreted Canon 20 of the American Bar Association's Canons of Professional Ethics to prohibit such statements. Being advised of the great public interest in the case, the mass coverage of the press, and the potential prejudicial impact of publicity, the court could also have requested the appropriate city and county officials to promulgate a regulation with respect to dissemination of information about the case by their employees. In addition, reporters who wrote or broadcast prejudicial stories, could have been warned as to the impropriety of publishing material not introduced in the proceedings. The judge was put on notice of such events by defense counsel's complaint about the WHK broadcast on the second day of trial. See p. 1513, supra. In this manner, Sheppard's right to a trial free from outside interference would have been given added protection without corresponding curtailment of the news media. Had the judge, the other officers of the court, and the police placed the interest of justice first, the news media would have soon learned to be content with the task of reporting the case as it unfolded in the courtroom--not pieced together from extrajudicial statements.

From the cases coming here we note that unfair and prejudicial news comment on pending trials has become increasingly prevalent. Due process requires that the accused receive a trial by an impartial jury free from outside influences. Given the pervasiveness of modern communications and the difficulty of effacing prejudicial publicity from the minds of the jurors, the trial courts must take strong measures to ensure that the balance is never weighed against the accused. And appellate tribunals have the duty to make an independent evaluation of the circumstances. Of course, there is nothing that proscribes the press from reporting events that transpire in the courtroom. But where there is a reasonable likelihood that prejudicial news prior to trial will prevent a fair trial, the judge should continue the case until the threat abates, or transfer it to another county not so permeated with publicity. In addition, sequestration of the jury was something the judge should have raised sua sponte with counsel. If publicity during the proceedings threatens the fairness of the trial, a new trial should be ordered. But we must remember that reversals are but palliatives; the cure lies in those remedial measures that will prevent the prejudice at its inception. The courts must take such steps by rule and regulation that will protect their processes from prejudicial outside interferences. Neither prosecutors, counsel for defense, the accused, witnesses, court staff nor enforcement officers coming under the jurisdiction of the court should be permitted to frustrate its function. Collaboration between counsel and the press as to information affecting the fairness of a criminal trial is not only subject to regulation, but is highly censurable and worthy of disciplinary measures.

Since the state trial judge did not fulfill his duty to protect Sheppard from the inherently prejudicial publicity which saturated the community and to control disruptive influences in the courtroom, we must reverse the denial of the habeas petition. The case is remanded to the District Court with instructions to issue the writ and order that Sheppard be released from custody unless the State puts him to its charges again within a reasonable time.

It is so ordered.

Mr. Justice BLACK dissents.

NEBRASKA PRESS ASSOCIATION et al., Petitioners,
v.
Hugh STUART, Judge, District Court of Lincoln County, Nebraska, et al.

427 U.S. 539

Supreme Court of the United States

Decided June 30, 1976.

Mr. Chief Justice BURGER delivered the opinion of the Court.

The respondent State District Judge entered an order restraining the petitioners from publishing or broadcasting accounts of confessions or admission made by the accused or facts "strongly implicative" of the accused in a widely reported murder of six persons. We granted certiorari to decide whether the entry of such an order on the showing made before the state court violated the constitutional guarantee of freedom of the press.

I

On the evening of October 18, 1975, local police found the six members of the Henry Kellie family murdered in their home in Sutherland, Neb., a town of about 850 people. Police released the description of a suspect, Erwin Charles Simants, to the reporters who had hastened to the scene of the crime. Simants was arrested and arraigned in Lincoln County Court the following morning, ending a tense night for this small rural community.

The crime immediately attracted widespread news coverage, by local, regional, and national newspapers, radio and television stations. Three days after the crime, the County Attorney and Simants' attorney joined in asking the County Court to enter a restrictive order relating to "matters that may or may not be publicly reported or disclosed to the public," because of the "mass coverage by news media" and the "reasonable likelihood of prejudicial news which would make difficult, if not impossible, the impaneling of an impartial jury and tend to prevent a fair trial." The County Court heard oral argument but took no evidence; no attorney for members of the press appeared at this stage. The County Court granted the prosecutor's motion for a restrictive order and entered it the next day, October 22. The order prohibited everyone in attendance from "releas(ing) or authoriz(ing) the release for public dissemination in any form or manner whatsoever any testimony given or evidence adduced"; the order also required members of the press to observe the Nebraska Bar-Press Guidelines. [FN1]

FN1. These Guidelines are voluntary standards adopted by members of the state bar and news media to deal with the reporting of crimes and criminal trials. They outline the matters of fact that may appropriately be reported, and also list what items are not generally appropriate for reporting, including confessions, opinions on guilt or innocence, statements that would influence the outcome of a trial, the results of tests or examinations, comments on the credibility of witnesses, and evidence presented in the jury's absence. The publication of an accused's criminal record should, under the Guidelines, be "considered very carefully." The Guidelines also set out standards for taking and publishing photographs, and set up a joint bar-press committee to foster cooperation in resolving particular problems that emerge.

Simants' preliminary hearing was held the same day, open to the public but subject to the order. The County Court bound over the defendant for trial to the State District Court. The charges, as amended to reflect the autopsy findings, were that Simants had committed the murders in the course of a sexual assault.

Petitioners several press and broadcast associations, publishers, and individual reporters moved on October 23 for leave to intervene in the District Court, asking that the restrictive order imposed by the County Court be vacated. The District Court conducted a hearing, at which the County Judge testified and newspaper articles about the Simants case were admitted in evidence. The District Judge granted petitioners' motion to intervene and, on October 27, entered his own restrictive order. The judge found "because of the nature of the crimes charged in the complaint that there is a clear and present danger that pre-trial publicity could impinge upon the defendant's right to a fair trial." The order applied only until the jury was impaneled, and specifically prohibited petitioners from reporting five subjects: (1) the existence or contents of a confession Simants had made to law enforcement officers, which had been introduced in open court at arraignment; (2) the fact or nature of statements Simants had made to other persons; (3) the contents of a note he had written the night of the crime; (4) certain aspects of the medical testimony at the preliminary hearing; and (5) the identity of the victims of the alleged sexual assault and the nature of the assault. It also prohibited reporting the exact nature of the restrictive order itself. Like the County Court's order, this order incorporated the Nebraska Bar-Press Guidelines. Finally, the order set out a plan for attendance, seating, and courthouse traffic control during the trial.

Four days later, on October 31, petitioners asked the District Court to stay its order. At the same time, they applied to the Nebraska Supreme Court for a writ of mandamus, a stay, and an expedited appeal from the order. The State of Nebraska and the defendant Simants intervened in these actions. The Nebraska Supreme Court heard oral argument on November 25, and issued its Per curiam opinion December 1. State v. Simants, 194 Neb. 783, 236 N.W.2d 794 (1975).

The Nebraska Supreme Court balanced the "heavy presumption against . . . constitutional validity" that an order restraining publication bears, New York Times Co. v. United States, 403 U.S. 713, 714, 91 S.Ct. 2140, 2141, 29 L.Ed.2d 822 (1971), against the importance of the defendant's right to trial by an impartial jury. Both society and the individual defendant, the court held, had a vital interest in assuring that Simants be tried by an impartial jury. Because of the publicity surrounding the crime, the court determined that this right was in jeopardy. The court noted that Nebraska statutes required the District Court to try Simants within six months of his arrest, and that a change of venue could move the trial only to adjoining counties, which had been subject to essentially the same publicity as Lincoln County. The Nebraska Supreme Court held that "(u)nless the absolutist position of the relators was constitutionally correct, it would appear that the District Court acted properly." 194 Neb., at 797, 236 N.W.2d, at 803.

The Nebraska Supreme Court rejected that "absolutist position," but modified the District Court's order to accommodate the defendant's right to a fair trial and the petitioners' interest in reporting pretrial events. The order as modified prohibited reporting of only three matters: (a) the existence and nature of any confessions or admissions made by the defendant to law enforcement officers, (b) any confessions or admissions made to any third parties, except members of the press, and (c) other facts "strongly implicative" of the accused. The Nebraska Supreme Court did not rely on the Nebraska Bar-Press Guidelines. See n. 1, Supra. After construing Nebraska law to permit closure in certain circumstances, the court remanded the case to the District Judge for reconsideration of the issue whether pretrial hearings should be closed to the press and public.

We granted certiorari to address the important issues raised by the District Court order as modified by the Nebraska Supreme Court, but we denied the motion to expedite review or to stay entirely the order of the State District Court pending Simants' trial. 423 U.S. 1027, 96 S.Ct. 557, 46 L.Ed.2d 401 (1975). We are informed by the parties that since we granted certiorari, Simants has been convicted of murder and sentenced to death. His appeal is pending in the Nebraska Supreme Court.

## III

The problems presented by this case are almost as old as the Republic. Neither in the Constitution nor in contemporaneous writings do we find that the conflict between these two important rights was anticipated, yet it is inconceivable that the authors of the Constitution were unaware of the potential conflicts between the right to an unbiased jury and the guarantee of freedom of the press. The unusually able lawyers who helped write the Constitution and later drafted the Bill of Rights were familiar with the historic episode in which John Adams defended British soldiers charged with homicide for firing into a crowd of Boston demonstrators; they were intimately familiar with the clash of the adversary system and the part that passions of the populace sometimes play in influencing potential jurors. They did not address themselves directly to the situation presented by this case; their chief concern was the need for freedom of expression in the political arena and the dialogue in ideas. But they recognized that there were risks to private rights from an unfettered press. Jefferson, for example, writing from Paris in 1786 concerning press attacks on John Jay, stated:

> "In truth it is afflicting that a man who has past his life in serving the public . . . should yet be liable to have his peace of mind so much disturbed by any individual who shall think proper to

arraign him in a newspaper. It is however an evil for which there is no remedy. Our liberty depends on the freedom of the press, and that cannot be limited without being lost. . . ." 9 Papers of Thomas Jefferson 239 (J. Boyd ed. 1954).

See also F. Mott, Jefferson and the Press 21, 38-46 (1943).

The trial of Aaron Burr in 1807 presented Mr. Chief Justice Marshall, presiding as a trial judge, with acute problems in selecting an unbiased jury. Few people in the area of Virginia from which jurors were drawn had not formed some opinions concerning Mr. Burr or the case, from newspaper accounts and heightened discussion both private and public. The Chief Justice conducted a searching Voir dire of the two panels eventually called, and rendered a substantial opinion on the purposes of Voir dire and the standards to be applied. See 1 Causes Celebres, Trial of Aaron Burr for Treason 404-427, 473- 481 (1879); United States v. Burr, 25 Fed.Cas.No. 14,692g, p. 49 (CC Va.1807). Burr was acquitted, so there was no occasion for appellate review to examine the problem of prejudicial pretrial publicity. Mr. Chief Justice Marshall's careful voir dire inquiry into the matter of possible bias makes clear that the problem is not a new one . . . .

The state trial judge in the case before us acted responsibly, out of a legitimate concern, in an effort to protect the defendant's right to a fair trial. What we must decide is not simply whether the Nebraska courts erred in seeing the possibility of real danger to the defendant's rights, b whether in the circumstances of this case the means employed were foreclosed by another provision of the Constitution.

V

The First Amendment provides that "Congress shall make no law . . . abridging the freedom . . . of the press," and it is "no longer open to doubt that the liberty of the press and of speech, is within the liberty safeguarded by the due process clause of the Fourteenth Amendment from invasion by state action." Near v. Minnesota ex rel. Olson, 283 U.S. 697, 707, 51 S.Ct. 625, 628, 75 L.Ed. 1357 (1931). See also Grosjean v. American Press Co., 297 U.S. 233, 244, 56 S.Ct. 444, 446, 80 L.Ed. 660 (1936). The Court has interpreted these guarantees to afford special protection against orders that prohibit the publication or broadcast of particular information or commentary orders that impose a "previous" or "prior" restraint on speech. None of our decided cases on prior restraint involved restrictive orders entered to protect a defendant's right to a fair and impartial jury, but the opinions on prior restraint have a common thread relevant to this case . . . .

The thread running through all these cases is that prior restraints on speech and publication are the most serious and the least tolerable infringement on First Amendment rights. A criminal penalty or a judgment in a defamation case is subject to the whole panoply of protections afforded by deferring the impact of the judgment until all avenues of appellate review have been exhausted. Only after judgment has become final, correct or otherwise, does the law's sanction become fully operative.

A prior restraint, by contrast and by definition, has an immediate and irreversible sanction. If it can be said that a threat of criminal or civil sanctions after publication "chills" speech, prior restraint "freezes" it at least for the time . . . .

## VI

We turn now to the record in this case to determine whether, as Learned Hand put it, "the gravity of the 'evil,' discounted by its improbability, justifies such invasion of free speech as is necessary to avoid the danger." United States v. Dennis, 183 F.2d 201, 212 (CA2 1950), aff'd, 341 U.S. 494, 71 S.Ct. 857, 95 L.Ed. 1137 (1951); see also L. Hand, The Bill of Rights 58-61 (1958). To do so, we must examine the evidence before the trial judge when the order was entered to determine (a) the nature and extent of pretrial news coverage; (b) whether other measures would be likely to mitigate the effects of unrestrained pretrial publicity; and (c) how effectively a restraining order would operate to prevent the threatened danger. The precise terms of the restraining order are also important. We must then consider whether the record supports the entry of a prior restraint on publication, one of the most extraordinary remedies known to our jurisprudence.

### A

In assessing the probable extent of publicity, the trial judge had before him newspapers demonstrating that the crime had already drawn intensive news coverage, and the testimony of the County Judge, who had entered the initial restraining order based on the local and national attention the case had attracted. The District Judge was required to assess the probable publicity that would be given these shocking crimes prior to the time a jury was selected and sequestered. He then had to examine the probable nature of the publicity and determine how it would affect prospective jurors.

Our review of the pretrial record persuades us that the trial judge was justified in concluding that there would be intense and pervasive pretrial publicity concerning this case. He could also reasonably conclude, based on common man experience, that publicity might impair the defendant's right to a fair trial. He did not purport to say more, for he found only "a clear and present danger that pre-trial publicity Could Impinge upon the defendant's right to a fair trial." (Emphasis added.) His conclusion as to the impact of such publicity on prospective jurors was of necessity speculative, dealing as he was with factors unknown and unknowable.

### B

We find little in the record that goes to another aspect of our task, determining whether measures short of an order retraining all publication would have insured the defendant a fair trial. Although the entry of the order might be read as a judicial determination that other measures would not suffice, the trial court made no express findings to that effect; the Nebraska Supreme Court referred to the issue only by implication. See 194 Neb., at 797-798, 236 N.W.2d, at 803.

Most of the alternatives to prior restraint of publication in these circumstances were discussed with obvious approval in Sheppard v. Maxwell, 384 U.S., at 357-362, 86 S.Ct., at 1519-1522: (a) change of trial venue to a place less exposed to the intense publicity that seemed imminent in Lincoln County; (b) postponement of the trial to allow public attention to subside; (c) searching questioning of prospective jurors, as Mr. Chief Justice Marshall used in the Burr Case, to screen out those with fixed opinions as to guilt or innocence; (d) the use of emphatic and clear instructions on the sworn duty of each juror to decide the issues only on evidence presented in open court. Sequestration of jurors is, of course, always available. Although that measure insulates jurors only after they are sworn, it also enhances the likelihood of dissipating the impact of pretrial publicity and emphasizes the elements of the jurors' oaths.

This Court has outlined other measures short of prior restraints on publication tending to blunt the impact of pretrial publicity. See Sheppard v. Maxwell, supra, at 361-362, 86 S.Ct., at 1521-1522. Professional studies have filled out these suggestions, recommending that trial courts in appropriate cases limit what the contending lawyers, the police, and witnesses may say to anyone. See American Bar Association Project on Standards for Criminal Justice, Fair Trial and Free Press 2-15 (App. Draft 1968).

We have noted earlier that pretrial publicity, even if pervasive and concentrated, cannot be regarded as leading automatically and in every kind of criminal case to an unfair trial. The decided cases "cannot be made to stand for the proposition that juror exposure to information about a state defendant's prior convictions or to news accounts of the crime with which he is charged alone presumptively deprives the defendant of due process." Murphy v. Florida, 421 U.S., at 799, 95 S.Ct., at 2036. Appellate evaluations as to the impact of publicity take into account what other measures were used to mitigate the adverse effects of publicity. The more difficult prospective or predictive assessment that a trial judge must make also calls for a judgment as to whether other precautionary steps will suffice.

We have therefore examined this record to determine the probable efficacy of the measures short of prior restraint on the press and speech. There is no finding that alternative measures would not have protected Simants' rights, and the Nebraska Supreme Court did no more than imply that such measures might not be adequate. Moreover, the record is lacking in evidence to support such a finding.

C

We must also assess the probable efficacy of prior restraint on publication as a workable method of protecting Simants' right to a fair trial, and we cannot ignore the reality of the problems of managing and enforcing pretrial restraining orders . . . .

Finally, we note that the events disclosed by the record took place in a community of 850 people. It is reasonable to assume that, without any news accounts being printed or broadcast, rumors would travel swiftly by word of mouth. One can only speculate on the accuracy of such reports, given the generative propensities of rumors; they could well be more damaging than reasonably accurate news accounts. But plainly a whole community cannot be restrained from discussing a subject intimately affecting life within it.

Given these practical problems, it is far from clear that prior restraint on publication would have protected Simants' rights.

D

Finally, another feature of this case leads us to conclude that the restrictive order entered here is not supportable. At the outset the County Court entered a very broad restrictive order, the terms of which are not before us; it then held a preliminary hearing open to the public and the press. There was testimony concerning at least two incriminating statements made by Simants to private persons; the statement evidently a confession that he gave to law enforcement officials was also introduced. The State District Court's later order was entered after this public hearing and, as modified by the Nebraska Supreme Court, enjoined reporting of (1) "(c)onfessions or admissions against interests made by the accused to law enforcement officials"; (2) "(c) onfessions or admissions against interest, oral or written, if any, made by the accused to third parties, excepting any statements, if any, made by the accused to representatives of the news media"; and (3) all "(o)ther information strongly implicative of the accused as the perpetrator of the slayings." 194 Neb., at 801, 236 N.W.2d, at 805.

To the extent that this order prohibited the reporting of evidence adduced at the open preliminary hearing, it plainly violated settled principles: "(T)here is nothing that proscribes the press from reporting events that transpire in the courtroom." Sheppard v. Maxwell, 384 U.S., at 362-363, 86 S.Ct., at 1522. See also Cox Broadcasting Corp. v. Cohn, 420 U.S. 469, 95 S.Ct. 1029, 43 L.Ed.2d 328 (1975); Craig v. Harney, 331 U.S. 367, 67 S.Ct. 1249, 91 L.Ed.2d 1546 (1947). The County Court could not know that closure of the preliminary hearing was an alternative open to it until the Nebraska Supreme Court so construed state law; but once a public hearing had been held, what transpired there could not be subject to prior restraint . . . .

Our analysis ends as it began, with a confrontation between prior restraint imposed to protect one vital constitutional guarantee and the explicit command of another that the freedom to speak and publish shall not be abridged. We reaffirm that the guarantees of freedom of expression are not an absolute prohibition under all circumstances, but the barriers to prior restraint remain high and the presumption against its use continues intact. We hold that, with respect to the order entered in this case prohibiting reporting or commentary on judicial proceedings held in public, the barriers have not been overcome; to the extent that this order restrained publication of such material, it is clearly invalid. To the extent that it prohibited publication based on information gained from other sources, we conclude that the heavy burden imposed as a condition to securing a prior restraint was not met and the judgment of the Nebraska Supreme Court is therefore

Reversed.

RICHMOND NEWSPAPERS, INC., et al., Appellants,
v.
Commonwealth of VIRGINIA et al.

448 U.S. 555

Supreme Court of the United States

Decided July 2, 1980.

Mr. Chief Justice BURGER announced the judgment of the Court . . . .

The narrow question presented in this case is whether the right of the public and press to attend criminal trials is guaranteed under the United States Constitution.

I

In March 1976, one Stevenson was indicted for the murder of a hotel manager who had been found stabbed to death on December 2, 1975. Tried promptly in July 1976, Stevenson was convicted of second-degree murder in the Circuit Court of Hanover County, Va. The Virginia Supreme Court reversed the conviction in October 1977, holding that a bloodstained shirt purportedly belongingto Stevenson had been improperly admitted into evidence. Stevenson v. Commonwealth, 218 Va. 462, 237 S.E.2d 779.

Stevenson was retried in the same court. This second trial ended in a mistrial on May 30, 1978, when a juror asked to be excused after trial had begun and no alternate was available.

A third trial, which began in the same court on June 6, 1978, also ended in a mistrial. It appears that the mistrial may have been declared because a prospective juror had read about Stevenson's previous trials in a newspaper and had told other prospective jurors about the case before the retrial began. See App. 35a-36a.

Stevenson was tried in the same court for a fourth time beginning on September 11, 1978. Present in the courtroom when the case was called were appellants Wheeler and McCarthy, reporters for appellant Richmond Newspapers, Inc. Before the trial began, counsel for the defendant moved that it be closed to the public:

"[T]here was this woman that was with the family of the deceased when we were here before. She had sat in the Courtroom. I would like to ask that everybody be excluded from the Courtroom because I don't want any information being shuffled back and forth when we have a recess as to what--who testified to what." Tr. of Sept. 11, 1978 Hearing on Defendant's Motion to Close Trial to the Public 2-3.

The trial judge, who had presided over two of the three previous trials, asked if the prosecution had any objection to clearing the courtroom. The prosecutor stated he had no objection and would leave it to the discretion of the court. Id., at 4. Presumably referring to Va.Code § 19.2-266 (Supp.1980), the trial judge then announced: "[T]he statute gives me that power specifically and the defendant has made the motion." He then ordered "that the Courtroom be kept clear of all parties except the witnesses when they testify." Tr., supra, at 4-5. [FN2] The record does not show that any objections to the closure order were made by anyone present at the time, including appellants Wheeler and McCarthy.

> FN2. Virginia Code § 19.2-266 (Supp.1980) provides in part:
> "In the trial of all criminal cases, whether the same be felony or misdemeanor cases, the court may, in its discretion, exclude from the trial any persons whose presence would impair the conduct of a fair trial, provided that the right of the accused to a public trial shall not be violated."

Later that same day, however, appellants sought a hearing on a motion to vacate the closure order. The trial judge granted the request and scheduled a hearing to follow the close of the day's proceedings. When the hearing began, the court ruled that the hearing was to be treated as part of the trial; accordingly, he again ordered the reporters to leave the courtroom, and they complied.

At the closed hearing, counsel for appellants observed that no evidentiary findings had been made by the court prior to the entry of its closure order and pointed out that the court had failed to consider any other, less drastic measures within its power to ensure a fair trial. Tr. of Sept. 11, 1978 Hearing on Motion to Vacate 11-12. Counsel for appellants argued that constitutional considerations mandated that before ordering closure, the court should first decide that the rights of the defendant could be protected in no other way.

Counsel for defendant Stevenson pointed out that this was the fourth time he was standing trial. He also referred to "difficulty with information between the jurors," and stated that he "didn't want information to leak out," be published by the media, perhaps inaccurately, and then be seen by the jurors. Defense counsel argued that these things, plus the fact that "this is a small community," made this a proper case for closure. Id., at 16-18.

The trial judge noted that counsel for the defendant had made similar statements at the morning hearing. The court also stated:

"[O]ne of the other points that we take into consideration in this particular Courtroom is layout of the Courtroom. I think that having people in the Courtroom is distracting to the jury. Now, we have to have certain people in here and maybe that's not a very good reason. When we get into our new Court Building, people can sit in the audience so the jury can't see them. The rule of the Court may be different under those circumstances. . . ." Id., at 19.

The prosecutor again declined comment, and the court summed up by saying:

"I'm inclined to agree with [defense counsel] that, if I feel that the rights of the defendant are infringed in any way, [when] he makes the motion to do something and it doesn't completely override all rights of everyone else, then I'm inclined to go along with the defendant's motion." Id., at 20.

The court denied the motion to vacate and ordered the trial to continue the following morning "with the press and public excluded." Id., at 27; App. 21a.

What transpired when the closed trial resumed the next day was disclosed in the following manner by an order of the court entered September 12, 1978:

"[I]n the absence of the jury, the defendant by counsel made a Motion that a mis-trial be declared, which motion was taken under advisement.

"At the conclusion of the Commonwealth's evidence, the attorney for the defendant moved the Court to strike the Commonwealth's evidence on grounds stated to the record, which Motion was sustained by the Court.

"And the jury having been excused, the Court doth find the accused NOT GUILTY of Murder, as charged in the Indictment, and he was allowed to depart." Id., at 22a.

On September 27, 1978, the trial court granted appellants' motion to intervenenunc pro tunc in the Stevenson case. Appellants then petitioned the Virginia Supreme Court for writs of mandamus and prohibition and filed an appeal from the trial court's closure order. On July 9, 1979, the Virginia Supreme court dismissed the mandamus and prohibition petitions and, finding no reversible error, denied the petition for appeal. Id., at 23a-28a . . . .

II

We begin consideration of this case by noting that the precise issue presented here has not previously been before this Court for decision. In Gannett Co. v. DePasquale, supra, the Court was not required to decide whether a right of access to trials, as distinguished from hearings on pre trial motions, was constitutionally guaranteed. The Court held that the Sixth Amendment's guarantee to the accused of a public trial gave neither the public nor the press an enforceable right of access to a pre trial suppression hearing. One concurring opinion specifically emphasized that "a hearing on a motion before trial to suppress evidence is not a trial . . . ." 443 U.S., at 394, 99 S.Ct., at 2913 (BURGER, C. J., concurring). Moreover, the Court did not decide whether the First and Fourteenth Amendments guarantee a right of the public to attend trials, id., at 392 and n. 24, 99 S.Ct., at 2912, and n. 24; nor did the dissenting opinion reach this issue. Id., at 447, 99 S.Ct., at 2940 (opinion of BLACKMUN, J.) . . . .

A

The origins of the proceeding which has become the modern criminal trial in Anglo-American justice can be traced back beyond reliable historical records. We need not here review all details of its development, but a summary of that history is instructive. What is significant for present purposes is that throughout its evolution, the trial has been open to all who care to observe.

In the days before the Norman Conquest, cases in England were generally brought before moots, such as the local court of the hundred or the county court, which were attended by the freemen of the community. Pollock, English Law Before the Norman Conquest, in 1 Select Essays in Anglo-American Legal History 88, 89 (1907). Somewhat like modern jury duty, attendance at these early meetings was compulsory on the part of the freemen, who were called upon to render judgment. Id., at 89-90; see also 1 W. Holdsworth, A History of English Law 10, 12 (1927).

With the gradual evolution of the jury system in the years after the Norman Conquest, see, e. g., id., at 316, the duty of all freemen to attend trials to render judgment was relaxed, but there is no indication that criminal trials did not remain public. When certain groups were excused from compelled attendance, see the Statute of Marlborough, 52 Hen. 3, ch. 10 (1267); 1 Holdsworth, supra, at 79, and n. 4, the statutory exemption did not prevent them from attending; Lord Coke observed that those excused "are not compellable to come, but left to their own liberty." 2 E. Coke, Institutes of the Laws of England 121 (6th ed. 1681).

Although there appear to be a few contemporary statements on the subject, reports of the Eyre of Kent, a general court held in 1313- 1314, evince a recognition of the importance of public attendance apart from the "jury duty" aspect. It was explained that

"the King's will was that all evil doers should be punished after their deserts, and that justice should be ministered indifferently to rich as to poor; and for the better accomplishing of this, he prayed the community of the county by their attendance there to lend him their aid in the establishing of a happy and certain peace that should be both for the honour of the realm and for their own welfare." 1 Holdsworth, supra, at 268, quoting from the S. S. edition of the Eyre of Kent, vol. i., p. 2 (emphasis added).

From these early times, although great changes in courts and procedures took place, one thing remained constant: the public character of the trial at which guilt or innocence was decided. Sir Thomas Smith, writing in 1565 about "the definitive proceedings in causes criminall," explained that, while the indictment was put in writing as in civil law countries:

"All the rest is doone openlie in the presence of the Judges, the Justices, the enquest, the prisoner, and so manie as will or can come so neare as to heare it, and all depositions and witnesses given aloude, that all men may heare from the mouth of the depositors and witnesses what is saide." T. Smith, De Republica Anglorum 101 (Alston ed. 1972) (emphasis added).

Three centuries later, Sir Frederick Pollock was able to state of the "rule of publicity" that, "[h]ere we have one tradition, at any rate, which has persisted through all changes." F. Pollock, the Expansion of the Common Law 31-32 (1904). See also E. Jenks, The Book of English Law 73-74 (6th ed. 1967): "[O]ne of the most conspicuous features of English justice, that all judicial trials are held in open court, to which the public have free access, . . . appears to have been the rule in England from time immemorial."

We have found nothing to suggest that the presumptive openness of the trial, which English courts were later to call "one of the essential qualities of a court of justice," Daubney v. Cooper, 10 B. & C. 237, 240, 109 Eng.Rep. 438, 440 (K. B. 1829), was not also an attribute of the judicial systems of colonial America. In Virginia, for example, such records as there are of early criminal trials indicate that they were open, and nothing to the contrary has been cited. See A. Scott, Criminal Law in Colonial Virginia 128-129 (1930); Reinsch, The English Common Law in the Early American Colonies, in 1 Select Essays in Anglo-American Legal History 367, 405 (1907). Indeed, when in the mid-1600's the Virginia Assembly felt that the respect due the courts was "by the clamorous unmannerlynes of the people lost, and order, gravity and decoram which should manifest the authority of a court in the court it selfe neglected," the response was not to restrict the openness of the trials to the public, but instead to prescribe rules for the conduct of those attending them . . . .

B

As we have shown, and as was shown in both the Court's opinion and the dissent in Gannett, 443 U.S., at 384, 386, n. 15, 418-425, 99 S.Ct., at 2908, 2909, n. 15, 2925-2929, the historical evidence demonstrates conclusively that at the time when our organic laws were adopted, criminal trials both here and in England had long been presumptively open. This is no quirk of history; rather, it has long been recognized as an indispensible attribute of an Anglo- American trial. Both Hale in the 17th century and Blackstone in the 18th saw the importance of openness to the proper functioning of a trial; it gave assurance that the proceedings were conducted fairly to all concerned, and it discouraged perjury, the misconduct of participants, and decisions based on secret bias or partiality. See, e. g., M. Hale, The History of the Common Law of England 343-345 (6th ed. 1820); 3 W. Blackstone, Commentaries *372-* 373. Jeremy Bentham not only recognized the therapeutic value of open justice but regarded it as the keystone:

"Without publicity, all other checks are insufficient: in comparison of publicity, all other checks are of small account. Recordation, appeal, whatever other institutions might present themselves in the character of checks, would be found to operate rather as cloaks than checks; as cloaks in reality, as checks only in appearance." 1 J. Bentham, Rationale of Judicial Evidence 524 (1827).

Panegyrics on the values of openness were by no means confined to self-praise by the English. Foreign observers of English criminal procedure in the 18th and early 19th centuries came away impressed by the very fact that they had been freely admitted to the courts, as many were not in their own homelands. See L. Radzinowicz, A History of English Criminal Law 715, and n. 96 (1948). They marveled that "the whole juridical procedure passes in public," 2 P. Grosley, A Tour to London; or New Observations on England 142 (Nugent trans. 1772), quoted in Radzinowicz, supra, at 717, and one commentator declared:

"The main excellence of the English judicature consists in publicity, in the free trial by jury, and in the extraordinary despatch with which business is transacted. The publicity of their proceedings is indeed astonishing. Free access to the courts is universally granted." C. Goede, A Foreigner's Opinion of England 214 (Horne trans. 1822). (Emphasis added.)

The nexus between openness, fairness, and the perception of fairness was not lost on them: "[T]he judge, the counsel, and the jury, are constantly exposed to public animadversion; and this greatly tends to augment the extraordinary confidence, which the English repose in the administration of justice." Id., at 215.

This observation raises the important point that "[t]he publicity of a judicial proceeding is a requirement of much broader bearing than its mere effect upon the quality of testimony." 6 J. Wigmore, Evidence § 1834, p. 435 (J. Chadbourn rev. 1976). The early history of open trials in part reflects the widespread acknowledgment, long before there were behavioral scientists, that public trials had significant community therapeutic value. Even without such experts to frame the concept in words, people sensed from experience and observation that, especially in the administration of criminal justice, the means used to achieve justice must have the support derived from public acceptance of both the process and its results . . . .

People in an open society do not demand infallibility from their institutions, but it is difficult for them to accept what they are prohibited from observing. When a criminal trial is conducted in the open, there is at least an opportunity both for understanding the system in general and its workings in a particular case:

"The educative effect of public attendance is a material advantage. Not only is respect for the law increased and intelligent acquaintance acquired with the methods of government, but a strong confidence in judicial remedies is secured which could never be inspired by a system of secrecy." 6 Wigmore, supra, at 438. See also 1 J. Bentham, Rationale of Judicial Evidence, at 525.

In earlier times, both in England and America, attendance at court was a common mode of "passing the time." See, e. g., 6 Wigmore, supra, at 436; Mueller, supra, at 6. With the press, cinema, and electronic media now supplying the representations or reality of the real life drama once available only in the courtroom, attendance at court is no longer a widespread pastime. Yet "[i]t is not unrealistic even in this day to believe that public inclusion affords citizens a form of legal education and hopefully promotes confidence in the fair administration of justice." State v. Schmit, 273 Minn. 78, 87-88, 139 N.W.2d 800, 807 (1966). Instead of acquiring information about trials by firsthand observation or by word of mouth from those who attended, people now acquire it chiefly through the print and electronic media. In a sense, this validates the media claim of functioning as surrogates for the public . . . .

C

From this unbroken, uncontradicted history, supported by reasons as valid today as in centuries past, we are bound to conclude that a presumption of openness inheres in the very nature of a criminal trial under our system of justice . . . .

III

C

The State argues that the Constitution nowhere spells out a guarantee for the right of the public to attend trials, and that accordingly no such right is protected. The possibility that such a contention could be made did not escape the notice of the Constitution's draftsmen; they were concerned that some important rights might be thought disparaged because not specifically guaranteed. It was even argued that because of this danger no Bill of Rights should be adopted. See, e. g., The Federalist No. 84 (A. Hamilton). In a letter to Thomas Jefferson in October 1788, James Madison explained why he, although "in favor of a bill of rights," had "not viewed it in an important light" up to that time: "I conceive that in a certain degree . . . the rights in question are reserved by the manner in which the federal powers are granted." He went on to state that "there is great reason to fear that a positive declaration of some of the most essential rights could not be obtained in the requisite latitude." 5 Writings of James Madison 271 (G. Hunt ed. 1904).

But arguments such as the State makes have not precluded recognition of important rights not enumerated. Notwithstanding the appropriate caution against reading into the Constitution rights not explicitly defined, the Court has acknowledged that certain unarticulated rights are implicit in enumerated guarantees. For example, the rights of association and of privacy, the right to be presumed innocent, and the right to be judged by a standard of proof beyond a reasonable doubt in a criminal trial, as well as the right to travel, appear nowhere in the Constitution or Bill of Rights. Yet these important but unarticulated rights have nonetheless been found to share constitutional protection in common with explicit guarantees. The concerns expressed by Madison and others have thus been resolved; fundamental rights, even though not expressly guaranteed, have been recognized by the Court as indispensable to the enjoyment of rights explicitly defined.

We hold that the right to attend criminal trials is implicit in the guarantees of the First Amendment; without the freedom to attend such trials, which people have exercised for centuries, important aspects of freedom of speech and "of the press could be eviscerated." Branzburg, 408 U.S., at 681, 92 S.Ct., at 2656.

D

Having concluded there was a guaranteed right of the public under the First and Fourteenth Amendments to attend the trial of Stevenson's case, we return to the closure order challengedby appellants. The Court in Gannett made clear that although the Sixth Amendment guarantees the accused a right to a public trial, it does not give a right to a private trial. 443 U.S., at 382, 99 S.Ct., at 2907. Despite the fact that this was the fourth trial of the accused, the trial judge made no findings to support closure; no inquiry was made as to whether alternative solutions would have met the need to ensure fairness; there was no recognition of any right under the Constitution for the public or press to attend the trial. In contrast to the pretrial proceeding dealt with in Gannett, there exist in the context of the trial itself various tested alternatives to satisfy the constitutional demands of fairness. See e. g., Nebraska Press Assn. v. Stuart, 427 U.S., at 563-565, 96 S.Ct., at 2804-2805; Sheppard v. Maxwell, 384 U.S., at 357-362, 86 S.Ct., at 1519-1522. There was no suggestion that any problems with witnesses could not have been dealt with by their exclusion from the courtroom or their sequestration during the trial. See id., at 359, 86 S.Ct., at 1520. Nor is there anything to indicate that sequestration of the jurors would not have guarded against their being subjected to any improper information. All of the alternatives admittedly present difficulties for trial courts, but none of the factors relied on here was beyond the realm of the manageable. Absent an overriding interest articulated in findings, the trial of a criminal case must be open to the public. Accordingly, the judgment under review is

Reversed.

Mr. Justice POWELL took no part in the consideration or decision of this case.

PRESS-ENTERPRISE COMPANY, etc., Petitioner

v.

SUPERIOR COURT OF CALIFORNIA FOR the COUNTY OF RIVERSIDE.

478 U.S. 1

Supreme Court of the United States

Decided June 30, 1986.

Chief Justice BURGER delivered the opinion of the Court.

We granted certiorari to decide whether petitioner has a First Amendment right of access to the transcript of a preliminary hearing growing out of a criminal prosecution.

I

On December 23, 1981, the State of California filed a complaint in the Riverside County Municipal Court, charging Robert Diaz with 12 counts of murder and seeking the death penalty. The complaint alleged that Diaz, a nurse, murdered 12 patients by administering massive doses of the heart drug lidocaine. The preliminary hearing on the complaint commenced on July 6, 1982. Diaz moved to exclude the public from the proceedings under Cal. Penal Code Ann. § 868 (West 1985), which requires such proceedings to be open unless "exclusion of the public is necessary in order to protect the defendant's right to a fair and impartial trial." The Magistrate granted the unopposed motion, finding that closure was necessary because the case had attracted national publicity and "only one side may get reported in the media." App. 22a.

The preliminary hearing continued for 41 days. Most of the testimony and the evidence presented by the State was medical and scientific; the remainder consisted of testimony by personnel who worked with Diaz on the shifts when the 12 patients died. Diaz did not introduce any evidence, but his counsel subjected most of the witnesses to vigorous cross-examination. Diaz was held to answer on all charges. At the conclusion of the hearing, petitioner Press-Enterprise Company asked that the transcript of the proceedings be released. The Magistrate refused and sealed the record.

On January 21, 1983, the State moved in Superior Court to have the transcript of the preliminary hearing released to the public; petitioner later joined in support of the motion. Diaz opposed the motion, contending that release of the transcript would result in prejudicial pretrial publicity. The Superior Court found that the information in the transcript was "as factual as it could be," and that the facts were neither "inflammatory" nor "exciting," but that there was, nonetheless, "a reasonable likelihood that release of all or any part of the transcripts might prejudice defendant's right to a fair and impartial trial." Id., at 60a-61a.

Petitioner then filed a peremptory writ of mandate with the Court of Appeal. That court originally denied the writ but, after being so ordered by the California Supreme Court, set the matter for a hearing. Meanwhile, Diaz waived his right to a jury trial and the Superior Court released the transcript. After holding that the controversy was not moot, the Court of Appeal denied the writ of mandate.

The California Supreme Court thereafter denied petitioner's peremptory writ of mandate, holding that there is no general First Amendment right of access to preliminary hearings. 37 Cal.3d 772, 209 Cal.Rptr. 360, 691 P.2d 1026 (1984). The court reasoned that the right of access to criminal proceedings recognized in Press-Enterprise Co. v. Superior Court, 464 U.S. 501, 104 S.Ct. 819, 78 L.Ed.2d 629 (1984) (Press-Enterprise I), and Globe Newspaper Co. v. Superior Court, 457 U.S. 596, 102 S.Ct. 2613, 73 L.Ed.2d 248 (1982), extended only to actual criminal trials. 37 Cal.3d, at 776, 209 Cal.Rptr., at 362, 691 P.2d, at 1028. Furthermore, the reasons that had been asserted for closing the proceedings in Press-Enterprise I and Globe--the interests of witnesses and other third parties--were not the same as the right asserted in this case--the defendant's right to a fair and impartial trial by a jury uninfluenced by news accounts.

Having found no general First Amendment right of access, the court then considered the circumstances in which the closure would be proper under the California access statute, Cal.Penal Code Ann. § 868 (West 1985). Under the statute, the court reasoned, if the defendant establishes a "reasonable likelihood of substantial prejudice" the burden shifts to the prosecution or the media to show by a preponderance of the evidence that there is no such reasonable probability of prejudice. 37 Cal.3d, at 782, 209 Cal.Rptr., at 366, 691 P.2d, at 1032.

We granted certiorari. 474 U.S. 899, 106 S.Ct. 224, 88 L.Ed.2d 223 (1985). We reverse.

II

We must first consider whether we have jurisdiction under Article III, § 2, of the Constitution. In this Court, petitioner challenges the Superior Court's original refusal to release the transcript of the preliminary hearing. As noted above, the specific relief petitioner seeks has already been granted--the transcript of the preliminary hearing was released after Diaz waived his right to a jury trial. However, as in Globe Newspaper, supra, 457 U.S., at 603, 102 S.Ct., at 2618, and Gannett Co. v. DePasquale, 443 U.S. 368, 377-378, 99 S.Ct. 2898, 2904-05, 61 L.Ed.2d 608 (1979), this controversy is " 'capable of repetition, yet evading review.' " It can reasonably be assumed that petitioner will be subjected to a similar closure order and, because criminal proceedings are typically of short duration, such an order will likely evade review. Globe and Gannett, therefore, require the conclusion that this case is not moot. Accordingly, we turn to the merits.

III

It is important to identify precisely what the California Supreme Court decided:

"[W]e conclude that the magistrate shall close the preliminary hearing upon finding a reasonable likelihood of substantial prejudice which would impinge upon the right to a fair trial. Penal code section 868 makes clear that the primary right is the right to a fair trial and that the public's right of access must give way when there is conflict." 37 Cal.3d, at 781, 209 Cal.Rptr., at 366, 691 P.2d, at 1032.

It is difficult to disagree in the abstract with that court's analysis balancing the defendant's right to a fair trial against the public right of access. It is also important to remember that these interests are not necessarily inconsistent. Plainly, the defendant has a right to a fair trial but, as we have repeatedly recognized, one of the important means of assuring a fair trial is that the process be open to neutral observers.

The right to an open public trial is a shared right of the accused and the public, the common concern being the assurance of fairness. Only recently, in Waller v. Georgia, 467 U.S. 39, 104 S.Ct. 2210, 81 L.Ed.2d 31 (1984), for example, we considered whether the defendant's Sixth Amendment right to an open trial prevented the closure of a suppression hearing over the defendant's objection. We noted that the First Amendment right of access would in most instances attach to such proceedings and that "the explicit Sixth Amendment right of the accused is no less protective of a public trial than the implicit First Amendment right of the press and public." Id., at 46, 104 S.Ct., at 2215. When the defendant objects to the closure of a suppression hearing, therefore, the hearing must be open unless the party seeking to close the hearing advances an overriding interest that is likely to be prejudiced. Id., at 47, 104 S.Ct., at 2216.

Here, unlike Waller, the right asserted is not the defendant's Sixth Amendment right to a public trial since the defendant requested a closed preliminary hearing. Instead, the right asserted here is that of the public under the First Amendment. See Gannett, supra, 443 U.S., at 397, 99 S.Ct., at 2914 (POWELL, J., concurring). The California Supreme Court concluded that the First Amendment was not implicated because the proceeding was not a criminal trial, but a preliminary hearing. However, the First Amendment question cannot be resolved solely on the label we give the event, i.e., "trial" or otherwise, particularly where the preliminary hearing functions much like a full-scale trial.

In cases dealing with the claim of a First Amendment right of access to criminal proceedings, our decisions have emphasized two complementary considerations. First, because, a " 'tradition of accessibility implies the favorable judgment of experiences' " Globe Newspaper, 457 U.S., at 605, 102 S.Ct., at 2619 (quoting Richmond Newspapers, Inc. v. Virginia, 448 U.S. 555, 589, 100 S.Ct. 2814, 2834, 65 L.Ed.2d 973 (1980) (BRENNAN, J., concurring in judgment)), we have considered whether the place and process have historically been open to the press and general public.

In Press-Enterprise I, for example, we observed that "since the development of trial by jury, the process of selection of jurors has presumptively been a public process with exceptions only for good cause shown." 464 U.S., at 505, 104 S.Ct., at 822. In Richmond Newspapers, we reviewed some of the early history of England's open trials from the day when a trial was much like a "town meeting." In the days before the Norman Conquest, criminal cases were brought before "moots," a collection of the freemen in the community. The public trial, "one of the essential qualities of a court of justice" in England, was recognized early on in the Colonies. There were risks, of course, inherent in such a "town meeting" trial--the risk that it might become a gathering moved by emotions or passions growing from the nature of a crime; a "lynch mob" ambience is hardly conducive to calm, reasoned decision-makingbased on evidence. Plainly the modern trial with jurors open to interrogation for possible bias is a far cry from the "town meeting trial" of ancient English practice. Yet even our modern procedural protections have their origin in the ancient common-law principle which provided, not for closed proceedings, but rather for rules of conduct for those who attend trials. Richmond Newspapers, supra, 448 U.S. at 567, 100 S.Ct., at 2822.

Second, in this setting the Court has traditionally considered whether public access plays a significant positive role in the functioning of the particular process in question. Globe Newspaper, supra, 457 U.S., at 606, 102 S.Ct., at 2619. Although many governmental processes operate best under public scrutiny, it takes little imagination to recognize that there are some kinds of government operations that would be totally frustrated if conducted openly. A classic example is that "the proper functioning of our grand jury system depends upon the secrecy of grand jury proceedings." Douglas Oil Co. v. Petrol Stops Northwest, 441 U.S. 211, 218, 99 S.Ct. 1667, 1672, 60 L.Ed.2d 156 (1979). Other proceedings plainly require public access. In Press-Enterprise I, we summarized the holdings of prior cases, noting that openness in criminal trials, including the selection of jurors, "enhances both the basic fairness of the criminal trial and the appearance of fairness so essential to public confidence in the system." 464 U.S., at 501, 104 S.Ct., at 820.

These considerations of experience and logic are, of course, related, for history and experience shape the functioning of governmental processes. If the particular proceeding in question passes these tests of experience and logic, a qualified First Amendment right of public access attaches. But even when a right of access attaches, it is not absolute. Globe Newspaper Co. v. Superior Court, supra, 457 U.S., at 606, 102 S.Ct., at 2619. While open criminal proceedings give assurances of fairness to both the public and the accused, there are some limited circumstances in which the right of the accused to a fair trial might be undermined by publicity. In such cases, the trial court must determine whether the situation is such that the rights of the accused override the qualified First Amendment right of access. In Press-Enterprise I we stated:

> "[T]he presumption may be overcome only by an overriding interest based on findings that closure is essential to preserve higher values and is narrowly tailored to serve that interest. The interest is to be articulated along with findings specific enough that a reviewing court can determine whether the closure order was properly entered." 464 U.S., at 510, 104 S.Ct... 824.

IV

A

The considerations that led the Court to apply the First Amendment right of access to criminal trials in Richmond Newspapers and Globe and the selection of jurors in Press-Enterprise I lead us to conclude that the right of access applies to preliminary hearings as conducted in California.

First, there has been a tradition of accessibility to preliminary hearings of the type conducted in California. Although grand jury proceedings have traditionally been closed to the public and the accused, preliminary hearings conducted before neutral and detached magistrates have been open to the public. Long ago in the celebrated trial of Aaron Burr for treason, for example, with Chief Justice Marshall sitting as trial judge, the probable-cause hearing was held in the Hall of the House of Delegates in Virginia, the courtroom being too small to accommodate the crush of interested citizens. United States v. Burr, 25 F.Cas. 1 (No. 14,692) (CC Va.1807). From Burr until the present day, the near uniform practice of state and federal courts has been to conduct preliminary hearings in open court. As we noted in Gannett, several States following the original New York Field Code of Criminal Procedure published in 1850 have allowed preliminary hearings to be closed on the motion of the accused. 443 U.S., at 390-391, 99 S.Ct., at 2911. But even in these States the proceedings are presumptively open to the public and are closed only for cause shown. Open preliminary hearings, therefore, have been accorded " 'the favorable judgment of experience.' " Globe, supra, 457 U.S., at 605, 102 S.Ct., at 2619.

The second question is whether public access to preliminary hearings as they are conducted in California plays a particularly significant positive role in the actual functioning of the process. We have already determined in Richmond Newspapers, Globe, and Press-Enterprise I that public access to criminal trials and the selection of jurors is essential to the proper functioning of the criminal justice system. California preliminary hearings are sufficiently like a trial to justify the same conclusion.

In California, to bring a felon to trial, the prosecutor has a choice of securing a grand jury indictment or a finding of probable cause following a preliminary hearing. Even when the accused has been indicted by a grand jury, however, he has an absolute right to an elaborate preliminary hearing before a neutral magistrate. Hawkins v. Superior Court, 22 Cal.3d 584, 150 Cal.Rptr. 435, 437, 586 P.2d 916, 918 (1978). The accused has the right to personally appear at the hearing, to be represented by counsel, to cross-examine hostile witnesses, to present exculpatory evidence, and to exclude illegally obtained evidence. Cal.Penal Code Ann. §§ 859-866 (West 1985), § 1538.5 (West Supp.1986). If the magistrate determines that probable cause exists, the accused is bound over for trial; such a finding leads to a guilty plea in the majority of cases.

It is true that unlike a criminal trial, the California preliminary hearing cannot result in the conviction of the accused and the adjudication is before a magistrate or other judicial officer without a jury. But these features, standing alone, do not make public access any less essential to the proper functioning of the proceedings in the overall criminal justice process. Because of its extensive scope, the preliminary hearing is often the final and most important step in the criminal proceeding. See Waller v. Georgia, 467 U.S., at 46-47, 104 S.Ct., at 2215-2216. As the California Supreme Court stated in San Jose Mercury-News v. Municipal Court, 30 Cal.3d 498, 511, 179 Cal.Rptr. 772, 780, 638 P.2d 655, 663 (1982), the preliminary hearing in many cases provides "the sole occasion for public observation of the criminal justice system." See also Richmond Newspapers, 448 U.S., at 572, 100 S.Ct., at 2825.

Similarly, the absence of a jury, long recognized as "an inestimable safeguard against the corrupt or overzealous prosecutor and against the complaint, biased, or eccentric judge," Duncan v. Louisiana, 391 U.S. 145, 156, 88 S.Ct. 1444, 1451, 20 L.Ed.2d 491 (1968), makes the importance of public access to a preliminary hearing even more significant. "People in an open society do not demand infallibility from their institutions, but it is difficult for them to accept what they are prohibited from observing." Richmond Newspapers, 448 U.S., at 572, 100 S.Ct., at 2825.

Denying the transcript of a 41-day preliminary hearing would frustrate what we have characterized as the "community therapeutic value" of openness. Id., at 570, 100 S.Ct., at 2824. Criminal acts, especially certain violent crimes, provoke public concern, outrage, and hostility. "When the public is aware that the law is being enforced and the criminal justice system is functioning, an outlet is provided for these understandable reactions and emotions." Press-Enterprise I, 464 U.S., at 509, 104 S.Ct., at 823. See also H. Weihofen, The Urge to Punish 130-131 (1956); T. Reik, The Compulsion to Confess (1959). In sum:

> "The value of openness lies in the fact that people not actually attending trials can have confidence that standards of fairness are being observed; the sure knowledge that anyone is free to attend gives assurance that established procedures are being followed and that deviations will become known. Openness thus enhances both the basic fairness of the criminal trial and the appearance of fairness so essential to public confidence in the system." Press- Enterprise I, supra, at 508, 104 S.Ct., at 823 (emphasis in original).

We therefore conclude that the qualified First Amendment right of access to criminal proceedings applies to preliminary hearings as they are conducted in California.

B

Since a qualified First Amendment right of access attaches to preliminary hearings in California under Cal.Penal Code Ann. § 858 et seq. (West 1985), the proceedings cannot be closed unless specific, on the record findings are made demonstrating that "closure is essential to preserve higher values and is narrowly tailored to serve that interest." Press- Enterprise I, supra, at 510, 104 S.Ct., at 824. . . . If the interest asserted is the right of the accused to a fair trial, the preliminary hearing shall be closed only if specific findings are made demonstrating that, first, there is a substantial probability that the defendant's right to a fair trial will be prejudiced by publicity that closure would prevent and, second, reasonable alternatives to closure cannot adequately protect the defendant's fair trial rights. See Press-Enterprise I, supra; Richmond Newspapers, supra, 448 U.S., at 581, 100 S.Ct., at 2829.

The California Supreme Court, interpreting its access statute, concluded that "the magistrate shall close the preliminary hearing upon finding a reasonable likelihood of substantial prejudice." 37 Cal.3d, at 781, 209 Cal.Rptr., at 366, 691 P.2d, at 1032. As the court itself acknowledged, the "reasonable likelihood" test places a lesser burden on the defendant than the "substantial probability" test which we hold is called for by the First Amendment. See ibid.; see also id., at 783, 209 Cal.Rptr., at 367, 691 P.2d, at 1033 (Lucas, J., concurring and dissenting). Moreover, the court failed to consider whether alternatives short of complete closure would have protected the interests of the accused.

In Gannett we observed:

"Publicity concerning pretrial suppression hearings such as the one involved in the present case poses special risks of unfairness. The whole purpose of such hearings is to screen out unreliable or illegally obtained evidence and insure that this evidence does not become known to the jury. Cf. Jackson v. Denno, 378 U.S. 368 [84 S.Ct. 1774, 12 L.Ed.2d 908]. Publicity concerning the proceedings at a pretrial hearing, however, could influence public opinion against a defendant and inform potential jurors of inculpatory information wholly inadmissible at the actual trial." 443 U.S., at 378, 99 S.Ct., at 2905.

But this risk of prejudice does not automatically justify refusing public access to hearings on every motion to suppress. Through voir dire, cumbersome as it is in some circumstances, a court can identify those jurors whose prior knowledge of the case would disable them from rendering an impartial verdict. And even if closure were justified for the hearings on a motion to suppress, closure of an entire 41-day proceeding would rarely be warranted. The First Amendment right of access cannot be overcome by the conclusory assertion that publicity might deprive the defendant of that right. And any limitation must be "narrowly tailored to serve that interest." Press-Enterprise I, supra, 464 U.S., at 510, 104 S.Ct., at 824.

The standard applied by the California Supreme Court failed to consider the First Amendment right of access to criminal proceedings. Accordingly, the judgment of the California Supreme Court is reversed.

It is so ordered.

Justice STEVENS, with whom Justice REHNQUIST joins as to Part II, dissenting.

Billie Sol ESTES, Petitioner,
v.
STATE OF TEXAS.

381 U.S. 532

Supreme Court of the United States

Decided June 7, 1965.

Mr. Justice CLARK delivered the opinion of the Court.

The question presented here is whether the petitioner, who stands convicted in the District Court for the Seventh Judicial District of Texas at Tyler for swindling, was deprived of his right under the Fourteenth Amendment to due process by the televising and broadcasting of his trial. Both the trial court and the Texas Court of Criminal Appeals found against the petitioner. We hold to the contrary and reverse his conviction.

I.

While petitioner recites his claim in the framework of Canon 35 of the Judicial Canons of the American Bar Association he does not contend that we should enshrine Canon 35 in the Fourteenth Amendment, but only that the time honored principles of a fair trial were not followed in his case and that he was thus convicted without due process of law. Canon 35, of course, has of itself no binding effect on the courts but merely expresses the view of the Association in opposition to the broadcasting, televising and photographing of court proceedings. Likewise, Judicial Canon 28 of the Integrated State Bar of Texas, 27 Tex.B.J. 102 (1964), which leaves to the trial judge's sound discretion the telecasting and photographing of court proceedings, is of itself not law. In short, the question here is not the validity of either Canon 35 of the American Bar Association or Canon 28 of the State Bar of Texas, but only whether petitioner was tried in a manner which comports with the due process requirement of the Fourteenth Amendment.

Petitioner's case was originally called for trial on September 24, 1962, in Smith County after a change of venue from Reeves County, some 500 miles west. Massive pretrial publicity totaling 11 volumes of press clippings, which are on file with the Clerk, had given it national notoriety. All available seats in the courtroom were taken and some 30 persons stood in the aisles. However, at that time a defense motion to prevent telecasting, broadcasting by radio and news photography and a defense motion for continuance were presented, and after a two-day hearing the former was denied and the latter granted.

These initial hearings were carried live by both radio and television, and news photography was permitted throughout. The videotapes of these hearings clearly illustrate that the picture presented was not one of that judicial serenity and calm to which petitioner was entitled. Cf. Wood v. Georgia, 370 U.S. 375, 383, 82 S.Ct. 1364, 1369, 8 L.Ed.2d 569 (1962); Turner v. State of Louisiana, 379 U.S. 466, 472, 85 S.Ct. 546, 549, 13 L.Ed.2d 424 (1965); Cox v. State of Louisiana, 379 U.S. 559, 562, 85 S.Ct. 476, 479, 13 L.Ed.2d 487 (1965). Indeed, at least 12 cameramen were engaged in the courtroom throughout the hearing taking motion and still pictures and televising the proceedings. Cables and wires were snaked across the courtroom floor, three microphones were on the judge's bench and others were beamed at the jury box and the counsel table. It is conceded that the activities of the television crews and news photographers led to considerable disruption of the hearings. Moreover, veniremen had been summoned and were present in the courtroom during the entire hearing but were later released after petitioner's motion for continuance had been granted. The court also had the names of the witnesses called; some answered but the absence of others led to a continuance of the case until October 22, 1962. It is contended that this two-day pretrial hearing cannot be considered in determining the question before us. We cannot agree. Pretrial can create a major problem for the defendant in a criminal case. Indeed, it may be more harmful than publicity during the trial for it may well set the community opinion as to guilt or innocence. Though the September hearings dealt with motions to prohibit television coverage and to postpone the trial, they are unquestionably relevant to the issue before us. All of this two-day affair was highly publicized and could only have impressed those present, and also the community at large, with the notorious character of the petitioner as well as the proceeding. The trial witnesses present at the hearing, as well as the original jury panel, were undoubtedly made aware of the peculiar public importance of the case by the press and television coverage being provided, and by the fact that they themselves were televised live and their pictures rebroadcast on the evening show.

When the case was called for trial on October 22 the scene had been altered. A booth had been constructed at the back of the courtroom which was painted to blend with the permanent structure of the room. It had an aperture to allow the lens of the cameras an unrestricted view of the courtroom. All television cameras and newsreel photographers were restricted to the area of the booth when shooting film or telecasting.

Because of continual objection, the rules governing live telecasting, as well as radio and still photos, were changed as the exigencies of the situation seemed to require. As a result, live telecasting was prohibited during a great portion of the actual trial. Only the opening and closing arguments of the State, the return of the jury's verdict and its receipt by the trial judge were carried live with sound. Although the order allowed videotapes of the entire proceeding without sound, the cameras operated only intermittently, recording various portions of the trial for broadcast on regularly scheduled newscasts later in the day and evening. At the request of the petitioner, the trial judge prohibited coverage of any kind, still or television, of the defense counsel during their summations to the jury.

Because of the varying restrictions placed on sound and live telecasting the telecasts of the trial were confined largely to film clips shown on the stations' regularly scheduled news programs. The news commentators would use the film of a particular part of the day's trial activities as a backdrop for their reports. Their commentary included excerpts from testimony and the usual reportorial remarks. On one occasion the videotapes of the September hearings were rebroadcast in place of the 'late movie' . . . .

VI.

As has been said, the chief function of our judicial machinery is to ascertain the truth. The use of television, however, cannot be said to contribute materially to this objective. Rather its use amounts to the injection of an irrelevant factor into court proceedings. In addition experience teaches that there are numerous situations in which it might cause actual unfairness--some so subtle as to defy detection by the accused or control by the judge. We enumerate some in summary:

1. The potential impact of television on the jurors is perhaps of the greatest significance. They are the nerve center of the fact-finding process. It is true that in States like Texas where they are required to be sequestered in trials of this nature the jurors will probably not see any of the proceedings as televised from the courtroom. But the inquiry cannot end there. From the moment the trial judge announces that a case will be televised it becomes a cause ce le bre. The whole community, including prospective jurors, becomes interested in all the morbid details surrounding it. The approaching trial immediately assumes an important status in the public press and the accused is highly publicized along with the offense with which he is charged. Every juror carries with him into the jury box these solemn facts and thus increases the change of prejudice that is present in every criminal case. And we must remember that realistically it is only the notorious trial which will be broadcast, because of the necessity for paid sponsorship. The conscious or unconscious effect that this may have on the juror's judgment cannot be evaluated, but experience indicates that it is not only possible but highly probable that it will have a direct bearing on his vote as to guilt or innocence. Where pretrial publicity of all kinds has created intense public feeling which is aggravated by the telecasting or picturing of the trial the televised jurors cannot help but feel the pressures of knowing that friends and neighbors have their eyes upon them. If the community be hostile to an accused a televised juror, realizing that he must return to neighbors who saw the trial themselves, may well be led 'not to hold the balance nice, clear and true between the State and the accused. * * *'

Moreover, while it is practically impossible to assess the effect of television on jury attentiveness, those of us who know juries realize the problem of jury 'distraction.' The State argues this is de minimis since the physical disturbances have been eliminated. But we know that distractions are not caused solely by the physical presence of the camera and its telltale red lights. It is the awareness of the fact of telecasting that is felt by the juror throughout the trial. We are all self-conscious and uneasy when being televised. Human nature being what it is, not only will a juror's eyes be fixed on the camera, but also his mind will be preoccupied with the telecasting rather than with the testimony.

Furthermore, in many States the jurors serving in the trial may see the broadcasts of the trial proceedings. Admittedly, the Texas sequestration rule would prevent this occurring there. In other States following no such practice jurors would return home and turn on the TV if only to see how they appeared upon it. They would also be subjected to reenactment and emphasis of the selected parts of the proceedings which the requirements of the broadcasters determined would be telecast and would be subconsciously influenced the more by that testimony. Moreover, they would be subjected to the broadest commentary and criticism and perhaps the well-meant advice of friends, relatives and inquiring strangers who recognized them on the streets. Finally, new trials plainly would be jeopardized in that potential jurors will often have seen and heard the original trial when it was telecast. Yet viewers may later be called upon to sit in the jury box during the new trial. These very dangers are illustrated in this case where the court, due to the defendant's objections, permitted only the State's opening and closing arguments to be broadcast with sound to the public.

2. The quality of the testimony in criminal trials will often be impaired. The impact upon a witness of the knowledge that he is being viewed by a vast audience is simply incalculable. Some may be demoralized and frightened, some cocky and given to overstatement; memories may falter, as with anyone speaking publicly, and accuracy of statement may be severely undermined. Embarrassment may impede the search for the truth, as may a natural tendency toward overdramatization. Furthermore, inquisitive strangers and 'cranks' might approach witnesses on the street with jibes, advice or demands for explanation of testimony. There is little wonder that the defendant cannot 'prove' the existence of such factors. Yet we all know from experience that they exist.

In addition the invocation of the rule against witnesses is frustrated. In most instances witnesses would be able to go to their homes and view broadcasts of the day's trial proceedings, notwithstanding the fact that they had been admonished not to do so. They could view and hear the testimony of preceding witnesses, and so shape their own testimony as to make its impact crucial. And even in the absence of sound, the influences of such viewing on the attitude of the witness toward testifying, his frame of mind upon taking the stand or his apprehension of withering cross-examination defy objective assessment. Indeed, the mere fact that the trial is to be televised might render witnesses reluctant to appear and thereby impede the trial as well as the discovery of the truth.

While some of the dangers mentioned above are present as well in newspaper coverage of any important trial, the circumstances and extraneous influences intruding upon the solemn decorum of court procedure in the televised trial are far more serious than in cases involving only newspaper coverage.

3. A major aspect of the problem is the additional responsibilities the presence of television places on the trial judge. His job is to make certain that the accused receives a fair trial. This most difficult task requires his undivided attention. Still when television comes into the

courtroom he must also supervise it. In this trial, for example, the judge on several different occasions--aside from the two days of pretrial--was obliged to have a hearing or enter an order made necessary solely because of the presence of television. Thus, where telecasting is restricted as it was here, and as even the State concedes it must be, his task is made much more difficult and exacting. And, as happened here, such rulings may unfortunately militate against the fairness of the trial. In addition, laying physical interruptions aside, there is the ever-present distraction that the mere awareness of television's presence prompts. Judges are human beings also and are subject to the same psychological reactions as laymen. Telecasting is particularly bad where the judge is elected, as is the case in all save a half dozen of our States. The telecasting of a trial becomes a political weapon, which, along with other distractions inherent in broadcasting, diverts his attention from the task at hand--the fair trial of the accused.

But this is not all. There is the initial decision that must be made as to whether the use of television will be permitted. This is perhaps an even more crucial consideration. Our judges are highminded men and women. But it is difficult to remain oblivious to the pressures that the news media can bring to bear on them both directly and through the shaping of public opinion. Moreover, where one judge in a district or even in a State permits telecasting, the requirement that the others do the same is almost mandatory. Especially is this true where the judge is selected at the ballot box.

4. Finally, we cannot ignore the impact of courtroom television on the defendant. Its presence is a form of mental--if not physical--harassment, resembling a police line-up or the third degree. The inevitable close-ups of his gestures and expressions during the ordeal of his trial might well transgress his personal sensibilities, his dignity, and his ability to concentrate on the proceedings before him--sometimes the difference between life and death--dispassionately, freely and without the distraction of wide public surveillance. A defendant on trial for a specific crime is entitled to his day in court, not in a stadium, or a city or nationwide arena. The heightened public clamor resulting from radio and television coverage will inevitably result in prejudice. Trial by television is, therefore, foreign to our system. Furthermore, telecasting may also deprive an accused of effective counsel. The distractions, intrusions into confidential attorney-client relationships and the temptation offered by television to play to the public audience might often have a direct effect not only upon the lawyers, but the judge, the jury and the witnesses. See Pye, The Lessons of Dallas--Threats to Fair Trial and Free Press, National Civil Liberties Clearing House, 16th Annual Conference.

The television camera is a powerful weapon. Intentionally or inadvertently it can destroy an accused and his case in the eyes of the public. While our telecasters are honorable men, they too are human. The necessity for sponsorship weighs heavily in favor of the televising of only notorious cases, such as this one, and invariably focuses the lens upon the unpopular or infamous accused. Such a selection is necessary in order to obtain a sponsor willing to pay a sufficient fee to cover the costs and return a profit. We have already examined the ways in which public sentiment can affect the trial participants. To the extent that television shapes that sentiment, it can strip the accused of a fair trial . . . .

It is said that the ever-advancing techniques of public communication and the adjustment of the public to its presence may bring about a change in the effect of telecasting upon the fairness of criminal trials. But we are not dealing here with future developments in the field of electronics. Our judgment cannot be rested on the hypothesis of tomorrow but must take the facts as they are presented today.

The judgment is therefore reversed.

Mr. Justice STEWART, whom Mr. Justice BLACK, Mr. Justice BRENNAN, and Mr. Justice WHITE join, dissenting.

I cannot agree with the Court's decision that the circumstances of this trial led to a denial of the petitioner's Fourteenth Amendment rights. I think that the introduction of television into a courtroom, is, at least in the present state of the art, an extremely unwise policy. It invites many constitutional risks, and it detracts from the inherent dignity of a courtroom. But I am unable to escalate this personal view into a per se constitutional rule. And I am unable to find, on the specific record of this case, that the circumstances attending the limited televising of the petitioner's trial resulted in the denial of any right guaranteed to him by the United States Constitution . . . .

Noel CHANDLER and Robert Granger, Appellants,
v.
State of FLORIDA.

449 U.S. 560

Supreme Court of the United States

Decided Jan. 26, 1981.

Chief Justice BURGER delivered the opinion of the Court.

The question presented on this appeal is whether, consistent with constitutional guarantees, a state may provide for radio, television, and still photographic coverage of a criminal trial for public broadcast, notwithstanding the objection of the accused.

I

A

Background. Over the past 50 years, some criminal cases characterized as "sensational" have been subjected to extensive coverage by news media, sometimes seriously interfering with the conduct of the proceedings and creating a setting wholly inappropriate for the administration of justice. Judges, lawyers, and others soon became concerned, and in 1937, after study, the American Bar Association House of Delegates adopted Judicial Canon 35, declaring that all photographic and broadcast coverage of courtroom proceedings should be prohibited. [FN1] In 1952, the House of Delegates amended Canon 35 to proscribe television coverage as well. 77 A.B.A.Rep. 610-611 (1952). The Canon's proscription was reaffirmed in 1972 when the Code of Judicial Conduct replaced the Canons of Judicial Ethics and Canon 3A(7) superseded Canon 35. E. Thode, Reporter's Notes to Code of Judicial Conduct 56-59 (1973). Cf. Fed.Rules Crim.Proc. 53. A majority of the states, including Florida, adopted the substance of the ABA provision and its amendments. In Florida, the rule was embodied in Canon 3A(7) of the Florida Code of Judicial Conduct. [FN2]

FN1. 62 A.B.A.Rep. 1134-1135 (1937). As adopted on September 30, 1937, Judicial Canon 35 read:
"Proceedings in court should be conducted with fitting dignity and decorum. The taking of photographs in the courtroom, during sessions of the court or recesses between sessions, and the broadcasting of court proceedings are calculated to detract from the essential dignity of the proceedings, degrade the court and create misconceptions with respect thereto in the mind of the public and should not be permitted."

FN2. As originally adopted in Florida, Canon 3A(7) provided:
"A judge should prohibit broadcasting, televising, recording, or taking photographs in the courtroom and areas immediately adjacent thereto during sessions of court or recesses between sessions, except that a judge may authorize:
"(a) the use of electronic or photographic means for the presentation of evidence, for the perpetuation of a record, or for other purposes of judicial administration;
"(b) the broadcasting, televising, recording, or photographing of investitive, ceremonial, or naturalization proceedings;
"(c) the photographic or electronic recording and reproduction of appropriate court proceedings under the following conditions;
"(i) the means of recording will not distract participants or impair the dignity of the proceedings;
"(ii) the parties have consented, and the consent to being depicted or recorded has been obtained from each witness appearing in the recording and reproduction;
"(iii) the reproduction will not be exhibited until after the proceeding has been concluded and all direct appeals have been exhausted; and
"(iv) the reproduction will be exhibited only for instructional purposes in educational institutions."

In February 1978, the American Bar Association Committee on Fair Trial-Free Press proposed revised standards. These included a provision permitting courtroom coverage by the electronic media under conditions to be established by local rule and under the control of the trial judge, but only if such coverage was carried out unobtrusively and without affecting the conduct of the trial. The revision was endorsed by the ABA's Standing Committee on Standards for Criminal Justice and by its Committee on Criminal Justice and the Media, but it was rejected by the House of Delegates on February 12, 1979. 65 A.B.A.J. 304 (1979).

In 1978, based upon its own study of the matter, the Conference of State Chief Justices, by a vote of 44 to 1, approved a resolution to allow the highest court of each state to promulgate standards and guidelines regulating radio, television, and other photographic coverage of court proceedings . . . .

B

In July 1977, appellants were charged with conspiracy to commit burglary, grand larceny, and possession of burglary tools. The counts covered breaking and entering a well-known Miami Beach restaurant.

The details of the alleged criminal conduct are not relevant to the issue before us, but several aspects of the case distinguish it from a routine burglary. At the time of their arrest, appellants were Miami Beach policemen. The State's principal witness was John Sion, an amateur radio operator who, by sheer chance, had overheard and recorded conversations between the appellants over their police walkie-talkie radios during the burglary. Not surprisingly, these novel factors attracted the attention of the media.

By pretrial motion, counsel for the appellants sought to have experimental Canon 3A(7) declared unconstitutional on its face and as applied. The trial court denied relief but certified the issue to the Florida Supreme Court. However, the Supreme Court declined to rule on the question, on the ground that it was not directly relevant to the criminal charges against the appellants. State v. Granger, 352 So.2d 175 (1977).

After several additional fruitless attempts by the appellants to prevent electronic coverage of the trial, the jury was selected. At voir dire, the appellants' counsel asked each prospective juror whether he or she would be able to be "fair and impartial" despite the presence of a television camera during some, or all, of the trial. Each juror selected responded that such coverage would not affect his or her consideration in any way. A television camera recorded the voir dire.

A defense motion to sequester the jury because of the television coverage was denied by the trial judge. However, the court instructed the jury not to watch or read anything about the case in the media and suggested that jurors "avoid the local news and watch only the national news on television." App. 13. Subsequently, defense counsel requested that the witnesses be instructed not to watch any television accounts of testimony presented at trial. The trial court declined to give such an instruction, for "no witness' testimony was [being] reported or televised [on the evening news] in any way." Id., at 14.

A television camera was in place for one entire afternoon, during which the State presented the testimony of Sion, its chief witness. No camera was present for the presentation of any part of the case for the defense. The camera returned to cover closing arguments. Only 2 minutes and 55 seconds of the trial below were broadcast--and those depicted only the prosecution's side of the case.

The jury returned a guilty verdict on all counts. Appellants moved for a new trial, claiming that because of the television coverage, they had been denied a fair and impartial trial. No evidence of specific prejudice was tendered.

The Florida District Court of Appeal affirmed the convictions . . . the Florida Supreme Court denied review . . . .

III

Appellants rely chiefly on Estes v. Texas, 381 U.S. 532, 85 S.Ct. 1628, 14 L.Ed.2d 543 (1965), and Chief Justice Warren's separate concurring opinion in that case. They argue that the televising of criminal trials is inherently a denial of due process, and they read Estes as announcing a per se constitutional rule to that effect . . . .

Justice STEWART, joined by Justices BLACK, BRENNAN, and WHITE in dissent, concluded that no prejudice had been shown and that Estes' Fourteenth Amendment rights had not been violated. While expressing reservations not unlike those of Justice Harlan and those of Chief Justice Warren, the dissent expressed unwillingness to "escalate this personal view into a per se constitutional rule." Id., at 601, 85 S.Ct. at 1669. The four dissenters disagreed both with the per se rule embodied in the plurality opinion of Justice Clark and with the judgment of the Court that "the circumstances of [that] trial led to a denial of [Estes'] Fourteenth Amendment rights." Ibid. (emphasis added).

Parsing the six opinions in Estes, one is left with a sense of doubt as to precisely how much of Justice Clark's opinion was joined in, and supported by, Justice Harlan. In an area charged with constitutional nuances, perhaps more should not be expected. Nonetheless, it is fair to say that Justice Harlan viewed the holding as limited to the proposition that "what was done in this case infringed the fundamental right to a fair trial assured by the Due Process Clause of the Fourteenth Amendment," id., 587, 85 S.Ct., at 1662 (emphasis added), he went on:

> "At the present juncture I can only conclude that televised trials, at least in cases like this one, possess such capabilities for interfering with the even course of the judicial process that they are constitutionally banned" . . . .

## IV

Since we are satisfied that Estes did not announce a constitutional rule that all photographic or broadcast coverage of criminal trials is inherently a denial of due process, we turn to consideration, as a matter of first impression, of the appellants' suggestion that we now promulgate such a per se rule.

### A

Any criminal case that generates a great deal of publicity presents some risks that the publicity may compromise the right of the defendant to a fair trial. Trial courts must be especially vigilant to guard against any impairment of the defendant's right to a verdict based solely upon the evidence and the relevant law. Over the years, courts have developed a range of curative devices to prevent publicity about a trial from infecting jury deliberations. See, e. g., Nebraska Press Assn. v. Stuart, 427 U.S. 539, 563-565, 96 S.Ct. 2791, 2804, 2805, 49 L.Ed.2d 683 (1976).

An absolute constitutional ban on broadcast coverage of trials cannot be justified simply because there is a danger that, in some cases, prejudicial broadcast accounts of pretrial and trial events may impair the ability of jurors to decide the issue of guilt or innocence uninfluenced by extraneous matter. The risk of juror prejudice in some cases does not justify an absolute ban on news coverage of trials by the printed media; so also the risk of such prejudice does not warrant an absolute constitutional ban on all broadcast coverage. A case attracts a high level of public attention because of its intrinsic interest to the public and the manner of reporting the event. The risk of juror prejudice is present in any publication of a trial, but the appropriate safeguard against such prejudice is the defendant's right to demonstrate that the media's coverage of his case--be it printed or broadcast-- compromised the ability of the particular jury that heard the case to adjudicate fairly . . . .

Whatever may be the "mischievous potentialities [of broadcast coverage] for intruding upon the detached atmosphere which should always surround the judicial process," Estes v. Texas, 381 U.S., at 587, 85 S.Ct., at 1662, at present no one has been able to present empirical data sufficient to establish that the mere presence of the broadcast media inherently has an adverse effect on that process. See n. 11, supra. The appellants have offered nothing to demonstrate that their trial was subtly tainted by broadcast coverage--let alone that all broadcast trials would be so tainted . . . .

D

To say that the appellants have not demonstrated that broadcast coverage is inherently a denial of due process is not to say that the appellants were in fact accorded all of the protections of due process in their trial. As noted earlier, a defendant has the right on review to show that the media's coverage of his case--printed or broadcast--compromised the ability of the jury to judge him fairly. Alternatively, a defendant might show that broadcast coverage of his particular case had an adverse impact on the trial participants sufficient to constitute a denial of due process. Neither showing was made in this case.

To demonstrate prejudice in a specific case a defendant must show something more than juror awareness that the trial is such as to attract the attention of broadcasters. Murphy v. Florida, 421 U.S. 794, 800, 95 S.Ct. 2031, 2036, 44 L.Ed.2d 589 (1975). No doubt the very presence of a camera in the courtroom made the jurors aware that the trial was thought to be of sufficient interest to the public to warrant coverage. Jurors, forbidden to watch all broadcasts, would have had no way of knowing that only fleeting seconds of the proceeding would be reproduced. But the appellants have not attempted to show with any specificity that the presence of cameras impaired the ability of the jurors to decide the case on only the evidence before them or that their trial was affected adversely by the impact on any of the participants of the presence of cameras and the prospect of broadcast.

Although not essential to our holding, we note that at voir dire, the jurors were asked if the presence of the camera would in any way compromise their ability to consider the case. Each answered that the camera would not prevent him or her from considering the case solely on the merits. App. 8-12. The trial court instructed the jurors not to watch television accounts of the trial, id., at 13-14, and the appellants do not contend that any juror violated this instruction. The appellants have offered no evidence that any participant in this case was affected by the presence of cameras. In short, there is no showing that the trial was compromised by television coverage, as was the case in Estes.

V.

It is not necessary either to ignore or to discount the potential danger to the fairness of a trial in a particular case in order to conclude that Florida may permit the electronic media to cover trials in its state courts. Dangers lurk in this, as in most experiments, but unless we were to conclude that television coverage under all conditions is prohibited by the Constitution, the states must be free to experiment. We are not empowered by the Constitution to oversee or harness state procedural experimentation; only when the state action infringes fundamental guarantees are we authorized to intervene. We must assume state courts will be alert to any factors that impair the fundamental rights of the accused.

The Florida program is inherently evolutional in nature; the initial project has provided guidance for the new canons which can be changed at will, and application of which is subject to control by the trial judge. The risk of prejudice to particular defendants is ever present and must be examined carefully as cases arise. Nothing of the "Roman circus" or "Yankee Stadium" atmosphere, as in Estes, prevailed here, however, nor have appellants attempted to show that the unsequestered jury was exposed to "sensational" coverage, in the sense of Estes or of Sheppard v. Maxwell, 384 U.S. 333, 86 S.Ct. 1507, 16 L.Ed.2d 600 (1966). Absent a showing of prejudice of constitutional dimensions to these defendants, there is no reason for this Court either to endorse or to invalidate Florida's experiment.

In this setting, because this Court has no supervisory authority over state courts, our review is confined to whether there is a constitutional violation. We hold that the Constitution does not prohibit a state from experimenting with the program authorized by revised Canon 3A(7).

Affirmed.

Justice STEVENS took no part in the decision of this case.

# Part IV: Protection of News Sources

Dan COHEN, Petitioner
v.
COWLES MEDIA COMPANY, dba Minneapolis Star and Tribune Company, et al.

501 U.S. 663

Supreme Court of the United States

Decided June 24, 1991.

Justice WHITE delivered the opinion of the Court.

The question before us is whether the First Amendment prohibits a plaintiff from recovering damages, under state promissory estoppel law, for a newspaper's breach of a promise of confidentiality given to the plaintiff in exchange for information. We hold that it does not.

During the closing days of the 1982 Minnesota gubernatorial race, Dan Cohen, an active Republican associated with Wheelock Whitney's Independent-Republican gubernatorial campaign, approached reporters from the St. Paul Pioneer Press Dispatch (Pioneer Press) and the Minneapolis Star and Tribune (Star Tribune) and offered to provide documents relating to a candidate in the upcoming election. Cohen made clear to the reporters that he would provide the information only if he was given a promise of confidentiality. Reporters from both papers promised to keep Cohen's identity anonymous and Cohen turned over copies of two public court records concerning Marlene Johnson, the Democratic- Farmer-Labor candidate for Lieutenant Governor. The first record indicated that Johnson had been charged in 1969 with three counts of unlawful assembly, and the second that she had been convicted in 1970 of petit theft. Both newspapers interviewed Johnson for her explanation and one reporter tracked down the person who had found the records for Cohen. As it turned out, the unlawful assembly charges arose out of Johnson's participation in a protest of an alleged failure to hire minority workers on municipal construction projects, and the charges were eventually dismissed. The petit theft conviction was for leaving a store without paying for $6 worth of sewing materials. The incident apparently occurred at a time during which Johnson was emotionally distraught, and the conviction was later vacated.

After consultation and debate, the editorial staffs of the two newspapers independently decided to publish Cohen's name as part of their stories concerning Johnson. In their stories, both papers identified Cohen as the source of the court records, indicated his connection to the Whitney campaign, and included denials by Whitney campaign officials of any role in the matter. The same day the stories appeared, Cohen was fired by his employer.

Cohen sued respondents, the publishers of the Pioneer Press and Star Tribune, in Minnesota state court, alleging fraudulent misrepresentation and breach of contract. The trial court rejected respondents' argument that the First Amendment barred Cohen's lawsuit. A jury returned a verdict in Cohen's favor, awarding him $200,000 in compensatory damages and $500,000 in punitive damages. The Minnesota Court of Appeals, in a split decision, reversed the award of punitive damages after concluding that Cohen had failed to establish a fraud claim, the only claim which would support such an award. 445 N.W.2d 248, 260 (1989). However, the court upheld the finding of liability for breach of contract and the $200,000 compensatory damages award. Id., at 262.

A divided Minnesota Supreme Court reversed the compensatory damages award. 457 N.W.2d 199 (1990). After affirming the Court of Appeals' determination that Cohen had not established a claim for fraudulent misrepresentation, the court considered his breach-of-contract claim and concluded that "a contract cause of action is inappropriate for these particular circumstances." Id., at 203. The court then went on to address the question whether Cohen could establish a cause of action under Minnesota law on a promissory estoppel theory. Apparently, a promissory estoppel theory was never tried to the jury, nor briefed nor argued by the parties; it first arose during oral argument in the Minnesota Supreme Court when one of the justices asked a question about equitable estoppel. See App. 38.

In addressing the promissory estoppel question, the court decided that the most problematic element in establishing such a cause of action here was whether injustice could be avoided only by enforcing the promise of confidentiality made to Cohen. The court stated: "Under a promissory estoppel analysis there can be no neutrality towards the First Amendment. In deciding whether it would be unjust not to enforce the promise, the court must necessarily weigh the same considerations that are weighed for whether the First Amendment has been violated. The court must balance the constitutional rights of a free press against the common law interest in protecting a promise of anonymity." 457 N.W.2d, at 205. After a brief discussion, the court concluded that "in this case enforcement of the promise of confidentiality under a promissory estoppel theory would violate defendants' First Amendment rights." Ibid.

We granted certiorari to consider the First Amendment implications of this case. 498 U.S. 1011, 111 S.Ct. 578, 112 L.Ed.2d 583 (1990).

Respondents initially contend that the Court should dismiss this case without reaching the merits because the promissory estoppel theory was not argued or presented in the courts below and because the Minnesota Supreme Court's decision rests entirely on the interpretation of state law. These contentions do not merit extended discussion. It is irrelevant to this Court's jurisdiction whether a party raised below and argued a federal-law issue that the state supreme court actually considered and decided .... Moreover, that the Minnesota Supreme Court rested its holding on federal law could not be made more clear than by its conclusion that "in this case enforcement of the promise of confidentiality under a promissory estoppel theory would violate defendants' First Amendment rights." 457 N.W.2d, at 205. It can hardly be said that there is no First Amendment issue present in the case when respondents have defended against this suit all along by arguing that the First Amendment barred the enforcement of the reporters' promises to Cohen. We proceed to consider whether that Amendment bars a promissory estoppel cause of action against respondents . . . .

Respondents rely on the proposition that "if a newspaper lawfully obtains truthful information about a matter of public significance then state officials may not constitutionally punish publication of the information, absent a need to further a state interest of the highest order." Smith v. Daily Mail Publishing Co., 443 U.S. 97, 103, 99 S.Ct. 2667, 2671, 61 L.Ed.2d 399 (1979). That proposition is unexceptionable, and it has been applied in various cases that have found insufficient the asserted state interests in preventing publication of truthful, lawfully obtained information . . .

This case, however, is not controlled by this line of cases but, rather, by the equally well-established line of decisions holding that generally applicable laws do not offend the First Amendment simply because their enforcement against the press has incidental effects on its ability to gather and report the news. As the cases relied on by respondents recognize, the truthful information sought to be published must have been lawfully acquired. The press may not with impunity break and enter an office or dwelling to gather news. Neither does the First Amendment relieve a newspaper reporter of the obligation shared by all citizens to respond to a grand jury subpoena and answer questions relevant to a criminal investigation, even though the reporter might be required to reveal a confidential source. Branzburg v. Hayes, 408 U.S. 665, 92 S.Ct. 2646, 33 L.Ed.2d 626 (1972). The press, like others interested in publishing, may not publish copyrighted material without obeying the copyright laws. See Zacchini v. Scripps-Howard Broadcasting Co., 433 U.S. 562, 576-579, 97 S.Ct. 2849, 2857-2859, 53 L.Ed.2d 965 (1977). Similarly, the media must obey the National Labor Relations Act, Associated Press v. NLRB, 301 U.S. 103, 57 S.Ct. 650, 81 L.Ed. 953 (1937), and the Fair Labor Standards Act, Oklahoma Press Publishing Co. v. Walling, 327 U.S. 186, 192-193, 66 S.Ct. 494, 497, 90 L.Ed. 614 (1946); may not restrain trade in violation of the antitrust laws, Associated Press v. United States, 326 U.S. 1, 65 S.Ct. 1416, 89 L.Ed. 2013 (1945); Citizen Publishing Co. v. United States, 394 U.S. 131, 139, 89 S.Ct. 927, 931, 22 L.Ed.2d 148 (1969); and must pay non-discriminatory taxes, Murdock v. Pennsylvania, 319 U.S. 105, 112, 63 S.Ct. 870, 874, 87 L.Ed. 1292 (1943); Minneapolis Star & Tribune Co. v. Minnesota Comm'r of Revenue, 460 U.S. 575, 581-583, 103 S.Ct. 1365, 1369-1371, 75 L.Ed.2d 295 (1983). Cf. University of Pennsylvania v. EEOC, 493 U.S. 182, 201-202, 110 S.Ct. 577, 588-589, 107 L.Ed.2d 571 (1990). It is, therefore, beyond dispute that "[t]he publisher of a newspaper has no special immunity from the application of general laws. He has no special privilege to invade the rights and liberties of others." Associated Press v. NLRB, supra, 301 U.S., at 132-133, 57 S.Ct., at 655-656. Accordingly, enforcement of such general laws against the press is not subject to stricter scrutiny than would be applied to enforcement against other persons or organizations.

There can be little doubt that the Minnesota doctrine of promissory estoppel is a law of general applicability. It does not target or single out the press. Rather, insofar as we are advised, the doctrine is generally applicable to the daily transactions of all the citizens of Minnesota. The First Amendment does not forbid its application to the press.

Justice BLACKMUN suggests that applying Minnesota promissory estoppel doctrine in this case will "punish" respondents for publishing truthful information that was lawfully obtained. Post, at 2521-2522. This is not strictly accurate because compensatory damages are not a form of punishment, as were the criminal sanctions at issue in Smith v. Daily Mail, supra. If the contract between the parties in this case had contained a liquidated damages provision, it would be perfectly clear that the payment to petitioner would represent a cost of acquiring newsworthy material to be published at a profit, rather than a punishment imposed by the State. The payment of compensatory damages in this case is constitutionally indistinguishable from a generous bonus paid to a confidential news source. In any event, as indicated above, the characterization of the payment makes no difference for First Amendment purposes when the law being applied is a general law and does not single out the press. Moreover, Justice BLACKMUN's reliance on cases like Florida Star v. B.J.F., supra, and Smith v. Daily Mail is misplaced. In those cases, the State itself defined the content of publications that would trigger liability. Here, by contrast, Minnesota law simply requires those making promises to keep them. The parties themselves, as in this case, determine the scope of their legal obligations, and any restrictions that may be placed on the publication of truthful information are self-imposed.

Also, it is not at all clear that respondents obtained Cohen's name "lawfully" in this case, at least for purposes of publishing it. Unlike the situation in Florida Star, where the rape victim's name was obtained through lawful access to a police report, respondents obtained Cohen's name only by making a promise that they did not honor. The dissenting opinions suggest that the press should not be subject to any law, including copyright law for example, which in any fashion or to any degree limits or restricts the press' right to report truthful information. The First Amendment does not grant the press such limitless protection.

Nor is Cohen attempting to use a promissory estoppel cause of action to avoid the strict requirements for establishing a libel or defamation claim. As the Minnesota Supreme Court observed here, "Cohen could not sue for defamation because the information disclosed [his name] was true." 457 N.W.2d, at 202. Cohen is not seeking damages for injury to his reputation or his state of mind. He sought damages in excess of $50,000 for breach of a promise that caused him to lose his job and lowered his earning capacity. Thus, this is not a case like Hustler Magazine, Inc. v. Falwell, 485 U.S. 46, 108 S.Ct. 876, 99 L.Ed.2d 41 (1988), where we held that the constitutional libel standards apply to a claim alleging that the publication of a parody was a state-law tort of intentional infliction of emotional distress.

Respondents and amici argue that permitting Cohen to maintain a cause of action for promissory estoppel will inhibit truthful reporting because news organizations will have legal incentives not to disclose a confidential source's identity even when that person's identity is itself newsworthy.

Justice SOUTER makes a similar argument. But if this is the case, it is no more than the incidental, and constitutionally insignificant, consequence of applying to the press a generally applicable law that requires those who make certain kinds of promises to keep them. Although we conclude that the First Amendment does not confer on the press a constitutional right to disregard promises that would otherwise be enforced under state law, we reject Cohen's request that in reversing the Minnesota Supreme Court's judgment we reinstate the jury verdict awarding him $200,000 in compensatory damages. See Brief for Petitioner 31. The Minnesota Supreme Court's incorrect conclusion that the First Amendment barred Cohen's claim may well have truncated its consideration of whether a promissory estoppel claim had otherwise been established under Minnesota law and whether Cohen's jury verdict could be upheld on a promissory estoppel basis. Or perhaps the State Constitution may be construed to shield the press from a promissory estoppel cause of action such as this one. These are matters for the Minnesota Supreme Court to address and resolve in the first instance on remand. Accordingly, the judgment of the Minnesota Supreme Court is reversed, and the case is remanded for further proceedings not inconsistent with this opinion.

So ordered.

Justice BLACKMUN, with whom Justice MARSHALL and Justice SOUTER join, dissenting.

. . . To the extent that truthful speech may ever be sanctioned consistent with the First Amendment, it must be in furtherance of a state interest "of the highest order." Smith, 443 U.S., at 103, 99 S.Ct., at 2671. Because the Minnesota Supreme Court's opinion makes clear that the State's interest in enforcing its promissory estoppel doctrine in this case was far from compelling, see 457 N.W.2d, at 204-205, I would affirm that court's decision.

I respectfully dissent.

Justice SOUTER, with whom Justice MARSHALL, Justice BLACKMUN, and Justice O'CONNOR join, dissenting.

I agree with Justice BLACKMUN that this case does not fall within the line of authority holding the press to laws of general applicability where commercial activities and relationships, not the content of publication, are at issue. See ante, at 2520-2521. Even such general laws as do entail effects on the content of speech, like the one in question, may of course be found constitutional, but only, as Justice Harlan observed,

> "when [such effects] have been found justified by subordinating valid governmental interests, a prerequisite to constitutionality which has necessarily involved a weighing of the governmental interest involved.... Whenever, in such a context, these constitutional protections are asserted against the exercise of valid governmental powers a reconciliation must be effected, and that perforce requires an appropriate weighing of the respective interests involved." Konigsberg v. State Bar of California, 366 U.S. 36, 51, 81 S.Ct. 997, 1007, 6 L.Ed.2d 105 (1961).

Paul M. BRANZBURG, Petitioner,
v.
John P. HAYES, Judge, etc., et al.
In the Matter of Paul PAPPAS, Petitioner.
UNITED STATES, Petitioner,
v.
Earl CALDWELL.

408 U.S. 665

Supreme Court of the United States

Decided June 29, 1972.

Mr. Justice Powell filed concurring opinion; Mr. Justice Douglas dissented and filed opinion, see 92 S.Ct. 2686; Mr. Justice Stewart dissented and filed opinion in which Mr. Justice Brennan and Mr. Justice Marshall joined.

Opinion of the Court by Mr. Justice WHITE, announced by THE CHIEF JUSTICE.

The issue in these cases is whether requiring newsmen to appear and testify before state or federal grand juries abridges the freedom of speech and press guaranteed by the First Amendment. We hold that it does not.

I

The writ of certiorari in No. 70--85, Branzburg v. Hayes and Meigs, brings before us two judgments of the Kentucky Court of Appeals, both involving petitioner Branzburg, a staff reporter for the Courier-Journal, a daily newspaper published in Louisville, Kentucky.

On November 15, 1969, the Courier-Journal carried a story under petitioner's by-line describing in detail his observations of two young residents of Jefferson County synthesizing hashish from marihuana, an activity which, they asserted, earned them about $5,000 in three weeks. The article included a photograph of a pair of hands working above a laboratory table on which was a substance identified by the caption as hashish. The article stated that petitioner had promised not to reveal the identity of the two hashish makers. [FN1] Petitioner was shortly subpoenaed by the Jefferson County grand jury; he appeared, but refused to identify the individuals he had seen possessing marihuana or the persons he had seen making hashish from marihuana. [FN2] A state trial court judge ordered petitioner to answer these questions and rejected his contention that the Kentucky reporters' privilege statute, Ky.Rev.Stat. s 421.100 (1962), [FN4] the First Amendment of the United States Constitution, or ss 1, 2 and 8 of the Kentucky Constitution authorized his refusal to answer. Petitioner then sought prohibition and mandamus in the Kentucky Court of Appeals on the same grounds, but the Court of Appeals denied the petition. Branzburg v. Pound, 461 S.W.2d 345 (1970), as modified on denial of rehearing, Jan. 22, 1971. It held that petitioner had abandoned his First Amendment argument in a supplemental memorandum he had filed and tacitly rejected his argument based on the Kentucky Constitution. It also construed Ky.Rev.Stat. s 421.100 as affording a newsman the privilege of refusing to divulge the identity of an informant who supplied him with information, but held that the statute did not permit a reporter to refuse to testify about events he had observed personally, including the identities of those persons he had observed.

FN1. The article contained the following paragraph: "I don't know why I'm letting you do this story,' (one informant) said quietly. 'To make the narcs (narcotics detectives) mad, I guess. That's the main reason.' However, Larry and his partner asked for and received a promise that their names would be changed.' App. 3--4.

FN2. The Foreman of the grand jury reported that petitioner Branzburg had refused to answer the following two questions: '#1. On November 12, or 13, 1969, who was the person or persons you observed in possession of Marijuana, about which you wrote an article in the Courier-Journal on November 15, 1969? #2. On Novebmer 12, or 13, 1969, who was the person or persons you observed compounding Marijuana, producing same to a compound known as Hashish?' App. 6.

FN4. Ky.Rev.Stat. s 421.100 provides:
'No person shall be compelled to disclose in any legal proceeding or trial before any court, or before any grand or petit jury, or before the presiding officer of any tribunal, or his agent or agents, or before the General Assembly, or any committee thereof, or before any city or county legislative body, or any committee thereof, or elsewhere, the source of any information procured or obtained by him, and published in a newspaper or by a radio or television broadcasting station by which he is engaged or employed, or with which he is connected.'

The second case involving petitioner Branzburg arose out of his later story published on January 10, 1971, which described in detail the use of drugs in Frankfort, Kentucky. The article reported that in order to provide a comprehensive survey of the 'drug scene' in Frankfort, petitioner had 'spent two weeks interviewing several dozen drug users in the capital city' and had seen some of them smoking marihuana. A number of conversations with and observations of several unnamed drug users were recounted. Subpoenaed to appear before a Franklin County grand jury 'to testify in the matter of violation of statutes concerning use and sale of drugs,' petitioner Branzburg moved to quash the summons; the motion was denied, although an order was issued protecting Branzburg from revealing 'confidential associations, sources or information' but requiring that he 'answer any questions which concern or pertain to any criminal act, the commission of which was actually observed by (him).' Prior to the time he was slated to appear before the grand jury, petitioner sought mandamus and prohibition from the Kentucky Court of Appeals, arguing that if he were forced to go before the grand jury or to answer questions regarding the identity of informants or disclose information given to him in confidence, his effectiveness as a reporter would be greatly damaged. The Court of Appeals once again denied the requested writs, reaffirming its construction of Ky.Rev.Stat. s 421.100, and rejecting petitioner's claim of a First Amendment privilege. It distinguished Caldwell v. United States, 434 F.2d 1081 (CA9 1970), and it also announced its 'misgivings' about that decision, asserting that it represented 'a drastic departure from the generally recognized rule that the sources of information of a newspaper reporter are not privileged under the First Amendment.' It characterized petitioner's fear that his ability to obtain news would be destroyed as 'so tenuous that it does not, in the opinion of this court, present an issue of abridgement of the freedom of the press within the meaning of that term as used in the Constitution of the United States.'

Petitioner sought a writ of certiorari to review both judgments of the Kentucky Court of Appeals, and we granted the writ. 402 U.S. 942, 91 S.Ct. 1616, 29 L.Ed.2d 109 (1971).

In re Pappas, No. 70--94, originated when petitioner Pappas, a television newsman-photographer working out of the Providence, Rhode Island, office of a New Bedford, Massachusetts, television station, was called to New Bedford on July 30, 1970, to report on civil disorders there which involved fires and other turmoil. He intended to cover a Black Panther news conference at that group's headquarters in a boarded-up store. Petitioner found the streets around the store barricaded, but he ultimately gained entrance to the area and recorded and photographed a prepared statement read by one of the Black Panther leaders at about 3 p.m. He then asked for and received permission to re-enter the area. Returning at about 9 o'clock, he was allowed to enter and remain inside Panther headquarters. As a condition of entry, Pappas agreed not to disclose anything he saw or heard inside the store except an anticipated police raid, which Pappas, 'on his own,' was free to photograph and report as he wished . . . .

United States v. Caldwell, No. 70--57, arose from subpoenas issued by a federal grand jury in the Northern District of California to respondent Earl Caldwell, a reporter for the New York Times assigned to cover the Black Panther Party and other black militant groups. A subpoena duces tecum was served on respondent on February 2, 1970, ordering him to appear before the grand jury to testify and to bring with him notes and tape recordings of interviews given him for publication by officers and spokesmen of the Black Panther Party concerning the aims, purposes, and activities of that organization. Respondent objected to the scope of this subpoena, and an agreement between his counsel and the Government attorneys resulted in a continuance. A second subpoena, served on March 16, omitted the documentary requirement and simply ordered Caldwell 'to appear . . . to testify before the Grand Jury.' Respondent and his employer, the New York Times, moved to quash on the ground that the unlimited breadth of the subpoenas and the fact that Caldwell would have to appear in secret before the grand jury would destroy his working relationship with the Black Panther Party and 'suppress vital First Amendment freedoms . . . .

## II

Petitioners Branzburg and Pappas and respondent Caldwell press First Amendment claims that may be simply put: that to gather news it is often necessary to agree either not to identify the source of information published or to publish only part of the facts revealed, or both; that if the reporter is nevertheless forced to reveal these confidences to a grand jury, the source so identified and other confidential sources of other reporters will be measurably deterred from furnishing publishable information, all to the detriment of the free flow of information protected by the First Amendment. Although the newsmen in these cases do not claim an absolute privilege against official interrogation in all circumstances, they assert that the reporter should not be forced either to appear or to testify before a grand jury or at trial until and unless sufficient grounds are shown for believing that the reporter possesses information relevant to a crime the grand jury is investigating, that the information the reporter has is unavailable from other sources, and that the need for the information is sufficiently compelling to overide the claimed invasion of First Amendment interests occasioned by the disclosure. Principally relied upon are prior cases emphasizing the importance of the First Amendment guarantees to individual development and to our system of representative government, decisions requiring that official action with adverse impact on First Amendment rights be justified by a public interest that is 'compelling' or 'paramount,' and those precedents establishing the principle that justifiable governmental goals may not be achieved by unduly broad means having an unnecessary impact on protected rights of speech, press, or association. The heart of the claim is that the burden on news gathering resulting from compelling reporters to disclose confidential information outweighs any public interest in obtaining the information.

We do not question the significance of free speech, press, or assembly to the country's welfare. Nor is it suggested that news gathering does not quality for First Amendment protection; without some protection for seeking out the news, freedom of the press could be eviscerated. But these cases involve no intrusions upon speech or assemby, no prior restraint or restriction on what the press may publish, and no express or implied command that the press publish what it prefers to withhold. No exaction or tax for the privilege of publishing, and no penalty, civil or criminal, related to the content of published material is at issue here. The use of confidential sources by the press is not forbidden or restricted; reporters remain free to seek news from any source by means within the law. No attempt is made to require the press to publish its sources of information or indiscriminately to disclose them on request.

The sole issue before us is the obligation of reporters to respond to grand jury subpoenas as other citizens do and to answer questions relevant to an investigation into the commission of crime. Citizens generally are not constitutionally immune from grand jury subpoenas; and neither the First Amendment nor any other constitutional provision protects the average citizen from disclosing to a grand jury information that he has received in confidence. The claim is, however, that reporters are exempt from these obligations because if forced to respond to subpoenas and identify their sources or disclose other confidences, their informants will refuse or be reluctant to furnish newsworthy information in the future. This asserted burden on news gathering is said to make compelled testimony from newsmen constitutionally suspect and to require a privileged position for them.

It is clear that the First Amendment does not invalidate every incidental burdening of the press that may result from the enforcement of civil or criminal statutes of general applicability. Under prior cases, otherwise valid laws serving substantial public interests may be enforced against the press as against others, despite the possible burden that may be imposed. The Court has emphasized that '(t)he publisher of a newspaper has no special immunity from the application of general laws. He has no special privilege to invade the rights and liberties of others.' Associated Press v. NLRB, 301 U.S. 103, 132--133, 57 S.Ct. 650, 656, 81 L.Ed. 953 (1937) . . . .

It is thus not surprising that the great weight of authority is that newsmen are not exempt from the normal duty of appearing before a grand jury and answering questions relevant to a criminal investigation. At common law, courts consistently refused to recognize the existence of any privilege authorizing a newsman to refuse to reveal confidential information to a grand jury . . . . In 1958, a news gatherer asserted for the first time that the First Amendment exempted confidential information from public disclosure pursuant to a subpoena issued in a civil suit, Garland v. Torre, 259 F.2d 545 (CA2), cert. denied, 358 U.S. 910, 79 S.Ct. 237, 3 L.Ed.2d 231 (1958), but the claim was denied, and this argument has been almost uniformly rejected since then although there are occasional dicta that, in circumstances not presented here, a newsman might be excused. In re Goodfader, 45 Haw. 317, 367 P.2d 472 (1961); In re Taylor, 412 Pa. 32, 193 A.2d 181 (1963); State v. Buchanan, 250 Or. 244, 436 P.2d 729, cert. denied, 392 U.S. 905, 88 S.Ct. 2055, 20 L.Ed.2d 1363 (1968); Murphy v. Colorado (No. 19604 Sup.Ct.Colo.), cert. denied, 365 U.S. 843, 81 S.Ct. 802, 5 L.Ed.2d 810 (1961) (unreported, discussed in In re Goodfader, supra, 45 Haw., at 366, 367 P.2d, at 498 (Mizuha, J., dissenting)). These courts have applied the presumption against the existence of an asserted testimonial privilege, United States v. Bryan, 339 U.S. 323, 331, 70 S.Ct. 724, 730, 94 L.Ed. 884 (1950), and have concluded that the First Amendment interest asserted by the newsman was outweighed by the general obligation of a citizen to appear before a grand jury or at trial, pursuant to a subpoena, and give what information he possesses. The opinions of the state courts in Branzburg and Pappas are typical of the prevailing view, although a few recent cases, such as Caldwell, have recognized and given effect to some form of constitutional newsman's privilege ....

The prevailing constitutional view of the newsman's privilege is very much rooted in the ancient role of the grand jury that has the dual function of determining if there is probable cause to believe that a crime has been committed and of protecting citizens against unfounded criminal prosecutions. Grand jury proceedings are constitutionally mandated for the institution of federal criminal prosecutions for capital or other serious crimes, and 'its constitutional prerogatives are rooted in long centuries of Anglo-American history.' Hannah v. Larche, 363 U.S. 420, 489--490, 80 S.Ct. 1502, 1544, 4 L.Ed.2d 1307 (1960). (Frankfurter, J., concurring in result). The Fifth Amendment provides that '(n)o person shall be held to answer for a capital, or otherwise infamous crime, unless on a presentment or indictment of a Grand Jury.' The adoption of the grand jury 'in our Constitution as the sole method for preferring charges in serious criminal cases shows the high place it held as an instrument of justice.' Costello v. United States, 350 U.S. 359, 362, 76 S.Ct. 406, 408, 100 L.Ed. 397 (1956). Although state systems of criminal procedure differ greatly among themselves, the grand jury is similarly guaranteed by many state constitutions and plays an important role in fair and effective law enforcement in the overwhelming majority of the States . . . .

A number of States have provided newsmen a statutory pvivilege of varying breadth, but the majority have not done so, and none has been provided by federal statute. Until now the only testimonial privilege for unofficial witnesses that is rooted in the Federal Constitution is the Fifth Amendment privilege against compelled self- incrimination. We are asked to create another by interpreting the First Amendment to grant newsmen a testimonial privilege that other citizens do not enjoy. This we decline to do. Fair and effective law enforcement aimed at providing security for the person and property of the individual is a fundamental function of government, and the grand jury plays an important, constitutionally mandated role in this process. On the records now before us, we perceive no basis for holding that the public interest in law enforcement and in ensuring effective grand jury proceedings is insufficient to override the consequential, but uncertain, burden on news gathering that is said to result from insisting that reporters, like other citizens, respond to relevant questions put to them in the course of a valid grand jury investigation or criminal trial.

This conclusion itself involves no restraint on what newspapers may publish or on the type or quality of information reporters may seek to acquire, nor does it threaten the vast bulk of confidential relationships between reporters and their sources. Grand juries address themselves to the issues of whether crimes have been committed and who committed them. Only where news sources themselves are implicated in crime or possess information relevant to the grand jury's task need they or the reporter be concerned about grand jury subpoenas. Nothing before us indicates that a large number or percentage of all confidential news sources falls into either category and would in any way be deterred by our holding that the Constitution does not, as it never has, exempt the newsman from performing the citizen's normal duty of appearing and furnishing information relevant to the grand jury's task.

The preference for anonymity of those confidential informants involved in actual criminal conduct is presumably a product of their desire to escape criminal prosecution, and this preference, while understandable, is hardly deserving of constitutional protection. It would be frivolous to assert--and no one does in these cases--that the First Amendment, in the interest of securing news or otherwise, confers a license on either the reporter or his news sources to violate valid criminal laws. Although stealing documents or private wiretapping could provide newsworthy information, neither reporter nor source is immune from conviction for such conduct, whatever the impact on the flow of news. Neither is immume, on First Amendment grounds, from testifying against the other, before the grand jury or at a criminal trial. The Amendment does not reach so far as to override the interest of the public in ensuring that neither reporter nor source is invading the rights of other citizens through reprehensible conduct forbidden to all other persons. To assert the contrary proposition . . . .

Thus, we cannot seriously entertain the notion that the First Amendment protects a newsman's agreement to conceal the criminal conduct of his source, or evidence thereof, on the theory that it is better to write about crime than to do something about it. Insofar as any reporter in these cases undertook not to reveal or testify about the crime he witnessed, his claim of privilege under the First Amendment presents no substantial question. The crimes of news sources are no less reprehensible and threatening to the public interest when witnessed by a reporter than when they are not.

There remain those situations where a source is not engaged in criminal conduct but has information suggesting illegal conduct by others. Newsmen frequently receive information from such sources pursuant to a tacit or express agreement to withhold the source's name and suppress any information that the source wishes not published. Such informants presumably desire anonymity in order to avoid being entangled as a witness in a criminal trial or grand jury investigation. They may fear that disclosure will threaten their job security or personal safety or that it will simply result in dishonor or embarassment.

The argument that the flow of news will be diminished by compelling reporters to aid the grand jury in a criminal investigation is not irrational, nor are the records before us silent on the matter. But we remain unclear how often and to what extent informers are actually deterred from furnishing information when newsmen are forced to testify before a grand jury. The available data indicate that some newsmen rely a great deal on confidential sources and that some informants are particularly sensitive to the threat of exposure and may be silenced if it is held by this Court that, ordinarily, newsmen must testify pursuant to subpoenas, but the evidence fails to demonstrate that there would be a significant construction of the flow of news to the public if this Court reaffirms the prior common-law and constitutional rule regarding the testimonial obligations of newsmen. Estimates of the inhibiting effect of such subpoenas on the willingness of informants to make disclosures to newsmen are widely divergent and to a great extent speculative . . . .

Accepting the fact, however, that an undetermined number of informants not themselves implicated in crime will nevertheless, for whatever reason, refuse to talk to newsmen if they fear identification by a reporter in an official investigation, we cannot accept the argument that the public interest in possible future news about crime from undisclosed, unverified sources must take precedence over the public interest in pursuing and prosecuting those crimes reported to the press by informants and in thus deterring the commission of such crimes in the future . . . .

It is said that currently press subpoenas have multiplied, that mutual distrust and tension between press and officialdom have increased, that reporting styles have changed, and that there is now more need for confidential sources, particularly where the press seeks news about minority cultural and political groups or dissident organizations suspicious of the law and public officials. These developments, even if true, are treacherous grounds for a far-reaching interpretation of the First Amendment fastening a nationwide rule on courts, grand juries, and prosecuting officials everywhere. The obligation to testify in response to grand jury subpoenas will not threaten these sources not involved with criminal conduct and without information relevant to grand jury investigations, and we cannot hold that the Constitution places the sources in these two categories either above the law or beyond its reach . . . .

We are unwilling to embark the judiciary on a long and difficult journey to such an uncertain destination. The administration of a constitutional newsman's privilege would present practical and conceptual difficulties of a high order. Sooner or later, it would be necessary to define those categories of newsmen who qualified for the privilege, a questionable procedure in light of the traditional doctrine that liberty of the press is the right of the lonely pamphleteer who uses carbon paper or a mimeograph just as much as of the large metropolitan publisher who utilizes the latest photocomposition methods. Cf. In re Grand Jury Witnesses, 322 F.Supp. 573, 574 (ND Cal.1970). Freedom of the press is a 'fundamental personal right' which 'is not confined to newspapers and periodicals. It necessarily embraces pamphlets and leaflets. . . . The press in its historic connotation comprehends every sort of publication which affords a vehicle of information and opinion.' Lovell v. City of Griffin, 303 U.S. 444, 450, 452, 58 S.Ct. 666, 669, 82 L.Ed. 949 (1938). See also Mills v. Alabama, 384 U.S. 214, 219, 86 S.Ct. 1434, 1437, 16 L.Ed.2d 484 (1966); Murdock v. Pennsylvania, 319 U.S. 105, 111, 63 S.Ct. 870, 874, 87 L.Ed. 1292 (1943). The informative function asserted by representatives of the organized press in the present cases is also performed by lecturers, political pollsters, novelists, academic researchers, and dramatists. Almost any author may quite accurately assert that he is contributing to the flow of information to the public, that he relies on confidential sources of information, and that these sources will be silenced if he is forced to make disclosures before a grand jury.

In each instance where a reporter is subpoenaed to testify, the courts would also be embroiled in preliminary factual and legal determinations with respect to whether the proper predicate had been laid for the reporter's appearance: Is there probable cause to believe a crime has been committed? Is it likely that the reporter has useful information gained in confidence? Could the grand jury obtain the information elsewhere? Is the official interest sufficient to outweigh the claimedprivilege?

Thus, in the end, by considering whether enforcement of a particular law served a 'compelling' governmental interest, the courts would be inextricably involved in distinguishing between the value of enforcing different criminal laws. By requiring testimony from a reporter in investigations involving some crimes but not in others, they would be making a value judgment that a legislature had declined to make, since in each case the criminal law involved would represent a considered legislative judgment, not constitutionally suspect, of what conduct is liable to criminal prosecution. The task of judges, like other officials outside the legislative branch, is not to make the law but to uphold it in accordance with their oaths.

At the federal level, Congress has freedom to determine whether a statutory newsman's privilege is necessary and desirable and to fashion standards and rules as narrow or broad as deemed necessary to deal with the evil discerned and, equally important, to refashion those rules as experience from time to time may dictate. There is also merit in leaving state legislatures free, within First Amendment limits, to fashion their own standards in light of the conditions and problems with respect to the relations between law enforcement officials and press in their own areas. It goes without saying, of course, that we are powerless to bar state courts from responding in their own way and construing their own constitutions so as to recognize a newsman's privilege, either qualified or absolute.

In addition, there is much force in the pragmatic view that the press has at its disposal powerful mechanisms of communication and is far from helpless to protect itself from harassment or substantial harm. Furthermore, if what the newsmen urged in these cases is true--that law enforcement cannot hope to gain and may suffer from subpoenaing newsmen before grand juries--prosecutors will be loath to risk so much for so little. Thus, at the federal level the Attorney General has already fashioned a set of rules for federal officials in connection with subpoenaing members of the press to testify before grand juries or at criminal trials. These rules are a major step in the direction the reporters herein desire to move. They may prove wholly sufficient to resolve the bulk of disagreements and controversies between press and federal officials.

Finally, as we have earlier indicated, news gathering is not without its First Amendment protections, and grand jury investigations if instituted or conducted other than in good faith, would pose wholly different issues for resolution under the First Amendment. Official harassment of the press undertaken not for purposes of law enforcement but to disrupt a reporter's relationship with his news sources would have no justification. Grand juries are subject to judicial control and subpoenas to motions to quash. We do not expect courts will forget that grand juries must operate within the limits of the First Amendment as well as the Fifth.

## III

We turn, therefore, to the disposition of the cases before us. From what we have said, it necessarily follows that the decision in United States v. Caldwell, No. 70--57, must be reversed. If there is no First Amendment privilege to refuse to answer the relevant and material questions asked during a good-faith grand jury investigation, then it is a fortiori true that there is no privilege to refuse to appear before such a grand jury until the Government demonstrates some 'compelling need' for a newsman's testimony. Other issues were urged upon us, but since they were not passed upon by the Court of Appeals, we decline to address them in the first instance.

The decisions in No. 70--85, Branzburg v. Hayes and Branzburg v. Meigs, must be affirmed. Here, petitioner refused to answer questions that directly related to criminal conduct that he had observed and written about. The Kentucky Court of Appeals noted that marihuana is defined as a narcotic drug by statute, Ky.Rev.Stat. s 218.010(14) (1962), and that unlicensed possession or compounding of it is a felony punishable by both fine and imprisonment. Ky.Rev.Stat. s 218.210 (1962). It held that petitioner 'saw the commission of the statutory felonies of unlawful possession of marijuana and the unlawful conversion of it into hashish,' in Branzburg v. Pound,

461 S.W.2d, at 346. Petitioner may be presumed to have observed similar violations of the state narcotics laws during the research he did for the story that forms the basis of the subpoena in Branzburg v. Meigs. In both cases, if what petitioner wrote was true, he had direct information to provide the grand jury concerning the ommission of serious crimes.

The only question presented at the present time in In re Pappas, No. 70--94, is whether petitioner Pappas must appear before the grand jury to testify pursuant to subpoena. The Massachusetts Supreme Judicial Court characterized the record in this case as 'meager,' and it is not clear what petitioner will be asked by the grand jury. It is not even clear that he will be asked to divulge information received in confidence. We affirm the decision of the Massachusetts Supreme Judicial Court and hold that petitioner must appear before the grand jury to answer the questions put to him, subject, of course, to the supervision of the presiding judge as to 'the propriety, purposes, and scope of the grand jury inquiry and the pertinence of the probable testimony.' 358 Mass., at 614, 266 N.E.2d, at 303--304.

So ordered.

Mr. Justice POWELL, concurring.

I add this brief statement to emphasize what seems to me to be the limited nature of the Court's holding. The Court does not hold that newsmen, subpoenaed to testify before a grand jury, are without constitutional rights with respect to the gathering of news or in safeguarding their sources. Certainly, we do not hold, as suggested in Mr. Justice STEWART's dissenting opinion, that state and federal authorities are free to 'annex' the news media as 'an investigative arm of government.' The solicitude repeatedly shown by this Court for First Amendment freedoms should be sufficient assurance against any such effort, even if one seriously believed that the media--properly free and untrammeled in the fullest sense of these terms--were not able to protect themselves.

As indicated in the concluding portion of the opinion, the Court states that no harassment of newsmen will be tolerated. If a newsman believes that the grand jury investigation is not being conducted in good faith he is not without remedy. Indeed, if the newsman is called upon to give information bearing only a remote and tenuous relationship to the subject of the investigation, or if he has some other reason to believe that his testimony implicates confidential source relationship without a legitimate need of law enforcement, he will have access to the court on a motion to quash and an appropriate protective order may be entered. The asserted claim to privilege should be judged on its facts by the striking of a proper balance between freedom of the press and the obligation of all citizens to give relevant testimony with respect to criminal conduct. The balance of these vital constitutional and societal interests on a case-by-case basis accords with the tried and traditional way of adjudicating such questions.

In short, the courts will be available to newsmen under circumstances where legitimate First Amendment interests require protection.

Mr. Justice STEWART, with whom Mr. Justice BRENNAN and Mr. Justice MARSHALL join, dissenting.

The Court's crabbed view of the First Amendment reflects a disturbing insensitivity to the critical role of an independent press in our society. The question whether a reporter has a constitutional right to a confidential relationship with his source is of first impression here, but the principles that should guide our decision are as basic as any to be found in the Constitution. While Mr. Justice POWELL'S enigmatic concurring opinion gives some hope of a more flexible view in the future, the Court in these cases holds that a newsman has no First Amendment right to protect his sources when called before a grand jury. The Court thus invites state and federal authorities to undermine the historic independence of the press by attempting to annex the journalistic profession as an investigative arm of government. Not only will this decision impair performance of the press' constitutionally protected functions, but it will, I am convinced, in the long run, harm rather than help the administration of justice.

I respectfully dissent.

I

The reporter's constitutional right to a confidential relationship with his source stems from the broad societal interest in a full and free flow of information to the public. It is this basic concern that underlies the Constitution's protection of a free press, Grosjean v. American Press Co., 297 U.S. 233, 250, 56 S.Ct. 444, 449, 80 L.Ed. 660; New York Times Co. v. Sullivan, 376 U.S. 254, 269, 84 S.Ct. 710, 720, 11 L.Ed.2d 686, because the guarantee is 'not for the benefit of the press so much as for the benefit of all of us.' Time, Inc. v. Hill, 385 U.S. 374, 389, 87 S.Ct. 534, 543, 17 L.Ed.2d 456.

Enlightened choice by an informed citizenry is the basic ideal upon which an open society is premised, and a free press is thus indispensable to a free society. Not only does the press enhance personal self-fulfillment by providing the people with the widest possible range of fact and opinion, but it also is an incontestable precondition of self-government. The press 'has been a mighty catalyst in awakening public interest in governmental affairs, exposing corruption among public officers and employees and generally informing the citizenry of public events and occurrences . . ..' Estes v. Texas, 381 U.S. 532, 539, 85 S.Ct. 1628, 1631, 14 L.Ed.2d 543; Mills v. Alabama, 384 U.S. 214, 219, 86 S.Ct. 1434, 1437, 16 L.Ed.2d 484; Grosjean, supra, 297 U.S. at 250, 56 S.Ct. at 449. As private and public aggregations of power burgeon in size and the pressures for conformity necessarily mount, there is obviously a continuing need for an independent press to disseminate a robust variety of information and opinion through reportage, investigation, and criticism, if we are to preserve our constitutional tradition of maximizing freedom of choice by encouraging diversity of expression.

A

In keeping with this tradition, we have held that the right to publish is central to the First Amendment and basic to the existence of constitutional democracy. Grosjean, supra, at 250, 56 S.Ct. at 449; New York Times, supra, 376 U.S. at 270, 84 S.Ct. at 720.

A corollary of the right to publish must be the right to gather news. The full flow of information to the public protected by the free-press guarantee would be severely curtailed if no protection whatever were afforded to the process by which news is assembled and disseminated. We have, therefore, recognized that there is a right to publish without prior governmental approval, Near v. Minnesota, 283 U.S. 697, 51 S.Ct. 625, 75 L.Ed. 1357; New York Times Co. v. United States, 403 U.S. 713, 91 S.Ct. 2140, 29 L.Ed.2d 822, a right to distribute information, see, e.g., Lovell v. Griffin, 303 U.S., 444, 452, 58 S.Ct. 666, 669, 82 L.Ed. 949; Marsh v. Alabama, 326 U.S. 501, 66 S.Ct. 276, 90 L.Ed. 265; Martin v. City of Struthers, 319 U.S. 141, 63 S.Ct. 862, 87 L.Ed. 1313; Grosjean, supra, and a right to receive printed matter, Lamont v. Postmaster General, 381 U.S. 301, 85 S.Ct. 1493, 14 L.Ed.2d 398.

No less important to the news dissemination process is the gathering of information. News must not be unnecessarily cut off at its source, for without freedom to acquire information the right to publish would be impermissibly compromised. Accordingly, a right to gather news, of some dimensions, must exist. Zemel v. Rusk, 381 U.S. 1, 85 S.Ct. 1271, 14 L.Ed.2d 179. Note, The Right of the Press to Gather Information, 71 Col.L.Rev. 838 (1971). As Madison wrote: 'A popular Government, without popular information, or the means of acquiring it, is but a Prologue to a Farce or a Tragedy; or perhaps both.' 9 Writings of James Madison 103 (G. Hunt ed. 1910).

B

The right to gather news implies, in turn, a right to a confidential relationship between a reporter and his source. This proposition follows as a matter of simple logic once three factual predicates are recognized: (1) newsmen require informants to gather news; (2) confidentiality--the promise or understanding that names or certain aspects of communications will be kept off the record--is essential to the creation and maintenance of a news-gathering relationship with informants; and (3) an unbridled subpoena power--the absence of a constitutional right protecting, in any way, a confidential relationship from compulsary process--will either deter sources from divulging information or deter reporters from gathering and publishing information.

It is obvious that informants are necessary to the news-gathering process as we know it today. If it is to perform its constitutional mission, the press must do far more than merely print public statements or publish prepared handouts. Familiarity with the people and circumstances involved in the myriad background activities that result in the final product called 'news' is vital to complete and responsible journalism, unless the press is to be a captive mouthpiece of 'newsmakers.'

It is equally obvious that the promise of confidentiality may be a necessary prerequisite to a productive relationship between a newsman and his informants. An officeholder may fear his superior; a member of the bureaucracy, his associates; a dissident, the scorn of majority opinion. All may have information valuable to the public discourse, yet each may be willing to relate that information only in confidence to a reporter whom he trusts, either because of excessive caution or because of a reasonable fear of reprisals or censure for unorthodox views. The First Amendment concern must not be with the motives of any particular news source, but rather with the conditions in which informants of all shades of the spectrum may make information available through the press to the public. Cf. Talley v. California, 362 U.S. 60, 65, 80 S.Ct. 536, 539, 4 L.Ed.2d 559; Bates v. City of Little Rock, 361 U.S. 516, 80 S.Ct. 412, 4 L.Ed.2d 480; NAACP v. Alabama, 357 U.S. 449, 78 S.Ct. 1163, 2 L.Ed.2d 1488.

In Caldwell, the District Court found that 'confidential relationships . . . are commonly developed and maintained by professional journalists, and are indispensable to their work of gathering, analyzing and publishing the news.' Commentators and individual reporters have repeatedly noted the importance of confidentiality. And surveys among reporters and editors indicate that the promise of nondisclosure is necessary for many types of news gathering.

Finally, and most important, when governmental officials possess an unchecked power to compel newsmen to disclose information received in confidence, sources will clearly be deterred from giving information, and reporters will clearly be deterred from publishing it, because uncertainty about exercise of the power will lead to 'self-censorship.' Smith v. California, 361 U.S. 147, 149-- 154, 80 S.Ct. 215, 216--219, 4 L.Ed.2d 205; New York Times Co. v. Sullivan, 376 U.S., at 279, 84 S.Ct., at 725. The uncertainty arises, of course, because the judiciary has traditionally imposed virtually no limitations on the grand jury's broad investigatory powers. See Antell, The Modern Grand Jury: Benighted Supergovernment, 51 A.B.A.J. 153 (1965). See also Part II, infra.

After today's decision, the potential informant can never be sure that his identity or off-the-record communications will not subsequently be revealed through the compelled testimony of a newsman. A public-spirited person inside government, who is not implicated in any crime, will now be fearful of revealing corruption or other governmental wrongdoing, because he will now know he can subsequently be identified by use of compulsory process. The potential source must, therefore, choose between risking exposure by giving information or avoiding the risk by remaining silent.

The reporter must speculate about whether contact with a controversial source or publication of controversial material will lead to a subpoena. In the event of a subpoena, under today's decision, the newsman will know that he must choose between being punished for contempt if he refuses to testify, or violating his profession's ethics and impairing his resourcefulness as a reporter if he discloses confidential information.

Again, the commonsense understanding that such deterrence will occur is buttressed by concrete evidence. The existence of deterrent effects through fear and self-censorship was impressively developed in the District Court in Caldwell. Individual reporters and commentators have noted such effects. Surveys have verified that an unbridled subpoena power will substantially impair the flow of news to the public, especially in sensitive areas involving governmental officials, financial affairs, political figures, dissidents, or minority groups that require in-depth, investigative reporting. And the Justice Department has recognized that 'compulsory process in some circumstances may have a limiting effect on the exercise of First Amendment right.' No evidence contradicting the existence of such deterrent effects was offered at the trials or in the briefs here by the petitioner in Caldwell or by the respondents in Branzburg and Pappas.

The impairment of the flow of news cannot, of course, be proved with scientific precision, as the Court seems to demand. Obviously, not every news- gathering relationship requires confidentiality. And it is difficult to pinpoint precisely how many relationship do require a promise or understanding of nondisclosure. But we have never before demanded that First Amendment rights rest on elaborate empirical studies demonstrating beyond any conceivable doubt that deterrent effects exist; we have never before required proof of the exact number of people potentially affected by governmental action, who would actually be dissuaded from engaging in First Amendment activity . . . .

II

Posed against the First Amendment's protection of the newsman's confidential relationships in these cases is society's interest in the use of the grand jury to administer justice fairly and effectively. The grand jury serves two important functions: 'to examine into the commission of crimes' and 'to stand between the prosecutor and the accused, and to determine whether the charge was founded upon credible testimony or was dictated by malice or personal ill will.' Hale v. Henkel, 201 U.S. 43, 59, 26 S.Ct. 370, 373, 50 L.Ed. 652. And to perform these functions the grand jury must have available to it every man's relevant evidence. See Blair v. United States, 250 U.S 273, 281, 39 S.Ct. 468, 471, 63 L.Ed. 979; Blackmer v. United States, 284 U.S. 421, 438, 52 S.Ct. 252, 255, 76 L.Ed. 375.

Yet the longstanding rule making every person's evidence available to the grand jury is not absolute. The rule has been limited by the Fifth Amendment, the Fourth Amendment, and the evidentiary privileges of the common law. So it was that in Blair, supra, after recognizing that the right against compulsory self-incrimination prohibited certain inquiries, the Court noted that 'some confidential matters are shielded from considerations of policy, and perhaps in other cases for special reasons a witness may be excused from telling all that he knows.' Id., 250 U.S. at 281, 39 S.Ct. at 471 (emphasis supplied). And in United States v. Bryan, 339 U.S. 323, 70 S.Ct. 724, 94 L.Ed. 844, the Court observed that any exemption from the duty to testify before the grand jury 'presupposes a very real interest to be protected.' Id., at 332, 70 S.Ct. at 731.

Such an interest must surely be the First Amendment protection of a confidential relationship that I have discussed above in Part I. As noted there, this protection does not exist for the purely private interests of the newsman or his informant, nor even, at bottom, for the First Amendment interests of either partner in the news-gathering relationship. Rather, it functions to insure nothing less than democratic decisionmaking through the free flow of information to the public, and it serves, thereby, to honor the 'profound national commitment to the principle that debate on public issues should be uninhibited, robust, and wide-open.' New York Times Co. v. Sullivan, 376 U.S., at 270, 84 S.Ct., at 721.

In striking the proper balance between the public interest in the efficient administration of justice and the First Amendment guarantee of the fullest flow of information, we must begin with the basic proposition that because of their 'delicate and vulnerable' nature, NAACP v. Button, 371 U.S., at 433, 83 S.Ct., at 338, and their transcendent importance for the just functioning of our society, First Amendment rights require special safeguards . . . .

A

. . . Accordingly, when a reporter is asked to appear before a grand jury and reveal confidences, I would hold that the government must (1) show that there is probable cause to believe that the newsman has information that is clearly relevant to a specific probable violation of law; (2) demonstrate that the information sought cannot be obtained by alternative means less destructive of First Amendment rights; and (3) demonstrate a compelling and overriding interest in the information.

This is not to say that a grand jury could not issue a subpoena until such a showing were made, and it is not to say that a newsman would be in any way privileged to ignore any subpoena that was issued. Obviously, before the government's burden to make such a showing were triggered, the reporter would have to move to quash the subpoena, asserting the basis on which he considered the particular relationship a confidential one.

B

The crux of the Court's rejection of any newsman's privilege is its observation that only 'where news sources themselves are implicated in crime or possess information relevant to the grand jury's task need they or the reporter be concerned about grand jury subpoenas.' See ante, at 2661 (emphasis supplied). But this is a most misleading construct. For it is obviously not true that the only persons about whom reporters will be forced to testify will be those 'confidential informants involved in actual criminal conduct' and those having 'information suggesting illegal conduct by others.' See ante, at 2661, 2662. As noted above, given the grand jury's extraordinarily broad investigative powers and the weak standards of relevance and materiality that apply during such inquiries, reporters, if they have no testimonial privilege, will be called to give information about informants who have neither committed crimes nor have information about crime. It is to avoid deterrence of such sources and thus to prevent needless injury to First Amendment values that I think the government must be required to show probable cause that the newsman has information that is clearly relevant to a specific probable violation of criminal law.

SEAN PATRICK DELANEY et al., Petitioners,
v.
THE SUPERIOR COURT OF LOS ANGELES COUNTY, Respondent; ROXANA KOPETMAN et al.,
Real Parties in Interest

50 Cal.3d 785

Supreme Court of California.

May 3, 1990.

EAGLESON, J.

The issues in this case are: (1) whether the term 'unpublished information' in the California newsperson's shield law (Cal. Const., art. I, § 2, subd. (b); Evid. Code, § 1070) includes a newsperson's nonconfidential, eyewitness observations of an occurrence in a public place; and, (2) if so, whether a newsperson can nevertheless be held in contempt for refusing to disclose such information in a criminal proceeding.

As we shall explain, we hold the shield law's broad definition of 'unpublished information' does not require a showing by the newsperson that the information was obtained in confidence. We further hold, however, that a newsperson's protection under the shield law must yield to a criminal defendant's constitutional right to a fair trial when the newsperson's refusal to disclose information would unduly infringe on that right. In this case, the trial court correctly determined that the balance between the rights of the newspersons and the defendant weighs in favor of compelled disclosure. We affirm the judgment of the Court of Appeal.

## Facts

### Underlying Facts

Real parties in interest, Los Angeles Times reporter Roxana Kopetman and photographer Roberto Santiago Bertero, were accompanying members of a Long Beach Police Department task force on patrol. (For convenience we will sometimes refer collectively to Kopetman and Bertero as the reporters.) The officers observed Sean Patrick Delaney and a companion seated on a bench in the Long Beach Plaza Mall. A plastic bag of a type often used to store narcotics was protruding from Delaney's shirt pocket. The officers inquired about the contents of the bag, and Delaney removed it from his pocket to show that it contained a piece of gold and a piece of jewelry. He told the officers he intended to pawn the items at the mall. Because no pawnshops were in the mall, the officers became suspicious and asked Delaney for his identification. Delaney reached for a jacket lying next to him on the bench as if to get his wallet. According to the officers, they asked Delaney before he picked up the jacket if they could check it for weapons. He allegedly consented to the search. An officer ran his fingers along the outside of the jacket and felt a hard object in its pocket. He reached inside and retrieved a set of brass knuckles, which Delaney claimed was a key chain.

Four days later, the Los Angeles Times (hereafter the Times) published an article about the police task force. The article included information regarding the police contact with Delaney but did not refer to whether he had consented to the search of his jacket pocket.

### Procedural History

Delaney was charged in a misdemeanor complaint with possession of brass knuckles in violation of Penal Code section 12020, subdivision (a). He moved to suppress evidence of the brass knuckles, arguing that he had not consented to the patdown search of his jacket and that the resulting seizure of the brass knuckles was therefore illegal because the officers had lacked a reasonable suspicion that he was armed. Delaney subpoenaed the reporters to testify at the suppression hearing in municipal court. The reporters moved to quash the subpoenas, contending they could not be compelled to testify because their eyewitness observations of the public search and seizure constituted 'unpublished information' protected by the newspersons' shield law from disclosure. The motions were denied.

Following testimony by the officers at the suppression hearing, the reporters were called to testify by the prosecution to demonstrate the legality of the seizure. Their testimony established that each of them observed the events leading to the seizure and that each was situated in a position to observe whether Delaney had consented to the search of his jacket. The reporters, however, refused to answer any questions relating to whether Delaney had consented. The municipal court concluded that the shield law did not apply to the reporters' eyewitness observations of the nonconfidential, public circumstances of the search and seizure. The court further found that, even if the shield law applied, the need for the reporters' presumably disinterested testimony on the consent issue outweighed their claim of immunity under the shield law. The court cited both reporters for contempt.

The reporters filed petitions for writs of habeas corpus in the superior court. That court found the shield law provided the reporters with immunity from contempt and granted their petitions.

Delaney and the People of the State of California (through the Long Beach City Prosecutor) filed a joint petition in the Court of Appeal seeking to vacate the orders of the superior court that granted the reporters' habeas corpus petitions. (Delaney's misdemeanor prosecution has been suspended pending final resolution of the reporters' contempt citations.) The Court of Appeal held the shield law does not give a newsperson the right to refuse to testify as to his observations of a public event and ordered the superior court to vacate its orders granting the petitions for writs of habeas corpus. The Court of Appeal's decision was initially unanimous but, after real parties petitioned for rehearing, one justice changed her position and filed a dissenting opinion.

Discussion

I. History of California's Shield Law

Newspersons had no privilege or immunity under common law to refuse to disclose the identity of their confidential sources. (Ex Parte Lawrence and Levings (1897) 116 Cal. 298, 300 [48 P. 124] [upholding contempt citations issued to a newspaper reporter and editor for refusing to disclose confidential sources to the state Senate]; Mitchell v. Superior Court (1984) 37 Cal.3d 268, 274, fn. 3 [208 Cal.Rptr. 152, 690 P.2d 625] [noting prohibition in Evidence Code section 911 of common law privileges]; Tent. Recommendation and Study Relating to the Uniform Rules of Evidence, art. V, Privileges (Feb. 1964) 6 Cal. Law Revision Com. Rep. (1964) p. 488 [noting that 'the newsmen's privilege is entirely alien to the common law'].)

In 1935 the Legislature passed the first shield law. (Stats. 1935, ch. 532, § 1, pp. 1608-1610.) The statute, which was codified as Code of Civil Procedure section 1881, subdivision 6, provided that newspaper employees could not be adjudged in contempt for refusal to disclose their sources to courts or legislative or administrative bodies. Subsequent amendments extended the immunity to employees of radio and television stations, press associations, and wire services. (Stats. 1961, ch. 629, § 1, pp. 1797-1798.) In 1965 the Legislature transferred these statutory provisions to Evidence Code section 1070, which became effective in 1967. (Stats. 1965, ch. 299, § 2, pp. 1297, 1323-1335; Evid. Code, § 12.)

In 1972, a plurality of the United States Supreme Court concluded that the First Amendment to the federal Constitution does not provide newspersons with even a qualified privilege against appearing before a grand jury and being compelled to answer questions as to either the identity of news sources or information received from those sources. (Branzburg v. Hayes (1972) 408 U.S. 665 [33 L.Ed.2d 626, 92 S.Ct. 2646].) The high court made clear, however, that state legislatures are 'free, within First Amendment limits, to fashion their own standards.' ( Id., at p. 706.) [FN3]

FN3 There has been considerable debate as to whether the court as a whole in Branzburg v. Hayes, supra, 408 U.S. 665, recognized a qualified privilege. Four justices dissented from the plurality opinion. Three of them (Justices Brennan, Marshall, and Stewart) would have recognized a qualified privilege; the fourth (Justice Douglas) advocated an absolute privilege. Justice Powell joined the plurality in finding no privilege on the facts before the court but stated his view that the question of privilege should be determined on a case-by-case basis. Justice Stewart subsequently observed that, in light of Justice Powell's concurring opinion, the decision was 'perhaps by a vote of four and a half to four and a half.' (Stewart, Or of the Press (1975) 26 Hastings L.J. 631, 635.) Similarly, counsel for the New York Times in one of the consolidated cases decided in Branzburg later acknowledged that '... Justice Powell's opinion is singularly opaque ....' (Goodale, Branzburg v. Hayes and the Developing Qualified Privilege for Newsmen (1975) 26 Hastings L.J. 709.) Despite this lack of clear guidance, '... lower federal courts have consistently read the case to support some kind of qualified privilege for reporters.'

(Tribe, American Constitutional Law (2d ed. 1988) § 12-22, p. 972.) Several state courts have done likewise. In Mitchell v. Superior Court, supra, 37 Cal.3d 268, 277, we concurred in the observation by some other courts that Justice Powell's position was the 'minimum common denominator' of Branzburg and that the decision therefore does not preclude a qualified privilege. We did not decide the question of whether Branzburg requires a privilege in some cases. Because Branzburg is not dispositive of the present case, we need not linger over the troublesome question of its scope and meaning.

In 1974 the California Legislature amended section 1070 to its present form, apparently in response to Branzburg, supra, 408 U.S. 665. (Stats. 1974, ch. 1323, § 1, p. 2877; Stats. 1974, ch. 1456, § 2, p. 3184.) That amendment expanded the scope of the shield law to protect against the compelled disclosure of 'unpublished information' as well as sources.

In June 1980, California voters approved Proposition 5, a state constitutional amendment proposed by the Assembly. (Assem. Const. Amend. No. 4, Stats. 1978 (1977-1978 Reg. Sess.) res. ch. 77, pp. 4819-4820.) The proposition incorporated language virtually identical to section 1070 into the California Constitution, as article I, section 2, subdivision (b). [FN4]

FN4 For convenience and brevity we refer in the remainder of this opinion to the constitutional provision as article I, section 2(b). It states in its entirety: 'A publisher, editor, reporter, or other person connected with or employed upon a newspaper, magazine, or other periodical publication, or by a press association or wire service, or any person who has been so connected or employed, shall not be adjudged in contempt by a judicial, legislative, or administrative body, or any other body having the power to issue subpoenas, for refusing to disclose the source of any information procured while so connected or employed for publication in a newspaper, magazine or other periodical publication, or for refusing to disclose any unpublished information obtained or prepared in gathering, receiving or processing of information for communication to the public.

'Nor shall a radio or television news reporter or other person connected with or employed by a radio or television station, or any person who has been so connected or employed, be so adjudged in contempt for refusing to disclose the source of any information procured while so connected or employed for news or news commentary purposes on radio or television, or for refusing to disclose any unpublished information obtained or prepared in gathering, receiving or processing of information for communication to the public.

'As used in this subdivision, 'unpublished information' includes information not disseminated to the public by the person from whom disclosure is sought, whether or not related information has been disseminated and includes, but is not limited to, all notes, outtakes, photographs, tapes or other data of whatever sort not itself disseminated to the public through a medium of communication, whether or not published information based upon or related to such material has been disseminated.'

## II. Scope of the Shield Law

Article I, section 2(b) provides that a newsperson 'shall not be adjudged in contempt ... for refusing to disclose the source of any information procured while so connected or employed [as a newsperson] ... or for refusing to disclose any unpublished information obtained or prepared in gathering, receiving or processing of information for communication to the public.' (Italics added.) (1) Stated more simply, article I, section 2(b) protects a newsperson from being adjudged in contempt for refusing to disclose either: (1) unpublished information, or (2) the source of information, whether published or unpublished.

The parties agree there is no attempt to compel the reporters to reveal the identity of a source. Delaney was the source of whatever information the reporters may have as to whether he consented to the police search of his jacket, and his identity is of course already known. Rather, Delaney seeks only the reporters' testimony as to whether he consented to the search. The reporters do not contend they promised to keep confidential any information they obtained or observations they made while preparing their article on the Long Beach Police Department's task force. (2a) The question therefore is whether the shield law's definition of 'unpublished information' includes a newsperson's unpublished, nonconfidential eyewitness observations of an occurrence in a public place. (3) We conclude that it does . . . .

## III. Delaney's Constitutional Rights

Our determination that the reporters' observations of the police search are 'unpublished information' within the scope of article I, section 2(b) does not decide the issue of whether the municipal court properly held the reporters in contempt for refusing to disclose that information. (15) The reporters themselves concede, as they must, that the shield law's protection is overcome in a criminal proceeding on a showing that nondisclosure would deprive the defendant of his federal constitutional right to a fair trial. Although this court has not decided a case involving the application of the shield law in a criminal prosecution, the principle is beyond question. (CBS, Inc. v. Superior Court, supra, 85 Cal.App.3d 241, 251; Hallissy v. Superior Court, supra, 200 Cal.App.3d 1038; Playboy Enterprises, Inc. v. Superior Court, supra, 154 Cal.App.3d 14, 24-25; Hammarley v. Superior Court, supra, 89 Cal.App.3d 388, 402; cf. People v. Borunda (1974) 11 Cal.3d 523, 527 [113 Cal.Rptr. 825, 522 P.2d 1] [defendant seeking identity of anonymous informant].) The incorporation of the shield law into the California Constitution cannot restrict a criminal defendant's federal constitutional right to a fair trial. (Mulkey v. Reitman (1966) 64 Cal.2d 529, 533 [50 Cal.Rptr. 881, 413 P.2d 825], affd. (1967) 387 U.S. 369 [18 L.Ed.2d 830, 87 S.Ct. 1627] [explaining that California constitutional amendment adopted by ballot must conform to the United States Constitution].) Such result would violate the supremacy clauses of the federal and state Constitutions. (U.S. Const., art. VI, cl. 2; Cal. Const., art. III, § 1; Hammarley v. Superior Court, supra, 89 Cal.App.3d 388, 399, fn. 4.)

The parties disagree, however, as to the nature of the showing a criminal defendant must make to overcome a claim of immunity under the shield law. Delaney contends he need establish only a reasonable possibility that the evidence sought to be discovered might result in his exoneration. The reporters propose a more complex, four-part test under which a defendant would have to show the following: (1) The information must go to the heart of defendant's case. (2) The information must have a significant effect on the outcome of the case. (This proposed element seems to be the same as the 'heart-of-the-case' element.) (3) The information is not available from alternative sources. (4) The infringement on the defendant's rights caused by nondisclosure must outweigh the newsperson's interests. (This element seems to be the conclusion a court would reach under the test rather than an element of the test.) As we will explain, precedent and principle lead us to conclude that neither test is entirely warranted.

### A. The proper test for accommodating conflicting constitutional rights

To formulate the proper test we begin with our decision in Mitchell v. Superior Court, supra, 37 Cal.3d 268, in which we set forth a balancing test to determine when a reporter must disclose confidential information. We identified four relevant factors for a trial court to consider when making that determination. First, we noted the nature of the proceeding and observed that, 'In general, disclosure is appropriate in civil cases, especially when a reporter is a party to the litigation.' ( Id., at p. 279.) Second, the Mitchell court stated the information must be more than merely relevant and that it must go to 'the heart of the case' for the party seeking discovery. ( Id., at pp. 280-282.) Third, the court stated that discovery should generally be denied unless it is shown that all alternative sources of the information have been exhausted. ( Id., at p. 282.) Fourth, Mitchell stated that the trial court should consider the importance of protecting confidentiality in the case at hand. ( Id., at pp. 282-283.)

Although Mitchell, a defamation action, helps to illustrate the competing concerns that arise when a litigant seeks information from a newsperson, an identical approach is not entirely appropriate in a criminal proceeding. We were careful to emphasize in Mitchell that 'In criminal proceedings, both the interest of the state in law enforcement, recognized as a compelling interest in Branzburg (see 408 U.S. 665, 700 [33 L.Ed.2d 626, 650]), and the interest of the defendant in discovering exonerating evidence outweigh any interest asserted in ordinary civil litigation.' ( Mitchell, supra, 37 Cal.3d at p. 278.) We did not consider the factors a court should consider in a criminal case.

#### 1. Threshold showing required

In now deciding the issue, we must first consider the threshold showing a criminal defendant must make. The reporters claim Delaney must show their testimony would go to the 'heart of his case.' He contends he need show only a reasonable possibility the evidence might result in his exoneration. On this point, Delaney has the better view. In CBS, Inc. v. Superior Court, supra, 85 Cal.App.3d 241, the court explained, 'Against this right [of a free press] we are obliged to measure the threat to defendants' right to a fair trial. The existence of such a right is clear .... [I]t has resulted in the rule that, where a criminal defendant has demonstrated a reasonable possibility that evidence sought to be discovered might result in his exoneration, he is entitled to its discovery.' ( Id., at p. 251, italics in original; Hallissy v. Superior Court, supra, 200 Cal.App.3d 1038, 1045.) Similarly, in Hammarley v. Superior Court, supra, 89 Cal.App.3d 388, the court stated, "Allowing an accused the right to discover is based on the fundamental proposition that he is entitled to a fair trial and an intelligent defense in light of all relevant and reasonably accessible information." ( Id., at pp. 398-399, quoting Pitchess v. Superior Court (1974) 11 Cal.3d 531, 535 [113 Cal.Rptr. 897, 522 P.2d 305], italics added.)

We hold that, to overcome a prima facie showing by a newsperson that he is entitled to withhold information under the shield law, a criminal defendant must show a reasonable possibility the information will materially assist his defense. A criminal defendant is not required to show that the information goes to the heart of his case . . . .

2. Factors to consider

By meeting the threshold requirement, a defendant is not necessarily entitled to a newsperson's unpublished information. The trial court must then consider the importance of protecting the unpublished information. ( Mitchell, supra, 37 Cal.3d at pp. 282-283.) This determination may properly be characterized as a balancing of the defendant's and newsperson's respective, perhaps conflicting, interests. The factors to be considered in making this determination are as follows:

(a) Whether the unpublished information is confidential or sensitive

If the information is not confidential, the court should consider whether it is nevertheless sensitive, that is, whether its disclosure would somehow unduly restrict the newsperson's access to future sources and information. (We hereafter refer to this type of nonconfidential information as 'sensitive information.') Generally, nonconfidential or nonsensitive information will be less worthy of protection than confidential or sensitive information. Disclosure of the latter types of information will more likely have a significant effect on the newsperson's future ability to gather news. (U.S. v. LaRouche Campaign (1st Cir. 1988) 841 F.2d 1176, 1180-1182 [noting slight deference due nonconfidential information].) The protection of that ability is the primary purpose of the shield law. (Ballot Pamp., Proposed Amends. to Cal. Const. with arguments to voters, Primary Elec., supra, p. 19; see ante, at p. 802, fn. 13.)

(b) The interests sought to be protected by the shield law

Even if the information was sensitive or obtained in confidence, other circumstances may, as a practical matter, render moot the need to avoid disclosure. If, as in this case, the criminal defendant seeking disclosure is himself the source of the information, it cannot be seriously argued that the source (the defendant) will feel that his confidence has been breached. The reporter's news-gathering ability will not be prejudiced. Other circumstances may also mitigate or eliminate the adverse consequences of disclosure. We do not purport to decide the significance to be given to any future set of facts before a trial court. The point is simply that a trial court must determine whether the policy of the shield law will in fact be thwarted by disclosure.

(c) The importance of the information to the criminal defendant

A defendant in a given case may be able not only to meet but to exceed the threshold 'reasonable possibility' requirement. For example, he may be able to show that the evidence would be dispositive in his favor, i.e., to use the reporters' phrase, that it goes to 'the heart of defendant's case.' If so, the balance will weigh more heavily in favor of disclosure than if he could show only a reasonable possibility the evidence would assist his defense.

(d) Whether there is an alternative source for the unpublished information

We stated in Mitchell, supra, 37 Cal.3d 268, 282, that discovery of a reporter's confidential information should be denied unless the party seeking it 'has exhausted all alternative sources of obtaining the needed information.' This requirement has also been imposed on criminal defendants. (Hammarley v. Superior Court, supra, 89 Cal.App.3d 388, 399; Hallissy v. Superior Court, supra, 200 Cal.App.3d 1038, 1045-1046.) Whether there is an alternative source is indeed a factor for the trial court to consider in a criminal proceeding. In light of a defendant's constitutional right to a fair trial, however, Mitchell, a civil case, does not mandate a rigid alternative-source requirement in criminal proceedings.

The facts in Mitchell, supra, 37 Cal.3d 268, also suggest the alternative-source requirement may not always be appropriate. In Mitchell, the plaintiff sought documents that would reveal confidential sources of information. ( Id., at p. 272.) The obvious purpose of the alternative-source requirement is to protect against unnecessary disclosure of a newsperson's confidential or sensitive information. Where the information is shown to be not confidential or sensitive, the primary basis for the requirement is not present and imposing a rigid requirement would be to sustain a rule without a reason. As we have explained above, the proper balancing in a criminal case must take into account whether the unpublished information is confidential or sensitive and, if so, the importance of protecting the information in a given case. (Ante, at pp. 810-811.) For the same reason, a trial court should consider the nature of the information in determining whether to impose an absolute alternative-source requirement in a given case.

We also note that in Mitchell, supra, 37 Cal.3d 268, the information request was for documents that would reveal the identity of possible witnesses. We noted that the names of these persons likely could be obtained from sources other than the newsperson. Objective evidence of that nature is likely unaffected by its source. The contents of a document do not depend on the source of the document (assuming no alteration). Similarly, the name of a witness is the same regardless of who provides the name. The evidence sought by Delaney in this case, however, is qualitatively different from that sought in Mitchell. Delaney seeks the reporters' testimony as to their percipient observations of the events leading to his search and arrest. Two witnesses to an act may - indeed, likely do - see it differently, and even when their perceptions are substantially the same, their recollection of the event may differ. Moreover, even if their testimony is substantively similar, one witness may have more credibility with a jury. Likewise, two witnesses may convince the jury of a fact where one witness by himself would not do so.

Finally, we note a significant practical difference between this case and Mitchell, supra, 37 Cal.3d 268. That case arose out of a pretrial discovery order in a civil case. In light of the wide range of procedures available for pretrial discovery in civil litigation, it is not unreasonable to require a party seeking information from a newsperson to look elsewhere first. There are no similar procedures available to a criminal defendant. For example, he cannot compel a witness's attendance at a deposition and, if unsuccessful in obtaining information, subpoena a different witness. Moreover, the economic reality of the criminal justice system is such that a criminal defendant will generally have less opportunity than a civil litigant to obtain information before trial.

For all the foregoing reasons, we conclude that a universal and inflexible alternative-source requirement is inappropriate in a criminal proceeding. In considering whether the requirement is appropriate in a given case, the trial court should consider the type of information being sought (e.g., names of potential witnesses, documents, a reporter's eyewitness observations), the quality of the alternative source, and the practicality of obtaining the information from the alternative source. The trial court must also consider the other balancing factors set forth above: whether the information is confidential or sensitive, the interests sought to be protected by the shield law, and the importance of the information to the criminal defendant. In short, whether an alternative-source requirement applies will depend on the facts of each case.

3. Balancing the factors

Although a trial court must consider the foregoing factors, their relative importance will likely vary from case to case. In some cases, as in the present one, all the factors may weigh strongly in favor of disclosure. In others, the balance may be more even, and in some cases one factor may be so compelling as to outweigh all the others. We decline to hold in the abstract that any factor or combination of factors must be determinative. A mechanistic, checklist approach would not in the long run (nor perhaps even in a particular case) serve the best interests of either newspersons or criminal defendants . . . .

B. Application of the proper test to this case

Under the proper balancing test set forth above, Delaney was clearly entitled to the reporters' testimony as to whether he consented to the police search of his jacket.

Threshold showing - Even under the test advocated by the reporters (heart of the case), Delaney would be entitled to their testimony. The municipal court explained to the reporters' counsel the lack of probable cause for the search: 'If there were probable cause for the search, I guarantee you the prosecutor would not be introducing the matter of [Delaney's] consent.' The court explained that if there was no consent the search was therefore illegal, and the charge against Delaney would have to be dismissed. Conversely, if he consented to the search, it was legal, the brass knuckles would be admitted into evidence, and Delaney would have little chance of an acquittal. As the court put it, the case 'will rise or fall on the admission or not of those metal knuckles.' We agree. It is an understatement to say, in the words of the test we adopt, that there is a reasonable possibility the reporters' testimony will assist Delaney in his defense. There is a substantial certainty that the reporters' testimony will materially affect the outcome of the criminal proceeding. Delaney has met and surpassed the required threshold showing.

Balancing factors - The balance weighs overwhelmingly in favor of requiring the reporters to testify. A brief review of the factors to be balanced makes this clear.

(1) Whether the unpublished information is confidential or senstitive - As we have already noted, the reporters do not claim their percipient observations of Delaney's search and arrest in a public place were made in confidence or were sensitive.

(2) The interests sought to be protected by the shield law - There is not even a suggestion in this case that the reporters' testimony would impinge on their future news-gathering ability or other interest, if any, sought to be protected by the shield law. Both parties who were observed by the reporters (Delaney and the police) are seeking their testimony. Thus, it cannot be said the parties or anyone else would be reluctant to provide these reporters with future information based on a belief that the reporters had breached a confidence or divulged sensitive information.

(3) The importance of the information to the criminal defendant - As explained above, the reporters' testimony will likely be determinative of the outcome of this case.

(4) Whether there is an alternative source for the unpublished information - We have explained that a criminal defendant need not always show the lack of an alternative source for a newsperson's unpublished information. We need not consider whether such a showing was required in this case because the municipal court implicitly assumed that it was required, and Delaney made a satisfactory showing. At the hearing on the motion to suppress, the reporters' counsel suggested that Delaney be required to take the stand and testify as to whether he had consented to the search. The court promptly advised counsel as to a defendant's constitutional right not to do so. Counsel also urged as alternative sources Delaney's companion, who was present at the time of the search, and four other officers who might have been within hearing distance of the search. The court correctly explained that neither the companion nor the other officers would be disinterested witnesses. The only two persons fitting that description are the two reporters. Thus, contrary to their assertion, their testimony would not be merely cumulative to that of the other potential witnesses. We concur in the municipal court's determination that there was no meaningful alternative source for the reporters' testimony.

In short, the court struck the correct balance. Delaney's personal liberty is at stake. The reporters are not being asked to breach a confidence or to disclose sensitive information that would in any way even remotely restrict their news-gathering ability. All that is being required of them is to accept the civic responsibility imposed on all persons who witness alleged criminal conduct . . . .

Disposition

The judgment of the Court of Appeal is affirmed . . .

In re Beth WILLON, et al., on Habeas Corpus.

47 Cal.App.4th 1080, 55 Cal.Rptr.2d 245

Court of Appeal, Sixth District, California.

July 25, 1996.

Writ issued.

Premo, Acting P.J., filed a concurring opinion.

ELIA, Associate Justice.

In this writ proceeding, a reporter and news director of a local television station seek relief from contempt after they refused to disclose the identity of a person who provided information about a pending criminal prosecution in violation of a protective ("gag") order. Petitioners contend that California's shield law, California Constitution, article I, section 2, subdivision (b) (hereafter, article I, section (2)(b)), immunizes them from contempt under these circumstances. Respondent, the Santa Clara County Superior Court, maintains that the contempt order was necessary to deter future violations and thereby protect the defendant's right to a fair trial. We hold that the shield law protects the news media from contempt absent a specific showing that nondisclosure of the source will create a substantial probability of injury to the criminal defendant's right to a fair trial. Accordingly, we will grant petitioners' request for a writ of habeas corpus or certiorari and annul the judgment of contempt.

Background

Petitioner Beth Willon is a news reporter for KNTV Channel 11 in San Jose. Petitioner Terrence McElhatton is the news director of KNTV. On February 14, 1996, jury selection began in the trial of Richard Allen Davis, who was accused of the kidnapping and murder of 12-year-old Polly Klaas. Polly's disappearance from her Petaluma home and the subsequent arrest of Davis had generated widespread publicity and extensive local community involvement. Although the preliminary hearing was open to the public, the Sonoma County Superior Court closed some of the pretrial proceedings and issued a protective order prohibiting court staff, participants and witnesses from discussing what had transpired at those hearings. Nevertheless, due to the magnitude of public attention to the case in Sonoma County, the court was unable to obtain an impartial jury, and eventually it granted a motion for a change of venue to Santa Clara County.

On January 10, 1996, the superior court in Santa Clara County expressed its concern that selection of an unbiased jury would be frustrated if facts were disclosed about the upcoming trial. The court observed that the case was "one of considerable public interest which may result in substantial publicity and that there is a reasonable likelihood that public dissemination by any means of extrajudicial statements relating to this case may interfere with a fair trial, and may otherwise prejudice the due administration of justice." Accordingly, the court issued another protective order which prohibited court officers, law enforcement officers and other public officials, and prospective trial witnesses from releasing to the public any evidence that had not yet been ruled admissible by the court, as well as any comments about the evidence gathered, testimony already heard or expected, and the identity of prospective witnesses. Subsequently, the trial court denied a request by representatives of the news media to make transcripts of the prior closed hearings available to the public before a jury was seated, citing its duty to protect the defendant's right to a fair trial.

On February 14, 1996, the first day of jury selection, KNTV broadcast a report prepared by petitioner Beth Willon. During the 6:00 p.m. newscast, anchor Doug Moore stated, "KNTV news has learned the entire videotaped confession of accused killer Richard Allen Davis will be used as evidence in the Polly Klaas murder trial." Co-anchor Maggi Scura added, "This development comes from a source close to the investigation." Willon then related the details of the events to which Davis had confessed, as described by "a source close to the case." The "source" also told Willon that there were no witnesses to two stops the defendant had made after kidnapping Polly, and that Davis was not asked about sexual assault when his confession was taped. Willon commented that "because Polly Klaas' body was so badly decomposed, it will probably never be known if she was sexually assaulted." Scura and Willon added that most of the contents of the statement had already been made public; the new information was that the entire statement would be admitted into evidence at trial.

Later that day, during the 11 p.m. newscast, Doug Moore repeated that Davis's confession would be used as evidence in the trial. Willon again related details of the kidnapping and murder as described in Davis's statement, punctuated by introductory phrases such as "Our source says ..." and "Our source tells us...." At the conclusion of Willon's report, Moore added, "And our source says it will likely never be known if Polly Klaas was still alive when the deputies stopped Davis on Pithian Road. Along with the kidnap and murder charges, Davis is charged with lewd and lascivious conduct, but because Polly Klaas' body was so badly decomposed, it will probably never be known if she was sexually assaulted. Our source tells us there were no questions about sexual assault when Davis' confession was taped."

The following day, February 15, 1996, the trial court played a videotape of the newscasts and asked the parties to address its concern that the contents of the KNTV newscasts might have been obtained in violation of the court's protective order. The district attorney believed that all of the information reported was available from the preliminary hearing transcript and from other media coverage. The court noted, however, that several of the statements were prefaced by references to their "source close to the case." If these statements were in fact obtained from a person subject to the order, the reporter involved would have "no privilege to refuse to disclose this so-called confidential source." The court had an "obligation" to discover who had violated the protective order; otherwise, "a court order means nothing." The court added that the timing of the broadcast "could not be worse," since jury selection had just begun; in the court's view it appeared to be an attempt to contaminate the jury pool in Santa Clara County and "ensure that the parties don't receive a fair trial."

On February 21, 1996, the trial court issued subpoenas ordering petitioners to appear in court the following week. On February 28, 1996, petitioners appeared with counsel. The court commenced the hearing by stating it had a "mandatory duty" to protect defendants from the effects of prejudicial publicity "by censuring and disciplining those who violate protective orders." The court expressed "significant concerns" that the material in the KNTV newscasts was obtained from a person subject to the existing protective order, "and that this information could have the reasonable likelihood of tainting the potential jurors and depriving this defendant of his right to a fair trial."

The court identified several statements by KNTV that it believed were derived from material encompassed within the protective order: (1) the announcement that the defendant's confession would be used as evidence at trial; (2) the narration of Davis's confession in detail; (3) the statement that there were no witnesses to either of the stops Davis made after kidnapping Polly; (4) the statement that Davis was not asked about sexual assault when his confession was taped; and (5) the comment that the body was so badly decomposed it probably will never be known if she was sexually assaulted.

Each of these statements, the court found, was a violation of the previous orders sealing records and prohibiting comment or disclosure regarding the case. The court emphasized the importance of ascertaining who had violated its protective orders, not only to punish the violation, but "to ensure that no future violations occur." The court reminded the parties that "[t]he need to prevent the dissemination of prejudicial publicity during jury selection is not only paramount, but goes to the heart of the right of this defendant to receive a fair trial in Santa Clara County." In the court's view, "this is exactly the type of prejudicial pre-trial publicity which taints the jury pools."

The trial court recognized the protection afforded news reporters under article I, section (2)(b), but it opined that the protection was of a limited immunity which was outweighed by the defendant's right to a fair trial. In order to protect that right, the court reasoned, it was "both bound and empowered" to explore the violations of the protective order as an exercise of its "preeminent federal constitutionally compelled duty to control its own officers," and thereby to forestall additional pretrial publicity. The court also found that questioning up to 1500 individuals who were subject to the order would entail a needless delay of the trial and therefore was "not a reasonable alternative."

Through county counsel the trial court proceeded to question petitioners individually regarding the identity of their source. On each occasion the court admonished them that the question was "constitutionally permissible" and ordered them to answer. To every question but one, petitioners declined to answer, citing the shield law and the First Amendment of the federal Constitution. Petitioners did respond when county counsel asked whether they had promised confidentiality to the source; Willon had made such a promise, and McElhatton had not.

At the conclusion of the hearing the trial court informed petitioners that they were being cited for contempt, based on the following findings: "You have been informed that the qualified immunity set forth in Evidence Code section 1070 and the California Constitution, Article One, Section 2(b), does not apply to the circumstances before the court in which the court has a duty to determine those individuals who have violated the court's protective order in order to ensure the defendant's right to a fair trial." The court observed that petitioners had the ability to comply with the order but "chose not to do so." Accordingly, the court found petitioners to be in direct contempt within the meaning of Code of Civil Procedure section 1209, subdivisions (a)(5) and (a)(9), and ordered them imprisoned until they agreed to answer the court's questions. At the request of petitioners' counsel, the court granted a five-day stay until Monday, March 4, 1996.

On February 29, 1996, petitioners applied in this court for a temporary stay of execution of the trial court's contempt order. On March 1, this court granted a temporary stay of execution, and granted petitioners 10 days to file a formal petition for review. On March 29, 1996, after receiving the petition, opposition, and an amicus curiae brief from various media representatives, we issued an order directing the trial court to show cause for denial of the requested relief.

## Discussion

### 1. Standard of Review

The standard of this court's review is governed by established principles. The question before us is whether the trial court had jurisdiction to impose the contempt order. We examine the entire record to determine whether there is substantial evidence to sustain the order. (In re Buckley (1973) 10 Cal.3d 237, 247, 110 Cal.Rptr. 121, 514 P.2d 1201; Mitchell v. Superior Court (1989) 49 Cal.3d 1230, 1256, 265 Cal.Rptr. 144, 783 P.2d 731.) In this case, the trial court punished petitioners for direct contempt, since their refusal to answer questions occurred in the court's immediate presence. A direct contempt order may be punished summarily, but the court must state the facts on which it is based with sufficient particularity to demonstrate on its face, without the aid of speculation, that petitioner's conduct constituted a legal contempt. (Ibid.; McCann v. Municipal Court (1990) 221 Cal.App.3d 527, 536, 270 Cal.Rptr. 640.) Although the power to weigh evidence is solely that of the trial court, the reviewing court does not presume in support of the contempt order. (McCann v. Municipal Court, supra, 221 Cal.App.3d at p. 537, 270 Cal.Rptr. 640.) If the record of the proceedings fails to demonstrate on its face the existence of all the necessary facts upon which jurisdiction depended, the contempt order cannot be sustained. (Mitchell v. Superior Court, supra, 49 Cal.3d at p. 1256, 265 Cal.Rptr. 144, 783 P.2d 731.)

There is no dispute about the facts underlying the contempt order in this case. Petitioners refused to answer questions about the identity of the person on whom they apparently relied in gathering information for their broadcasts about Davis's trial. The trial court's conclusion that petitioners' refusal to disclose their source was a sufficient ground for contempt was based on the court's concern that future violations of its protective order would taint the jury pool and thus preclude a trial by an impartial jury. This determination presents a mixed question of law and fact which is subject to independent appellate review. (People v. Louis (1986) 42 Cal.3d 969, 984, 232 Cal.Rptr. 110, 728 P.2d 180; cf. People v. Sanders (1995) 11 Cal.4th 475, 506, 46 Cal.Rptr.2d 751, 905 P.2d 420 [in motions for change of venue, reasonable likelihood of a fair and impartial trial is mixed question of law and fact, reviewed de novo].) Before we can make this determination, however, we must address the overarching question of what showing is necessary to override the constitutional protection of article I, section 2(b) and compel disclosure of news sources during a pending criminal proceeding.

2. Application of the Shield Law

California's shield law has been in existence since 1935, when it was added to Code of Civil Procedure section 1881 as subdivision (6). (Stats 1935, ch. 532, § 1, p. 1608.) Over the next 40 years the statute was amended numerous times. In 1961 the Legislature expanded the class of protected individuals beyond those connected with newspapers to persons associated with magazines, television, radio, and wire services. In 1965, the Legislature incorporated the shield into the newly adopted Evidence Code, where it was enacted as section 1070. (Stats.1965, ch. 299, § 2, p. 1335.) Evidence Code section 1070 (hereafter, "section 1070") was amended several more times, most notably in 1974, when the Legislature added a protection for the refusal to disclose unpublished information. (Stats.1974, ch. 1323, § 1, p. 2877; ch. 1456, § 2, p. 3184.)

The most significant development in the evolution of California's shield law took place in 1980, when the voters passed Proposition 5, thereby incorporating the shield law into the state Constitution. In languagenearly identical to section 1070, article I, section 2(b) provides that persons currently or formerly employed in the news media "shall not be adjudged in contempt" for refusing to disclose either (1) the source of information obtained while associated with the newsgathering organization, or (2) materials such as notes, photographs, or tapes acquired or prepared in gathering news, but not disseminated to the public. . . . .

On its face, article I, section 2(b) does appear to provide absolute protection to those engaged in the newsgathering process; it is couched in clear mandatory language without qualification. Indeed, in civil proceedings the provision has been construed to provide "the highest possible level of protection" from disclosure of materials sought by a civil litigant. (Playboy Enterprises, Inc. v. Superior Court, supra, 154 Cal.App.3d at p. 27-28, 201 Cal.Rptr. 207; Mitchell v. Superior Court, supra, 37 Cal.3d at p. 274, 208 Cal.Rptr. 152, 690 P.2d 625; New York Times Co. v. Superior Court, supra, 51 Cal.3d 453, 456, 273 Cal.Rptr. 98, 796 P.2d 811.)

In the context of criminal proceedings, however, it is settled that the protection "must yield to a criminal defendant's constitutional right to a fair trial when the newsperson's refusal to disclose information would unduly infringe on that right." (Delaney v. Superior Court, supra, 50 Cal.3d at p. 793.) . . . .

This test, however, is inapplicable here. Unlike Delaney, we are not confronted with a request by a defendant for information that would directly assist in his or her defense; here it is the trial court that seeks disclosure in order to preserve its ability to control the judicial process and maintain an unbiased jury pool. Furthermore, petitioners have not been ordered to testify as observers of a public event, as were the reporters in Delaney, but as holders of confidential information respecting the identity of their news source. We thus agree with the parties that the threshold showing and balancing test formulated in Delaney are not controlling here . . . .

Petitioners' argument is well taken. Article I, section 2(b) offers no real protection if it can be overridden merely by a conclusive presumption that nondisclosure will be harmful to the accused. "[P]retrial publicity, even if pervasive and concentrated, cannot be regarded as leading automatically and in every kind of criminal case to an unfair trial." (Nebraska Press Assn. v. Stuart, supra, 427 U.S. at p. 565, 96 S.Ct. at p. 2805.) Nor is it sufficient to state, as did the trial court here, that the newsperson had the ability to answer the court's questions and refused to do so. In our view, a newsperson should not be held in contempt for refusing to disclose news sources or unpublished information absent specific findings demonstrating that disclosure of the information sought is necessary to avert an actual threat to the defendant's right to a fair trial.

This conclusion, however, calls for more precise guidelines. By what standard should the underlying facts be examined to determine whether disclosure is necessary to avoid prejudice to defendant? Furthermore, what criteria should guide a trial court's application of that standard?

In Sheppard v. Maxwell, supra, 384 U.S. 333, 86 S.Ct. 1507, 16 L.Ed.2d 600, the United States Supreme Court used a "reasonable likelihood" test for determining the necessity of measures to guard against prejudicial publicity. Accordingly, where there is a "reasonable likelihood that prejudicial news prior to trial will prevent a fair trial," a trial judge must take whatever steps are necessary to protect the proceedings from such interference. (Id. at p. 363, 86 S.Ct. at 1522.) Similarly, Penal Code 1033 requires the court to grant a motion for change of venue "when it appears that there is a reasonable likelihood that a fair and impartial trial cannot be had in the county." (Pen.Code, § 1033, emphasis added.) Appellate courts of this state also use this standard in ascertaining the effect of certain trial court errors; those errors will be considered prejudicial only if it is "reasonably probable" that a result more favorable to the defendant would have been reached absent the error. (People v. Watson (1956) 46 Cal.2d 818, 836, 299 P.2d 243.)

We believe this standard is inadequate to preserve the newsperson's constitutional immunity under article 1, section 2(b). The "reasonable probability" test generally imparts a meaning greater than "merely possible," but less than "more likely than not." (People v. Bonin (1988) 46 Cal.3d 659, 673, 250 Cal.Rptr. 687, 758 P.2d 1217; College Hospital, Inc. v. Superior Court

(1994) 8 Cal.4th 704, 715, 34 Cal.Rptr.2d 898, 882 P.2d 894 [term "probability" in the Watson test means "merely a reasonable chance, more than an abstract possibility"]; see also Strickland v. Washington (1984) 466 U.S. 668, 693, 694, 104 S.Ct. 2052, 2067-2068, 2068, 80 L.Ed.2d 674 [to establish reasonable probability of prejudice arising from ineffective assistance of counsel, defendant need not show counsel's deficient performance "more likely than not" altered result, but only probability "sufficient to undermine confidence in the outcome."] ) Here, however, the defendant's right to a fair trial must be considered not in isolation but in relation to a competing constitutional interest, albeit a subordinate one. In such cases a stronger showing than a reasonable likelihood of prejudice should be required to overcome the protection of the shield law.

Petitioners advocate a "substantial probability" test, a more demanding level of scrutiny than the "reasonable likelihood" test. (Press- Enterprise II, supra, 478 U.S. at p. 14, 106 S.Ct. at p. 2743; Press- Enterprise v. Superior Court, supra, 22 Cal.App.4th 498, 27 Cal.Rptr.2d 708; People v. Clair (1992) 2 Cal.4th 629, 668, 7 Cal.Rptr.2d 564, 828 P.2d 705.) This is the same standard used to review judicial restrictions on public access to criminal proceedings. Jury voir dire, preliminary examination, and trial must remain open absent specific, express findings demonstrating that exclusion of the public "is essential to preserve higher values and is narrowly tailored to serve that interest." (Press-Enterprise I, supra, 464 U.S. 501, 510, 104 S.Ct. 819, 824, 78 L.Ed.2d 629; Globe Newspaper Co. v. Superior Court, supra, 457 U.S. 596, 607, 102 S.Ct. 2613, 2620, 73 L.Ed.2d 248; Press-Enterprise II, supra, 478 U.S. 1, 13-14, 106 S.Ct. 2735, 2742- 2743, 92 L.Ed.2d 1.) If the interest asserted is the right of the accused to a fair trial, the preliminary hearing may be closed "only if specific findings are made demonstrating that, first, there is a substantial probability that the defendant's right to a fair trial will be prejudiced by publicity that closure would prevent and, second, reasonable alternatives to closure cannot adequately protect the defendant's fair trial rights." (Press-Enterprise II, supra, 478 U.S. at p. 14, 106 S.Ct. at p. 2743, emphasis added.)

The "substantial probability" test has been applied in a variety of procedural contexts in which a defendant's right to a fair trial is the dominant interest to be protected, even when no competing individual interests are involved . . . .

We believe that a substantial probability standard both protects the defendant's fair trial rights and recognizes the importance of the immunity conferred by article I, section 2(b). Accordingly, where a violation of a protective or "gag" order has already occurred, a court should determine the necessity of disclosure of the newsperson's source by addressing two principal considerations in light of all the relevant circumstances: (1) If the newsperson does not disclose the identity of the source, is there a substantial probability of future violations, or "leaks," that will impair the defendant's ability to obtain a fair trial? and (2) Are there reasonable alternatives to disclosure that will protect the interests asserted by both the newsperson and the defendant?

The first inquiry suggests two secondary questions: (a) is there any indication that further leaks are likely to occur; and (b) will those leaks, if published, make it impossible to obtain an impartial jury in the chosen venue? Factors relevant to these determinations include the nature and extent of the publicity, the amount of information already in the public domain, the existence of prejudicial information not yet released to the public, the size of the county from which prospective jurors will be drawn, and the potential of voir dire or other measures to eliminate any prejudice caused by the publicity.

The second inquiry entails consideration of the feasibility of alternative methods of obtaining the information and the confidentiality or sensitivity of the information. Disclosure of confidential or sensitive information is more likely to have a significant effect on the newsperson's future ability to gather news, the protection of which is the primary purpose of the shield law. (Delaney v. Superior Court, supra, 50 Cal.3d at p. 810, 268 Cal.Rptr. 753, 789 P.2d 934.) By the same token, the importance of finding alternatives to disclosure is diminished where the identity of the source is not confidential, since "[t]he obvious purpose of the alternative-source requirement is to protect against unnecessary disclosure of a newsperson's confidential or sensitive information." (Id. at pp. 811-812, 268 Cal.Rptr. 753, 789 P.2d 934.)

We initially consider the facts pertaining to the first inquiry--whether there is a substantial probability that failure to identify petitioners' source will facilitate additional leaks that will jeopardize the fairness of Davis's trial. As noted earlier, this is a mixed question of law and fact subject to our independent judgment. We enter into this analysis keeping in mind that assessing the likely effect of an event by its nature calls for speculation. (See People v. Cooper, supra, 53 Cal.3d 771, 839, 281 Cal.Rptr. 90, 809 P.2d 865; see also Nebraska Press Assn. v. Stuart, supra, 427 U.S. at p. 563, 96 S.Ct. at 2804 [finding that publicity could affect prospective jurors was necessarily speculative, since it dealt with "factors unknown and unknowable."] )

At the beginning of the contempt hearing the trial court stated that the KNTV newscasts "could have the reasonable likelihood of tainting the potential jurors." In its written contempt order, the court found that the dissemination of information subject to the protective order "poses a substantial likelihood of interfering with the defendant's basic constitutional right to a fair trial." This finding is predicated on the assumptions that unless petitioners disclose their source, future leaks will occur, and those leaks will prejudicially influence prospective jurors in Santa Clara County.

There is no evidence to support these assumptions. Although publicity surrounding this case was high, much of that attention had already resulted in the public's awareness of the salient details of the crime and Davis's participation in it. Davis's confession to the kidnapping and murder, for example, had been reported by several of the news media. Moreover, the details of the confession were revealed during the preliminary examination through the testimony of police sergeant Michael Meese, who had obtained the confession during his interrogation of Davis. The news that the confession would be admitted at trial added little to the public's knowledge of the case. If the court had ruled the confession inadmissible, or if Davis had retracted his statements before trial, we would be more inclined to view the release of information regarding the confession as potentially harmful. But in this situation, any impact on the community caused by the admissibility ruling would be alleviated by asking questions at voir dire regarding the effect of a confession on the prospective jurors' ability to be fair and impartial.

In addition to the details of the confession and the admissibility ruling, the trial court expressed disapproval of the source's alleged statements that there were no witnesses to either of the stops Davis made after kidnapping Polly and that the videotaped interview did not include questions about sexual assault. The only inference the court drew from these statements, however, was that they were made in violation of the protective order. The court did not suggest, nor do we perceive, any prejudice that could result from these statements. Viewed in the context of the entire newscast, which related the salient details of the crime and the recovery of the victim's body, these two points pertaining to the absence of evidence appear relatively insignificant.

Finally, the court took exception to the KNTV comment that "because Polly Klaas' body was so badly decomposed, it will probably never be known if she was sexually assaulted." Although this statement was not directly attributed to the source, the court found that it "purports to report information that could only be known to persons subject to the court's protective and seal orders." We disagree. At the preliminary hearing, which was open to the public, the prosecution examined Jay Chapman, the forensic pathologist, regarding the condition of the victim's body. During Dr. Chapman's testimony the public learned that the decomposition of the body precluded medical conclusions regarding sexual abuse. Furthermore, like the two statements discussed above, this one pertained to the absence of evidence, not a matter excluded from evidence. Any anticipated effect this information might have on selection of an impartial jury could be controlled by appropriate voir dire questions eliciting the prospective jurors' reactions to learning about a decomposed body.

In each of these instances of concern to the trial court, the material reported by KNTV was already in the public domain, of minimal significance to the case, or remediable by effective voir dire. There was no evidence that Santa Clara County was permeated by prejudicial views regarding the crime, or that the KNTV newscast was heard by a large portion of the community. Thus, even assuming that petitioners obtained information for the newscasts from their source, we see no substantial or even reasonable probability that the source's violation would have influenced the entire jury pool. Since the record does not indicate that there is additional evidence that the court sought to withhold from the public pending jury selection, we have no basis for finding a substantial likelihood of any future violations of the protective order that would create impermissible juror bias.

We therefore conclude there are insufficient grounds for finding a substantial probability of prejudice from nondisclosure of petitioners' source. Since disclosure has not been shown to be necessary to assure Davis a fair trial under this first step of the inquiry, we need not address the second question, whether there are reasonable alternatives to compelled disclosure. We also need not discuss petitioners' claim of protection under the First Amendment, their argument that the court violated their due process right to notice and an opportunity to be heard, or the contention of amicus curiae that the gag order was unconstitutionally overbroad.

James ZURCHER, etc., et al., Petitioners,
v.
The STANFORD DAILY et al.

436 U.S. 547

Supreme Court of the United States

Decided May 31, 1978.

Mr. Justice WHITE delivered the opinion of the Court.

The terms of the Fourth Amendment, applicable to the States by virtue of the Fourteenth Amendment, are familiar:

> "The right of the people to be secure in their persons, houses, papers, and effects, against unreasonable searches and seizures, shall not be violated, and no Warrants shall issue, but upon probable cause, supported by Oath or affirmation, and particularly describing the place to be searched, and the persons or things to be seized."

As heretofore understood, the Amendment has not been a barrier to warrants to search property on which there is probable cause to believe that fruits, instrumentalities, or evidence of crime is located, whether or not the owner or possessor of the premises to be searched is himself reasonably suspected of complicity in the crime being investigated. We are now asked to reconstrue the Fourth Amendment and to hold for the first time that when the place to be searched is occupied by a person not then a suspect, a warrant to search for criminal objects and evidence reasonably believed to be located there should not issue except in the most unusual circumstances, and that except in such circumstances, a subpoena duces tecum must be relied upon to recover the objects or evidence sought.

I

Late in the day on Friday, April 9, 1971, officers of the Palo Alto Police Department and of the Santa Clara County Sheriff's Department responded to a call from the director of the Stanford University Hospital requesting the removal of a large group of demonstrators who had seized the hospital's administrative offices and occupied them since the previous afternoon. After several futile efforts to persuade the demonstrators to leave peacefully, more drastic measures were employed. The demonstrators had barricaded the doors at both ends of a hall adjacent to the administrative offices. The police chose to force their way in at the west end of the corridor. As they did so, a group of demonstrators emerged through the doors at the east end and, armed with sticks and clubs, attacked the group of nine police officers stationed there. One officer was knocked to the floor and struck repeatedly on the head; another suffered a broken shoulder. All nine were injured. There were no police photographers at the east doors, and most bystanders and reporters were on the west side. The officers themselves were able to identify only two of their assailants, but one of them did see at least one person photographing the assault at the east doors.

On Sunday, April 11, a special edition of the Stanford Daily (Daily), a student newspaper published at Stanford University, carried articles and photographs devoted to the hospital protest and the violent clash between demonstrators and police. The photographs carried the byline of a Daily staff member and indicated that he had been at the east end of the hospital hallway where he could have photographed the assault on the nine officers. The next day, the Santa Clara County District Attorney's Office secured a warrant from the Municipal Court for an immediate search of the Daily's offices for negatives, film, and pictures showing the events and occurrences at the hospital on the evening of April 9. The warrant issued on a finding of "just, probable and reasonable cause for believing that: Negatives and photographs and films, evidence material and relevant to the identity of the perpetrators of felonies, to wit, Battery on a Peace Officer, and Assault with Deadly Weapon, will be located [on the premises of the Daily]." App. 31-32. The warrant affidavit contained no allegation or indication that members of the Daily staff were in any way involved in unlawful acts at the hospital.

The search pursuant to the warrant was conducted later that day by four police officers and took place in the presence of some members of the Daily staff. The Daily's photographic laboratories, filing cabinets, desks, and wastepaper baskets were searched. Locked drawers and rooms were not opened. The officers apparently had opportunity to read notes and correspondence during the search; but, contrary to claims of the staff, the officers denied that they had exceeded the limits of the warrant. They had not been advised by the staff that the areas they were searching contained confidential materials. The search revealed only the photographs that had already been published on April 11, and no materials were removed from the Daily's office.

A month later the Daily and various members of its staff, respondents here, brought a civil action in the United States District Court for the Northern District of California seeking declaratory and injunctive relief under 42 U.S.C. § 1983 against the police officers who conducted the search, the chief of police, the district attorney and one of his deputies, and the judge who had issued the warrant. The complaint alleged that the search of the Daily's office had deprived respondents under color of state law of rights secured to them by the First, Fourth, and Fourteenth Amendments of the United States Constitution.

The District Court denied the request for an injunction but, on respondents' motion for summary judgment, granted declaratory relief. 353 F.Supp. 124 (1972). The court did not question the existence of probable cause to believe that a crime had been committed and to believe that relevant evidence would be found on the Daily's premises. It held, however, that the Fourth and Fourteenth Amendments forbade the issuance of a warrant to search for materials in possession of one not suspected of crime unless there is probable cause to believe, based on facts presented in a sworn affidavit, that a subpoena duces tecum would be impracticable. Moreover, the failure to honor a subpoena would not alone justify a warrant; it must also appear that the possessor of the objects sought would disregard a court order not to remove or destroy them. The District Court further held that where the innocent object of the search is a newspaper, First Amendment interests are also involved and that such a search is constitutionally permissible "only in the rare circumstance where there is a clear showing that (1) important materials will be destroyed or removed from the jurisdiction; and (2) a restraining order would be futile." Id., at 135. Since these preconditions to a valid warrant had not been satisfied here, the search of the Daily's offices was declared to have been illegal. The Court of Appeals affirmed per curiam, adopting the opinion of the District Court. 550 F.2d 464 (CA9 1977). We issued the writs of certiorari requested by petitioners. 434 U.S. 816, 98 S.Ct. 52, 54 L.Ed.2d 71 (1977). We reverse.

II

The issue here is how the Fourth Amendment is to be construed and applied to the "third party" search, the recurring situation where state authorities have probable cause to believe that fruits, instrumentalities, or other evidence of crime is located on identified property but do not then have probable cause to believe that the owner or possessor of the property is himself implicated in the crime that has occurred or is occurring. Because under the District Court's rule impracticability can be shown only by furnishing facts demonstrating that the third party will not only disobey the subpoena but also ignore a restraining order not to move or destroy the property, it is apparent that only in unusual situations could the State satisfy such a severe burden and that for all practical purposes the effect of the rule is that fruits, instrumentalities, and evidence of crime may be recovered from third parties only by subpoena, not by search warrant. At least, we assume that the District Court did not intend its rule to be toothless and anticipated that only subpoenas would be available in many cases where without the rule a search warrant would issue.

It is an understatement to say that there is no direct authority in this or any other federal court for the District Court's sweeping revision of the Fourth Amendment. Under existing law, valid warrants may be issued to search any property, whether or not occupied by a third party, at which there is probable cause to believe that fruits, instrumentalities, or evidence of a crime will be found. Nothing on the face of the Amendment suggests that a third-party search warrant should not normally issue. The Warrant Clause speaks of search warrants issued on "probable cause" and "particularly describing the place to be searched, and the persons or things to be seized." In situations where the State does not seek to seize "persons" but only those "things" which there is probable cause to believe are located on the place to be searched, there is no apparent basis in the languageof the Amendment for also imposing the requirements for a valid arrest--probable cause to believe that the third party is implicated in the crime . . . .

## IV

The District Court held, and respondents assert here, that whatever may be true of third-party searches generally, where the third party is a newspaper, there are additional factors derived from the First Amendment that justify a nearly per se rule forbidding the search warrant and permitting only the subpoena duces tecum. The general submission is that searches of newspaper offices for evidence of crime reasonably believed to be on the premises will seriously threaten the ability of the press to gather, analyze, and disseminate news. This is said to be true for several reasons: First, searches will be physically disruptive to such an extent that timely publication will be impeded. Second, confidential sources of information will dry up, and the press will also lose opportunities to cover various events because of fears of the participants that press files will be readily available to the authorities. Third, reporters will be deterred from recording and preserving their recollections for future use if such information is subject to seizure. Fourth, the processing of news and its dissemination will be chilled by the prospects that searches will disclose internal editorial deliberations. Fifth, the press will resort to self-censorship to conceal its possession of information of potential interest to the police.

It is true that the struggle from which the Fourth Amendment emerged "is largely a history of conflict between the Crown and the press," Stanford v. Texas, 379 U.S. 476, 482, 85 S.Ct. 506, 510, 13 L.Ed.2d 431 (1965), and that in issuing warrants and determining the reasonableness of a search, state and federal magistrates should be aware that "unrestricted power of search and seizure could also be an instrument for stifling liberty of expression." Marcus v. Search Warrant, 367 U.S. 717, 729, 81 S.Ct. 1708, 1715, 6 L.Ed.2d 1127 (1961). Where the materials sought to be seized may be protected by the First Amendment, the requirements of the Fourth Amendment must be applied with "scrupulous exactitude." Stanford v. Texas, supra, 379 U.S., at 485, 85 S.Ct., at 511. "A seizure reasonable as to one type of material in one setting may be unreasonable in a different setting or with respect to another kind of material." Roaden v. Kentucky, 413 U.S. 496, 501, 93 S.Ct. 2796, 2800, 37 L.Ed.2d 757 (1973). Hence, in Stanford v. Texas, the Court invalidated a warrant authorizing the search of a private home for all books, records, and other materials relating to the Communist Party, on the ground that whether or not the warrant would have been sufficient in other contexts, it authorized the searchers to rummage among and make judgments about books and papers and was the functional equivalent of a general warrant, one of the principal targets of the Fourth Amendment. Where presumptively protected materials are sought to be seized, the warrant requirement should be administered to leave as little as possible to the discretion or whim of the officer in the field.

Similarly, where seizure is sought of allegedly obscene materials, the judgment of the arresting officer alone is insufficient to justify issuance of a search warrant or a seizure without a warrant incident to arrest. The procedure for determining probable cause must afford an opportunity for the judicial officer to "focus searchingly on the question of obscenity." Marcus v. Search Warrant, supra, 367 U.S., at 732, 81 S.Ct., at 1716; A Quantity of Books v. Kansas, 378 U.S. 205, 210, 84 S.Ct. 1723, 1725, 12 L.Ed.2d 809 (1964); Lee Art Theatre, Inc. v. Virginia, 392 U.S. 636, 637, 88 S.Ct. 2103, 2104, 20 L.Ed.2d 1313 (1968 . . .

Neither the Fourth Amendment nor the cases requiring consideration of First Amendment values in issuing search warrants, however, call for imposing the regime ordered by the District Court. Aware of the long struggle between Crown and press and desiring to curb unjustified official intrusions, the Framers took the enormously important step of subjecting searches to the test of reasonableness and to the general rule requiring search warrants issued by neutral magistrates. They nevertheless did not forbid warrants where the press was involved, did not require special showings that subpoenas would be impractical, and did not insist that the owner of the place to be searched, if connected with the press, must be shown to be implicated in the offense being investigated. Further, the prior cases do no more than insist that the courts apply the warrant requirements with particular exactitude when First Amendment interests would be endangered by the search. As we see it, no more than this is required where the warrant requested is for the seizure of criminal evidence reasonably believed to be on the premises occupied by a newspaper. Properly administered, the preconditions for a warrant--probable cause, specificity with respect to the place to be searched and the things to be seized, and overall reasonableness--should afford sufficient protection against the harms that are assertedly threatened by warrants for searching newspaper offices.

There is no reason to believe, for example, that magistrates cannot guard against searches of the type, scope, and intrusiveness that would actually interfere with the timely publication of a newspaper. Nor, if the requirements of specificity and reasonableness are properly applied, policed, and observed, will there be any occasion or opportunity for officers to rummage at large in newspaper files or to intrude into or to deter normal editorial and publication decisions. The warrant issued in this case authorized nothing of this sort. Nor are we convinced, any more than we were in Branzburg v. Hayes, 408 U.S. 665, 92 S.Ct. 2646, 33 L.Ed.2d 626 (1972), that confidential sources will disappear and that the press will suppress news because of fears of warranted searches. Whatever incremental effect there may be in this regard if search warrants, as well as subpoenas, are permissible in proper circumstances, it does not make a constitutional difference in our judgment.

The fact is that respondents and amici have pointed to only a very few instances in the entire United States since 1971 involving the issuance of warrants for searching newspaper premises. This reality hardly suggests abuse; and if abuse occurs, there will be time enough to deal with it. Furthermore, the press is not only an important, critical, and valuable asset to society, but it is not easily intimidated--nor should it be.

Respondents also insist that the press should be afforded opportunity to litigate the State's entitlement to the material it seeks before it is turned over or seized and that whereas the search warrant procedure is defective in this respect, resort to the subpoena would solve the problem. The Court has held that a restraining order imposing a prior restraint upon free expression is invalid for want of notice and opportunity for a hearing, Carroll v. Princess Anne, 393 U.S. 175, 89 S.Ct. 347, 21 L.Ed.2d 325 (1968), and that seizures not merely for use as evidence but entirely removing arguably protected materials from circulation may be effected only after an adversary hearing and a judicial finding of obscenity. A Quantity of Books v. Kansas, supra. But presumptively protected materials are not necessarily immune from seizure under warrant for use at a criminal trial. Not every such seizure, and not even most, will impose a prior restraint. Heller v. New York, supra. And surely a warrant to search newspaper premises for criminal evidence such as the one issued here for news photographs taken in a public place carries no realistic threat of prior restraint or of any direct restraint whatsoever on the publication of the Daily or on its communication of ideas. The hazards of such warrants can be avoided by a neutral magistrate carrying out his responsibilities under the Fourth Amendment, for he has ample tools at his disposal to confine warrants to search within reasonable limits.

We note finally that if the evidence sought by warrant is sufficiently connected with the crime to satisfy the probable-cause requirement, it will very likely be sufficiently relevant to justify a subpoena and to withstand a motion to quash. Further, Fifth Amendment and state shield-law objections that might be asserted in opposition to compliance with a subpoena are largely irrelevant to determining the legality of a search warrant under the Fourth Amendment. Of course, the Fourth Amendment does not prevent or advise against legislative or executive efforts to establish nonconstitutional protections against possible abuses of the search warrant procedure, but we decline to reinterpret the Amendment to impose a general constitutional barrier against warrants to search newspaper premises, to require resort to subpoenas as a general rule, or to demand prior notice and hearing in connection with the issuance of search warrants.

V

We accordingly reject the reasons given by the District Court and adopted by the Court of Appeals for holding the search for photographs at the Stanford Daily to have been unreasonable within the meaning of the Fourth Amendment and in violation of the First Amendment. Nor has anything else presented here persuaded us that the Amendments forbade this search. It follows that the judgment of the Court of Appeals is reversed.

So ordered.

Mr. Justice STEWART, with whom Mr. Justice MARSHALL joins, dissenting.

Believing that the search by the police of the offices of the Stanford Daily infringed the First and Fourteenth Amendments' guarantee of a free press, I respectfully dissent.

I

It seems to me self-evident that police searches of newspaper offices burden the freedom of the press. The most immediate and obvious First Amendment injury caused by such a visitation by the police is physical disruption of the operation of the newspaper. Policemen occupying a newsroom and searching it thoroughly for what may be an extended period of time will inevitably interrupt its normal operations, and thus impair or even temporarily prevent the processes of newsgathering, writing, editing, and publishing. By contrast, a subpoena would afford the newspaper itself an opportunity to locate whatever material might be requested and produce it.

But there is another and more serious burden on a free press imposed by an unannounced police search of a newspaper office: the possibility of disclosure of information received from confidential sources, or of the identity of the sources themselves. Protection of those sources is necessary to ensure that the press can fulfill its constitutionally designated function of informing the public, because important information can often be obtained only by an assurance that the source will not be revealed. Branzburg v. Hayes, 408 U.S. 665, 725-736, 92 S.Ct. 2646, 2671-2677, 33 L.Ed.2d 626 (dissenting opinion). And the Court has recognized that " 'without some protection for seeking out the news, freedom of the press could be eviscerated.' " Pell v. Procunier, 417 U.S. 817, 833, 94 S.Ct. 2800, 2809, 41 L.Ed.2d 495.

Today the Court does not question the existence of this constitutional protection, but says only that it is not "convinced . . . that confidential sources will disappear and that the press will suppress news because of fears of warranted searches." Ante, at 1982. This facile conclusion seems to me to ignore common experience. It requires no blind leap of faith to understand that a person who gives information to a journalist only on condition that his identity will not be revealed will be less likely to give that information if he knows that, despite the journalist's assurance his identity may in fact be disclosed. And it cannot be denied that confidential information may be exposed to the eyes of police officers who execute a search warrant by rummaging through the files, cabinets, desks, and wastebaskets of a newsroom. [FN5] Since the indisputable effect of such searches will thus be to prevent a newsman from being able to promise confidentiality to his potential sources, it seems obvious to me that a journalist's access to information, and thus the public's will thereby be impaired.

# Part V: Broadcast-Cable-Internet

TELECOMMUNICATIONS RESEARCH AND ACTION CENTER (TRAC)
and Media Access Project,
Petitioners,
v.
FEDERAL COMMUNICATIONS COMMISSION and the United States of America,
Respondents,
National Association of Broadcasters, Public Broadcasting Service, American
Newspaper Publishers Association, Intervenors.

801 F.2d 501

United States Court of Appeals,
District of Columbia Circuit.

Decided Sept. 19, 1986.

BORK, Circuit Judge:

Petitioners challenge the Federal Communications Commission's decision not to apply three forms of political broadcast regulation to a new technology, teletext. Teletext provides a means of transmitting textual and graphic material to the television screens of home viewers.

The Communications Act of 1934, 47 U.S.C. § 312(a)(7) (1982), requires broadcast licensees to "allow reasonable access ... for the use of a broadcasting station by a legally qualified candidate for Federal elective office on behalf of his candidacy." In addition, under 47 U.S.C. § 315(a) (1982), if the licensee "permit[s] any person who is a legally qualified candidate for any public office to use a broadcasting station," he or she incurs the additional obligation of "afford[ing] equal opportunities to all other such candidates for that office." Complementing these statutory provisions, there exists a form of political broadcast regulation that the Commission created early in its history in the name of its mandate to ensure the use of the airwaves in the "public 'convenience, interest, or necessity.' " See Red Lion Broadcasting v. FCC, 395 U.S. 367, 376-77, 89 S.Ct. 1794, 1799, 23 L.Ed.2d 371 (1969). The "fairness doctrine," as this policy is known, "provides that broadcasters have certain obligations to afford reasonable opportunity for the discussion of conflicting views on issues of public importance." 47 C.F.R. § 73.1910 (1985).

The case before us presents the question whether the Commission erred in determining that these three political broadcast provisions do not apply to teletext. Because we find that the

Commission acted reasonably with respect to section 312(a)(7) and the fairness doctrine, but erroneously held section 315 not to apply to teletext, we affirm in part and reverse in part, and remand to the Commission for further proceedings.

I.

. . . On June 3, 1985, the Telecommunications Research and Action Center and the Media Access Project ("TRAC/MAP") filed a petition for review in this court, largely renewing the substantive legal arguments asserted in the petitions for reconsideration below. Because the Commission's interpretation of the first amendment affects its analysis of political broadcasting regulation and teletext at several points, we discuss that interpretation first. We then address the petitioners' contentions with respect to section 312(a)(7), section 315, and the fairness doctrine in that order.

II.

In the Commission's view the regulation of teletext's "unique blend of the print medium with radio technology" raises first amendment problems not associated with the regulation of traditional broadcasting. Thus, the argument goes, existing Supreme Court precedent upholding political content regulation of traditional broadcasting does not necessarily justify the application of such regulation to the new medium of teletext. While not concluding that this application to a "print medium" like teletext would violate the first amendment, the Commission suggested that its application of that regulation would be sufficiently suspect to justify not imputing to Congress an intent to apply "section 315 and similar statutory provisions, and ... associated rules and policies, to the teletext medium." 101 F.C.C.2d at 834. To appreciate the Commission's argument, a brief discussion of the case law will be useful.

In Red Lion Broadcasting Co. v. FCC, 395 U.S. 367, 89 S.Ct. 1794, 23 L.Ed.2d 371 (1969), the Supreme Court rejected a first amendment challenge to the fairness doctrine and related rules governing personal attacks and political editorials by licensees. In reasoning that applies generally to political broadcasting regulation, the Court found justification for limiting first amendment protection of broadcasting in the "scarcity doctrine." Given the fact of a limited number of broadcast frequencies and the "massive" problem of broadcast interference, the Court remarked that "only a tiny fraction of those with resources and intelligence can hope to communicate by radio at the same time if intelligible communication is to be had, even if the entire radio spectrum is utilized in the present state of commercially acceptable technology." Id. at 388, 89 S.Ct. at 1805. The Court observed that this necessitated the division of the radio spectrum into usable portions, the assignment of subdivisions of the frequency to individual users, and regulation under which the "Government ... tell[s] some applicants that they [cannot] ... broadcast at all because there [is] room for only a few." Id. Therefore, the Court asserted, because "there are substantially more individuals who want to broadcast than there are frequencies to allocate, it is idle to posit an unabridgeable First Amendment right to broadcast comparable to the right of every individual to speak, write or publish." Id.

Observing that licensees and those who can obtain no license have identical first amendment rights, the Court in Red Lion further concluded that

> [t]here is nothing in the First Amendment which prevents the Government from requiring a licensee to share his frequency with others and to conduct himself as a proxy or fiduciary with obligations to present those views and voices which are representative of his community and which would otherwise, by necessity, be barred from the airwaves.

395 U.S. at 389, 89 S.Ct. at 1806. The Court then enunciated the classic formulation of the scarcity doctrine:

> Because of the scarcity of radio frequencies, the Government is permitted to put restraints on licensees in favor of others whose views should be expressed on this unique medium. But the people as a whole retain their interest in free speech by radio and their collective right to have the medium function consistently with the ends and purposes of the First Amendment. It is the right of the viewers and listeners, not the right of the broadcasters, which is paramount.

Id. at 390, 89 S.Ct. at 1806. It was on this principle that the Court found no first amendment infirmity in political broadcast regulation.

The Commission believes, however, that the regulation of teletext falls not within the permissive approach of Red Lion, but rather within the strict first amendment rule applied to content regulation of the print media. In Miami Herald Publishing Co. v. Tornillo, 418 U.S. 241, 94 S.Ct. 2831, 41 L.Ed.2d 730 (1974), the Court struck down an editorial right-of-reply statute that applied to newspapers. The content regulation in Tornillo bore a strong resemblance to that upheld in Red Lion. In Tornillo the Court held that such regulation impermissibly interfered with the newspapers' "editorial control and judgment." Id. at 258, 94 S.Ct. at 2840. The Court made the broad assertion that "[i]t has yet to be demonstrated how governmental regulation of this crucial [editorial] process can be exercised consistent with the First Amendment guarantees of a free press." Id. If the Commission's view is correct, and Tornillo rather than Red Lion applies to teletext, that service is entitled to greater first amendment protections than ordinary broadcasting and it would be proper, at a minimum, to construe political broadcasting provisions narrowly to avoid constitutionally suspect results.

The Commission has offered two grounds for its view that Tornillo rather than Red Lion is pertinent. Both reasons relate to the textual nature of teletext service. First, the Commission read an "immediacy" component into the scarcity doctrine:

> Implicit in the "scarcity" rationale ... is an assumption that broadcasters, through their access to the radio spectrum, possess a power to communicate ideas through sound and visual images in a manner that is significantly different from traditional avenues of communication because of the immediacy of the medium.

53 Rad.Reg.2d (P & F) at 1324. Second, the Commission held that the print nature of teletext "more closely resembles, and will largely compete with, other print communication media such as newspapers and magazines." Id. Under this analysis, scarcity of alternative first amendment resources does not exist with respect to teletext. We address these points in turn.

With respect to the first argument, the deficiencies of the scarcity rationale as a basis for depriving broadcasting of full first amendment protection, have led some to think that it is the immediacy and the power of broadcasting that causes its differential treatment. Whether or not that is true, we are unwilling to endorse an argument that makes the very effectiveness of speech the justification for according it less first amendment protection. More important, the Supreme Court's articulation of the scarcity doctrine contains no hint of any immediacy rationale. The Court based its reasoning entirely on the physical scarcity of broadcasting frequencies, which, it thought, permitted attaching fiduciary duties to the receipt of a license to use a frequency. This "immediacy" distinction cannot, therefore, be employed to affect the ability of the Commission to regulate public affairs broadcasting on teletext to ensure "the right of the public to receive suitable access to social, political, esthetic, moral, and other ideas and experiences." Red Lion, 395 U.S. at 390, 89 S.Ct. at 1807.

The Commission's second distinction--that a textual medium is not scarce insofar as it competes with other "print media"--also fails to dislodge the hold of Red Lion. The dispositive fact is that teletext is transmitted over broadcast frequencies that the Supreme Court has ruled scarce and this makes teletext's content regulable. We can understand, however, why the Commission thought it could reason in this fashion. The basic difficulty in this entire area is that the line drawn between the print media and the broadcast media, resting as it does on the physical scarcity of the latter, is a distinction without a difference. Employing the scarcity concept as an analytic tool, particularly with respect to new and unforeseen technologies, inevitably leads to strained reasoning and artificial results.

It is certainly true that broadcast frequencies are scarce but it is unclear why that fact justifies content regulation of broadcasting in a way that would be intolerable if applied to the editorial process of the print media. All economic goods are scarce, not least the newsprint, ink, delivery trucks, computers, and other resources that go into the production and dissemination of print journalism. Not everyone who wishes to publish a newspaper, or even a pamphlet, may do so. Since scarcity is a universal fact, it can hardly explain regulation in one context and not another. The attempt to use a universal fact as a distinguishing principle necessarily leads to analytical confusion.

Neither is content regulation explained by the fact that broadcasters face the problem of interference, so that the government must define useable frequencies and protect those frequencies from encroachment. This governmental definition of frequencies is another instance of a universal fact that does not offer an explanatory principle for differing treatment. A publisher can deliver his newspapers only because government provides streets and regulates traffic on the streets by allocating rights of way. Yet no one would contend that the necessity for these governmental functions, which are certainly analogous to the government's function in allocating broadcast frequencies, could justify regulation of the content of a newspaper to ensure that it serves the needs of the citizens.

There may be ways to reconcile Red Lion and Tornillo but the "scarcity" of broadcast frequencies does not appear capable of doing so. Perhaps the Supreme Court will one day revisit this area of the law and either eliminate the distinction between print and broadcast media, surely by pronouncing Tornillo applicable to both, or announce a constitutional distinction that is more usable than the present one. In the meantime, neither we nor the Commission are free to seek new rationales to remedy the inadequacy of the doctrine in this area. The attempt to do that has led the Commission to find "implicit" considerations in the law that are not really there. The Supreme Court has drawn a first amendment distinction between broadcast and print media on a premise of the physical scarcity of broadcast frequencies. Teletext, whatever its similarities to print media, uses broadcast frequencies, and that, given Red Lion, would seem to be that.

## Excerpts from: "Filthy Words," recording by George Carlin*

(*From Appendix, FCC v. Pacifica)

The following is a verbatim transcript of "Filthy Words" prepared by the Federal Communications Commission.

Aruba-du, ruba-tu, ruba-tu. I was thinking about the curse words and the swear words, the cuss words and the words that you can't say, that you're not supposed to say all the time, [']cause words or people into words want to hear your words. Some guys like to record your words and sell them back to you if they can, (laughter) listen in on the telephone, write down what words you say. A guy who used to be in Washington, knew that his phone was tapped, used to answer, Fuck Hoover, yes, go ahead. (laughter) Okay, I was thinking one night about the words you couldn't say on the public, ah, airwaves, um, the ones you definitely wouldn't say, ever, [']cause I heard a lady say bitch one night on television, and it was cool like she was talking about, you know, ah, well, the bitch is the first one to notice that in the litter Johnie right (murmur) Right. And, uh, bastard you can say, and hell and damn so I have to figure out which ones you couldn't and ever and it came down to seven but the list is open to amendment, and in fact, has been changed, uh, by now, ha, a lot of people pointed things out to me, and I noticed some myself. The original seven words were, shit, piss, fuck, cunt, cocksucker, motherfucker, and tits. Those are the ones that will curve your spine, grow hair on your hands and (laughter) maybe, even bring us, God help us, peace without honor (laughter) um, and a bourbon. (laughter) And now the first thing that we noticed was that work fuck was really repeated in there because the word motherfucker is a compound word and it's another form of the word fuck. (laughter) You want to be a purist it doesn't really--it can't be on the list of basic words. Also, cocksucker is a compound word and neither half of that is really dirty. The word--the half sucker that's merely suggestive (laughter) and the word cock is a half-way dirty word, 50% dirty--dirty half the time, depending on what you mean by it. (laughter) Uh, remember when you first heard it, like in 6th grade, you used to giggle. And the cock crowed three times, heh (laughter) the cock--three times. It's in the Bible, cock in the Bible. (laughter) And the first time you heard about a cock-fight, remember--What? Huh? naw. It ain't that, are you stupid? man. (laughter, clapping) It's chickens, you know, (laughter) Then you have the four letter words from the old Angle-Saxon fame. Uh, shit and fuck. The word shit, uh, is an interesting kind of word in that the middle class has never really accepted it and approved it. They use it like, crazy but it's not really okay. It's still a rude, dirty, old kind of gushy word. (laughter) They don't like that, but they say it, like, they say it like, a lady now in a middle-class home, you'll hear most of the time she says it as an expletive, you know, it's out of her mouth before she knows. She says, Oh shit oh shit, (laughter) oh shit. If she drops something, Oh, the shit hurt the broccoli. Shit. Thank you. (footsteps fading away) (papers ruffling)

Read it! (from audience)

Shit! (laughter) I won the Grammy, man, for the comedy album. Isn't that groovy? (clapping, whistling) (murmur) That's true. Thank you. Thank you man. Yeah. (murmer) (continuous clapping) Thank you man. Thank you. Thank you very much, man. Thank, no, (end of continuous clapping) for that and for the Grammy, man, [']cause (laughter) that's based on people liking it man, yeh, that's ah, that's okay man. (laughter) Let's let that go, man. I got my Grammy. I can let my hair hang down now, shit. (laughter) Ha! So! Now the word shit is okay for the man. At work you can say it like crazy. Mostly figuratively, Get that shit out of here, will ya? I don't want to see that shit anymore. I can't cut that shit, buddy. I've had that shit up to here. I think you're full of shit myself. (laughter) He don't know shit from Shinola. (laughter) you know that? (laughter) Always wondered how the Shinola people felt about that (laughter) Hi, I'm the new man from Shinola, (laughter) Hi, how are ya? Nice to see ya. (laughter) How are ya? (laughter) Boy, I don't know whether to shit or wind my watch. (laughter) Guess, I'll shit on my watch. (laughter) Oh, the shit is going to hit de fan. (laughter). Built like a brick shit-house. (laughter) Up, he's up shit's creek. (laughter) He's had it. (laughter) He hit me, I'm sorry. (laughter) Hot shit, holy shit, tough shit, eat shit. (laughter) shit-eating grin. Uh, whoever thought of that was ill. (murmur laughter) He had a shit- eating grin! He had a what? (laughter) Shit on a stick. (laughter) Shit in a handbag. I always like that. He ain't worth shit in a handbag. (laughter) Shitty. He acted real shitty. (laughter) You know what I mean? (laughter) I got the money back, but a real shitty attitude. Heh, he had a shit-fit. (laughter) Wow! Shit-fit. Whew! Glad I wasn't there. (murmur, laughter) All the animals--Bull shit, horseshit, cow shit, rat shit, bat shit. (laughter) First time I heard bat shit, I really came apart. A guy in Oklahoma, Boggs, said it, man. Aw! Bat shit. (laughter) Vera reminded me of that last night, ah (murmur). Snake shit, slicker than owl shit. (laughter) Get your shit together. Shit or get off the pot. (laughter) I got a shit- load full of them. (laughter) I got a shit-pot full, all right. Shit-head, shit-heel, shit in your heart, shit for brains, (laughter) shit-face, heh (laughter) I always try to think how that could have originated; the first guy that said that. Somebody got drunk and fell in some shit, you know. (laughter) Hey, I'm shit-face. (laughter) Shit-face, today. (laughter) Anyway, enough of that shit. (laughter) . . . .

FEDERAL COMMUNICATIONS COMMISSION, Petitioner,
v.
PACIFICA FOUNDATION.

438 U.S. 726

Supreme Court of the United States

Decided July 3, 1978.
Rehearing Denied Oct. 2, 1978.

Mr. Justice STEVENS delivered the opinion of the Court (Parts I, II, III and IV-C) and an opinion in which THE CHIEF JUSTICE and Mr. Justice REHNQUIST joined (Parts IV-A and IV-B).

This case requires that we decide whether the Federal Communications Commission has any power to regulate a radio broadcast that is indecent but not obscene.

A satiric humorist named George Carlin recorded a 12-minute monologue entitled "Filthy Words" before a live audience in a California theater. He began by referring to his thoughts about "the words you couldn't say on the public, ah, airwaves, um, the ones you definitely wouldn't say, ever." He proceeded to list those words and repeat them over and over again in a variety of colloquialisms. The transcript of the recording, which is appended to this opinion, indicates frequent laughter from the audience.

At about 2 o'clock in the afternoon on Tuesday, October 30, 1973, a New York radio station, owned by respondent Pacifica Foundation, broadcast the "Filthy Words" monologue. A few weeks later a man, who stated that he had heard the broadcast while driving with his young son, wrote a letter complaining to the Commission. He stated that, although he could perhaps understand the "record's being sold for private use, I certainly cannot understand the broadcast of same over the air that, supposedly, you control."

The complaint was forwarded to the station for comment. In its response, Pacifica explained that the monologue had been played during a program about contemporary society's attitude toward language and that, immediately before its broadcast, listeners had been advised that it included "sensitive language which might be regarded as offensive to some." Pacifica characterized George Carlin as "a significant social satirist" who "like Twain and Sahl before him, examines the language of ordinary people. . . . Carlin is not mouthing obscenities, he is merely using words to satirize as harmless and essentially silly our attitudes towards those words." Pacifica stated that it was not aware of any other complaints about the broadcast.

On February 21, 1975, the Commission issued a declaratory order granting the complaint and holding that Pacifica "could have been the subject of administrative sanctions." 56 F.C.C.2d 94, 99. The Commission did not impose formal sanctions, but it did state that the order would be "associated with the station's license file, and in the event that subsequent complaints are received, the Commission will then decide whether it should utilize any of the available sanctions it has been granted by Congress."

In its memorandum opinion the commission stated that it intended to "clarify the standards which will be utilized in considering" the growing number of complaints about indecent speech on the airwaves. Id., at 94. Advancing several reasons for treating broadcast speech differently from other forms of expression, [FN2] the Commission found a power to regulate indecent broadcasting in two statutes: 18 U.S.C. § 1464 (1976 ed.), which forbids the use of "any obscene, indecent, or profane language by means of radio communications," [FN3] and 47 U.S.C. § 303(g), which requires the Commission to "encourage the larger and more effective use of radio in the public interest." [FN4]

FN2. Broadcasting requires special treatment because of four important considerations: (1) children have access to radios and in many cases are unsupervised by parents; (2) radio receivers are in the home, a place where people's privacy interest is entitled to extra deference, see Rowan v. Post Office Dept., 397 U.S. 728 [90 S.Ct. 1484, 25 L.Ed.2d 736] (1970); (3) unconsenting adults may tune in a station without any warning that offensive languageis being or will be broadcast; and (4) there is a scarcity of spectrum space, the use of which the government must therefore license in the public interest. Of special concern to the Commission as well as parents is the first point regarding the use of radio by children." Id., at 97.

FN3. Title 18 U.S.C. § 1464 (1976 ed.) provides:
"Whoever utters any obscene, indecent, or profane language by means of radio communication shall be fined not more than $10,000 or imprisoned not more than two years, or both."

FN4. Section 303(g) of the Communications Act of 1934, 48 Stat. 1082, as amended, as set forth in 47 U.S.C. § 303(g), in relevant part, provides:
"Except as otherwise provided in this chapter, the Commission from time to time, as public convenience, interest, or necessity requires, shall--

* * *

"(g) . . . generally encourage the larger and more effective use of radio in the public interest."

The Commission characterized the language used in the Carlin monologue as "patently offensive," though not necessarily obscene, and expressed the opinion that it should be regulated by principles analogous to those found in the law of nuisance where the "law generally speaks to channeling behavior more than actually prohibiting it. . . . [T]he concept of 'indecent' is intimately connected with the exposure of children to language that describes, in terms patently offensive as measured by contemporary community standards for the broadcast medium, sexual or excretory activities and organs at times of the day when there is a reasonable risk that children may be in the audience." 56 F.C.C.2d, at 98.

Applying these considerations to the language used in the monologue as broadcast by respondent, the Commission concluded that certain words depicted sexual and excretory activities in a patently offensive manner, noted that they "were broadcast at a time when children were undoubtedly in the audience (i. e., in the early afternoon)," and that the prerecorded language, with these offensive words "repeated over and over," was "deliberately broadcast." Id., at 99. In summary, the Commission stated: "We therefore hold that the language as broadcast was indecent and prohibited by 18 U.S.C. [§] 1464." Ibid. . . . .

The United States Court of Appeals for the District of Columbia Circuit reversed, with each of the three judges on the panel writing separately. 181 U.S.App.D.C. 132, 556 F.2d 9. Judge Tamm concluded that the order represented censorship and was expressly prohibited by § 326 of the Communications Act. Alternatively, Judge Tamm read the Commission opinion as the functional equivalent of a rule and concluded that it was "overbroad." 181 U.S.App.D.C., at 141, 556 F.2d, at 18. Chief Judge Bazelon's concurrence rested on the Constitution. He was persuaded that § 326's prohibition against censorship is inapplicable to broadcasts forbidden by § 1464. However, he concluded that § 1464 must be narrowly construed to cover only language that is obscene or otherwise unprotected by the First Amendment. 181 U.S.App.D.C., at 140-153, 556 F.2d, at 24-30. Judge Leventhal, in dissent, stated that the only issue was whether the Commission could regulate the language "as broadcast." Id., at 154, 556 F.2d, at 31. Emphasizing the interest in protecting children, not only from exposure to indecent language, but also from exposure to the idea that such language has official approval, id., at 160, and n.18, 556 F.2d, at 37, and n. 18, he concluded that the Commission had correctly condemned the daytime broadcast as indecent.

Having granted the Commission's petition for certiorari, 434 U.S. 1008, 98 S.Ct. 715, 54 L.Ed.2d 749, we must decide: (1) whether the scope of judicial review encompasses more than the Commission's determination that the monologue was indecent "as broadcast"; (2) whether the Commission's order was a form of censorship forbidden by § 326; (3) whether the broadcast was indecent within the meaning of § 1464; and (4) whether the order violates the First Amendment of the United States Constitution . . . .

Entirely apart from the fact that the subsequent review of program content is not the sort of censorship at which the statute was directed, its history makes it perfectly clear that it was not intended to limit the Commission's power to regulate the broadcast of obscene, indecent, or profane language. A single section of the 1927 Act is the source of both the anticensorship provision and the Commission's authority to impose sanctions for the broadcast of indecent or obscene language. Quite plainly, Congress intended to give meaning to both provisions. Respect for that intent requires that the censorship language be read as inapplicable to the prohibition on broadcasting obscene, indecent, or profane language.

There is nothing in the legislative history to contradict this conclusion. The provision was discussed only in generalities when it was first enacted. In 1934, the anticensorship provision and the prohibition against indecent broadcasts were re-enacted in the same section, just as in the 1927 Act. In 1948, when the Criminal Code was revised to include provisions that had previously been located in other Titles of the United States Code, the prohibition against obscene, indecent, and profane broadcasts was removed from the Communications Act and re-enacted as § 1464 of Title 18. 62 Stat. 769 and 866. That rearrangement of the Code cannot reasonably be interpreted as having been intended to change the meaning of the anticensorship provision. H.R.Rep.No. 304, 80th Cong., 1st Sess., A106 (1947). Cf. Tidewater Oil Co. v. United States, 409 U.S. 151, 162, 93 S.Ct. 408, 415, 34 L.Ed.2d 375.

We conclude, therefore, that § 326 does not limit the Commission's authority to impose sanctions on licensees who engage in obscene, indecent, or profane broadcasting.

III

The only other statutory question presented by this case is whether the afternoon broadcast of the "Filthy Words" monologue was indecent within the meaning of § 1464. Even that question is narrowly confined by the arguments of the parties.

The Commission identified several words that referred to excretory or sexual activities or organs, stated that the repetitive, deliberate use of those words in an afternoon broadcast when children are in the audience was patently offensive, and held that the broadcast was indecent. Pacifica takes issue with the Commission's definition of indecency, but does not dispute the Commission's preliminary determination that each of the components of its definition was present. Specifically, Pacifica does not quarrel with the conclusion that this afternoon broadcast was patently offensive. Pacifica's claim that the broadcast was not indecent within the meaning of the statute rests entirely on the absence of prurient appeal.

The plain languageof the statute does not support Pacifica's argument. The words "obscene, indecent, or profane" are written in the disjunctive, implying that each has a separate meaning. Prurient appeal is an element of the obscene, but the normal definition of "indecent" merely refers to nonconformance with accepted standards of morality . . . .
Because neither our prior decisions nor the language or history of § 1464 supports the conclusion that prurient appeal is an essential component of indecent language, we reject Pacifica's construction of the statute. When that construction is put to one side, there is no basis for disagreeing with the Commission's conclusion that indecent language was used in this broadcast.

IV

Pacifica makes two constitutional attacks on the Commission's order. First, it argues that the Commission's construction of the statutory language broadly encompasses so much constitutionally protected speech that reversal is required even if Pacifica's broadcast of the "Filthy Words" monologue is not itself protected by the First Amendment. Second, Pacifica argues that inasmuch as the recording is not obscene, the Constitution forbids any abridgment of the right to broadcast it on the radio.

A

The first argument fails because our review is limited to the question whether the Commission has the authority to proscribe this particular broadcast. As the Commission itself emphasized, its order was "issued in a specific factual context." 59 F.C.C.2d, at 893. That approach is appropriate for courts as well as the Commission when regulation of indecency is at stake, for indecency is largely a function of context--it cannot be adequately judged in the abstract . . . .

B

When the issue is narrowed to the facts of this case, the question is whether the First Amendment denies government any power to restrict the public broadcast of indecent language in any circumstances. For if the government has any such power, this was an appropriate occasion for its exercise.

The words of the Carlin monologue are unquestionably "speech" within the meaning of the First Amendment. It is equally clear that the Commission's objections to the broadcast were based in part on its content. The order must therefore fall if, as Pacifica argues, the First Amendment prohibits all governmental regulation that depends on the content of speech. Our past cases demonstrate, however, that no such absolute rule is mandated by the Constitution.

The classic exposition of the proposition that both the content and the context of speech are critical elements of First Amendment analysis is Mr. Justice Holmes' statement for the Court in Schenck v. United States, 249 U.S. 47, 52, 39 S.Ct. 247, 248, 63 L.Ed. 470:

> "We admit that in many places and in ordinary times the defendants in saying all that was said in the circular would have been within their constitutional rights. But the character of every act depends upon the circumstances in which it is done. . . . The most stringent protection of free speech would not protect a man in falsely shouting fire in a theatre and causing a panic. It does not even protect a man from an injunction against uttering words that may have all the effect of force. . . . The question in every case is whether the words used are used in such circumstances and are of such a nature as to create a clear and present danger that they will bring about the substantive evils that Congress has a right to prevent."

Other distinctions based on content have been approved in the years since Schenck. The government may forbid speech calculated to provoke a fight. See Chaplinsky v. New Hampshire, 315 U.S. 568, 62 S.Ct. 766, 86 L.Ed. 1031. It may pay heed to the " 'commonsense differences' between commercial speech and other varieties." Bates v. State Bar of Arizona, supra, 433 U.S., at 381, 97 S.Ct., at 2707. It may treat libels against private citizens more severely than libels against public officials. See Gertz v. Robert Welch, Inc., 418 U.S. 323, 94 S.Ct. 2997, 41 L.Ed.2d 789. Obscenity may be wholly prohibited. Miller v. California, 413 U.S. 15, 93 S.Ct. 2607, 37 L.Ed.2d 419. And only two Terms ago we refused to hold that a "statutory classification is unconstitutional because it is based on the content of communication protected by the First Amendment." Young v. American Mini Theatres, Inc., supra, 427 U.S., at 52, 96 S.Ct., at 2443.

The question in this case is whether a broadcast of patently offensive words dealing with sex and excretion may be regulated because of its content. Obscene materials have been denied the protection of the First Amendment because their content is so offensive to contemporary moral standards. Roth v. United States, 354 U.S. 476, 77 S.Ct. 1304, 1 L.Ed.2d 1498. But the fact that society may find speech offensive is not a sufficient reason for suppressing it. Indeed, if it is the speaker's opinion that gives offense, that consequence is a reason for according it constitutional protection. For it is a central tenet of the First Amendment that the government must remain neutral in the marketplace of ideas. If there were any reason to believe that the Commission's characterization of the Carlin monologue as offensive could be traced to its political content--or even to the fact that it satirized contemporary attitudes about four-letter words [FN22]--First Amendment protection might be required. But that is simply not this case. These words offend for the same reasons that obscenity offends. [FN23] Their place in the hierarchy of First Amendment values was aptly sketched by Mr. Justice Murphy when he said: "Such utterances are no essential part of any exposition of ideas, and are of such slight social value as a step to truth that any benefit that may be derived from them is clearly outweighed by the social interest in order and morality." Chaplinsky v. New Hampshire, 315 U.S., at 572, 62 S.Ct., at 769.

FN22. The monologue does present a point of view; it attempts to show that the words it uses are "harmless" and that our attitudes toward them are "essentially silly." See supra, at 3030. The Commission objects, not to this point of view, but to the way in which it is expressed. The belief that these words are harmless does not necessarily confer a First Amendment privilege to use them while proselytizing, just as the conviction that obscenity is harmless does not license one to communicate that conviction by the indiscriminate distribution of an obscene leaflet.

FN23. The Commission stated: "Obnoxious, gutter language describing these matters has the effect of debasing and brutalizing human beings by reducing them to their mere bodily functions . . . ." 56 F.C.C.2d, at 98. Our society has a tradition of performing certain bodily functions in private, and of severely limiting the public exposure or discussion of such matters. Verbal or physical acts exposing those intimacies are offensive irrespective of any message that may accompany the exposure.

Although these words ordinarily lack literary, political, or scientific value, they are not entirely outside the protection of the First Amendment. Some uses of even the most offensive words are unquestionably protected. See, e. g., Hess v. Indiana, 414 U.S. 105, 94 S.Ct. 326, 38 L.Ed.2d 303. Indeed, we may assume, arguendo, that this monologue would be protected in other contexts. Nonetheless, the constitutional protection accorded to a communication containing such patently offensive sexual and excretory language need not be the same in every context. It is a characteristic of speech such as this that both its capacity to offend and its "social value," to use Mr. Justice Murphy's term, vary with the circumstances. Words that are commonplace in one setting are shocking in another. To paraphrase Mr. Justice Harlan, one occasion's lyric is another's vulgarity. Cf. Cohen v. California, 403 U.S. 15, 25, 91 S.Ct. 1780, 1788, 29 L.Ed.2d 284. [FN25]

FN25. The importance of context is illustrated by the Cohen case. That case arose when Paul Cohen entered a Los Angeles courthouse wearing a jacket emblazoned with the words "Fuck the Draft." After entering the courtroom, he took the jacket off and folded it. 403 U.S., at 19 n. 3, 91 S.Ct., at 1785. So far as the evidence showed, no one in the courthouse was offended by his jacket. Nonetheless, when he left the courtroom, Cohen was arrested, convicted of disturbing the peace, and sentenced to 30 days in prison.

In holding that criminal sanctions could not be imposed on Cohen for his political statement in a public place, the Court rejected the argument that his speech would offend unwilling viewers; it noted that "there was no evidence that persons powerless to avoid [his] conduct did in fact object to it." Id., at 22, 91 S.Ct., at 1786. In contrast, in this case the Commission was responding to a listener's strenuous complaint, and Pacifica does not question its determination that this afternoon broadcast was likely to offend listeners. It should be noted that the Commission imposed a far more moderate penalty on Pacifica than the state court imposed on Cohen. Even the strongest civil penalty at the Commission's command does not include criminal prosecution. See n. 1, supra.

In this case it is undisputed that the content of Pacifica's broadcast was "vulgar," "offensive," and "shocking." Because content of that character is not entitled to absolute constitutional protection under all circumstances, we must consider its context in order to determine whether the Commission's action was constitutionally permissible.

C

We have long recognized that each medium of expression presents special First Amendment problems. Joseph Burstyn, Inc. v. Wilson, 343 U.S. 495, 502-503, 72 S.Ct. 777, 780-781, 96 L.Ed. 1098. And of all forms of communication, it is broadcasting that has received the most limited First Amendment protection. Thus, although other speakers cannot be licensed except under laws that carefully define and narrow official discretion, a broadcaster may be deprived of his license and his forum if the Commission decides that such an action would serve "the public interest, convenience, and necessity." Similarly, although the First Amendment protects newspaper publishers from being required to print the replies of those whom they criticize,

Miami Herald Publishing Co. v. Tornillo, 418 U.S. 241, 94 S.Ct. 2831, 41 L.Ed.2d 730, it affords no such protection to broadcasters; on the contrary, they must give free time to the victims of their criticism. Red Lion Broadcasting Co. v. FCC, 395 U.S. 367, 89 S.Ct. 1794, 23 L.Ed.2d 371.

The reasons for these distinctions are complex, but two have relevance to the present case. First, the broadcast media have established a uniquely pervasive presence in the lives of all Americans. Patently offensive, indecent material presented over the airwaves confronts the citizen, not only in public, but also in the privacy of the home, where the individual's right to be left alone plainly outweighs the First Amendment rights of an intruder. Rowan v. Post Office Dept., 397 U.S. 728, 90 S.Ct. 1484, 25 L.Ed.2d 736. Because the broadcast audience is constantly tuning in and out, prior warnings cannot completely protect the listener or viewer from unexpected program content. To say that one may avoid further offense by turning off the radio when he hears indecent language is like saying that the remedy for an assault is to run away after the first blow. One may hang up on an indecent phone call, but that option does not give the caller a constitutional immunity or avoid a harm that has already taken place. [FN27]

FN27. Outside the home, the balance between the offensive speaker and the unwilling audience may sometimes tip in favor of the speaker, requiring the offended listener to turn away. See Erznoznik v. Jacksonville, 422 U.S. 205, 95 S.Ct. 2268, 45 L.Ed.2d 125. As we noted in Cohen v. California:
"While this Court has recognized that government may properly act in many situations to prohibit intrusion into the privacy of the home of unwelcome views and ideas which cannot be totally banned from the public dialogue . . . , we have at the same time consistently stressed that 'we are often "captives" outside the sanctuary of the home and subject to objectionable speech.' " 403 U.S., at 21, 91 S.Ct., at 1786.
The problem of harassing phone calls is hardly hypothetical. Congress has recently found it necessary to prohibit debt collectors from "plac[ing] telephone calls without meaningful disclosure of the caller's identity"; from "engaging any person in telephone conversation repeatedly or continuously with intent to annoy, abuse, or harass any person at the called number"; and from "us[ing] obscene or profane language or language the natural consequence of which is to abuse the hearer or reader." Consumer Credit Protection Act Amendments, 91 Stat.

Second, broadcasting is uniquely accessible to children, even those too young to read. Although Cohen's written message might have been incomprehensible to a first grader, Pacifica's broadcast could have enlarged a child's vocabulary in an instant. Other forms of offensive expression may be withheld from the young without restricting the expression at its source. Bookstores and motion picture theaters, for example, may be prohibited from making indecent material available to children. We held in Ginsberg v. New York, 390 U.S. 629, 88 S.Ct. 1274, 20 L.Ed.2d 195, that the government's interest in the "well-being of its youth" and in supporting "parents' claim to authority in their own household" justified the regulation of otherwise protected expression. Id., at 640 and 639, 88 S.Ct., at 1280. [FN28] The ease with which children may obtain access to broadcast material, coupled with the concerns recognized in Ginsberg, amply justify special treatment of indecent broadcasting.

FN28. The Commission's action does not by any means reduce adults to hearing only what is fit for children. Cf. Butler v. Michigan, 352 U.S. 380, 383, 77 S.Ct. 524, 526, 1 L.Ed.2d 412. Adults who feel the need may purchase tapes and records or go to theaters and nightclubs to hear these words. In fact, the Commission has not unequivocally closed even broadcasting to speech of this sort; whether broadcast audiences in the late evening contain so few children that playing this monologue would be permissible is an issue neither the Commission nor this Court has decided.

It is appropriate, in conclusion, to emphasize the narrowness of our holding. This case does not involve a two-way radio conversation between a cab driver and a dispatcher, or a telecast of an Elizabethan comedy. We have not decided that an occasional expletive in either setting would justify any sanction or, indeed, that this broadcast would justify a criminal prosecution. The Commission's decision rested entirely on a nuisance rationale under which context is all-important. The concept requires consideration of a host of variables. The time of day was emphasized by the Commission. The content of the program in which the languageis used will also affect the composition of the audience, and differences between radio, television, and perhaps closed-circuit transmissions, may also be relevant. As Mr. Justice Sutherland wrote a "nuisance may be merely a right thing in the wrong place,--like a pig in the parlor instead of the barnyard." Euclid v. Ambler Realty Co., 272 U.S. 365, 388, 47 S.Ct. 114, 118, 71 L.Ed. 303. We simply hold that when the Commission finds that a pig has entered the parlor, the exercise of its regulatory power does not depend on proof that the pig is obscene.

The judgment of the Court of Appeals is reversed.
It is so ordered.

Mr. Justice POWELL, with whom Mr. Justice BLACKMUN joins, concurring in part and concurring in the judgment.

I join Parts I, II, III, and IV-C of Mr. Justice STEVENS' opinion. The Court today reviews only the Commission's holding that Carlin's monologue was indecent "as broadcast" at two o'clock in the afternoon, and not the broad sweep of the Commission's opinion. Ante, at 3032-3033. In addition to being consistent with our settled practice of not deciding constitutional issues unnecessarily, see ante, at 3032; Ashwander v. TVA, 297 U.S. 288, 345-348, 56 S.Ct. 466, 482-484, 80 L.Ed. 688 (1936) (Brandeis, J., concurring), this narrow focus also is conducive to the orderly development of this relatively new and difficult area of law, in the first instance by the Commission, and then by the reviewing courts. See 181 U.S.App.D.C. 132, 158-160, 556 F.2d 9, 35-37 (1977) (Leventhal, J., dissenting).

I also agree with much that is said in Part IV of Mr. Justice STEVENS' opinion, and with its conclusion that the Commission's holding in this case does not violate the First Amendment. Because I do not subscribe to all that is said in Part IV, however, I state my views separately . . .

Mr. Justice BRENNAN, with whom Mr. Justice MARSHALL joins, dissenting.

I agree with Mr. Justice STEWART that, under Hamling v. United States, 418 U.S. 87, 94 S.Ct. 2887, 41 L.Ed.2d 590 (1974), and United States v. 12 200- ft. Reels of Film, 413 U.S. 123, 93 S.Ct. 2665, 37 L.Ed.2d 500 (1973), the word "indecent" in 18 U.S.C. § 1464 (1976 ed.) must be construed to prohibit only obscene speech. I would, therefore, normally refrain from expressing my views on any constitutional issues implicated in this case. However, I find the Court's misapplication of fundamental First Amendment principles so patent, and its attempt to impose its notions of propriety on the whole of the American people so misguided, that I am unable to remain silent.

I

For the second time in two years, see Young v. American Mini Theatres, Inc., 427 U.S. 50, 96 S.Ct. 2440, 49 L.Ed.2d 310 (1976), the Court refuses to embrace the notion, completely antithetical to basic First Amendment values, that the degree of protection the First Amendment affords protected speech varies with the social value ascribed to that speech by five Members of this Court. See opinion of Mr. Justice POWELL, ante, at 3046-3047. Moreover, as do all parties, all Members of the Court agree that the Carlin monologue aired by Station WBAI does not fall within one of the categories of speech, such as "fighting words," Chaplinsky v. New Hampshire, 315 U.S. 568, 62 S.Ct. 766, 86 L.Ed. 1031 (1942), or obscenity, Roth v. United States, 354 U.S. 476, 77 S.Ct. 1304, 1 L.Ed.2d 1498 (1957), that is totally without First Amendment protection. This conclusion, of course, is compelled by our cases expressly holding that communications containing some of the words found condemnable here are fully protected by the First Amendment in other contexts. See Eaton v. Tulsa, 415 U.S. 697, 94 S.Ct. 1228, 39 L.Ed.2d 693 (1974); Papish v. University of Missouri Curators, 410 U.S. 667, 93 S.Ct. 1197, 35 L.Ed.2d 618 (1973); Brown v. Oklahoma, 408 U.S. 914, 92 S.Ct. 2507, 33 L.Ed.2d 326 (1972); Lewis v. New Orleans, 408 U.S. 913, 92 S.Ct. 2499, 33 L.Ed.2d 321 (1972); Rosenfeld v. New Jersey, 408 U.S. 901, 92 S.Ct. 2479, 33 L.Ed.2d 321 (1972); Cohen v. California, 403 U.S. 15, 91 S.Ct. 1780, 29 L.Ed.2d 284 (1971). Yet despite the Court's refusal to create a sliding scale of First Amendment protection calibrated to this Court's perception of the worth of a communication's content, and despite our unanimous agreement that the Carlin monologue is protected speech, a majority of the Court nevertheless finds that, on the facts of this case, the FCC is not constitutionally barred from imposing sanctions on Pacifica for its airing of the Carlin monologue. This majority apparently believes that the FCC's disapproval of Pacifica's afternoon broadcast of Carlin's "Dirty Words" recording is a permissible time, place, and manner regulation. Kovacs v. Cooper, 336 U.S. 77, 69 S.Ct. 448, 93 L.Ed. 513 (1949). Both the opinion of my Brother STEVENS and the opinion of my Brother POWELL rely principally on two factors in reaching this conclusion: (1) the capacity of a radio broadcast to intrude into the unwilling listener's home, and (2) the presence of children in the listening audience. Dispassionate analysis, removed from individual notions as to what is proper and what is not, starkly reveals that these justifications, whether individually or together, simply do not support even the professedly moderate degree of governmental homogenization of radio communications--if, indeed, such homogenization can ever be moderate given the pre-eminent status of the right of free speech in our constitutional scheme-- that the Court today permits.

A

Without question, the privacy interests of an individual in his home are substantial and deserving of significant protection. In finding these interests sufficient to justify the content regulation of protected speech, however, the Court commits two errors. First, it misconceives the nature of the privacy interests involved where an individual voluntarily chooses to admit radio communications into his home. Second, it ignores the constitutionally protected interests of both those who wish to transmit and those who desire to receive broadcasts that many--including the FCC and this Court--might find offensive . . . .

III

It is quite evident that I find the Court's attempt to unstitch the warp and woof of First Amendment law in an effort to reshape its fabric to cover the patently wrong result the Court reaches in this case dangerous as well as lamentable. Yet there runs throughout the opinions of my Brothers POWELL and STEVENS another vein I find equally disturbing: a depressing inability to appreciate that in our land of cultural pluralism, there are many who think, act, and talk differently from the Members of this Court, and who do not share their fragile sensibilities. It is only an acute ethnocentric myopia that enables the Court to approve the censorship of communications solely because of the words they contain . . . .

Mr. Justice STEWART, with whom Mr. Justice BRENNAN, Mr. Justice WHITE, and Mr. Justice MARSHALL join, dissenting.

The Court today recognizes the wise admonition that we should "avoid the unnecessary decision of [constitutional] issues." Ante, at 3033. But it disregards one important application of this salutary principle--the need to construe an Act of Congress so as to avoid, if possible, passing upon its constitutionality. It is apparent that the constitutional questions raised by the order of the Commission in this case are substantial. Before deciding them, we should be certain that it is necessary to do so.

The statute pursuant to which the Commission acted, 18 U.S.C. § 1464 (1976 ed.), makes it a federal offense to utter "any obscene, indecent, or profane language by means of radio communication." The Commission held, and the Court today agrees, that "indecent" is a broader concept than "obscene" as the latter term was defined in Miller v. California, 413 U.S. 15, 93 S.Ct. 2607, 37 L.Ed.2d 419, because language can be "indecent" although it has social, political, or artistic value and lacks prurient appeal. 56 F.C.C.2d 94, 97-98. ] But this construction of § 1464, while perhaps plausible, is by no means compelled. To the contrary, I think that "indecent" should properly be read as meaning no more than "obscene." Since the Carlin monologue concededly was not "obscene," I believe that the Commission lacked statutory authority to ban it. Under this construction of the statute, it is unnecessary to address the difficult and important issue of the Commission's constitutional power to prohibit speech that would be constitutionally protected outside the context of electronic broadcasting . . . .

I would hold, therefore, that Congress intended, by using the word "indecent" in § 1464, to prohibit nothing more than obscene speech. [FN8] Under that reading of the statute, the Commission's order in this case was not authorized, and on that basis I would affirm the judgment of the Court of Appeals.

ACTION FOR CHILDREN'S TELEVISION; American Civil Liberties Union; The Association of Independent Television Stations, Inc.; Capital City/American Broadcasting Co., Inc.; CBS, Inc.; Fox Television Stations, Inc.; Greater Media, Inc.; Infinity Broadcasting Corporation; Motion Picture Association of America, Inc.; National Association of Broadcasters; National Public Radio; People for the American Way; Post-Newsweek Stations, Inc.; Public Broadcasting Service; Radio-Television News Directors Association; Reporters Committee for Freedom of the Press; Society of Professional Journalists, Petitioners,

v.

FEDERAL COMMUNICATIONS COMMISSION; United States of America, Respondents.

PACIFICA FOUNDATION; National Federation of Community Broadcasters; American Public Radio; National Association of College Broadcasters; Intercollegiate Broadcast System; Pen American Center; Allen Ginsberg, Petitioners,

v.

FEDERAL COMMUNICATIONS COMMISSION; United States of America, Respondents.

58 F.3d 654

United States Court of Appeals,
District of Columbia Circuit.

Decided June 30, 1995.

BUCKLEY, Circuit Judge:

We are asked to determine the constitutionality of section 16(a) of the Public Telecommunications Act of 1992, which seeks to shield minors from indecent radio and television programs by restricting the hours within which they may be broadcast. Section 16(a) provides that, with one exception, indecent materials may only be broadcast between the hours of midnight and 6:00 a.m. The exception permits public radio and television stations that go off the air at or before midnight to broadcast such materials after 10:00 p.m.

We find that the Government has a compelling interest in protecting children under the age of 18 from exposure to indecent broadcasts. We are also satisfied that, standing alone, the "channeling" of indecent broadcasts to the hours between midnight and 6:00 a.m. would not unduly burden the First Amendment. Because the distinction drawn by Congress between the two categories of broadcasters bears no apparent relationship to the compelling Government interests that section 16(a) is intended to serve, however, we find the more restrictive limitation unconstitutional. Accordingly, we grant the petitions for review and remand the cases to the Federal Communications Commission with instructions to revise its regulations to permit the broadcasting of indecent material between the hours of 10:00 p.m. and 6:00 a.m.

## I. BACKGROUND

The Radio Act of 1927 provides that "[w]hoever utters any obscene, indecent, or profane language by means of radio communication shall be fined not more than $10,000 or imprisoned not more than two years, or both." 18 U.S.C. § 1464 (1988). While all obscene speech is indecent, not all indecent speech is obscene. The Supreme Court has defined obscene material as

works which, taken as a whole, appeal to the prurient interest in sex, which portray sexual conduct in a patently offensive way, and which, taken as a whole, do not have serious literary, artistic, political, or scientific value. Miller v. California, 413 U.S. 15, 24, 93 S.Ct. 2607, 2615, 37 L.Ed.2d 419 (1973). In enforcing section 1464 of the Radio Act, the Federal Communications Commission defines "broadcast indecency" aslanguage or material that, in context, depicts or describes, in terms patently offensive as measured by contemporary community standards for the broadcast medium, sexual or excretory activities or organs.

In re Enforcement of Prohibitions Against Broadcast Indecency in 18 U.S.C. § 1464, 8 F.C.C.R. 704, 705 n. 10 (1993) ("1993 Report and Order "). This definition has remained substantially unchanged since it was first enunciated in In re Pacifica Foundation, 56 F.C.C.2d 94, 98 (1975).

While obscene speech is not accorded constitutional protection, "[s]exual expression which is indecent but not obscene is protected by the First Amendment...." Sable Communications of California, Inc. v. FCC, 492 U.S. 115, 126, 109 S.Ct. 2829, 2836, 106 L.Ed.2d 93 (1989). "The Government may, however, regulate the content of [such] constitutionally protected speech in order to promote a compelling interest if it chooses the least restrictive means to further the articulated interest." Id. Noting that broadcasting has received the most limited First Amendment protection because of its unique pervasiveness and accessibility to children, the Supreme Court has held that the FCC may, in appropriate circumstances, place restrictions on the broadcast of indecent speech. See FCC v. Pacifica Foundation, 438 U.S. 726, 750-51, 98 S.Ct. 3026, 3041, 57 L.Ed.2d 1073 (1978) ("when the Commission finds that a pig has entered the parlor, the exercise of its regulatory power does not depend on proof that the pig is obscene.").

In In re Infinity Broadcasting Corp. of Pa., 3 F.C.C.R. 930 (1987) ( "Reconsideration Order "), the Commission reviewed its decisions in three cases: In re Infinity Broadcasting Corp. of Pa., 2 F.C.C.R. 2705 (1987), In re Pacifica Foundation, Inc., 2 F.C.C.R. 2698 (1987), and In re Regents of the University of California, 2 F.C.C.R. 2703 (1987). One of these cases involved a morning broadcast; the other two dealt with programs that were aired after 10:00 p.m. In each of them, the agency found that a radio station had introduced particularly offensive pigs into American parlors in violation of section 1464. The offending morning broadcast, for example, contained "explicit references to masturbation, ejaculation, breast size, penis size, sexual intercourse, nudity, urination, oral-genital contact, erections, sodomy, bestiality, menstruation and testicles." Reconsideration Order, 3 F.C.C.R. at 932 (internal quotation marks omitted). The remaining two were similarly objectionable. See id. at 932-33.

The FCC reaffirmed the Government interest in safeguarding children from exposure to such speech and placed broadcasters on notice that because

> at least with respect to the particular markets involved, available evidence suggested there were still significant numbers of children in the audience at 10:00 p.m. ... broadcasters should no longer assume that 10:00 p.m. is automatically the time after which indecent broadcasts may safely be aired. Rather, ... indecent material would be actionable (that is, would be held in violation of 18 U.S.C. § 1464) if broadcast when there is a reasonable risk that children may be in the audience....

Id. at 930-31. The Commission noted, however, that it was its "current thinking" that midnight marked the time after which it is reasonable to expect that it is late enough to ensure that the risk of children in the audience is minimized and to rely on parents to exercise increased supervision over whatever children remain in the viewing and listening audience.

In our review of the Reconsideration Order in Action for Children's Television v. FCC, 852 F.2d 1332 (D.C.Cir.1988) ("ACT I" ), we rejected the argument that the Commission's definition of indecency was unconstitutionally vague and overbroad. Id. at 1338-40. But although we affirmed the declaratory ruling that found portions of the morning broadcast to be in violation of section 1464, id. at 1341, we vacated the Commission's rulings with respect to the two post-10:00 p.m. broadcasts. Id. In those instances, we considered the findings on which the Commission rested its decision to be "more ritual than real," id., because the Commission had relied on data as to the number of teenagers in the total radio audience rather than the number of them who listened to the radio stations in question. We were also troubled by the FCC's failure to explain why it identified the relevant age group as children aged 12 to 17 when it had earlier proposed legislation for the protection of only those under 12. Id. at 1341-42. We further concluded that "the FCC's midnight advice, indeed its entire position on channeling, was not adequately thought through." Id. at 1342.

Two months after our decision in ACT I, Congress instructed the Commission to promulgate regulations "enforc[ing] the provisions of ... section [1464] on a 24 hour per day basis." Pub.L. No. 100-459, § 608, 102 Stat. 2186, 2228 (1988). The Commission complied by issuing a regulation banning all broadcasts of indecent material, which was immediately challenged by Action for Children's Television and others. The following year, we remanded the record to the Commission to enable it to solicit information relevant to the congressionally mandated 24-hour ban; and in 1989, the FCC issued a "Notice of Inquiry" for that purpose. In re Enforcement of Prohibitions Against Broadcast Indecency in 18 U.S.C. § 1464, 4 F.C.C.R. 8358 (1989) ("1989 NOI ").

After analyzing the public comment received in response to the 1989 NOI, the Commission reported its conclusions in In re Enforcement of Prohibitions Against Broadcast Indecency in 18 U.S.C. § 1464, 5 F.C.C.R. 5297 (1990) ( "1990 Report "). In the 1990 Report, the FCC defined the category of persons to be protected under section 1464 as "children ages 17 and under." Id. at 5301. It then found that because the narrowness with which courts have

> interpreted "obscenity" has commensurably broadened the range of patently offensive material that could be deemed "indecent" if broadcast ... [and in light of the evidence] that there is a reasonable risk that significant numbers of children ages 17 and under listen to radio and view television at all times of day and night[,] ... the compelling government interest in protecting children from indecent broadcasts would not be promoted effectively by any means more narrowly tailored than a 24-hour prohibition.

Id. at 5297.

We reviewed the 24-hour ban in Action for Children's Television v. FCC, 932 F.2d 1504 (D.C.Cir.1991) ("ACT II ). We again rejected petitioners' vagueness and overbreadth arguments, but we struck down the total ban on indecent broadcasts because "[o]ur previous holding in ACT I that the Commission must identify some reasonable period of time during which indecent material may be broadcast necessarily means that the Commission may not ban such broadcasts entirely." Id. at 1509.

Shortly after the Supreme Court denied certiorari in ACT II, 503 U.S. 913, 112 S.Ct. 1281, 117 L.Ed.2d 507 (1992), Congress again intervened, passing the Public Telecommunications Act of 1992, Pub.L. No. 102-356, 106 Stat. 949 (1992). Section 16(a) of the Act requires the Commission to

> promulgate regulations to prohibit the broadcasting of indecent programming--
> (1) between 6 a.m. and 10 p.m. on any day by any public radio station or public television station that goes off the air at or before 12 midnight; and
> (2) between 6 a.m. and 12 midnight on any day for any radio or television broadcasting station not described in paragraph (1).

47 U.S.C. § 303 note (Supp. IV 1992). Pursuant to this congressional mandate, the Commission published a notice of proposed rulemaking, In re Enforcement of Prohibitions Against Broadcast Indecency in 18 U.S.C. § 1464, 7 F.C.C.R. 6464 (1992), and, in 1993, it issued regulations implementing section 16(a). 1993 Report and Order, 8 F.C.C.R. at 711; 47 C.F.R. § 73.3999 (1994). These are challenged in the petition now before us.

## II. DISCUSSION

Petitioners present three challenges to the constitutionality of section 16(a) and its implementing regulations: First, the statute and regulations violate the First Amendment because they impose restrictions on indecent broadcasts that are not narrowly tailored to further the Government's interest, which petitioners define as the promotion of parental authority by shielding unsupervised children from indecent speech in the broadcast media; second, section 16(a) unconstitutionally discriminates among categories of broadcasters by distinguishing the times during which certain public and commercial broadcasters may air indecent material; and third, the Commission's generic definition of indecency is unconstitutionally vague. Petitioners also assert that our decisions in ACT I and ACT II compel the rejection of the newly enacted restrictions both because there are insufficient data to justify the new statutory ban and because the Commission continues to include children ages 12 to 17 in the protected class.

The Commission argues that the Government's interests extend beyond facilitating parental supervision to include protecting children from exposure to indecent broadcasts and safeguarding the home from unwanted intrusion by such broadcasts. The Commission asserts that restricting indecent broadcasts to the hours between midnight and 6:00 a.m. is narrowly tailored to achieve these compelling governmental interests. It defends the exception allowing public stations that go off the air at or before midnight to broadcast such materials after 10:00 p.m. on the basis that these stations would otherwise have no opportunity to air indecent programs.

At the outset, we dismiss petitioners' vagueness challenge as meritless. The FCC's definition of indecency in the new regulations is identical to the one at issue in ACT II, where we stated that "the Supreme Court's decision in Pacifica dispelled any vagueness concerns attending the [Commission's] definition," as did our holding in ACT I. 932 F.2d at 1508. Petitioners fail to provide any convincing reasons why we should ignore this precedent.

We now proceed to petitioners' remaining constitutional arguments.

A. The First Amendment Challenge

> It is common ground that "[s]exual expression which is indecent but not obscene is protected by the First Amendment." Sable, 492 U.S. at 126, 109 S.Ct. at 2836. The Government may, however, regulate the content of constitutionally protected speech in order to promote a compelling interest if it chooses the least restrictive means to further the articulated interest.

Id. Thus, a restriction on indecent speech will survive First Amendment scrutiny if the "Government's ends are compelling [and its] means [are] carefully tailored to achieve those ends."

The Supreme Court has "long recognized that each medium of expression presents special First Amendment problems.... [O]f all forms of communication, it is broadcasting that has received the most limited First Amendment protection." Pacifica, 438 U.S. at 748, 98 S.Ct. at 3039-40. (citation omitted). The Court has identified two reasons for this distinction that are relevant here:

> First, the broadcast media have established a uniquely pervasive presence in the lives of all Americans. Patently offensive, indecent material presented over the airwaves confronts the citizen, not only in public, but also in the privacy of the home, where the individual's right to be left alone plainly outweighs the First Amendment rights of an intruder. ... Because the broadcast audience is constantly tuning in and out, prior warnings cannot completely protect the listener or viewer from unexpected program content. ...
>
> Second, broadcasting is uniquely accessible to children.... Other forms of offensive expression may be withheld from the young without restricting the expression at its source. Bookstores and motion picture theaters, for example, may be prohibited from making indecent material available to children. ... The ease with which children may obtain access to broadcast material, coupled with the concerns [over the well-being of youths] recognized in Ginsberg [v. New York, 390 U.S. 629, 88 S.Ct. 1274, 20 L.Ed.2d 195 (1968) ], amply justifies special treatment of indecent broadcasting.

Id. at 748-50, 98 S.Ct. at 3040-41. As Justice Powell observed in Pacifica,

> [t]he difficulty is that ... a physical separation of the audience [such as that possible in bookstores and movie theaters] cannot be accomplished in the broadcast media. ... This ... is one of the distinctions between the broadcast and other media ... [that] justif[ies] a different treatment of the broadcast media for First Amendment purposes.

438 U.S. at 758-59, 98 S.Ct. at 3045 (Powell, J., concurring in part and concurring in the judgment). Despite the increasing availability of other means of receiving television, such as cable (which is not immune to the concerns we address today, see Alliance for Community Media v. FCC, 56 F.3d 105, 123-125 (D.C.Cir.1995)), there can be no doubt that the traditional broadcast media are properly subject to more regulation than is generally permissible under the First Amendment.

Unlike cable subscribers, who are offered such options as "pay-per-view" channels, broadcast audiences have no choice but to "subscribe" to the entire output of traditional broadcasters. Thus they are confronted without warning with offensive material. See Pacifica, 438 U.S. at 748-49, 98 S.Ct. at 3039-40. This is "manifestly different from a situation" where a recipient "seeks and is willing to pay for the communication...." Sable, 492 U.S. at 128, 109 S.Ct. at 2837; see also Cruz v. Ferre, 755 F.2d 1415, 1420 (11th Cir.1985) (distinguishing Pacifica from cases in which cable subscriber affirmatively elects to have specific cable service come into home).

In light of these differences, radio and television broadcasts may properly be subject to different--and often more restrictive--regulation than is permissible for other media under the First Amendment. While we apply strict scrutiny to regulations of this kind regardless of the medium affected by them, our assessment of whether section 16(a) survives that scrutiny must necessarily take into account the unique context of the broadcast medium.

1. The compelling Government interests

In examiningthe Government's interests in protecting children from broadcast indecency, it is important to understand that hard-core pornography may be deemed indecent rather than obscene if it is "not patently offensive" under the relevant contemporary community standards. The Second Circuit, for example, has found that the "detailed portrayals of genitalia, sexual intercourse, fellatio, and masturbation" contained in a grab bag of pornographic materials (which included such notorious films as "Deep Throat") are not obscene in light of the community standards prevailing in New York City. United States v. Various Articles of Obscene Merchandise, Schedule No. 2102, 709 F.2d 132, 134, 137 (2d Cir.1983). Therefore, as Justice Scalia has observed,

> [t]he more narrow the understanding of what is "obscene," and hence the more pornographic what is embraced within the residual category of "indecency," the more reasonable it becomes to insist upon greater assurance of insulation from minors.

Sable, 492 U.S. at 132, 109 S.Ct. at 2840 (Scalia, J., concurring).

The Commission identifies three compelling Government interests as justifying the regulation of broadcast indecency: support for parental supervision of children, a concern for children's well-being, and the protection of the home against intrusion by offensive broadcasts. Because we find the first two sufficient to support such regulation, we will not address the third.

Petitioners do not contest that the Government has a compelling interest in supporting parental supervision of what children see and hear on the public airwaves. Indeed, the Court has repeatedly emphasized the Government's fundamental interest in helping parents exercise their "primary responsibility for [their] children's well-being" with "laws designed to aid [in the] discharge of that responsibility." Ginsberg v. New York, 390 U.S. 629, 639, 88 S.Ct. 1274, 1280, 20 L.Ed.2d 195 (1968). This interest includes "supporting parents' claim to authority in their own household" through "regulation of otherwise protected expression." Pacifica, 438 U.S. at 749, 98 S.Ct. at 3040 (internal quotation marks omitted).

Although petitioners disagree, we believe the Government's own interest in the well-being of minors provides an independent justification for the regulation of broadcast indecency . . . .

The Government's dual interests in assisting parents and protecting minors necessarily extends beyond merely channeling broadcast indecency to those hours when parents can be at home to supervise what their children see and hear. It is fanciful to believe that the vast majority of parents who wish to shield their children from indecent material can effectively do so without meaningful restrictions on the airing of broadcast indecency . . . .

## III. CONCLUSION

"If there is a bedrock principle underlying the First Amendment, it is that the government may not prohibit the expression of an idea simply because society finds the idea itself offensive or disagreeable." Texas v. Johnson, 491 U.S. 397, 414, 109 S.Ct. 2533, 2545, 105 L.Ed.2d 342 (1989). The Constitution, however, permits restrictions on speech where necessary in order to serve a compelling public interest, provided that they are narrowly tailored. We hold that section 16(a) serves such an interest. But because Congress imposed different restrictions on each of two categories of broadcasters while failing to explain how this disparate treatment advanced its goal of protecting young minds from the corrupting influences of indecent speech, we must set aside the more restrictive one. Accordingly, we remand this case to the Federal Communications Commission with instructions to limit its ban on the broadcasting of indecent programs to the period from 6:00 a.m. to 10:00 p.m.

It is so ordered.

GILLETT COMMUNICATIONS OF ATLANTA, INC., d/b/a WAGA-TV5, Plaintiff,

v.

Daniel BECKER, Daniel Becker for Congress Committee, and the Federal Communications Committee. Defendants.

807 F.Supp. 757

United States District Court,
N.D. Georgia,
Atlanta Division.

Oct. 30, 1992.

ROBERT H. HALL, District Judge.

This case is before the Court on Gillett Communications of Atlanta, Inc., d/b/a WAGA-TV5's ("WAGA-TV") Application for Temporary Restraining Order and Petition for Declaratory Judgment, filed on October 28, 1992. A hearing was held on October 29, 1992. The Court GRANTS IN PART and DENIES IN PART the Application and Petition.

## BACKGROUND

WAGA-TV is engaged in the business of television broadcasting in Atlanta and the surrounding area and operates under a license granted by the Federal Communications Commission ("FCC"). Defendant Daniel Becker is a legally qualified candidate for the United States Congress in Georgia's Ninth Congressional District. Defendant Federal Communications Commission is an agency of the United States government and has regulatory authority over WAGA- TV as a broadcast licensee. This case arises out of the Becker Campaign Committee's ongoing attempt to purchase air time on WAGA-TV for paid political advertising.

On October 26, 1992, Defendant Becker presented to WAGA-TV for airing a paid political advertising videotape, which is approximately thirty minutes in length. Defendant Becker has requested WAGA-TV to air the videotape between 4:00 and 5:00 p.m. on Sunday, November 1, 1992, immediately following the broadcast of the National Football League game between the Atlanta Falcons and the Los Angeles Rams.

At issue in this case is one particular segment of the videotape entitled "Abortion in America: The Real Story." WAGA-TV contends that the videotape is indecent, and therefore, it should not be required to air it during the requested hours. WAGA-TV seeks declaratory and injunctive relief.

DISCUSSION

B. Declaratory Ruling

WAGA-TV petitions this Court for a declaratory ruling that WAGA-TV may "channel" the videotape to the "safe harbor" hours between 12:00 midnight and 6:00 a.m., without violating the "reasonable access" and "no censorship" provisions of the Federal Communications Act. The Court so rules.

This suit involves two different statutory provisions regulating WAGA-TV's broadcasting of Mr. Becker's political advertisement. First, 47 U.S.C. §§ 312(a) and 315(a) provide:

> The Commission may revoke any station license or construction permit--
>
> (7) for willful or repeated failure to allow reasonable access to or to permit purchase of reasonable amounts of time for the use of a broad-casting station by a legally qualified candidate for Federal elective office on behalf of his candidacy.
>
> 47 U.S.C. § 312(a).
>
> If any licensee shall permit any person who is a legally qualified candidate for any public office to use a broadcasting station, he shall afford equal opportunities to all other such candidates for that office in the use of such broadcasting station: Provided, That such licensee shall have no power of censorship over the material broadcast under the provisions of this section.
>
> 47 U.S.C. § 315.

Second, 18 U.S.C. § 1464 provides:

> Whoever utters any obscene, indecent or profane language by means of radio communications shall be fined not more than $10,000 or imprisoned not more than two years, or both.

Violation of either statute constitutes grounds for revocation of a broadcaster's FCC license. 47 U.S.C. §§ 312(a)(6) and (7), 315.

With regard to these statutory provisions, the Court faces the following issues: (1) Does the prohibition against the broadcasting of indecent material constitute an exception to the requirements of reasonable access, equal opportunities and no censorship? (2) Is the videotape indecent under 18 U.S.C. § 1464? (3) If so, may WAGA-TV channel the videotape into the safe harbor hours of 12:00 midnight and 6:00 a.m.? (4) Does this violate the First Amendment? The Court will address each in turn.

1. Does the prohibition against the broadcasting of indecent material constitute an exception to the requirements of reasonable access, equal opportunities and no censorship?

Yes. Apparently, there is no reported decision concerning this issue. However, it is the FCC's position that:

> A broadcaster would be justified in refusing access to a candidate who intended to utter obscene

> or indecent language, because Section 312(a)(6) ... must be granted to carve an exception to Section 312(a)(7).... The application of both traditional norms of statutory construction as well as an analysis of the legislative evolution of Section 315 [of the Communications Act] militate in favor or reading [18 USC] section 1464 as an exception to Section 315.

Memorandum by FCC Staff, Jan. 6, 1984, attached as exhibit to Plaintiff's Memorandum.

The Court gives due deference to a reasonable construction of the statutes put forth by the agency charged with implementing the acts. RJR Nabisco, Inc. v. United States, 955 F.2d 1457, 1464 (11th Cir.1992). Furthermore, the Court finds that this conclusion does not significantly undercut the purpose of the "reasonable access" and "no censorship" provisions of the Communications Act: namely to prevent discrimination against candidates and to allow candidates a full opportunity to relate to the public their political stand. KVUE, Inc. v. Austin Broadcasting Corp., 709 F.2d 922 (5th Cir.1983), aff'd, 465 U.S. 1092, 104 S.Ct. 1580, 80 L.Ed.2d 114 (1984); Flory v. FCC, 528 F.2d 124 (7th Cir.1975).

2. Is the videotape indecent under 18 U.S.C. § 1464?

Upon careful consideration of all of the evidence, the Court answers this question in the affirmative.

The FCC defines indecency as:

> language or material that, in context, depicts or describes, in terms patently offensive as measured by contemporary community standards for the broadcast medium, sexual or excretory activities or organs.

In re Goodrich Broadcasting, Inc., 6 FCC Rcd 7484 (1991). In FCC v. Pacifica Foundation, 438 U.S. 726, 98 S.Ct. 3026, 57 L.Ed.2d 1073 (1978), the Supreme Court ultimately affirmed the FCC's application of this definition in regulating the broadcast under review. "[T]he linchpin of indecency enforcement is the protection of children from inappropriate broadcast material." In the Matter of Liability of Sagittarius Broadcasting Corporation, (available on WESTLAW, FCOM-FCC database), 1992 FCC LEXIS 6042, at *4 (October 23, 1992) (citing Action for Children's Television v. F.C.C., 852 F.2d 1332, 1340 (D.C.1988)). The extent to which a broadcast is indecent focuses on whether it is readily understandable to children in the audience.

The Court has viewed the videotape in its entirety and found that it contains descriptions and depictions in violation of § 1464. Specifically, beginning with the segment "Abortion in America: The Real Story," the videotape depicts the actual surgical procedure for abortion. During a short segment, approximately four minutes in length, the videotape contains graphic depictions and descriptions of female genitalia, the uterus, excreted uterine fluid, dismembered fetal body parts, and aborted fetuses. This portion of the videotape depicts these activities and materials in a manner which is patently offensive according to contemporary community standards. This is so in light of the context of the entire video. The Court further concludes that the evidence shows that the images, words, and depictions in the videotape would be readily understandable to children in the audience.

In addition to the video, WAGA-TV provided testimony concerning viewer reactions to the previous one-minute spot. Many calls were taken; they were longer and more involved than those which the station usually receives in response to programming. The evidence supports the conclusion that the previous video was much less graphic and did not contain views of the female sexual organ. WAGA-TV also presented expert testimony of two psychiatrists concerning the effect of the video on children. Both psychiatrists testified that the videotape would have a negative impact on children in the viewing audience. Thus, the Court determines upon viewing the evidence in its entirety, there is ample support for the conclusion that the videotape contains indecent materials, the broadcasting of which is prescribed by 18 U.S.C. § 1464.

3. May WAGA-TV channel the Videotape into the safe harbor hours of 12:00 midnight and 6:00 a.m.?

In Action for Children's Television v. F.C.C., 932 F.2d 1504 (D.C.1991), the court rejected a twenty-four hour ban on the broadcasting of indecent materials. However, the court also made clear that some regulation will withstand constitutional scrutiny. Id. The court directed the FCC to develop a "safe harbor" exception to its regulation of indecent broadcasts; that is, a time in which indecent material may be broadcast.

Congress has also directed the FCC to create regulations designating the hours between 12:00 midnight and 6:00 a.m. as safe harbor hours. The FCC has begun to implement the Congressional mandate. See FCC Proceeding to Implement Regulations to Restrict Broadcasting of Indecent Programming, 1992 FCC LEXIS 5392 (September 17, 1991). Mr. Sander, president of WAGA-TV, testified that significant numbers of children would be watching television between 4:00 and 5:00 p.m. on Sunday. Mr. Sander further testified that between the hours of nine and ten, the percentage of viewers between the ages of 2 and 17 would still be significant, although there may be more supervision of children. The number of children in the audience would decline as the evening progresses. WAGA-TV also presented the testimony of two psychiatrists who stated that although parental supervision may lessen the detrimental effects on children, it may also exacerbate them. Jack Sander further testified that during the time slot of 12:00 midnight to 6:00 A.M., everyone is not asleep. Rather, late night ratings are comparable to weekend day programming with regard to the adult viewing audience.

The Court concludes that WAGA-TV has presented sufficient evidence to support the conclusion that the videotape should be shown between 12:00 midnight and 6:00 a.m. The Court is convinced that this time slot best accommodates the two competing interests and rights: the interest in protecting children from indecent materials and Mr. Becker's right to broadcast his political advertisement.

4. First Amendment Concerns

Neither this Court's order, nor Plaintiff's compliance therewith act as prior restraints on Defendant's speech in violation of the First Amendment. A content-based restriction on speech, especially political speech, must be "a precisely drawn means of serving a compelling state interest" to withstand constitutional scrutiny. Action for Children's Television v. FCC, 852 F.2d 1332, 1343 n. 18 (D.C.Cir.1988). The Supreme Court has found the government's interest in "safeguarding the physical and psychological well- being of a minor" to be compelling. New York v. Ferber, 458 U.S. 747, 756- 57, 102 S.Ct. 3348, 3354, 73 L.Ed.2d 1113 (1982). Accordingly, the Circuit Court for the District of Columbia recognized that the FCC may regulate indecent material, so long as it does so with "due respect for the high value our Constitution places on freedom and choice in what the people say and hear." Action, 852 F.2d at 1344.

This Court's order does not deprive Defendant of the ability to air his advertisement on Plaintiff's programing. It merely channels what is decidedly indecent material to a time slot that sufficiently reduces the chances of injury to the "psychological well-being" of minors in the community. Thus, this Court's order does not violate Defendant's First Amendment rights.

C. Injunctive Relief

WAGA-TV seeks injunctive relief against Becker, the Becker Campaign and the FCC. The Court concludes that WAGA-TV has met its burden with respect to Becker, and the Becker campaign. First, WAGA-TV has proven that it will prevail on the merits of its claim, as discussed above. Second, WAGA-TV has proven that it faces a substantial threat of irreparable injury. WAGA-TV faces the dilemma of choosing between seemingly conflicting obligations as a broadcaster, and the failure to comply with either one could result in revocation of its license. Furthermore, and perhaps most importantly, WAGA-TV faces the possibility of substantial public disapproval of its broadcasting the videotape during hours in which children are very likely to see it. The evidence demonstrates that WAGA-TV received numerous phone calls in response to Defendant Becker's last advertisement, and testimony supports the conclusion that any effort to explain that WAGA-TV was under a legal obligation to broadcast the material was ineffective in diminishing the disapproval. The objectionable portion of this video is over four times as long as the previous video, and testimony supports the conclusion that this video is also much more graphic and contains images and descriptions absent in the last video. Third, WAGA-TV has proven that its own injury outweighs the injury to Defendant Becker and the Becker campaign. The two Defendants are still free to air the political campaign video; it simply must be aired during a time in which children are less likely to see the indecent material contained within it. Finally, the Court concludes that a strong public interest supports injunctive relief: protecting children from indecent materials, an interest recognized by many courts and by the legislative body as compelling.

The Court's conclusion, however, is different with respect to the FCC. First, as discussed above, under normal circumstances, this Court would have invoked the primary jurisdiction doctrine, thus allowing the FCC to pass on the issues at hand. Given the circumstances, the Court believes it would be improper to enjoin the activities of the FCC. To do so would upset the balance of power the primary jurisdiction doctrine is designed to protect. Second, this Court questions whether it has the authority to enjoin the FCC from exercising its administrative powers. Clearly, judicial review of FCC's decisions and orders, including the power to enjoin enforcement of orders, lies with the courts of appeal. See 47 U.S.C. § 402 and 28 U.S.C. § 2342. Finally, the Court remains convinced that WAGA-TV has an adequate remedy with respect to any action taken by the FCC which may be contrary to this Order: review by the court of appeals.

Thus, with respect to injunctive relief, the Court HEREBY ORDERS:
Defendants Daniel Becker and the Daniel Becker for Congress Committee are enjoined and restrained from requiring WAGA-TV to air the Becker videotape at any time other than between the hours of 12:00 midnight and 6:00 A.M.

## CONCLUSION

In conclusion, the Court GRANTS WAGA-TV's request for declaratory relief. The Court GRANTS WAGA-TV's request for injunctive relief against Defendant Becker and Becker's Campaign. The Court DENIES WAGA-TV's request for injunctive relief against the FCC.

Furthermore, the Court has been informed by counsel for the FCC that they expect to rule on the issues presented in this Order by 5:00 today. In the event that the FCC does issue an order specifically ruling on each of the issues presented in this case as follows:

(1) Does the prohibition against the broadcasting of indecent material constitute an exception to the requirements of reasonable access, equal opportunities and no censorship?

(2) Is the videotape indecent under 18 U.S.C. § 1464?

(3) May WAGA-TV channel the videotape into the safe harbor hours of 12:00 midnight and 6:00 A.M.?

this order shall become MOOT.

So ORDERED this 30th day of October, 1992.

## The FCC Response

In 1994, the FCC issued an order allowing broadcasters to protect children from disturbing images, consistent with the 1992 ruling.

## The Becker Appeal

In 1996, the FCC order was overturned by the U.S. Court of Appeals in Washington D.C., which ruled that broadcasters may not refuse to broadcast a candidate's political advertisements or air them only in off hours just because they contain graphic images of aborted fetuses. The appeals court ruled that FCC regulations give candidates the right to seek the widest possible audience for the message they seek to convey. The court noted that Becker's ads were not "indecent" or "obscene." Broadcasters do have the right to reject "indecent' or "obscene" advertisements.

In Re Complaint by ATLANTA NAACP, ATLANTA, GA. Concerning Section 315 Political Broadcast by J. B. Stoner

36 F.C.C.2d 635

AUGUST 3, 1972

MR. LONNIE KING, Atlanta NAACP, 859 1/2 Hunter Street, Atlanta, Ga. 30314
DEAR MR. KING: This will refer to your letter of August 2, 1972, which was also signed by Reverend Joe Boone, Community Coalition on Broadcasting, and Mr. Stuart Lowengrub, Anti-Defamation League, concerning the broadcast of a political announcement by Mr. J. B. Stoner, one of 17 candidates entered in the Democratic primary for U.S. Senator from Georgia.

You request that the Commission '(1) recognize that when a broadcast licensee has in hand strong evidence to the effect that broadcasting of specific political advertisements with racial slurs contained therein poses an imminent and immediate threat to the safety and security of the public it serves, such a licensee should be free to, and it is the responsibility of such licensee under the public interest standard to, withhold such announcement or advertisement, pending further review by an authorized body, without incurring either sanction or penalty of this Commission; and (2)... make known to its licensees in the State of Georgia that application of the foregoing standard, or any other reasonable standard the Commission may choose to employ, subject to fuller briefing and argument, means that no penalty or sanction will be applied to said licensees for refusing to telecast or broadcast the aforementioned advertisement of J. B. Stoner.'

You state that the primary election is to be held on August 8, 1972; and that Mr. Stoner, 'Chairman of the neo-Nazi National States Rights Party, is a white supremacist candidate... whose often stated goal is to rid the U.S. of all Blacks and Jews...'; that he is purchasing radio and television advertising time in several Georgia communities; that while under normal circumstances the broadcast licensee is prohibited by Section 315 of the Communications Act from exercising any censorship over the nature or substance of a candidate's presentation, the substance of one of Mr. Stoner's recently broadcast political announcements is such that it poses a serious and imminent threat to the safety and well being of the stations which air it and to the community at large; that the telecast of the advertisement has already resulted in threats of bombing and violence against broadcasting stations in Augusta (WRDW-TV) and Savannah (WTOC-TV), Georgia; and that Mr. Stoner intends to have the advertisement telecast and broadcast in Atlanta as well as in several other Georgia communities. You further state that in your judgment the continued broadcasting of the advertisement will pose a very serious threat to the welfare of your city and state and to the safety of both its black and white citizens; that 'the clear and intended effect of this advertisement is to incite racial hatred and violence, to exacerbate fears, and to reverse the tide of understanding and progress between the races by provoking the ugly image of violence and terror'; that there are extremists who would welcome a violent confrontation and that Mr. Stoner's advertisement provides the kind of fuel that can ignite such a fire; that you recognize that the purpose of the no-censorship clause of Section 315 of the Communications Act is to protect the right of political candidates to engage in open and free discussion of the issues and to insure that the public will be allowed to hear all divergent points of view of such candidates without interference or influenceby the broadcast licensees; and that while you heartily endorse the concept of non-censorship as well as the constitutional right of freedom of speech, even the latter has certain limitations such as the prohibition of yelling fire in a crowded theatre and that Mr. Stoner is yelling fire in the crowded theatre.

Attached to your letter was a copy of an Executive Order issued by Mayor Sam Massell of Atlanta which urges radio and television stations and other mass media not to accept advertising using language such as that in Mr. Stoner's advertisements on the ground that it is 'calculated to incite hearers of such language to take violent action....'

You state that the political announcement in question is as follows:
I am J. B. Stoner. I am the only candidate for U.S. Senator who is for the white people. I am the only candidate who is against integration. All of the other candidates are race mixers to one degree or another. I say we must repeal Gambrell's civil rights law. Gambrell's law takes jobs from us whites and gives those jobs to the niggers. The main reason why niggers want integration is because the niggers want our white women. I am for law and order with the knowledge that you cannot have law and order and niggers too. Vote white. This time vote your convictions by voting white racist J. B. Stoner into the run-off election for U.S. Senator. Thank you.

The basic question here is whether the Commission should advise the affected licensees that they may refuse to carry the Stoner announcements. As you recognize, Section 315 of the Communications Act of 1934, as amended, 47 U.S.C. 315, prohibits licensee censorship of broadcasts by legally qualified candidates for public office. It states in pertinent part that a 'licensee shall have no power of censorship over the material broadcast under the provisions of this section.' In addition, Section 326 of the Act, 47 U.S.C., 326, prohibits the Commission from censoring broadcast matter or interfering with the right of free speech by means of radio communication. The Supreme Court in Farmers Union v. WDAY, 360 U.S. 525, has held that in view of the no- censorship provision of Section 315, licensees are immune to suit for defamatory statements contained in candidates' broadcasts, and has pointed out that permitting censorship for libel would 'undermine the basic purpose for which Section 315 was passed -- full and unrestricted discussion of political issues by legally qualified candidates.' (360 U.S. at 529).

The relief requested in your letter would amount to an advance approval by the Commission of licensee censorship of a candidate's remarks. By way of background, we note that Constitutional guarantees do not permit the proscription of even the advocacy of force or of law violation 'except where such advocacy is directed to inciting or producing imminent lawless action and is likely to incite or produce such action.' Brandenburg v. Ohio, 395 U.S. 444, 447. And a prior restraint bears a heavy presumption against its constitutional validity. Carroll v. Princess Anne,

393 U.S. 175, 181. While there may be situations where speech is 'so interlaced with burgeoning violence that it is not protected,' Carroll v. Princess Anne, 393 U.S. at 180, and while a similar approach might warrant overriding the no-censorship command of Section 315, we need not resolve that difficult issue here, for we conclude on the basis of the information before us that there is no factual basis for the relief you request. Despite your report of threats of bombing and violence, there does not appear to be that clear and present danger of imminent violence which might warrant interfering with speech which does not contain any direct incitement to violence. A contrary conclusion here would permit anyone to prevent a candidate from exercisinghis rights under Section 315 by threatening a violent reaction. In view of the precise commands of Sections 315 and 326, we are constrained to deny your requests.

However abhorent some speech might be to the Commission, we deem it best to adhere to what we stated in another context in Anti-Defamation League of B'nai B'rith, 4 F.C.C. 2d 190, 191 (1966), affirmed, Anti-Defamation League of B'nai B'rith v. F.C.C., 131 U.S. App. D.C. 146, 403 F.2d 169, (1968), cert. den. 394 U.S. 930 (1969):

It is the judgment of the Commission, as it has been the judgment of those who drafted our Constitution and of the overwhelming majority of our legislators and judges over the years, that the public interest is best served by permitting the expression of any views that do not involve 'a clear and present danger of serious substantive evil that rises far above public inconvenience, annoyance, or unrest.' Terminiello v. Chicago, 337 US 1, 4 (1949); Chaplinsky v. New Hampshire, 315 US 568; Ashton v. Kentucky [384 US 195], 34 LW 4398 (1966). This most assuredly does not mean that those who uphold this principle approve of the opinions that are expressed under its protection. On the contrary, this principle insures that the most diverse and opposing opinions will be expressed, many of which may be even highly offensive to those officials who thus protect the rights of others to free speech. If there is to be free speech, it must be free for speech that we abhor and hate as well as for speech that we find tolerable or congenial.

Accordingly, your request IS DENIED.

Commissioners Robert E. Lee, Acting Chairman; H. Rex Lee and Wiley acting as a Board.
BY DIRECTION OF THE COMMISSION, BEN F. WAPLE, Secretary.

POLISH AMERICAN CONGRESS and Thaddeus L. Kowalski, Petitioners,
v.
FEDERAL COMMUNICATIONS COMMISSION and United States of America, Respondents,
American Broadcasting Companies, Inc., Intervenor.

520 F.2d 1248

United States Court of Appeals,
Seventh Circuit.

Decided July 23, 1975.

Before HASTINGS, Senior Circuit Judge, and CUMMINGS and STEVENS, Circuit Judges.

CUMMINGS, Circuit Judge.

This petition asks us to set aside an order of the Federal Communications Commission denying the complaint of petitioners that American Broadcasting Companies, Inc. ("ABC") violated the Federal Communications Commission's fairness doctrine and personal attack rule by refusing petitioners air-time to respond to an August 10, 1972, broadcast of the Dick Cavett Show containing Polish jokes.

During the program in question, comedian Bob Einstein, masquerading as Gil Drabowski, president of an imaginary Polish Anti-Defamation League, told four "Polish jokes," all denigrating the intellectual or motor skills or personal hygiene standards of Poles. The show was hosted by comedian Steve Allen. The setting was an interview of Einstein by Allen regarding a fictitious lawsuit against the three television networks brought by Drabowski on behalf of his organization, demanding a public apology for Polish jokes told on the networks and endeavoring to make sure that there would be no more Polish jokes broadcast by the networks. Thereafter, in jest, Drabowski gave the four objectionable jokes assailed by petitioners, as examples of those shown by the networks for which his organization thought an apology was required. As a result of a protest by petitioners and others, on the following evening Steve Allen explained that Einstein's comedy sketch involving Polish jokes was intended to amuse "just as the 'All in the Family' show, which is the No. 1 show in the country, intends to amuse when it does jokes about the Polish, Italians, and every group in the world." Allen then stated that he, Bob Einstein and ABC apologized to those who were offended. Although Allen indicated that he had invited a spokesman for a protesting Polish American organization to "speak his piece" during the August 11th show, no such spokesman appeared.

On October 4, 1972, petitioners wrote ABC requesting "equal time" to reply "under Federal Communications Commission Regulations" to the August 10th telecast. ABC replied as follows on October 31st:

"We are sorry that anything said or done by either Steve Allen or Bob Einstein offended you. The following evening Steve Allen apologized on behalf of himself, Mr. Einstein and the ABC Television Network.

"No harm or malice towards Polish-Americans was intended and we are most sincerely regretful that you were hurt or offended.

"For your information, 'equal time' under Section 315 of the Communications Act is limited in scope to candidates for public office and, accordingly, we respectfully decline your 'equal time' request."

Eight months thereafter, petitioners filed a complaint with the Commission, requesting it to rule under the personal attack rule of the fairness doctrine and under the fairness doctrine itself that petitioners were entitled to equal time or a reasonable opportunity to respond free of charge on the ABC network "to the personal attacks on the character, intelligence, hygiene or appearance of members of the Polish American community, an identifiable group," on the August 10th telecast. The complaint contended that demeaning and defamatory attacks in the guise of ethnic humor constituted a controversial issue of public importance "because such programming represents a single warped and negative point of view which has an enormous influence on the viewing audience."

On September 26, 1973, the Commission's Broadcast Bureau denied petitioners' complaint, noting at the outset that Section 326 of the Federal Communications Act (47 U.S.C. s 326) prohibits the Commission from censoring broadcast material. Under the fairness doctrine, the Broadcast Bureau acknowledged that if a station presents one side of a controversial issue of public importance, it is required to afford reasonable opportunity for the presentation of contrasting views. The Bureau's ruling further stated:

"It is the responsibility of the broadcast licensee to determine whether a controversial issue of public importance has been presented and, if so, how best to present contrasting views on the issue. The Commission will review complaints to determine whether the licensee can be said to have acted reasonably and in good faith.

"In support of your contention that the broadcast of Polish jokes constitutes a controversial issue of public importance, you state that the jokes 'belittle a large segment of the population' by perpetuating a 'dumb Polack image.' However, you have not shown that there is any controversy in this country concerning the intelligence or other qualities of Polish Americans. (Footnote omitted.) Accordingly, we are unable to find from the evidence presently before us that ABC was unreasonable in concluding that the broadcast of the jokes and attendant remarks did not constitute the discussion of a controversy of public importance.

"Since we have determined that the network was not unreasonable in concluding that no controversial issue of public importance was involved, the broadcast of the Polish jokes could not constitute, under the Commission's rules, a personal attack. In order for the personal attack rule to be applicable, the attack must occur during the discussion of a controversial issue of public importance. Section 73.123(a) of the Commission's Rules and Regulations. Even had a controversial issue of public importance been involved here, it does not appear that these jokes and attendant remarks could have constituted a personal attack under the Commission's rules. The statement of a particular view, however strongly or forcefully made, does not necessarily constitute a personal attack. The Port of New York Authority, 25 FCC 2d 417 (1970). To qualify under the Commission's rule, the attack must reflect upon the 'honesty, character, integrity or like personal qualities' of a person or group, and not merely reflect upon ability, knowledge or like intellectual or motor skills."

Subsequently, the petitioners applied to the full Commission for a review of the Broadcast Bureau's ruling. The application was denied. 46 F.C.C.2d 124 (1974). Again the Commission reminded petitioners that Section 326 of the Act prohibits it from interfering with broadcasters' rights of free speech. After expressing its approval of the Broadcast Bureau's ruling that no controversial issue of public importance had been shown, the Commission echoed the Bureau's alternate rationale that the personal attack rule only applies where an attack is made "upon the honesty, character, integrity or like personal qualities of an identified person or group." Even assuming that a controversial issue of public importance had been involved, the Commission held that the personal attack rule does not apply to these jokes because there was no "attack on those personal qualities bearing on the moral rectitude or personal credibility of the named individual or group," citing Rome Hospital and Murphy Memorial Hospital, 40 F.C.C.2d 452, 453 (1973). This petition for review followed.

Fairness Doctrine and Personal Attack Rule

. . . The rule on personal attacks, like that on political editorials, is a Commission rule setting out an aspect of the fairness doctrine. See Red Lion, supra, 395 U.S. at 383-386, 89 S.Ct. 1794. The personal attack rule's application is specifically confined to a situation where the attack occurs "during the presentation of views on a controversial issue of public importance." [FN4] The confinement of the rule's application to "controversial issues of public importance" parallels an identical limitation on the application of the more general fairness doctrine. See Columbia Broadcasting System, supra, 412 U.S. at 111-112, 93 S.Ct. 2080; Healey v. Federal Communications Commission, 148 U.S.App.D.C. 409, 460 F.2d 917, 920, 922 (1972); Democratic National Committee, supra, at 900-901; Green v. Federal Communications Commission, 144 U.S.App.D.C. 353, 447 F.2d 323, 327, 329 (1971); Obligations of Broadcast Licensees, supra, at 28; Loevinger, "Free Speech, Fairness and Fiduciary Duty in Broadcasting," 34 Law and Contemp.Prob. 278, 285 (1969). Therefore, in order for petitioners to establish the right to a reply under either the general fairness doctrine or the particular personal attack rule, they must show that views on a controversial issue of public importance were set forth in the assailed broadcast.

FN4. The personal attack facet of the fairness doctrine was incorporated into a rule in 1967 and provides in pertinent part:
"(a) When, during the presentation of views on a controversial issue of public importance, an attack is made upon the honesty, character, integrity or like personal qualities of an identified person or group, the licensee shall, within a reasonable time and in no event later than one week after the attack, transmit to the person or group attacked (1) notification of the date, time and identification of the broadcast; (2) a script or tape (or an accurate summary if a script or tape is not available) of the attack; and (3) an offer of a reasonable opportunity to respond over the licensee's facilities." 47 C.F.R. s 73.679 (1974). See 47 C.F.R. ss 73.123, 73.300 and 73.598 (all identical to s 73.679). The obligations upon the broadcaster under the personal attack rule differ from those imposed by the general fairness doctrine in that under the former "the broadcaster does not have the option of presenting the attacked party's side himself or choosing a third party to present that side." Red Lion, supra, at 378, 89 S.Ct. at 1800. The attacked party himself must be given an opportunity to respond. See Democratic National Committee, supra, at 902 . . . .

The Commission's Determination that ABC Acted Reasonably and in Good Faith

In the present case, ABC decided that the Polish joke material contained in the August 10th Dick Cavett Show did not present a controversial issue of public importance. Thus in its opposition to the application for review before the full Commission, ABC formally contended that the comedy skit on the August 10th show did not represent a controversial issue of public importance. The Commission concluded that ABC acted reasonably and in good faith in making this determination because petitioners had not shown there was any controversy in this country concerning the intelligence or other qualities of Polish Americans. Even petitioners recognize "that broadcasters have discretion in deciding whether a controversial issue of public importance exists and their latitude may be wide" (Reply Br. at 6). Neither the Commission nor we should encroach upon this determination by ABC in the absence of an abuse of its discretion. Democratic National Committee, supra, at 906.

Petitioners do not assert that ABC lacked good faith. Thus the thrust of their argument is that the network's determination that there was no discussion of a controversial issue of public importance in the August 10th Polish joke skit was unreasonable.

In order to invoke the fairness doctrine, a petitioner must first define the issue which it maintains is a controversial one of public importance. Green v. Federal Communications Commission, supra, at 329. In the complaint and application for review before the Commission, in the briefs here, and at oral argument we searched in vain for petitioners' statement of the issue. We have found no clear statement of a question that could serve as an issue around which an important public controversy could form. In petitioners' letter to ABC, they simply requested "equal time" to reply to the August 10th show wherein Steve Allen and Bob Einstein allegedly "defamed Polish Americans." In the July 2, 1973, complaint to the Commission, the attempts to state the issue were as follows:

"Under the Fairness Doctrine, the broadcasting of personal attacks, the depiction of Polish persons or culture in a demeaning manner, the broadcasting of ethnic 'humor' that is insulting to the intelligence, character, hygiene, or appearance of these persons is a controversial issue of public importance because such programming represents a single warped and negative point of view which has an enormous influence on the viewing audience. The televising of so- called 'Polack jokes' is per se a controversial issue of public importance, harmful and insulting to a considerable segment of the American population.

"The Federal Communications Commission is therefore requested to rule that the 'Polack jokes' on the Dick Cavett Show, hosted by Steve Allen, on August 10 and 11, 1972 constitute a controversial issue of public importance because such jokes in and of themselves belittle a large segment of the population, both young and adult."

After the Bureau's ruling that there was no discussion of a controversial issue of public importance on the August 10th show, the application for review before the full Commission was filed, containing these statements about the issue:

"The Staff action supported the view of the licensee that promulgating such humor (Polish jokes) is not a controversial issue of public importance, and that complainants did not present evidence that the issue is such a controversy of public importance.

"The group attacked is large, in excess of ten million Polish Americans. The issue is one of public importance as a result of mere numbers alone. It is controversial because the unanswered 'Polack joke' does, tends to, or is likely to belittle the Polish American in our society."

Reading the pleadings before the Commission leniently, two possible issues are suggested by these excerpts: (1) whether Poles or Polish Americans are inferior to other human beings in terms of intelligence, personal hygiene, etc.; or (2) whether "promulgating" Polish jokes by broadcasting them (if promulgation can be inferred from mere broadcasting) is desirable. Nowhere in the complaint or application for review before the Commission is there a clear statement of the issue which is alleged to be both controversial and of public importance. It would be improper to require the licensee and the Commission to ferret out the critical issue, since petitioners bear the burden of putting the issue forward in a manner that makes it possible for the exercise of discretion as to whether the fairness doctrine or personal attack rule has been properly invoked. Nevertheless, we need not rely on petitioners' failure to state the issue clearly, because the Commission was correct in ruling that ABC did not overstep its discretion in failing to find a controversial issue of public importance, even if we regard the above two issues as properly suggested in the complaint and application for review.

Petitioners allege nothing that would support a contention that there is a controversy over the issue whether Poles or Polish Americans are less intelligent, less clean, less coordinated, etc. than other people. If some people do seriously assert the inferiority of Poles and Polish Americans, it was not unreasonable for ABC to decide that they have not generated enough support for their position to raise a controversial issue of public importance. Even if such a debate existed, we could not say that a determination by ABC that the broadcast of the skit in question did not constitute a discussion of this issue was unreasonable. In any event, the record satisfies us that petitioners did not seek to convince the Commission that the skit presented views on such a question.

Assuming that petitioners asserted the question whether broadcasting Polish jokes is desirable, they still failed to demonstrate that there is a controversy of public importance over that issue. In an attempt to show that a controversial issue of public importance was aired on August 10th, petitioners cite the news coverage afforded the filing of the complaint in this case. Many newspapers across the country carried a wire service story describing the action filed with the Commission. All newsworthy events do not constitute controversial issues of public importance. Healey v. Federal Communications Commission, supra, at 922. Moreover, the newsworthy event covered by the papers was not the Polish joke skit, but a filing of a complaint by petitioners before the Commission. The complaint was filed almost eleven months after the broadcast. To the extent that news stories might reflect on the existence of a controversial issue of public importance, the "fairness doctrine requires a current judgment," so that the passage of the eleven months from the broadcast might well have caused the Commission to discount the relevance of the news stories. Larus & Brother Co., supra, at 881, 883.

In assailing the licensee's decision, petitioners also rely on the denunciation of Polish jokes by various individuals and groups, including resolutions by the city government of Hartford, Connecticut, and the United States House of Representatives. Such condemnations do not cause a skit containing Polish jokes to become a discussion of a controversial issue of public importance. No contrary resolutions or other disagreements with the essence of the resolutions are cited from which the Commission or ABC might deduce that a controversy existed over the desirability of broadcasting Polish jokes. Even if we assume that the skit constituted a statement favoring the broadcasting of Polish jokes, it was reasonable to conclude that such an endorsement does not create a public issue requiring a response, where nothing suggests that such an issue existed before the broadcast . . . .

Since we cannot agree with petitioners that the broadcast of these jokes constituted a presentation of views on a controversial issue of public importance, the Commission's order is affirmed.

TURNER BROADCASTING SYSTEM, INC., et al., Appellants
v.
FEDERAL COMMUNICATIONS COMMISSION et al.

117 S.Ct. 1174

Supreme Court of the United States

Decided March 31, 1997.

Justice Stevens concurred and filed opinion.

Justice Breyer concurred in part and filed opinion.

Justice O'Connor dissented and filed opinion in which Justices Scalia, Thomas, and Ginsburg joined.

Justice KENNEDY delivered the opinion of the Court, except as to a portion of Part II-A-1.

Sections 4 and 5 of the Cable Television Consumer Protection and Competition Act of 1992 require cable television systems to dedicate some of their channels to local broadcast television stations. Earlier in this case, we held the so-called "must-carry" provisions to be content-neutral restrictions on speech, subject to intermediate First Amendment scrutiny under United States v. O'Brien, 391 U.S. 367, 377, 88 S.Ct. 1673, 1679, 20 L.Ed.2d 672 (1968). A plurality of the Court considered the record as then developed insufficient to determine whether the provisions were narrowly tailored to further important governmental interests, and we remanded the case to the District Court for the District of Columbia for additional factfinding.

On appeal from the District Court's grant of summary judgment for appellees, the case now presents the two questions left open during the first appeal: First, whether the record as it now stands supports Congress' predictive judgment that the must-carry provisions further important governmental interests; and second, whether the provisions do not burden substantially more speech than necessary to further those interests. We answer both questions in the affirmative, and conclude the must-carry provisions are consistent with the First Amendment.

I

An outline of the Cable Act, Congress' purposes in adopting it, and the facts of the case are set out in detail in our first opinion, see Turner Broadcasting System, Inc. v. FCC, 512 U.S. 622, 114 S.Ct. 2445, 129 L.Ed.2d 497 (1994) (Turner), and a more abbreviated summary will suffice here. Soon after Congress enacted the Cable Television Consumer Protection and Competition Act of

1992, Pub.L. 102-385, 106 Stat. 1460 (Cable Act), appellants brought suit against the United States and the Federal Communications Commission (both referred to here as the Government) in the United States District Court for the District of Columbia, challengingthe constitutionality of the must-carry provisions under the First Amendment. The three-judge District Court, in a divided opinion, granted summary judgment for the Government and intervenor- defendants. A majority of the court sustained the must-carry provisions under the intermediate standard of scrutiny set forth in United States v. O'Brien, supra, concludingthe must-carry provisions were content-neutral "industry- specific antitrust and fair trade" legislation narrowly tailored to preserve local broadcasting beset by monopoly power in most cable systems, growing concentration in the cable industry, and concomitant risks of programming decisions driven by anticompetitive policies. 819 F.Supp. 32, 40, 45-47 (D.D.C 1993).

On appeal, we agreed with the District Court that must-carry does not "distinguish favored speech from disfavored speech on the basis of the ideas or views expressed," 512 U.S., at 643, 114 S.Ct., at 2459, but is a content- neutral regulation designed "to prevent cable operators from exploiting their economic power to the detriment of broadcasters," and "to ensure that all Americans, especially those unable to subscribe to cable, have access to free television programming--whateverits content." Id., at 649, 114 S.Ct., at 2462. We held that, under the intermediate level of scrutiny applicable to content-neutral regulations, must-carry would be sustained if it were shown to further an important or substantial governmental interest unrelated to the suppression of free speech, provided the incidental restrictions did not "burden substantially more speech than is necessary to further" those interests. Id., at 662, 114 S.Ct., at 2469 (quoting Ward v. Rock Against Racism, 491 U.S. 781, 799, 109 S.Ct. 2746, 2758, 105 L.Ed.2d 661 (1989)). Although we "ha[d] no difficulty concluding" the interests must-carry was designed to serve were important in the abstract, 512 U.S., at 663, 114 S.Ct., at 2469-2470, a four-Justice plurality concluded genuine issues of material fact remained regardingwhether "the economic health of local broadcasting is in genuine jeopardy and need of the protections afforded by must-carry," and whether must-carry " 'burden[s] substantially more speech than is necessary to further the government's legitimate interests.' " Id., at 665, 114 S.Ct., at 2470 (quoting Ward, supra, at 799, 109 S.Ct., at 2758). Justice STEVENS would have found the statute valid on the record then before us; he agreed to remand the case to ensure a judgment of the Court, and the case was returned to the District Court for further proceedings. 512 U.S., at 673-674, 114 S.Ct., at 2474-2475 (STEVENS, J., concurring in part and concurring in judgment); id., at 667-668, 114 S.Ct., at 2471-2472.

The District Court oversaw another 18 months of factual development on remand "yielding a record of tens of thousands of pages" of evidence, Turner Broadcasting v. FCC, 910 F.Supp. 734, 755 (D.D.C.1995), comprised of materials acquired during Congress' three years of preenactment hearings, see Turner, supra, at 632-634, 114 S.Ct., at 2453-2455, as well as additional expert submissions, sworn declarations and testimony, and industry documents obtained on remand. Upon consideration of the expanded record, a divided panel of the District Court again granted summary judgment to appellees. 910 F.Supp., at 751. The majority determined "Congress drew reasonable inferences" from substantial evidence before it to conclude that "in the absence of must-carry rules, 'significant' numbers of broadcast stations would be refused carriage." Id., at 742. The court found Congress drew on studies and anecdotal evidence indicating "cable operators had already dropped, refused to carry, or adversely repositioned significant numbers of local broadcasters," and suggesting that in the vast majority of cases the broadcasters were not restored to carriage in their prior position. Ibid. Noting evidence in the record before Congress and the testimony of experts on remand, id., at 743, the court decided the noncarriage problem would grow worse without must-carry because cable operators had refrained from dropping broadcast stations during Congress' investigation and the pendency of this litigation, id., at 742-743, and possessed increasing incentives to use their growing economic power to capture broadcasters' advertising revenues and promote affiliated cable programmers. Ibid. The court concluded "substantial evidence before Congress" supported the predictive judgment that a local broadcaster denied carriage "would suffer financial harm and possible ruin." Id., at 743-744. It cited evidence that adverse carriage actions decrease broadcasters' revenues by reducing audience levels, id., at 744-745, and evidence that the invalidation of the FCC's prior must-carry regulations had contributed to declining growth in the broadcast industry. Id., at 744, and n. 34.

The court held must-carry to be narrowly tailored to promote the Government's legitimate interests. It found the effects of must-carry on cable operators to be minimal, noting evidence that: most cable systems had not been required to add any broadcast stations since the rules were adopted; only 1.2 percent of all cable channels had been devoted to broadcast stations added because of must-carry; and the burden was likely to diminish as channel capacity expanded in the future. Id., at 746-747. The court proceeded to consider a number of alternatives to must-carry that appellants had proposed, including: a leased-access regime, under which cable operators would be required to set aside channels for both broadcasters and cable programmers to use at a regulated price; use of so-called A/B switches, giving consumers a choice of both cable and broadcast signals; a more limited set of must-carry obligations modeled on those earlier used by the FCC; and subsidies for broadcasters. The court rejected each in turn, concluding that "even assuming that [the alternatives] would be less burdensome" on cable operators' First Amendment interests, they "are not in any respect as effective in achieving the government's [interests]." Id., at 747. Judge Jackson would have preferred a trial to summary judgment, but concurred in the judgment of the court. Id., at 751-754.

Judge Williams dissented. His review of the record, and particularly evidence concerning growth in the number of broadcasters, industry advertising revenues, and per-station profits during the period without must-carry, led him to conclude the broadcast industry as a whole would not be " 'seriously jeopardized' " in the absence of must-carry. Id., at 759-767. Judge Williams acknowledged the Government had a legitimate interest in preventing anticompetitive behavior, and accepted that cable operators have incentives to discriminate against broadcasters in favor of their own vertically integrated cable programming. Id., at 772, 775, 779. He would have granted summary judgment for appellants nonetheless on the ground must-carry is not narrowly tailored. In his view, must-carry constitutes a significant (though "diminish [ing]," id., at 782) burden on cable operators' and programmers' rights, ibid., and the Cable Act's must-carry provisions suppress more speech than necessary because "less-restrictive" alternatives exist to accomplish the Government's legitimate objectives. Id., at 782-789.

This direct appeal followed. See 47 U.S.C. § 555(c)(1); 28 U.S.C. § 1253. We noted probable jurisdiction, 516 U.S. ----, 116 S.Ct. 907, 133 L.Ed.2d 839 (1996), and we now affirm.

II

We begin where the plurality ended in Turner, applying the standards for intermediate scrutiny enunciated in O'Brien. A content- neutral regulation will be sustained under the First Amendment if it advances important governmental interests unrelated to the suppression of free speech and does not burden substantially more speech than necessary to further those interests. O'Brien, 391 U.S., at 377, 88 S.Ct., at 1679. As noted in Turner, must-carry was designed to serve "three interrelated interests: (1) preserving the benefits of free, over-the-air local broadcast television, (2) promoting the widespread dissemination of information from a multiplicity of sources, and (3) promoting fair competition in the market for television programming." 512 U.S., at 662, 114 S.Ct., at 2469. We decided then, and now reaffirm, that each of those is an important governmental interest. We have been most explicit in holding that " 'protecting noncable households from loss of regular television broadcasting service due to competition from cable systems' is an important federal interest." Id., at 663, 114 S.Ct., at 2470 (quoting Capital Cities Cable, Inc. v. Crisp, 467 U.S. 691, 714, 104 S.Ct. 2694, 2708, 81 L.Ed.2d 580 (1984)). Forty percent of American households continue to rely on over-the-air signals for television programming. Despite the growing importance of cable television and alternative technologies, " 'broadcasting is demonstrably a principal source of information and entertainment for a great part of the Nation's population.' " Turner, supra, at 663, 114 S.Ct., at 2469 (quoting United States v. Southwestern Cable Co., 392 U.S. 157, 177, 88 S.Ct. 1994, 2005, 20 L.Ed.2d 1001 (1968)). We have identified a corresponding "governmental purpose of the highest order" in ensuring public access to "a multiplicity of information sources," 512 U.S., at 663, 114 S.Ct., at 2469. And it is undisputed the Government has an interest in "eliminating restraints on fair competition ..., even when the individuals o entities subject to particular regulations are engaged in expressive activity protected by the First Amendment." Ibid.

On remand, and again before this Court, both sides have advanced new interpretations of these interests in an attempt to recast them in forms "more readily proven." 910 F.Supp., at 759 (Williams, J., dissenting). The Government downplays the importance of showing a risk to the broadcast industry as a whole and suggests the loss of even a few broadcast stations "is a matter of critical importance." Tr. of Oral Arg. 23. Taking the opposite approach, appellants argue Congress' interest in preserving broadcasting is not implicated unless it is shown the industry as a whole would fail without must- carry, Brief for Appellant National Cable Television Association, Inc. 18-23 (NCTA Brief), Brief for Appellant Time Warner Entertainment Co., L.P. 8-10 (Time Warner Brief), and suggest Congress' legitimate interest in "assuring that the public has access to a multiplicity of information sources," Turner, supra, at 663, 114 S.Ct., at 2470, extends only as far as preserving "a minimum amount of television broadcast service." Time Warner Brief 28; NCTA Brief 40; Reply Brief for Appellant NCTA 12.

These alternative formulations are inconsistent with Congress' stated interests in enacting must-carry. The congressional findings do not reflect concern that, absent must-carry, "a few voices," Tr. of Oral Arg. 23, would be lost from the television marketplace. In explicit factual findings, Congress expressed clear concern that the "marked shift in market share from broadcast television to cable television services," Cable Act § 2(a)(13), note following 47 U.S.C. § 521, resulting from increasing market penetration by cable services, as well as the expanding horizontal concentration and vertical integration of cable operators, combined to give cable systems the incentive and ability to delete, reposition, or decline carriage to local broadcasters in an attempt to favor affiliated cable programmers. §§ 2a(2)-(5), (15). Congress predicted that "absent the reimposition of [must-carry], additional local broadcast signals will be deleted, repositioned, or not carried" (§ 2(a)(15); see also § 2(a)(8)(D)), with the end result that "the economic viability of free local broadcast television and its ability to originate quality local programming will be seriously jeopardized." § 2(a)(16).

At the same time, Congress was under no illusion that there would be a complete disappearance of broadcast television nationwide in the absence of must-carry. Congress recognized broadcast programming (and network programming in particular) "remains the most popular programming on cable systems," § 2(a)(19). Indeed, reflecting the popularity and strength of some broadcasters, Congress included in the Cable Act a provision permitting broadcasters to charge cable systems for carriage of the broadcasters' signals. See § 6, codified at 47 U.S.C. § 325. Congress was concerned not that broadcast television would disappear in its entirety without must-carry, but that without it, "significant numbers of broadcast stations will be refused carriage on cable systems," and those "broadcast stations denied carriage will either deteriorate to a substantial degree or fail altogether." 512 U.S., at 666, 114 S.Ct., at 2471. See, e.g., H.R.Rep. No. 102-628, p. 51 (1992) (House Report) (the absence of must-carry "will result in a weakening of the over-the- air television industry and a reduction in competition"); id., at 64 ("The Committee wishes to make clear that its concerns are not limited to a situation where stations are dropped wholesale by large numbers of cable systems"); S.Rep. No. 102-92, p. 62 (1991) (Senate Report) ("Without congressional action, ... the role of local television broadcasting in our system of communications will steadily decline ..."); see also Brief for Federal Appellees in Turner Broadcasting System, Inc. v. FCC, No. 93-44 p. 32, n. 22 (the question is not whether "the evidence shows that broadcast television is likely to be totally eliminated" but "whether the broadcast services available to viewers [without cable] ... are likely to be reduced to a significant extent, because of either loss of some stations altogether or curtailment of services by others").

Nor do the congressional findings support appellants' suggestion that legitimate legislative goals would be satisfied by the preservation of a rump broadcasting industry providing a minimum of broadcast service to Americans without cable. We have noted that " 'it has long been a basic tenet of national communications policy that "the widest possible dissemination of information from diverse and antagonistic sources is essential to the welfare of the public." ' " Turner, 512 U.S., at 663-664, 114 S.Ct., at 2470 (quoting United States v. Midwest Video Corp., 406 U.S. 649, 668, n. 27, 92 S.Ct. 1860, 1870-1871, n. 27, 32 L.Ed.2d 390 (1972)) (plurality opinion) (quoting Associated Press v. United States, 326 U.S. 1, 20, 65 S.Ct. 1416, 1424-1425, 89 L.Ed. 2013

(1945)); see also FCC v. WNCN Listeners Guild, 450 U.S. 582, 594, 101 S.Ct. 1266, 1274, 67 L.Ed.2d 521 (1981). " '[I]ncreasing the number of outlets for community self-expression' " represents a " 'long-established regulatory goa[l] in the field of television broadcasting.' " United States v. Midwest Video Corp., supra, at 667-668, 92 S.Ct., at 1870 (plurality opinion). Consistent with this objective, the Cable Act's findings reflect a concern that congressional action was necessary to prevent "a reduction in the number of media voices available to consumers." § 2(a)(4). Congress identified a specific interest in "ensuring [the] continuation" of "the local origination of [broadcast] programming," § 2(a)(10), an interest consistent with its larger purpose of promoting multiple types of media, § 2(a)(6), and found must-carry necessary "to serve the goals" of the original Communications Act of 1934 of "providing a fair, efficient, and equitable distribution of broadcast services" (§ 2(a)(9)). In short, Congress enacted must-carry to "preserve the existing structure of the Nation's broadcast television medium while permitting the concomitant expansion and development of cable television." 512 U.S., at 652, 114 S.Ct., at 2464.

Although Congress set no definite number of broadcast stations sufficient for these purposes, the Cable Act's requirement that all cable operators with more than 12 channels set aside one-third of their channel capacity for local broadcasters, § 4, 47 U.S.C. § 534(b)(1)(B), refutes the notion that Congress contemplated preserving only a bare minimum of stations. Congress' evident interest in "preserv[ing] the existing structure," 512 U.S., at 652, 114 S.Ct., at 2464, of the broadcast industry discloses a purpose to prevent any significant reduction in the multiplicity of broadcast programming sources available to noncable households. To the extent the appellants question the substantiality of the Government's interest in preserving something more than a minimum number of stations in each community, their position is meritless. It is for Congress to decide how much local broadcast television should be preserved for noncable households, and the validity of its determination " 'does not turn on a judge's agreement with the responsible decisionmaker concerning' ... the degree to which [the Government's] interests should be promoted." Ward, 491 U.S., at 800, 109 S.Ct., at 2758 (quoting United States v. Albertini, 472 U.S. 675, 689, 105 S.Ct. 2897, 2906-2907, 86 L.Ed.2d 536 (1985)); accord, Clark v. Community for Creative Non-Violence, 468 U.S. 288, 299, 104 S.Ct. 3065, 3071-3072, 82 L.Ed.2d 221 (1984) ("We do not believe ... [that] United States v. O'Brien ... endow[s] the judiciary with the competence to judge how much protection of park lands is wise").

The dissent proceeds on the assumption that must-carry is designed solely to be (and can only be justified as) a measure to protect broadcasters from cable operators' anticompetitive behavior. See post, at 1215, 1216, 1219. Federal policy, however, has long favored preserving a multiplicity of broadcast outlets regardless of whether the conduct that threatens it is motivated by anticompetitive animus or rises to the level of an antitrust violation. See Capital Cities Cable, Inc. v. Crisp, 467 U.S., at 714, 104 S.Ct., at 2708; United States v. Midwest Video Corp., supra, at 665, 92 S.Ct., at 1869-1870 (plurality opinion) (FCC regulations "were ... avowedly designed to guard broadcast services from being undermined by unregulated [cable] growth"); National Broadcasting Co. v. United States, 319 U.S. 190, 223-224, 63 S.Ct. 997, 1012-1013, 87 L.Ed. 1344 (1943) (" 'While many of the network practices raise serious questions under the antitrust laws, ... [i]t is not [the FCC's] function to apply the antitrust laws as such' ") (quoting FCC Report on Chain Broadcasting Regulations (1941)). Broadcast television is an important source of information to many Americans. Though it is but one of many means for communication, by tradition and use for decades now it has been an essential part of the national discourse on subjects across the whole broad spectrum of speech, thought, and expression. See Turner, supra, at 663, 114 S.Ct., at 2469-2470; FCC v. National Citizens Committee for Broadcasting, 436 U.S. 775, 783, 98 S.Ct. 2096, 2106, 56 L.Ed.2d 697 (1978) (referring to studies "showing the dominant role of television stations ... as sources of local news and other information"). Congress has an independent interest in preserving a multiplicity of broadcasters to ensure that all households have access to information and entertainment on an equal footing with those who subscribe to cable.

A

On our earlier review, we were constrained by the state of the record to assessing the importance of the Government's asserted interests when "viewed in the abstract," Turner, 512 U.S., at 663, 114 S.Ct., at 2469-2470. The expanded record now permits us to consider whether the must-carry provisions were designed to address a real harm, and whether those provisions will alleviate it in a material way. Id., at 663-664, 114 S.Ct., at 2469-2470. We turn first to the harm or risk which prompted Congress to act. The Government's assertion that "the economic health of local broadcasting is in genuine jeopardy and in need of the protections afforded by must-carry," id., at 664-665, 114 S.Ct., at 2470, rests on two component propositions: First, "significant numbers of broadcast stations will be refused carriage on cable systems" absent must-carry, id., at 666, 114 S.Ct., at 2471. Second, "the broadcast stations denied carriage will either deteriorate to a substantial degree or fail altogether." Ibid.

In reviewing the constitutionality of a statute, "courts must accord substantial deference to the predictive judgments of Congress" . . . .

1

We have no difficulty in finding a substantial basis to support Congress' conclusion that a real threat justified enactment of the must-carry provisions. We examine first the evidence before Congress and then the further evidence presented to the District Court on remand to supplement the congressional determination.

As to the evidence before Congress, there was specific support for its conclusion that cable operators had considerable and growing market power over local video programming markets. Cable served at least 60 percent of American households in 1992, see Cable Act § 2(a)(3), and evidence indicated cable market penetration was projected to grow beyond 70 percent. See Cable TV Consumer Protection Act of 1991: Hearing on S. 12 before the Subcommittee on Communications of the Senate Committee on Commerce, Science, and Transportation, 102d Cong., 1st Sess., 259 (1991) (statement of Edward O. Fritts) (App.1253); see also Defendants' Joint Statement of Evidence Before Congress ¶¶ 9, 10 (JSCR) (App.1252-1253). As Congress noted (§ 2(a)(2)), cable operators possess a local monopoly over cable households. Only one percent of communities are served by more than one cable system, JSCR ¶¶ 31-40 (App.1262-1266). Even in communities with two or more cable systems, in the typical case each system has a local monopoly over its subscribers. See Comments of NAB before the FCC on MM Docket No. 85-349, ¶ 47 (April 25, 1986) (App.26). Cable operators thus exercise "control over most (if not all) of the television programming that is channeled into the subscriber's home .... [and] can thus silence the voice of competing speakers with a mere flick of the switch." Turner, 512 U.S., at 656, 114 S.Ct., at 2466.

Evidence indicated the structure of the cable industry would give cable operators increasing ability and incentive to drop local broadcast stations from their systems, or reposition them to a less-viewed channel. Horizontal concentration was increasing as a small number of multiple system operators (MSO's) acquired large numbers of cable systems nationwide. § 2(a)(4). The trend was accelerating, giving the MSO's increasing market power. In 1985, the 10 largest MSO's controlled cable systems serving slightly less than 42 percent of all cable subscribers; by 1989, the figure was nearly 54 percent. JSCR ¶ 77 (App.1282); Competitive Problems in the Cable Television Industry, Hearing before the Subcommittee on Antitrust, Monopolies and Business Rights of the Senate Committee on the Judiciary, 101st Cong., 1st Sess., 74 (1990) (Hearing on Competitive Problems in the Cable Television Industry) (statement of Gene Kimmelman and Dr. Mark N. Cooper).

Vertical integration in the industry also was increasing. As Congress was aware, many MSO's owned or had affiliation agreements with cable programmers. § 2(a)(5); Senate Report, at 24-29. Evidence indicated that before 1984 cable operators had equity interests in 38 percent of cable programming networks. In the late 1980's, 64 percent of new cable programmers were held in vertical ownership. JSCR ¶ 197 (App.1332-1333). Congress concluded that "vertical integration gives cable operators the incentive and ability to favor their affiliated programming services" (§ 2(a)(5); Senate Report, at 25) a conclusion that even Judge Williams' dissent conceded to be reasonable. See 910 F.Supp., at 775. Extensive testimony indicated that cable operators would have an incentive to drop local broadcasters and to favor affiliated programmers . . . .

In addition, evidence before Congress, supplemented on remand, indicated that cable systems would have incentives to drop local broadcasters in favor of other programmers less likely to compete with them for audience and advertisers. Independent local broadcasters tend to be the closest substitutes for cable programs, because their programming tends to be similar, see JSCR ¶¶ 269, 274, 276 (App.1367, 1368-1370), and because both primarily target the same type of advertiser: those interested in cheaper (and more frequent) ad spots than are typically available on network affiliates. Second Declaration of Tom Meek ¶ 32 (Second Meek Declaration) (App.1866); Reply Declaration of James N. Dertouzos ¶ 26 (App.2023); Carriage of Television Broadcast Signals by Cable Television Systems, Reply Comment of the Staff of the Bureau of Economics and the San Francisco Regional Office of the Federal Trade Commission, p. 19 (Nov. 26, 1991) (Reply Comment of FTC) (App.176). The ability of broadcast stations to compete for advertising is greatly increased by cable carriage, which increases viewership substantially.

See Second Meek Declaration ¶ 34 (App.1866-1867). With expanded viewership, broadcast presents a more competitive medium for television advertising. Empirical studies indicate that cable-carried broadcasters so enhance competition for advertising that even modest increases in the numbers of broadcast stations carried on cable are correlated with significant decreases in advertising revenue to cable systems. Dertouzos Declaration ¶¶ 20, 25-28 (App.966, 969-971); see also Reply Comment of FTC, at 18 (App.175). Empirical evidence also indicates that demand for premium cable services (such as pay-per-view) is reduced when a cable system carries more independent broadcasters. Hearing on Competitive Problems in the Cable Television Industry, at 323 (statement of Michael O. Wirth). Thus, operators stand to benefit by dropping broadcast stations. Dertouzos Declaration ¶ 6b (App.959).

Cable systems also have more systemic reasons for seeking to disadvantage broadcast stations: Simply stated, cable has little interest in assisting, through carriage, a competing medium of communication. As one cable-industry executive put it, " 'our job is to promote cable television, not broadcast television.' " Hearing on Competitive Issues, at 658 (quoting Multichannel News, Channel Realignments: United Cable Eyes Plan to Bump Network Affils to Upper Channels, Nov. 3, 1986, p. 39); see also id., at 661 (" 'Shouldn't we give more ... shelf space to cable? Why have people trained to view UHF?' ") (vice president of operations at Comcast, an MSO, quoted in Multichannel News, Cable Operators begin to Shuffle Channel Lineups, Sept. 8, 1986, p. 38)). The incentive to subscribe to cable is lower in markets with many over-the-air viewing options. See JSCR ¶ 275 (App.1369); Dertouzos Declaration ¶¶ 27, 32 (App.970, 972). Evidence adduced on remand indicated cable systems have little incentive to carry, and a significant incentive to drop, broadcast stations that will only be strengthened by access to the 60% of the television market that cable typically controls. Dertouzos Declaration ¶¶ 29, 35 (App.971, 973); Noll Declaration ¶ 43 (App.1029). Congress could therefore reasonably conclude that cable systems would drop broadcasters in favor of programmers--even unaffiliated ones--less likely to compete with them for audience and advertisers. The cap on carriage of affiliates included in the Cable Act, 47 U.S.C. § 533(f)(1)(B); 47 CFR § 76.504) (1995), and relied on by the dissent, post, at 1210, 1216, is of limited utility in protecting broadcasters.

The dissent contends Congress could not reasonably conclude cable systems would engage in such predation because cable operators, whose primary source of revenue is subscriptions, would not risk dropping a widely viewed broadcast station in order to capture advertising revenues. Post, at 1210. However, if viewers are faced with the choice of sacrificing a handful of broadcast stations to gain access to dozens of cable channels (plus network affiliates), it is likely they would still subscribe to cable even if they would prefer the dropped television stations to the cable programming that replaced them. Substantial evidence introduced on remand bears this out: With the exception of a handful of very popular broadcast stations (typically network affiliates), a cable system's choice between carrying a cable programmer or broadcast station has little or no effect on cable subscriptions, and subscribership thus typically does not bear on carriage decisions. Noll Declaration ¶ 29 (App.1018-1019); Rebuttal Declaration of Roger G. Noll ¶ 20 (App.1798); Reply Declaration of Roger G. Noll ¶¶ 3-4, and n. 3 (App.2003-2004); see also Declaration of John R. Haring ¶ 37 (Haring Declaration) (App.1106).

It was more than a theoretical possibility in 1992 that cable operators would take actions adverse to local broadcasters; indeed, significant numbers of broadcasters had already been dropped. The record before Congress contained extensive anecdotal evidence about scores of adverse carriage decisions against broadcast stations . . . .

This is not a case in which we are called upon to give our best judgment as to the likely economic consequences of certain financial arrangements or business structures, or to assess competing economic theories and predictive judgments, as we would in a case arising, say, under the antitrust laws. "Statutes frequently require courts to make policy judgments. The Sherman Act, for example, requires courts to delve deeply into the theory of economic organization." See Holder v. Hall, 512 U.S. 874, 966, 114 S.Ct. 2581, 2629-2630, 129 L.Ed.2d 687 (1994) (separate opinion of STEVENS, J.). The issue before us is whether, given conflicting views of the probable development of the television industry, Congress had substantial evidence for making the judgment that it did. We need not put our imprimatur on Congress' economic theory in order to validate the reasonableness of its judgment.

2

The harm Congress feared was that stations dropped or denied carriage would be at a "serious risk of financial difficulty," 512 U.S., at 667, 114 S.Ct., at 2472, and would "deteriorate to a substantial degree or fail altogether." Id., at 666, 114 S.Ct., at 2471. Congress had before it substantial evidence to support its conclusion. Congress was advised the viability of a broadcast station depends to a material extent on its ability to secure cable carriage . . . .

To be sure, the record also contains evidence to support a contrary conclusion. Appellants (and the dissent in the District Court) make much of the fact that the number of broadcast stations and their advertising revenue continued to grow during the period without must-carry, albeit at a diminished rate. Evidence introduced on remand indicated that only 31 broadcast stations actually went dark during the period without must-carry (one of which failed after a tornado destroyed its transmitter), and during the same period some 263 new stations signed on the air. Meek Declaration ¶¶ 76-77 (App.627-628). New evidence appellants produced on remand indicates the average cable system voluntarily carried local broadcast stations accounting for about 97 percent of television ratings in noncable households. Declaration of Stanley Besen, Part III-D (App.808). Appellants, as well as the dissent in the District Court, contend that in light of such evidence, it is clear "the must-carry law is not necessary to assure the economic viability of the broadcast system as a whole." NCTA Brief 18.

This assertion misapprehends the relevant inquiry. The question is not whether Congress, as an objective matter, was correct to determine must-carry is necessary to prevent a substantial number of broadcast stations from losing cable carriage and suffering significant financial hardship. Rather, the question is whether the legislative conclusion was reasonable and supported by substantial evidence in the record before Congress. Turner, 512 U.S., at 665-666,

114 S.Ct., at 2470-2471. In making that determination, we are not to "re-weigh the evidence de novo, or to replace Congress' factual predictions with our own." Id., at 666, 114 S.Ct., at 2471. Rather, we are simply to determine if the standard is satisfied. If it is, summary judgment for defendants-appellees is appropriate regardless of whether the evidence is in conflict. We have noted in another context, involving less deferential review than is at issue here, that " 'the possibility of drawing two inconsistent conclusions from the evidence does not prevent ... [a] finding from being supported by substantial evidence.' " American Textile Mfrs. Institute, Inc. v. Donovan, 452 U.S. 490, 523, 101 S.Ct. 2478, 2497, 69 L.Ed.2d 185 (1981) (citation omitted) (quoting Consolo v. Federal Maritime Comm'n, 383 U.S. 607, 620, 86 S.Ct. 1018, 1026, 16 L.Ed.2d 131 (1966)).

Although evidence of continuing growth in broadcast could have supported the opposite conclusion, a reasonable interpretation is that expansion in the cable industry was causing harm to broadcasting. . . . .

We think it apparent must-carry serves the Government's interests "in a direct and effective way." Ward, 491 U.S., at 800, 109 S.Ct., at 2759. Must-carry ensures that a number of local broadcasters retain cable carriage, with the concomitant audience access and advertising revenues needed to support a multiplicity of stations. Appellants contend that even were this so, must-carry is broader than necessary to accomplish its goals. We turn to this question.

B

The second portion of the O'Brien inquiry concerns the fit between the asserted interests and the means chosen to advance them. Content-neutral regulations do not pose the same "inherent dangers to free expression," Turner, supra, at 661, 114 S.Ct., at 2469, that content-based regulations do, and thus are subject to a less rigorous analysis, which affords the Government latitude in designing a regulatory solution. See, e.g., Ward, 491 U.S., at 798-799, n. 6, 109 S.Ct., at 2758, n. 6. Under intermediate scrutiny, the Government may employ the means of its choosing " 'so long as the ... regulation promotes a substantial governmental interest that would be achieved less effectively absent the regulation,' " and does not " 'burden substantially more speech than is necessary to further' " that interest. Turner, supra, at 662, 114 S.Ct., at 2469 (quoting Ward, supra, at 799, 109 S.Ct., at 2758).

The must-carry provisions have the potential to interfere with protected speech in two ways. First, the provisions restrain cable operators' editorial discretion in creating programming packages by "reduc[ing] the number of channels over which [they] exercise unfettered control." Turner, 512 U.S., at 637, 114 S.Ct., at 2456. Second, the rules "render it more difficult for cable programmers to compete for carriage on the limited channels remaining." Ibid.

Appellants say the burden of must-carry is great, but the evidence adduced on remand indicates the actual effects are modest. Significant evidence indicates the vast majority of cable operators have not been affected in a significant manner by must-carry. Cable operators have been able to satisfy their must- carry obligations 87 percent of the time using previously unused channel capacity (Declaration of Harry Shooshan III, ¶ 14 (App.692)); 94.5 percent of the 11,628 cable systems nationwide have not had to drop any programming in order to fulfill their must-carry obligations; the remaining 5.5 percent have had to drop an average of only 1.22 services from their programming, id., ¶ 15 (App.692); and cable operators nationwide carry 99.8 percent of the programming they carried before enactment of must-carry. Id., ¶ 21 (App.694-695). Appellees note that only 1.18 percent of the approximately 500,000 cable channels nationwide is devoted to channels added because of must- carry, see id., ¶ 11(b) (App.688-689); weighted for subscribership, the figure is 2.4 percent. 910 F.Supp., at 780 (Williams, J., dissenting). Appellees contend the burdens of must-carry will soon diminish as cable channel capacity increases, as is occurring nationwide. NAB Brief 45; see also 910 F.Supp., at 746-747.

We do not understand appellants to dispute in any fundamental way the accuracy of those figures, only their significance. See NCTA Brief 46; id., at 44-49; Time Warner Brief 38-45; Turner Brief 33-42. They note national averages fail to account for greater crowding on certain (especially urban) cable systems, see Time Warner Brief 41, 43; Turner Brief 41, and contend that half of all cable systems, serving two-thirds of all cable subscribers, have no available capacity, NCTA Brief 45; Turner Brief 34; Time Warner Brief 42, n. 58. Appellants argue that the rate of growth in cable programming outstrips cable operators' creation of new channel space, that the rate of cable growth is lower than claimed, Turner Brief 39, and that must- carry infringes First Amendment rights now irrespective of future growth. Turner Brief 40; Reply Brief for Appellants Turner Broadcasting System, Inc., et al. 12-13. Finally, they say that regardless of the percentage of channels occupied, must-carry still represents "thousands of real and individual infringements of speech." Time Warner Brief 44.

While the parties' evidence is susceptible of varying interpretations, a few definite conclusions can be drawn about the burdens of must-carry. It is undisputed that broadcast stations gained carriage on 5,880 channels as a result of must-carry. While broadcast stations occupy another 30,006 cable channels nationwide, this carriage does not represent a significant First Amendment harm to either system operators or cable programmers because those stations were carried voluntarily before 1992, and even appellants represent, Tr. of Oral Arg. 6, that the vast majority of those channels would continue to be carried in the absence of any legal obligation to do so. See Turner, supra, at 673, n. 6, 114 S.Ct., at 2475, n. 6 (STEVENS, J., concurring in part and concurring in judgment). The 5,880 channels occupied by added broadcasters represent the actual burden of the regulatory scheme. Appellants concede most of those stations would be dropped in the absence of must-carry, Tr. of Oral Arg. 6, so the figure approximates the benefits of must-carry as well.

Because the burden imposed by must-carry is congruent to the benefits it affords, we conclude must-carry is narrowly tailored to preserve a multiplicity of broadcast stations for the 40 percent of American households without cable . . . .

Appellants say the must-carry provisions are overbroad because they require carriage in some instances when the Government's interests are not implicated: the must-carry rules prohibit a cable system operator from dropping a broadcaster "even if the operator has no anticompetitive motives, and even if the broadcaster that would have to be dropped ... would survive without cable access." 512 U.S., at 683, 114 S.Ct., at 2480 (O'CONNOR, J., dissenting). See also NCTA Brief 25-26. We are not persuaded that either possibility is so prevalent that must-carry is substantially overbroad. As discussed supra, at 1192, cable systems serving 70 percent of subscribers are vertically integrated with cable programmers, so anti competitive motives may be implicated in a majority of systems' decisions not to carry broadcasters. Some broadcasters will opt for must-carry although they would not suffer serious financial harm in its absence . . . .

Appellants posit a number of alternatives in an effort to demonstrate a less-restrictive means to achieve the Government's aims. They ask us, in effect, to "sif[t] through all the available or imagined alternative means of regulating [cable television] in order to determine whether the [Government's] solution was 'the least intrusive means' of achieving the desired end," an approach we rejected in Ward v. Rock Against Racism, 491 U.S., at 797, 109 S.Ct., at 2757. This " 'less-restrictive-alternative analysis ... has never been a part of the inquiry into the validity' " of content-neutral regulations on speech. Ibid. (quoting Regan v. Time, Inc., 468 U.S. 641, 657, 104 S.Ct. 3262, 3271, 82 L.Ed.2d 487 (1984) (plurality opinion) (ellipses in original)). Our precedents establish that when evaluating a content-neutral regulation which incidentally burdens speech, we will not invalidate the preferred remedial scheme because some alternative solution is marginally less intrusive on a speaker's First Amendment interests. "So long as the means chosen are not substantially broader than necessary to achieve the government's interest, ... the regulation will not be invalid simply because a court concludes that the government's interest could be adequately served by some less-speech-restrictive alternative." Ward, supra, at 800, 109 S.Ct., at 2758 . . . .

III

Judgments about how competing economic interests are to be reconciled in the complex and fast-changing field of television are for Congress to make. Those judgments "cannot be ignored or undervalued simply because [appellants] cas[t] [their] claims under the umbrella of the First Amendment." Columbia Broadcasting v. Democratic National Committee, 412 U.S., at 103, 93 S.Ct., at 2087. Appellants' challenges to must-carry reflect little more than disagreement over the level of protection broadcast stations are to be afforded and how protection is to be attained. We cannot displace Congress' judgment respecting content-neutral regulations with our own, so long as its policy is grounded on reasonable factual findings supported by evidence that is substantial for a legislative determination. Those requirements were met in this case, and in these circumstances the First Amendment requires nothing more. The judgment of the District Court is affirmed.

It is so ordered.

Justice BREYER, concurring in part.

I join the opinion of the Court except insofar as Part II-A-1 relies on an anticompetitive rationale. I agree with the majority that the statute must be "sustained under the First Amendment if it advances important governmental interests unrelated to the suppression of free speech and does not burden substantially more speech than necessary to further those interests." Ante, at 1186 (citing United States v. O'Brien, 391 U.S. 367, 377, 88 S.Ct. 1673, 1679, 20 L.Ed.2d 672 (1968)). I also agree that the statute satisfies this standard. My conclusion rests, however, not upon the principal opinion's analysis of the statute's efforts to "promot[e] fair competition," see post, at 1206-1207, 1209-1210, but rather upon its discussion of the statute's other objectives, namely " '(1) preserving the benefits of free, over-the-air local broadcast television,' " and " '(2) promoting the widespread dissemination of information from a multiplicity of sources.' " Ante, at 1186 (quoting Turner Broadcasting System, Inc. v. FCC, 512 U.S. 622, 662, 114 S.Ct. 2445, 2446, 129 L.Ed.2d 497 (1994) (Turner) ). Whether or not the statute does or does not sensibly compensate for some significant market defect, it undoubtedly seeks to provide over-the-air viewers who lack cable with a rich mix of over-the-air programming by guaranteeing the over-the- air stations that provide such programming with the extra dollars that an additional cable audience will generate. I believe that this purpose--to assure the over-the-air public "access to a multiplicity of information sources," id., at 663, 114 S.Ct., at 2469--provides sufficient basis for rejecting appellants' First Amendment claim.

I do not deny that the compulsory carriage that creates the "guarantee" extracts a serious First Amendment price. It interferes with the protected interests of the cable operators to choose their own programming; it prevents displaced cable program providers from obtaining an audience; and it will sometimes prevent some cable viewers from watching what, in its absence, would have been their preferred set of programs. Ante, at 1197-1198; post, at 1215. This "price" amounts to a "suppression of speech."

But there are important First Amendment interests on the other side as well. The statute's basic noneconomic purpose is to prevent too precipitous a decline in the quality and quantity of programming choice for an ever-shrinking non- cable-subscribing segment of the public. Ante, at 1186, 1187-1189. This purpose reflects what "has long been a basic tenet of national communications policy," namely that "the widest possible dissemination of information from diverse and antagonistic sources is essential to the welfare of the public." Turner, supra, at 663, 114 S.Ct., at 2470 (quoting United States v. Midwest Video Corp., 406 U.S. 649, 668, n. 27, 92 S.Ct. 1860, 1870-1871, n. 27, 32 L.Ed.2d 390 (1972)) (plurality opinion) (quoting Associated Press v. United States, 326 U.S. 1, 20, 65 S.Ct. 1416, 1424-1425, 89 L.Ed. 2013 (1945) (internal quotation marks omitted)); see also FCC v. WNCN Listeners Guild, 450 U.S. 582, 594, 101 S.Ct. 1266, 1274, 67 L.Ed.2d 521 (1981). That policy, in turn, seeks to facilitate the public discussion and informed deliberation, which, as Justice Brandeis pointed out many years ago, democratic government presupposes and the First Amendment seeks to achieve. Whitney v. California, 274 U.S. 357, 375-376, 47 S.Ct. 641, 648, 71 L.Ed. 1095 (1927) (Brandeis, J., concurring). See also New York Times Co. v. Sullivan, 376 U.S. 254, 270, 84 S.Ct. 710, 720-721,

11 L.Ed.2d 686 (1964); Red Lion Broadcasting Co. v. FCC, 395 U.S. 367, 390, 89 S.Ct. 1794, 1806, 23 L.Ed.2d 371 (1969); Associated Press v. United States, supra, at 20, 65 S.Ct., at 1424-1425. Indeed, Turner rested in part upon the proposition that "assuring that the public has access to a multiplicity of information sources is a governmental purpose of the highest order, for it promotes values central to the First Amendment." 512 U.S., at 663, 114 S.Ct., at 2470.

With important First Amendment interests on both sides of the equation, the key question becomes one of proper fit. That question, in my view, requires a reviewing court to determine both whether there are significantly less restrictive ways to achieve Congress' over-the-air programming objectives, and also to decide whether the statute, in its effort to achieve those objectives, strikes a reasonable balance between potentially speech-restricting and speech-enhancing consequences. Ward v. Rock Against Racism, 491 U.S. 781, 799-800, 109 S.Ct. 2746, 2758-2759, 105 L.Ed.2d 661 (1989); ante, at 1200. The majority's opinion analyzes and evaluates those consequences, and I agree with its conclusions in respect to both of these matters.

In particular, I note (and agree) that a cable system, physically dependent upon the availability of space along city streets, at present (perhaps less in the future) typically faces little competition, that it therefore constitutes a kind of bottleneck that controls the range of viewer choice (whether or not it uses any consequent economic power for economically predatory purposes), and that some degree--at least a limited degree--of governmental intervention and control through regulation can prove appropriate when justified under O'Brien (at least when not "content based"). Ante, at 1190, 1193-1194, 1195-1198; see also Defendants' Joint Statement of Evidence before Congress ¶¶ 12-21, 31-59 (App.1254-1258, 1262- 1274) (JSCR); Cable Act, § 2(a)(2), P.L. 102-385, 106 Stat. 1460. Cf. Red Lion, supra, at 377-378, 387-401, 89 S.Ct., at 1799-1800, 1805-1812; 47 C.F.R. §§ 73.123, 73.300, 73.598, 73.679 (1969) (FCC regulations upheld in Red Lion ); United Broadcasting Co., 10 F.C.C. 515 (1945); New Broadcasting Co., 6 P & F Radio Reg. 258 (1950). I also agree that, without the statute, cable systems would likely carry significantly fewer over-the-air stations, ante, at 1187, 1192-1193, that station revenues would therefore decline, ante, at 1195-1198, and that the quality of over-the-air programming on such stations would almost inevitably suffer, e.g., JSCR ¶¶ 596, 704-706 (App.1544, 1600-1601); Rebuttal Declaration of Roger G. Noll ¶¶ 5, 11, 34, 38 (App.1790, 1793, 1804-1805, 1806). I agree further that the burden the statute imposes upon the cable system, potential cable programmers, and cable viewers, is limited and will diminish as typical cable system capacity grows over time.

Finally, I believe that Congress could reasonably conclude that the statute will help the typical over-the-air viewer (by maintaining an expanded range of choice) more than it will hurt the typical cable subscriber (by restricting cable slots otherwise available for preferred programming). The latter's cable choices are many and varied, and the range of choice is rapidly increasing. The former's over-the-air choice is more restricted; and, as cable becomes more popular, it may well become still more restricted insofar as the over-the- air market shrinks and thereby, by itself, becomes less profitable. In these circumstances, I do not believe the First Amendment dictates a result that favors the cable viewers' interests.

These and other similar factors discussed by the majority, lead me to agree that the statute survives "intermediate scrutiny," whether or not the statute is properly tailored to Congress' purely economic objectives.

Justice O'CONNOR, with whom Justice SCALIA, Justice THOMAS, and Justice GINSBURG join, dissenting.

In sustaining the must-carry provisions of the Cable Television Protection and Competition Act of 1992, Pub.L. 102-385, §§ 4-5, 106 Stat. 1460 (Cable Act), against a First Amendment challenge by cable system operators and cable programmers, the Court errs in two crucial respects. First, the Court disregards one of the principal defenses of the statute urged by appellees on remand: that it serves a substantial interest in preserving "diverse," "quality" programming that is "responsive" to the needs of the local community. The course of this litigation on remand and the proffered defense strongly reinforce my view that the Court adopted the wrong analytic framework in the prior phase of this case. See Turner Broadcasting System, Inc. v. FCC, 512 U.S. 622, 643-651, 114 S.Ct. 2445, 2460-2464, 129 L.Ed.2d 497 (1994) (Turner); id., at 675-680, 114 S.Ct., at 2475-2478 (O'CONNOR, J., concurring in part and dissenting in part). Second, the Court misapplies the "intermediate scrutiny" framework it adopts. Although we owe deference to Congress' predictive judgments and its evaluation of complex economic questions, we have an independent duty to identify with care the Government interests supporting the scheme, to inquire into the reasonableness of congressional findings regarding its necessity, and to examine the fit between its goals and its consequences. Edenfield v. Fane, 507 U.S. 761, 770-771, 113 S.Ct. 1792, 1799-1801, 123 L.Ed.2d 543 (1993); Sable Communications of Cal., Inc. v. FCC, 492 U.S. 115, 129, 109 S.Ct. 2829, 2838, 106 L.Ed.2d 93 (1989); Los Angeles v. Preferred Communications, Inc., 476 U.S. 488, 496, 106 S.Ct. 2034, 2038, 90 L.Ed.2d 480 (1986); Landmark Communications, Inc. v. Virginia, 435 U.S. 829, 843, 98 S.Ct. 1535, 1543, 56 L.Ed.2d 1 (1978). The Court fails to discharge its duty here ....

II

The principal opinion goes to great lengths to avoid acknowledging that preferences for "quality," "diverse," and "responsive" local programming underlie the must-carry scheme, although the partial concurrence's reliance on such preferences is explicit. See ante, at 1204 (BREYER, J., concurring in part). I take the principal opinion at its word and evaluate the claim that the threat of anticompetitive behavior by cable operators supplies a content- neutral basis for sustaining the statute. It does not.

The Turner Court remanded the case for a determination whether the must- carry provisions satisfy intermediate scrutiny under United States v. O'Brien, 391 U.S. 367, 88 S.Ct. 1673, 20 L.Ed.2d 672 (1968). Under that standard, appellees must demonstrate that the must-carry provisions (1) "furthe [r] an important or substantial government interest"; and (2) burden speech no more "than is essential to the furtherance of that interest." Id., at 377, 88 S.Ct., at

1679; see also Ward v. Rock Against Racism, 491 U.S. 781, 799, 109 S.Ct. 2746, 2758, 105 L.Ed.2d 661 (1989). The Turner plurality found that genuine issues of material fact remained as to both parts of the O'Brien analysis. On whether must-carry furthers a substantial governmental interest, the Turner Court remanded the case to test two essential and unproven propositions: "(1) that unless cable operators are compelled to carry broadcast stations, significant numbers of broadcast stations will be refused carriage on cable systems; and (2) that the broadcast stations denied carriage will either deteriorate to a substantial degree or fail altogether." 512 U.S., at 666, 114 S.Ct., at 2471 (emphasis added). As for whether must-carry restricts no more speech than essential to further Congress' asserted purpose, the Turner plurality found evidence lacking on the extent of the burden that the must-carry provisions would place on cable operators and cable programmers. Id., at 667-668, 114 S.Ct., at 2471-2472 . . . .

A

2

Under the standard articulated by the Turner plurality, the conclusion that must-carry serves a substantial governmental interest depends upon the "essential propositio[n]" that, without must-carry, "significant numbers of broadcast stations will be refused carriage on cable systems." 512 U.S., at 666, 114 S.Ct., at 2471. In analyzing whether this undefined standard is satisfied, the Court focuses almost exclusively on raw numbers of stations denied carriage or "repositioned"--that is, shifted out of their traditional channel positions . . . .

In any event, the larger problem with the Court's approach is that neither the FCC study nor the additional evidence on remand canvassed by the Court, ante, at 1193-1195, says anything about the broadcast markets in which adverse carriage decisions take place. The Court accepts Congress' stated concern about preserving the availability of a "multiplicity" of broadcast stations, but apparently thinks it sufficient to evaluate that concern in the abstract, without considering how much local service is already available in a given broadcast market. Ante, at 1197; see also ante, at 1203-1204 (BREYER, J., concurring in part). I address this gap in the Court's discussion at greater length below, infra, at 1213-1215, by examiningthe reasonableness of Congress' prediction that adverse carriage decisions will inflict severe harm on broadcast stations.

Nor can we evaluate whether must-carry is necessary to serve an interest in preserving broadcast stations without examiningthe value of the stations protected by the must-carry scheme to viewers in noncable households. By disregarding the distribution and viewership of stations not carried on cable, the Court upholds the must-carry provisions without addressing the interests of the over-the-air television viewers that Congress purportedly seeks to protect. See Turner, 512 U.S., at 647, 114 S.Ct., at 2461 (describing interest in "protecting noncable households from loss of regular television broadcasting service" (emphasis added; internal quotation marks omitted)); id., at 652, 114 S.Ct., at 2464 (describing interest in ensuring that broadcast television remains available as a source of video programming for those without cable (emphasis added)); ante, at 1188 (describing interest in preventing "any significant reduction in the multiplicity of broadcast programming sources available to noncable households" (emphasis added)). The Court relies on analyses suggesting that, as of 1992, the typical independent commercial broadcaster was being denied carriage on cable systems serving 47 percent of subscribers in its local market, and the typical noncommercial station was denied carriage on cable systems serving 36 percent of subscribers in its local market. Ante, at 1193. The only analysis in the record of the relationship between carriage and noncable viewership favors the appellants. A 1991 study by Federal Trade Commission staff concluded that most cable systems voluntarily carried broadcast stations with any reportable ratings in noncable households and that most instances of noncarriage involved "relatively remote (and duplicated) network stations, or local stations that few viewers watch." Carriage of Television Broadcast Signals by Cable Television Systems, Reply Comment of the Staff of the Bureau of Economics and the San Francisco Regional Office of the Federal Trade Commission, p. 3 (Nov. 26, 1991) (App.163); see also Declaration of Stanley M. Besen (Besen Declaration) (App.808, 818); Second Declaration of Stanley M. Besen (App.1812) (presenting data that (1) the typical cable subscriber was served by a cable system carrying local broadcast stations accounting for 97 percent of viewing in noncable households; and (2) the typical cable subscriber was served by a cable system carrying 90 percent of all local broadcast stations with any reportable ratings and 30 percent of all local broadcast stations with no reportable ratings).

Appellees claim there are various methodological flaws in each study, including appellants' expert's reliance on Nielsen data to measure viewership shares. A protective order entered by the District Court in this case prevents the parties from contesting the accuracy of such data. App. 321. But appellees--who bear the burden of proof in this case--offer no alternative measure of the viewership in noncable households of stations dropped or denied carriage. Instead, appellees and their experts repeatedly emphasize the importance of preserving "vulnerable" or "marginal" independent stations serving "relatively small" audiences . . . .

3

I turn now to the evidence of harm to broadcasters denied carriage or repositioned. The Court remanded for a determination whether broadcast stations denied carriage would be at " 'serious risk of financial difficulty' " and would " 'deteriorate to a substantial degree or fail altogether.' " Ante, at 1195 (quoting Turner, supra, at 667, 666, 114 S.Ct., at 2472, 2471). The Turner plurality noted that there was no evidence that "local broadcast stations have fallen into bankruptcy, turned in their broadcast licenses, curtailed their broadcast operations, or suffered a serious reduction in operating revenues" because of adverse carriage decisions. 512 U.S., at 667, 114 S.Ct., at 2472. The record on remand does not permit the conclusion, at the summary judgment stage, that Congress could reasonably have predicted serious harm to a significant number of stations in the absence of must-carry.

The purported link between an adverse carriage decision and severe harm to a station depends on yet another untested premise. Even accepting the conclusion that a cable system operator has a monopoly over cable services to the home, supra, at 1209, it does not necessarily follow that the operator also has a monopoly over all video services to cabled households. Cable subscribers using an input selector switch and an antenna can receive broadcast signals. Widespread use of such switches would completely eliminate any cable system "monopoly" over sources of video input. See 910 F.Supp., at 786 (Williams, J., dissenting). Growing use of direct-broadcast satellite television also tends to undercut the notion that cable operators have an inevitable monopoly over video services entering cable households. See, e.g., Farhi, Dishing Out the Competition to Cable TV, Washington Post, Oct. 12, 1996, p. H1, col. 3.

In the Cable Act, Congress rejected the wisdom of any "substantial societal investment" in developing input selector switch technology. § 2(a)(18). In defending this choice, the Court purports to identify "substantial evidence of technological shortcomings" that prevent widespread, efficient use of such devices. But nearly all of the "data" in question are drawn from sources predating the enactment of must-carry by roughly six years . . . . The Court notes the importance of deferring to congressional judgments about the "interaction of industries undergoing rapid economic and technological change." Ante, at 1189. But this principle does not require wholesale deference to judgments about rapidly changing technologies that are based on unquestionably outdated information.

The Court concludes that the evidence on remand meets the threshold of harm established in Turner. The Court begins with the "[c]onsiderable evidence" that broadcast stations denied carriage have fallen into bankruptcy. Ante, at 1195. The analysis, however, does not focus on features of the market in which these stations were located or on the size of the audience they commanded. The "considerable evidence" relied on by the Court consists of repeated references to the bankruptcies of the same 23 commercial independent stations--apparently, new stations. See JSCR ¶¶ 659, 671-672, 676, 681 (App.1576, 1581-1582, 1584, 1587); Hearing on Competitive Issues, at 548 (statement of Milton Maltz) (CR Vol. I.C, Exh. 8, p. CR 01887). Because the must-carry provisions have never been justified as a means of enhancing broadcast television, I do not understand the relevance of this evidence, or of the evidence concerning the difficulties encountered by new stations seeking financing. See ante, at 1195-1196 (citing JSCR ¶¶ 643-658 (App.1564-1576)).

The Court also claims that the record on remand reflects "considerable evidence" of stations curtailing their broadcast operations or suffering reductions in operating revenues. Most of the anecdotal accounts of harm on which the Court relies are sharply disputed . . . .

The principal opinion disavows a need to closely scrutinize the logic of the regulatory scheme at issue on the ground that it "need not put [its] imprimatur on Congress' economic theory in order to validate the reasonableness of its judgment." Ante, at 1195. That approach trivializes the First Amendment issue at stake in this case. A highly dubious economic theory has been advanced as the "substantial interest" supporting a First Amendment burden on cable operators and cable programmers. In finding that must-carry serves a substantial interest, the principal opinion necessarily accepts that theory. The partial concurrence does not, but neither does it articulate what threat to the availability of a "multiplicity" of broadcast stations would exist in a perfectly competitive market.

B

I turn now to the second portion of the O'Brien inquiry, which concerns the fit between the Government's asserted interests and the means chosen to advance them. The Court observes that "broadcast stations gained carriage on 5,880 channels as a result of must-carry," and recognizes that this forced carriage imposes a burden on cable system operators and cable programmers. Ante, at 1198. But the Court also concludes that the other 30,006 cable channels occupied by broadcast stations are irrelevant to measuring the burden of the must-carry scheme. The must-carry rules prevent operators from dropping these broadcast stations should other more desirable cable programming become available, even though operators have carried these stations voluntarily in the past. The must-carry requirements thus burden an operator's First Amendment freedom to exercise unfettered control over a number of channels in its system, whether or not the operator's present choice is aligned with that of the Government.

Even assuming that the Court is correct that the 5,880 channels occupied by added broadcasters "represent the actual burden of the regulatory scheme," ante, at 1199, the Court's leap to the conclusion that must-carry "is narrowly tailored to preserve a multiplicity of broadcast stations," ante, at 1198-1199, is nothing short of astounding. The Court's logic is circular. Surmising that most of the 5,880 channels added by the regulatory scheme would be dropped in its absence, the Court concludes that the figure also approximates the "benefit" of must-carry. Finding the scheme's burden "congruent" to the benefit it affords, the Court declares the statute narrowly tailored. The Court achieves this result, however, only by equating the effect of the statute--requiring cable operators to add 5,880 stations--with the governmental interest sought to be served. The Court's citation of Ward v. Rock Against Racism, 491 U.S. 781, 109 S.Ct. 2746, 105 L.Ed.2d 661 (1989), reveals the true nature of the interest at stake. The "evi[l] the Government seeks to eliminate," id., at 799, n. 7, 109 S.Ct., at 2758, n. 7, is not the failure of cable operators to carry these 5,880 stations. Rather, to read the first half of the principal opinion, the "evil" is anticompetitive behavior by cable operators. As a factual matter, we do not know whether these stations were not carried because of anticompetitive impulses. Positing the effect of a statute as the governmental interest "can sidestep judicial review of almost any statute, because it makes all statutes look narrowly tailored." Simon & Schuster, Inc. v. Members of N.Y. State Crime Victims Bd., 502 U.S. 105, 120, 112 S.Ct. 501, 510, 116 L.Ed.2d 476 (1991). Without a sense whether most adverse carriage decisions are anticompetitively motivated, it is improper to conclude that the statute is narrowly tailored simply because it prevents some adverse carriage decisions. See Board of Trustees of State Univ. of N.Y. v. Fox, 492 U.S. 469, 480, 109 S.Ct. 3028, 3035, 106 L.Ed.2d 388 (1989) (scope of law must be "in proportion to the interest served") (internal quotation marks omitted).

In my view, the statute is not narrowly tailored to serve a substantial interest in preventing anticompetitive conduct . . . .

Finally, I note my disagreement with the Court's suggestion that the availability of less-speech-restrictive alternatives is never relevant to O'Brien's narrow tailoring inquiry. Ante, at 1199-1200. The Turner Court remanded this case in part because a plurality concluded that "judicial findings concerning the availability and efficacy of constitutionally acceptable less restrictive means of achieving the Government's asserted interests" were lacking in the original record. 512 U.S., at 668, 114 S.Ct., at 2472 (internal quotation marks omitted). The Court's present position on this issue is puzzling.

Our cases suggest only that we have not interpreted the narrow tailoring inquiry to "require elimination of all less restrictive alternatives." Fox, supra, at 478, 109 S.Ct., at 3033. Put another way, we have refrained from imposing a least-restrictive-means requirement in cases involving intermediate First Amendment scrutiny. Ward, 491 U.S., at 798, 109 S.Ct., at 2757 (time, place, and manner restriction); Clark v. Community for Creative Non- Violence, 468 U.S. 288, 293, 104 S.Ct. 3065, 3068-3069, 82 L.Ed.2d 221 (1984) (same); Fox, supra, at 478, 109 S.Ct., at 3033 (commercial speech). It is one thing to say that a regulation need not be the least-speech- restrictive means of serving an important governmental objective. It is quite another to suggest, as I read the majority to do here, that the availability of less-speech-restrictive alternatives cannot establish or confirm that a regulation is substantially broader than necessary to achieve the Government's goals. While the validity of a Government regulation subject to intermediate First Amendment scrutiny does not turn on our "agreement with the responsible decisionmaker concerning the most appropriate method for promoting significant government interests," United States v. Albertini, 472 U.S. 675, 689, 105 S.Ct. 2897, 2907, 86 L.Ed.2d 536 (1985), the availability of less intrusive approaches to a problem serves as a benchmark for assessing the reasonableness of the fit between Congress' articulated goals and the means chosen to pursue them. Rubin v. Coors Brewing Co., 514 U.S. 476, 490-491, 115 S.Ct. 1585, ---- - ----, 131 L.Ed.2d 532 (1995).

As shown above, supra, at 1215-1216, in this case it is plain without reference to any alternatives that the must-carry scheme is "substantially broader than necessary," Ward, supra, at 800, 109 S.Ct., at 2758, to serve the only governmental interest that the principal opinion fully explains-- preventing unfair competition. If Congress truly sought to address anticompetitive behavior by cable system operators, it passed the wrong law. See Turner, supra, at 682, 114 S.Ct., at 2479 (O'CONNOR, J., concurring in part and dissenting in part) ("That some speech within a broad category causes harm ... does not justify restricting the whole category"). Nevertheless, the availability of less restrictive alternatives--a leased-access regime and subsidies--reinforces my conclusion that the must-carry provisions are overbroad.

Consider first appellants' proposed leased-access scheme, under which a cable system operator would be required to make a specified proportion of the system's channels available to broadcasters and independent cable programmers alike at regulated rates. Leased access would directly address both vertical integration and predatory behavior, by placing broadcasters and cable programmers on a level playing field for access to cable. The principal opinion never explicitly identifies any threat to the availability of broadcast television to noncable households other than anticompetitive conduct, nor does Justice BREYER's partial concurrence. Accordingly, to the extent that leased access would address problems of anticompetitive behavior, I fail to understand why it would not achieve the goal of "ensuring that significant programming remains available" for noncable households....

## IV

In sustaining the must-carry provisions of the Cable Act, the Court ignores the main justification of the statute urged by appellees and subjects restrictions on expressive activity to an inappropriately lenient level of scrutiny. The principal opinion then misapplies the analytic framework it chooses, exhibiting an extraordinary and unwarranted deference for congressional judgments, a profound fear of delving into complex economic matters, and a willingness to substitute untested assumptions for evidence. In light of gaps in logic and evidence, it is improper to conclude, at the summary judgment stage, that the must-carry scheme serves a significant governmental interest "in a direct and effective way." Ward, 491 U.S., at 800, 109 S.Ct., at 2759. Moreover, because the undisputed facts demonstrate that the must-carry scheme is plainly not narrowly tailored to serving the only governmental interest the principal opinion fully explains and embraces-- preventing anticompetitive behavior--appellants are entitled to summary judgment in their favor.

Justice BREYER disavows the principal opinion's position on anticompetitive behavior, and instead treats the must-carry rules as a "speech-enhancing" measure designed to ensure access to "quality" programming for noncable households. Neither the principal opinion nor the partial concurrence explains the nature of the alleged threat to the availability of a "multiplicity of broadcast programming sources," if that threat does not arise from cable operators' anticompetitive conduct. Such an approach makes it impossible to discern whether Congress was addressing a problem that is "real, not merely conjectural," and whether must-carry addresses the problem in a "direct and material way." Turner, supra, at 664, 114 S.Ct., at 2470 (plurality opinion).

I therefore respectfully dissent, and would reverse the judgment below.

Janet RENO, Attorney General of the United States, et al., Appellants
v.
AMERICAN CIVIL LIBERTIES UNION et al.

117 S.Ct. 2329

Supreme Court of the United States

Decided June 26, 1997.

Justice STEVENS delivered the opinion of the Court.

At issue is the constitutionality of two statutory provisions enacted to protect minors from "indecent" and "patently offensive" communications on the Internet. Notwithstanding the legitimacy and importance of the congressional goal of protecting children from harmful materials, we agree with the three- judge District Court that the statute abridges "the freedom of speech" protected by the First Amendment.

I

The District Court made extensive findings of fact, most of which were based on a detailed stipulation prepared by the parties. See 929 F.Supp. 824, 830-849 (E.D.Pa.1996). The findings describe the character and the dimensions of the Internet, the availability of sexually explicit material in that medium, and the problems confronting age verification for recipients of Internet communications. Because those findings provide the underpinnings for the legal issues, we begin with a summary of the undisputed facts.

The Internet

The Internet is an international network of interconnected computers. It is the outgrowth of what began in 1969 as a military program called "ARPANET," which was designed to enable computers operated by the military, defense contractors, and universities conducting defense-related research to communicate with one another by redundant channels even if some portions of the network were damaged in a war. While the ARPANET no longer exists, it provided an example for the development of a number of civilian networks that, eventually linking with each other, now enable tens of millions of people to communicate with one another and to access vast amounts of information from around the world. The Internet is "a unique and wholly new medium of worldwide human communication."

The Internet has experienced "extraordinary growth." The number of "host" computers--those that store information and relay communications-- increased from about 300 in 1981 to approximately 9,400,000 by the time of the trial in 1996. Roughly 60% of these hosts are located in the United States. About 40 million people used the Internet at the time of trial, a number that is expected to mushroom to 200 million by 1999.

Individuals can obtain access to the Internet from many different sources, generally hosts themselves or entities with a host affiliation. Most colleges and universities provide access for their students and faculty; many corporations provide their employees with access through an office network; many communities and local libraries provide free access; and an increasing number of storefront "computer coffee shops" provide access for a small hourly fee. Several major national "online services" such as America Online, CompuServe, the Microsoft Network, and Prodigy offer access to their own extensive proprietary networks as well as a link to the much larger resources of the Internet. These commercial online services had almost 12 million individual subscribers at the time of trial.

Anyone with access to the Internet may take advantage of a wide variety of communication and information retrieval methods. These methods are constantly evolving and difficult to categorize precisely. But, as presently constituted, those most relevant to this case are electronic mail ("e-mail"), automatic mailing list services ("mail exploders," sometimes referred to as "listservs"), "newsgroups," "chat rooms," and the "World Wide Web." All of these methods can be used to transmit text; most can transmit sound, pictures, and moving video images. Taken together, these tools constitute a unique medium-- known to its users as "cyberspace"--located in no particular geographical location but available to anyone, anywhere in the world, with access to the Internet.

E-mail enables an individual to send an electronic message--generally akin to a note or letter--to another individual or to a group of addressees. The message is generally stored electronically, sometimes waiting for the recipient to check her "mailbox" and sometimes making its receipt known through some type of prompt. A mail exploder is a sort of e-mail group. Subscribers can send messages to a common e-mail address, which then forwards the message to the group's other subscribers. Newsgroups also serve groups of regular participants, but these postings may be read by others as well. There are thousands of such groups, each serving to foster an exchange of information or opinion on a particular topic running the gamut from, say, the music of Wagner to Balkan politics to AIDS prevention to the Chicago Bulls. About 100,000 new messages are posted every day. In most newsgroups, postings are automatically purged at regular intervals. In addition to posting a message that can be read later, two or more individuals wishing to communicate more immediately can enter a chat room to engage in real-time dialogue--in other words, by typing messages to one another that appear almost immediately on the others' computer screens. The District Court found that at any given time "tens of thousands of users are engaging in conversations on a huge range of subjects." It is "no exaggeration to conclude that the content on the Internet is as diverse as human thought."

The best known category of communication over the Internet is the World Wide Web, which allows users to search for and retrieve information stored in remote computers, as well as, in some cases, to communicate back to designated sites. In concrete terms, the Web consists of a vast number of documents stored in different computers all over the world. Some of these documents are simply files containing information. However, more elaborate documents, commonly known as Web "pages," are also prevalent. Each has its own address--"rather like a telephone number." Web pages frequently contain information and sometimes allow the viewer to communicate with the page's (or "site's") author. They generally also contain "links" to other documents created by that site's author or to other (generally) related sites. Typically, the links are either blue or underlined text--sometimes images.

Navigating the Web is relatively straightforward. A user may either type the address of a known page or enter one or more keywords into a commercial "search engine" in an effort to locate sites on a subject of interest. A particular Web page may contain the information sought by the "surfer," or, through its links, it may be an avenue to other documents located anywhere on the Internet. Users generally explore a given Web page, or move to another, by clicking a computer "mouse" on one of the page's icons or links. Access to most Web pages is freely available, but some allow access only to those who have purchased the right from a commercial provider. The Web is thus comparable, from the readers' viewpoint, to both a vast library including millions of readily available and indexed publications and a sprawling mall offering goods and services.

From the publishers' point of view, it constitutes a vast platform from which to address and hear from a world-wide audience of millions of readers, viewers, researchers, and buyers. Any person or organization with a computer connected to the Internet can "publish" information. Publishers include government agencies, educational institutions, commercial entities, advocacy groups, and individuals. Publishers may either make their material available to the entire pool of Internet users, or confine access to a selected group, such as those willing to pay for the privilege. "No single organization controls any membership in the Web, nor is there any centralized point from which individual Web sites or services can be blocked from the Web."

Sexually Explicit Material

Sexually explicit material on the Internet includes text, pictures, and chat and "extends from the modestly titillating to the hardest-core." These files are created, named, and posted in the same manner as material that is not sexually explicit, and may be accessed either deliberately or unintentionally during the course of an imprecise search. "Once a provider posts its content on the Internet, it cannot prevent that content from entering any community." Thus, for example,

> "when the UCR/California Museum of Photography posts to its Web site nudes by Edward Weston and Robert Mapplethorpe to announce that its new exhibit will travel to Baltimore and New York City, those images are available not only in Los Angeles, Baltimore, and New York City, but also in Cincinnati, Mobile, or Beijing--wherever Internet users live. Similarly, the safer sex instructions that Critical Path posts to its Web site, written in street languageso that

the teenage receiver can understand them, are available not just in Philadelphia, but also in Provo and Prague."

Some of the communications over the Internet that originate in foreign countries are also sexually explicit.

Though such material is widely available, users seldom encounter such content accidentally. "A document's title or a description of the document will usually appear before the document itself ... and in many cases the user will receive detailed information about a site's content before he or she need take the step to access the document. Almost all sexually explicit images are preceded by warnings as to the content." For that reason, the "odds are slim" that a user would enter a sexually explicit site by accident. Unlike communications received by radio or television, "the receipt of information on the Internet requires a series of affirmative steps more deliberate and directed than merely turning a dial. A child requires some sophistication and some ability to read to retrieve material and thereby to use the Internet unattended."

Systems have been developed to help parents control the material that may be available on a home computer with Internet access. A system may either limit a computer's access to an approved list of sources that have been identified as containing no adult material, it may block designated inappropriate sites, or it may attempt to block messages containing identifiable objectionable features. "Although parental control software currently can screen for certain suggestive words or for known sexually explicit sites, it cannot now screen for sexually explicit images." Nevertheless, the evidence indicates that "a reasonably effective method by which parents can prevent their children from accessing sexually explicit and other material which parents may believe is inappropriate for their children will soon be available."

Age Verification

The problem of age verification differs for different uses of the Internet. The District Court categorically determined that there "is no effective way to determine the identity or the age of a user who is accessing material through e-mail, mail exploders, newsgroups or chat rooms." The Government offered no evidence that there was a reliable way to screen recipients and participants in such fora for age. Moreover, even if it were technologically feasible to block minors' access to newsgroups and chat rooms containing discussions of art, politics or other subjects that potentially elicit "indecent" or "patently offensive" contributions, it would not be possible to block their access to that material and "still allow them access to the remaining content, even if the overwhelming majority of that content was not indecent."

Technology exists by which an operator of a Web site may condition access on the verification of requested information such as a credit card number or an adult password. Credit card verification is only feasible, however, either in connection with a commercial transaction in which the card is used, or by payment to a verification agency. Using credit card possession as a surrogate for proof of age would impose costs on non-commercial Web sites that would require many of them to shut down. For that reason, at the time of the trial, credit card verification was "effectively unavailable to a substantial number of Internet content providers." Id., at 846 (finding 102). Moreover, the imposition of such a requirement "would completely bar adults who do not have a credit card and lack the resources to obtain one from accessing any blocked material."

In sum, the District Court found:

> "Even if credit card verification or adult password verification were implemented, the Government presented no testimony as to how such systems could ensure that the user of the password or credit card is in fact over 18. The burdens imposed by credit card verification and adult password verification systems make them effectively unavailable to a substantial number of Internet content providers." Ibid. (finding 107).

## II

The Telecommunications Act of 1996, Pub.L. 104-104, 110 Stat. 56, was an unusually important legislative enactment. As stated on the first of its 103 pages, its primary purpose was to reduce regulation and encourage " the rapid deployment of new telecommunications technologies." The major components of the statute have nothing to do with the Internet; they were designed to promote competition in the local telephone service market, the multichannel video market, and the market for over-the-air broadcasting. The Act includes seven Titles, six of which are the product of extensive committee hearings and the subject of discussion in Reports prepared by Committees of the Senate and the House of Representatives. By contrast, Title V--known as the "Communications Decency Act of 1996" (CDA)--contains provisions that were either added in executive committee after the hearings were concluded or as amendments offered during floor debate on the legislation. An amendment offered in the Senate was the source of the two statutory provisions challenged in this case. They are informally described as the "indecent transmission" provision and the "patently offensive display" provision.

The first, 47 U.S.C.A. § 223(a) (Supp.1997), prohibits the knowing transmission of obscene or indecent messages to any recipient under 18 years of age. It provides in pertinent part:

> "(a) Whoever--
>
> "(1) in interstate or foreign communications--
>
> . . . . .
>
> "(B) by means of a telecommunications device knowingly--
>
> "(i) makes, creates, or solicits, and
>
> "(ii) initiates the transmission of,
>
> "any comment, request, suggestion, proposal, image, or other communication which is obscene or indecent, knowing that the recipient of the communication is under 18 years of age, regardless of whether the maker of such communication placed the call or initiated the communication;
>
> . . . . .

"(2) knowingly permits any telecommunications facility under his control to be used for any activity prohibited by paragraph (1) with the intent that it be used for such activity,
"shall be fined under Title 18, or imprisoned not more than two years, or both."

The second provision, § 223(d), prohibits the knowing sending or displaying of patently offensive messages in a manner that is available to a person under 18 years of age. It provides:
"(d) Whoever--
"(1) in interstate or foreign communications knowingly--
"(A) uses an interactive computer service to send to a specific person or persons under 18 years of age, or
"(B) uses any interactive computer service to display in a manner available to a person under 18 years of age,
"any comment, request, suggestion, proposal, image, or other communication that, in context, depicts or describes, in terms patently offensive as measured by contemporary community standards, sexual or excretory activities or organs, regardless of whether the user of such service placed the call or initiated the communication; or
"(2) knowingly permits any telecommunications facility under such person's control to be used for an activity prohibited by paragraph (1) with the intent that it be used for such activity,
"shall be fined under Title 18, or imprisoned not more than two years, or both."

The breadth of these prohibitions is qualified by two affirmative defenses. See § 223(e)(5). [FN26] One covers those who take "good faith, reasonable, effective, and appropriate actions" to restrict access by minors to the prohibited communications. § 223(e)(5)(A). The other covers those who restrict access to covered material by requiring certain designated forms of age proof, such as a verified credit card or an adult identification number or code. § 223(e)(5)(B).

FN26. In full, § 223(e)(5) provides:
"(5) It is a defense to a prosecution under subsection (a)(1)(B) or (d) of this section, or under subsection (a)(2) of this section with respect to the use of a facility for an activity under subsection (a)(1)(B) of this section that a person--
"(A) has taken, in good faith, reasonable, effective, and appropriate actions under the circumstances to restrict or prevent access by minors to a communication specified in such subsections, which may involve any appropriate measures to restrict minors from such communications, including any method which is feasible under available technology; or
"(B) has restricted access to such communication by requiring use of a verified credit card, debit account, adult access code, or adult personal identification number."

III

On February 8, 1996, immediately after the President signed the statute, 20 plaintiffs [FN27] filed suit against the Attorney General of the United States and the Department of Justice challenging the constitutionality of §§ 223(a)(1) and 223(d). A week later, based on his conclusion that the term "indecent" was too vague to provide the basis for a criminal prosecution, District Judge Buckwalter entered a temporary restraining order against enforcement of § 223(a)(1)(B)(ii) insofar as it applies to indecent communications. A second suit was then filed by 27 additional plaintiffs, [FN28] the two cases were consolidated, and a three-judge District Court was convened pursuant to § 561 of the Act. After an evidentiary hearing, that Court entered a preliminary injunction against enforcement of both of the challenged provisions. Each of the three judges wrote a separate opinion, but their judgment was unanimous.

FN27. American Civil Liberties Union; Human Rights Watch; Electronic Privacy Information Center; Electronic Frontier Foundation; Journalism Education Association; Computer Professionals for Social Responsibility; National Writers Union; Clarinet Communications Corp.; Institute for Global Communications; Stop Prisoner Rape; AIDS Education Global Information System; Bibliobytes; Queer Resources Directory; Critical Path AIDS Project, Inc.; Wildcat Press, Inc.; Declan McCullagh dba Justice on Campus; Brock Meeks dba Cyberwire Dispatch; John Troyer dba The Safer Sex Page; Jonathan Wallace dba The Ethical Spectacle; and Planned Parenthood Federation of America, Inc.

FN28. American Library Association; America Online, Inc.; American Booksellers Association, Inc.; American Booksellers Foundation for Free Expression; American Society of Newspaper Editors; Apple Computer, Inc.; Association of American Publishers, Inc.; Association of Publishers, Editors and Writers; Citizens Internet Empowerment Coalition; Commercial Internet Exchange Association; CompuServe Incorporated; Families Against Internet Censorship; Freedom to Read Foundation, Inc.; Health Sciences Libraries Consortium; Hotwired Ventures LLC; Interactive Digital Software Association; Interactive Services Association; Magazine Publishers of America; Microsoft Corporation; The Microsoft Network, L.L. C.; National Press Photographers Association; Netcom On-Line Communication Services, Inc.; Newspaper Association of America; Opnet, Inc.; Prodigy Services Company; Society of Professional Journalists; Wired Ventures, Ltd.

Chief Judge Sloviter doubted the strength of the Government's interest in regulating "the vast range of online material covered or potentially covered by the CDA," but acknowledged that the interest was "compelling" with respect to some of that material. 929 F.Supp., at 853. She concluded, nonetheless, that the statute "sweeps more broadly than necessary and thereby chills the expression of adults" and that the terms "patently offensive" and "indecent" were "inherently vague." Id., at 854. She also determined that the affirmative defenses were not "technologically or economically feasible for most providers," specifically considering and rejecting an argument that providers could avoid liability by "tagging" their material in a manner that would allow potential readers to screen out unwanted transmissions. Id., at 856. Chief Judge Sloviter also rejected the Government's suggestion that the scope of the statute could be narrowed by construing it to apply only to commercial pornographers. Id., at 854-855.

Judge Buckwalter concluded that the word "indecent" in § 223(a)(1)(B) and the terms "patently offensive" and "in context" in § 223(d)(1) were so vague that criminal enforcement of either section would violate the "fundamental constitutional principle" of "simple fairness," id., at 861, and the specific protections of the First and Fifth Amendments, id., at 858. He found no statutory basis for the Government's argument that the challenged provisions would be applied only to "pornographic" materials, noting that, unlike obscenity, "indecency has not been defined to exclude works of serious literary, artistic, political or scientific value." Id., at 863. Moreover, the Government's claim that the work must be considered patently offensive "in context" was itself vague because the relevant context might "refer to, among other things, the nature of the communication as a whole, the time of day it was conveyed, the medium used, the identity of the speaker, or whether or not it is accompanied by appropriate warnings." Id., at 864. He believed that the unique nature of the Internet aggravated the vagueness of the statute. Id., at 865, n. 9.

Judge Dalzell's review of "the special attributes of Internet communication" disclosed by the evidence convinced him that the First Amendment denies Congress the power to regulate the content of protected speech on the Internet. Id., at 867. His opinion explained at length why he believed the Act would abridge significant protected speech, particularly by noncommercial speakers, while "[p]erversely, commercial pornographers would remain relatively unaffected." Id., at 879. He construed our cases as requiring a "medium- specific" approach to the analysis of the regulation of mass communication, id., at 873, and concluded that the Internet--as "the most participatory form of mass speech yet developed," id., at 883--is entitled to "the highest protection from governmental intrusion," ibid.

The judgment of the District Court enjoins the Government from enforcing the prohibitions in § 223(a)(1)(B) insofar as they relate to "indecent" communications, but expressly preserves the Government's right to investigate and prosecute the obscenity or child pornography activities prohibited therein. The injunction against enforcement of §§ 223(d)(1) and (2) is unqualified because those provisions contain no separate reference to obscenity or child pornography.

The Government appealed under the Act's special review provisions, § 561, 110 Stat.142-143, and we noted probable jurisdiction, see 519 U.S. ----, 117 S.Ct. 554, 136 L.Ed.2d 436 (1996). In its appeal, the Government argues that the District Court erred in holding that the CDA violated both the First Amendment because it is overbroad and the Fifth Amendment because it is vague. While we discuss the vagueness of the CDA because of its relevance to the First Amendment overbreadth inquiry, we conclude that the judgment should be affirmed without reaching the Fifth Amendment issue. We begin our analysis by reviewing the principal authorities on which the Government relies. Then, after describing the overbreadth of the CDA, we consider the Government's specific contentions, including its submission that we save portions of the statute either by severance or by fashioning judicial limitations on the scope of its coverage.

## IV

In arguing for reversal, the Government contends that the CDA is plainly constitutional under three of our prior decisions: (1) Ginsberg v. New York, 390 U.S. 629, 88 S.Ct. 1274, 20 L.Ed.2d 195 (1968); (2) FCC v. Pacifica Foundation, 438 U.S. 726, 98 S.Ct. 3026, 57 L.Ed.2d 1073 (1978); and (3) Renton v. Playtime Theatres, Inc., 475 U.S. 41, 106 S.Ct. 925, 89 L.Ed.2d 29 (1986). A close look at these cases, however, raises--rather than relieves--doubts concerning the constitutionality of the CDA.

In Ginsberg, we upheld the constitutionality of a New York statute that prohibited selling to minors under 17 years of age material that was considered obscene as to them even if not obscene as to adults. We rejected the defendant's broad submission that "the scope of the constitutional freedom of expression secured to a citizen to read or see material concerned with sex cannot be made to depend on whether the citizen is an adult or a minor." 390 U.S., at 636, 88 S.Ct., at 1279. In rejecting that contention, we relied not only on the State's independent interest in the well-being of its youth, but also on our consistent recognition of the principle that "the parents' claim to authority in their own household to direct the rearing of their children is basic in the structure of our society."

In four important respects, the statute upheld in Ginsberg was narrower than the CDA. First, we noted in Ginsberg that "the prohibition against sales to minors does not bar parents who so desire from purchasing the magazines for their children." Id., at 639, 88 S.Ct., at 1280. Under the CDA, by contrast, neither the parents' consent--nor even their participation-- in the communication would avoid the application of the statute. Second, the New York statute applied only to commercial transactions, id., at 647, 88 S.Ct., at 1284-1285, whereas the CDA contains no such limitation. Third, the New York statute cabined its definition of material that is harmful to minors with the requirement that it be "utterly without redeeming social importance for minors." Id., at 646, 88 S.Ct., at 1284. The CDA fails to provide us with any definition of the term "indecent" as used in § 223(a)(1) and, importantly, omits any requirement that the "patently offensive" material covered by § 223(d) lack serious literary, artistic, political, or scientific value. Fourth, the New York statute defined a minor as a person under the age of 17, whereas the CDA, in applying to all those under 18 years, includes an additional year of those nearest majority.

In Pacifica, we upheld a declaratory order of the Federal Communications Commission, holding that the broadcast of a recording of a 12-minute monologue entitled "Filthy Words" that had previously been delivered to a live audience "could have been the subject of administrative sanctions." 438 U.S., at 730, 98 S.Ct., at 3030 (internal quotations omitted). The Commission had found that the repetitive use of certain words referring to excretory or sexual activities or organs "in an afternoon broadcast when children are in the audience was patently offensive" and concluded that the monologue was indecent "as broadcast." Id., at 735, 98 S.Ct., at 3033. The respondent did not quarrel with the finding that the afternoon broadcast was patently offensive, but contended that it was not "indecent" within the meaning of the relevant statutes because it contained no prurient appeal. After rejecting respondent's statutory arguments, we confronted its two constitutional arguments: (1) that the Commission's construction of its authority to ban indecent speech was so broad that its order had to be set aside even if the broadcast at issue was unprotected; and (2) that since the recording was not obscene, the First Amendment forbade any abridgement of the right to broadcast it on the radio.

In the portion of the lead opinion not joined by Justices Powell and Blackmun, the plurality stated that the First Amendment does not prohibit all governmental regulation that depends on the content of speech. Id., at 742- 743, 98 S.Ct., at 3036-3037. Accordingly, the availability of constitutional protection for a vulgar and offensive monologue that was not obscene depended on the context of the broadcast. Id., at 744-748, 98 S.Ct., at 3037-3040. Relying on the premise that "of all forms of communication" broadcasting had received the most limited First Amendment protection, id., at 748-749, 98 S.Ct., at 3039-3040, the Court concluded that the ease with which children may obtain access to broadcasts, "coupled with the concerns recognized in Ginsberg," justified special treatment of indecent broadcasting. Id., at 749-750, 98 S.Ct., at 3040-3041.

As with the New York statute at issue in Ginsberg, there are significant differences between the order upheld in Pacifica and the CDA. First, the order in Pacifica, issued by an agency that had been regulating radio stations for decades, targeted a specific broadcast that represented a rather dramatic departure from traditional program content in order to designate when--rather than whether--it would be permissible to air such a program in that particular medium. The CDA's broad categorical prohibitions are not limited to particular times and are not dependent on any evaluation by an agency familiar with the unique characteristics of the Internet. Second, unlike the CDA, the Commission's declaratory order was not punitive; we expressly refused to decide whether the indecent broadcast "would justify a criminal prosecution." Id., at 750, 98 S.Ct., at 3041. Finally, the Commission's order applied to a medium which as a matter of history had "received the most limited First Amendment protection," id., at 748, 98 S.Ct., at 3040, in large part because warnings could not adequately protect the listener from unexpected program content. The Internet, however, has no comparable history. Moreover, the District Court found that the risk of encountering indecent material by accident is remote because a series of affirmative steps is required to access specific material.

In Renton, we upheld a zoning ordinance that kept adult movie theatres out of residential neighborhoods. The ordinance was aimed, not at the content of the films shown in the theaters, but rather at the "secondary effects"--such as crime and deteriorating property values--that these theaters fostered: " 'It is th[e] secondary effect which these zoning ordinances attempt to avoid, not the dissemination of "offensive" speech.' " 475 U.S., at 49, 106 S.Ct., at 930 (quoting Young v. American Mini Theatres, Inc., 427 U.S. 50, 71, n. 34, 96 S.Ct. 2440, 2453, n. 34, 49 L.Ed.2d 310 (1976)). According to the Government, the CDA is constitutional because it constitutes a sort of "cyberzoning" on the Internet. But the CDA applies broadly to the entire universe of cyberspace. And the purpose of the CDA is to protect children from the primary effects of "indecent" and "patently offensive" speech, rather than any "secondary" effect of such speech. Thus, the CDA is a content-based blanket restriction on speech, and, as such, cannot be "properly analyzed as a form of time, place, and manner regulation." 475 U.S., at 46, 106 S.Ct., at 928. See also Boos v. Barry, 485 U.S. 312, 321, 108 S.Ct. 1157, 1163, 99 L.Ed.2d 333 (1988) ("Regulations that focus on the direct impact of speech on its audience" are not properly analyzed under Renton ); Forsyth County v. Nationalist Movement, 505 U.S. 123, 134, 112 S.Ct. 2395, 2403, 120 L.Ed.2d 101 (1992) ("Listeners' reaction to speech is not a content-neutral basis for regulation").

These precedents, then, surely do not require us to uphold the CDA and are fully consistent with the application of the most stringent review of its provisions.

V

In Southeastern Promotions, Ltd. v. Conrad, 420 U.S. 546, 557, 95 S.Ct. 1239, 1245-1246, 43 L.Ed.2d 448 (1975), we observed that "[e]ach medium of expression ... may present its own problems." Thus, some of our cases have recognized special justifications for regulation of the broadcast media that are not applicable to other speakers, see Red Lion Broadcasting Co. v. FCC, 395 U.S. 367, 89 S.Ct. 1794, 23 L.Ed.2d 371 (1969); FCC v. Pacifica Foundation, 438 U.S. 726, 98 S.Ct. 3026, 57 L.Ed.2d 1073 (1978). In these cases, the Court relied on the history of extensive government regulation of the broadcast medium, see, e.g., Red Lion, 395 U.S., at 399-400, 89 S.Ct., at 1811-1812; the scarcity of available frequencies at its inception, see, e.g., Turner Broadcasting System, Inc. v. FCC, 512 U.S. 622, 637-638, 114 S.Ct. 2445, 2456-2457, 129 L.Ed.2d 497 (1994); and its "invasive" nature, see Sable Communications of Cal., Inc. v. FCC, 492 U.S. 115, 128, 109 S.Ct. 2829, 2837-2838, 106 L.Ed.2d 93 (1989).

Those factors are not present in cyberspace. Neither before nor after the enactment of the CDA have the vast democratic fora of the Internet been subject to the type of government supervision and regulation that has attended the broadcast industry. Moreover, the Internet is not as "invasive" as radio or television. The District Court specifically found that "[c]ommunications over the Internet do not 'invade' an individual's home or appear on one's computer screen unbidden. Users seldom encounter content 'by accident.' " 929 F.Supp., at 844 (finding 88). It also found that "[a]lmost all sexually explicit images are preceded by warnings as to the content," and cited testimony that " 'odds are slim' that a user would come across a sexually explicit sight by accident." Ibid.

We distinguished Pacifica in Sable, 492 U.S., at 128, 109 S.Ct., at 2837-2838, on just this basis. In Sable, a company engaged in the business of offering sexually oriented prerecorded telephone messages (popularly known as "dial-a-porn") challenged the constitutionality of an amendment to the Communications Act that imposed a blanket prohibition on indecent as well as obscene interstate commercial telephone messages. We held that the statute was constitutional insofar as it applied to obscene messages but invalid as applied to indecent messages. In attempting to justify the complete ban and criminalization of indecent commercial telephone messages, the Government relied on Pacifica, arguing that the ban was necessary to prevent children from gaining access to such messages. We agreed that "there is a compelling interest in protecting the physical and psychological well-being of minors" which extended to shielding them from indecent messages that are not obscene by adult standards, 492 U.S., at 126, 109 S.Ct., at 2836-2837, but distinguished our "emphatically narrow holding" in Pacifica because it did not involve a complete ban and because it involved a different medium of communication, id., at 127, 109 S.Ct., at 2837. We explained that "the dial-it medium requires the listener to take affirmative steps to receive the communication." Id., at 127-128, 109 S.Ct., at 2837. "Placing a telephone call," we continued, "is not the same as turning on a radio and being taken by surprise by an indecent message." Id., at 128, 109 S.Ct., at 2837.

Finally, unlike the conditions that prevailed when Congress first authorized regulation of the broadcast spectrum, the Internet can hardly be considered a "scarce" expressive commodity. It provides relatively unlimited, low-cost capacity for communication of all kinds. The Government estimates that "[a]s many as 40 million people use the Internet today, and that figure is expected to grow to 200 million by 1999." This dynamic, multifaceted category of communication includes not only traditional print and news services, but also audio, video, and still images, as well as interactive, real-time dialogue. Through the use of chat rooms, any person with a phone line can become a town crier with a voice that resonates farther than it could from any soapbox. Through the use of Web pages, mail exploders, and newsgroups, the same individual can become a pamphleteer. As the District Court found, "the content on the Internet is as diverse as human thought." 929 F.Supp., at 842 (finding 74). We agree with its conclusion that our cases provide no basis for qualifying the level of First Amendment scrutiny that should be applied to this medium.

## VI

Regardless of whether the CDA is so vague that it violates the Fifth Amendment, the many ambiguities concerning the scope of its coverage render it problematic for purposes of the First Amendment. For instance, each of the two parts of the CDA uses a different linguistic form. The first uses the word "indecent," 47 U.S.C.A. § 223(a) (Supp.1997), while the second speaks of material that "in context, depicts or describes, in terms patently offensive as measured by contemporary community standards, sexual or excretory activities or organs," § 223(d). Given the absence of a definition of either term, this difference in language will provoke uncertainty among speakers about how the two standards relate to each other and just what they mean. Could a speaker confidently assume that a serious discussion about birth control practices, homosexuality, the First Amendment issues raised by the Appendix to our Pacifica opinion, or the consequences of prison rape would not violate the CDA? This uncertainty undermines the likelihood that the CDA has been carefully tailored to the congressional goal of protecting minors from potentially harmful materials.

The vagueness of the CDA is a matter of special concern for two reasons. First, the CDA is a content-based regulation of speech. The vagueness of such a regulation raises special First Amendment concerns because of its obvious chilling effect on free speech. See, e.g., Gentile v. State Bar of Nev., 501 U.S. 1030, 1048-1051, 111 S.Ct. 2720, 2731-2733, 115 L.Ed.2d 888

(1991). Second, the CDA is a criminal statute. In addition to the opprobrium and stigma of a criminal conviction, the CDA threatens violators with penalties including up to two years in prison for each act of violation. The severity of criminal sanctions may well cause speakers to remain silent rather than communicate even arguably unlawful words, ideas, and images. See, e.g., Dombrowski v. Pfister, 380 U.S. 479, 494, 85 S.Ct. 1116, 1125, 14 L.Ed.2d 22 (1965). As a practical matter, this increased deterrent effect, coupled with the "risk of discriminatory enforcement" of vague regulations, poses greater First Amendment concerns than those implicated by the civil regulation reviewed in Denver Area Ed. Telecommunications Consortium, Inc. v. FCC, 518 U.S. ----, 116 S.Ct. 2374, 135 L.Ed.2d 888 (1996).

The Government argues that the statute is no more vague than the obscenity standard this Court established in Miller v. California, 413 U.S. 15, 93 S.Ct. 2607, 37 L.Ed.2d 419 (1973). But that is not so. In Miller, this Court reviewed a criminal conviction against a commercial vendor who mailed brochures containing pictures of sexually explicit activities to individuals who had not requested such materials. Id., at 18, 93 S.Ct., at 2611-2612. Having struggled for some time to establish a definition of obscenity, we set forth in Miller the test for obscenity that controls to this day:

> "(a) whether the average person, applying contemporary community standards would find that the work, taken as a whole, appeals to the prurient interest; (b) whether the work depicts or describes, in a patently offensive way, sexual conduct specifically defined by the applicable state law; and (c) whether the work, taken as a whole, lacks serious literary, artistic, political, or scientific value." Id., at 24, 93 S.Ct., at 2615 (internal quotation marks and citations omitted).

Because the CDA's "patently offensive" standard (and, we assume arguendo, its synonymous "indecent" standard) is one part of the three-prong Miller test, the Government reasons, it cannot be unconstitutionally vague.

The Government's assertion is incorrect as a matter of fact. The second prong of the Miller test--the purportedly analogous standard--contains a critical requirement that is omitted from the CDA: that the proscribed material be "specifically defined by the applicable state law." This requirement reduces the vagueness inherent in the open-ended term "patently offensive" as used in the CDA. Moreover, the Miller definition is limited to "sexual conduct," whereas the CDA extends also to include (1) "excretory activities" as well as (2) "organs" of both a sexual and excretory nature.

The Government's reasoning is also flawed. Just because a definition including three limitations is not vague, it does not follow that one of those limitations, standing by itself, is not vague. [FN38] Each of Miller 's additional two prongs--(1) that, taken as a whole, the material appeal to the "prurient" interest, and (2) that it "lac[k] serious literary, artistic, political, or scientific value"--critically limits the uncertain sweep of the obscenity definition. The second requirement is particularly important because, unlike the "patently offensive" and "prurient interest" criteria, it is not judged by contemporary community standards. See Pope v. Illinois, 481 U.S. 497, 500, 107 S.Ct. 1918, 1920-1921, 95 L.Ed.2d 439 (1987). This "societal value" requirement, absent in the CDA, allows appellate courts to impose some limitations and regularity on the definition by setting, as a matter of law, a national floor for socially redeeming value. The Government's contention that courts will be able to give such legal limitations to the CDA's standards is belied by Miller's own rationale for having juries determine whether material is "patently offensive" according to community standards: that such questions are essentially ones of fact. [FN39]

FN38. Even though the word "trunk," standing alone, might refer to luggage,a swimming suit, the base of a tree, or the long nose of an animal, its meaning is clear when it is one prong of a three-part description of a species of gray animals.

FN39. 413 U.S., at 30, 93 S.Ct., at 2618 (Determinations of "what appeals to the 'prurient interest' or is 'patently offensive' .... are essentially questions of fact, and our Nation is simply too big and too diverse for this Court to reasonably expect that such standards could be articulated for all 50 States in a single formulation, even assuming the prerequisite consensus exists"). The CDA, which implements the "contemporary community standards" language of Miller, thus conflicts with the Conferees' own assertion that the CDA was intended "to establish a uniform national standard of content regulation." S. Conf. Rep., at 191.

In contrast to Miller and our other previous cases, the CDA thus presents a greater threat of censoring speech that, in fact, falls outside the statute's scope. Given the vague contours of the coverage of the statute, it unquestionably silences some speakers whose messages would be entitled to constitutional protection. That danger provides further reason for insisting that the statute not be overly broad. The CDA's burden on protected speech cannot be justified if it could be avoided by a more carefully drafted statute.

## VII

We are persuaded that the CDA lacks the precision that the First Amendment requires when a statute regulates the content of speech. In order to deny minors access to potentially harmful speech, the CDA effectively suppresses a large amount of speech that adults have a constitutional right to receive and to address to one another. That burden on adult speech is unacceptable if less restrictive alternatives would be at least as effective in achieving the legitimate purpose that the statute was enacted to serve.

In evaluating the free speech rights of adults, we have made it perfectly clear that "[s]exual expression which is indecent but not obscene is protected by the First Amendment." Sable, 492 U.S., at 126, 109 S.Ct., at 2836. See also Carey v. Population Services Int'l, 431 U.S. 678, 701, 97 S.Ct. 2010, 2024, 52 L.Ed.2d 675 (1977) ("[W]here obscenity is not involved, we have consistently held that the fact that protected speech may be offensive to some does not justify its suppression"). Indeed, Pacifica itself admonished that "the fact that society may find speech offensive is not a sufficient reason for suppressing it." 438 U.S., at 745, 98 S.Ct., at 3038.

It is true that we have repeatedly recognized the governmental interest in protecting children from harmful materials. See Ginsberg, 390 U.S., at 639, 88 S.Ct., at 1280; Pacifica, 438 U.S., at 749, 98 S.Ct., at 3040. But that interest does not justify an unnecessarily broad suppression of speech addressed to adults. As we have explained, the Government may not "reduc[e] the adult population ... to ... only what is fit for children." Denver, 518 U.S., at ----, 116 S.Ct., at 2393 (internal quotation marks omitted) (quoting Sable, 492 U.S., at 128, 109 S.Ct., at 2837-2838). "[R]egardless of the strength of the government's interest" in protecting children, "[t]he level of discourse reaching a mailbox simply cannot be limited to that which would be suitable for a sandbox." Bolger v. Youngs Drug Products Corp., 463 U.S. 60, 74-75 ...

The District Court was correct to conclude that the CDA effectively resembles the ban on "dial-a-porn" invalidated in Sable. 929 F.Supp., at 854. In Sable, 492 U.S., at 129, 109 S.Ct., at 2838, this Court rejected the argument that we should defer to the congressional judgment that nothing less than a total ban would be effective in preventing enterprising youngsters from gaining access to indecent communications. Sable thus made clear that the mere fact that a statutory regulation of speech was enacted for the important purpose of protecting children from exposure to sexually explicit material does not foreclose inquiry into its validity. As we pointed out last Term, that inquiry embodies an "over-arching commitment" to make sure that Congress has designed its statute to accomplish its purpose "without imposing an unnecessarily great restriction on speech." Denver, 518 U.S., at ----, 116 S.Ct., at 2385.

In arguing that the CDA does not so diminish adult communication, the Government relies on the incorrect factual premise that prohibiting a transmission whenever it is known that one of its recipients is a minor would not interfere with adult-to-adult communication. The findings of the District Court make clear that this premise is untenable. Given the size of the potential audience for most messages, in the absence of a viable age verification process, the sender must be charged with knowing that one or more minors will likely view it. Knowledge that, for instance, one or more members of a 100-person chat group will be minor--and therefore that it would be a crime to send the group an indecent message--would surely burden communication among adults.

The District Court found that at the time of trial existing technology did not include any effective method for a sender to prevent minors from obtaining access to its communications on the Internet without also denying access to adults. The Court found no effective way to determine the age of a user who is accessing material through e-mail, mail exploders, newsgroups, or chat rooms. 929 F.Supp., at 845 (findings 90-94). As a practical matter, the Court also found that it would be prohibitively expensive for noncommercial--as well as some commercial--speakers who have Web sites to verify that their users are adults. Id., at 845-848 (findings 95-116). These limitations must inevitably curtail a significant amount of adult communication on the Internet. By contrast, the District Court found that "[d]espite its limitations, currently available user-based software suggests that a reasonably effective method by which parents can prevent their children from accessing sexually explicit and other material which parents may believe is inappropriate for their children will soon be widely available." Id., at 842 (finding 73) (emphases added).

The breadth of the CDA's coverage is wholly unprecedented. Unlike the regulations upheld in Ginsberg and Pacifica, the scope of the CDA is not limited to commercial speech or commercial entities. Its open-ended prohibitions embrace all nonprofit entities and individuals posting indecent messages or displaying them on their own computers in the presence of minors. The general, undefined terms "indecent" and "patently offensive" cover large amounts of nonpornographic material with serious educational or other value. Moreover, the "community standards" criterion as applied to the Internet means that any communication available to a nation-wide audience will be judged by the standards of the community most likely to be offended by the message. The regulated subject matter includes any of the seven "dirty words" used in the Pacifica monologue, the use of which the Government's expert acknowledged could constitute a felony. See Olsen Test., Tr. Vol. V, 53:16-54:10. It may also extend to discussions about prison rape or safe sexual practices, artistic images that include nude subjects, and arguably the card catalogue of the Carnegie Library.

For the purposes of our decision, we need neither accept nor reject the Government's submission that the First Amendment does not forbid a blanket prohibition on all "indecent" and "patently offensive" messages communicated to a 17-year old--no matter how much value the message may contain and regardless of parental approval. It is at least clear that the strength of the Government's interest in protecting minors is not equally strong throughout the coverage of this broad statute. Under the CDA, a parent allowing her 17-year- old to use the family computer to obtain information on the Internet that she, in her parental judgment, deems appropriate could face a lengthy prison term. See 47 U.S.C.A. § 223(a)(2) (Supp.1997). Similarly, a parent who sent his 17-year-old college freshman information on birth control via e-mail could be incarcerated even though neither he, his child, nor anyone in their home community, found the material "indecent" or "patently offensive," if the college town's community thought otherwise.

The breadth of this content-based restriction of speech imposes an especially heavy burden on the Government to explain why a less restrictive provision would not be as effective as the CDA. It has not done so. The arguments in this Court have referred to possible alternatives such as requiring that indecent material be "tagged" in a way that facilitates parental control of material coming into their homes, making exceptions for messages with artistic or educational value, providing some tolerance for parental choice, and regulating some portions of the Internet--such as commercial web sites-- differently than others, such as chat rooms. Particularly in the light of the absence of any detailed findings by the Congress, or even hearings addressing the special problems of the CDA, we are persuaded that the CDA is not narrowly tailored if that requirement has any meaning at all.

## VIII

In an attempt to curtail the CDA's facial overbreadth, the Government advances three additional arguments for sustaining the Act's affirmative prohibitions: (1) that the CDA is constitutional because it leaves open ample "alternative channels" of communication; (2) that the plain meaning of the Act's "knowledge" and "specific person" requirement significantly restricts its permissible applications; and (3) that the Act's prohibitions are "almost always" limited to material lacking redeeming social value.

The Government first contends that, even though the CDA effectively censors discourse on many of the Internet's modalities--such as chat groups, newsgroups, and mail exploders--it is nonetheless constitutional because it provides a "reasonable opportunity" for speakers to engage in the restricted speech on the World Wide Web. Brief for Appellants 39. This argument is unpersuasive because the CDA regulates speech on the basis of its content. A "time, place, and manner" analysis is therefore inapplicable. See Consolidated Edison Co. of N.Y. v. Public Serv. Comm'n of N.Y., 447 U.S. 530, 536, 100 S.Ct. 2326, 2332-2333, 65 L.Ed.2d 319 (1980). It is thus immaterial whether such speech would be feasible on the Web (which, as the Government's own expert acknowledged, would cost up to $10,000 if the speaker's interests were not accommodated by an existing Web site, not including costs for database management and age verification). The Government's position is equivalent to arguing that a statute could ban leaflets on certain subjects as long as individuals are free to publish books. In invalidating a number of laws that banned leafletting on the streets regardless of their content--we explained that "one is not to have the exercise of his liberty of expression in appropriate places abridged on the plea that it may be exercised in some other place." Schneider v. State of N.J. (Town of Irvington), 308 U.S. 147, 163, 60 S.Ct. 146, 151-152, 84 L.Ed. 155 (1939).

The Government also asserts that the "knowledge" requirement of both §§ 223(a) and (d), especially when coupled with the "specific child" element found in § 223(d), saves the CDA from overbreadth. Because both sections prohibit the dissemination of indecent messages only to persons known to be under 18, the Government argues, it does not require transmitters to "refrain from communicating indecent material to adults; they need only refrain from disseminating such materials to persons they know to be under 18." Brief for Appellants 24.

This argument ignores the fact that most Internet fora--including chat rooms, newsgroups, mail exploders, and the Web--are open to all comers. The Government's assertion that the knowledge requirement somehow protects the communications of adults is therefore untenable. Even the strongest reading of the "specific person" requirement of § 223(d) cannot save the statute. It would confer broad powers of censorship, in the form of a "heckler's veto," upon any opponent of indecent speech who might simply log on and inform the would-be discoursers that his 17-year-old child--a "specific person ... under 18 years of age," 47 U.S.C.A. § 223(d)(1)(A) (Supp.1997)--would be present.

Finally, we find no textual support for the Government's submission that material having scientific, educational, or other redeeming social value will necessarily fall outside the CDA's "patently offensive" and "indecent" prohibitions. See also n. 37, supra.

## IX

The Government's three remaining arguments focus on the defenses provided in § 223(e)(5). First, relying on the "good faith, reasonable, effective, and appropriate actions" provision, the Government suggests that "tagging" provides a defense that saves the constitutionality of the Act. The suggestion assumes that transmitters may encode their indecent communications in a way that would indicate their contents, thus permitting recipients to block their reception with appropriate software. It is the requirement that the good faith action must be "effective" that makes this defense illusory. The Government recognizes that its proposed screening software does not currently exist. Even if it did, there is no way to know whether a potential recipient will actually block the encoded material. Without the impossible knowledge that every guardian in America is screening for the "tag," the transmitter could not reasonably rely on its action to be "effective."

For its second and third arguments concerning defenses--which we can consider together--the Government relies on the latter half of § 223(e)(5), which applies when the transmitter has restricted access by requiring use of a verified credit card or adult identification. Such verification is not only technologically available but actually is used by commercial providers of sexually explicit material. These providers, therefore, would be protected by the defense. Under the findings of the District Court, however, it is not economically feasible for most noncommercial speakers to employ such verification. Accordingly, this defense would not significantly narrow the statute's burden on noncommercial speech. Even with respect to the commercial pornographers that would be protected by the defense, the Government failed to adduce any evidence that these verification techniques actually preclude minors from posing as adults. Given that the risk of criminal sanctions "hovers over each content provider, like the proverbial sword of Damocles," the District Court correctly refused to rely on unproven future technology to save the statute. The Government thus failed to prove that the proffered defense would significantly reduce the heavy burden on adult speech produced by the prohibition on offensive displays.

We agree with the District Court's conclusion that the CDA places an unacceptably heavy burden on protected speech, and that the defenses do not constitute the sort of "narrow tailoring" that will save an otherwise patently invalid unconstitutional provision. In Sable, 492 U.S., at 127, 109 S.Ct., at 2837, we remarked that the speech restriction at issue there amounted to " 'burn[ing] the house to roast the pig.' " The CDA, casting a far darker shadow over free speech, threatens to torch a large segment of the Internet community.

## X

At oral argument, the Government relied heavily on its ultimate fall- back position: If this Court should conclude that the CDA is insufficiently tailored, it urged, we should save the statute's constitutionality by honoring the severability clause, see 47 U.S.C. § 608, and construing nonseverable terms narrowly. In only one respect is this argument acceptable.

A severability clause requires textual provisions that can be severed. We will follow § 608's guidance by leaving constitutional textual elements of the statute intact in the one place where they are, in fact, severable. The "indecency" provision, 47 U.S.C.A. § 223(a) (Supp.1997), applies to "any comment, request, suggestion, proposal, image, or other communication which is obscene or indecent." (Emphasis added.) Appellees do not challenge the application of the statute to obscene speech, which, they acknowledge, can be banned totally because it enjoys no First Amendment protection. See Miller, 413 U.S., at 18, 93 S.Ct., at 2611-2612. As set forth by the statute, the restriction of "obscene" material enjoys a textual manifestation separate from that for "indecent" material, which we have held unconstitutional. Therefore, we will sever the term "or indecent" from the statute, leaving the rest of § 223(a) standing. In no other respect, however, can § 223(a) or § 223(d) be saved by such a textual surgery.

The Government also draws on an additional, less traditional aspect of the CDA's severability clause, 47 U.S.C., § 608, which asks any reviewing court that holds the statute facially unconstitutional not to invalidate the CDA in application to "other persons or circumstances" that might be constitutionally permissible. It further invokes this Court's admonition that, absent "countervailing considerations," a statute should "be declared invalid to the extent it reaches too far, but otherwise left intact." Brockett v. Spokane Arcades, Inc., 472 U.S. 491, 503-504, 105 S.Ct. 2794, 2801-2802, 86 L.Ed.2d 394 (1985). There are two flaws in this argument.

First, the statute that grants our jurisdiction for this expedited review, 47 U.S.C.A. § 561 (Supp.1997), limits that jurisdictional grant to actions challenging the CDA "on its face." Consistent with § 561, the plaintiffs who brought this suit and the three-judge panel that decided it treated it as a facial challenge. We have no authority, in this particular posture, to convert this litigation into an "as-applied" challenge. Nor, given the vast array of plaintiffs, the range of their expressive activities, and the vagueness of the statute, would it be practicable to limit our holding to a judicially defined set of specific applications.

Second, one of the "countervailing considerations" mentioned in Brockett is present here. In considering a facial challenge, this Court may impose a limiting construction on a statute only if it is "readily susceptible" to such a construction. Virginia v. American Bookseller's Assn., Inc., 484 U.S. 383, 397, 108 S.Ct. 636, 645, 98 L.Ed.2d 782 (1988). See also Erznoznik, v. Jacksonville, 422 U.S. 205, 216, 95 S.Ct. 2268, 2276, 45 L.Ed.2d 125 (1975) ("readily subject" to narrowing construction). The open- ended character of the CDA provides no guidance what ever for limiting its coverage.

This case is therefore unlike those in which we have construed a statute narrowly because the text or other source of congressional intent identified a clear line that this Court could draw. Cf., e.g., Brockett, 472 U.S., at 504-505, 105 S.Ct., at 2802 (invalidating obscenity statute only to the extent that word "lust" was actually or effectively excised from statute); United States v. Grace, 461 U.S. 171, 180-183, 103 S.Ct. 1702, 1708-1710, 75 L.Ed.2d 736 (1983) (invalidating federal statute banning expressive displays only insofar as it extended to public sidewalks when clear line could be drawn between sidewalks and other grounds that comported with congressional purpose of protecting the building, grounds, and people therein). Rather, our decision in United States v. National Treasury Employees Union, 513 U.S. 454, 479, n. 26, 115 S.Ct. 1003, 1019, n. 26, 130 L.Ed.2d 964 (1995), is applicable. In that case, we declined to "dra[w] one or more lines between categories of speech covered by an overly broad statute, when Congress has sent inconsistent signals as to where the new line or lines should be drawn" because doing so "involves a far more serious invasion of the legislative domain." This Court "will not rewrite a ... law to conform it to constitutional requirements." American Booksellers, 484 U.S., at 397, 108 S.Ct., at 645.

XI

In this Court, though not in the District Court, the Government asserts that-- in addition to its interest in protecting children--its "[e]qually significant" interest in fostering the growth of the Internet provides an independent basis for upholding the constitutionality of the CDA. Brief for Appellants 19. The Government apparently assumes that the unregulated availability of "indecent" and "patently offensive" material on the Internet is driving countless citizens away from the medium because of the risk of exposing themselves or their children to harmful material.

We find this argument singularly unpersuasive. The dramatic expansion of this new marketplace of ideas contradicts the factual basis of this contention. The record demonstrates that the growth of the Internet has been and continues to be phenomenal. As a matter of constitutional tradition, in the absence of evidence to the contrary, we presume that governmental regulation of the content of speech is more likely to interfere with the free exchange of ideas than to encourage it. The interest in encouraging freedom of expression in a democratic society outweighs any theoretical but unproven benefit of censorship.

For the foregoing reasons, the judgment of the district court is affirmed.
It is so ordered.

Justice O'CONNOR, with whom THE CHIEF JUSTICE joins, concurring in the judgment in part and dissenting in part.

# Part VI: Advertising Regulation

CENTRAL HUDSON GAS & ELECTRIC CORPORATION, Appellant,
v.
PUBLIC SERVICE COMMISSION OF NEW YORK.

447 U.S. 557

Supreme Court of the United States

Decided June 20, 1980.

Mr. Justice POWELL delivered the opinion of the Court.

This case presents the question whether a regulation of the Public Service Commission of the State of New York violates the First and Fourteenth Amendments because it completely bans promotional advertising by an electrical utility.

I

In December 1973, the Commission, appellee here, ordered electric utilities in New York State to cease all advertising that "promot[es] the use of electricity." App. to Juris. Statement 31a. The order was based on the Commission's finding that "the interconnected utility system in New York State does not have sufficient fuel stocks or sources of supply to continue furnishing all customer demands for the 1973-1974 winter." Id., at 26a.

Three years later, when the fuel shortage had eased, the Commission requested comments from the public on its proposal to continue the ban on promotional advertising. Central Hudson Gas & Electric Corp., the appellant in this case, opposed the ban on First Amendment grounds. App. A10. After reviewing the public comments, the Commission extended the prohibition in a Policy Statement issued on February 25, 1977.

The Policy Statement divided advertising expenses "into two broad categories: promotional--advertising intended to stimulate the purchase of utility services--and institutional and informational, a broad category inclusive of all advertising not clearly intended to promote sales." App. to Juris. Statement 35a. The Commission declared all promotional advertising contrary to the national policy of conserving energy. It acknowledged that the ban is not a perfect vehicle for conserving energy. For example, the Commission's order prohibits promotional advertising to develop consumption during periods when demand for electricity is low. By limiting growth in "off- peak" consumption, the ban limits the "beneficial side effects" of such growth in terms of more efficient use of existing power-plants. Id., at 37a. And since oil dealers are not under the Commission's jurisdiction and thus remain free to advertise, it was recognized that the ban can achieve only "piecemeal conservationism." Still, the Commission adopted the restriction because it was deemed likely to "result in some dampening of unnecessary growth" in energy consumption. Ibid.

The Commission's order explicitly permitted "informational" advertising designed to encourage "shifts of consumption" from peak demand times to periods of low electricity demand. Ibid. (emphasis in original). Informational advertising would not seek to increase aggregate consumption, but would invite a leveling of demand throughout any given 24-hour period. The agency offered to review "specific proposals by the companies for specifically described [advertising] programs that meet these criteria." Id., at 38a.

When it rejected requests for rehearing on the Policy Statement, the Commission supplemented its rationale for the advertising ban. The agency observed that additional electricity probably would be more expensive to produce than existing output. Because electricity rates in New York were not then based on marginal cost, the Commission feared that additional power would be priced below the actual cost of generation. This additional electricity would be subsidized by all consumers through generally higher rates. Id., at 57a-58a. The state agency also thought that promotional advertising would give "misleading signals" to the public by appearing to encourage energy consumption at a time when conservation is needed. Id., at 59a.

Appellant challenged the order in state court, arguing that the Commission had restrained commercial speech in violation of the First and Fourteenth Amendments. The Commission's order was upheld by the trial court and at the intermediate appellate level. The New York Court of Appeals affirmed. It found little value to advertising in "the noncompetitive market in which electric corporations operate." Consolidated Edison Co. v. Public Service Comm'n, 47 N.Y.2d 94, 110, 417 N.Y.S.2d 30, 39, 390 N.E.2d 749, 757 (1979). Since consumers "have no choice regarding the source of their electric power," the court denied that "promotional advertising of electricity might contribute to society's interest in 'informed and reliable' economic decisionmaking." Ibid. The court also observed that by encouraging consumption, promotional advertising would only exacerbate the current energy situation. Id., at 110, 417 N.Y.S.2d, at 39, 390 N.E.2d, at 758. The court concluded that the governmental interest in the prohibition outweighed the limited constitutional value of the commercial speech at issue. We noted probable jurisdiction, 444 U.S. 962, 100 S.Ct. 446, 62 L.Ed.2d 374 (1979), and now reverse.

II

The Commission's order restricts only commercial speech, that is, expression related solely to the economic interests of the speaker and its audience. Virginia Pharmacy Board v. Virginia Citizens Consumer Council, 425 U.S. 748, 762, 96 S.Ct. 1817, 1825, 48 L.Ed.2d 346 (1976); Bates v. State Bar of Arizona, 433 U.S. 350, 363-364, 97 S.Ct. 2691, 2698-2699, 53 L.Ed.2d 810 (1977); Friedman v. Rogers, 440 U.S. 1, 11, 99 S.Ct. 887, 895, 59 L.Ed.2d 100 (1979). The First Amendment, as applied to the States through the Fourteenth Amendment, protects commercial speech from unwarranted governmental regulation. Virginia Pharmacy Board, 425 U.S., at 761-762, 96 S.Ct., at 1825. Commercial expression not only serves the economic interest of the speaker, but also assists consumers and furthers the societal interest in the fullest possible dissemination of information. In applying the First Amendment to this area, we have rejected the "highly paternalistic" view that government has complete power to suppress or regulate commercial speech. "[P]eople will perceive their own best interests if only they are well enough informed, and . . . the best means to that end is to open the channels of communication rather than to close them. . . ." Id., at 770, 96 S.Ct., at 1829, see Linmark Associates, Inc. v. Willingboro, 431 U.S. 85, 92, 97 S.Ct. 1614, 1618, 50 L.Ed.2d 155 (1977). Even when advertising communicates only an incomplete version of the relevant facts, the First Amendment presumes that some accurate information is better than no information at all. Bates v. State Bar of Arizona, supra, at 374, 97 S.Ct., at 2704.

Nevertheless, our decisions have recognized "the 'commonsense' distinction between speech proposing a commercial transaction, which occurs in an area traditionally subject to government regulation, and other varieties of speech." Ohralik v. Ohio State Bar Assn., 436 U.S. 447, 455-456, 98 S.Ct. 1912, 1918, 56 L.Ed.2d 444 (1978); see Bates v. State Bar of Arizona, supra, 433 U.S., at 381, 97 S.Ct., at 2707; see also Jackson & Jeffries, Commercial Speech: Economic Due Process and the First Amendment, 65 Va.L.Rev. 1, 38-39 (1979). The Constitution therefore accords a lesser protection to commercial speech than to other constitutionally guaranteed expression. 436 U.S., at 456, 457, 98 S.Ct., at 1918, 1919. The protection available for particular commercial expression turns on the nature both of the expression and of the governmental interests served by its regulation.

The First Amendment's concern for commercial speech is based on the informational function of advertising. See First National Bank of Boston v. Bellotti, 435 U.S. 765, 783, 98 S.Ct. 1407, 1419, 55 L.Ed.2d 707 (1978). Consequently, there can be no constitutional objection to the suppression of commercial messages that do not accurately inform the public about lawful activity. The government may ban forms of communication more likely to deceive the public than to inform it, Friedman v. Rogers, supra, at 13, 15-16, 99 S.Ct., at 896, 897; Ohralik v. Ohio State Bar Assn., supra, at 464-465, 98 S.Ct., at 1923-1925, or commercial speech related to illegal activity, Pittsburgh Press Co. v. Human Relations Comm'n, 413 U.S. 376, 388, 93 S.Ct. 2553, 2560, 37 L.Ed.2d 669 (1973).

If the communication is neither misleading nor related to unlawful activity, the government's power is more circumscribed. The State must assert a substantial interest to be achieved by restrictions on commercial speech. Moreover, the regulatory technique must be in proportion to that interest. The limitation on expression must be designed carefully to achieve the State's goal. Compliance with this requirement may be measured by two criteria. First, the restriction must directly advance the state interest involved; the regulation may not be sustained if it provides only ineffective or remote support for the government's purpose. Second, if the governmental interest could be served as well by a more limited restriction on commercial speech, the excessive restrictions cannot survive.

Under the first criterion, the Court has declined to uphold regulations that only indirectly advance the state interest involved. In both Bates and Virginia Pharmacy Board, the Court concluded that an advertising ban could not be imposed to protect the ethical or performance standards of a profession. The Court noted in Virginia Pharmacy Board that "[t]he advertising ban does not directly affect professional standards one way or the other." 425 U.S., at 769, 96 S.Ct., at 1829. In Bates, the Court overturned an advertising prohibition that was designed to protect the "quality" of a lawyer's work. "Restraints on advertising . . . are an ineffective way of deterring shoddy work." 433 U.S., at 378, 97 S.Ct., at 2706.

The second criterion recognizes that the First Amendment mandates that speech restrictions be "narrowly drawn." In re Primus, 436 U.S. 412, 438, 98 S.Ct. 1893, 1908, 56 L.Ed.2d 417 (1978). The regulatory technique may extend only as far as the interest it serves. The State cannot regulate speech that poses no danger to the asserted state interest, see First National Bank of Boston v. Bellotti, supra, at 794-795, 98 S.Ct., at 1425-1426, nor can it completely suppress information when narrower restrictions on expression would serve its interest as well. For example, in Bates the Court explicitly did not "foreclose the possibility that some limited supplementation, by way of warning or disclaimer or the like, might be required" in promotional materials. 433 U.S., at 384, 97 S.Ct., at 2709. See Virginia Pharmacy Board, supra, at 773, 96 S.Ct., at 1831. And in Carey v. Population Services International, 431 U.S. 678, 701-702, 97 S.Ct. 2010, 2025, 52 L.Ed.2d 675 (1977), we held that the State's "arguments ... do not justify the total suppression of advertising concerning contraceptives." This holding left open the possibility that the State could implement more carefully drawn restrictions. See id., at 712, 97 S.Ct., at 2030 (POWELL, J., concurring in part and in judgment); id., at 716-717, 97 S.Ct., at 2032 (STEVENS, J., concurring in part and in judgment).

In commercial speech cases, then, a four-part analysis has developed. At the outset, we must determine whether the expression is protected by the First Amendment. For commercial speech to come within that provision, it at least must concern lawful activity and not be misleading. Next, we ask whether the asserted governmental interest is substantial. If both inquiries yield positive answers, we must determine whether the regulation directly advances the governmental interest asserted, and whether it is not more extensive than is necessary to serve that interest.

III

We now apply this four-step analysis for commercial speech to the Commission's arguments in support of its ban on promotional advertising.

A

The Commission does not claim that the expression at issue either is inaccurate or relates to unlawful activity. Yet the New York Court of Appeals questioned whether Central Hudson's advertising is protected commercial speech. Because appellant holds a monopoly over the sale of electricity in its service area, the state court suggested that the Commission's order restricts no commercial speech of any worth. The court stated that advertising in a "noncompetitive market" could not improve the decisionmaking of consumers. 47 N.Y.2d, at 110, 417 N.Y.S.2d, at 39, 390 N.E.2d, at 757. The court saw no constitutional problem with barring commercial speech that it viewed as conveying little useful information.

This reasoning falls short of establishing that appellant's advertising is not commercial speech protected by the First Amendment. Monopoly over the supply of a product provides no protection from competition with substitutes for that product. Electric utilities compete with suppliers of fuel oil and natural gas in several markets, such as those for home heating and industrial power. This Court noted the existence of interfuel competition 45 years ago, see West Ohio Gas Co. v. Public Utilities Comm'n, 294 U.S. 63, 72, 55 S.Ct. 316, 321, 79 L.Ed. 761 (1935). Each energy source continues to offer peculiar advantages and disadvantages that may influence consumer choice. For consumers in those competitive markets, advertising by utilities is just as valuable as advertising by unregulated firms.

Even in monopoly markets, the suppression of advertising reduces the information available for consumer decisions and thereby defeats the purpose of the First Amendment. The New York court's argument appears to assume that the providers of a monopoly service or product are willing to pay for wholly ineffective advertising. Most businesses--even regulated monopolies--are unlikely to underwrite promotional advertising that is of no interest or use to consumers. Indeed, a monopoly enterprise legitimately may wish to inform the public that it has developed new services or terms of doing business. A consumer may need information to aid his decision whether or not to use the monopoly service at all, or how much of the service he should purchase. In the absence of factors that would distort the decision to advertise, we may assume that the willingness of a business to promote its products reflects a belief that consumers are interested in the advertising. Since no such extraordinary conditions have been identified in this case, appellant's monopoly position does not alter the First Amendment's protection for its commercial speech.

B

The Commission offers two state interests as justifications for the ban on promotional advertising. The first concerns energy conservation. Any increase in demand for electricity--during peak or off-peak periods--means greater consumption of energy. The Commission argues, and the New York court agreed, that the State's interest in conserving energy is sufficient to support suppression of advertising designed to increase consumption of electricity. In view of our country's dependence on energy resources beyond our control, no one can doubt the importance of energy conservation. Plainly, therefore, the state interest asserted is substantial.

The Commission also argues that promotional advertising will aggravate inequities caused by the failure to base the utilities' rates on marginal cost. The utilities argued to the Commission that if they could promote the use of electricity in periods of low demand, they would improve their utilization of generating capacity. The Commission responded that promotion of off-peak consumption also would increase consumption during peak periods. If peak demand were to rise, the absence of marginal cost rates would mean that the rates charged for the additional power would not reflect the true costs of expanding production. Instead, the extra costs would be borne by all consumers through higher overall rates. Without promotional advertising, the Commission stated, this inequitable turn of events would be less likely to occur. The choice among rate structures involves difficult and important questions of economic supply and distributional fairness. The State's concern that rates be fair and efficient represents a clear and substantial governmental interest.

C

Next, we focus on the relationship between the State's interests and the advertising ban. Under this criterion, the Commission's laudable concern over the equity and efficiency of appellant's rates does not provide a constitutionally adequate reason for restricting protected speech. The link between the advertising prohibition and appellant's rate structure is, at most, tenuous. The impact of promotional advertising on the equity of appellant's rates is highly speculative. Advertising to increase off-peak usage would have to increase peak usage, while other factors that directly affect the fairness and efficiency of appellant's rates remained constant. Such conditional and remote eventualities simply cannot justify silencing appellant's promotional advertising.

In contrast, the State's interest in energy conservation is directly advanced by the Commission order at issue here. There is an immediate connection between advertising and demand for electricity. Central Hudson would not contest the advertising ban unless it believed that promotion would increase its sales. Thus, we find a direct link between the state interest in conservation and the Commission's order.

D

We come finally to the critical inquiry in this case: whether the Commission's complete suppression of speech ordinarily protected by the First Amendment is no more extensive than necessary to further the State's interest in energy conservation. The Commission's order reaches all promotional advertising, regardless of the impact of the touted service on overall energy use. But the energy conservation rationale, as important as it is, cannot justify suppressing information about electric devices or services that would cause no net increase in total energy use. In addition, no showing has been made that a more limited restriction on the content of promotional advertising would not serve adequately the State's interests.

Appellant insists that but for the ban, it would advertise products and services that use energy efficiently. These include the "heat pump," which both parties acknowledge to be a major improvement in electric heating, and the use of electric heat as a "backup" to solar and other heat sources. Although the Commission has questioned the efficiency of electric heating before this Court, neither the Commission's Policy Statement nor its order denying rehearing made findings on this issue. In the absence of authoritative findings to the contrary, we must credit as within the realm of possibility the claim that electric heat can be an efficient alternative in some circumstances.

The Commission's order prevents appellant from promoting electric services that would reduce energy use by diverting demand from less efficient sources, or that would consume roughly the same amount of energy as do alternative sources. In neither situation would the utility's advertising endanger conservation or mislead the public. To the extent that the Commission's order suppresses speech that in no way impairs the State's interest in energy conservation, the Commission's order violates the First and Fourteenth Amendments and must be invalidated. See First National Bank of Boston v. Bellotti, 435 U.S. 765, 98 S.Ct. 1407, 55 L.Ed.2d 707 (1978).

The Commission also has not demonstrated that its interest in conservation cannot be protected adequately by more limited regulation of appellant's commercial expression. To further its policy of conservation, the Commission could attempt to restrict the format and content of Central Hudson's advertising. It might, for example, require that the advertisements include information about the relative efficiency and expense of the offered service, both under current conditions and for the foreseeable future. Cf. Banzhaf v. FCC, 132 U.S.App.D.C. 14, 405 F.2d 1082 (1968), cert. denied sub nom. Tobacco Institute, Inc. v. FCC, 396 U.S. 842, 90 S.Ct. 50, 24 L.Ed.2d 93 (1969). In the absence of a showing that more limited speech regulation would be ineffective, we cannot approve the complete suppression of Central Hudson's advertising.

IV

Our decision today in no way disparages the national interest in energy conservation. We accept without reservation the argument that conservation, as well as the development of alternative energy sources, is an imperative national goal. Administrative bodies empowered to regulate electric utilities have the authority--and indeed the duty--to take appropriate action to further this goal. When, however, such action involves the suppression of speech, the First and Fourteenth Amendments require that the restriction be no more extensive than is necessary to serve the state interest. In this case, the record before us fails to show that the total ban on promotional advertising meets this requirement.

Accordingly, the judgment of the New York Court of Appeals is

Reversed.

Robert E. RUBIN, Secretary of the Treasury, Petitioner
v.
COORS BREWING COMPANY, Respondent.

514 U.S. 476

Supreme Court of the United States

Decided April 19, 1995.

Justice Stevens, filed an opinion concurring in the judgment.

Justice THOMAS delivered the opinion of the Court.

Section 5(e)(2) of the Federal Alcohol Administration Act of 1935 prohibits beer labels from displaying alcohol content. We granted certiorari in this case to review the Tenth Circuit's holding that the labeling ban violates the First Amendment because it fails to advance a governmental interest in a direct and material way. Because § 5(e)(2) is inconsistent with the protections granted to commercial speech by the First Amendment, we affirm.

I

Respondent brews beer. In 1987, respondent applied to the Bureau of Alcohol, Tobacco and Firearms (BATF), an agency of the Department of the Treasury, for approval of proposed labels and advertisements that disclosed the alcohol content of its beer. BATF rejected the application on the ground that the Federal Alcohol Administration Act (FAAA or Act), 49 Stat. 977, 27 U.S.C. § 201 et seq., prohibited disclosure of the alcohol content of beer on labels or in advertising. Respondent then filed suit in the District Court for the District of Colorado seeking a declaratory judgment that the relevant provisions of the Act violated the First Amendment; respondent also sought injunctive relief barring enforcement of these provisions. The Government took the position that the ban was necessary to suppress the threat of "strength wars" among brewers, who, without the regulation, would seek to compete in the marketplace based on the potency of their beer.

The District Court granted the relief sought, but a panel of the Court of Appeals for the Tenth Circuit reversed and remanded. Adolph Coors Co. v. Brady, 944 F.2d 1543 (1991). Applying the framework set out in Central Hudson Gas & Electric Corp. v. Public Serv. Comm'n of N.Y., 447 U.S. 557, 100 S.Ct. 2343, 65 L.Ed.2d 341 (1980), the Court of Appeals found that the Government's interest in suppressing alcoholic "strength wars" was "substantial." Brady, supra, at 1547-1549. It further held, however, that the record provided insufficient evidence to determine whether the FAAA's ban on disclosure "directly advanced" that interest. Id., at 1549-1551. The court remanded for further proceedings to ascertain whether a " 'reasonable fit' " existed between the ban and the goal of avoiding strength wars. Id., at 1554.

After further factfinding, the District Court upheld the ban on the disclosure of alcohol content in advertising but invalidated the ban as it applied to labels. Although the Government asked the Tenth Circuit to review the invalidation of the labeling ban, respondent did not appeal the court's decision sustaining the advertising ban. On the case's second appeal, the Court of Appeals affirmed the District Court. Adolph Coors Co. v. Bentsen, 2 F.3d 355 (1993). Following our recent decision in Edenfield v. Fane, 507 U.S. 761, 113 S.Ct. 1792, 123 L.Ed.2d 543 (1993), the Tenth Circuit asked whether the Government had shown that the " 'challenged regulation advances [the government's] interests in a direct and material way.' " 2 F.3d, at 357 (quoting Edenfield, supra, 507 U.S., at ---- - ----, 113 S.Ct., at 1798). After reviewing the record, the Court of Appeals concluded that the Government had failed to demonstrate that the prohibition in any way prevented strength wars. The court found that there was no evidence of any relationship between the publication of factual information regarding alcohol content and competition on the basis of such content. 2 F.3d, at 358-359.

We granted certiorari, 512 U.S. 1203, 114 S.Ct. 2671, 129 L.Ed.2d 807 (1994), to review the Tenth Circuit's decision that § 205(e)(2) violates the First Amendment. We conclude that the ban infringes respondent's freedom of speech, and we therefore affirm.

## II

### A

Soon after the ratification of the Twenty-first Amendment, which repealed the Eighteenth Amendment and ended the Nation's experiment with Prohibition, Congress enacted the FAAA. The statute establishes national rules governing the distribution, production, and importation of alcohol and established a Federal Alcohol Administration to implement these rules. Section 5(e)(2) of the Act prohibits any producer, importer, wholesaler, or bottler of alcoholic beverages from selling, shipping, or delivering in interstate or foreign commerce any malt beverages, distilled spirits, or wines in bottles

> "unless such products are bottled, packaged, and labeled in conformity with such regulations, to be prescribed by the Secretary of the Treasury, with respect to packaging, marking, branding, and labeling and size and fill of container ... as will provide the consumer with adequate information as to the identity and quality of the products, the alcoholic content thereof (except that statements of, or statements likely to be considered as statements of, alcoholic content of malt beverages are prohibited unless required by State law and except that, in case of wines, statements of alcoholic content shall be required only for wines containing more than 14 per centum of alcohol by volume), the net contents of the package, and the manufacturer or bottler or importer of the product." 27 U.S.C. § 205(e)(2) (emphasis added).

The Act defines " 'malt beverage[s]' " in such a way as to include all beers and ales. § 211(a)(7).

Implementing regulations promulgated by BATF (under delegation of authority from the Secretary of the Treasury) prohibit the disclosure of alcohol content on beer labels. 27 CFR § 7.26(a) (1994). In addition to prohibiting numerical indications of alcohol content, the labeling regulations proscribe descriptive terms that suggest high content, such as "strong," "full strength," "extra strength," "high test," "high proof," "pre-war strength," and "full oldtime alcoholic strength." § 7.29(f). The prohibitions do not preclude labels from identifying a beer as "low alcohol," "reduced alcohol," "non-alcoholic," or "alcohol-free." Ibid.; see also § 7.26(b)-(d). By statute and by regulation, the labeling ban must give way if state law requires disclosure of alcohol content.

B

Both parties agree that the information on beer labels constitutes commercial speech. Though we once took the position that the First Amendment does not protect commercial speech, see Valentine v. Chrestensen, 316 U.S. 52, 62 S.Ct. 920, 86 L.Ed. 1262 (1942), we repudiated that position in Virginia State Bd. of Pharmacy v. Virginia Citizens Consumer Council, Inc., 425 U.S. 748, 96 S.Ct. 1817, 48 L.Ed.2d 346 (1976). There we noted that the free flow of commercial information is "indispensable to the proper allocation of resources in a free enterprise system" because it informs the numerous private decisions that drive the system. Id., at 765, 96 S.Ct., at 1827. Indeed, we observed that a "particular consumer's interest in the free flow of commercial information ... may be as keen, if not keener by far, than his interest in the day's most urgent political debate." Id., at 763, 96 S.Ct., at 1826.

Still, Virginia Board of Pharmacy suggested that certain types of restrictions might be tolerated in the commercial speech area because of the nature of such speech. See id., at 771-772, n. 24, 96 S.Ct., at 1830-1831, n. 24. In later decisions we gradually articulated a test based on " 'the "commonsense" distinction between speech proposing a commercial transaction, which occurs in an area traditionally subject to government regulation, and other varieties of speech.' " Central Hudson Gas & Electric Corp. v. Public Serv. Comm'n of N.Y., 447 U.S. 557, 562, 100 S.Ct. 2343, 2349, 65 L.Ed.2d 341 (1980) (quoting Ohralik v. Ohio State Bar Assn., 436 U.S. 447, 455-456, 98 S.Ct. 1912, 1918-1919, 56 L.Ed.2d 444 (1978)). Central Hudson identified several factors that courts should consider in determining whether a regulation of commercial speech survives First Amendment scrutiny:

> "For commercial speech to come within [the First Amendment], it at least must concern lawful activity and not be misleading. Next, we ask whether the asserted governmental interest is substantial. If both inquiries yield positive answers, we must determine whether the regulation directly advances the governmental interest asserted, and whether it is not more extensive than is necessary to serve that interest." 447 U.S., at 566, 100 S.Ct., at 2351.

We now apply Central Hudson's test to § 205(e)(2).

III

Both the lower courts and the parties agree that respondent seeks to disclose only truthful, verifiable, and nonmisleading factual information about alcohol content on its beer labels. Thus, our analysis focuses on the substantiality of the interest behind § 205(e)(2) and on whether the labeling ban bears an acceptable fit with the Government's goal. A careful consideration of these factors indicates that § 205(e)(2) violates the First Amendment's protection of commercial speech.

A

The Government identifies two interests it considers sufficiently "substantial" to justify § 205(e)(2)'s labeling ban. First, the Government contends that § 205(e)(2) advances Congress' goal of curbing "strength wars" by beer brewers who might seek to compete for customers on the basis of alcohol content. According to the Government, the FAAA's restriction prevents a particular type of beer drinker--one who selects a beverage because of its high potency--from choosing beers solely for their alcohol content. In the Government's view, restricting disclosure of information regarding a particular product characteristic will decrease the extent to which consumers will select the product on the basis of that characteristic.

Respondent counters that Congress actually intended the FAAA to achieve the far different purpose of preventing brewers from making inaccurate claims concerning alcohol content. According to respondent, when Congress passed the FAAA in 1935, brewers did not have the technology to produce beer with alcohol levels within predictable tolerances--a skill that modern beer producers now possess. Further, respondent argues that the true policy guiding federal alcohol regulation is not aimed at suppressing strength wars. If such were the goal, the Government would not pursue the opposite policy with respect to wines and distilled spirits. Although § 205(e)(2) requires BATF to promulgate regulations barring the disclosure of alcohol content on beer labels, it also orders BATF to require the disclosure of alcohol content on the labels of wines and spirits. See 27 CFR § 4.36 (1994) (wines); § 5.37 (distilled spirits).

Rather than suppressing the free flow of factual information in the wine and spirits markets, the Government seeks to control competition on the basis of strength by monitoring distillers' promotions and marketing. The respondent quite correctly notes that the general thrust of federal alcohol policy appears to favor greater disclosure of information, rather than less. This also seems to be the trend in federal regulation of other consumer products as well. See, e.g., Nutrition Labeling and Education Act of 1990, Pub.L.101-535, 104 Stat. 2353, as amended (requiring labels of food products sold in the United States to display nutritional information).

Respondent offers a plausible reading of the purpose behind § 205(e)(2), but the prevention of misleading statements of alcohol content need not be the exclusive government interest served by § 205(e)(2). In Posadas de Puerto Rico Associates v. Tourism Co. of Puerto Rico, 478 U.S. 328, 341, 106 S.Ct. 2968, 2976, 92 L.Ed.2d 266 (1986), we found that the Puerto Rico Legislature's interest in promoting the health, safety, and welfare of its citizens by reducing their demand for gamblingprovided a sufficiently "substantial" governmental interest to justify the regulation of gamblingadvertising. So too the Government here has a significant interest in protecting the health, safety, and welfare of its citizens by preventing brewers from competing on the basis of alcohol strength, which could lead to greater alcoholism and its attendant social costs. Both panels of the Court of Appeals that heard this case concluded that the goal of suppressing strength wars constituted a substantial interest, and we cannot say that their conclusion is erroneous. We have no reason to think that strength wars, if they were to occur, would not produce the type of social harm that the Government hopes to prevent.

The Government attempts to bolster its position by arguing that the labeling ban not only curbs strength wars, but also "facilitates" state efforts to regulate alcohol under the Twenty-first Amendment. The Solicitor General directs us to United States v. Edge Broadcasting Co., 509 U.S. 418, 113 S.Ct. 2696, 125 L.Ed.2d 345 (1993), in which we upheld a federal law that prohibited lottery advertising by radio stations located in States that did not operate lotteries. That case involved a station located in North Carolina (a nonlottery state) that broadcast lottery advertisements primarily into Virginia(a State with a lottery). We upheld the statute against First Amendment challenge in part because it supported North Carolina's antigambling policy without unduly interfering with States that sponsored lotteries. Id., at ---- - ----, 113 S.Ct., at ---- - ----. (slip op., at 12-15). In this case, the Government claims that the interest behind § 205(e)(2) mirrors that of the statute in Edge Broadcasting because it prohibits disclosure of alcohol content only in States that do not affirmatively require brewers to provide that information. In the Government's view, this saves States that might wish to ban such labels the trouble of enacting their own legislation, and it discourages beer drinkers from crossing state lines to buy beer they believe is stronger.

We conclude that the Government's interest in preserving state authority is not sufficiently substantial to meet the requirements of Central Hudson. Even if the Federal Government possessed the broad authority to facilitate state powers, in this case the Government has offered nothing that suggests that States are in need of federal assistance. States clearly possess ample authority to ban the disclosure of alcohol content--subject, of course, to the same First Amendment restrictions that apply to the Federal Government. Unlike the situation in Edge Broadcasting, the policies of some States do not prevent neighboring States from pursuing their own alcohol-related policies within their respective borders. One State's decision to permit brewers to disclose alcohol content on beer labels will not preclude neighboring States from effectively banning such disclosure of that information within their borders.

### B

The remaining Central Hudson factors require that a valid restriction on commercial speech directly advance the governmental interest and be no more extensive than necessary to serve that interest. We have said that "[t]he last two steps of the Central Hudson analysis basically involve a consideration of the 'fit' between the legislature's ends and the means chosen to accomplish those ends." Posadas, supra, 478 U.S., at 341, 106 S.Ct., at 2977. The Tenth Circuit found that § 205(e)(2) failed to advance the interest in suppressing strength wars sufficiently to justify the ban. We agree.

Just two Terms ago, in Edenfeld v. Fane, 507 U.S. 761, 113 S.Ct. 1792, 123 L.Ed.2d 543 (1993), we had occasion to explain the Central Hudson factor concerning whether the regulation of commercial speech "directly advances the governmental interest asserted." In Edenfield, we decided that the Government carries the burden of showing that the challenged regulation advances the Government's interest "in a direct and material way." Id., at ----, 113 S.Ct., at 1798. That burden "is not satisfied by mere speculation and conjecture; rather, a governmental body seeking to sustain a restriction on commercial speech must demonstrate that the harms it recites are real and that its restriction will in fact alleviate them to a material degree." Id., at ----, 113 S.Ct., at 1800. We cautioned that this requirement was critical; otherwise, "a State could with ease restrict commercial speech in the service of other objectives that could not themselves justify a burden on commercial expression." Ibid.

The Government attempts to meet its burden by pointing to current developments in the consumer market. It claims that beer producers are already competing and advertising on the basis of alcohol strength in the "malt liquor" segment of the beer market. The Government attempts to show that this competition threatens to spread to the rest of the market by directing our attention to respondent's motives in bringing this litigation. Respondent allegedly suffers from consumer misperceptions that its beers contain less alcohol than other brands. According to the Government, once respondent gains relief from § 205(e)(2), it will use its labels to overcome this handicap.

Under the Government's theory, § 205(e)(2) suppresses the threat of such competition by preventing consumers from choosing beers on the basis of alcohol content. It is assuredly a matter of "common sense," Brief for Petitioner 27, that a restriction on the advertising of a product characteristic will decrease the extent to which consumers select a product on the basis of that trait. In addition to common sense, the Government urges us to turn to history as a guide. According to the Government, at the time Congress enacted the FAAA, the use of labels displaying alcohol content had helped produce a strength war. Section 205(e)(2) allegedly relieved competitive pressures to market beer on the basis of alcohol content, resulting over the long term in beers with lower alcohol levels.

We conclude that § 205(e)(2) cannot directly and materially advance its asserted interest because of the overall irrationality of the Government's regulatory scheme. While the laws governing labeling prohibit the disclosure of alcohol content unless required by state law, federal regulations apply a contrary policy to beer advertising. 27 U.S.C. § 205(f)(2); 27 CFR § 7.50 (1994). Like § 205(e)(2), these restrictions prohibit statements of alcohol content in advertising, but, unlike § 205(e)(2), they apply only in States that affirmatively prohibit such advertisements. As only 18 States at best prohibit disclosure of content in advertisements, App. to Brief for Respondent 1a-12a, brewers remain free to disclose alcohol content in advertisements, but not on labels, in much of the country. The failure to prohibit the disclosure of alcohol content in advertising, which would seem to constitute a more influential weapon in any strength war than labels, makes no rational sense if the government's true aim is to suppress strength wars.

Other provisions of the FAAA and its regulations similarly undermine § 205(e)(2)'s efforts to prevent strength wars. While § 205(e)(2) bans the disclosure of alcohol content on beer labels, it allows the exact opposite in the case of wines and spirits. Thus, distilled spirits may contain statements of alcohol content, 27 CFR § 5.37 (1994), and such disclosures are required for wines with more than 14 percent alcohol, 27 CFR § 4.36 (1994). If combatting strength wars were the goal, we would assume that Congress would regulate disclosure of alcohol content for the strongest beverages as well as for the weakest ones. Further, the Government permits brewers to signal high alcohol content through use of the term "malt liquor." Although the Secretary has proscribed the use of various colorful terms suggesting high alcohol levels, 27 CFR § 7.29(f) (1994), manufacturers still can distinguish a class of stronger malt beverages by identifying them as malt liquors. One would think that if the Government sought to suppress strength wars by prohibiting numerical disclosures of alcohol content, it also would preclude brewers from indicating higher alcohol beverages by using descriptive terms.

While we are mindful that respondent only appealed the constitutionality of § 205(e)(2), these exemptions and inconsistencies bring into question the purpose of the labelling ban. To be sure, the Government's interest in combatting strength wars remains a valid goal. But the irrationality of this unique and puzzling regulatory framework ensures that the labeling ban will fail to achieve that end. There is little chance that § 205(e)(2) can directly and materially advance its aim, while other provisions of the same act directly undermine and counteract its effects.

This conclusion explains the findings of the courts below. Both the District Court and the Court of Appeals found that the Government had failed to present any credible evidence showing that the disclosure of alcohol content would promote strength wars. In the District Court's words, "none of the witnesses, none of the depositions that I have read, no credible evidence that I have heard, lead[s] me to believe that giving alcoholic content on labels will in any way promote ... strength wars." App. to Pet. for Cert. A-38. See also Bentsen, 2 F.3d, at 359. Indeed, the District Court concluded that "[p]rohibiting the alcoholic content disclosure of malt beverages on labels has little, if anything, to do with the type of advertising that promotes strength wars." App. to Pet. for Cert. A-36. As the FAAA's exceptions and regulations would have counteracted any effect the labeling ban had exerted, it is not surprising that the lower courts did not find any evidence that § 205(e)(2) had suppressed strength wars.

The Government's brief submits anecdotal evidence and educated guesses to suggest that competition on the basis of alcohol content is occurring today and that § 205(e)(2)'s ban has constrained strength wars that otherwise would burst out of control. These various tidbits, however, cannot overcome the irrationality of the regulatory scheme and the weight of the record. The Government did not offer any convincing evidence that the labeling ban has inhibited strength wars. Indeed, it could not, in light of the effect of the FAAA's other provisions. The absence of strength wars over the past six decades may have resulted from any number of factors.

Nor do we think that respondent's litigating positions can be used against it as proof that the Government's regulation is necessary. That respondent wishes to disseminate factual information concerning alcohol content does not demonstrate that it intends to compete on the basis of alcohol content. Brewers may have many different reasons--only one of which might be a desire to wage a strength war--why they wish to disclose the potency of their beverages.

Even if § 205(e)(2) did meet the Edenfield standard, it would still not survive First Amendment scrutiny because the Government's regulation of speech is not sufficiently tailored to its goal. The Government argues that a sufficient "fit" exists here because the labeling ban applies to only one product characteristic and because the ban does not prohibit all disclosures of alcohol content--it applies only to those involving labeling and advertising. In response, respondent suggests several alternatives, such as directly limiting the alcohol content of beers, prohibiting marketing efforts emphasizing high alcohol strength (which is apparently the policy in some other Western nations), or limiting the labeling ban only to malt liquors, which is the segment of the market that allegedly is threatened with a strength war. We agree that the availability of these options, all of which could advance the Government's asserted interest in a manner less intrusive to respondent's First Amendment rights, indicates that § 205(e)(2) is more extensive than necessary.

## IV

In sum, although the Government may have a substantial interest in suppressing strength wars in the beer market, the FAAA's countervailing provisions prevent § 205(e)(2) from furthering that purpose in a direct and material fashion. The FAAA's defects are further highlighted by the availability of alternatives that would prove less intrusive to the First Amendment's protections for commercial speech. Because we find that § 205(e)(2) fails the Central Hudson test, we affirm the decision of the court below.

It is so ordered.

FEDERAL TRADE COMMISSION, Petitioner,

v.

COLGATE-PALMOLIVE CO. et al.

380 U.S. 374

Supreme Court of the United States

Decided April 5, 1965.

Mr. Chief Justice WARREN delivered the opinion of the Court.

The basic question before us is whether it is a deceptive trade practice, prohibited by s 5 of the Federal Trade Commission Act, to represent falsely that a televised test, experiment, or demonstration provides a viewer with visual proof of a product claim, regardless of whether the product claim is itself true.

The case arises out of an attempt by respondent Colgate-Palmolive Company to prove to the television public that its shaving cream, 'Rapid Shave,' out- shaves them all. Respondent Ted Bates & Company, Inc., an advertising agency, prepared for Colgate three one-minute commercials designed to show that Rapid Shave could soften even the toughness of sandpaper. Each of the commercials contained the same 'sandpaper test.' The announcer informed the audience that, 'To prove RAPID SHAVE'S super-moisturizing power, we put it right from the can onto this tough, dry sandpaper. It was apply * * * soak * * * and off in a stroke.' While the announcer was speaking, Rapid Shave was applied to a substance that appeared to be sandpaper, and immediately thereafter a razor was shown shaving the substance clean.

The Federal Trade Commission issued a complaint against respondents Colgate and Bates charging that the commercials were false and deceptive. The evidence before the hearing examiner disclosed that sandpaper of the type depicted in the commercials could not be shaved immediately following the application of Rapid Shave, but required a substantial soaking period of approximately 80 minutes. The evidence also showed that the substance resembling sandpaper was in fact a simulated prop, or 'mock-up,' made of plexiglass to which sand had been applied. However, the examiner found that Rapid Shave could shave sandpaper, even though not in the short time represented by the commercials, and that if real sandpaper had been used in the commercials the inadequacies of television transmission would have made it appear to viewers to be nothing more than plain, colored paper. The examiner dismissed the complaint because neither misrepresentation--concerning the actual moistening time or the identity of the shaved substance--was in his opinion a material one that would mislead the public.

The Commission, in an opinion dated December 29, 1961, reversed the hearing examiner. It found that since Rapid Shave could not shave sandpaper within the time depicted in the commercials, respondents had misrepresented the product's moisturizing power. Moreover, the Commission found that the undisclosed use of a plexiglass substitute for sandpaper was an additional material misrepresentation that was a deceptive act separate and distinct from the misrepresentation concerning Rapid Shave's underlying qualities. Even if the sandpaper could be shaved just as depicted in the commercials, the Commission found that viewers had been misled into believing they had seen it done with their own eyes. As a result of these findings the Commission entered a cease-and-desist order against the respondents.

An appeal was taken to the Court of Appeals for the First Circuit which rendered an opinion on November 20, 1962, 310 F.2d 89. That court sustained the Commission's conclusion that respondents had misrepresented the qualities of Rapid Shave, but it would not accept the Commission's order forbidding the future use of undisclosed simulations in television commercials. It set aside the Commission's order and directed that a new order be entered. On May 7, 1963, the Commission, over the protest of respondents, issued a new order narrowing and clarifying its original order to comply with the court's mandate. The Court of Appeals again found unsatisfactory that portion of the order dealing with simulated props and refused to enforce it, 326 F.2d 517. We granted certiorari, 377 U.S. 942, 84 S.Ct. 1352, 12 L.Ed.2d 306, to consider this aspect of the case and do not have before us any question concerning the misrepresentation that Rapid Shave could shave sandpaper immediately after application, that being conceded . . . .

II.

In reviewing the substantive issues in the case, it is well to remember the respective roles of the Commission and the courts in the administration of the Federal Trade Commission Act. When the Commission was created by Congress in 1914, it was directed by s 5 to prevent '(u)nfair methods of competition in commerce.' Congress amended the Act in 1938 to extend the Commission's jurisdiction to include 'unfair or deceptive acts or practices in commerce'--a significant amendment showing Congress' concern for consumers as well as for competitors. It is important to note the generality of these standards of illegality; the proscriptions in s 5 are flexible, 'to be defined with particularity by the myriad of cases from the field of business.' Federal Trade Comm. v. Motion Picture Advertising Service Co., 344 U.S. 392, 394, 73 S.Ct. 361, 363, 97 L.Ed. 426.

This statutory scheme necessarily gives the Commission an influential role in interpreting s 5 and in applying it to the facts of particular cases arising out of unprecedented situations. Moreover, as an administrative agency which deals continually with cases in the area, the Commission is often in a better position than are courts to determine when a practice is 'deceptive' within the meaning of the Act. This Court has frequently stated that the Commission's judgment is to be given great weight by reviewing courts. This admonition is especially true with respect to allegedly deceptive advertising since the finding of a s 5 violation in this field rests so heavily on inference and pragmatic judgment. Nevertheless, while informed judicial determination is dependent upon enlightenment gained from administrative experience, in the last analysis the words 'deceptive practices' set forth a legal standard and they must get their final meaning from judicial construction. Cf. Federal Trade Comm. v. R. F. Keppel & Bro., Inc., 291 U.S. 304, 314, 54 S.Ct. 423, 427, 78 L.Ed. 814.

We are not concerned in this case with the clear misrepresentation in the commercials concerning the speed with which Rapid Shave could shave sandpaper, since the Court of Appeals upheld the Commission's finding on that matter and the respondents have not challenged the finding here. We granted certiorari to consider the Commission's conclusion that even if an advertiser has himself conducted a test, experiment or demonstration which he honestly believes will prove a certain product claim, he may not convey to television viewers the false impression that they are seeing the test, experiment or demonstration for themselves, when they are not because of the undisclosed use of mock-ups.

We accept the Commission's determination that the commercials involved in this case contained three representations to the public: (1) that sandpaper could be shaved by Rapid Shave; (2) that an experiment had been conducted which verified this claim; and (3) that the viewer was seeing this experiment for himself. Respondents admit that the first two representations were made, but deny that the third was. The Commission, however, found to the contrary, and, since this is a matter of fact resting on an inference that could reasonably be drawn from the commercials themselves, the Commission's finding should be sustained. For the purposes of our review, we can assume that the first two representations were true; the focus of our consideration is on the third which was clearly false. The parties agree that s 5 prohibits the intentional misrepresentation of any fact which would constitute a material factor in a purchaser's decision whether to buy. They differ, however, in their conception of what 'facts' constitute a 'material factor' in a purchaser's decision to buy. Respondents submit, in effect, that the only material facts are those which deal with the substantive qualities of a product. The Commission, on the other hand, submits that the misrepresentation of any fact so long as it materially induces a purchaser's decision to buy is a deception prohibited by s 5.

The Comission's interpretation of what is a deceptive practice seems more in line with the decided cases than that of respondents. This Court said in Federal Trade Comm. v. Algoma Lumber Co., 291 U.S. 67, 78, 54 S.Ct. 315, 320, 78 L.Ed. 655: '(T)he public is entitled to get what it chooses, though the choice may be dictated by caprice or by fashion or perhaps by ignorance.' It has long been considered a deceptive practice to state falsely that a product ordinarily sells for an inflated price but that it is being offered at a special reduced price, even if the offered price represents the actual value of the product and the purchaser is receiving his money's worth. Applying respondents' arguments to these cases, it would appear that so long as buyers paid no more than the product was actually worth and the product contained the qualities advertised, the misstatement of an inflated original price was immaterial.

It has also been held a violation of s 5 for a seller to misrepresent to the public that he is in a certain line of business, even though the misstatement in no way affects the qualities of the product. As was said in Federal Trade Comm. v. Royal Milling Co., 288 U.S. 212, 216, 53 S.Ct. 335, 336, 77 L.Ed. 706:

> 'If consumers or dealers prefer to purchase a given article because it was made by a particular manufacturer or class of manufacturers, they have a right to do so, and this right cannot be satisfied by imposing upon them an exactly similar article, or one equally as good, but having a different origin.'

The courts of appeals have applied this reasoning to the merchandising of reprocessed products that are as good as new, without a disclosure that they are in fact reprocessed. And it has also been held that it is a deceptive practice to misappropriate the trade name of another.

Respondents claim that all these cases are irrelevant to our decision because they involve misrepresentations related to the product itself and not merely to the manner in which an advertising message is communicated. This distinction misses the mark for two reasons. In the first place, the present case is not concerned with a mode of communication, but with a misrepresentation that viewers have objective proof of a seller's product claim over and above the seller's word. Secondly, all of the above cases, like the present case, deal with methods designed to get a consumer to purchase a product, not with whether the product, when purchased, will perform up to expectations. We find an especially strong similarity between the present case and those cases in which a seller induces the public to purchase an arguably good product by misrepresenting his line of business, by concealing the fact that the product is reprocessed, or by misappropriating another's trademark. In each the seller has used a misrepresentation to break down what he regards to be an annoying or irrational habit of the buying public--the preference for particular manufacturers or known brands regardless of a product's actual qualities, the prejudice against reprocessed goods, and the desire for verification of a product claim. In each case the seller reasons that when the habit is broken the buyer will be satisfied with the performance of the product he receives. Yet, a misrepresentation has been used to break the habit and, as was stated in Algoma Lumber, a misrepresentation for such an end is not permitted.

We need not limit ourselves to the cases already mentioned because there are other situations which also illustrate the correctness of the Commission's finding in the present case. It is generally accepted that it is a deceptive practice to state falsely that a product has received a testimonial from a respected source. In addition, the Commission has consistently acted to prevent sellers from falsely stating that their product claims have been 'certified.' We find these situations to be indistinguishable from the present case. We can assume that in each the underlying product claim is true and in each the seller actually conducted an experiment sufficient to prove to himself the truth of the claim. But in each the seller has told the public that it could rely on something other than his word concerning both the truth of the claim and the validity of his experiment. We find it an immaterial difference that in one case the viewer is told to rely on the word of a celebrity or authority he respects, in another on the word of a testing agency, and in the present case on his own perception of an undisclosed simulation.

Respondents again insist that the present case is not like any of the above, but is more like a case in which a celebrity or independent testing agency has in fact submitted a written verification of an experiment actually observed, but, because of the inability of the camera to transmit accurately an impression of the paper on which the testimonial is written, the seller reproduces it on another substance so that it can be seen by the viewing audience. This analogy ignores the finding of the Commission that in the present case the seller misrepresented to the public that it was being given objective proof of a product claim. In respondents' hypothetical the objective proof of the product claim that is offered, the word of the celebrity or agency that the experiment was actually conducted, does exist; while in the case before us the objective proof offered, the viewer's own perception of an actual experiment, does not exist. Thus, in respondents' hypothetical, unlike the present case, the use of the undisclosed mock-up does not conflict with the seller's claim that there is objective proof.

We agree with the Commission, therefore, that the undisclosed use of plexiglass in the present commercials was a material deceptive practice, independent and separate from the other misrepresentation found. We find unpersuasive respondents' other objections to this conclusion. Respondents claim that it will be impractical to inform the viewing public that it is not seeing an actual test, experiment or demonstration, but we think it inconceivable that the ingenious advertising world will be unable, if it so desires, to conform to the Commission's insistence that the public be not misinformed. If, however, it becomes impossible or impractical to show simulated demonstrations on television in a truthful manner, this indicates that television is not a medium that lends itself to this type of commercial, not that the commercial must survive at all costs. Similarly unpersuasive is respondents' objection that the Commission's decision discriminates against sellers whose product claims cannot be 'verified' on television without the use of simulations. All methods of advertising do not equally favor every seller. If the inherent limitations of a method do not permit its use in the way a seller desires, the seller cannot by material misrepresentation compensate for those limitations.

Respondents also claim that the Commission reached out to decide a question not properly before it and has presented this Court with an abstract question. They argue that since the commercials in the present case misrepresented the time element involved in shaving sandpaper, this Court should not consider the additional misrepresentation that the public had objective proof of the seller's claim. As we have already said, these misrepresentations are separate and distinct, and we fail to see why respondents should be sheltered from a cease-and-desist order with respect to one deceptive practice merely because they also engaged in another.

Respondents finally object to what they consider to be the absence of an adequate record to sustain the Commission's finding. It is true that in its initial stages the case was concerned more with the misrepresentation about the product's underlying qualities than with the misrepresentation that objective proof was being given. Nevertheless, both misrepresentations were in the case from the beginning, and respondents were never prejudicially misled into believing that the second question was not being considered. Nor was it necessary for the Commission to conduct a survey of the viewing public before it could determine that the commercials had a tendency to mislead, for when the Commission finds deception it is also authorized, within the bounds of reason, to infer that the deception will constitute a material factor in a purchaser's decision to buy. See Federal Trade Comm. v. Raladam Co., 316 U.S. 149, 152, 62 S.Ct. 966, 968, 86 L.Ed. 1336. We find the record in this case sufficient to support the Commission's findings.

III.

We turn our attention now to the order issued by the Commission. It has been repeatedly held that the Commission has wide discretion in determining the type of order that is necessary to cope with the unfair practices found, e.g., Jacob Siegel Co. v. Federal Trade Comm., 327 U.S. 608, 611, 66 S.Ct. 758, 759, 90 L.Ed. 888, and that Congress has placed the primary responsibility for fashioning orders upon the Commission, Federal Trade Comm. v. National Lead Co., 352 U.S. 419, 429, 77 S.Ct. 502, 509, 1 L.Ed.2d 438. For these reasons the courts should not 'lightly modify' the Commission's orders. Federal Trade Comm. v. Cement Institute, 333 U.S. 683, 726, 68 S.Ct. 793, 815, 92 L.Ed. 1010. However, this Court has also warned that an order's prohibitions 'should be clear and precise in order that they may be understood by those against whom they are directed,' Federal Trade Comm. v. Cement Institute, supra, at 726, 68 S.Ct. at 815, and that '(t)he severity of possible penalties prescribed * * * for violations of orders which have become final underlines the necessity for fashioning orders which are, at the outset, sufficiently clear and precise to avoid raising serious questions as to their meaning and application.' Federal Trade Comm. v. Henry Broch & Co., 368 U.S. 360, 367--368, 82 S.Ct. 431, 436, 7 L.Ed.2d 353.

The Court of Appeals has criticized the reference in the Commission's order to 'test, experiment or demonstration' as not capable of practical interpretation. It could find no difference between the Rapid Shave commercial and a commercial which extolled the goodness of ice cream while giving viewers a picture of a scoop of mashed potatoes appearing to be ice cream. We do not understand this difficulty. In the ice cream case the mashed potato prop is not being used for additional proof of the product claim, while the purpose of the Rapid Shave commercial is to give the viewer objective proof of the claims made. If in the ice cream hypothetical the focus of the commercial becomes the undisclosed potato prop and the viewer is invited, explicitly or by implication, to see for himself the truth of the claims about the ice cream's rich texture and full color, and perhaps compare it to a 'rival product,' then the commercial has become similar to the one now before us. Clearly, however, a commercial which depicts happy actors delightedly eating ice cream that is in fact mashed potatoes or drinking a product appearing to be coffee but which is in fact some other substance is not covered by the present order.

The crucial terms of the present order--'test, experiment or demonstration * * * represented * * * as actual proof of a claim'--are as specific as the circumstances will permit. If respondents in their subsequent commercials attempt to come as close to the line of misrepresentation as the Commission's order permits, they may without specifically intending to do so cross into the area proscribed by this order. However, it does not seem 'unfair to require that one who deliberately goes perilously close to an area of proscribed conduct shall take the risk that he may cross the line.' Boyce Motor Lines, Inc. v. United States, 342 U.S. 337, 340, 72 S.Ct. 329, 331, 96 L.Ed. 367. In commercials where the emphasis is on the seller's word, and not on the viewer's own perception, the respondents need not fear that an undisclosed use of props is prohibited by the present order. On the other hand, when the commercial not only makes a claim, but also invites the viewer to rely on his own perception, for demonstrative proof of the claim, the respondents will be aware that the use of undisclosed props in strategic places might be a material deception. We believe that respondents will have no difficulty applying the Commission's order to the vast majority of their contemplated future commercials. If, however, a situation arises in which respondents are sincerely unable to determine whether a proposed course of action would violate the present order, they can, by complying with the Commission's rules, oblige the Commission to give them definitive advice as to whether their proposed action, if pursued, would constitute compliance with the order.

Finally, we find no defect in the provision of the order which prohibits respondents from engagingin similar practices with respect to 'any product' they advertise. The propriety of a broad order depends upon the specific circumstances of the case, but the courts will not interfere except where the remedy selected has no reasonable relation to the unlawful practices found to exist. In this case the respondents produced three different commercials which employed the same deceptive practice. This we believe gave the Commission a sufficient basis for believing that the respondents would be inclined to use similar commercials with respect to the other products they advertise. We think it reasonable for the Commission to frame its order broadly enough to prevent respondents from engaging in similarly illegal practices in future advertisements. As was said in Federal Trade Comm. v. Ruberoid Co., 343 U.S. 470, 473, 72 S.Ct. 800, 803, 96 L.Ed. 1081: '(T)he Commission is not limited to prohibiting the illegal practice in the precise form in which it is found to have existed in the past.' Having been caught violating the Act, respondents 'must expect some fencing in.' Federal Trade Comm. v. National Lead Co., 352 U.S. 419, 431, 77 S.Ct. 502, 510, 1 L.Ed.2d 438.

The judgment of the Court of Appeals is reversed and the case remanded for the entry of a judgment enforcing the Commission's order.

Reversed and remanded.

Mr. Justice HARLAN, whom Mr. Justice STEWART joins, dissenting in part.

Under the limited grant of certiorari in this case, the Court must assume that the advertiser can perform the experiment in question and that the demonstration is as simple to execute as it appears on television. The only question here is what techniques the advertiser may use to convey essential truth to the television viewer. If the claim is true and valid, then the technique for projecting that claim, within broad boundaries, falls purely within the advertiser's art. The warrant to the Federal Trade Commission is to police the verity of the claim itself.

I do not agree that the use of 'mock-ups' by the television advertiser is of itself a deceptive trade practice. Further, while there was an independent deceptive element in this commercial, I do not think this record justifies the broad remedial order issued by the Commission. I would remand the case to the Commission for further proceedings.

## I.
## 'MOCK-UPS' AS SUCH.

The faulty prop in the Court's reasoning is that it focuses entirely on what is taking place in the studio rather than on what the viewer is seeing on his screen. That which the viewer sees with his own eyes is not, however, what is taking place in the studio, but an electronic image. If the image he sees on the screen is an accurate reproduction of what he would see with the naked eyes were the experiment performed before him with sandpaper in his home or in the studio, there can hardly be a misrepresentation in any legally significant sense. While the Commission undoubtedly possesses broad authority to give content to the proscriptions of the Act, its discretion, as the Court recognizes, is not unbridled, and 'in the last analysis the words 'deceptive practices' set forth a legal standard and they must get their final meaning from judicial construction' (ante, p. 1043). In this case, assuming that Rapid Shave could soften sandpaper as quickly as it does sand-covered plexiglass, a viewer who wants to entertain his friends by duplicating the actual experiment could do so by buying a can of Rapid Shave and some sandpaper. If he wished to shave himself, and his beard were really as tough as sandpaper, he could perform this part of his morning ablutions with Rapid Shave in the same way as he saw the plexiglass shaved on television.

I do not see how such a commercial can be said to be 'deceptive' in any legally acceptable use of that term. The Court attempts to distinguish the case where a 'celebrity' has written a testimonial endorsing some product, but the original testimonial cannot be seen over television and a copy is shown over the air by the manufacturer. The Court states of this 'hypothetical': 'In respondents' hypothetical the objective proof of the product claim that is offered, the word of the celebrity or agency that the experiment was actually conducted, does exist; while in the case before us the objective proof offered, the viewer's own perception of an actual experiment, does not exist.' Ante, at 1045. But in both cases the viewer is told to 'see for himself,' in the one case that the celebrity has endorsed the product; in the other, that the product can shave sandpaper; in neither case is the viewer actually seeing the proof; and in both cases the objective proof does exist, be it the original testimonial or the sandpaper test actually conducted by the manufacturer. In neither case, however, is there a material misrepresentation, because what the viewer sees is an accurate image of the objective proof.

Nor can I readily understand how the accurate portrayal of an experiment by means of a mock-up can be considered more deceptive than the use of mashed potatoes to convey the glamorous qualities of a particular ice cream (ante, pp. 1046--1047); indeed, to a potato-lover 'the smile on the face of the tiger' might come more naturally than if he were actually being served ice cream.

It is commonly known that television presents certain distortions in transmission for which the broadcasting industry must compensate. Thus, a white towel will look a dingy gray over television, but a blue towel will look a sparkling white. On the Court's analysis, an advertiser must achieve accuracy in the studio even though it results in an inaccurate image being projected on the home screen. This led the Court of Appeals to question whether it would be proper for an advertiser to show a product on television that somehow, because of the medium, looks better on the screen than it does in real life. 310 F.2d 89, 94; 326 F.2d 517, 523, n. 16.

John R. BATES and Van O'Steen, Appellants,

v.

STATE BAR OF ARIZONA.

433 U.S. 350

Supreme Court of the United States

Decided June 27, 1977.

Mr. Justice BLACKMUN delivered the opinion of the Court.

As part of its regulation of the Arizona Bar, the Supreme Court of that State has imposed and enforces a disciplinary rule that restricts advertising by attorneys. This case presents two issues: whether ss 1 and 2 of the Sherman Act, 15 U.S.C. ss 1 and 2, forbid such state regulation, and whether the operation of the rule violates the First Amendment, made applicable to the State through the Fourteenth.

I

Appellants John R. Bates and Van O'Steen are attorneys licensed to practice law in the State of Arizona. As such, they are members of the appellee, the State Bar of Arizona. After admission to the bar in 1972, appellants worked as attorneys with the Maricopa County Legal Aid Society. App. 221.

In March 1974, appellants left the Society and opened a law office, which they call a 'legal clinic,' in Phoenix. Their aim was to provide legal services at modest fees to persons of moderate income who did not qualify for governmental legal aid. Id., at 75. In order to achieve this end, they would accept only routine matters, such as uncontested divorces, uncontested adoptions, simple personal bankruptcies, and changes of name, for which costs could be kept down by extensive use of paralegals, automatic typewriting equipment, and standardized forms and office procedures. More complicated cases, such as contested divorces, would not be accepted. Id., at 97. Because appellants set their prices so as to have a relatively low return on each case they handled, they depended on substantial volume. Id., at 122- 123.

After conducting their practice in this manner for two years, appellants concluded that their practice and clinical concept could not survive unless the availability of legal services at low cost was advertised and in particular, fees were advertised. Id., at 120-123. Consequently, in order to generate the necessary flow of business, that is, 'to attract clients,' id., at 121; Tr. of Oral Arg. 4, appellants on February 22, 1976, placed an advertisement (reproduced in the Appendix to this opinion, infra, at 2710) in the Arizona Republic, a daily newspaper of general circulation in the Phoenix metropolitan area. As may be seen, the advertisement stated that appellants were offering 'legal services at very reasonable fees,' and listed their fees for certain services.

Appellants concede that the advertisement constituted a clear violation of Disciplinary Rule 2-101(B), incorporated in Rule 29(a) of the Supreme Court of Arizona, 17A Ariz.Rev.Stat., p. 26 (Supp. 1976). The disciplinary rule provides in part:
'(B) A lawyer shall not publicize himself, or his partner, or associate, or any other lawyer affiliated with him or his firm, as a lawyer through newspaper or magazine advertisements, ratio or television announcements, display advertisements in the city or telephone directories or other means of commercial publicity, nor shall he authorize or permit others to do so in his behalf.' [FN5]

FN5. The remainder of subdivision (B) states exceptions to the general prohibition:
'However, a lawyer recommended by, paid by, or whose legal services are furnished by, a qualified legal assistance organization may authorize or permit or assist such organization to use means of dignified commercial publicity, which does not identify any lawyer by name, to describe the availability or nature of its legal services or legal service benefits. This rule does not prohibit limited and dignified identification of a lawyer as a lawyer as well as by name:
'(1) In political advertisements when his professional status is germane to the political campaign or to a political issue.
'(2) In public notices when the name and profession of a lawyer are required or authorized by law or are reasonably pertinent for a purpose other than the attraction of potential clients.
'(3) In routine reports and announcements of a bona fide business, civic, professional, or political organization in which he serves as a director or officer. '(4) In and on legal documents prepared by him.
'(5) In and on legal textbooks, treatises, and other legal publications, and in dignified advertisements thereof.
'(6) In communications by a qualified legal assistance organization, along with the biographical information permitted under DR 2- 102(A)(6) (biographical information that may be listed 'in a reputable law list or legal directory'), directed to a member of beneficiary of such organization.'

Upon the filing of a complaint initiated by the president of the State Bar, App. 350, a hearing was held before a three-member Special Local Administrative Committee, as prescribed by Arizona Supreme Court Rule 33. App. 16. Although the committee took the position that it could not consider an attack on the validity of the rule, it allowed the parties to develop a record on which such a challenge could be based. The committee recommended that each of the appellants be suspended from the practice of law for not less than six months. Id., at 482. Upon further review by the Board of Governors of the State Bar, pursuant to the Supreme Court's Rule 36, the Board recommended only a one-week suspension for each appellant, the weeks to run consecutively. App. 486-487.

Appellants, as permitted by the Supreme Court's Rule 37, then sought review in the Supreme Court of Arizona, arguing, among other things, that the disciplinary rule violated ss 1 and 2 of the Sherman Act because of its tendency to limit competition, and that the rule infringed their First Amendment rights. The court rejected both claims. In re Bates, 113 Ariz. 394, 555 P.2d 640 (1976). The plurality may have viewed with some skepticism the claim that a restraint on advertising might have an adverse effect on competition. But, even if the rule might otherwise violate the Act, the plurality concluded that the regulation was exempt from Sherman Act attack because the rule 'is an activity of the State of Arizona acting as sovereign.' Id., at 397, 555 P.2d at 643. The regulation thus was held to be shielded from the Sherman Act by the state-action exemption of Parker v. Brown, 317 U.S. 341, 63 S.Ct. 307, 87 L.Ed. 315 (1943).

Turning to the First Amendment issue, the plurality noted that restrictions on professional advertising have survived constitutional challenge in the past, citing, along with other cases, Williamson v. Lee Optical Co., 348 U.S. 483, 75 S.Ct. 461, 99 L.Ed. 563 (1955), and Semler v. Dental Examiners, 294 U.S. 608, 55 S.Ct. 570, 79 L.Ed. 1086 (1935). Although recognizing that Virginia Pharmacy Board v. Virginia Consumer Council, 425 U.S. 748, 96 S.Ct. 1817, 48 L.Ed.2d 346 (1976), and Bigelow v. Virginia, 421 U.S. 809, 95 S.Ct. 2222, 44 L.Ed.2d 600 (1975), held that commercial speech was entitled to certain protection under the First Amendment, the plurality focused on passages in those opinions acknowledging that special considerations might bear on the advertising of professional services by lawyers. See Virginia Pharmacy Board v. Virginia Consumer Council, 425 U.S., at 773 n. 25, 96 S.Ct., at 1831; id., at 773-775, 96 S.Ct. at 1831-1832 (concurring opinion); Bigelow v. Virginia, 421 U.S., at 825 n. 10, 95 S.C., at 2234. The plurality apparently was of the view that the older decisions dealing with professional advertising survived these recent cases unscathed, and held that Disciplinary Rule 2-101(B) passed First Amendment muster. Because the court, in agreement with the Board of Governors, felt that appellants' advertising 'was done in good faith to test the constitutionality of DR 2-101(B),' it reduced the sanction to censure only. 113 Ariz., at 400, 555 P.2d, at 646.

Of particular interest here is the opinion of Mr. Justice Holohan in dissent. In his view, the case should have been framed in terms of 'the right of the public as consumers and citizens to know about the activities of the legal profession,' id., at 402, 555 P.2d, at 648, rather than as one involving merely the regulation of a profession. Observed in this light, he felt that the rule performed a substantial disservice to the public:

> 'Obviously the information of what lawyers charge is important for private economic decisions by those in need of legal services. Such information is also helpful, perhaps indispensable, to the formation of an intelligent opinion by the public on how well the legal system is working and whether it should be regulated or even altered. . . . The rule at issue prevents access to such information by the public.' Id., at 402-403, 555 P.2d, at 648-649.

Although the dissenter acknowledged that some types of advertising might cause confusion and deceptin, he felt that the remedy was to ban that form, rather than all advertising. Thus, despite his 'personal dislike of the concept of advertising by attorneys,' id., at 402, 555 P.2d, at 648, he found the ban unconstitutional.

We noted probable jurisdiction. 429 U.S. 813, 97 S.Ct. 53, 50 L.Ed.2d 73 (1976).

## III

## The First Amendment

### A

Last Term, in VirginiaPharmacy Board v. VirginiaConsumer Council, 425 U.S. 748, 96 S.Ct. 1817, 48 L.Ed.2d 346 (1976), the Court considered the validity under the First Amendment of a Virginia statute declaring that a pharmacist was guilty of 'unprofessional conduct' if he advertised prescription drug prices. The pharmacist would then be subject to a monetary penalty or the suspension or revocation of his license. The statute thus effectively prevented the advertising of prescription drug price information. We recognized that the pharmacist who desired to advertise did not wish to report any particularly newsworthy fact or to comment on any cultural, philosophical, or political subject; his desired communication was characterized simply: "I will sell you the X prescription drug at the Y price." Id., at 761, 96 S.Ct., at 1825. Nonetheless, we held that commercial speech of that kind was entitled to the protection of the First Amendment.

Our analysis began, ibid., with the observation that our cases long have protected speech even though it is in the form of a paid advertisement, Buckley v. Valeo, 424 U.S. 1, 96 S.Ct. 612, 46 L.Ed.2d 659 (1976); New York Times Co. v. Sullivan, 376 U.S. 254, 84 S.Ct. 710, 11 L.Ed.2d 686 (1964); in a form that is sold for profit, Smith v. California, 361 U.S. 147, 80 S.Ct. 215, 4 L.Ed.2d 205 (1959); Murdock v. Pennsylvania, 319 U.S. 105, 63 S.Ct. 870, 87 L.Ed. 1292 (1943); or in the form of a solicitation to pay or contribute money, New York Times Co. v. Sullivan, supra; Cantwell v. Connecticut, 310 U.S. 296, 60 S.Ct. 900, 84 L.Ed. 1213 (1940). If commercial speech is to be distinguished, it 'must be distinguished by its content.' 425 U.S., at 761, 96 S.Ct., at 1825. But a consideration of competing interests reinforced our view that such speech should not be withdrawn from protection merely because it proposed a mundane commercial transaction. Even though the speaker's interest is largely economic, the Court has protected such speech in certain contexts. See, e. g., NLRB v. Gissel Packing Co., 395 U.S. 575, 89 S.Ct. 1918, 23 L.Ed.2d 547 (1969); Thornhill v. Alabama, 310 U.S. 88, 60 S.Ct. 736, 84 L.Ed. 1093 (1940). The listener's interest is substantial: the consumer's concern for the free flow of commercial speech often may be far keener than his concern for urgent political dialogue. Moreover, significant societal interests are served by such speech. Advertising, though entirely commercial, may often carry information of import to significant issues of the day. See Bigelow v. Virginia, 421 U.S. 809, 95 S.Ct. 2222, 44 L.Ed.2d 600 (1975). And commercial speech serves to inform the public of the availability, nature, and prices of products and services, and thus performs an indispensable role in the allocation of resources in a free enterprise system. See FTC v. Procter & Gamble Co., 386 U.S. 568, 603-604, 87 S.Ct. 1224, 1242-1243, 18 L.Ed.2d 303 (1967) (Harlan, J., concurring). In short, such speech serves individual and societal interests in assuring informed and reliable decisionmaking. 425 U.S., at 761-765, 96 S.Ct., at 1825-1827.

Arrayed against these substantial interests in the free flow of commercial speech were a number of proffered justifications for the advertising ban. Central among them were claims that the ban was essential to the maintenance of professionalism among licensed pharmacists. It was asserted that advertising would create price competition that might cause the pharmacist to economize at the customer's expense. He might reduce or eliminate the truly professional portions of his services: the maintenance and packaging of drugs so as to assure their effectiveness, and the supplementation on occasion of the prescribing physician's advice as to use. Moreover, it was said, advertising would cause consumers to price-shop, thereby undermining the pharmacist's effort to monitor the drug use of a regular customer so as to ensure that the prescribed drug would not provoke an allergic reaction or be incompatible with another substance the customer was consuming. Finally, it was argued that advertising would reduce the image of the pharmacist as a skilled and specialized craftsman an image that was said to attract talent to the profession and to reinforce the good habits of those in it to that of a mere shopkeeper. Id., at 766-768, 96 S.Ct., at 1828-1829.

Although acknowledging that the State had a strong interest in maintaining professionalism among pharmacists, this Court concluded that the proffered justifications were inadequate to support the advertising ban. High professional standards were assured in large part by the close regulation to which pharmacists in Virginia were subject. Id., at 768, 96 S.Ct., at 1829. And we observed that 'on close inspection it is seen that the State's protectiveness of its citizens rests in large measure on the advantages of their being kept in ignorance.' Id., at 769, 96 S.Ct., at 1829. But we noted the presence of a potent alternative to this 'highly paternalistic' approach: 'That alternative is to assume that this information is not in itself harmful, that people will perceive their own best interests if only they are well enough informed, and that the best means to that end is to open the channels of communication rather than to close them.' Id., at 770, 96 S.Ct., at 1829. The choice between the dangers of suppressing information and the dangers arising from its free flow was seen as precisely the choice 'that the First Amendment makes for us.' Ibid. See also linmark Associates, Inc. v. Willingboro, 431 U.S. 85, 97, 97 S.Ct. 1614, 52 L.Ed.2d 155 (1977).

We have set out this detailed summary of the Pharmacy opinion because the conclusion that Arizona's disciplinary rule is violative of the First Amendment might be said to flow a fortiori from it. Like the Virginia statutes, the disciplinary rule serves to inhibit the free flow of commercial information and to keep the public in ignorance. Because of the possibility, however, that the differences among professions might bring different constitutional considerations into play, we specifically reserved judgment as to other professions.

In the instant case we are confronted with the arguments directed explicitly toward the regulation of advertising by licensed attorneys.

B

The issue presently before us is a narrow one. First, we need not address the peculiar problems associated with advertising claims relating to the quality of legal services. Such claims probably are not susceptible of precise measurement or verification and, under some circumstances, might well be deceptive or misleading to the public, or even false. Appellee does not suggest, nor do we perceive, that appellants' advertisement contained claims, extravagant or otherwise, as to the quality of services. Accordingly, we leave that issue for another day. Second, we also need not resolve the problems associated with in- person solicitation of clients at the hospital room or the accident site, or in any other situation that breeds undue influence by attorneys or their agents or 'runners.' Activity of that kind might well pose dangers of overreaching and misrepresentation not encountered in newspaper announcement advertising. Hence, this issue also is not before us. Third, we note that appellee's criticism of advertising by attorneys does not apply with much force to some of the basic factual content of advertising: information as to the attorney's name, address, and telephone number, office hours, and the like. The American Bar Association itself has a provision in its current Code of Professional Responsibility that would allow the disclosure of such information, and more, in the classified section of the telephone directory. DR 2-102(A)(6) (1976). We recognize, however, that an advertising diet limited to such spartan fare would provide scant nourishment.

The heart of the dispute before us today is whether lawyers also may constitutionally advertise the prices at which certain routine services will be performed. Numerous justifications are proffered for the restriction of such price advertising. We consider each in turn:

1. The Adverse Effect on Professionalism. Appellee places particular emphasis on the adverse effects that it feels price advertising will have on the legal profession. The key to professionalism, it is argued, is the sense of pride that involvement in the discipline generates. It is claimed that price advertising will bring about commercialization, which will undermine the attorney's sense of dignity and self-worth. The hustle of the marketplace will adversely affect the profession's service orientation, and irreparably damage the delicate balance between the lawyer's need to earn and his obligation selflessly to serve. Advertising is also said to erode the client's trust in his attorney: Once the client perceives that the lawyer is motivated by profit, his confidence that the attorney is acting out of a commitment to the client's welfare is jeopardized. And advertising is said to tarnish the dignified public image of the profession.

We recognize, of course, and commend the spirit of public service with which the profession of law is practiced and to which it is dedicated. The present Members of this Court, licensed attorneys all, could not feel otherwise. And we would have reason to pause if we felt that our decision today would undercut that spirit. But we find the postulated connection between advertising and the erosion of true professionalism to be severely strained. At its core, the argument presumes that attorneys must conceal from themselves and from their clients the real-life fact that lawyers earn their livelihood at the bar. We suspect that few attorneys engage in such self-deception. And rare is the client, moreover, even one of the modest means, who enlists the aid of an attorney with the expectation that his services will be rendered free of charge. See B. Christensen, Lawyers for People of Moderate Means 152-153 (1970). In fact, the American Bar Association advises that an attorney should reach 'a clear agreement with his client as to the basis of the fee charges to be made,' and that this is to be done '(a)s soon as feasible after a lawyer has been employed.' Code of Professional Responsibility EC 2-19 (1976). If the commercial basis of the relationship is to be promptly disclosed on ethical grounds, once the client is in the office, it seems inconsistent to condemn the candid revelation of the same information before he arrives at that office.

Moreover, the assertion that advertising will diminish the attorney's reputation in the community is open to question. Bankers and engineers advertise, and yet these professions are not regarded as undignified. In fact, it has been suggested that the failure of lawyers to advertise creates public disillusionment with the profession. The absence of advertising may be seen to reflect the profession's failure to reach out and serve the community: Studies reveal that many persons do not obtain counsel even when they perceive a need because of the feared price of services or because of an inability to locate a competent attorney. Indeed, cynicism with regard to the profession may be created by the fact that it long has publicly eschewed advertising, while condoning the actions of the attorney who structures his social or civic associations so as to provide contacts with potential clients.

It appears that the ban on advertising originated as a rule of etiquette and not as a rule of ethics. Early lawyers in Great Britain viewed the law as a form of public service, rather than as a means of earning a living, and they looked down on 'trade' as unseemly. See H. Drinker, Legal Ethics, 5, 210-211 (1953). Eventually, the attitude toward advertising fostered by this view evolved into an aspect of the ethics of the profession. Id., at 211. But habit and tradition are not in themselves an adequate answer to a constitutional challenge. In this day, we do not belittle the person who earns his living by the strength of his arm or the force of his mind. Since the belief that lawyers are somehow 'above' trade has become an anachronism, the historical foundation for the advertising restraint has crumbled.

2. The Inherently Misleading Nature of Attorney Advertising. It is argued that advertising of legal services inevitably will be misleading (a) because such services are so individualized with regard to content and quality as to prevent informed comparison on the basis of an advertisement, (b) because the consumer of legal services is unable to determine in advance just what services he needs, and (c) because advertising by attorneys will highlight irrelevant factors and fail to show the relevant factor of skill.

We are not persuaded that restrained professional advertising by lawyers inevitably will be misleading. Although many services performed by attorneys are indeed unique, it is doubtful that any attorney would or could advertise fixed prices for services of that type. The only services that lend themselves to advertising are the routine ones: the uncontested divorce, the simple adoption, the uncontested personal bankruptcy, the change of name, and the like the very services advertised by appellants. Although the precise service demanded in each task may vary slightly, and although legal services are not fungible, these facts do not make advertising misleading so long as the attorney does the necessary work at the advertised price. The argument that legal services are so unique that fixed rates cannot meaningfully be established is refuted by the record in this case: The appellee, State Bar itself sponsors a Legal Services Program in which the participating attorneys agree to perform services like those advertised by the appellants at standardized rates. App. 459-478. Indeed, until the decision of this Court in Goldfarb v. Virginia State Bar, 421 U.S. 773, 95 S.Ct. 2004, 44 L.Ed.2d 572 (1975), the Maricopa County Bar Association apparently had a schedule of suggested minimum fees for standard legal tasks. App. 355. We thus find of little force the assertion that advertising is misleading because of an inherent lack of standardization in legal services.

The second component of the argument that advertising ignores the diagnostic role fares little better. It is unlikely that many people go to an attorney merely to ascertain if they have a clean bill of legal health. Rather, attorneys are likely to be employed to perform specific tasks. Although the client may not know the detail involved in performing the task, he no doubt is able to identify the service he desires at the level of generality to which advertising lends itself.

The third component is not without merit: Advertising does not provide a complete foundation on which to select an attorney. But it seems peculiar to deny the consumer, on the ground that the information is incomplete, at least some of the relevant information needed to reach an informed decision. The alternative the prohibition of advertising serves only to restrict the information that flows to consumers. Moreover, the argument assumes that the public is not sophisticated enough to realize the limitations of advertising, and that the public is better kept in ignorance than trusted with correct but incomplete information. We suspect the argument rests on an underestimation of the public. In any event, we view as dubious any justification that is based on the benefits of public ignorance. See Virginia Pharmacy Board v. Virginia Consumer Council, 425 U.S., at 769-770, 96 S.Ct., at 1829-1830. Although, of course, the bar retains the power to correct omissions that have the effect of presenting an inaccurate picture, the preferred remedy is more disclosure, rather than less. If the naivete $ of the public will cause advertising by attorneys to be misleading, then it is the bar's role to assure that the populace is sufficiently informed as to enable it to place advertising in its proper perspective.

3. The Adverse Effect on the Administration of Justice. Advertising is said to have the undesirable effect of stirring up litigation. The judicial machinery is designed to serve those who feel sufficiently aggrieved to bring forward their claims. Advertising, it is argued, serves to encourage the assertion of legal rights in the courts, thereby undesirably unsettling societal repose. There is even a suggestion of barratry. See, e. g., Comment, A Critical Analysis of Rules Against Solicitation by Lawyers, 25 U.Chi.L.Rev. 674, 675-676 (1958).

But advertising by attorneys is not an unmitigated source of harm to the administration of justice. It may offer great benefits. Although advertising might increase the use of the judicial machinery, we cannot accept the notion that it is always better for a person to suffer a wrong silently than to redress it by legal action. As the bar acknowledges, 'the middle 70% of our population is not being reached or served adequately by the legal profession.' ABA, Revised Handbook on Prepaid Legal Services 2 (1972). Among the reasons for this underutilization is fear of the cost, and an inability to locate a suitable lawyer. See nn. 22 and 23, supra. Advertising can help to solve this acknowledged problem: Advertising is the traditional mechanism in a free-market economy for a supplier to inform a potential purchaser of the availability and terms of exchange. The disciplinary rule at issue likely has served to burden access to legal services, particularly for the not-quite-poor and the unknowledgeable. A rule allowing restrained advertising would be in accord with the bar's obligation to 'facilitate the process of intelligent selection of lawyers, and to assist in making legal services fully available.' ABA Code of Professional Responsibility EC 2-1 (1976).

4. The Undesirable Economic Effects of Advertising. It is claimed that advertising will increase the overhead costs of the profession, and that these costs then will be passed along to consumers in the form of increased fees. Moreover, it is claimed that the additional cost of practice will create a substantial entry barrier, deterring or preventing young attorneys from penetrating the market and entrenching the position of the bar's established members.

These two arguments seem dubious at best. Neither distinguishes lawyers from others, see Virginia Pharmacy Board v. Virginia Consumer Council, 425 U.S., at 768, 96 S.Ct., at 1828, and neither appears relevant to the First Amendment. The ban on advertising serves to increase the difficulty of discovering the lowest cost seller of acceptable ability. As a result, to this extent attorneys are isolated from competition, and the incentive to price competitively is reduced. Although it is true that the effect of advertising on the price of services has not been demonstrated, there is revealing evidence with regard to products; where consumers have the benefit of price advertising, retail prices often are dramatically lower than they would be without advertising. It is entirely possible that advertising will serve to reduce, not advance, the cost of legal services to the consumer.

The entry-barrier argument is equally unpersuasive. In the absence of advertising, an attorney must rely on his contacts with the community to generate a flow of business. In view of the time necessary to develop such contacts, the ban in fact serves to perpetuate the market position of established attorneys. Consideration of entry-barrier problems would urge that advertising be allowed so as to aid the new competitor in penetrating the market.

5. The Adverse Effect of Advertising on the Quality of Service. It is argued that the attorney may advertise a given 'package' of service at a set price, and will be inclined to provide, by indiscriminate use, the standard package regardless of whether it fits the client's needs.

Restraints on advertising, however, are an ineffective way of deterring shoddy work. An attorney who is inclined to cut quality will do so regardless of the rule on advertising. And the advertisement of a standardized fee does not necessarily mean that the services offered are undesirably standardized. Indeed, the assertion that an attorney who advertises a standard fee will cut quality is substantially undermined by the fixed-fee schedule of appellee's own prepaid Legal Services Program. Even if advertising leads to the creation of 'legal clinics' like that of appellants' clinics that emphasize standardized procedures for routine problems it is possible that such clinics will improve service by reducing the likelihood of error.

6. The Difficulties of Enforcement. Finally, it is argued that the wholesale restriction is justified by the problems of enforcement if any other course is taken. Because the public lacks sophistication in legal matters, it may be particularly susceptible to misleading or deceptive advertising by lawyers. After-the-fact action by the consumer lured by such advertising may not provide a realistic restraint because of the inability of the layman to assess whether the service he has received meets professional standards. Thus, the vigilance of a regulatory agency will be required. But because of the numerous purveyors of services, the overseeing of advertising will be burdensome.

It is at least somewhat incongruous for the opponents of advertising to extol the virtues and altruism of the legal profession at one point, and, at another, to assert that its members will seize the opportunity to mislead and distort. We suspect that, with advertising, most lawyers will behave as they always have: They will abide by their solemn oaths to uphold the integrity and honor of their profession and of the legal system. For every attorney who overreaches through advertising, there will be thousands of others who will be candid and honest and straightforward. And, of course, it will be in the latter's interest, as in other cases of misconduct at the bar, to assist in weeding out those few who abuse their trust.

In sum, we are not persuaded that any of the proffered justifications rise to the level of an acceptable reason for the suppression of all advertising by attorneys.

C

In the usual case involving a restraint on speech, a showing that the challenged rule served unconstitutionally to suppress speech would end our analysis. In the First Amendment context, the Court has permitted attacks on overly broad statutes without requiring that the person making the attack demonstrate that in fact his specific conduct was protected. See, e. g., Bigelow v. Virginia, 421 U.S., at 815-816, 95 S.Ct., at 2229; Gooding v. Wilson, 405 U.S. 518, 521-522, 92 S.Ct. 1103, 1105-1106, 31 L.Ed.2d 408 (1972); Dombrowski v. Pfister, 380 U.S. 479, 486, 85 S.Ct. 1116, 1120, 14 L.Ed.2d 22 (1965). Having shown that the disciplinary rule interferes with protected speech, appellants ordinarily could expect to benefit regardless of the nature of their acts.

The First Amendment overbreadth doctrine, however, represents a departure from the traditional rule that a person may not challenge a statute on the ground that it might be applied unconstitutionally in circumstances other than those before the court. See, e. g., Broadrick v. Oklahoma, 413 U.S. 601, 610, 93 S.Ct. 2908, 2914, 37 L.Ed.2d 830 (1973); United States v. Raines, 362 U.S. 17, 21, 80 S.Ct. 519, 522, 4 L.Ed.2d 524 (1960); Ashwander v. TVA, 297 U.S. 288, 347, 56 S.Ct. 466, 483, 80 L.Ed. 688 (1936) (Brandeis, J., concurring). The reason for the special rule in First Amendment cases is apparent: An overbroad statute might serve to chill protected speech. First Amendment interests are fragile interests, and a person who contemplates protected activity might be discouraged by the in terrorem effect of the statute. See NAACP v. Button, 371 U.S. 415, 433, 83 S.Ct. 328, 338, 9 L.Ed.2d 405 (1963). Indeed, such a person might choose not to speak because of uncertainty whether his claim of privilege would prevail if challenged. The use of overbreadth analysis reflects the conclusion that the possible harm to society from allowing unprotected speech to go unpunished is outweighed by the possibility that protected speech will be muted.

But the justification for the application of overbreadth analysis applies weakly, if at all, in the ordinary commercial context. As was acknowledged in Virginia Pharmacy Board v. Virginia Consumer Council, 425 U.S., at 771 n. 24, 96 S.Ct., at 1830, there are 'commonsense differences' between commercial speech and other varieties. See also id., at 775-781, 96 S.Ct., at 1832-1835 (concurring opinion). Since advertising is linked to commercial well-being, it seems unlikely that such speech is particularly susceptible to being crushed by overbroad regulation. See id., at 771-772 n. 24, 96 S.Ct. at 1830-1831. Moreover, concerns for uncertainty in determining the scope of protection are reduced; the advertiser seeks to disseminate information about a product or service that he provides, and presumably he can determine more readily than others whether his speech is truthful and protected. Ibid. Since overbreadth has been described by this Court as 'strong medicine,' which 'has been employed . . . sparingly and only as a last resort,' Broadrick v. Oklahoma, 413 U.S., at 613, 93 S.Ct., at 2916, we decline to apply it to professional advertising, a context where it is not necessary to further its intended objective. Cf. Bigelow v. Virginia, 421 U.S., at 817-818, 95 S.Ct., at 2230.

Is, then, appellants' advertisement outside the scope of basic First Amendment protection? Aside from general claims as to the undesirability of any advertising by attorneys, a matter considered above, appellee argues that appellants' advertisement is misleading, and hence unprotected, in three particulars: (a) the advertisement makes reference to a 'legal clinic,' an allegedly undefined term; (b) the advertisement claims that appellants offer services at 'very reasonable' prices, and, at least with regard to an uncontested divorce, the advertised price is not a bargain; and (c) the advertisement does not inform the consumer that he may obtain a name change without the services of an attorney. Tr. of Oral Arg. 56-57. On this record, these assertions are unpersuasive. We suspect that the public would readily understand the term 'legal clinic' if, indeed, it focused on the term at all to refer to an operation like that of appellants' that is geared to provide standardized and multiple services. In fact, in his deposition the president of the State Bar of Arizona observed that there was a committee of the bar 'exploring the ways in which the legal clinic concept can be properly developed.' App. 375; see id., at 401. See also id., at 84-85 (testimony of appellants). And the clinical concept in the sister profession of medicine surely by now is publicly acknowledged and understood.

As to the cost of an uncontested divorce, appellee's counsel stated at oral argument that this runs from $150 to $300 in the area. Tr. of Oral Arg. 58. Appellants advertised a fee of $175 plus a $20 court filing fee, a rate that seems 'very reasonable' in light of the customary charge. Appellee's own Legal Services Program sets the rate for an uncontested divorce at $250. App. 473. Of course, advertising will permit the comparison of rates among competitors, thus revealing if the rates are reasonable.

As to the final argument the failure to disclose that a name change might be accomplished by the client without the aid of an attorney we need only note that most legal services may be performed legally by the citizen for himself. See Faretta v. California, 422 U.S. 806, 95 S.Ct. 2525, 45 L.Ed.2d 562 (1975); ABA Code of Professional Responsibility EC 3-7 (1976). The record does not unambiguously reveal some of the relevant facts in determining whether the nondisclosure is misleading, such as how complicated the procedure is and whether the State provides assistance for laymen. The deposition of one appellant, however, reflects that when he ascertained that a name change required only the correction of a record or the like, he frequently would send the client to effect the change himself. App. 112.

We conclude that it has not been demonstrated that the advertisement at issue could be suppressed.

## IV

In holding that advertising by attorneys may not be subjected to blanket suppression, and that the advertisement at issue is protected, we, of course, do not hold that advertising by attorneys may not be regulated in any way. We mention some of the clearly permissible limitations on advertising not foreclosed by our holding.

Advertising that is false, deceptive, or misleading of course is subject to restraint. See Virginia Pharmacy Board v. Virginia Citizens Consumer Council, 425 U.S., at 771-772, and n. 24, 96 S.Ct., at 1830-1831. Since the advertiser knows his product and has a commercial interest in its dissemination, we have little worry that regulation to assure truthfulness will discourage protected speech. Id., at 771-772, n. 24, 96 S.Ct. at 1830. And any concern that strict requirements for truthfulness will undesirably inhibit spontaneity seems inapplicable because commercial speech generally is calculated. Indeed, the public and private benefits from commercial speech derive from confidence in its accuracy and reliability. Thus, the leeway for untruthful or misleading expression that has been allowed in other contexts has little force in the commercial arena. Compare Gertz v. Robert Welch, Inc., 418 U.S. 323, 339-341, 94 S.Ct. 2997, 3006-3007, 41 L.Ed.2d 789 (1974), and Cantwell v. Connecticut, 310 U.S., at 310, 60 S.Ct., at 906, with NLRB v. Gissel Packing Co., 395 U.S., at 618, 89 S.Ct., at 1942. In fact, because the public lacks sophistication concerning legal services, misstatements that might be overlooked or deemed unimportant in other advertising may be found quite inappropriate in legal advertising. For example, advertising claims as to the quality of services a matter we do not address today are not susceptible of measurement or verification; accordingly, such claims may be so likely to be misleading as to warrant restriction. Similar objections might justify restraints on in-person solicitation. We do not foreclose the possibility that some limited supplementation, by way of warning or disclaimer or the like, might be required of even an advertisement of the kind ruled upon today so as to assure that the consumer is not misled. In sum, we recognize that many of the problems in defining the boundary between deceptive and nondeceptive advertising remain to be resolved, and we expect that the bar will have a special role to play in assuring that advertising by attorneys flows both freely and cleanly.

As with other varieties of speech, it follows as well that there may be reasonable restrictions on the time, place, and manner of advertising. See Virginia Pharmacy Board v. Virginia Consumer Council, 425 U.S., at 771, 96 S.Ct., at 1830. Advertising concerning transactions that are themselves illegal obviously may be suppressed. See Pittsburgh Press Co. v. Human Relations Comm'n, 413 U.S. 376, 388, 93 S.Ct. 2553, 37 L.Ed.2d 669 (1973). And the special problems of advertising on the electronic broadcast media will warrant special consideration. Cf. Capital Broadcasting Co. v. Mitchell, 333 F.Supp. 582 (DC 1971), summarily aff'd sub nom. Capital Broadcasting Co. v. Acting Attorney General, 405 U.S. 1000, 92 S.Ct. 1289, 31 L.Ed.2d 472 (1972).

The constitutional issue in this case is only whether the State may prevent the publication in a newspaper of appellants' truthful advertisement concerning the availability and terms of routine legal services. We rule simply that the flow of such information may not be restrained, and we therefore hold the present application of the disciplinary rule against appellants to be violative of the First Amendment.

The judgment of the Supreme Court of Arizona is therefore affirmed in part and reversed in part.

It is so ordered.

Mr. Chief Justice BURGER, concurring in part and dissenting in part.

I am in general agreement with Mr. Justice POWELL'S analysis and with Part II of the Court's opinion. I particularly agree with Mr. Justice POWELL'S statement that 'today's decision will effect profound changes in the practice of law.' Post, at 2712. Although the exact effect of those changes cannot now be known, I fear that they will be injurious to those whom the ban on legal advertising was designed to protect the members of the general public in need of legal services.

Some Members of the Court apparently believe that the present case is controlled by our holding one year ago in Virginia State Board of Pharmacy v. Virginia Consumer Council, Inc., 425 U.S. 748, 96 S.Ct. 1817, 48 L.Ed.2d 346 (1976). However, I had thought that we made most explicit that our holding there rested on the fact that the advertisement of standardized, prepackaged, name-brand drugs was at issue. Id., at 773 n. 25, 96 S.Ct., at 1831. In that context, the prohibition on price advertising, which had served a useful function in the days of individually compounded medicines, was no longer tied to the conditions which had given it birth. The same cannot be said with respect to legal services which, by necessity, must vary greatly from case to case. Indeed, I find it difficult, if not impossible, to identify categories of legal problems or services which are fungible in nature. For example, Mr. Justice POWELL persuasively demonstrates the fallacy of any notion that even an uncontested divorce can be 'standard.' Post, at 2713. A 'reasonable charge' for such a divorce could be $195, as the appellants wish to advertise, or it could reasonably be a great deal more, depending on such variables as child custody, alimony, support, or any property settlement. Because legal services can rarely, if ever, be 'standardized' and because potential clients rarely know in advance what services they do in fact need, price advertising can never give the public an accurate picture on which to base its selection of an attorney. Indeed, in the context of legal services, such incomplete information could be worse than no information at all. It could become a trap for the unwary . . . .

To be sure, the public needs information concerning attorneys, their work, and their fees. At the same time, the public needs protection from the unscrupulous or the incompetent practitioner anxious to prey on the uninformed . . . .

Unfortunately, the legal profession in the past has approached solutions for the protection of the public with too much caution, and, as a result, too little progress has been made. However, as Mr. Justice POWELL points out, post, at 2716, the organized bar has recently made some reforms in this sensitive area and more appear to be in the offing. Rather than allowing these efforts to bear fruit, the Court today opts for a Draconian 'solution' which I believe will only breed more problems than it can conceivably resolve.

Mr. Justice POWELL, with whom Mr. Justice STEWART joins, concurring in part and dissenting in part.

I agree with the Court that appellants' Sherman Act claim is barred by the Parker v. Brown, 317 U.S. 341, 63 S.Ct. 307, 87 L.Ed.2d 315 (1943), exemption and therefore join Part II of the Court's opinion. But I cannot join the Court's holding that under the First Amendment 'truthful' newspaper advertising of a lawyer's prices for 'routine legal services' may not be restrained. Ante, at 2709. Although the Court appears to note some reservations (mentioned below), it is clear that within undefined limits today's decision will effect profound changes in the practice of law, viewed for centuries as a learned profession. The supervisory power of the courts over members of the bar, as officers of the courts, and the authority of the respective States to oversee the regulation of the profession have been weakened. Although the Court's opinion professes to be framed narrowly, and its reach is subject to future clarification, the holding is explicit and expansive with respect to the advertising of undefined 'routine legal services.' In my view, this result is neither required by the First Amendment, nor in the public interest . . . .

Mr. Justice REHNQUIST, dissenting in part.

. . . I dissent from Part III because I cannot agree that the First Amendment is infringed by Arizona's regulation of the essentially commercial activity of advertising legal services. . .

I continue to believe that the First Amendment speech provision, long regarded by this Court as a sanctuary for expressions of public importance or intellectual interest, is demeaned by invocation to protect advertisements of goods and services. I would hold quite simply that the appellants' advertisement, however truthful or reasonable it may be, is not the sort of expression that the Amendment was adopted to protect.

IN THE MATTER OF
MERCK & CO., INC., TRADING AS QUINTON COMPANY ET AL.

ORDER, OPINION, ETC., IN REGARD TO THE ALLEGED VIOLATION OF THE

FEDERAL TRADE COMMISSION ACT

69 F.T.C. 526
Docket 8635.

Decision, April 8, 1966

## INITIAL DECISION BY EDGAR A. BUTTLE, HEARING EXAMINER

This proceeding arises from a complaint issued by the Federal Trade Commission on August 7, 1964, charging respondents with falsely advertising 'Sucrets' and 'Children's Sucrets.' The statutory theory is that such advertising participated in by Merck & Co., Inc., the manufacturing advertiser, and Doherty, Clifford, Steers & Shenfield, Inc., its advertising agent, constitutes unfair and deceptive acts and practices in commerce, in violation of Sections 5 and 12 of the Federal Trade Commission Act. The complaint is premised upon the further theory that both the principal and its advertising agent are equally responsible even though there was final approval of the advertising by the principal . . . .

## CONCLUSIONS

It is apparent from the evidence that the representations made by respondents are literally true. Hexylresorcinol contained in 'Sucrets' and 'Children's Sucrets' does kill germs, including streptococci and staphylococci, on contact. Although the wording on the packages gives this forewarning, the representations considered herein reflected in TV commercials are without qualification. It is merely stated that 'when minor sore throat strikes and brings fiery pain, 'Sucrets' relieves sore throat pain and kills even Staph and Strep germs,' and that 'Children's Sucrets' (unqualifiedly) 'relieve pain fast and held fight infection.' The difficulty is that infections within the tissues of the throat are not reached by the hexylresorcinol which can only make external contact in the throat. There is some evidence that hexylresorcinol does penetrate the epithelial layer, but certain infections involving germs, including streptococci and staphylococci, are usually more deeply seated than in that layer. The penetration, therefore, at best is extremely limited and the evidence does not justify respondents' unqualified representations.

The fact that the advertising may be literally true in the sense that hexylresorcinol will kill germs on contact in the throat does not warrant a dismissal of the complaint. The implication from the language used in the advertising is that 'Sucrets' or 'Children's Sucrets' are materially curative because the germs are killed or rendered ineffectual. A person with a sore throat, upon hearing these representations, may reasonably assume that if such germs are killed, the product advertised is a cure for an existing throat infection. This is all the buyer of such a product is interested in, aside from relief of pain, which the evidence indicates 'Sucrets' do afford, not permanently, but temporarily. It is well recognized that 'words and sentences may be literally and technically true and yet be framed in such a setting as to mislead or deceive.' Bockenstette, et al. v. F.T.C., 134 F.2d 369, 371; D.D.D. Corporation v. F.T.C., 125 F.2d 679, 682.

Furthermore, 'advertisements are not to be judged by their effect on the scientific or legal mind which will dissect and analyze each phrase, but rather by their effect upon the average member of the public.' Ward Laboratories, Inc., v. F.T.C., 276 F.2d 952.
Respondent Doherty, Clifford, Steers & Shenfield, Inc., urges that it was merely the agent of Merck, could not act without its approval, and that it initiated advertising subsequently reviewed and approved by Merck, which was reflective of its understanding of the facts that had been presented to it by Merck concerning 'Sucrets.' However, the advertising formulated by the advertising agent was clearly conceived to present to the public not only the advantages of the product sought to be sold as literally stated, but also to work upon the public imagination. It is common knowledge that those who are ill seek cures with hope. This stimulates their imagination into optimistically believing what they read without analytical caution. It is therefore important and in the public interest that extreme care be exercised to make sure that deception will not result from lack of caution in describing the effectiveness of drugs. Misrepresentation by implication may be as detrimental to the public welfare and health as direct misstatements. In the instant case the public interest is clearly contravened.

On the other hand, the inadvertence or lack of caution exercised by the respondents herein should not in any way undermine the public confidence in highly ethical pharmaceutical companies and leaders in medical research such as the respondent Merck. It would appear to the hearing examiner that in reviewing the advertising prepared for Merck by its advertising agent, that Merck inadvertently approved an advertising format without thoroughly considering its implications, aside from its correct literal meaning. Every manufacturer has a subjective sense about his own product which makes objective analysis difficult where imaginative advertising is prescribed by an advertising agent. In this case, of course, it may be, although there is no evidence to this effect, that the advertising agent itself believed that there was no implied falsity in the advertising they disseminated on behalf of, and with the approval of, Merck & Co., Inc. Nevertheless, they were a participant in the preparation of the advertising and the same required caution must be imposed upon them as would be imposed upon their client or advertiser. The public interest and protection, therefore, clearly necessitates that an order be issued against the advertising agent as well as its client, the product manufacturer.

Although intent is not in issue in determining whether or not any cease and desist order should be issued, the evidence does not suggest that there was any sinister intent on the part of Merck & Co., Inc., or its advertising agent, to misrepresent its product, i.e., 'Sucrets' and 'Children's Sucrets' to the public. A conservative order limited to restricting the implied misrepresentations is therefore justified.

With regard to the nature of the order to be issued, complaint counsel proposes that respondents be enjoined from representing that 'Sucrets' or 'Children's Sucrets':

(a) Will reach of kill streptococcal, staphylococcal, or other germs causing an existing throat infection, or otherwise that it is effective in the treatment of any kind of throat infection;

(b) Will have any beneficial effect on:

(1) Severe pain of a sore throat, or

(2) Sore throat in excess of affording temporary relief of the pain of a minor sore throat.

This order, however, appears to be ambiguous with regard to part (a), particularly in the use of the word 'effective,' which has devious meanings. Furthermore, this portion of the order is inconsistent with the evidence adduced, since the primary question is whether or not 'Sucrets' are materially curative insofar as throat infection is concerned. The generality of the language used also would make such an order difficult to apply because its construction leaves much to conjecture. The evidence establishes that 'Sucrets' will not kill or render ineffectual germs in the throat tissues that are contributing to an existing throat infection. An order precluding the representation that 'Sucrets' will kill or render ineffectual such germs which specifically relates to the deceptive practice would, therefore, appear to be more understandable and therefore preferable in the public interest.

As regards the second part of the proposed order identified as (b), this also seeks relief inconsistent with the evidence. It has been well established that 'Sucrets' containing hexylresorcinol, which is an antiseptic having an anesthetic effect, will not afford permanent relief of sore throat pain. Nevertheless, the evidence does establish that this product will afford temporary relief. The reference to a minor sore throat, under the proposed order, has the effect of creating an ambiguity and makes the order difficult to apply, since the evidence establishes there is no relationship between the amount of pain and a minor or major sore throat. In fact, the complaint counsel's evidence thoroughly establishes that severe pain may accompany a minor sore throat condition and minor pain may accompany a major sore throat condition such as streptococcal and staphylococcal infection. The proposed order, therefore, seems inappropriate. The respondents, however, should be enjoined from representing that 'Sucrets' will afford premanent or long lasting relief of sore throat pain. Such relief would be entirely consistent with the evidence in this case.

In accordance with the limitations indicated, the dissemination by the respondents of the false advertising, as aforesaid, constituted, and now constitutes, unfair and deceptive acts and practices in commerce, in violation of sections 5 and 12 of the Federal Trade Commission Act. Accordingly, the following order shall issue:

## ORDER

It is ordered, That respondents Merck & Co., Inc., a corporation trading as Quinton Company or under any other name, and Doherty, Clifford, Steers & Shenfield, Inc., a corporation, and their officers, and respondents' representatives, agents and employees, directly or through any corporate or other device, in connection with the offering for sale, sale or distribution of 'Sucrets' throat lozenges, or 'Children's Sucrets' throat lozenges, or any other preparation of similar chemical composition or properties, do forthwith cease and desist from, directly or indirectly:

1. Disseminating, or causing to be disseminated, by means of the United States mails or by any means in commerce, as 'commerce' is defined in the Federal Trade Commission Act, any advertisement which represents directly or by implication that any of the aforementioned preparations, by virtue of their hexylresorcinol content, or otherwise:

(a) Will kill or render ineffectual, germs in the throat tissues that are contributing to an existing throat infection;

(b) Will afford permanent or long lasting relief of sore throat pain.

2. Disseminating, or causing to be disseminated, by any means, for the purpose of inducing, or which is likely to induce, directly or indirectly, the purchase of any such preparation, in commerce, as 'commerce' is defined in the Federal Trade Commission Act, any advertisement which contains any of the representations prohibited in Paragraph 1 hereof.

## OPINION OF THE COMMISSION

APRIL 8, 1966

BY REILLY, Commissioner:

This matter is before the Commission on cross appeals of counsel supporting the complaint and respondent Merck & Co., Inc. (trading as Quinton Company), and an appeal by the respondent advertising agency, Doherty, Clifford, Steers & Shenfield, Inc., from an initial decision holding that respondents had violated Sections 5 and 12 of the Federal Trade Commission Act.

The complaint charges respondents with the dissemination of false advertisements in connection with the sale and distribution of Sucrets throat lozenges and Children's Sucrets throat lozenges (hereinafter sometimes referred to as Sucrets). More specifically, it charges that respondents falsely represented in television commercials (1) that these preparations reach and kill germs causing existing throat infections and thus are effective in the treatment of throat infections, including those caused by streptococcal and staphylococcal germs; and (2) that they are effective in relieving severe pain of sore throat . . . .

The following oral representations are made in the Sucrets commercial:

When sore throat strikes and brings fiery pain, what do you do for relief? Millions of people depend on SUCRETS for relief of minor sore throat pain. Individually foil wrapped, remarkable SUCRETS lozenges relieve sore throat pain fast and kill even Staph and Strep germs with a special pain relieving antiseptic, HEXYLRESORCINOL. So, when minor sore throat strikes and brings fiery pain, SUCRETS relieve sore throat pain and kill even Staph and Strep germs.

SUCRETS are fast. Within minutes you can talk, swallow, even smoke in comfort. So, when sore throat strikes, relieve pain fast and kill even Staph and Strep germs.

The following oral representations are made in the Children's Sucrets advertisement:

When your child has a sore throat . . . It can made you feel helpless. What do you do to relieve the pain? If he's too young to gargle . . . and you want something more effective than candy cough drops . . . try new CHILDREN'S SUCRETS . . . specially flavored for youngsters . . . by the makers of regular SUCRETS. CHILDREN'S SUCRETS contain hexylresorcinol--the gentle antiseptic. And, CHILDREN'S SUCRETS relieve pain fast and help fight infection. These lozenges are made especially for children. Look: When minor sore throat strikes and brings burning pain . . . CHILDREN'S SUCRETS gently . . . safely . . . take care of the pain . . . and help fight infection. In no time at all . . . your child's like himself again. So next time your child has sore throat . . . if he's too young to gargle . . . and you want something more effective than candy cough drops . . . Relieve pain fast . . . help fight infection. Get new CHILDREN'S SUCRETS!

Included in both advertisements and appearing simultaneously with the above representations are pictures of flame being extinguished in the throat of a person using Sucrets or Children's Sucrets, as the case may be. The video portion of each commercial also portrays a person recovering from sore throat. For example, the Children's Sucrets advertisement depicts an obviously ill child suffering from the pain of sore throat. After taking a lozenge he is shown to be feeling well again, playing normally without any indication of sore throat pain . . . .

The respondent advertising agency has filed a separate appeal from the initial decision contending that the hearing examiner erred in holding it equally liable with Merck for the advertising claims found to be deceptive and placing it under an order to cease and desist. The principal argument made by the agency is that in developing the advertising it acted in good faith in reliance upon information furnished by Merck, and that mere participation in the preparation of advertising claims is not a sufficient basis for imposing liability on an advertising agency.

The examiner found in effect that while the agency should have known that the advertising claims were deceptive (Initial Decision, par. 14) the record did not establish that the agency had actual knowledge of the falsity of these claims (Initial Decision, conclusion, pp. 544-545). His decision did not turn on the question of knowledge or intent, however. He specifically held that the agency was a 'participant in the preparation of the advertising and the same required caution must be imposed upon them as would be imposed upon their client or advertiser.'

We agree with the conclusion of the hearing examiner that the agency should be held but not solely because it was a mere 'participant in the preparation of the advertising.' We believe that the record in this case establishes that the agency was at least equally responsible with its principal for the deception found to be implicit in the advertising under consideration. Moreover, we believe that the agency should have been aware of the deceptive capacity of such advertising. Although the agency contends, in this connection, that it relied on information furnished by Merck, the deception found to exist stems not from the falsity of this information but from the use made of it by the agency.

Marjorie A. EIMANN, Individually, as Next Friend of Gary Wayne Black, and as Representative of the Estate of Sandra Kay Black, Deceased, and Glenn G. Eimann, Plaintiffs-Appellees,

v.

SOLDIER OF FORTUNE MAGAZINE, INC. and Omega Group, Inc., Defendants-Appellants.

880 F.2d 830

United States Court of Appeals,
Fifth Circuit.

Aug. 17, 1989.

Before GARWOOD, JOLLY and DAVIS, Circuit Judges.

W. EUGENE DAVIS, Circuit Judge:

Soldier of Fortune Magazine, Inc. appeals a $9.4 million jury verdict against it in a wrongful death action brought by the son and mother of a murder victim. The jury found that Soldier of Fortune acted with negligence and gross negligence in publishing a personal services classified advertisement through which the victim's husband hired an assassin to kill her. We reverse the judgment entered on the jury's verdict.

## I. FACTS

John Wayne Hearn shot and killed Sandra Black at the behest of her husband, Robert, who offered to pay Hearn $10,000 for doing so. Robert Black contacted Hearn through a classified advertisement that Hearn ran in Soldier of Fortune Magazine, Inc. (SOF), a publication that focuses on mercenary activities and military affairs.

The ad, which ran in the September, October and November 1984 issues of SOF, read:

> EX-MARINES--67-69 'Nam Vets, Ex-DI, weapons specialist--jungle warfare, pilot, M.E., high risk assignments, U.S. or overseas. (404) 991-2684.

Hearn testified that "Ex-DI" meant ex-drill instructor; "M.E." meant multi- engine planes; and "high risk assignments" referred to work as a bodyguard or security specialist. Hearn testified that he and another former Marine placed the ad to recruit Vietnam veterans for work as bodyguards and security men for executives. Hearn's partner testified that they also hoped to train troops in South America. This partner never participated in any ad-related jobs and quit the venture shortly after the ad first ran.

Hearn and his partner testified that they did not place the ad with an intent to solicit criminal employment. However, Hearn stated that about 90 percent of the callers who responded to the ad sought his participation in illegal activities including beatings, kidnappings, jailbreaks, bombings and murders. It also generated at least one lawful inquiry from an oil conglomerate in Lebanon seeking ten bodyguards; Hearn received a commission for placing seven men with the company.

Between early 1982 and January 1984, Black had asked at least four friends or coworkers from Bryan, Texas to kill Sandra Black or help him kill her. All four refused. Black called Hearn in October 1984 after seeing his ad in SOF.

Hearn testified that his initial conversations with Black focused on Black's inquiries about getting bodyguard work through Hearn. In later calls they discussed the sale of Black's gun collection to Hearn. Hearn testified that he traveled from his home in Atlanta to Black's home in Bryan on January 9, 1985 to look at Black's gun collection. Hearn stated that Black discussed his plans for murdering his wife during the meeting and "hinted" that he wanted Hearn to participate, but did not ask Hearn directly to kill his wife. Hearn did not act on the hint and returned to Atlanta.

Black called Hearn repeatedly after Hearn returned to Atlanta. During one call Black spoke with Hearn's girlfriend, Debbie Bannister. Hearn and Bannister met after she called him in response to his SOF ad.

Black proposed directly that Hearn kill his wife during the call to Bannister. She passed the proposal on to Hearn, who called Black and said he would consider doing it. The two talked by phone several times in the following weeks. After an aborted murder attempt about three weeks later-- during which Hearn was to help Black himself kill his wife--Hearn killed Sandra Black on February 21, 1985. By that time Hearn also had killed the ex-husband of Bannister's sister on January 6, 1985 and Bannister's husband on February 2, 1985.

Neither Hearn, who was sentenced to concurrent life sentences for the murders, nor his partner had criminal records when they placed their ad in SOF. Neither had received a dishonorable discharge from the Marines. Further, Hearn included his real name and correct address in submitting the ad to SOF; the ad itself listed Hearn's correct home telephone number.

Sandra Black's son, Gary Wayne Black, and her mother, Marjorie Eimann, sued SOF and its parent, Omega Group, Ltd., for wrongful death under Texas law on the theory that SOF negligently published Hearn's classified ad.

Eimann introduced into evidence about three dozen personal service classified ads selected from the 2,000 or so classified ads that SOF had printed from its inception in 1975 until September 1984. Some ads offered services as a "Mercenary for Hire," "bounty hunter" or "mechanic"; others promised to perform "dirty work," "high risk contracts" or to "do anything, anywhere at the right price."

Eimann presented evidence that seven and perhaps as many as nine classified ads had been tied to crimes or criminal plots. Eimann introduced stories from sources including the Associated Press, United Press International, The Rocky Mountain News, The Denver Post, Time and Newsweek that reported on links between SOF classified ads and at least five of these crimes.

Eimann also presented evidence that law enforcement officials had contacted SOF staffers during investigations of two crimes linked to SOF personal service classifieds. In one case, SOF had provided correspondence from its files-- along with two affidavits signed by SOF's managing editor--that were used in the 1982 criminal trial of a Houston man who was convicted of soliciting the murder of his wife; during his effort the man had tried to hire a poisons expert by placing a classified ad in the October 1981 issue of SOF. Eimann also presented testimony from a New Jersey detective, who stated that in April 1984, SOF's advertising manager had helped him to identify a man who placed a classified ad in SOF.

In addition, Eimann presented expert testimony from Dr. Park Dietz, a forensic psychiatrist who had studied SOF, its ads and readership. Dietz testified that an average SOF subscriber--a male who owns camouflage clothing and more than one gun--would understand some phrases in SOF's classified ads as solicitations for illegal activity given the "context" of those ads.

That context included other classified ads in SOF, display ads for semiautomatic rifles and books with titles such as "How to Kill," and SOF articles including "Harassing the Bear, New Afghan Tactics Stall Soviet Victory," "Pipestone Canyon, Summertime in 'Nam and the Dyin' was Easy," and "Night Raiders on Russia's Border." Dietz also described his visit to a SOF convention in summer 1987, where he photographed exhibits of weapons and tactical gear.

Based on his studies, Dietz concluded that the Hearn ad "or any other personal service ad in Soldier of Fortune in 1984 foreseeably is related to the commission of domestic crimes." He suggested that classified ads such as Hearn's would not carry such connotations if they appeared in Esquire or Vanity Fair.

Dietz conceded, however, that he had abandoned an effort to distinguish lawful SOF classified ads from criminal ones on the basis of specific code words such as "gun for hire," "mechanic" and "hunter" because some ads were too ambiguous to assign an illegal meaning to them with any certainty. He also noted that crimes had been linked to SOF classified ads that "seemed relatively innocuous." For example, one ad tied to a kidnapping and extortion plot read:

> Recovery and collection. International agents guarantee results on any type of recover[y]. Reply to Delta Enterprises, P.O. Box 5241, Rockford, Illinois 61125.

As Dietz stated, "The code system doesn't work."

SOF relied primarily on the testimony of its president, Robert K. Brown, who stated he did not know or suspect in 1984 that some of the SOF classified ads had been linked to criminal plots. Other SOF staffers and readers echoed these denials. SOF's advertising manager, Joan Steele, testified that she understood the phrase "high risk assignments" in Hearn's ad to mean "gun for hire," but in the sense of a professional bodyguard or security consultant rather than a contract killer.

The district court's first special interrogatory asked the jury whether Hearn's ad "related to" illegal activity. The court's second interrogatory asked, "Did [SOF] ... know or should it have known from the face or the context of the Hearn advertisement that the advertisement could reasonably be interpreted as an offer to engage in illegal activity?"

The court's instructions charged SOF with knowledge that Hearn's ad reasonably could be interpreted as such an offer when (1) the relation to illegal activity appears on the ad's face; or (2) "the advertisement, embroidered by its context, would lead a reasonable publisher of ordinary prudence under the same or similar circumstances to conclude that the advertisement could reasonably be interpreted" as an offer to commit crimes. The court went on to define "context" as the magazine's (1) "nature"; (2) other advertisements; (3) articles; (4) readership; and (5) knowledge, if any, that other advertisements in the magazine could reasonably be interpreted as an offer to engage in illegal activity.

The jury answered "yes" to the first two interrogatories, and found that SOF's negligence was a proximate cause of Sandra Black's death in response to Interrogatory Three. The court then asked the jury whether SOF's negligence constituted "gross negligence," defined as "conscious indifference." The jury answered "yes" to this interrogatory as well. The jury awarded Eimann $1.9 million in compensatory damages and $7.5 million in punitive damages; the district court entered judgment on the verdict. SOF appeals.

## II. ANALYSIS

### A. Overview

Eimann presented this case as a straightforward negligence action revolving around one primary issue: whether SOF knew or should have known from the face or context of Hearn's ad that it represented an offer to perform illegal acts. Based on evidence that SOF knew of links between other classified ads and other criminal plots, she contends that SOF owed a duty to recognize ads such as Hearn's that reasonably might be interpreted as criminal solicitations and refrain from publishing them.

SOF argues first that no liability can attach under these facts because the criminal activities of Hearn and Robert Black, rather than Hearn's ad, were the proximate cause of Sandra Black's murder. SOF also argues that imposition of tort liability here contravenes first amendment protection for commercial speech because (1) the judgment below impermissibly imposed a duty on publishers to investigate its advertisers and their ads; and (2) the district court's all-encompassing definition of "context," combined with Dietz's testimony, allowed the jury to penalize SOF for the mercenary and military focus of the magazine's articles and other ads.

We need not address SOF's first amendment attacks on the judgment to resolve this appeal. Assuming without deciding that a Texas court would apply general negligence principles to this case, we conclude that no liability can attach under these principles as a matter of law. SOF owed no duty to refrain from publishing a facially innocuous classified advertisement when the ad's context--at most--made its message ambiguous.

Under Texas law, negligence liability requires the existence of a duty, breach of that duty, and an injury proximately resulting from that breach. City of Gladewater v. Pike, 727 S.W.2d 514, 517 (Tex.1987). The existence of a duty presents a threshold question of law for the court; the jury determines breach and proximate cause only after the court concludes that a duty exists. See Otis Engineering Corp. v. Clark, 668 S.W.2d 307, 309 (Tex.1983); Abalos v. Oil Dev. Co., 544 S.W.2d 627, 633 (Tex.1976). Our resolution of this case hinges on the initial duty question.

B. Duty

In essence, a duty represents a legally enforceable obligation to conform to a particular standard of conduct. W. Keeton, D. Dobbs, R. Keeton & D. Owen, Prosser and Keeton on Torts § 53 at 356 (5th Ed.1984). Whether the defendant in a negligence action owes a duty involves consideration of two related issues: (1) whether the defendant owes an obligation to this particular plaintiff to act as a reasonable person would in the circumstances; and (2) the standard of conduct required to satisfy that obligation. Id. . . . .
Our analysis here assumes that SOF owes a duty of reasonable care to the public; we focus on the second prong of the duty issue: whether SOF's decision to print Hearn's ad violated the standard of conduct . . . .

1. The Probability and Gravity of the Threatened Harm

In assessing the threatened harm we note that "nearly all human acts ... carry some recognizable but remote possibility of harm to another." Prosser Keeton, supra, § 31 at 170. The SOF classified ads presented more than a remote risk. Of the 2,000 or so personal service classified ads that SOF printed between 1975 and 1984, Eimann's evidence established that as many as nine had served as links in criminal plots. Of these nine, the evidence revealed that SOF staffers had participated in at least two police investigations of crimes in which classified ads played a role; other crimes tied to the ads received varying amounts of media coverage.

As noted above, the gravity of the threatened harm may require precautions against even unlikely events. Id. For example, the standard of care may require those who own oil storage tanks to take precautions against fires caused by an unpredictable lightning strike. See, e.g., Tex-Jersey Oil Corp. v. Beck, 292 S.W.2d 803, 807-09 (Tex.Civ.App.--Texarkana 1956), aff'd in part and rev'd in part on other grounds, 157 Tex. 541, 305 S.W.2d 162 (Tex.1957), overruled on other grounds in Sanchez v. Schindler, 651 S.W.2d 249, 251 (Tex.1983). The prospect of ad-inspired crime represents a threat of serious harm. Eimann presented evidence that SOF classified ads played a role in other crimes ranging from extortion to jailbreaks. Sandra Black's murder illustrates one aspect of the crime linked to SOF classified advertisements.

### 2. The Burden of Preventing the Harm

SOF contends that the standard of conduct applied by the district court impermissibly required the magazine to guard against criminal solicitation by investigating its advertisers and their ads. It relies on a series of cases holding that newspaper publishers owe no duty in tort to investigate their advertisers for the accuracy of ads placed for publication. See Pittman v. Dow Jones & Co., 662 F.Supp. 921, 923 (E.D.La.1987).

However, in our view the standard of conduct against which the jury measured SOF's actions was more exacting than a duty to investigate; it requires publishers to recognize ads that "reasonably could be interpreted as an offer to engage in illegal activity" based on their words or "context" and refrain from printing them. Based on evidence that SOF knew other ads had been tied to crimes, Eimann's counsel contended at oral argument that SOF should have refrained from publishing Hearn's ad and all other personal service classified ads--suggestive ones and bland ones alike. This represents an especially heavy burden given (1) the ambiguous nature of Hearn's ad; and (2) the pervasiveness of advertising in our society.

At most, the evidence reveals that Hearn submitted a facially innocuous ad. Standing alone, the phrase "high risk assignments" plausibly encompassed Hearn's professed goal of recruiting candidates for bodyguard jobs. Hearn performed precisely that function for at least one client who contacted him through the ad . . . .

### 3. Balancing the Burdens and Risks

We conclude that the standard of conduct imposed by the district court does not strike the proper balance between the risks of harm from ambiguous advertisement and the burden of preventing harm from this source under these facts. The appreciable risk that ads such as Hearn's will cause harm, combined with the gravity of that harm, does not outweigh the onerous burden Eimann asks us to endorse.

Hearn's ad presents a risk of serious harm. But everyday activities, such as driving on high-speed, closed access roadways, also carry definite risks that we as a society choose to accept in return for the activity's usefulness and convenience. See Restatement (Second) of Torts § 291 comment e at 56 (1965). To take a more extreme example, courts have almost uniformly rejected efforts to hold handgun manufacturers liable under negligence or strict liability theories to gunshot victims injured during crimes, despite the real possibility that such products can be used for criminal purposes. See Perkins v. F.I.E. Corp., 762 F.2d 1250, 1275 (5th Cir.1985) (applying Louisiana law); Armijo v. Ex Cam, Inc., 656 F.Supp. 771, 775 (D.N.M.1987) (applying New Mexico law); Caveny v. Raven Arms Co., 665 F.Supp. 530, 536 (S.D.Ohio 1987) (applying Ohio law); Patterson v. Gesellschaft, 608 F.Supp. 1206 (N.D.Tex.1985) (applying Texas law). Given the pervasiveness of advertising in our society and the important role it plays, we decline to impose on publishers the obligation to reject all ambiguous advertisements for products or services that might pose a threat of harm.

## III. CONCLUSION

The standard of conduct imposed by the district court against SOF is too high; it allows a jury to visit liability on a publisher for untoward consequences that flow from his decision to publish any suspicious, ambiguous ad that might cause serious harm. The burden on a publisher to avoid liability from suits of this type is too great: he must reject all such advertisements.

The range of foreseeable misuses of advertised products and services is as limitless as the forms and functions of the products themselves. Without a more specific indication of illegal intent than Hearn's ad or its context provided, we conclude that SOF did not violate the required standard of conduct by publishing an ad that later played a role in criminal activity.

The judgment of the district court is REVERSED and RENDERED.

# Part VII: Copyright

Hugo ZACCHINI, Petitioner,
v.
SCRIPPS-HOWARD BROADCASTING COMPANY.

433 U.S. 562

Supreme Court of the United States

Decided June 28, 1977.

Mr. Justice WHITE delivered the opinion of the Court.

Petitioner, Hugo Zacchini, is an entertainer. He performs a 'human cannonball' act in which he is shot from a cannon into a net some 200 feet away. Each performance occupies some 15 seconds. In August and September 1972, petitioner was engaged to perform his act on a regular basis at the Geauga County Fair in Burton, Ohio. He performed in a fenced area, surrounded by grandstands, at the fair grounds. Members of the public attending the fair were not charged a separate admission fee to observe his act.

On August 30, a freelance reporter for Scripps-Howard Broadcasting Co., the operator of a television broadcasting station and respondent in this case, attended the fair. He carried a small movie camera. Petitioner noticed the reporter and asked him not to film the performance. The reporter did not do so on that day; but on the instructions of the producer of respondent's daily newscast, he returned the following day and videotaped the entire act. This film clip approximately 15 seconds in length, was shown on the 11 o'clock news program that night, together with favorable commentary. [FN1]

FN1. The script of the commentary accompanying the film clip read as follows:
'This . . . now . . . is the story of a true spectator sport . . . the sport of human cannonballing . . . in fact, the great Zacchini is about the only human cannonball around, these days . . . just happens that, where he is, is the Great Geauga County Fair, in Burton . . . and believe me, although it's not a long act, it's a thriller . . . and you really need to see it in person . . . to appreciate it. . . .' (Emphasis in original.) App. 12.

Petitioner then brought this action for damages, alleging that he is 'engaged in the entertainment business,' that the act he performs is one 'invented by his father and . . . performed only by his family for the last fifty years,' that respondent 'showed and commercialized the film of his act without his consent,' and that such conduct was an 'unlawful appropriation of plaintiff's professional property.' App. 4-5. Respondent answered and moved for summary judgment, which was granted by the trial court.

The Court of Appeals of Ohio reversed. The majority held that petitioner's complaint stated a cause of action for conversion and for infringement of a common-law copyright, and one judge concurred in the judgment on the ground that the complaint stated a cause of action for appropriation of petitioner's 'right of publicity' in the film of his act. All three judges agreed that the First Amendment did not privilege the press to show the entire performance on a news program without compensating petitioner for any financial injury he could prove at trial.

Like the concurring judge in the Court of Appeals, the Supreme Court of Ohio rested petitioner's cause of action under state law on his 'right to the publicity value of his performance.' 47 Ohio St.2d 224, 351 N.E.2d 454, 455 (1976). The opinion syllabus, to which we are to look for the rule of law used to decide the case, declared first that one may not use for his own benefit the name or likeness of another, whether or not the use or benefit is a commercial one, and second that respondent would be liable for the appropriation over petitioner's objection and in the absence of license or privilege, of petitioner's right to the publicity value of his performance. Ibid. The court nevertheless gave judgment for respondent because, in the words of the syllabus:

> 'A TV station has a privilege to report in its newscasts matters of legitimate public interest which would otherwise be protected by an individual's right of publicity, unless the actual intent of the TV station was to appropriate the benefit of the publicity for some non-privileged private use, or unless the actual intent was to injure the individual.' Ibid.

We granted certiorari, 429 U.S. 1037, 97 S.Ct. 730, 50 L.Ed.2d 747 (1977), to consider an issue unresolved by this Court: whether the First and Fourteenth Amendments immunized respondent from damages for its alleged infringement of petitioner's statelaw 'right of publicity.' Pet. for Cert. 2. Insofar as the Ohio Supreme Court held that the First and Fourteenth Amendments of the United States Constitution required judgment for respondent, we reverse the judgment of that court.

II

The Ohio Supreme Court held that respondent is constitutionally privileged to include in its newscasts matters of public interest that would otherwise be protected by the right of publicity, absent an intent to injure or to appropriate for some nonprivileged purpose. If under this standard respondent had merely reported that petitioner was performing at the fair and described or commented on his act, with or without showing his picture on television, we would have a very different case. But petitioner is not contending that his appearance at the fair and his performance could not be reported by the press as newsworthy items. His complaint is that respondent filmed his entire act and displayed that film on television for the public to see and enjoy. This, he claimed, was an appropriation of his professional property. The Ohio Supreme Court agreed that petitioner had 'a right of publicity' that gave him 'personal control over commercial display and exploitation of his personality and the exercise of his talents.' This right of 'exclusive control over the publicity given to his performances' was said to be such a 'valuable part of the benefit which may be attained by his talents and efforts' that it was entitled to legal protection. It was also observed, or at least expressly assumed, that petitioner had not abandoned his rights by performing under the circumstances present at the Geauga County Fair Grounds.

The Ohio Supreme Court nevertheless held that the challenged invasion was privileged, saying that the press 'must be accorded broad latitude in its choice of how much it presents of each story or incident, and of the emphasis to be given to such presentation. No fixed standard which would bar the press from reporting or depicting either an entire occurrence or an entire discrete part of a public performance can be formulated which would not unduly restrict the 'breathing room' in reporting which freedom of the press requires.' 47 Ohio St.2d, at 235, 351 N.E.2d, at 461. Under this view, respondent was thus constitutionally free to film and display petitioner's entire act . . . .

The broadcast of a film of petitioner's entire act poses a substantial threat to the economic value of that performance. As the Ohio court recognized, this act is the product of petitioner's own talents and energy, the end result of much time, effort, and expense. Much of its economic value lies in the 'right of exclusive control over the publicity given to his performance'; if the public can see the act free on television, it will be less willing to pay to see it at the fair. The effect of a public broadcast of the performance is similar to preventing petitioner from charging an admission fee. 'The rationale for (protecting the right of publicity) is the straightforward one of preventing unjust enrichment by the theft of good will. No social purpose is served by having the defendant get free some aspect of the plaintiff that would have market value and for which he would normally pay.' Kalven, Privacy in Tort Law Were Warren and Brandeis Wrong?, 31 Law & Contemp. Prob. 326, 331 (1966). Moreover, the broadcast of petitioner's entire performance, unlike the unauthorized use of another's name for purposes of trade or the incidental use of a name or picture by the press, goes to the heart of petitioner's ability to earn a living as an entertainer. Thus, in this case, Ohio has recognized what may be the strongest case for a 'right of publicity' involving, not the appropriation of an entertainer's reputation to enhance the attractiveness of a commercial product, but the appropriation of the very activity by which the entertainer acquired his reputation in the first place.

Of course, Ohio's decision to protect petitioner's right of publicity here rests on more than a desire to compensate the performer for the time and effort invested in his act; the protection provides an economic incentive for him to make the investment required to produce a performance of interest to the public. This same consideration underlies the patent and copyright laws long enforced by this Court. As the Court stated in Mazer v. Stein, 347 U.S. 201, 219, 74 S.Ct. 460, 471, 98 L.Ed. 630 (1954):

> 'The economic philosophy behind the clause empowering Congress to grant patents and copyrights is the conviction that encouragement of individual effort by personal gain is the best way to advance public welfare through the talents of authors and inventors in 'Science and useful Arts.' Sacrificial days devoted to such creative activities deserve rewards commensurate with the services rendered.'

These laws perhaps regard the 'reward to the owner (as) a secondary consideration,' United States v. Paramount Pictures, 334 U.S. 131, 158, 68 S.Ct. 915, 929, 92 L.Ed. 1260 (1948), but they were 'intended definitely to grant valuable, enforceable rights' in order to afford greater encouragement to the production of works of benefit to the public. Washingtonian Publishing Co. v. Pearson, 306 U.S. 30, 36, 59 S.Ct. 397, 400, 83 L.Ed. 470 (1939). The Constitution does not prevent Ohio from making a similar choice here in deciding to protect the entertainer's incentive in order to encourage the production of this type of work. Cf. Goldstein v. California, 412 U.S. 546, 93 S.Ct. 2303, 37 L.Ed.2d 163 (1973); Kewanee Oil Co. v. Bicron Corp., 416 U.S. 470, 94 S.Ct. 1879, 40 L.Ed.2d 315 (1974).

There is no doubt that entertainment, as well as news, enjoys First Amendment protection. It is also true that entertainment itself can be important news. Time, Inc. v. Hill. But it is important to note that neither the public nor respondent will be deprived of the benefit of petitioner's performance as long as his commercial stake in his act is appropriately recognized. Petitioner does not seek to enjoin the broadcast of his performance; he simply wants to be paid for it. Nor do we think that a state-law damages remedy against respondent would represent a species of liability without fault contrary to the letter or spirit of Gertz v. Robert Welch, Inc., 418 U.S. 323, 94 S.Ct. 2997, 41 L.Ed.2d 789 (1974). Respondent knew that petitioner objected to televising his act, but nevertheless displayed the entire film.

We conclude that although the State of Ohio may as a matter of its own law privilege the press in the circumstances of this case, the First and Fourteenth Amendments do not require it to do so.

Reversed.

Mr. Justice POWELL, with whom Mr. Justice BRENNAN and Mr. Justice MARSHALL join, dissenting.

Disclaiming any attempt to do more than decide the narrow case before us, the Court reverses the decision of the Supreme Court of Ohio based on repeated incantation of a single formula: 'a performer's entire act.' The holding today is summed up in one sentence:

> 'Wherever the line in particular situations is to be drawn between media reports that are protected and those that are not, we are quite sure that the First and Fourteenth Amendments do not immunize the media when they broadcast a performer's entire act without his consent.' Ante, at 2856. I doubt that this formula provides a standard clear enough even for resolution of this case. In any event, I am not persuaded that the Court's opinion is appropriately sensitive to the First Amendment values at stake, and I therefore dissent.

FEIST PUBLICATIONS, INC., Petitioner
v.
RURAL TELEPHONE SERVICE COMPANY, INC.

499 U.S. 340

Supreme Court of the United States

Decided March 27, 1991.

Justice O'CONNOR delivered the opinion of the Court.

This case requires us to clarify the extent of copyright protection available to telephone directory white pages.

I

Rural Telephone Service Company, Inc., is a certified public utility that provides telephone service to several communities in northwest Kansas. It is subject to a state regulation that requires all telephone companies operating in Kansas to issue annually an updated telephone directory. Accordingly, as a condition of its monopoly franchise, Rural publishes a typical telephone directory, consisting of white pages and yellow pages. The white pages list in alphabetical order the names of Rural's subscribers, together with their towns and telephone numbers. The yellow pages list Rural's business subscribers alphabetically by category and feature classified advertisements of various sizes. Rural distributes its directory free of charge to its subscribers, but earns revenue by selling yellow pages advertisements.

Feist Publications, Inc., is a publishing company that specializes in area- wide telephone directories. Unlike a typical directory, which covers only a particular calling area, Feist's area-wide directories cover a much larger geographical range, reducing the need to call directory assistance or consult multiple directories. The Feist directory that is the subject of this litigation covers 11 different telephone service areas in 15 counties and contains 46,878 white pages listings--compared to Rural's approximately 7,700 listings. Like Rural's directory, Feist's is distributed free of charge and includes both white pages and yellow pages. Feist and Rural compete vigorously for yellow pages advertising.

As the sole provider of telephone service in its service area, Rural obtains subscriber information quite easily. Persons desiring telephone service must apply to Rural and provide their names and addresses; Rural then assigns them a telephone number. Feist is not a telephone company, let alone one with monopoly status, and therefore lacks independent access to any subscriber information. To obtain white pages listings for its area-wide directory, Feist approached each of the 11 telephone companies operating in northwest Kansas and offered to pay for the right to use its white pages listings.

Of the 11 telephone companies, only Rural refused to license its listings to Feist. Rural's refusal created a problem for Feist, as omitting these listings would have left a gaping hole in its area-wide directory, rendering it less attractive to potential yellow pages advertisers. In a decision subsequent to that which we review here, the District Court determined that this was precisely the reason Rural refused to license its listings. The refusal was motivated by an unlawful purpose "to extend its monopoly in telephone service to a monopoly in yellow pages advertising." Rural Telephone Service Co. v. Feist Publications, Inc., 737 F.Supp. 610, 622 (Kan.1990).

Unable to license Rural's white pages listings, Feist used them without Rural's consent. Feist began by removing several thousand listings that fell outside the geographic range of its area-wide directory, then hired personnel to investigate the 4,935 that remained. These employees verified the data reported by Rural and sought to obtain additional information. As a result, a typical Feist listing includes the individual's street address; most of Rural's listings do not. Notwithstanding these additions, however, 1,309 of the 46,878 listings in Feist's 1983 directory were identical to listings in Rural's 1982-1983 white pages. App. 54 (¶ 15-16), 57. Four of these were fictitious listings that Rural had inserted into its directory to detect copying.

Rural sued for copyright infringement in the District Court for the District of Kansas taking the position that Feist, in compiling its own directory, could not use the information contained in Rural's white pages. Rural asserted that Feist's employees were obliged to travel door-to-door or conduct a telephone survey to discover the same information for themselves. Feist responded that such efforts were economically impractical and, in any event, unnecessary because the information copied was beyond the scope of copyright protection. The District Court granted summary judgment to Rural, explaining that "[c]ourts have consistently held that telephone directories are copyrightable" and citing a string of lower court decisions. 663 F.Supp. 214, 218 (1987). In an unpublished opinion, the Court of Appeals for the Tenth Circuit affirmed "for substantially the reasons given by the district court." App. to Pet. for Cert. 4a, judgt. order reported at 916 F.2d 718 (1990). We granted certiorari, 498 U.S. 808, 111 S.Ct. 40, 112 L.Ed.2d 17 (1990), to determine whether the copyright in Rural's directory protects the names, towns, and telephone numbers copied by Feist.

## II

### A

This case concerns the interaction of two well-established propositions. The first is that facts are not copyrightable; the other, that compilations of facts generally are. Each of these propositions possesses an impeccable pedigree. That there can be no valid copyright in facts is universally understood. The most fundamental axiom of copyright law is that "[n]o author may copyright his ideas or the facts he narrates." Harper & Row, Publishers, Inc. v. Nation

Enterprises, 471 U.S. 539, 556, 105 S.Ct. 2218, 2228, 85 L.Ed.2d 588 (1985). Rural wisely concedes this point, noting in its brief that "[f]acts and discoveries, of course, are not themselves subject to copyright protection." Brief for Respondent 24. At the same time, however, it is beyond dispute that compilations of facts are within the subject matter of copyright. Compilations were expressly mentioned in the Copyright Act of 1909, and again in the Copyright Act of 1976.

There is an undeniable tension between these two propositions. Many compilations consist of nothing but raw data--i.e., wholly factual information not accompanied by any original written expression. On what basis may one claim a copyright in such a work? Common sense tells us that 100 uncopyrightable facts do not magically change their status when gathered together in one place. Yet copyright law seems to contemplate that compilations that consist exclusively of facts are potentially within its scope.

The key to resolving the tension lies in understanding why facts are not copyrightable. The sine qua non of copyright is originality. To qualify for copyright protection, a work must be original to the author. See Harper & Row, supra, at 547-549, 105 S.Ct., at 2223-2224. Original, as the term is used in copyright, means only that the work was independently created by the author (as opposed to copied from other works), and that it possesses at least some minimal degree of creativity. 1 M. Nimmer & D. Nimmer, Copyright §§ 2.01[A], [B] (1990) (hereinafter Nimmer). To be sure, the requisite level of creativity is extremely low; even a slight amount will suffice. The vast majority of works make the grade quite easily, as they possess some creative spark, "no matter how crude, humble or obvious" it might be. Id., § 1.08[C] [1]. Originality does not signify novelty; a work may be original even though it closely resembles other works so long as the similarity is fortuitous, not the result of copying. To illustrate, assume that two poets, each ignorant of the other, compose identical poems. Neither work is novel, yet both are original and, hence, copyrightable. See Sheldon v. Metro-Goldwyn Pictures Corp., 81 F.2d 49, 54 (CA2 1936).

Originality is a constitutional requirement. The source of Congress' power to enact copyright laws is Article I, § 8, cl. 8, of the Constitution, which authorizes Congress to "secur[e] for limited Times to Authors ... the exclusive Right to their respective Writings." In two decisions from the late 19th century--The Trade-Mark Cases, 100 U.S. 82, 25 L.Ed. 550 (1879); and Burrow-Giles Lithographic Co. v. Sarony, 111 U.S. 53, 4 S.Ct. 279, 28 L.Ed. 349 (1884)--this Court defined the crucial terms "authors" and "writings." In so doing, the Court made it unmistakably clear that these terms presuppose a degree of originality . . . .

It is this bedrock principle of copyright that mandates the law's seemingly disparate treatment of facts and factual compilations. "No one may claim originality as to facts." Id., § 2.11[A], p. 2-157. This is because facts do not owe their origin to an act of authorship. The distinction is one between creation and discovery: The first person to find and report a particular fact has not created the fact; he or she has merely discovered its existence. To borrow from Burrow-Giles, one who discovers a fact is not its "maker" or "originator." 111 U.S., at 58, 4 S.Ct., at 281. "The discoverer merely finds and records." Nimmer § 2.03[E]. Census takers, for example, do not "create" the population figures that emerge from their efforts; in a sense, they copy these figures from the world around them. Denicola, Copyright in Collections of Facts: A Theory for the Protection of Nonfiction Literary Works, 81 Colum.L.Rev. 516, 525 (1981) (hereinafter Denicola). Census data therefore do not trigger copyright because these data are not "original" in the constitutional sense. Nimmer § 2.03[E]. The same is true of all facts--scientific, historical, biographical, and news of the day. "[T]hey may not be copyrighted and are part of the public domain available to every person." Miller, supra, at 1369.

Factual compilations, on the other hand, may possess the requisite originality. The compilation author typically chooses which facts to include, in what order to place them, and how to arrange the collected data so that they may be used effectively by readers. These choices as to selection and arrangement, so long as they are made independently by the compiler and entail a minimal degree of creativity, are sufficiently original that Congress may protect such compilations through the copyright laws. Nimmer §§ 2.11[D], 3.03; Denicola 523, n. 38. Thus, even a directory that contains absolutely no protectible written expression, only facts, meets the constitutional minimum for copyright protection if it features an original selection or arrangement. See Harper & Row, 471 U.S., at 547, 105 S.Ct., at 2223. Accord, Nimmer § 3.03.

This protection is subject to an important limitation. The mere fact that a work is copyrighted does not mean that every element of the work may be protected. Originality remains the sine qua non of copyright; accordingly, copyright protection may extend only to those components of a work that are original to the author. Patterson & Joyce 800-802; Ginsburg, Creation and Commercial Value: Copyright Protection of Works of Information, 90 Colum.L.Rev. 1865, 1868, and n. 12 (1990) (hereinafter Ginsburg). Thus, if the compilation author clothes facts with an original collocation of words, he or she may be able to claim a copyright in this written expression. Others may copy the underlying facts from the publication, but not the precise words used to present them. In Harper & Row, for example, we explained that President Ford could not prevent others from copying bare historical facts from his autobiography, see 471 U.S., at 556-557, 105 S.Ct., at 2228-2229, but that he could prevent others from copying his "subjective descriptions and portraits of public figures." Id., at 563, 105 S.Ct., at 2232. Where the compilation author adds no written expression but rather lets the facts speak for themselves, the expressive element is more elusive. The only conceivable expression is the manner in which the compiler has selected and arranged the facts. Thus, if the selection and arrangement are original, these elements of the work are eligible for copyright protection. See Patry, Copyright in Compilations of Facts (or Why the "White Pages" Are Not Copyrightable), 12 Com. & Law 37, 64 (Dec. 1990) (hereinafter Patry). No matter how original the format, however, the facts themselves do not become original through association. See Patterson & Joyce 776.

This inevitably means that the copyright in a factual compilation is thin. Notwithstanding a valid copyright, a subsequent compiler remains free to use the facts contained in another's publication to aid in preparing a competing work, so long as the competing work does not feature the same selection and arrangement. As one commentator explains it: "[N]o matter how much original authorship the work displays, the facts and ideas it exposes are free for the taking.... [T]he very same facts and ideas may be divorced from the context imposed by the author, and restated or reshuffled by second comers, even if the author was the first to discover the facts or to propose the ideas." Ginsburg 1868.

It may seem unfair that much of the fruit of the compiler's labor may be used by others without compensation. As Justice Brennan has correctly observed, however, this is not "some unforeseen byproduct of a statutory scheme." Harper & Row, 471 U.S., at 589, 105 S.Ct., at 2245 (dissenting opinion). It is, rather, "the essence of copyright," ibid., and a constitutional requirement. The primary objective of copyright is not to reward the labor of authors, but "[t]o promote the Progress of Science and useful Arts." Art. I, § 8, cl. 8. Accord, Twentieth Century Music Corp. v. Aiken, 422 U.S. 151, 156, 95 S.Ct. 2040, 2044, 45 L.Ed.2d 84 (1975). To this end, copyright assures authors the right to their original expression, but encourages others to build freely upon the ideas and information conveyed by a work. Harper & Row, supra, 471 U.S., at 556-557, 105 S.Ct., at 2228-2229. This principle, known as the idea/expression or fact/expression dichotomy, applies to all works of authorship. As applied to a factual compilation, assuming the absence of original written expression, only the compiler's selection and arrangement may be protected; the raw facts may be copied at will. This result is neither unfair nor unfortunate. It is the means by which copyright advances the progress of science and art . . . .

This, then, resolves the doctrinal tension: Copyright treats facts and factual compilations in a wholly consistent manner. Facts, whether alone or as part of a compilation, are not original and therefore may not be copyrighted. A factual compilation is eligible for copyright if it features an original selection or arrangement of facts, but the copyright is limited to the particular selection or arrangement. In no event may copyright extend to the facts themselves . . . .

Not every selection, coordination, or arrangement will pass muster. This is plain from the statute. It states that, to merit protection, the facts must be selected, coordinated, or arranged "in such a way" as to render the work as a whole original. This implies that some "ways" will trigger copyright, but that others will not. See Patry 57, and n. 76. Otherwise, the phrase "in such a way" is meaningless and Congress should have defined "compilation" simply as "a work formed by the collection and assembly of preexisting materials or data that are selected, coordinated, or arranged." That Congress did not do so is dispositive. In accordance with "the established principle that a court should give effect, if possible, to every clause and word of a statute," Moskal v. United States, 498 U.S. 103, 109- 110, 111 S.Ct. 461, 466, 112 L.Ed.2d 449 (1990) (internal quotation marks omitted), we conclude that the statute envisions that there will be some fact- based works in which the selection, coordination, and arrangement are not sufficiently original to trigger copyright protection . . . .

## III

There is no doubt that Feist took from the white pages of Rural's directory a substantial amount of factual information. At a minimum, Feist copied the names, towns, and telephone numbers of 1,309 of Rural's subscribers. Not all copying, however, is copyright infringement. To establish infringement, two elements must be proven: (1) ownership of a valid copyright, and (2) copying of constituent elements of the work that are original. See Harper & Row, 471 U.S., at 548, 105 S.Ct., at 2224. The first element is not at issue here; Feist appears to concede that Rural's directory, considered as a whole, is subject to a valid copyright because it contains some foreword text, as well as original material in its yellow pages advertisements. See Brief for Petitioner 18; Pet. for Cert. 9.

The question is whether Rural has proved the second element. In other words, did Feist, by taking 1,309 names, towns, and telephone numbers from Rural's white pages, copy anything that was "original" to Rural? Certainly, the raw data does not satisfy the originality requirement. Rural may have been the first to discover and report the names, towns, and telephone numbers of its subscribers, but this data does not " 'ow[e] its origin' " to Rural. Burrow-Giles, 111 U.S., at 58, 4 S.Ct., at 281. Rather, these bits of information are uncopyrightable facts; they existed before Rural reported them and would have continued to exist if Rural had never published a telephone directory. The originality requirement "rule[s] out protecting ... names, addresses, and telephone numbers of which the plaintiff by no stretch of the imagination could be called the author." Patterson & Joyce 776 . . . .

The question that remains is whether Rural selected, coordinated, or arranged these uncopyrightable facts in an original way. As mentioned, originality is not a stringent standard; it does not require that facts be presented in an innovative or surprising way. It is equally true, however, that the selection and arrangement of facts cannot be so mechanical or routine as to require no creativity whatsoever. The standard of originality is low, but it does exist. See Patterson & Joyce 760, n. 144 ("While this requirement is sometimes characterized as modest, or a low threshold, it is not without effect") (internal quotation marks omitted; citations omitted). As this Court has explained, the Constitution mandates some minimal degree of creativity, see The Trade-Mark Cases, 100 U.S., at 94; and an author who claims infringement must prove "the existence of ... intellectual production, of thought, and conception." Burrow-Giles, supra, 111 U.S., at 59-60, 4 S.Ct., at 281-282.

The selection, coordination, and arrangement of Rural's white pages do not satisfy the minimum constitutional standards for copyright protection. As mentioned at the outset, Rural's white pages are entirely typical. Persons desiring telephone service in Rural's service area fill out an application and Rural issues them a telephone number. In preparing its white pages, Rural simply takes the data provided by its subscribers and lists it alphabetically by surname. The end product is a garden-variety white pages directory, devoid of even the slightest trace of creativity . . . .

We conclude that the names, towns, and telephone numbers copied by Feist were not original to Rural and therefore were not protected by the copyright in Rural's combined white and yellow pages directory. As a constitutional matter, copyright protects only those constituent elements of a work that possess more than a de minimis quantum of creativity. Rural's white pages, limited to basic subscriber information and arranged alphabetically, fall short of the mark. As a statutory matter, 17 U.S.C. § 101 does not afford protection from copying to a collection of facts that are selected, coordinated, and arranged in a way that utterly lacks originality. Given that some works must fail, we cannot imagine a more likely candidate. Indeed, were we to hold that Rural's white pages pass muster, it is hard to believe that any collection of facts could fail.

Because Rural's white pages lack the requisite originality, Feist's use of the listings cannot constitute infringement. This decision should not be construed as demeaning Rural's efforts in compiling its directory, but rather as making clear that copyright rewards originality, not effort. As this Court noted more than a century ago, " 'great praise may be due to the plaintiffs for their industry and enterprise in publishing this paper, yet the law does not contemplate their being rewarded in this way.' " Baker v. Selden, 101 U.S., at 105.

The judgment of the Court of Appeals is

Reversed.

Justice BLACKMUN concurs in the judgment.

HARPER & ROW, PUBLISHERS, INC. and the Reader's Digest Association, Inc., Petitioners
v.
NATION ENTERPRISES and the Nation Associates, Inc.

471 U.S. 539

Supreme Court of the United States

Decided May 20, 1985.

Justice O'CONNOR delivered the opinion of the Court.

This case requires us to consider to what extent the "fair use" provision of the Copyright Revision Act of 1976, (hereinafter the Copyright Act) 17 U.S.C. § 107, sanctions the unauthorized use of quotations from a public figure's unpublished manuscript. In March 1979, an undisclosed source provided The Nation Magazine with the unpublished manuscript of "A Time to Heal: The Autobiography of Gerald R. Ford." Working directly from the purloined manuscript, an editor of The Nation produced a short piece entitled "The Ford Memoirs--Behind the Nixon Pardon." The piece was timed to "scoop" an article scheduled shortly to appear in Time Magazine. Time had agreed to purchase the exclusive right to print prepublication excerpts from the copyright holders, Harper & Row Publishers, Inc. (hereinafter Harper & Row), and Reader's Digest Association, Inc. (hereinafter Reader's Digest). As a result of The Nation article, Time canceled its agreement. Petitioners brought a successful copyright action against The Nation. On appeal, the Second Circuit reversed the lower court's finding of infringement, holding that The Nation's act was sanctioned as a "fair use" of the copyrighted material. We granted certiorari, 467 U.S. 1214, 104 S.Ct. 2655, 81 L.Ed.2d 362 (1984), and we now reverse.

I

In February 1977, shortly after leaving the White House, former President Gerald R. Ford contracted with petitioners Harper & Row and Reader's Digest, to publish his as yet unwritten memoirs. The memoirs were to contain "significant hitherto unpublished material" concerning the Watergate crisis, Mr. Ford's pardon of former President Nixon and "Mr. Ford's reflections on this period of history, and the morality and personalities involved." App. to Pet. for Cert. C-14--C-15. In addition to the right to publish the Ford memoirs in book form, the agreement gave petitioners the exclusive right to license prepublication excerpts, known in the trade as "first serial rights." Two years later, as the memoirs were nearing completion, petitioners negotiated a prepublication licensing agreement with Time, a weekly news magazine. Time agreed to pay $25,000, $12,500 in advance and an additional $12,500 at publication, in exchange for the right to excerpt 7,500 words from Mr. Ford's account of the Nixon pardon. The issue featuring the excerpts was timed to appear approximately one week before shipment of the full length book version to bookstores. Exclusivity was an important consideration; Harper & Row instituted procedures designed to maintain the confidentiality of the manuscript, and Time retained the right to renegotiate the second payment should the material appear in print prior to its release of the excerpts.

Two to three weeks before the Time article's scheduled release, an unidentified person secretly brought a copy of the Ford manuscript to Victor Navasky, editor of The Nation, a political commentary magazine. Mr. Navasky knew that his possession of the manuscript was not authorized and that the manuscript must be returned quickly to his "source" to avoid discovery. 557 F.Supp. 1067, 1069 (SDNY 1983). He hastily put together what he believed was "a real hot news story" composed of quotes, paraphrases, and facts drawn exclusively from the manuscript. Ibid. Mr. Navasky attempted no independent commentary, research or criticism, in part because of the need for speed if he was to "make news" by "publish[ing] in advance of publication of the Ford book." App. 416-417. The 2,250-word article, reprinted in the Appendix to this opinion, appeared on April 3, 1979. As a result of The Nation's article, Time canceled its piece and refused to pay the remaining $12,500.

Petitioners brought suit in the District Court for the Southern District of New York, alleging conversion, tortious interference with contract, and violations of the Copyright Act. After a 6-day bench trial, the District Judge found that "A Time to Heal" was protected by copyright at the time of The Nation publication and that respondents' use of the copyrighted material constituted an infringement under the Copyright Act, §§ 106(1), (2), and (3), protecting respectively the right to reproduce the work, the right to license preparation of derivative works, and the right of first distribution of the copyrighted work to the public. App. to Pet. for Cert. C-29--C- 30. The District Court rejected respondents' argument that The Nation's piece was a "fair use" sanctioned by § 107 of the Act. Though billed as "hot news," the article contained no new facts. The magazine had "published its article for profit," taking "the heart" of "a soon-to-be-published" work. This unauthorized use "caused the Time agreement to be aborted and thus diminished the value of the copyright." 557 F.Supp., at 1072. Although certain elements of the Ford memoirs, such as historical facts and memoranda, were not per se copyrightable, the District Court held that it was "the totality of these facts and memoranda collected together with Ford's reflections that made them of value to The Nation, [and] this ... totality ... is protected by the copyright laws." Id., at 1072-1073. The court awarded actual damages of $12,500.

A divided panel of the Court of Appeals for the Second Circuit reversed. The majority recognized that Mr. Ford's verbatim "reflections" were original "expression" protected by copyright. But it held that the District Court had erred in assuming the "coupling [of these reflections] with uncopyrightable fact transformed that information into a copyrighted 'totality.' " 723 F.2d 195, 205 (CA2 1983). The majority noted that copyright attaches to expression, not facts or ideas. It concluded that, to avoid granting a copyright monopoly over the facts underlying history and news, " 'expression' [in such works must be confined] to its barest elements--the ordering and choice of the words themselves." Id., at 204. Thus similarities between the original and the challenged work traceable to the copying or paraphrasing of uncopyrightable material, such as historical facts, memoranda and other public documents, and quoted remarks of third parties, must be disregarded in evaluating whether the second author's use was fair or infringing.

> "When the uncopyrighted material is stripped away, the article in The Nation contains, at most, approximately 300 words that are copyrighted. These remaining paragraphs and scattered phrases are all verbatim quotations from the memoirs which had not appeared previously in other publications. They include a short segment of Ford's conversations with Henry Kissinger and several other individuals. Ford's impressionistic depictions of Nixon, ill with phlebitis after the resignation and pardon, and of Nixon's character, constitute the major portion of this material. It is these parts of the magazine piece on which [the court] must focus in [its] examination of the question whether there was a 'fair use' of copyrighted matter." Id., at 206.

Examining the four factors enumerated in § 107, see infra, at 2224, n. 2, the majority found the purpose of the article was "news reporting," the original work was essentially factual in nature, the 300 words appropriated were insubstantial in relation to the 2,250-word piece, and the impact on the market for the original was minimal as "the evidence [did] not support a finding that it was the very limited use of expression per se which led to Time's decision not to print the excerpt." The Nation's borrowing of verbatim quotations merely "len[t] authenticity to this politically significant material ... complementing the reporting of the facts." 723 F.2d, at 208. The Court of Appeals was especially influenced by the "politically significant" nature of the subject matter and its conviction that it is not "the purpose of the Copyright Act to impede that harvest of knowledge so necessary to a democratic state" or "chill the activities of the press by forbidding a circumscribed use of copyrighted words." Id., at 197, 209.

## II

We agree with the Court of Appeals that copyright is intended to increase and not to impede the harvest of knowledge. But we believe the Second Circuit gave insufficient deference to the scheme established by the Copyright Act for fostering the original works that provide the seed and substance of this harvest. The rights conferred by copyright are designed to assure contributors to the store of knowledge a fair return for their labors. Twentieth Century Music Corp. v. Aiken, 422 U.S. 151, 156, 95 S.Ct. 2040, 2043, 45 L.Ed.2d 84 (1975).

Article I, § 8, of the Constitution provides:

> "The Congress shall have Power ... to Promote the Progress of Science and useful Arts, by securing for limited Times to Authors and Inventors the exclusive Right to their respective Writings and Discoveries."

As we noted last Term: "[This] limited grant is a means by which an important public purpose may be achieved. It is intended to motivate the creative activity of authors and inventors by the provision of a special reward, and to allow the public access to the products of their genius after the limited period of exclusive control has expired." Sony Corp. of America v. Universal City Studios, Inc., 464 U.S. 417, 429, 104 S.Ct. 774, 782, 78 L.Ed.2d 574 (1984). "The monopoly created by copyright thus rewards the individual author in order to benefit the public." Id., at 477, 104 S.Ct., at 807 (dissenting opinion). This principle applies equally to works of fiction and nonfiction. The book at issue here, for example, was two years in the making, and began with a contract giving the author's copyright to the publishers in exchange for their services in producing and marketing the work. In preparing the book, Mr. Ford drafted essays and word portraits of public figures and participated in hundreds of taped interviews that were later distilled to chronicle his personal viewpoint. It is evident that the monopoly granted by copyright actively served its intended purpose of inducing the creation of new material of potential historical value.

Section 106 of the Copyright Act confers a bundle of exclusive rights to the owner of the copyright. [FN1] Under the Copyright Act, these rights-- to publish, copy, and distribute the author's work--vest in the author of an original work from the time of its creation. § 106. In practice, the author commonly sells his rights to publishers who offer royalties in exchange for their services in producing and marketing the author's work. The copyright owner's rights, however, are subject to certain statutory exceptions. §§ 107- 118. Among these is § 107 which codifies the traditional privilege of other authors to make "fair use" of an earlier writer's work. [FN2] In addition, no author may copyright facts or ideas. § 102. The copyright is limited to those aspects of the work--termed "expression"--that display the stamp of the author's originality . . . .

FN1. Section 106 provides in pertinent part:
"Subject to sections 107 through 118, the owner of copyright under this title has the exclusive rights to do and authorize any of the following:
"(1) to reproduce the copyrighted work in copies ... ;
"(2) to prepare derivative works based upon the copyrighted work;
"(3) to distribute copies ... of the copyrighted work to the public...."

FN2. Section 107 states:
"Notwithstanding the provisions of section 106, the fair use of a copyrighted work ... for purposes such as criticism, comment, news reporting, teaching (including multiple copies for classroom use), scholarship, or research, is not an infringement of copyright. In determining whether the use made of a work in any particular case is a fair use the factors to be considered shall include--
"(1) the purpose and character of the use, including whether such use is of a commercial nature or is for nonprofit educational purposes;
"(2) the nature of the copyrighted work;
"(3) the amount and substantiality of the portion used in relation to the copyrighted work as a whole; and
"(4) the effect of the use upon the potential market for or value of the copyrighted work."

## IV

Fair use is a mixed question of law and fact. Pacific & Southern Co. v. Duncan, 744 F.2d 1490, 1495, n. 8 (CA11 1984). Where the district court has found facts sufficient to evaluate each of the statutory factors, an appellate court "need not remand for further factfinding ... [but] may conclude as a matter of law that [the challenged use] do[es] not qualify as a fair use of the copyrighted work." Id., at 1495. Thus whether The Nation article constitutes fair use under § 107 must be reviewed in light of the principles discussed above. The factors enumerated in the section are not meant to be exclusive: "[S]ince the doctrine is an equitable rule of reason, no generally applicable definition is possible, and each case raising the question must be decided on its own facts." House Report, at 65, U.S.Code Cong. & Admin.News 1976, p. 5678. The four factors identified by Congress as especially relevant in determining whether the use was fair are: (1) the purpose and character of the use; (2) the nature of the copyrighted work; (3) the substantiality of the portion used in relation to the copyrighted work as a whole; (4) the effect on the potential market for or value of the copyrighted work. We address each one separately.

Purpose of the Use. The Second Circuit correctly identified news reporting as the general purpose of The Nation's use. News reporting is one of the examples enumerated in § 107 to "give some idea of the sort of activities the courts might regard as fair use under the circumstances." Senate Report, at 61. This listing was not intended to be exhaustive, see ibid.; § 101 (definition of "including" and "such as"), or to single out any particular use as presumptively a "fair" use. The drafters resisted pressures from special interest groups to create presumptive categories of fair use, but structured the provision as an affirmative defense requiring a case-by-case analysis. See H.R.Rep. No. 83, 90th Cong., 1st Sess., 37 (1967); Patry 477, n. 4. "[W]hether a use referred to in the first sentence of section 107 is a fair use in a particular case will depend upon the application of the determinative factors, including those mentioned in the second sentence." Senate Report, at 62. The fact that an article arguably is "news" and therefore a productive use is simply one factor in a fair use analysis.

We agree with the Second Circuit that the trial court erred in fixing on whether the information contained in the memoirs was actually new to the public. As Judge Meskill wisely noted, "[c]ourts should be chary of deciding what is and what is not news." 723 F.2d, at 215 (dissenting). Cf. Gertz v. Robert Welch, Inc., 418 U.S. 323, 345-346, 94 S.Ct. 2997, 3009-3010, 41 L.Ed.2d 789 (1974). "The issue is not what constitutes 'news,' but whether a claim of newsreporting is a valid fair use defense to an infringement of copyrightable expression." Patry 119. The Nation has every right to seek to be the first to publish information. But The Nation went beyond simply reporting uncopyrightable information and actively sought to exploit the headline value of its infringement, making a "news event" out of its unauthorized first publication of a noted figure's copyrighted expression.

The fact that a publication was commercial as opposed to nonprofit is a separate factor that tends to weigh against a finding of fair use. "[E]very commercial use of copyrighted material is presumptively an unfair exploitation of the monopoly privilege that belongs to the owner of the copyright." Sony Corp. of America v. Universal City Studios, Inc., 464 U.S., at 451, 104 S.Ct., at 793. In arguing that the purpose of news reporting is not purely commercial, The Nation misses the point entirely. The crux of the profit/nonprofit distinction is not whether the sole motive of the use is monetary gain but whether the user stands to profit from exploitation of the copyrighted material without paying the customary price. See Roy Export Co. Establishment v. Columbia Broadcasting System, Inc., 503 F.Supp., at 1144; 3 Nimmer § 13.05[A][1], at 13-71, n. 25.3.

In evaluating character and purpose we cannot ignore The Nation's stated purpose of scooping the forthcoming hardcover and Time abstracts. App. to Pet. for Cert. C-27. The Nation's use had not merely the incidental effect but the intended purpose of supplanting the copyright holder's commercially valuable right of first publication. See Meredith Corp. v. Harper & Row, Publishers, Inc., 378 F.Supp. 686, 690 (SDNY) (purpose of text was to compete with original), aff'd, 500 F.2d 1221 (CA2 1974). Also relevant to the "character" of the use is "the propriety of the defendant's conduct." 3 Nimmer § 13.05[A], at 13-72. "Fair use presupposes 'good faith' and 'fair dealing.' " Time Inc. v. Bernard Geis Associates, 293 F.Supp. 130, 146 (SDNY 1968), quoting Schulman, Fair Use and the Revision of the Copyright Act, 53 Iowa L.Rev. 832 (1968). The trial court found that The Nation knowingly exploited a purloined manuscript. App. to Pet. for Cert. B-1, C-20--C-21, C-28--C-29. Unlike the typical claim of fair use, The Nation cannot offer up even the fiction of consent as justification. Like its competitor newsweekly, it was free to bid for the right of abstracting excerpts from "A Time to Heal." Fair use "distinguishes between 'a true scholar and a chiseler who infringes a work for personal profit.' " Wainwright Securities Inc. v. Wall Street Transcript Corp., 558 F.2d, at 94, quoting from Hearings on Bills for the General Revision of the Copyright Law before the House Committee on the Judiciary, 89th Cong., 1st Sess., ser. 8, pt. 3, p. 1706 (1966) (statement of John Schulman).

Nature of the Copyrighted Work. Second, the Act directs attention to the nature of the copyrighted work. "A Time to Heal" may be characterized as an unpublished historical narrative or autobiography. The law generally recognizes a greater need to disseminate factual works than works of fiction or fantasy. See Gorman, Fact or Fancy? The Implications for Copyright, 29 J. Copyright Soc. 560, 561 (1982).

> "[E]ven within the field of fact works, there are gradations as to the relative proportion of fact and fancy. One may move from sparsely embellished maps and directories to elegantly written biography. The extent to which one must permit expressive languageto be copied, in order to assure dissemination of the underlying facts, will thus vary from case to case." Id., at 563.

Some of the briefer quotes from the memoirs are arguably necessary adequately to convey the facts; for example, Mr. Ford's characterization of the White House tapes as the "smoking gun" is perhaps so integral to the idea expressed as to be inseparable from it. Cf. 1 Nimmer § 1.10[C]. But The Nation did not stop at isolated phrases and instead excerpted subjective descriptions and portraits of public figures whose power lies in the author's individualized expression. Such use, focusing on the most expressive elements of the work, exceeds that necessary to disseminate the facts.

The fact that a work is unpublished is a critical element of its "nature." 3 Nimmer § 13.05[A]; Comment, 58 St. John's L.Rev., at 613. Our prior discussion establishes that the scope of fair use is narrower with respect to unpublished works. While even substantial quotations might qualify as fair use in a review of a published work or a news account of a speech that had been delivered to the public or disseminated to the press, see House Report, at 65, the author's right to control the first public appearance of his expression weighs against such use of the work before its release. The right of first publication encompasses not only the choice whether to publish at all, but also the choices of when, where, and in what form first to publish a work.

In the case of Mr. Ford's manuscript, the copyright holders' interest in confidentiality is irrefutable; the copyright holders had entered into a contractual undertaking to "keep the manuscript confidential" and required that all those to whom the manuscript was shown also "sign an agreement to keep the manuscript confidential." App. to Pet. for Cert. C-19--C-20. While the copyright holders' contract with Time required Time to submit its proposed article seven days before publication, The Nation's clandestine publication afforded no such opportunity for creative or quality control. Id., at C- 18. It was hastily patched together and contained "a number of inaccuracies." App. 300b-300c (testimony of Victor Navasky). A use that so clearly infringes the copyright holder's interests in confidentiality and creative control is difficult to characterize as "fair."

Amount and Substantiality of the Portion Used. Next, the Act directs us to examine the amount and substantiality of the portion used in relation to the copyrighted work as a whole. In absolute terms, the words actually quoted were an insubstantial portion of "A Time to Heal." The District Court, however, found that "[T]he Nation took what was essentially the heart of the book." 557 F.Supp., at 1072. We believe the Court of Appeals erred in overruling the District Judge's evaluation of the qualitative nature of the taking. See, e.g., Roy Export Co. Establishment v. Columbia Broadcasting System, Inc., 503 F.Supp., at 1145 (taking of 55 seconds out of 1 hour and 29- minute film deemed qualitatively substantial). A Time editor described the chapters on the pardon as "the most interesting and moving parts of the entire manuscript." Reply Brief for Petitioners 16, n. 8. The portions actually quoted were selected by Mr. Navasky as among the most powerful passages in those chapters. He testified that he used verbatim excerpts because simply reciting the information could not adequately convey the "absolute certainty with which [Ford] expressed himself," App. 303; or show that "this comes from President Ford," id., at 305; or carry the "definitive quality" of the original, id., at 306. In short, he quoted these passages precisely because they qualitatively embodied Ford's distinctive expression.

As the statutory language indicates, a taking may not be excused merely because it is insubstantial with respect to the infringing work. As Judge Learned Hand cogently remarked, "no plagiarist can excuse the wrong by showing how much of his work he did not pirate." Sheldon v. Metro-Goldwyn Pictures Corp., 81 F.2d 49, 56 (CA2), cert. denied, 298 U.S. 669, 56 S.Ct. 835, 80 L.Ed. 1392 (1936). Conversely, the fact that a substantial portion of the infringing work was copied verbatim is evidence of the qualitative value of the copied material, both to the originator and to the plagiarist who seeks to profit from marketing someone else's copyrighted expression.

Stripped to the verbatim quotes, the direct takings from the unpublished manuscript constitute at least 13% of the infringing article. See Meeropol v. Nizer, 560 F.2d 1061, 1071 (CA2 1977) (copyrighted letters constituted less than 1% of infringing work but were prominently featured). The Nation article is structured around the quoted excerpts which serve as its dramatic focal points. See Appendix to this opinion, post, p. 2235. In view of the expressive value of the excerpts and their key role in the infringing work, we cannot agree with the Second Circuit that the "magazine took a meager, indeed an infinitesimal amount of Ford's original language." 723 F.2d, at 209.

Effect on the Market. Finally, the Act focuses on "the effect of the use upon the potential market for or value of the copyrighted work." This last factor is undoubtedly the single most important element of fair use. See 3 Nimmer § 13.05[A], at 13-76, and cases cited therein. "Fair use, when properly applied, is limited to copying by others which does not materially impair the marketability of the work which is copied." 1 Nimmer § 1.10[D], at 1-87. The trial court found not merely a potential but an actual effect on the market. Time's cancellation of its projected serialization and its refusal to pay the $12,500 were the direct effect of the infringement. The Court of Appeals rejected this factfinding as clearly erroneous, noting that the record did not establish a causal relation between Time's nonperformance and respondents' unauthorized publication of Mr. Ford's expression as opposed to the facts taken from the memoirs. We disagree. Rarely will a case of copyright infringement present such clear-cut evidence of actual damage. Petitioners assured Time that there would be no other authorized publication of any portion of the unpublished manuscript prior to April 23, 1979. Any publication of material from chapters 1 and 3 would permit Time to renegotiate its final payment. Time cited The Nation's article, which contained verbatim quotes from the unpublished manuscript, as a reason for its nonperformance. With respect to apportionment of profits flowing from a copyright infringement, this Court has held that an infringer who commingles infringing and noninfringing elements "must abide the consequences, unless he can make a separation of the profits so as to assure to the injured party all that justly belongs to him." Sheldon v. Metro-Goldwyn Pictures Corp., 309 U.S. 390, 406, 60 S.Ct. 681, 687, 84 L.Ed. 825 (1940). Cf. 17 U.S.C. § 504(b) (the infringer is required to prove elements of profits attributable to other than the infringed work). Similarly, once a copyright holder establishes with reasonable probability the existence of a causal connection between the infringement and a loss of revenue, the burden properly shifts to the infringer to show that this damage would have occurred had there been no taking of copyrighted expression. See 3 Nimmer § 14.02, at 14-7--14-8.1. Petitioners established a prima facie case of actual damage that respondents failed to rebut. See Stevens Linen Associates, Inc. v. Mastercraft Corp., 656 F.2d 11, 15 (CA2 1981). The trial court properly awarded actual damages and accounting of profits. See 17 U.S.C. § 504(b).

More important, to negate fair use one need only show that if the challenged use "should become widespread, it would adversely affect the potential market for the copyrighted work." Sony Corp. of America v. Universal City Studios, Inc., 464 U.S., at 451, 104 S.Ct., at 793 (emphasis added); id., at 484, and n. 36, 104 S.Ct., at 810, and n. 36 (collecting cases) (dissenting opinion). This inquiry must take account not only of harm to the original but also of harm to the market for derivative works. See Iowa State University Research Foundation, Inc. v. American Broadcasting Cos., 621 F.2d 57 (CA2 1980); Meeropol v. Nizer, supra, at 1070; Roy Export v. Columbia Broadcasting System, Inc., 503 F.Supp., at 1146. "If the defendant's work adversely affects the value of any of the rights in the copyrighted work (in this case the adaptation [and serialization] right) the use is not fair." 3 Nimmer § 13.05[B], at 13-77--13-78 (footnote omitted).

It is undisputed that the factual material in the balance of The Nation's article, besides the verbatim quotes at issue here, was drawn exclusively from the chapters on the pardon. The excerpts were employed as featured episodes in a story about the Nixon pardon--precisely the use petitioners had licensed to Time. The borrowing of these verbatim quotes from the unpublished manuscript lent The Nation's piece a special air of authenticity--as Navasky expressed it, the reader would know it was Ford speaking and not The Nation. App. 300c. Thus it directly competed for a share of the market for prepublication excerpts. The Senate Report states:

> "With certain special exceptions ... a use that supplants any part of the normal market for a copyrighted work would ordinarily be considered an infringement." Senate Report, at 65.

Placed in a broader perspective, a fair use doctrine that permits extensive prepublication quotations from an unreleased manuscript without the copyright owner's consent poses substantial potential for damage to the marketability of first serialization rights in general. "Isolated instances of minor infringements, when multiplied many times, become in the aggregate a major inroad on copyright that must be prevented." Ibid.

V

The Court of Appeals erred in concluding that The Nation's use of the copyrighted material was excused by the public's interest in the subject matter. It erred, as well, in overlooking the unpublished nature of the work and the resulting impact on the potential market for first serial rights of permitting unauthorized prepublication excerpts under the rubric of fair use. Finally, in finding the taking "infinitesimal," the Court of Appeals accorded too little weight to the qualitative importance of the quoted passages of original expression. In sum, the traditional doctrine of fair use, as embodied in the Copyright Act, does not sanction the use made by The Nation of these copyrighted materials. Any copyright infringer may claim to benefit the public by increasing public access to the copyrighted work. See Pacific & Southern Co. v. Duncan, 744 F.2d, at 1499-1500. But Congress has not designed, and we see no warrant for judicially imposing, a "compulsory license" permitting unfettered access to the unpublished copyrighted expression of public figures.

The Nation conceded that its verbatim copying of some 300 words of direct quotation from the Ford manuscript would constitute an infringement unless excused as a fair use. Because we find that The Nation's use of these verbatim excerpts from the unpublished manuscript was not a fair use, the judgment of the Court of Appeals is reversed, and the case is remanded for further proceedings consistent with this opinion.

It is so ordered.

Marvin FISHER d/b/a Marvin Music Company and Jack Segal, Plaintiffs-Appellants,
v.
Rick DEES, Atlantic Recording Corporation, Warner Communications, Inc., Defendants-Appellees.

794 F.2d 432

United States Court of Appeals,
Ninth Circuit.

Decided July 10, 1986.

Appeal from the United States District Court for the Central District of California.

Before WALLACE, SNEED, and KOZINSKI, Circuit Judges

SNEED, Circuit Judge:

The plaintiffs-appellants, Marvin Fisher and Jack Segal, appeal the district court's grant of summary judgment disposing of their federal claim for copyright infringement and their state-law claims for unfair competition, defamation, and product disparagement. We affirm.

## I.
## FACTUAL AND PROCEDURAL BACKGROUND

The plaintiffs-appellants, Marvin Fisher and Jack Segal (the composers), composed and own the copyright to the '50s standard "When Sunny Gets Blue" (the song). In late 1984, a law firm representing the defendants-appellees--disc jockey Rick Dees, Atlantic Recording Corp., and Warner Communications, Inc.--contacted Fisher and requested permission to use part or all of the music to "When Sunny Gets Blue" in order to create a comedic and inoffensive version of the song. Fisher refused the request.

A few months later, Dees released a comedy record album (also issued in cassette form) called Put It Where the Moon Don't Shine. One cut on the album, entitled "When Sonny Sniffs Glue" (the parody), is an obvious take-off on the composers' song. The parody copies the first six of the song's thirty-eight bars of music--its recognizable main theme. In addition, it changes the original's opening lyrics--"When Sunny gets blue, her eyes get gray and cloudy, then the rain begins to fall" to "When Sonny sniffs glue, her eyes get red and bulgy, then her hair begins to fall." The parody runs for 29 seconds of the approximately forty minutes of material on Dees's album.

The composers brought an action in federal district court for copyright infringement, unfair competition, product disparagement, and defamation. The complaint included a proper demand for a jury trial. Before the commencement of discovery, both sides filed motions for summary judgment. The district court granted summary judgment in favor of Dees on all the composers' claims and the composers timely filed this appeal.

## II.
## DISCUSSION

The district court did not reveal the bases for its decision. Nonetheless, we may affirm if the record, viewed in the light most favorable to the composers, discloses no genuine issues of material fact and if Dees was entitled to judgment as a matter of law. See Frederick S. Wyle Professional Corp. v. Texaco, Inc., 764 F.2d 604, 609 (9th Cir.1985).

### A. Copyright Infringement

Dees urges affirmance of summary judgment on the claim for copyright infringement on the ground that the copying of the song for purposes of parody constituted a fair use. We agree for the reasons discussed below.

#### 1. Overview of the fair-use doctrine

The fair-use doctrine was initially developed by courts as an equitable defense to copyright infringement. In effect, the doctrine creates a limited privilege in those other than the owner of a copyright to use the copyrighted material in a reasonable manner without the owner's consent. See Harper & Row, Publishers, Inc. v. Nation Enterprises, 471 U.S. ----, 105 S.Ct. 2218, 2225, 85 L.Ed.2d 588 (1985) (citing H. Ball, Law of Copyright and Literary Property 260 (1944)). Congress codified this judge-made doctrine in section 107 of the Copyrights Act of 1976, Pub.L.No. 94-553, § 107, 90 Stat. 2541, 2546 (codified at 17 U.S.C. § 107 (1982)); but that enactment did not freeze the fair-use doctrine in stone. Rather, Congress expressly sought to preserve the doctrine's common law character, leaving courts "free to adapt the doctrine to particular situations on a case-by-case basis." 17 U.S.C. § 107 historical and revision notes (1982).

In restating the fair-use doctrine in section 107, Congress enumerated four nonexclusive factors for courts to consider:

(1) the purpose and character of the use, including whether such use is of a commercial nature or is for nonprofit educational purposes;
(2) the nature of the copyrighted work;
(3) the amount and substantiality of the portion used in relation to the copyrighted work as a whole; and
(4) the effect of the use upon the potential market for or value of the copyrighted work.

17 U.S.C. § 107 (1982). In addition, in the legislative notes accompanying the provision, Congress listed examples "of the sort of activities the courts might regard as fair use under the circumstances." Id. § 107 historical and revision notes (1982).

Congress named parody as one of these activities. Nonetheless, parody was not classified as a presumptively fair use. See Harper & Row, 105 S.Ct. at 2231. Each assertion of the "parody defense" must be considered individually, in light of the statutory factors, reason, experience, and, of course, the general principles developed in past cases.

There have been few cases in this circuit involving the parody branch of the fair-use doctrine. An early case, Benny v. Loew's Inc., 239 F.2d 532 (9th Cir.1956), aff'd by an equally divided Court, 356 U.S. 43, 78 S.Ct. 667, 2 L.Ed.2d 583 (1958), held that " 'a parodized or burlesqued taking [was] to be treated no differently from any other [copyright] appropriation,' " id. at 537 (quoting lower court opinion, 131 F.Supp. 165, 183 (S.D.Cal.1955)). This decision was criticized by contemporary commentators, see Berlin v. E.C. Publications, Inc., 329 F.2d 541, 544-45 (2d Cir.) (listing critiques), cert. denied, 379 U.S. 822, 85 S.Ct. 46, 13 L.Ed.2d 33 (1964), and was essentially repudiated by Congress's recognition of parody in the notes to the Copyrights Act of 1976. See discussion, supra. Accordingly, in Walt Disney Productions v. Air Pirates, 581 F.2d 751 (9th Cir.1978), cert denied, 439 U.S. 1132, 99 S.Ct. 1054, 59 L.Ed.2d 94 (1979), we gave the Benny opinion a narrow interpretation and acknowledged that parody is a potential fair use subject to the multi-factor analysis codified in section 107. See id. at 756-58.

2. Applying the fair-use test

The composers advance five principal reasons why the parody before us is not a fair use: (1) the so-called parody is not actually a parody, or at least is not a parody of the composers' song; (2) Dees acted in bad faith; (3) Dees's use is commercial in nature; (4) the parody competes in the same market-- record albums and tapes--as the song; and (5) the taking is more substantial than was reasonably necessary to "conjure up" the original in the mind of the audience.

In addition, the composers assert that the question of fair use is an issue for the jury. Even if the material facts pertaining to each factor in the fair-use test are undisputed, they maintain, the ultimate issue, fair use or no, is appropriate for determination on summary judgment only when no reasonable jury could have decided the question differently.

(a) Judge or jury?

We dispose of this last argument first, because it is completely undercut by the Supreme Court's recent decision in Harper & Row, Publishers, Inc. v. Nation Enterprises, --- U.S. ----, 105 S.Ct. 2218, 85 L.Ed.2d 588 (1985). The Court held in that case that "[f]air use is a mixed question of law and fact", id. at 2231, and that "[w]here the District Court has found facts sufficient to evaluate each of the statutory factors," an appellate court may conclude as a matter of law--without remanding for further factfinding--" 'that [the challenged use] do[es] not qualify as a fair use of the copyrighted work,' " id. (quoting Pacific & Southern Co. v. Duncan, 744 F.2d 1490, 1495 n. 8 (11th Cir.1984), cert. denied, --- U.S. ----, 105 S.Ct. 1867, 85 L.Ed.2d 161 (1985)).

No material historical facts are at issue in this case. The parties dispute only the ultimate conclusions to be drawn from the admitted facts. Because, under Harper & Row, these judgments are legal in nature, we can make them without usurping the function of the jury.

(b) Substantive fair-use issues

We now turn to the composers' numerous substantive arguments as to why the fair-use defense is not available.

(1) The subject of the parody

The composers assert that the parody, although it borrows from the original work, was not "directed" at the original. That is, a humorous or satiric work deserves protection under the fair-use doctrine only if the copied work is at least partly the target of the work in question. See Walt Disney Productions v. Air Pirates, 581 F.2d 751, 758 n. 15 (9th Cir.1978), cert. denied, 439 U.S. 1132, 99 S.Ct. 1054, 59 L.Ed.2d 94 (1979). Otherwise, there is no need to "conjure up" the original in the audience's mind and no justification for borrowing from it. Id; accord MCA, Inc. v. Wilson, 677 F.2d 180, 185 (2d Cir.1981).

We requested counsel to provide us with tapes of both Dees's parody and the original (as sung by Johnny Mathis). Although we have no illusions of musical expertise, it was clear to us that Dees's version was intended to poke fun at the composers' song, and at Mr. Mathis's rather singular vocal range. We reject the notion that the song was used merely as a vehicle to achieve a comedic objective unrelated to the song, its place and time. Cf. id. at 183-85 (purpose of saving the effort of composing original music); infra note 5.

(2) The propriety of Dees's conduct

One theme running through the composers' briefs is that Dees's alleged bad conduct should bar his use of the equitable defense of fair use. The principle invoked is sound. Because " '[f]air use presupposes "good faith" and "fair dealing," ' " Harper & Row, 105 S.Ct. at 2232 (quoting Time Inc. v. Bernard Geis Associates, 293 F.Supp. 130, 146 (S.D.N.Y.1968)), courts may weigh "the propriety of the defendant's conduct" in the equitable balance of a fair use determination, 3 M. Nimmer, Nimmer on Copyright § 13.05 [A], at 13-72 to -73 (rev.ed. 1985).

Nonetheless, we conclude that the composers have failed to identify any conduct of Dees that is sufficiently blameworthy. For example, Fisher and Segal fault Dees for using the song after Fisher expressly refused him permission to do so. In their view, this shows bad faith on Dees's part. We cannot agree. Parodists will seldom get permission from those whose works are parodied. Self-esteem is seldom strong enough to permit the granting of permission even in exchange for a reasonable fee. See Note, The Parody Defense to Copyright Infringement: Productive Fair Use After Betamax, 97 Harv.L.Rev. 1395, 1397 n. 12 (1984) [hereinafter cited as Parody Defense ]. The parody defense to copyright infringement exists precisely to make possible a use that generally cannot be bought. See 3 M. Nimmer, supra, § 13.05[C], at 13-89; Gordon, Fair Use as Market Failure: A Structural and Economic Analysis of the Betamax Case and its Predecessors, 82 Colum.L.Rev. 1600, 1633 & n. 177. Moreover, to consider Dees blameworthy because he asked permission would penalize him for this modest show of consideration. Even though such gestures are predictably futile, we refuse to discourage them.

The composers also claim that the parody is immoral and thus unprotected by the fair-use doctrine. They cite the parody's irreverent references to drug addiction and its purported use of obscenities. Assuming without deciding that an obscene use is not a fair use, but see Pillsbury Co. v. Milky Way Productions, Inc., 215 U.S.P.Q. 124, 131 & n. 10 (N.D.Ga.1981), we conclude, after listening to it, that the parody is innocuous--silly perhaps, but surely not obscene or immoral.

(3) The purpose and character of the use

The first fair-use factor section 107 directs courts to consider is "the purpose and character of the use, including whether such use is of a commercial nature or is for nonprofit educational purposes." 17 U.S.C. § 107(1) (1982). The parties agree that the parody is a commercial use of the song. This fact "tends to weigh against a finding of fair use," Harper & Row, 105 S.Ct. at 2231, because "every commercial use of copyrighted material is presumptively an unfair exploitation of the monopoly privilege that belongs to the owner of the copyright." Sony Corp. v. Universal City Studios, Inc., 464 U.S. 417, 451, 104 S.Ct. 774, 793, 78 L.Ed.2d 574 (1984).

We recognize, however, that many parodies distributed commercially may be "more in the nature of an editorial or social commentary than ... an attempt to capitalize financially on the plaintiff's original work." Milky Way Productions, 215 U.S.P.Q. at 131 (footnote omitted). In such cases, of which this is one, the initial presumption need not be fatal to the defendant's cause. The defendant can rebut the presumption by convincing the court that the parody does not unfairly diminish the economic value of the original. See id. & n. 9.

(4) The economic effect of the use

Thus, we must turn our attention to the fourth factor in the fair-use analysis--"the effect of the use upon the potential market for or value of the copyrighted work," 17 U.S.C. § 107(4). This factor, not surprisingly, "is undoubtedly the single most important element of fair use." Harper & Row, 105 S.Ct. at 2234 (footnote omitted).

In assessing the economic effect of the parody, the parody's critical impact must be excluded. Through its critical function, a "parody may quite legitimately aim at garroting the original, destroying it commercially as well as artistically." B. Kaplan, An Unhurried View of Copyright

69 (1967). Copyright law is not designed to stifle critics. " 'Destructive' parodies play an important role in social and literary criticism and thus merit protection even though they may discourage or discredit an original author." Parody Defense, 96 Harv.L.Rev. at 1411. Accordingly, the economic effect of a parody with which we are concerned is not its potential to destroy or diminish the market for the original--any bad review can have that effect--but rather whether it fulfills the demand for the original. Biting criticism suppresses demand; copyright infringement usurps it. Thus, infringement occurs when a parody supplants the original in markets the original is aimed at, or in which the original is, or has reasonable potential to become, commercially valuable . . .

This is not a case in which commercial substitution is likely. "When Sunny Gets Blue" is "a lyrical song concerning or relating to a woman's feelings about lost love and her chance for ... happiness again." Appellants' Opening Brief at 3. By contrast, the parody is a 29-second recording concerning a woman who sniffs glue, which "ends with noise and laughter mixed into the song." Id. at 7. We do not believe that consumers desirous of hearing a romantic and nostalgic ballad such as the composers' song would be satisfied to purchase the parody instead. Nor are those fond of parody likely to consider "When Sunny Gets Blue" a source of satisfaction. The two works do not fulfill the same demand. Consequently, the parody has no cognizable economic effect on the original.

(5) The amount and substantiality of the taking

This court has also consistently focused on the third fair-use factor--the amount and substantiality of the taking, 17 U.S.C. § 107(3). See Air Pirates, 581 F.2d at 756. Thus far, however, we have provided few concrete guidelines; we have merely sketched the outer boundaries of the inquiry. On the one hand, "substantial copying by a defendant, combined with the fact that the portion copied constituted a substantial part of the defendant's work," does not automatically preclude the fair use defense. Id. On the other hand, "copying that is virtually complete or almost verbatim" will not be protected. Id.

In Air Pirates, we ultimately based our analysis on the so-called "conjure up" test. See Air Pirates, 581 F.2d at 757 (citing Berlin v. E.C. Publications, Inc., 329 F.2d 541 (2d Cir.), cert. denied, 379 U.S. 822, 85 S.Ct. 46, 13 L.Ed.2d 33 (1964), and Columbia Pictures Corp. v. National Broadcasting Co., 137 F.Supp. 348 (S.D.Cal.1955)). As the Air Pirates opinion articulated it, the test asks "whether the parodist has appropriated a greater amount of the original work than is necessary to 'recall or conjure up' the object of his satire." Id. The composers interpret this test to limit the amount of permissible copying to that amount necessary to evoke only initial recognition in the listener.

We disagree with this rigid view. As the Second Circuit stated in Elsmere Music, Inc. v. National Broadcasting Co., 623 F.2d 252 (2d Cir.1980) (per curiam):

> [T]he concept of "conjuring up" an original came into the copyright law not as a limitation on how much of an original may be used, but as a recognition that a parody frequently needs to be

more than a fleeting evocation of an original in order to make its humorous point. A parody is entitled at least to "conjure up" the original.

Id. at 253 n. 1 (citation omitted). Air Pirates does not compel a different view. In that case--which concerned the near-verbatim copying of Disney characters in the defendants' underground comic book--we concluded that the defendants "took more than was necessary to place firmly in the reader's mind the parodied work and those specific attributes that [were] to be satirized," 581 F.2d at 758. We did not set a fixed limit on copying, but merely expressed our judgment that that particular parody could easily have been accomplished through more restricted means.

We singled out three considerations that we thought important in determining whether a taking is excessive under the circumstances--the degree of public recognition of the original work, the ease of conjuring up the original work in the chosen medium, and the focus of the parody. See Air Pirates, 581 F.2d at 757-58. Because the Disney characters were familiar and graphics was a relatively easy medium for parody, we concluded that close copying was impermissible. See id. But we expressly noted that media other than the graphic arts might justify greater leeway. We observed: "[W]hen the medium involved is a comic book, a recognizable caricature is not difficult to draw, so that an alternative that involves less copying is more likely to be available than if a speech, for instance, is parodied." Id. at 758.

The unavailabity of viable alternatives is evident in the present case. Like a speech, a song is difficult to parody effectively without exact or near-exact copying. If the would-be parodist varies the music or meter of the original substantially, it simply will not be recognizable to the general audience. This "special need for accuracy," provides some license for "closer" parody. See id. To be sure, that license is not limitless: the parodist's desire to make the best parody must be "balanced against the rights of the copyright owner in his original expressions." Id. We think the balance tips in the parodists' favor here. In view of the parody's medium, its purposes, and its brevity, it takes no more from the original than is necessary to accomplish reasonably its parodic purpose.

(6) Summation

We conclude that "When Sonny Sniffs Glue" is a parody deserving of fair-use protection as a matter of law. Thus, we affirm the district court's grant of summary judgment on the copyright claim.

B. State Law Claims

1. Unfair competition

Dees's album, Put It Where the Moon Don't Shine, contains six musical numbers including the parody. The album cover's credits list Dees as the author of five of the songs, but no credits appear in connection with "When Sonny Sniffs Glue." Fisher and Segal assert that, in so designing the cover, Dees implicity represented that the music, words, and title of the parody were also authored by him. Thus, Fisher and Segal conclude, Dees engaged in unfair competition by deceiving the public as to the true source of the parody.

Under California law, a plaintiff claiming unfair competition must "prove a likelihood of confusion by purchasers as to source." Air Pirates, 581 F.2d at 760. Yet this confusion must be of a specific kind: the public must be misled into thinking that the defendant's product is actually the plaintiff's. In other words, the defendant must be guilty of "passing off" his product as the plaintiff's. See Sinatra v. Goodyear Tire & Rubber Co., 435 F.2d 711, 714 (9th Cir.1970), cert. denied, 402 U.S. 906 (1971). See generally W.P. Keeton, Prosser and Keeton on Torts § 130, at 1015 (5th ed. lawyer's ed. 1984) (discussing tort of "passing off"). Here, there is no "passing off." In fact, the composers allege the opposite situation--namely that Dees sells their work as if it were his.

Assuming arguendo that the false claiming of authorship constitutes a separate tort under California law, such a cause of action is nevertheless preempted by federal law. In Compco Corp. v. Day-Bright Lighting, Inc., 376 U.S. 234, 84 S.Ct. 779, 11 L.Ed.2d 669 (1964), and Sears, Roebuck & Co. v. Stiffel Co., 376 U.S. 225, 84 S.Ct. 784, 11 L.Ed.2d 661 (1964), the Supreme Court determined that the Supremacy Clause of the United States Constitution, U.S. Const., art. VI, precludes the states from protecting types of intellectual property that are already covered by the federal copyright or patent laws. Sears and Compco "ma[k]e it very clear that just as a state could not encroach upon the federal patent laws directly it could not do so indirectly under the guise of enforcing its laws against unfair competition where those laws would clash with the federal objectives." Sinatra v. Goodyear Tire & Rubber Co., 435 F.2d 711, 717 (9th Cir.1970), cert. denied, 402 U.S. 906, 91 S.Ct. 1376, 28 L.Ed.2d 646 (1971). The same applies to the copyright statute. Accordingly, the kind of misappropriation alleged by the composers can be redressed, if at all, only under federal law.

2. Defamation/Disparagement

Finally, the composers claim that Dees defamed them and disparaged their song by associating the song "with obscene, indecent and offensive words" and by causing it "to be reproduced, distributed and performed for and to the public in an offensive manner." See Excerpt of the Clerk's Record at 8-9 (reprinting the composers' third and fourth causes of action). A recent California case, Polygram Records, Inc. v. Superior Court, 170 Cal.App.3d 543, 216 Cal.Rptr. 252 (1985), persuades us that the composers cannot prevail. The court in Polygram, relying in part on the guarantees of free speech in the state constitution, held that defamation and product disparagement claims against comedic works may be dismissed summarily if the material the plaintiff complains of "is not fairly susceptible of a defamatory meaning." 170 Cal.App.3d at 551, 216 Cal.Rptr. at 256. Because Dees's parody cannot reasonably be understood in a defamatory sense by those who hear it, the composers' claims for defamation and disparagement must fail.

AFFIRMED.

# Part VIII: Obscenity

Marvin MILLER
v.
State of CALIFORNIA.

413 U.S. 15

Supreme Court of the United States

Decided June 21, 1973.

Mr. Chief Justice BURGER delivered the opinion of the Court.

This is one of a group of 'obscenity-pornography' cases being reviewed by the Court in a re-examination of standards enunciated in earlier cases involving what Mr. Justice Harlan called 'the intractable obscenity problem.' Interstate Circuit, Inc. v. Dallas, 390 U.S. 676, 704, 88 S.Ct. 1298, 1313, 20 L.Ed.2d 225 (1968) (concurring and dissenting).

Appellant conducted a mass mailing campaign to advertise the sale of illustrated books, euphemistically called 'adult' material. After a jury trial, he was convicted of violating California Penal Code s 311.2(a), a misdemeanor, by knowingly distributing obscene matter, [FN1] ***17** and the Appellate Department, Superior Court of California, County of Orange, summarily affirmed the judgment without opinion. Appellant's conviction was specifically based on his conduct in causing five unsolicited advertising brochures to be sent through the mail in an envelope addressed to a restaurant in Newport Beach, California. The envelope was opened by the manager of the restaurant and his mother. They had not requested the brochures; they complained to the police.

> FN1. At the time of the commission of the alleged offense, which was prior to June 25, 1969, ss 311.2(a) and 311 of the California Penal Code read in relevant part:
> 's 311.2 Sending or bringing into state for sale or distribution; printing, exhibiting, distributing or possessing within state
> '(a) Every person who knowingly: sends or causes to be sent, or brings or causes to be brought, into this state for sale or distribution, or in this state prepares, publishes, prints, exhibits, distributes, or offers to distribute, or has in his possession with intent to distribute or to exhibit or offer to distribute, any obscene matter is guilty of a misdemeanor. . . .'

's 311. Definitions

'As used in this chapter:

'(a) 'Obscene' means that to the average person, applying contemporary standards, the predominant appeal of the matter, taken as a whole, is to prurient interest, i.e., a shameful or morbid interest in nudity, sex, or excretion, which goes substantially beyond customary limits of candor in description or representation of such matters and is matter which is utterly without redeeming social importance.

'(b) 'Matter' means any book, magazine, newspaper, or other printed or written material or any picture, drawing, photograph, motion picture, or other pictorial represention or any statute or other figure, or any recording, transcription or mechanical, chemical or electrical reproduction or any other articles, equipment, machines or materials.

'(c) 'Person' means any individual, partnership, firm, association, corporation, or other legal entity.

'(d) 'Distribute' means to transfer possession of, whether with or without consideration.

'(e) 'Knowingly' means having knowledge that the matter is obscene.'

Section 311(e) of the California Penal Code, supra, was amended on June 25, 1969, to read as follows:

'(e) 'Knowingly' means being aware of the character of the matter' . . . .

The brochures advertise four books entitled 'Intercourse,' 'Man-Woman,' 'Sex Orgies Illustrated,' and 'An Illustrated History of Pornography,' and a film entitled 'Marital Intercourse.' While the brochures contain some descriptive printed material, primarily they consist of pictures and drawings very explicitly depicting men and women in groups of two or more engaging in a variety of sexual activities, with genitals often prominently displayed.

I

This case involves the application of a State's criminal obscenity statute to a situation in which sexually explicit materials have been thrust by aggressive sales action upon unwilling recipients who had in no way indicated any desire to receive such materials. This Court has recognized that the States have a legitimate interest in prohibiting dissemination or exhibition of obscene material when the mode of dissemination carries with it a significant danger of offending the sensibilities of unwilling recipients or of exposure to juveniles . . . . It is in this context that we are called on to define the standards which must be used to identify obscene material that a State may regulate without infringing on the First Amendment as applicable to the States through the Fourteenth Amendment.

The dissent of Mr. Justice BRENNAN reviews the background of the obscenity problem, but since the Court now undertakes to formulate standards more concrete than those in the past, it is useful for us to focus on two of the landmark cases in the somewhat tortured history of the Court's obscenity decisions. In Roth v. United States, 354 U.S. 476, 77 S.Ct. 1304, 1 L.Ed.2d 1498 (1957), the Court sustained a conviction under a federal statute punishing the mailing of 'obscene, lewd, lascivious or filthy . . .' materials. The key to that holding was the Court's rejection of the claim that obscene materials were protected by the First Amendment. Five Justices joined in the opinion stating:

> 'All ideas having even the slightest redeeming social importance--unorthodox ideas, controversial ideas, even ideas hateful to the prevailing climate of opinion--have the full protection of the (First Amendment) guaranties, unless excludable because they encroach upon the limited area of more important interests. But implicit in the history of the First Amendment is the rejection of obscenity as utterly without redeeming social importance. . . . This is the same judgment expressed by this Court in Chaplinsky v. New Hampshire, 315 U.S. 568, 571--572, 62 S.Ct. 766, 768--769, 86 L.Ed. 1031:
>
> ". . . There are certain well-defined and narrowly limited classes of speech, the prevention and punishment of which have never been thought to raise any Constitutional problem. These include the lewd and obscene . . .. It has been well observed that such utterances are no essential part of any exposition of ideas, and are of such slight social value as a step to truth that any benefit that may be derived from them is clearly outweighed by the social interest in order and morality. . . .' (Emphasis by Court in Roth opinion.)
>
> 'We hold that obscenity is not within the area of constitutionally protected speech or press.' 354 U.S., at 484--485, 77 S.Ct., 1309 (footnotes omitted).

Nine years later, in Memoirs v. Massachusetts, 383 U.S. 413, 86 S.Ct. 975, 16 L.Ed.2d 1 (1966), the Court veered sharply away from the Roth concept and, with only three Justices in the plurality opinion, articulated a new test of obscenity. The plurality held that under the Roth definition

> 'as elaborated in subsequent cases, three elements must coalesce: it must be established that (a) the dominant theme of the material taken as a whole appeals to a prurient interest in sex; (b) the material is patently offensive because if affronts contemporary community standards relating to the description or representation of sexual matters; and (c) the material is utterly without redeeming social value.' Id., at 418, 86 S.Ct., at 977.

The sharpness of the break with Roth, represented by the third element of the Memoirs test and emphasized by Mr. Justice White's dissent, id., at 460-- 462, 86 S.Ct., at 999, was further underscored when the Memoirs plurality went on to state:

> 'The Supreme Judicial Court erred in holding that a book need not be 'unqualifiedly worthless before it can be deemed obscene.' A book cannot be proscribed unless it is found to be utterly without redeeming social value.' Id., at 419, 86 S.Ct., at 978 (emphasis in original).

While Roth presumed 'obscenity' to be 'utterly without redeeming social importance,' Memoirs required that to prove obscenity it must be affirmatively established that the material is 'utterly without redeeming social value.' Thus, even as they repeated the words of Roth, the Memoirs plurality produced a drastically altered test that called on the prosecution to prove a negative, i.e., that the material was 'utterly without redeeming social value'--a burden virtually impossible to discharge under our criminal standards of proof. Such considerations caused Mr. Justice Harlan to wonder if the 'utterly without redeeming social value' test had any meaning at all. See Memoirs v. Massachusetts, id., at 459, 86 S.Ct., at 998 (Harlan, J., dissenting). See also id., at 461, 86 S.Ct., at 999 (White, J., dissenting) . . .

Apart from the initial formulation in the Roth case, no majority of the Court has at any given time been able to agree on a standard to determine what constitutes obscene, pornographic material subject to regulation under the States' police power. See, e.g., Redrup v. New York, 386 U.S., at 770--771, 87 S.Ct., at 1415--1416. We have seen 'a variety of views among the members of the Court unmatched in any other course of constitutional adjudication.' Interstate Circuit, Inc. v. Dallas, 390 U.S., at 704--705, 88 S.Ct., at 1314 (Harlan, J., concurring and dissenting) (footnote omitted). This is not remarkable, for in the area of freedom of speech and press the courts must always remain sensitive to any infringement on genuinely serious literary, artistic, political, or scientific expression. This is an area in which there are few eternal verities.

The case we now review was tried on the theory that the California Penal Code s 311 approximately incorporates the three-stage Memoirs test, supra. But now the Memoirs test has been abandoned as unworkable by its author, and no Member of the Court today supports the Memoirs formulation.

II

This much has been categorically settled by the Court, that obscene material is unprotected by the First Amendment. Kois v. Wisconsin, 408 U.S. 229, 92 S.Ct. 2245, 33 L.Ed.2d 312 (1972); United States v. Reidel, 402 U.S., at 354, 91 S.Ct., at 1411--1412; Roth v. United States, supra, 354 U.S., at 485, 77 S.Ct., at 1309. 'The First and Fourteenth Amendments have never been treated as absolutes (footnote omitted).' Breard v. Alexandria, 341 U.S., at 642, 71 S.Ct., at 932, and cases cited. See Times Film Corp. v. Chicago, 365 U.S. 43, 47--50, 81 S.Ct. 391, 393--395, 5 L.Ed.2d 403 (1961); Joseph Burstyn, Inc. v. Wilson, 343 U.S., at 502, 72 S.Ct., at 780. We acknowledge, however, the inherent dangers of undertaking to regulate any form of expression. State statutes designed to regulate obscene materials must be carefully limited. See Interstate Circuit, Inc. v. Dallas, supra, 390 U.S., at 682--685, 88 S.Ct., at 1302--1305. As a result, we now confine the permissible scope of such regulation to works which depict or describe sexual conduct. That conduct must be specifically defined by the applicable state law, as written or authoritatively construed. A state offense must also be limited to works which, taken as a whole, appeal to the prurient interest in sex, which portray sexual conduct in a patently offensive way, and which, taken as a whole, do not have serious literary, artistic, political, or scientific value.

The basic guidelines for the trier of fact must be: (a) whether 'the average person, applying contemporary community standards' would find that the work, taken as a whole, appeals to the prurient interest, Kois v. Wisconsin, supra, 408 U.S., at 230, 92 S.Ct., at 2246, quoting Roth v. United States, supra, 354 U.S., at 489, 77 S.Ct., at 1311; (b) whether the work depicts or describes, in a patently offensive way, sexual conduct specifically defined by the applicable state law; and (c) whether the work, taken as a whole, lacks serious literary, artistic, political, or scientific value. We do not adopt as a constituional standard the 'utterly without redeeming social value' test of Memoirs v. Massachusetts, 383 U.S., at 419, 86 S.Ct., at 977; that concept has never commanded the adherence of more than three Justices at one time. See supra, at 2613. If a state law that regulates obscene material is thus limited, as written or construed, the First Amendment values applicable to the States through the Fourteenth Amendment are adequately protected by the ultimate power of appellante courts to conduct an independent review of constitutional claims when necessary. See Kois v. Wisconsin, supra, 408 U.S., at 232, 92 S.Ct., at 2247; Memoirs v. Massachuetts, supra, 383 U.S., at 459--460, 86 S.Ct., at 998 (Harlan, J., dissenting); Jacobellis v. Ohio, 378 U.S., at 204, 84 S.Ct., at 1686 (Harlan, J., dissenting); New York Times Co. v. Sullivan, 376 U.S. 254, 284--285, 84 S.Ct. 710, 728, 11 L.Ed.2d 686 (1964); Roth v. United States, supra, 354 U.S., at 497--498, 77 S.Ct., at 1315--1316 (Harlan, J., concurring and dissenting).

We emphasize that it is not our function to propose regulatory schemes for the States. That must await their concrete legislative efforts. It is possible, however, to give a few plain examples of what a state statute could define for regulation under part (b) of the standard announced in this opinion, supra:

(a) Patently offensive representations or descriptions of ultimate sexual acts, normal or perverted, actual or simulated.

(b) Patently offensive representation or descriptions of masturbation, excretory functions, and lews exhibition of the genitals.

Sex and nudity may not be exploited without limit by films or pictures exhibited or sold in places of public accommodation any more than live sex and nudity can be exhibited or sold without limit in such public places. At a minimum, prurient, patently offensive depiction or description of sexual conduct must have serious literary, artistic, political, or scientific value to merit First Amendment protection. See Kois v. Wisconsin, supra, 408 U.S., at 230--232, 92 S.Ct., at 2246--2247; Roth v. United States, supra, 354 U.S., at 487, 77 S.Ct., at 1310; Thornhill v. Alabama, 310 U.S. 88, 101--102, 60 S.Ct. 736, 743--744, 84 L.Ed. 1093 (1940). For example, medical books for the education of physicians and related personnel necessarily use graphic illustrations and descriptions of human anatomy. In resolving the inevitably sensitive questions of fact and law, we must continue to rely on the jury system, accompanied by the safeguards that judges, rules of evidence, presumption of innocence, and other protective features provide, as we do with rape, murder, and a host of other offenses against society and its individual members . . . .

## III

Under a National Constitution, fundamental First Amendment limitations on the powers of the States do not vary from community to community, but this does not mean that there are, or should or can be, fixed, uniform national standards of precisely what appeals to the 'prurient interest' or is 'patently offensive.' These are essentially questions of fact, and our Nation is simply too big and too diverse for this Court to reasonably expect that such standards could be articulated for all 50 States in a single formulation, even assuming the prerequisite consensus exists. When triers of fact are asked to decide whether 'the average person, applying contemporary community standards' would consider certain materials 'prurient,' it would be unrealistic to require that the answer be based on some abstract formulation. The adversary system, with lay jurors as the usual ultimate factfinders in criminal prosecutions, has historically permitted triers of fact to draw on the standards of their community, guided always by limiting instructions on the law. To require a State to structure obscenity proceedings around evidence of a national 'community standard' would be an exercise in futility ....

It is neither realistic nor constitutionally sound to read the First Amendment as requiring that the people of Maine or Mississippi accept public depiction of conduct found tolerable in Las Vegas, or New York City. People in different States vary in their tastes and attitudes, and this diversity is not to be strangled by the absolutism of imposed uniformity. As the Court made clear in Mishkin v. New York, 383 U.S., at 508--509, 86 S.Ct., at 963, the primary concern with requiring a jury to apply the standard of 'the average person, applying contemporary community standards' is to be certain that, so far as material is not aimed at a deviant group, it will be judged by its impact on an average person, rather than a particularly susceptible or sensitive person--or indeed a totally insensitive one . . . .

In sum, we (a) reaffirm the Roth holding that obscene material is not protected by the First Amendment; (b) hold that such material can be regulated by the States, subject to the specific safeguards enunciated above, without a showing that the material is 'utterly without redeeming social value'; and (c) hold that obscenity is to be determined by applying 'contemporary community standards,' see Kois v. Wisconsin, supra, 408 U.S., at 230, 92 S.Ct., at 2246, and Roth v. United States, supra, 354 U.S., at 489, 77 S.Ct., at 1311, not 'national standards.' The judgment of the Appellate Department of the Superior Court, Orange County, California, is vacated and the case remanded to that court for further proceedings not inconsistent with the First Amendment standards established by this opinion. See United States v. 12 200-Foot Reels of Super 8mm. Film, 413 U.S. 123, at 130 n. 7, 93 S.Ct. 2665, at 2670 n. 7, 37 L.Ed.2d 500.

Vacated and remanded.

Mr. Justice DOUGLAS, dissenting.

I

Today we levae open the way for California to send a man to prison for distributing brochures that advertise books and a movie under freshly written standards defining obscenity which until today's decision were never the part of any law.

The Court has worked hard to define obscenity and concededly has failed. In Roth v. United States, 354 U.S. 476, 77 S.Ct. 1304, 1 L.Ed.2d 1498, it ruled that '(o)bscene material is material which deals with sex in a manner appealing to prurient interest.' Id., at 487, 77 S.Ct., at 1310. Obscenity, it was said, was rejected by the First Amendment because it is 'utterly without redeeming social importance.' Id., at 484, 77 S.Ct., at 1308. The presence of a 'prurient interest' was to be determined by 'contemporary community standards.' Id., at 489, 77 S.Ct., at 1311. That test, it has been said, could not be determined by one standard here and another standard there, Jacobellis v. Ohio, 378 U.S. 184, 194, 84 S.Ct. 1676, 1682, 12 L.Ed.2d 793, but 'on the basis of a national standard.' Id., at 195, 84 S.Ct., at 1682. My brother Stewart in Jacobellis commented that the difficulty of the Court in giving content to obscenity was that it was 'faced with the task of trying to define what may be indefinable.' Id., at 197, 84 S.Ct., at 1683 . . . .

If there are to be restraints on what is obscene, then a constitutional amendment should be the way of achieving the end. There are societies where religion and mathematics are the only free segments. It would be a dark day for America if that were our destiny. But the people can make it such if they choose to write obscenity into the Constitution and define it.

We deal with highly emotional, not rational, questions. To many the Song of Solomon is obscene. I do not think we, the judges, were ever given the constitutional power to make definitions of obscenity. If it is to be defined, let the people debate and decide by a constitutional amendment what they want to ban as obscene and what standards they want the legislatures and the courts to apply. Perhaps the people will decide that the path towards a mature, integrated society requires that all ideas competing for acceptance must have no censor. Perhaps they will decide otherwise. Whatever the choice, the courts will have some guidelines. Now we have none except our own predilections.

Mr. Justice BRENNAN, with whom Mr. Justice STEWART and Mr. Justice MARSHALL join, dissenting.

In my dissent in Paris Adult Theatre I v. Slaton, 413 U.S. 49, 73, 93 S.Ct. 2628, 2642, 37 L.Ed.2d 446, decided this date, I noted that I had no occasion to consider the extent of state power to regulate the distribution of sexually oriented material to juveniles or the offensive exposure of such material to unconsenting adults. In the case before us, appellant was convicted of distributing obscene matter in violation of California Penal Code s 311.2, on the basis of evidence that he had caused to be mailed unsolicited brochures advertising various books and a movie. I need not now decide whether a statute might be drawn to impose, within the requirements of the First Amendment, criminal penalties for the precise conduct at issue here. For it is clear that under my dissent in Paris Adult Theatre, I, the statute under which the prosecution was brought is unconstitutionally overbroad, and therefore invalid on its face.

NEW YORK, Petitioner
v.
Paul Ira FERBER.

458 U.S. 747

Supreme Court of the United States

Decided July 2, 1982.

Justice WHITE delivered the opinion of the Court.

At issue in this case is the constitutionality of a New York criminal statute which prohibits persons from knowingly promoting sexual performances by children under the age of 16 by distributing material which depicts such performances.

I

In recent years, the exploitive use of children in the production of pornography has become a serious national problem. [FN1] The Federal Government and 47 States have sought to combat the problem with statutes specifically directed at the production of child pornography. At least half of such statutes do not require that the materials produced be legally obscene. Thirty-five States and the United States Congress have also passed legislation prohibiting the distribution of such materials; 20 States prohibit the distribution of material depicting children engaged in sexual conduct without requiring that the material be legally obscene.

> FN1. "[C]hild pornography and child prostitution have become highly organized, multimillion dollar industries that operate on a nationwide scale." S.Rep.No.95-438, p. 5 (1977), U.S.Code Cong. & Admin.News 1978, pp. 40, 42. One researcher has documented the existence of over 260 different magazines which depict children engaging in sexually explicit conduct. Ibid. "Such magazines depict children, some as young as three to five years of age .... The activities featured range from lewd poses to intercourse, fellatio, cunnilingus, masturbation, rape, incest and sado- masochism." Id., at 6. In Los Angeles alone, police reported that 30,000 children have been sexually exploited. Sexual Exploitation of Children, Hearings before the Subcommittee on Select Education of the House Committee on Education and Labor, 95th Cong., 1st Sess., 41-42 (1977).

New York is one of the 20. In 1977, the New York Legislature enacted Article 263 of its Penal Law. N.Y. Penal Law, Art. 263 (McKinney 1980). Section 263.05 criminalizes as a class C felony the use of a child in a sexual performance:

"A person is guilty of the use of a child in a sexual performance if knowing the character and content thereof he employs, authorizes or induces a child less than sixteen years of age to engage in a sexual performance or being a parent, legal guardian or custodian of such child, he consents to the participation by such child in a sexual performance."

A "[s]exual performance" is defined as "any performance or part thereof which includes sexual conduct by a child less than sixteen years of age." § 263.00(1). "Sexual conduct" is in turn defined in § 263.00(3):

" 'Sexual conduct' means actual or simulated sexual intercourse, deviate sexual intercourse, sexual bestiality, masturbation, sado-masochistic abuse, or lewd exhibition of the genitals."

A performance is defined as "any play, motion picture, photograph or dance" or "any other visual representation exhibited before an audience." § 263.00(4).

At issue in this case is § 263.15, defining a class D felony: [FN3]

FN3. Class D felonies carry a maximum punishment of imprisonment for up to seven years as to individuals, and as to corporations a fine of up to $10,000. N.Y.Penal Law §§ 70.00, 80.10 (McKinney 1975). Respondent Ferber was sentenced to 45 days in prison.

"A person is guilty of promoting a sexual performance by a child when, knowing the character and content thereof, he produces, directs or promotes any performance which includes sexual conduct by a child less than sixteen years of age."

To "promote" is also defined:

" 'Promote' means to procure, manufacture, issue, sell, give, provide, lend, mail, deliver, transfer, transmute, publish, distribute, circulate, disseminate, present, exhibit or advertise, or to offer or agree to do the same." § 263.00(5).

A companion provision bans only the knowing dissemination of obscene material. § 263.10.

This case arose when Paul Ferber, the proprietor of a Manhattan bookstore specializing in sexually oriented products, sold two films to an undercover police officer. The films are devoted almost exclusively to depicting young boys masturbating. Ferber was indicted on two counts of violating § 263.10 and two counts of violating § 263.15, the two New York laws controlling dissemination of child pornography. After a jury trial, Ferber was acquitted of the two counts of promoting an obscene sexual performance, but found guilty of the two counts under § 263.15, which did not require proof that the films were obscene. Ferber's convictions were affirmed without opinion by the Appellate Division of the New York State Supreme Court. 74 A.D.2d 558, 424 N.Y.S.2d 967 (1980).

The New York Court of Appeals reversed, holding that § 263.15 violated the First Amendment. 52 N.Y.2d 674, 439 N.Y.S.2d 863, 422 N.E.2d 523 (1981). The court began by noting that in light of § 263.10's explicit inclusion of an obscenity standard, § 263.15 could not be construed to include such a standard. Therefore, "the statute would ... prohibit the promotion of materials which are traditionally entitled to constitutional protection from government interference under the First Amendment." 52 N.Y.2d, at 678, 439 N.Y.S.2d, at 865, 422 N.E.2d, at 525. Although the court recognized the State's "legitimate interest in protecting the welfare of minors" and noted that this "interest may transcend First Amendment concerns," id., at 679, 439 N.Y.S.2d, at 866, 422 N.E.2d, at 525-526, it nevertheless found two fatal defects in the New York statute. Section 263.15 was underinclusive because it discriminated against visual portrayals of children engaged in sexual activity by not also prohibiting the distribution of films of other dangerous activity. It was also overbroad because it prohibited the distribution of materials produced outside the State, as well as materials, such as medical books and educational sources, which "deal with adolescent sex in a realistic but nonobscene manner." 52 N.Y.2d, at 681, 439 N.Y.S.2d, at 866, 422 N.E.2d, at 526. Two judges dissented. We granted the State's petition for certiorari, 454 U.S. 1052, 102 S.Ct. 595, 70 L.Ed.2d 587 (1981), presenting the single question:

> "To prevent the abuse of children who are made to engage in sexual conduct for commercial purposes, could the New York State Legislature, consistent with the First Amendment, prohibit the dissemination of material which shows children engaged in sexual conduct, regardless of whether such material is obscene?"

II

The Court of Appeals proceeded on the assumption that the standard of obscenity incorporated in § 263.10, which follows the guidelines enunciated in Miller v. California, 413 U.S. 15, 93 S.Ct. 2607, 37 L.Ed.2d 419 (1973), constitutes the appropriate line dividing protected from unprotected expression by which to measure a regulation directed at child pornography. It was on the premise that "nonobscene adolescent sex" could not be singled out for special treatment that the court found § 263.15 "strikingly underinclusive." Moreover, the assumption that the constitutionally permissible regulation of pornography could not be more extensive with respect to the distribution of material depicting children may also have led the court to conclude that a narrowing construction of § 263.15 was unavailable.

The Court of Appeals' assumption was not unreasonable in light of our decisions. This case, however, constitutes our first examination of a statute directed at and limited to depictions of sexual activity involving children. We believe our inquiry should begin with the question of whether a State has somewhat more freedom in proscribing works which portray sexual acts or lewd exhibitions of genitalia by children . . . .

B

The Miller standard, like its predecessors, was an accommodation between the State's interests in protecting the "sensibilities of unwilling recipients" from exposure to pornographic material and the dangers of censorship inherent in unabashedly content-based laws. Like obscenity statutes, laws directed at the dissemination of child pornography run the risk of suppressing protected expression by allowing the hand of the censor to become unduly heavy. For the following reasons, however, we are persuaded that the States are entitled to greater leeway in the regulation of pornographic depictions of children.

First. It is evident beyond the need for elaboration that a State's interest in "safeguarding the physical and psychological well-being of a minor" is "compelling." Globe Newspaper Co. v. Superior Court, 457 U.S. 596, 607, 102 S.Ct. 2613, 2620, 73 L.Ed.2d 248 (1982). "A democratic society rests, for its continuance, upon the healthy, well-rounded growth of young people into full maturity as citizens." Prince v. Massachusetts, 321 U.S. 158, 168, 64 S.Ct. 438, 443, 88 L.Ed. 645 (1944). Accordingly, we have sustained legislation aimed at protecting the physical and emotional well-being of youth even when the laws have operated in the sensitive area of constitutionally protected rights. In Prince v. Massachusetts, supra, the Court held that a statute prohibiting use of a child to distribute literature on the street was valid notwithstanding the statute's effect on a First Amendment activity. In Ginsberg v. New York, supra, we sustained a New York law protecting children from exposure to nonobscene literature. Most recently, we held that the Government's interest in the "well-being of its youth" justified special treatment of indecent broadcasting received by adults as well as children. FCC v. Pacifica Foundation, 438 U.S. 726, 98 S.Ct. 3026, 57 L.Ed.2d 1073 (1978).

The prevention of sexual exploitation and abuse of children constitutes a government objective of surpassing importance. The legislative findings accompanying passage of the New York laws reflect this concern:

> "[T]here has been a proliferation of exploitation of children as subjects in sexual performances. The care of children is a sacred trust and should not be abused by those who seek to profit through a commercial network based upon the exploitation of children. The public policy of the state demands the protection of children from exploitation through sexual performances." 1977 N.Y.Laws, ch. 910, § 1.

We shall not second-guess this legislative judgment. Respondent has not intimated that we do so. Suffice it to say that virtually all of the States and the United States have passed legislation proscribing the production of or otherwise combating "child pornography." The legislative judgment, as well as the judgment found in the relevant literature, is that the use of children as subjects of pornographic materials is harmful to the physiological, emotional, and mental health of the child. That judgment, we think, easily passes muster under the First Amendment.

Second. The distribution of photographs and films depicting sexual activity by juveniles is intrinsically related to the sexual abuse of children in at least two ways. First, the materials produced are a permanent record of the children's participation and the harm to the child is exacerbated by their circulation. Second, the distribution network for child pornography must be closed if the production of material which requires the sexual exploitation of children is to be effectively controlled. Indeed, there is no serious contention that the legislature was unjustified in believing that it is difficult, if not impossible, to halt the exploitation of children by pursuing only those who produce the photographs and movies. While the production of pornographic materials is a low-profile, clandestine industry, the need to market the resulting products requires a visible apparatus of distribution. The most expeditious if not the only practical method of law enforcement may be to dry up the market for this material by imposing severe criminal penalties on persons selling, advertising, or otherwise promoting the product. Thirty-five States and

Congress have concluded that restraints on the distribution of pornographic materials are required in order to effectively combat the problem, and there is a body of literature and testimony to support these legislative conclusions . . .

Respondent does not contend that the State is unjustified in pursuing those who distribute child pornography. Rather, he argues that it is enough for the State to prohibit the distribution of materials that are legally obscene under the Miller test. While some States may find that this approach properly accommodates its interests, it does not follow that the First Amendment prohibits a State from going further. The Miller standard, like all general definitions of what may be banned as obscene, does not reflect the State's particular and more compelling interest in prosecuting those who promote the sexual exploitation of children. Thus, the question under the Miller test of whether a work, taken as a whole, appeals to the prurient interest of the average person bears no connection to the issue of whether a child has been physically or psychologically harmed in the production of the work. Similarly, a sexually explicit depiction need not be "patently offensive" in order to have required the sexual exploitation of a child for its production. In addition, a work which, taken on the whole, contains serious literary, artistic, political, or scientific value may nevertheless embody the hardest core of child pornography. "It is irrelevant to the child [who has been abused] whether or not the material ... has a literary, artistic, political or social value." Memorandum of Assemblyman Lasher in Support of § 263.15. We therefore cannot conclude that the Miller standard is a satisfactory solution to the child pornography problem.

Third. The advertising and selling of child pornography provide an economic motive for and are thus an integral part of the production of such materials, an activity illegal throughout the Nation. "It rarely has been suggested that the constitutional freedom for speech and press extends its immunity to speech or writing used as an integral part of conduct in violation of a valid criminal statute." Giboney v. Empire Storage & Ice Co., 336 U.S. 490, 498, 69 S.Ct. 684, 688, 93 L.Ed. 834 (1949). We note that were the statutes outlawing the employment of children in these films and photographs fully effective, and the constitutionality of these laws has not been questioned, the First Amendment implications would be no greater than that presented by laws against distribution: enforceable production laws would leave no child pornography to be marketed.

Fourth. The value of permitting live performances and photographic reproductions of children engaged in lewd sexual conduct is exceedingly modest, if not de minimis. We consider it unlikely that visual depictions of children performing sexual acts or lewdly exhibiting their genitals would often constitute an important and necessary part of a literary performance or scientific or educational work. As a state judge in this case observed, if it were necessary for literary or artistic value, a person over the statutory age who perhaps looked younger could be utilized. Simulation outside of the prohibition of the statute could provide another alternative. Nor is there any question here of censoring a particular literary theme or portrayal of sexual activity. The First Amendment interest is limited to that of rendering the portrayal somewhat more "realistic" by utilizing or photographing children.

Fifth. Recognizing and classifying child pornography as a category of material outside the protection of the First Amendment is not, incompatible with our earlier decisions. "The question whether speech is, or is not protected by the First Amendment often depends on the content of the speech." Young v. American Mini Theatres, Inc., 427 U.S. 50, 66, 96 S.Ct. 2440, 2450, 49 L.Ed.2d 310 (1976) (opinion of STEVENS, J., joined by BURGER, C.J., and WHITE and REHNQUIST, JJ.). See also FCC v. Pacifica Foundation, 438 U.S. 726, 742-748, 98 S.Ct. 3026, 3036-3039, 57 L.Ed.2d 1073 (1978) (opinion of STEVENS, J., joined by BURGER, C.J., and REHNQUIST, J.). "[I]t is the content of [an] utterance that determines whether it is a protected epithet or an unprotected 'fighting comment.' " Young v. American Mini Theatres, Inc., supra, 427 U.S., at 66, 96 S.Ct., at 2450. See Chaplinsky v. New Hampshire, 315 U.S. 568, 62 S.Ct. 766, 86 L.Ed. 1031 (1942). Leaving aside the special considerations when public officials are the target, New York Times Co. v. Sullivan, 376 U.S. 254 . . . (1964), a libelous publication is not protected by the Constitution. Beauharnais v. Illinois, 343 U.S. 250, 72 S.Ct. 725, 96 L.Ed. 919 (1952). Thus, it is not rare that a content-based classification of speech has been accepted because it may be appropriately generalized that within the confines of the given classification, the evil to be restricted so overwhelmingly outweighs the expressive interests, if any, at stake, that no process of case-by-case adjudication is required. When a definable class of material, such as that covered by § 263.15, bears so heavily and pervasively on the welfare of children engaged in its production, we think the balance of competing interests is clearly struck and that it is permissible to consider these materials as without the protection of the First Amendment.

C

There are, of course, limits on the category of child pornography which, like obscenity, is unprotected by the First Amendment. As with all legislation in this sensitive area, the conduct to be prohibited must be adequately defined by the applicable state law, as written or authoritatively construed. Here the nature of the harm to be combated requires that the state offense be limited to works that visually depict sexual conduct by children below a specified age. The category of "sexual conduct" proscribed must also be suitably limited and described.

The test for child pornography is separate from the obscenity standard enunciated in Miller, but may be compared to it for the purpose of clarity. The Miller formulation is adjusted in the following respects: A trier of fact need not find that the material appeals to the prurient interest of the average person; it is not required that sexual conduct portrayed be done so in a patently offensive manner; and the material at issue need not be considered as a whole . . . .

IV

Because § 263.15 is not substantially overbroad, it is unnecessary to consider its application to material that does not depict sexual conduct of a type that New York may restrict consistent with the First Amendment. As applied to Paul Ferber and to others who distribute similar material, the statute does not violate the First Amendment as applied to the States through the Fourteenth. The judgment of the New York Court of Appeals is reversed, and the case is remanded to that court for further proceedings not inconsistent with this opinion.

So ordered.

PLAYBOY ENTERPRISES, INC., et al., Plaintiffs,

v.

Edwin MEESE III, Attorney General of the United States, et al., Defendants.
MAGAZINE PUBLISHERS ASSOCIATION, Plaintiff,

v.

Edwin MEESE III, Attorney General of the United States, et al., Defendants.

639 F.Supp. 581

United States District Court,
District of Columbia.

July 3, 1986.

As Amended July 23, 1986.

JOHN GARRETT PENN, District Judge.

The plaintiffs in these consolidated actions seek to have the Court permanently enjoin the defendants, who are members of the Attorney General's Commission on Pornography (Commission), as members of the Commission and individually, from publicly disseminating a "blacklist" or from taking other action for the purpose of censoring and suppressing the distribution and sale of Playboy Magazine and other publications that are said to be lawfully and constitutionally protected. The case is now before the Court on the plaintiffs' motions for a preliminary injunction.

The plaintiffs in Civil Action No. 86-1346 are Playboy Enterprises, Inc. (PEI), American Booksellers Association, Inc. (ABA), a trade association of general interest bookstores said to represent 4,000 separate members operating approximately 7,000 book stores, Council for Periodical Distributors Associations, Inc. (CPDA) representing approximately 400 members who are engaged in the distribution of magazines, paperback books, comics, newspapers and other periodicals, and International Periodical Distributors Association, Inc. (IPDA), a trade association for the principal national periodical distributors engaged in the business of distributing or arranging for the distribution of paperback books and periodicals to wholesalers throughout the United States for ultimate distribution to retailers and the public.

I

Briefly stated, the underlying facts are as follows: On March 29, 1985, at the request of President Ronald Reagan and pursuant to the Federal Advisory Committee Act (FACA), 5

U.S.C.App. § 1 et. seq., the Attorney General, William French Smith, chartered the Attorney General's Commission on Pornography. The charter of the Commission states in part:

> The objectives of the Commission are to determine the nature, extent, and impact on society of pornography in the United States, and to make specific recommendations to the Attorney General concerning more effective ways in which the spread of pornography could be contained, consistent with constitutional guarantees.

The Commission held a series of six public hearings to obtain testimony from a variety of witnesses representing a broad spectrum of opinion, which included representatives of some of the plaintiffs. The Commission heard approximately 200 witnesses. Following the hearing, the Commission held public meetings at which the members discussed the testimony they had received and the shape the final report should take, and the further conduct of their undertaking. In subsequent public meetings, the Commission discussed the drafts of the chapters of the final report, and the substance of their discussions is reflected in minutes and transcripts that are also available to the public. In early May 1986, the Commission released a draft of the final report, which, the defendants represent that, except for some minor editorial changes, constitutes the substance of the final report. Defendants' Memorandum in Opposition to Motions for a Preliminary Injunction and Support of Defendants' Cross-Motion to Dismiss or, in the Alternative, for Summary Judgment (Defendants' Opposition) at 10. The Commission intends to issue and disseminate the report in early July 1986.

At a public hearing held on October 17, 1985, in Los Angeles, Reverend Donald Wildmon, the Executive Director of the National Federation of Decency testified before the Commission that certain corporations were engaged in the sale of pornography, which, in his view, included Playboy and Penthouse magazines. He also submitted a written statement setting forth his views. PEI Motion Exhibit C, MPA Motion Exhibit 4, Defendants' Opposition Exhibit B. At a public meeting held in January 1986, the Commission discussed the question of whether Reverend Wildmon's allegations should be included in the final report. Some of the members felt that before even addressing the question of whether his testimony or similar testimony should be included, corporations identified as being involved in the sale or distribution of pornography should be permitted the opportunity to respond. Eventually, it was decided to send a letter to those corporations. As a result, the subject letter was sent to those corporations. See Appendix.

The letter did not describe the "testimony", or state who gave the testimony, or advise the addressees that the letter had been based on the "testimony" and the written statement of one person, Reverend Wildmon. The Commission did attach a copy of Reverend Wildmon's written statement to each letter, but did not identify the author of the statement.

The Commission received a number of responses to their letters. Southland Corporation, the owners of 7-Eleven Stores, noted that the corporation had been following the work of the Commission, had sent observers to the hearings, and that while they had seen no conclusive evidence actually linking adult magazines to crime, violence and child abuse, that they were concerned with "growing public consciousness" and had decided to "discontinue the sale of any adult magazines." Southland noted that "In view of our decision to modify our policy and withdraw these magazines, we urge that any reference to Southland or 7-Eleven be deleted from your final report." Time, Inc. described the "accusations" in the letter as "outrageous". That corporation's response went on to state, "We cannot believe the U.S. Department of Justice would lend its name to this slipshod and misguided effort." It referred to the possible harm to Time, Inc. if the report contained its name. Some replies also noted inaccuracies or erroneous "facts" in the Wildmon statement. See Ennis Declaration dated June 3, 1986, and Exhibit A attached thereto.

The plaintiffs contend that as a result of the letter and the "threat" that the names of the corporations would be published in the report, that many stores pulled Playboy and similar magazines from their shelves. See Ennis Declaration dated June 3, 1986. Indeed, plaintiffs allege that some stores have pulled magazines such as American Photographer, Cosmopolitan and Texas Monthly out of an abundance of caution. American Photographer contained a picture of bare-breasted woman, Cosmopolitan and Texas Monthly contained an advertisement for "Obsession" perfume which depicted a woman with one breast partially exposed.

The plaintiffs asked for injunctive relief to include (1) that the Commission send a notice withdrawing its letter, (2) that the Commission not include a listing of the corporations in its final report and (3) that the Commission send a letter stating that Playboy and perhaps the other publications are not obscene.

II

In order to be entitled to injunctive relief, the plaintiffs must demonstrate that (1) they are likely to prevail on the merits, (2) they will suffer irreparable harm if injunctive relief is denied, (3) other persons would not suffer substantial injury if injunctive relief is granted, and (4) where lies the public interest. Washington Metropolitan Area Transit Commission v. Holiday Tours, Inc., 182 U.S.App.D.C. 220, 222, 559 F.2d 841, 843 (1977); Virginia Petroleum Jobbers Association v. FPC, 104 U.S.App.D.C. 106, 110, 259 F.2d 921, 925 (1958). Moreover, "[t]he necessary 'level' or 'degree' of possibility of success will vary according to the court's assessment of the other factors." Washington Metropolitan Area Transit Commission, 182 U.S.App.D.C. at 222, 559 F.2d at 843.

The Court considers first whether the plaintiffs have demonstrated that they are likely to prevail on the merits. In this connection, the parties are in agreement that the relevant, and perhaps controlling decision is Bantam Books, Inc. v. Sullivan, 372 U.S. 58, 83 S.Ct. 631, 9 L.Ed.2d 584 (1963). There, the Rhode Island legislature had established the "Rhode Island Commission to Encourage Morality in Youth". That Commission had established a practice of notifying distributors on official stationery that certain books and magazines were found to be "objectionable" for sale, distribution or display to youths under the age of 18. Notice of same would be sent to distributors, thanking them in advance for their cooperation and reminding them that the Commission had the duty to recommend prosecution for purveyors of "obscenity". A local police officer visited the distributors "shortly" after the distributor's receipt of the notice to determine what action the distributor had taken. The Supreme Court found that such activities of the Commission were unconstitutional and an abridgement to First Amendment liberties protected by the Fourteenth Amendment. The present plaintiffs make the same argument, but allege that their First Amendment rights are protected by the Fifth Amendment.

It hardly can be argued that the facts in Bantam Books and in the instant case are not similar. The Supreme Court found that it was informal censorship even though the Rhode Island Commission argued that it was doing no more than advising distributors of their legal rights.

The Court noted that, "[i]t would be naive to credit the State's assertion that these blacklists are in the nature of mere legal advice, when they plainly serve as instruments of regulation independent of the law against obscenity. 372 U.S. at 68-69, 83 S.Ct. at 638 (citation and footnote omitted). The Supreme Court observed that, although the Commission was limited to "informal sanctions ... the threat of invoking legal sanctions and other means of coercion, persuasion, and intimidation ... the record amply demonstrates that the Commission deliberately set about to achieve the suppression of publications deemed 'objectionable' and succeeded in its aim." 372 U.S. at 67, 83 S.Ct. at 637 (footnote omitted). And, the Supreme Court made clear that "informal censorship may sufficiently inhibit the circulation of publications to warrant injunctive relief." 372 U.S. at 67, 83 S.Ct. at 638 (footnote omitted). Included as informal censorship were "listings or notifications of supposedly obscene or objectionable publications or motion pictures." 372 U.S. at 67, n. 8, 83 S.Ct. at 638, n. 8. Finally, the Court noted that the term "objectionable" was vague and left distributors to speculate whether the Commission considered a particular publication to be obscene or simply harmful to juvenile morality. 372 U.S. at 71, 83 S.Ct. at 640.

The above references to Bantam Books gives the flavor of that decision and is sufficient to demonstrate that serious constitutional questions have been raised in the instant cases. Indeed, a reading of the above case against the brief record in the instant cases suggests that we may be venturing along the same path, and this being so, further supports the arguments that the plaintiffs have demonstrated that they may succeed on the merits. An in depth consideration must, of course, await a final hearing on the merits. In considering this prong on the issue of injunctive relief, the Court need not determine that the plaintiffs will succeed, only that they are likely to succeed, and the "level" or "degree" of possibility of success will vary according to the other facts.

The letters in the instant case were vague, in the sense that they did not define "pornography." Indeed, at oral argument the defendants conceded that "pornography" was not their word; rather, it was the word of Reverend Wildmon. He does not define the word, and his written submission to the Commission demonstrates that he may very well equate "pornography" with "obscenity". Of even greater concern is the fact that the letter is based on the testimony of one witness, when approximately 200 witnesses appeared before the Commission. Finally, the letter does appear to contain an implied threat to the addressees. It refers to "testimony alleging that your company is involved in the sale or distribution of pornography" and states that the Commission's letter is giving an opportunity to the corporations to respond to the allegations "prior to [the Commission] drafting its final section on identified distributors," and that if a company fails to respond that it will signal a "no objection" to be listed in the report as a distributor of pornography.

Turning to the issue of irreparable injury, the plaintiffs have presented affidavits and declarations through which they seek to demonstrate that they are suffering financial loss as the result of distributors refusing to sell their publications. This clearly applies to Playboy, for example, since a number of corporations no longer sell that magazine; Southland, for example. While the defendants argue that distributors voluntarily decided not to sell the magazine, it seems more than ironic that many of the decisions not to sell were made after the Commission's letters were sent out. Thus, there has been financial harm to the plaintiffs.

But, by far the most serious impact is with respect to the plaintiffs' First Amendment rights. It certainly can be argued, but the Court need not reach the issue at this time, that the effect of what the defendants have done amounts to a prior administrative restraint of material which even the defendants appear to concede is constitutionally protected matter. It is clear that something has occurred in the marketplace. A deprivation of a First Amendment right, that is a prior restraint on speech, a right so precious in this nation, constitutes irreparable injury. Dombrowski v. Pfister, 380 U.S. 479, 489, 85 S.Ct. 1116, 1122, 14 L.Ed.2d 22 (1965).

After weighing the above factors, the Court concludes that the plaintiffs have made a showing that they are likely to suffer irreparable injury.

III

With respect to the other two prongs relating to injunctive relief, the Court notes that courts must be extremely cautious when weighing whether to grant injunctive relief against an executive or legislative committee, for any such action may do violence to the separation of powers. Moreover, "[t]he courts avoid use of extraordinary remedies that involve needless friction with a coordinate branch of the government." Ansara v. Eastland, 143 U.S.App.D.C. 29, 31, 442 F.2d 751, 753 (1971) (citations omitted). See also Davis v. Ichord, 143 U.S.App.D.C. 183, 442 F.2d 1207 (1970). Stated differently, "[j]udicial inquiry into the matter of legislative purpose must be undertaken with caution and great deference to the regularity of action by a coordinate branch of government." Hentoff v. Ichord, 318 F.Supp. 1175, 1181 (D.D.C.1970).

A relevant inquiry then concerns the mandate given to the Commission and whether the action of the Commission went beyond that mandate. The beginning point for the consideration of this inquiry must be the Commission's Charter, and in particular, Paragraph Two which sets forth the "Objectives and Scope of Activity" of the Commission. The Court has already set out the first paragraph of Paragraph Two which states the objectives of the Commission. The second paragraph of Paragraph Two sets forth the "scope" of activity and reads:

> The scope of the Commission includes: a study of the dimensions of the problem of pornography, particularly visual and graphic pornography, including changes over the last several years in the nature of pornography, its volume, the impact of new technology, and pornography that relates to children; an examination of the means of production and distribution of pornographic materials, specifically including the role of organized crime in the pornography business; a review of the available empirical and scientific evidence on the relationship between exposure to pornographic materials and antisocial behavior, and on the impact of the creation and dissemination of both adult and child pornography upon children, including, as appropriate, the commissioning of new research on these subjects; a review of national, State, and local efforts, whether by the government or others, to curb pornography; and the exploration and, where appropriate, the recommendation of possible roles and initiatives that the Department of Justice and agencies of local, State, and Federal government could pursue in controlling, consistent with constitutional guarantees, the production and distribution of pornography.

When the Commission was directed to inquire and make "an examination of the means of production and distribution of pornographic materials", nothing in the charter suggested that the Commission was to publish lists of distributors, or seek to influence or persuade distributors not to sell so-called pornographic materials, or to recommend the prosecution of corporations or persons perceived to be distributors of pornography. Thus, the suggestion by the Commission that it will identify distributors of pornography goes beyond the Commission's mandate.

Even more questionable is what was to be gained by sending the letters. The transcript of the Commission meeting indicates that some members were concerned about including Reverend Wildmon's testimony and statement in the final report and that some felt that the corporations identified by Reverend Wildmon as distributors of pornography should have an opportunity to respond to those allegations. But, the Commission did not identify Reverend Wildmon even though there was no reason for it not to do so because as the defendants argue, the hearings and the reports are public. Reverend Wildmon was not entitled to an informer's privilege. The letter was poorly framed because it does not define what is meant by pornography. At oral argument the defendants conceded that they had no definition in mind and only used the words used by Reverend Wildmon, but if the defendants had no clear definition in mind, then there is no way they could have expected realistic responses.

The letter then only appears to have two purposes. First, if no response was received, then the Commission might very well conclude that the statement by Reverend Wildmon as to the non-answering corporation was admitted. Second, the corporations that did not wish to be included in the report could advise the Commission that the magazines, those identified by Reverend Wildmon, and perhaps other magazines not so identified, would no longer be sold. This is exactly what Southland did. And, this was the result reached in Bantam Books when the Rhode Island Commission sent out its notices. A possible third response would be to merely state that the corporation did not sell or distribute pornography based upon the corporation's own definition of pornography, but such a response would undoubtedly raise a question as to whether or not it would be accepted by the Commission. The letter exceeded the objectives and scope of the Commission and the responses would not appear to lend anything to the work of the Commission. In short, the letter does not appear to be in furtherance of the work of the Commission. This being so, it can be argued that the only purpose served by that letter was to discourage distributors from selling the publications; a form of pressure amounting to an administrative restraint of the plaintiffs' First Amendment rights. Similar findings had led to the granting of injunctive relief against a legislative committee. See Hentoff v. Ichord, supra.

Finally, the Court notes that it is in the public interest to uphold a constitutionally guaranteed right.

In sum, the plaintiffs have demonstrated a likelihood of success on the merits and have also demonstrated that they will suffer irreparable injury if injunctive relief is not granted. Moreover, the defendants will not suffer substantial injury if injunctive relief is granted because the actions challenged by the plaintiffs are not necessary or relevant to the Commission's mandate. The granting of injunctive relief is in the public interest.

IV

Having concluded that the plaintiffs are entitled to injunctive relief, the Court now turns to the task of determining the nature of the relief to be granted. The relief must take into consideration the First Amendment rights of the plaintiffs, but also must take into consideration the rights and obligations of the Commission consistent with its mandate and its obligation under the FACA. The Commission is required to conduct its business pursuant to the FACA. This means that the meetings are open to the public and that interested persons are invited to attend, appear before, or file statements before the Commission. 5 U.S.C.App. § 10(a)(1), (2) and, (3). The records, reports, transcripts, minutes, working papers, draft reports and similar documents are available to the public. 5 U.S.C.App. § 10(b). Thus, the testimony and statements of Reverend Wildmon like that of any other witness, are available to the public.

The plaintiffs do not seek to suppress the testimony of Reverend Wildmon or any other witness. What they do seek to avoid is an inclusion in the final report of a statement purporting to identify distributors of material which is alleged to be pornographic. While the defendants state that they do not now intend to publish such an identification in the final report, it is clear that the subject letter was designed to leave an impression that such a list would be included in the final report.

While the defendants have advised the Court that they will not publish the names of distributors of purported pornographic material in the final report, the record should be absolutely clear that they will not do so pending a final order in these cases. It seems likely that for at least some of the distributors, the concern over having their names published in the Commission report compelled them to withdraw the sale and distribution of some of plaintiffs' magazines and books. That issue should be put to rest; accordingly, the Court will enter a preliminary injunction to prohibit such publication.

The Court stresses that the injunction relating to publication of names goes no further than that, and relates back to the defendants' threat to identify the distributors of purported pornographic material in the final report. This part of the injunction does no more than to incorporate in an order what the defendants have stated in open court.

Plaintiffs also request that the defendants be required to furnish the plaintiffs with the names of the corporations sent copies of the subject letter. The Commission is required to do so under the terms of the FACA. 5 U.S.C.App. § 10(b). That requirement will be incorporated in the order with a requirement that the defendants do so within five days of the date of the order.

Plaintiffs also seek to have the Court direct the defendants to send a letter to each corporation or person who was sent a copy of the original letter, withdrawing the original letter and advising the addressee that the Commission will not publish a listing in the final report. Plaintiffs have also asked the Court to require the Commission to disavow the original letter and to include a statement that the Commission does not consider Playboy to be obscene, or to be linked to rape, or sexual violence, or organized crime.

The Court will direct the Commission to send a letter to each addressee of the original letter advising them that the original letter has been withdrawn and that no reply is required. In this way, the failure to answer the original letter cannot be interpreted as an admission by the addressee that the addressee is or was a distributor of pornography. The letter shall also advise the corporations that their names will not be included in the final report as sellers or distributors of pornographic materials. With respect to the remaining requests made by the plaintiffs, those requests are denied since to grant those requests would inject the Court into the determination process of the Commission.

Defendants have argued against any injunctive relief on the grounds that enjoining the report itself would be contrary to the First Amendment. The Court need not address this issue since it does not enjoin the issuance of the report, in fact, based upon the representations made by the defendants in open court, the Court's order does not affect the final report to be entered by the Commission. The defendants also argue that the Court cannot review the recommendations of an Executive Branch Advisory Committee that are to be made to the Attorney General and in turn to the President. This Court has not done so in its order.

An appropriate Order consistent with this Memorandum has been entered.

APPENDIX

Authorized Representative:

The Attorney General's Commission on Pornography has held six hearings across the United States during the past seven months on issues related to pornography. During the hearing in Los Angeles, in October 1985, the Commission received testimony alleging that your company is involved in the sale or distribution of pornography. The Commission has determined that it would be appropriate to allow your company an opportunity to respond to the allegations prior to drafting its final report section on identified distributors.

You will find a copy of the relevant testimony enclosed herewith. Please review the allegations and advise the Commission on or before March 3, 1986, if you disagree with the statements enclosed. Failure to respond will necessarily be accepted as an indication of no objection.

Please call Ms. Genny McSweeney, Attorney, at (202) 724-7837 if you have any questions.

Thank you for your assistance.

Truly yours,

Alan E. Sears

Executive Director

enc: Self-Addressed

Postage Paid Mailing Label

SKYYWALKER RECORDS, INC.; Luther Campbell; Mark Ross; David Hobbs; and Chris Wongwon, Plaintiffs,

v.

Nicholas NAVARRO, Defendant.

739 F.Supp. 578

United States District Court,
S.D. Florida,
Fort Lauderdale Division.

June 6, 1990.

## FINAL ORDER

GONZALEZ, District Judge.

This is a case between two ancient enemies: Anything Goes and Enough Already.

Justice Oliver Wendell Holmes, Jr. observed in Schenck v. United States, 249 U.S. 47, 39 S.Ct. 247, 63 L.Ed. 470 (1919), that the First Amendment is not absolute and that it does not permit one to yell "Fire" in a crowded theater. Today, this court decides whether the First Amendment absolutely permits one to yell another "F" word anywhere in the community when combined with graphic sexual descriptions.

Two distinct and narrow issues are presented: whether the recording As Nasty As They Wanna Be (Nasty ) is legally obscene; and second, whether the actions of the defendant Nicholas Navarro (Navarro), as Sheriff of Broward County, Florida, imposed an unconstitutional prior restaint upon the plaintiffs' right to free speech.

It is before the court following a trial on the merits held May 14 and May 15, 1990. The court has considered the pleadings, exhibits, the testimony of the witnesses, plus argument of able counsel. By the stipulation of the parties, the trial record also includes all evidence and argument presented at the plaintiffs' preliminary injunction hearing held April 19, 1990.

## THE PLAINTIFFS

The plaintiff Skyywalker Records, Inc. (Skyywalker) is a Florida corporation headquartered in Miami, Florida. The plaintiffs Luther Campbell, Mark Ross, David Hobbs, and Chris Wongwon, constitute the group known as "2 Live Crew" whose recording, As Nasty As They Wanna Be, is the subject of this lawsuit. Luther Campbell is also the President, Secretary, sole shareholder, and sole director of Skyywalker.

The plaintiffs have brought this action under section 1983, Title 42 of the United States Code, which provides a federal statutory remedy for unlawful deprivations of federal rights including those liberties guaranteed under the United States Constitution. The plaintiffs also seek a declaration of their legal rights, under the Federal Declaratory Judgment Act, 28 U.S.C. § 2201(a), and injunctive relief under section 2202(b) thereof. This court has previously denied the plaintiffs' motion for a preliminary injunction by ore tenus order entered April 19, 1990. There is no prayer for money damages.

Because this is a civil action, the party with the burden of proof must prevail by a preponderance of the evidence. On the issue of obscenity, the defendant Navarro has the burden of proof. As to the prior restraint claim, however, the plaintiffs have the burden to prove, beyond a preponderance of the evidence, that the defendant's actions were unconstitutional.

It must be emphasized at the outset that this decision does not criminalize the plaintiffs' conduct, nor does it charge anyone with a crime. That is a matter for the police and the criminal courts to determine. Whether the plaintiffs are guilty of a crime can only be decided if criminal charges are brought, a trial by jury conducted, and all other due process requirements have been met. Whether As Nasty as They Wanna Be is criminally obscene is left for the determination of another court on another day.

## THE FACTS

The recording As Nasty As They Wanna Be was released to the public by 2 Live Crew in 1989. To date, public sales have totalled approximately 1.7 million copies. The recording is available in various formats including phonograph records, cassette tapes, and compact discs. 2 Live Crew has also produced a recording entitled As Clean As They Wanna Be (Clean ) which has sold approximately 250,000 copies. Although neither party introduced Clean into evidence, it apparently contains the same music as Nasty but without the explicit sexual lyrics.

In mid-February 1990, the Broward County Sheriff's office began an investigation of the Nasty recording. The investigation began in response to complaints by South Florida residents.

Broward County Deputy Sheriff Mark Wichner was assigned to the case. On February 26, 1990, he traveled to Sound Warehouse, a Broward County retail music store, and purchased a cassette tape copy of the Nasty recording. The tape was purchased from an open display rack marked "Rap Music", easily accessible to all of Sound Warehouse's customers regardless of age.

Deputy Wichner listened to the Nasty recording, had six of the eighteen songs transcribed, and prepared an affidavit detailing these facts requesting that the Broward County Circuit Court find probable cause that the Nasty recording was legally obscene. On February 28, 1990, Deputy Wichner submitted the affidavit, an attached transcript of the six songs, and the tape cassette of the Nasty recording to the duty judge of the Broward County Circuit Court, the Honorable Mel Grossman. The communications between Deputy Wichner and Judge Grossman were limited to the filing of the affidavit, transcript, and tape cassette. Several days later, Judge Grossman's chambers contacted the deputy and requested further information concerning the location in Sound Warehouse of the Nasty recording and its accessibility to the public. Deputy Wichner communicated that information to the judge.

On March 9, Judge Grossman issued an order after reviewing the Nasty recording "in its entirety." The judge explicitly found probable cause to believe this recording was obscene under section 847.011 of the Florida Statutes and under applicable case law.

The Broward County Sheriff's office received and copied the order, and distributed it county wide to retail establishments that might be selling the Nasty recording. It decided to "warn the stores as a matter of courtesy" rather than make an initial arrest because, according to Deputy Wichner's testimony, such conduct would have been overaggressive. The Sheriff's office has not opened any investigations of other musical recordings because of the absence of citizen complaints.

Thereafter, Deputy Wichner re-visited the store where he had purchased the original recording plus another Sound Warehouse outlet and a store called Uncle Sam's Records. On these visits, the deputy wore a jacket marked "Broward County Sheriff" and displayed his badge in plain view. He spoke with a manager in each of the three stores, provided them with a copy of Judge Grossman's order, and told them, in a friendly conversational tone, that they should refrain from selling the Nasty recording. The managers were warned that further sales would result in arrest and that if convicted, the penalty for selling to a minor was a felony, and a misdemeanor if sold to an adult. Between fifteen and twenty different Broward County stores were personally visited by the Sheriff's office, and the evidence indicates that each of the visits was conducted in the same manner as were Deputy Wichner's three stops.

The Sheriff's office warnings were very effective. Within days, all retail stores in Broward County ceased offering the Nasty recording for sale. Those stores not directly visited by deputy sheriffs pulled the recording from their shelves after hearing about the visits from television and radio reports. Some stores continued to sell the Clean recording. Nasty was no longer sold even by stores having a policy of specially marking the recording with a warning, and of not selling it to minors. 2 Live Crew also includes a small statement on the front of the paper insert to their recording, as follows: "WARNING: EXPLICIT LANGUAGE CONTAINED".

The Broward County Sheriff's office took no further action because there was no information that any store was selling the Nasty recording.

On March 16, 1990, the plaintiffs filed this action in federal district court. On March 27, 1990, Sheriff Nicholas Navarro filed an in rem proceeding in Broward County Circuit Court against the Nasty recording seeking a judicial determination that it was obscene under state law. See Navarro

v. The Recording "As Nasty As They Wanna Be", case number 90-09324(12) (Reasbeck). There is no evidence of the status of the state case including whether a trial date has been set. No criminal proceedings against either the recording or the group 2 Live Crew have been instituted . . . .

The Florida Legislature has enacted a comprehensive set of laws. The primary provision is section 847.011 of the Florida Statutes. Subsection (1)(a) criminalizes the distribution, sale, or production of any obscene thing including a "recording" which can be "transmuted into auditory ... representations." Subsection (2) similarly makes it a crime for a person to knowingly have an obscene thing, including musical recordings, in his possession. Section 847.06 and 847.07 make it criminal to transport obscenity into the state or to create, deliver, or publish obscenity. There are several provisions which specifically apply to child pornography. See FLA.STAT.ANN. §§ 847.012, .0125, .013, .0135, .0145 (Supp.1990). Finally, sections 847.201 and 847.202 prohibit obscene programming on cable television during promotional periods and require ratings on video tapes rented and sold to the public.

An argument underlying the plaintiffs' position is that the obscenity or non-obscenity of any material should not be a concern of the criminal law, but rather should be left to the free market of ideas. Let each individual member of the public decide whether they wish to buy the material. 2 Live Crew has labeled their work with an explicit warning. They claim this label allows adults who would object to the recording's contents to exercise the consumer's right of free choice to not buy the product. To use the example of television, if the viewer does not like what he sees on Channel X, he may switch to Channel Y or turn off the set. In the case of obscene music, people who do not want to listen to obscenity do not have to buy it.

This is the argument of those absolutists who believe all speech, regardless of its content, is protected by the First Amendment. Such individuals label all regulation of speech as "censorship" and "paternalism". This absolutist view finds strength among those who believe rugged individualism is a valued virtue, if not a protected right that everyone should be permitted to "do their own thing."

This is a facially appealing argument. The problem is that it is not the law.

Florida has declared obscenity to be a crime. To repeat, violation of the laws against obscenity is as much against the law as assault, rape, kidnapping, robbery, or any other form of behavior which the legislature has declared criminal.

The absolutists and other members of the party of Anything Goes should address their petitions to the Florida Legislature, not to this court. If they are sincere let them say what they actually mean--Lets' Legalize Obscenity! . . . .

In sum, if persons subscribe to the view that obscenity should be legalized, they should take their petitions to Tallahassee, the Florida capital, not to the steps of the U.S. courthouse.

The people of Florida have made obscenity a crime. Individuals are not free to disobey or disregard the law. The law is not a smorgasbord where people are free to pick and choose among which laws they will obey and which they will reject. Neither is it a channel selector available to every member of the public to use as they deem fit. As noted in the Pattern Instructions of the Eleventh Circuit, jurors in deciding the rights and liberties of their fellow citizens "must ... follow the law ... whether.... [they] agree with that law or not."

Men and women in good faith may agree or disagree as to whether obscenity should be prohibited. They can argue that the obscenity statutes should or should not be repealed. In the meantime, however, the law must be obeyed and the Sheriff has a duty to enforce it. Indeed, Florida's Legislature has mandated that all sheriffs in the state are to "vigorously enforce" the obscenity laws. See FLA.STAT.ANN. § 847.011(9) (Supp.1990).

## THE MILLER V. CALIFORNIA TEST

In deciding whether a specific work is or is not obscene, the court must apply the controlling test enunciated in Miller v. California, 413 U.S. 15, 93 S.Ct. 2607, 37 L.Ed.2d 419 (1973). To be obscene, there must be proof of all three of the following factors: (1) the average person, applying contemporary community standards, would find that the work, taken as a whole, appeals to the prurient interest, (2) measured by contemporary community standards, the work depicts or describes, in a patently offensive way, sexual conduct specifically defined by the applicable state law, and (3) the work, taken as a whole, lacks serious literary, artistic, political, or scientific value. Id.; also see Memoirs, 383 U.S. at 419, 86 S.Ct. at 977 (to be obscene, all three elements must be met and each element must be "independently" evaluated); Penthouse International, Ltd. v. McAuliffe, 610 F.2d 1353, 1363 (5th Cir.1980) (same); United States v. Various Articles of Obscene Merchandise, 709 F.2d 132, 135 (2nd Cir.1983) (same).

## THE RELEVANT COMMUNITY

Both the first and second elements of Miller require application of "contemporary community standards." The issues of the size of the appropriate community, its composition, and the view of the average person in that group are all questions of fact to be decided by the trier of fact, which is the court in this case. See Miller, 413 U.S. at 30, 93 S.Ct. at 2618.

Both parties Apparently assumed that the relevant community was only Broward County, Florida. Neither litigant presented any evidence to support this assumption, which was apparently based upon the jurisdiction of the Broward County Sheriff and the County lines. However, the boundaries of the relevant community under Miller are a matter for judicial, not legislative, determination. See Smith, 431 U.S. 291, 303, 97 S.Ct. 1756, 1765, 52 L.Ed.2d 324 (1977).

This court finds that in assessing whether this work is obscene, the relevant community is the area of Palm Beach, Broward, and Dade Counties. In reaching this determination, the court has considered numerous factors. These three adjoining counties share common geography on the eastern coast of Florida. They also share beachfront on the Atlantic Ocean including all the common experiences that derive therefrom including the exposure to tourists. All three counties are open communities in the sense that visitors, from abroad and other states, come to South Florida to vacation and resettle. The area is also linked via common transportation. The three counties are connected by rail (Florida East Coast, Amtrak, and Tri-Rail), water (Atlantic Ocean and the Intracoastal Waterway), air, and highway (Federal Highway, Florida Turnpike, and Interstate 95). Through these transportation links, the labor forces of Broward and Dade on the one hand, and Broward and Palm Beach on the other, commingle. Each county has targeted media, but the three counties generally share access to the same radio and television stations and newspapers. Culturally, there is also a strong connection. Even though each county has a distinct mix of ethnic peoples, cultural events are advertised to and attended by the residents of all three. Because of the strong transportation ties, the area is also linked economically. Trade and industry in South Florida do not limit their business by county lines. Palm Beach, Broward, and Dade also share a similar composition of rural and urban areas, with the larger cities in the eastern portion of each county. Finally, there are political ties. Florida House and Senate Districts include areas within both Broward and Palm Beach . . . .

## THE AVERAGE PERSON STANDARD

The next inquiry is more difficult because this court must determine what are the standards for determining prurient interest and patent offensiveness in Palm Beach, Dade, and Broward Counties. The fact that the state legislature has enacted laws prohibiting obscenity is certainly relevant and entitled to great weight. The state's anti-obscenity stance as a whole, however, is overinclusive because other communities outside the three counties are included in the majority who passed the legislation.

In determining the views of the "average person" in this area, the court has not focused only on the views of the most tolerant or the most sensitive individuals. See Smith v. United States, 431 U.S. at 304-05, 97 S.Ct. at 1765-66 ("the most prudish or the most tolerant" or "the reactions of a sensitive or of a callous minority"). The "average person" does not necessarily represent any one segment of the community. It is a legal concept whereby a single perspective is derived from the aggregation or average of everyone's attitudes in the area including persons with differing degrees of tolerance. See Pinkus v. United States, 436 U.S. 293, 298-302, 98 S.Ct. 1808, 1812-14, 56 L.Ed.2d 293 (1978) (community under Miller is made up of all adults in the area including the most sensitive). The court has not considered minors in its considerations because there was not sufficient evidence adduced at trial that the music was targeted at such persons or that it actually reached children.

This court finds that the relevant community standard reflects a more tolerant view of obscene speech than would other communities within the state. This finding of fact is based upon this court's personal knowledge of the community. The undersigned judge has resided in Broward County since 1958. As a practicing attorney, state prosecutor, state circuit judge, and currently, a federal district judge, the undersigned has traveled and worked in Dade, Broward, and Palm Beach. As a member of the community, he has personal knowledge of this area's demographics, culture, economics, and politics. He has attended public functions and events in all three counties and is aware of the community's concerns as reported in the media and by word of mouth. In almost fourteen years as a state circuit judge, the undersigned gained personal knowledge of the nature of obscenity in the community while viewing dozens, if not hundreds of allegedly obscene films and other publications seized by law enforcement.

The court does not adopt the plaintiffs' position that these three counties can be labeled as "tolerant" per se as opposed to some degree thereof. Neither the trier of fact's personal knowledge nor the plaintiffs' evidence supports such a conclusion. The plaintiffs argue that the lack of written complaints in the Nasty investigation file created by the Broward Sheriff's office is evidence of a tolerant community standard. While this fact is entitled to some weight, it is far from significant. There may be many reasons why concerned citizens have not complained. For example, the Nasty recording was not released until 1989 and it takes time for even a popular musical release to reach the public consciousness. Although the Sheriff has the duty to enforce the obscenity laws regardless of community protest, Deputy Wichner's explanation of why this particular album was singled out can reasonably be linked to significant community discontent, whether communicated by telephone calls, anonymous messages, or letters to the police. Furthermore, the vast majority of complaints in the file, although not exclusively from Broward County, were residents of the relevant community . . . .

In deciding this case, the court's decision is not based upon the undersigned judge's personal opinion as to the obscenity of the work, but is an application of the law to the facts based upon the trier of fact's personal knowledge of community standards. In other works, even if the undersigned judge would not find As Nasty As They Wanna Be obscene, he would be compelled to do so if the community's standards so required . . . .

THE FIRST MILLER TEST: PRURIENT INTEREST

This court finds, as a matter of fact, that the recording As Nasty As They Wanna Be appeals to the prurient interest. The Supreme Court has defined prurient as "material having a tendency to excite lustful thoughts." Roth, 354 U.S. at 487 n. 20, 77 S.Ct. at 1310 n. 20. Appeals only to "normal, healthy sexual desires" are not adequate to meet the test. Brockett v. Spokane Arcades, Inc., 472 U.S. 491, 498, 105 S.Ct. 2794, 2798, 86 L.Ed.2d 394 (1985). The material must exhibit a "shameful or morbid interest in nudity, sex, or excretion". Id. (readopting definition in Roth, 354 U.S. at 487 n. 20, 77 S.Ct. at 1310 n. 20).

Nasty appeals to the prurient interest for several reasons. First, its lyrics and the titles of its songs are replete with references to female and male genitalia, human sexual excretion, oral-anal contact, fellatio, group sex, specific sexual positions, sado-masochism, the turgid state of the male sexual organ, masturbation, cunnilingus, sexual intercourse, and the sounds of moaning . . . .

## THE SECOND MILLER TEST: PATENTLY OFFENSIVE

The court also finds that the second element of the Miller test is satisfied in that the Nasty recording is patently offensive. This is a question of fact, which must be measured by contemporary community standards. See Miller, 413 U.S. at 30, 93 S.Ct. at 2618.

It is quite true that not all speech with sex as its topic is obscene. See Roth, 354 U.S. at 487, 77 S.Ct. at 1310. The As Nasty As They Wanna Be recording is another matter.

The recording depicts sexual conduct in graphic detail. The specificity of the descriptions makes the audio message analogous to a camera with a zoom lens, focusing on the sights and sounds of various ultimate sex acts. Furthermore, the frequency of the sexual lyrics must also be considered. With the exception of part B on Side 1, the entire Nasty recording is replete with explicit sexual lyrics. This is not a case of subtle references or innuendo, nor is it just "one particular scurrilous epithet" as in Cohen v. California, 403 U.S. 15, 22, 91 S.Ct. 1780, 1786, 29 L.Ed.2d 284 (1971) . . . .

## THE THIRD MILLER TEST: SOCIAL VALUE

The final factor under Miller is whether the Nasty recording, taken as a whole, lacks serious literary, artistic, political, or scientific value. This factor is not measured by community standards. The proper inquiry is whether a reasonable person would find serious social value in the material at issue. See Pope v. Illinois, 481 U.S. 497, 107 S.Ct. 1918, 1921, 95 L.Ed.2d 439 (1987). The plaintiffs correctly note that the value of a work can pass muster under Miller if it has serious merit, measured objectively, even if a majority of the community would not agree.

As a preliminary matter, it is again important to note what this case is not about. Neither the "Rap" or "Hip-Hop" musical genres are on trial. The narrow issue before this court is whether the recording entitled As Nasty As They Wanna Be is legally obscene.

This is also not a case about whether the group 2 Live Crew or any of its other music is obscene. The third element of the Miller test focuses upon the social value of the particular work, not its creators. The fact that individuals of whom we approve hold objectionable ideas or that people of whom we do not approve hold worthy ideas does not affect judicial review of the value of the ideas themselves.

The Phillistines are not always wrong, nor are the guardians of the First Amendment always right.

This court must examine the Nasty recording for its content; the inquiry is objective, not ad hominem.

Finally, this court's role is not to serve as a censor or an art and music critic. If the Nasty recording has serious literary, artistic, political, or scientific value, it is irrelevant that the work is not stylish, tasteful, or even popular.

The plaintiffs themselves testified that neither their music nor their lyrics were created to convey a political message.

The only witness testifying at trial that there was political content in the Nasty recording was Carlton Long, who was qualified as an expert on the culture of black Americans. This witness first stated that the recording was political because the 2 Live Crew, as a group of black Americans, used this medium to express themselves. While it is doubtless true that Nasty is a product of the group's background, including their heritage as black Americans, this fact does not convert whatever they say, or sing, into political speech. Professor Long also testified that the following passages from the recording contained political content: a four sentence phrase in the song "Dirty Nursery Rhymes" about Abraham Lincoln, the word "man" in the Georgie Porgie portion of the same song, and the use of the device of "boasting" to stress one's manhood. Even giving these isolated lyrics the meaning attributed by the expert, they are not sufficient in number or significance to give the Nasty recording, as a whole, any serious political value.

In terms of science, Professor Long also suggested that there is cultural content in 2 Live Crew's recording which rises to the level of serious sociological value. According to this witness, white Americans "hear" the Nasty recording in a different way than black Americans because of their different frames of references. Long identifies three cultural devices evident in the work here: "call and response", "doing the dozens", and "boasting". The court finds none of these arguments persuasive.

The only examples of "call and response" in the Nasty recording are portions where males and females yell, in repetitive verse, "Tastes Great--Less Filling" and, in another song, assail campus Greek-letter group. The phrases alone have no significant artistic merit nor are they examples of black American culture. In the case of "Tastes Great--Less Filling", this is merely a phrase lifted from a beer commercial.

The device of "doing the dozens" is a word game composed of a series of insults escalating in their satirical content. The "boasting" device is a way for persons to overstate their virtues such as sexual prowess.

While this court does not doubt that both "boasting" and "doing the dozens" are found in the culture of black Americans, these devices are also found in other cultures. "Doing the dozens" is commonly seen in adolescents, especially boys, of all races. "Boasting" seems to be part of the universal human condition.

Professor Long also cited to several different examples of literary devices such as rhyme and allusion which appear in Nasty, and points to the song title "Dick Almighty" as an example of the literary device of personification. This, of course, is nonsense regardless of the expert's credentials. "A quotation from Voltaire in the fly leaf of a book", noted the Supreme Court in Miller, "will not constitutionally redeem an otherwise obscene publication." 413 U.S. at 25 n. 7, 93 S.Ct. at 2615 n. 7 (quoting Kois v. Wisconsin, 408 U.S. 229, 231, 92 S.Ct. 2245, 2246, 33 L.Ed.2d 312 (1972)).

Prior to Miller, the government had to demonstrate that a work was utterly without redeeming social value to be judged obscene. See Memoirs, 383 U.S. at 419, 86 S.Ct. at 977. The present test is less stringent, only requiring proof of an absence of serious social worth. This leads to the plaintiffs' strongest argument: that the Nasty recording has serious artistic value. This category of social worth is broad enough to include the value contributed by the political, literary, and cultural aspects of the particular work.

The plaintiffs stress that the Nasty recording has value as comedy and satire. Certainly, people can and do laugh at obscenity. The plaintiffs point to the audience reaction at trial when the subject recording was played in open court. The audience giggled initially, but the court observed that after the initial titillation, it fell silent.

In a society where obscenity is forbidden, it is human nature to want taste forbidden fruit. It is quite another thing to say that this aspect of humanity forms the basis for finding that Nasty has serious artistic value. Furthermore, laughter can express much more than enjoyment and entertainment. It is also a means of hiding embarrassment, concealing shame, and releasing tension. The fact that laughter was only heard at the time that the first song of the tape was played is probative on what the audience's outbursts really meant. It cannot be reasonably argued that the violence, perversion, abuse of women, graphic depictions of all forms of sexual conduct, and miscroscopic descriptions of human genitilia contained on this recording are comedic art.

The Nasty recording is not comedy, but is first and foremost, music. Initially, it would appear very difficult to find a musical work obscene. As noted by the American Civil Liberties Union, the meaning of music is subjective and subject only to the limits of the listener's imagination. See ACLU Brief at 3.

Music nevertheless is not exempt from a state's obscenity statutes. Musical works are obscene if they meet the Miller test. Certainly it would be possible to compose an obscene oratoro or opera and it has probably been done . . . .

OBSCENITY? YES

The recording As Nasty As They Wanna Be, taken as a whole, is legally obscene . . . .

The court also finds As Nasty As They Wanna Be to be legally obscene under the Miller test by clear and convincing evidence, which standard the plaintiffs maintain is the correct burden of proof . . . .

And so our legal odyssey ends.

What began as a dispute between two ancient enemies concludes with the hope that they are reconciled by a mutual friend--The Constitution of the United States.

Having considered the above matters and the record in this cause, it is hereby

ORDERED AND ADJUDGED as follows:

(1) The recording As Nasty As They Wanna Be created by the group 2 Live Crew is hereby DECLARED obscene.

(2) The action of the Broward County Sheriff's office in threatening retail music stores with arrest for selling the Nasty recording and presenting them with a copy of a probable cause order is hereby DECLARED unconstitutional as an improper prior restraint of free speech in violation of the First and Fourteenth Amendments to the United States Constitution.

(3) The defendant, Sheriff Nicholas Navarro, and his deputies, agents, servants, employees, attorneys, and persons in active concert or participation with any of them who receive actual notice of this order are all hereby PERMANENTLY ENJOINED from threatening employees, managers, or owners of retail stores selling musical recordings with arrest for selling allegedly obscene materials. The same persons are also hereby PERMANENTLY ENJOINED from presenting or speaking about any probable cause order of obscenity to employees, managers, or owners of retail stores selling musical recordings. Nothing in this order shall be understood as prohibiting Sheriff Navarro or any of his deputies, agents, or employees from: (a) giving legal advice to any person who is suspected of violating a valid law prohibiting obscenity where such consultation is genuinely undertaken with the purpose of aiding the suspect to comply with the law and avoid prosecution under the obscenity laws, or (b) vigorously enforcing the obscenity laws of the state of Florida as mandated and required by section 847.011(9), Florida Statutes.

(4) The sole affirmative defense in the answer and the class action claims in the amended complaint are hereby DISMISSED. The plaintiffs amended their pleading to include class action allegations, but they never made a motion for certification of the class. Furthermore, the request to certify a class would be moot as this order awards the same relief which the class could conceivably seek. Judgment is not entered against the defendant on the affirmative defense

because the class portion of the case is moot. However, the court does find that the plaintiffs have standing and are "interested part[ies]" within the meaning of the Declaratory Judgment Act, 28 U.S.C. § 2201(a).

(5) Any party seeking costs or an award under section 1988, Title 42 of the U.S.Code, shall apply to the court within the time allowed by the Federal Rules of Civil Procedure, the local rules of this court, and other applicable law. The parties' applications, if any, shall include all appropriate factual and legal argument to support the request for an award.

(6) Judgment shall be ENTERED on the two counts of the amended complaint by separate order.

(7) The court shall RETAIN JURISDICTION to enforce the permanent injunction entered in this case.

DONE AND ORDERED.

LUKE RECORDS, INC., a Florida corporation formerly known as Skyywalker Records, Inc., et al., Plaintiffs-Appellants,

v.

Nick NAVARRO, Sheriff, Broward County, Florida, Defendant-Appellee.

960 F.2d 134

United States Court of Appeals,
Eleventh Circuit.

May 7, 1992.

Appeal from the United States District Court for the Southern District of Florida.

Before ANDERSON, Circuit Judge, RONEY and LIVELY, Senior Circuit Judges.

PER CURIAM:

In this appeal, appellants Luke Records, Inc., Luther Campbell, Mark Ross, David Hobbs, and Charles Wongwon seek reversal of the district court's declaratory judgment that the musical recording "As Nasty As They Wanna Be" is obscene under Fla.Stat. § 847.011 and the United States Constitution, contending that the district court misapplied the test for determining obscenity. We reverse.

Appellants Luther Campbell, David Hobbs, Mark Ross, and Charles Wongwon comprise the musical group "2 Live Crew," which recorded "As Nasty As They Wanna Be." In response to actions taken by the Broward County, Florida Sheriff's Office to discourage record stores from selling "As Nasty As They Wanna Be," appellants filed this action in federal district court to enjoin the Sheriff from interfering further with the sale of the recording. The district court granted the injunction, finding that the actions of the Sheriff's office were an unconstitutional prior restraint on free speech. The Sheriff does not appeal this determination.

In addition to injunctive relief, however, appellants sought a declaratory judgment pursuant to 28 U.S.C.A. § 2201 that the recording was not obscene. The district court found that "As Nasty As They Wanna Be" is obscene under Miller v. California.

This case is apparently the first time that a court of appeals has been asked to apply the Miller test to a musical composition, which contains both instrumental music and lyrics. Although we tend to agree with appellants' contention that because music possesses inherent artistic value, no work of music alone may be declared obscene, that issue is not presented in this case. The

Sheriff's contention that the work is not protected by the First Amendment is based on the lyrics, not the music. The Sheriff's brief denies any intention to put rap music to the test, but states "it is abundantly obvious that it is only the 'lyrical' content which makes "As Nasty As They Wanna Be" obscene." Assuming that music is not simply a sham attempt to protect obscene material, the Miller test should be applied to the lyrics and the music of "As Nasty As They Wanna Be" as a whole. The basic guidelines for the trier of fact must be: (a) whether "the average person, applying contemporary community standards" would find that the work, taken as a whole, appeals to the prurient interest; (b) whether the work depicts or describes, in a patently offensive way, sexual conduct specifically defined by the applicable state law; and (c) whether the work, taken as a whole, lacks serious literary, artistic, political, or scientific value. 413 U.S. at 24, 93 S.Ct. at 2615. This test is conjunctive. Penthouse Intern., Ltd. v. McAuliffe, 610 F.2d 1353, 1363 (5th Cir.1980). A work cannot be held obscene unless each element of the test has been evaluated independently and all three have been met. Id. ....

There are two problems with this case which make it unusually difficult to review. First, the Sheriff put in no evidence but the tape recording itself. The only evidence concerning the three-part Miller test was put in evidence by the plaintiffs. Second, the case was tried by a judge without a jury, and he relied on his own expertise as to the prurient interest community standard and artistic value prongs of the Miller test.

First, the Sheriff put in no evidence other than the cassette tape. He called no expert witnesses concerning contemporary community standards, prurient interest, or serious artistic value. His evidence was the tape recording itself.

The appellants called psychologist Mary Haber, music critics Gregory Baker, John Leland and Rhodes Scholar Carlton Long. Dr. Haber testified that the tape did not appeal to the average person's prurient interest . . . .

Second, the case was tried by a judge without a jury, and he relied on his own expertise as to the community standard and artistic prongs of the Miller test.

The district court found that the relevant community was Broward, Dade, and Palm Beach Counties . . . .

It is difficult for an appellate court to review value judgments. Although, generally, these determinations are made in the first instance by a jury, in this case the district judge served as the fact finder, which is permissible in civil cases. Because a judge served as a fact finder, however, and relied only on his own expertise, the difficulty of appellate review is enhanced. A fact finder, whether a judge or jury, is limited in discretion. "Our standard of review must be faithful to both Rule 52(a) and the rule of independent review." "The rule of independent review assigns to appellate judges a constitutional responsibility that cannot be delegated to the trier of fact," even where that fact finder is a judge.

In this case, it can be conceded without deciding that the judge's familiarity with contemporary community standards is sufficient to carry the case as to the first two prongs of the Miller test: prurient interest applying community standards and patent offensiveness as defined by Florida law. The record is insufficient, however, for this Court to assume the fact finder's artistic or literary knowledge or skills to satisfy the last prong of the Miller analysis, which requires determination of whether a work "lacks serious artistic, scientific, literary or political value" . . . .

> Just as the ideas a work represents need not obtain majority approval to merit protection, neither, insofar as the First Amendment is concerned, does the value of the work vary from community to community based on the degree of local acceptance it has won.

The Sheriff concedes that he has the burden of proof to show that the recording is obscene. Yet, he submitted no evidence to contradict the testimony that the work had artistic value. A work cannot be held obscene unless each element of the Miller test has been met. We reject the argument that simply by listening to this musical work, the judge could determine that it had no serious artistic value.

REVERSED.

# Part IX: National Security

NEW YORK TIMES COMPANY, Petitioner,
v.
UNITED STATES.
UNITED STATES, Petitioner,
v.
The WASHINGTON POST COMPANY et al.

403 U.S. 713

Supreme Court of the United States

Decided June 30, 1971.

PER CURIAM.

We granted certiorari, 403 U.S. 942, 943, 91 S.Ct. 2270, 2271, 29 L.Ed.2d 853 (1971) in these cases in which the United States seeks to enjoin the New York Times and the Washington Post from publishing the contents of a classified study entitled 'History of U.S. Decision-Making Process on Viet Nam Policy.'

'Any system of prior restraints of expression comes to this Court bearing a heavy presumption against its constitutional validity.' Bantam Books, Inc. v. Sullivan, 372 U.S. 58, 70, 83 S.Ct. 631, 639, 9 L.Ed.2d 584 (1963); see also Near v. Minnesota ex rel. Olson, 283 U.S. 697, 51 S.Ct. 625, 75 L.Ed. 1357 (1931). The Government 'thus carries a heavy burden of showing justification for the imposition of such a restraint.' Organization for a Better Austin v. Keefe, 402 U.S. 415, 419, 91 S.Ct. 1575, 1578, 29 L.Ed.2d 1 (1971). The District Court for the Southern District of New York in the New York Times case, 328 F.Supp. 324, and the District Court for the District of Columbia and the Court of Appeals for the District of Columbia Circuit, 446 F.2d 1327, in the Washington Post case held that the Government had not met that burden. We agree.

The judgment of the Court of Appeals for the District of Columbia Circuit is therefore affirmed. The order of the Court of Appeals for the Second Circuit is reversed, 444 F.2d 544, and the case is remanded with directions to enter a judgment affirming the judgment of the District Court for the Southern District of New York. The stays entered June 25, 1971, by the Court are vacated. The judgments shall issue forthwith.

So ordered.

Judgment of the Court of Appeals for the District of Columbia Circuit affirmed; order of the Court of Appeals for the Second Circuit reversed and case remanded with directions.

Mr. Justice BLACK, with whom Mr. Justice DOUGLAS joins, concurring. DP I adhere to the view that the Government's case against the Washington Post should have been dismissed and that the injunction against the New York Times should have been vacated without oral argument when the cases were first presented to this Court. I believe that every moment's continuance of the injunctions against these newspapers amounts to a flagrant, indefensible, and continuing violation of the First Amendment. Furthermore, after oral argument, I agree completely that we must affirm the judgment of the Court of Appeals for the District of Columbia Circuit and reverse the judgment of the Court of Appeals for the Second Circuit for the reasons stated by my Brothers DOUGLAS and BRENNAN. In my view it is unfortunate that some of my Brethren are apparently willing to hold that the publication of news may sometimes be enjoined. Such a holding would make a shambles of the First Amendment.

Our Government was launched in 1789 with the adoption of the Constitution. The Bill of Rights, including the First Amendment, followed in 1791. Now, for the first time in the 182 years since the founding of the Republic, the federal courts are asked to hold that the First Amendment does not mean what it says, but rather means that the Government can halt the publication of current news of vital importance to the people of this country.

In seeking injunctions against these newspapers and in its presentation to the Court, the Executive Branch seems to have forgotten the essential purpose and history of the First Amendment. When the Constitution was adopted, many people strongly opposed it because the document contained no Bill of Rights to safeguard certain basic freedoms. [FN1] They especially feared that the new powers granted to a central government might be interpreted to permit the government to curtail freedom of religion, press, assembly, and speech. In response to an overwhelming public clamor, James Madison offered a series of amendments to satisfy citizens that these great liberties would remain safe and beyond the power of government to abridge. Madison proposed what later became the First Amendment in three parts, two of which are set out below, and one of which proclaimed: 'The people shall not be deprived or abridged of their right to speak, to write, or to publish their sentiments; and the freedom of the press, as one of the great bulwarks of liberty, shall be inviolable.' [FN2] The amendments were offered to curtail and restrict the general powers granted to the Executive, Legislative, and Judicial Branches two years before in the original Constitution. The Bill of Rights changed the original Constitution into a new charter under which no branch of government could abridge the people's freedoms of press, speech, religion, and assembly. Yet the Solicitor General argues and some members of the Court appear to agree that the general powers of the Government adopted in the original Constitution should be interpreted to limit and restrict the specific and emphatic guarantees of the Bill of Rights adopted later. I can imagine no greater perversion of history. Madison and the other Framers of the First Amendment, able men that they were, wrote in language they earnestly believed could never be misunderstood: 'Congress shall make no law * * * abridging the freedom *

* * of the press * * *.' Both the history and languageof the First Amendment support the view that the press must be left free to publish news, whatever the source, without censorship, injunctions, or prior restraints.

FN1. In introducing the Bill of Rights in the House of Representatives, Madison said: '(B)ut I believe that the great mass of the people who opposed (the Constitution), disliked it because it did not contain effectual provisions against the encroachments on particular rights * * *.' 1 Annals of Cong. 433. Congressman Goodhue added: '(I)t is the wish of many of our constituents, that something should be added to the Constitution, to secure in a stronger manner their liberties from the inroads of power.' Id., at 426.

FN2. The other parts were:
'The civil rights of none shall be abridged on account of religious belief or worship, nor shall any national religion be established, nor shall the full and equal rights of conscience be in any manner, or on any pretext, infringed.'
'The people shall not be restrained from peaceably assembling and consulting for their common good; nor from applying to the Legislature by petitions, or remonstrances, for redress of their grievances.' 1 Annals of Cong. 434.

In the First Amendment the Founding Fathers gave the free press the protection it must have to fulfill its essential role in our democracy. The press was to serve the governed, not the governors. The Government's power to censor the press was abolished so that the press would remain forever free to censure the Government. The press was protected so that it could bare the secrets of government and inform the people. Only a free and unrestrained press can effectively expose deception in government. And paramount among the responsibilities of a free press is the duty to prevent any part of the government from deceiving the people and sending them off to distant lands to die of foreign fevers and foreign shot and shell. In my view, far from deserving condemnation for their courageous reporting, the New York Times, the Washington Post, and other newspapers should be commended for serving the purpose that the Founding Fathers saw so clearly. In revealing the workings of government that led to the Vietnam war, the newspapers nobly did precisely that which the Founders hoped and trusted they would do.

The Government's case here is based on premises entirely different from those that guided the Framers of the First Amendment. The Solicitor General has carefully and emphatically stated:

'Now, Mr. Justice (BLACK), your construction of * * * (the First Amendment) is well known, and I certainly respect it. You say that no law means no law, and that should be obvious. I can only say, Mr. Justice, that to me it is equally obvious that 'no law' does not mean 'no law', and I would seek to persuade the Court that that is true. * * * (T)here are other parts of the Constitution that grant powers and responsibilities to the Executive, and * * * the First Amendment was not intended to make it impossible for the Executive to function or to protect the security of the United States.'

And the Government argues in its brief that in spite of the First Amendment, '(t)he authority of the Executive Department to protect the nation against publication of information whose disclosure would endanger the national security stems from two interrelated sources: the constitutional power of the President over the conduct of foreign affairs and his authority as Commander-in-Chief.'

In other words, we are asked to hold that despite the First Amendment's emphatic command, the Executive Branch, the Congress, and the Judiciary can make laws enjoining publication of current news and abridging freedom of the press in the name of 'national security.' The Government does not even attempt to rely on any act of Congress. Instead it makes the bold and dangerously farreaching contention that the courts should take it upon themselves to 'make' a law abridging freedom of the press in the name of equity, presidential power and national security, even when the representatives of the people in Congress have adhered to the command of the First Amendment and refused to make such a law. [FN5] See concurring opinion of Mr. Justice DOUGLAS, post, at 2145. To find that the President has 'inherent power' to halt the publication of news by resort to the courts would wipe out the First Amendment and destroy the fundamental liberty and security of the very people the Government hopes to make 'secure.' No one can read the history of the adoption of the First Amendment without being convinced beyond any doubt that it was injunctions like those sought here that Madison and his collaborators intended to outlaw in this Nation for all time.

FN5. Compare the views of the Solicitor General with those of James Madison, the author of the First Amendment. When speaking of the Bill of Rights in the House of Representatives, Madison said: 'If they (the first ten amendments) are incorporated into the Constitution, independent tribunals of justice will consider themselves in a peculiar manner the guardians of those rights; they will be an impenetrable bulwark against every assumption of power in the Legislative or Executive; they will be naturally led to resist every encroachment upon rights expressly stipulated for in the Constitution by the declaration of rights.' 1 Annals of Cong. 439.

The word 'security' is a broad, vague generality whose contours should not be invoked to abrogate the fundamental law embodied in the First Amendment. The guarding of military and diplomatic secrets at the expense of informed representative government provides no real security for our Republic. The Framers of the First Amendment, fully aware of both the need to defend a new nation and the abuses of the English and Colonial Governments, sought to give this new society strength and security by providing that freedom of speech, press, religion, and assembly should not be abridged. This thought was eloquently expressed in 1937 by Mr. Chief Justice Hughes--great man and great Chief Justice that he was--when the Court held a man could not be punished for attending a meeting run by Communists.

> 'The greater the importance of safeguarding the community from incitements to the overthrow of our institutions by force and violence, the more imperative is the need to preserve inviolate the constitutional rights of free speech, free press and free assembly in order to maintain the opportunity for free political discussion, to the end that government may be responsive to the will of the people and that changes, if desired, may be obtained by peaceful means. Therein lies the security of the Republic, the very foundation of constitutional government.'

Mr. Justice DOUGLAS, with whom Mr. Justice BLACK joins, concurring.

While I join the opinion of the Court I believe it necessary to express my views more fully.

It should be noted at the outset that the First Amendment provides that 'Congress shall make no law * * * abridging the freedom of speech, or of the press.' That leaves, in my view, no room for governmental restraint on the press.

There is, moreover, no statute barring the publication by the press of the material which the Times and the Post seek to use. Title 18 U.S.C. s 793(e) provides that '(w)hoever having unauthorized possession of, access to, or control over any document, writing * * * or information relating to the national defense which information the possessor has reason to believe could be used to the injury of the United States or to the advantage of any foreign nation, willfully communicates * * * the same to any person not entitled to receive it * * * (s)hall be fined not more than $10,000 or imprisoned not more than ten years, or both.'

The Government suggests that the word 'communicates' is broad enough to encompass publication.

There are eight sections in the chapter on espionage and censorship, ss 792-- 799. In three of those eight 'publish' is specifically mentioned: s 794(b) applies to 'Whoever, in time of war, with intent that the same shall be communicated to the enemy, collects, records, publishes, or communicates * * * (the disposition of armed forces).'

Section 797 applies to whoever 'reproduces, publishes, sells, or gives away' photographs of defense installations.

Section 798 relating to cryptography applies to whoever: 'communicates, furnishes, transmits, or otherwise makes available * * * or publishes' the described materials. (Emphasis added.)

Thus it is apparent that Congress was capable of and did distinguish between publishing and communication in the various sections of the Espionage Act.

The other evidence that s 793 does not apply to the press is a rejected version of s 793. That version read: 'During any national emergency resulting from a war to which the United States is a party, or from threat of such a war, the President may, by proclamation, declare the existence of such emergency and, by proclamation, prohibit the publishing or communicating of, or the attempting to publish or communicate any information relating to the national defense which, in his judgment, is of such character that it is or might be useful to the enemy.' 55 Cong.Rec. 1763. During the debates in the Senate the First Amendment was specifically cited and that provision was defeated. 55 Cong.Rec. 2167.

Judge Gurfein's holding in the Times case that this Act does not apply to this case was therefore preeminently sound. Moreover, the Act of September 23, 1950, in amending 18 U.S.C. s 793 states in s 1(b) that:

> 'Nothing in this Act shall be construed to authorize, require, or establish military or civilian censorship or in any way to limit or infringe upon freedom of the press or of speech as guaranteed by the Constitution of the United States and no regulation shall be promulgated hereunder having that effect.' 64 Stat. 987.

Thus Congress has been faithful to the command of the First Amendment in this area.

So any power that the Government possesses must come from its 'inherent power.'

The power to wage war is 'the power to wage war successfully.' See Kiyoshi Hirabayashi v. United States, 320 U.S. 81, 93, 63 S.Ct. 1375, 1382, 87 L.Ed. 1774. But the war power stems from a declaration of war. The Constitution by Art. I, s 8, gives Congress, not the President, power '(t)o declare War.' Nowhere are presidential wars authorized. We need not decide therefore what leveling effect the war power of Congress might have.

These disclosures may have a serious impact. But that is no basis for sanctioning a previous restraint on the press. As stated by Chief Justice Hughes in Near v. Minnesota ex rel. Olson, 283 U.S. 697, 719-- 720, 51 S.Ct. 625, 632, 75 L.Ed. 1357:

> 'While reckless assaults upon public men, and efforts to bring obloquy upon those who are endeavoring faithfully to discharge official duties, exert a baleful influence and deserve the severest condemnation in public opinion, it cannot be said that this abuse is greater, and it is believed to be less, than that which characterized the period in which our institutions took shape. Meanwhile, the administration of government has become more complex, the opportunities for malfeasance and corruption have multiplied, crime has grown to most serious proportions, and the danger of its protection by unfaithful officials and of the impairment of the fundamental security of life and property by criminal alliances and official neglect, emphasizes the primary need of a vigilant and courageous press, especially in great cities. The fact that the liberty of the press may be abused by miscreant purveyors of scandal does not make any the less necessary the immunity of the press from previous restraint in dealing with official misconduct.'

As we stated only the other day in Organization for a Better Austin v. Keefe, 402 U.S. 415, 419, 91 S.Ct. 1575, 1578, 29 L.Ed.2d 1 '(a)ny prior restraint on expression comes to this Court with a 'heavy presumption' against its constitutional validity.'

The Government says that it has inherent powers to go into court and obtain an injunction to protect the national interest, which in this case is alleged to be national security.

Near v. Minnesota ex rel. Olson, 283 U.S. 697, 51 S.Ct. 625, 75 L.Ed. 1357, repudiated that expansive doctrine in no uncertain terms.

The dominant purpose of the First Amendment was to prohibit the widespread practice of governmental suppression of embarrassing information. It is common knowledge that the First Amendment was adopted against the widespread use of the common law of seditious libel to punish the dissemination of material that is embarrassing to the powers-that-be. See T. Emerson, The System of Freedom of Expression, c. V (1970); Z. Chafee, Free Speech in the United States, c. XIII (1941). The present cases will, I think, go down in history as the most dramatic illustration of that principle. A debate of large proportions goes on in the Nation over our posture in Vietnam. That debate antedated the disclosure of the contents of the present documents. The latter are highly relevant to the debate in progress.

Secrecy in government is fundamentally anti-democratic, perpetuating bureaucratic errors. Open debate and discussion of public issues are vital to our national health. On public questions there should be 'uninhibited, robust, and wide-open' debate. New York Times Co. v. Sullivan, 376 U.S. 254, 269-- 270, 84 S.Ct. 710, 720--721, 11 L.Ed.2d 686.

I would affirm the judgment of the Court of Appeals in the Post case, vacate the stay of the Court of Appeals in the Times case and direct that it affirm the District Court.

The stays is these cases that have been in effect for more than a week constitute a flouting of the principles of the First Amendment as interpreted in Near v. Minnesota ex rel. Olson.

Mr. Justice BRENNAN, concurring.

I

I write separately in these cases only to emphasize what should be apparent: that our judgments in the present cases may not be taken to indicate the propriety, in the future, of issuing temporary stays and restraining orders to block the publication of material sought to be suppressed by the Government. So far as I can determine, never before has the United States sought to enjoin a newspaper from publishing information in its possession. The relative novelty of the questions presented, the necessary haste with which decisions were reached, the magnitude of the interests asserted, and the fact that all the parties have concentrated their arguments upon the question whether permanent restraints were proper may have justified at least some of the restraints heretofore imposed in these cases. Certainly it is difficult to fault the several courts below for seeking to assure that the issues here involved were preserved for ultimate review by this Court. But even if it be assumed that some of the interim restraints were proper in the two cases before us, that assumption has no bearing upon the propriety of similar judicial action in the future. To begin with, there has now been ample time for reflection and judgment; whatever values there may be in the preservation of novel questions for appellate review may not support any restraints in the future. More important, the First Amendment stands as an absolute bar to the imposition of judicial restraints in circumstances of the kind presented by these cases.

II

The error that has pervaded these cases from the outset was the granting of any injunctive relief whatsoever, interim or otherwise. The entire thrust of the Government's claim throughout these cases has been that publication of the material sought to be enjoined 'could,' or 'might,' or 'may' prejudice the national interest in various ways. But the First Amendment tolerates absolutely no prior judicial restraints of the press predicated upon surmise or conjecture that untoward consequences may result. Our cases, it is true, have indicated that there is a single, extremely narrow class of cases in which the First Amendment's ban on prior judicial restraint may be overridden. Our cases have thus far indicated that such cases may arise only when the Nation 'is at war,' Schenck v. United States, 249 U.S. 47, 52, 39 S.Ct. 247, 249, 63 L.Ed. 470 (1919), during which times '(n)o one would question but that a government might prevent actual obstruction to its recruiting service or the publication of the sailing dates of transports or the number and location of troops.' Near v. Minnesota ex rel. Olson, 283 U.S. 697, 716, 51 S.Ct. 625, 631, 75 L.Ed. 1357 (1931). Even if the present world situation were assumed to be tantamount to a time of war, or if the power of presently available armaments would justify even in peacetime the suppression of information that would set in motion a nuclear holocaust, in neither of these actions has the Government presented or even alleged that publication of items from or based upon the material at issue would cause the happening of an event of that nature. '(T)he chief purpose of (the First Amendment's) guaranty (is) to prevent previous restraints upon publication.' Near v. Minnesota ex rel. Olson, supra, at 713, 51 S.Ct., at 630. Thus, only governmental allegation and proof that publication must inevitably, directly, and immediately cause the occurrence of an event kindred to imperiling the safety of a transport already at sea can support even the issuance of an interim restraining order. In no event may mere conclusions be sufficient: for if the Executive Branch seeks judicial aid in preventing publication, it must inevitably submit the basis upon which that aid is sought to scrutiny by the judiciary. And therefore, every restraint issued in this case, whatever its form, has violated the First Amendment--and not less so because that restraint was justified as necessary to afford the courts an opportunity to examine the claim more thoroughly. Unless and until the Government has clearly made out its case, the First Amendment commands that no injunction may issue.

Mr. Justice STEWART, with whom Mr. Justice WHITE joins, concurring.

In the governmental structure created by our Constitution, the Executive is endowed with enormous power in the two related areas of national defense and international relations. This power, largely unchecked by the Legislative and Judicial branches, has been pressed to the very hilt since the advent of the nuclear missile age. For better of for worse, the simple fact is that a President of the United States possesses vastly greater constitutional independence in these two vital areas of power than does, say, a prime minister of a country with a parliamentary form of government.

In the absence of the governmental checks and balances present in other areas of our national life, the only effective restraint upon executive policy and power in the areas of national defense and international affairs may lie in an enlightened citizenry--in an informed and critical public opinion which alone can here protect the values of democratic government. For this reason, it is perhaps here that a press that is alert, aware, and free most vitally serves the basic purpose of the First Amendment. For without an informed and free press there cannot be an enlightened people.

Yet it is elementary that the successful conduct of international diplomacy and the maintenance of an effective national defense require both confidentiality and secrecy. Other nations can hardly deal with this Nation in an atmosphere of mutual trust unless they can be assured that their confidences will be kept. And within our own executive departments, the development of considered and intelligent international policies would be impossible if those charged with their formulation could not communicate with each other freely, frankly, and in confidence. In the area of basic national defense the frequent need for absolute secrecy is, of course, self-evident.

I think there can be but one answer to this dilemma, if dilemma it be. The responsibility must be where the power is. If the Constitution gives the Executive a large degree of unshared power in the conduct of foreign affairs and the maintenance of our national defense, then under the Constitution the Executive must have the largely unshared duty to determine and preserve the degree of internal security necessary to exercise that power successfully. It is an awesome responsibility, requiring judgment and wisdom of a high order. I should suppose that moral, political, and practical considerations would dictate that a very first principle of that wisdom would be an insistence upon avoiding secrecy for its own sake. For when everything is classified, then nothing is classified, and the system becomes one to be disregarded by the cynical or the careless, and to be manipulated by those intent on self-protection or self-promotion. I should suppose, in short, that the hallmark of a truly effective internal security system would be the maximum possible disclosure, recognizing that secrecy can best be preserved only when credibility is truly maintained. But be that as it may, it is clear to me that it is the constitutional duty of the Executive--as a matter of sovereign prerogative and not as a matter of law as the courts know law--through the promulgation and enforcement of executive regulations, to protect the confidentiality necessary to carry out its responsibilities in the fields of international relations and national defense.

This is not to say that Congress and the courts have no role to play. Undoubtedly Congress has the power to enact specific and appropriate criminal laws to protect government property and preserve government secrets. Congress has passed such laws, and several of them are of very colorable relevance to the apparent circumstances of these cases. And if a criminal prosecution is instituted, it will be the responsibility of the courts to decide the applicability of the criminal law under which the charge is brought. Moreover, if Congress should pass a specific law authorizing civil proceedings in this field, the courts would likewise have the duty to decide the constitutionality of such a law as well as its applicability to the facts proved.

But in the cases before us we are asked neither to construe specific regulations nor to apply specific laws. We are asked, instead, to perform a function that the Constitution gave to the Executive, not the Judiciary. We are asked, quite simply, to prevent the publication by two newspapers of material that the Executive Branch insists should not, in the national interest, be published. I am convinced that the Executive is correct with respect to some of the documents involved. But I cannot say that disclosure of any of them will surely result in direct, immediate, and irreparable damage to our Nation or its people. That being so, there can under the First Amendment be but one judicial resolution of the issues before us. I join the judgments of the Court.

Mr. Justice WHITE, with whom Mr. Justice STEWART joins, concurring.

I concur in today's judgments, but only because of the concededly extraordinary protection against prior restraints enjoyed by the press under our constitutional system. I do not say that in no circumstances would the First Amendment permit an injunction against publishing information about government plans or operations. Nor, after examining the materials the Government characterizes as the most sensitive and destructive, can I deny that revelation of these documents will do substantial damage to public interests. Indeed, I am confident that their disclosure will have that result. But I nevertheless agree that the United States has not satisfied the very heavy burden that it must meet to warrant an injunction against publication in these cases, at least in the absence of express and appropriately limited congressional authorization for prior restraints in circumstances such as these.

The Government's position is simply stated: The responsibility of the Executive for the conduct of the foreign affairs and for the security of the Nation is so basic that the President is entitled to an injunction against publication of a newspaper story whenever he can convince a court that the information to be revealed threatens 'grave and irreparable' injury to the public interest; [FN2] and the injunction should issue whether or not the material to be published is classified, whether or not publication would be lawful under relevant criminal statutes enacted by Congress, and regardless of the circumstances by which the newspaper came into possession of the information.

FN2. The 'grave and irreparable danger' standard is that asserted by the Government in this Court. In remanding to Judge Gurfein for further hearings in the Times litigation, five members of the Court of Appeals for the Second Circuit directed him to determine whether disclosure of certain items specified with particularity by the Government would 'pose such grave and immediate danger to the security of the United States as to warrant their publication being enjoined.'

At least in the absence of legislation by Congress, based on its own investigations and findings, I am quite unable to agree that the inherent powers of the Executive and the courts reach so far as to authorize remedies having such sweeping potential for inhibiting publications by the press. Much of the difficulty inheres in the 'grave and irreparable danger' standard suggested by the United States. If the United States were to have judgment under such a standard in these cases, our decision would be of little guidance to other courts in other cases, for the material at issue here would not be available from the Court's opinion or from public records, nor would it be published by the press. Indeed, even today where we hold that the United States has not met its burden, the material remains sealed in court records and it is properly not discussed in today's opinions. Moreover, because the material poses substantial dangers to national interests and because of the hazards of criminal sanctions, a responsible press may choose never to publish the more sensitive materials. To sustain the Government in these cases would start the courts down a long and hazardous road that I am not willing to travel, at least without congressional guidance and direction.

It is not easy to reject the proposition urged by the United States and to deny relief on its good-faith claims in these cases that publication will work serious damage to the country. But that discomfiture is considerably dispelled by the infrequency of prior-restraint cases. Normally, publication will occur and the damage be done before the Government has either opportunity or grounds for suppression. So here, publication has already begun and a substantial part of the threatened damage has already occurred. The fact of a massive breakdown in security is known, access to the documents by many unauthorized people is undeniable, and the efficacy of equitable relief against these or other newspapers to avert anticipated damage is doubtful at best.

What is more, terminating the ban on publication of the relatively few sensitive documents the Government now seeks to suppress does not mean that the law either requires or invites newspapers or others to publish them or that they will be immune from criminal action if they do. Prior restraints require an unusually heavy justification under the First Amendment; but failure by the Government to justify prior restraints does not measure its constitutional entitlement to a conviction for criminal publication. That the Government mistakenly chose to proceed by injunction does not mean that it could not successfully proceed in another way.

When the Espionage Act was under consideration in 1917, Congress eliminated from the bill a provision that would have given the President broad powers in time of war to proscribe, under threat of criminal penalty, the publication of various categories of information related to the national defense. [FN3] Congress at that time was unwilling to clothe the President with such far-reaching powers to monitor the press, and those opposed to this part of the legislation assumed that a necessary concomitant of such power was the power to 'filter out the news to the people through some man.' 55 Cong.Rec. 2008 (remarks of Sen. Ashurst). However, these same members of Congress appeared to have little doubt that newspapers would be subject to criminal prosecution if they insisted on publishing information of the type Congress had itself determined should not be revealed. Senator Ashurst, for example, was quite sure that the editor of such a newspaper 'should be punished if he did publish information as to the movements of the fleet, the troops, the aircraft, the location of powder factories, the location of defense works, and all that sort of thing.' Id., at 2009.

FN3. 'Whoever, in time of war, in violation of reasonable regulations to be prescribed by the President, which he is hereby authorized to make and promulgate, shall publish any information with respect to the movement, numbers, description, condition, or disposition of any of the armed forces, ships, aircraft, or war materials of the United States, or with respect to the plans or conduct of any naval or military operations, or with respect to any works or measures undertaken for or connected with, or intended for the fortification or defense of any place, or any other information relating to the public defense calculated to be useful to the enemy, shall be punished by a fine * * * or by imprisonment * * *.' 55 Cong.Rec. 2100.

The Criminal Code contains numerous provisions potentially relevant to these cases. Section 797 [FN5] makes it a crime to publish certain photographs or drawings of military installations. Section 798, [FN6] also in precise language,proscribes knowing and willful publication of any classified information concerning the cryptographic systems or communication intelligence activities of the United States as well as any information obtained from communication intelligence operations. [FN7] If any of the material here at issue is of this nature, the newspapers are presumably now on full notice of the position of the United States and must face the consequences if they publish. I would have no difficulty in sustaining convictions under these sections on facts that would not justify the intervention of equity and the imposition of a prior restraint.

FN5. Title 18 U.S.C. s 797 provides:
'On and after thirty days from the date upon which the President defines any vital military or naval installation or equipment as being within the category contemplated under section 795 of this title, whoever reproduces, publishes, sells, or gives away any photograph, sketch, picture, drawing, map, or graphical representation of the vital military or naval installations or equipment so defined, without first obtaining permission of the commanding officer of the military or naval post, camp, or station concerned, or higher authority, unless such photograph, sketch, picture, drawing, map, or graphical representation has clearly indicated thereon that it has been censored by the proper military or naval authority, shall be fined not more than $1,000 or imprisoned not more than one year, or both.'

FN6. In relevant part 18 U.S.C. s 798 provides:
'(a) Whoever knowingly and willfully communicates, furnishes, transmits, or otherwise makes available to an unauthorized person, or publishes, or uses in any manner prejudicial to the safety or interest of the United States or for the benefit of any foreign government to the detriment of the United States any classified information--
'(1) concerning the nature, preparation, or use of any code, cipher, or cryptographic system of the United States or any foreign government; or
'(2) concerning the design, construction, use, maintenance, or repair of any device, apparatus, or appliance used or prepared or planned for use by the United States or any foreign government for cryptographic or communication intelligence purposes; or
'(3) concerning the communication intelligence activities of the United States or any foreign government; or

'(4) obtained by the process of communication intelligence from the communications of any foreign government, knowing the same to have been obtained by such processes--
'Shall be fined not more than $10,000 or imprisoned not more than ten years, or both.'

FN7. The purport of 18 U.S.C. s 798 is clear. Both the House and Senate Reports on the bill, in identical terms, speak of furthering the security of the United States by preventing disclosure of information concerning the cryptographic systems and the communication intelligence systems of the United States, and explaining that '(t)his bill make it a crime to reveal the methods, techniques, and mate riel used in the transmission by this Nation of enciphered or coded messages. * * * Further, it makes it a crime to reveal methods used by this Nation in breaking the secret codes of a foreign nation. It also prohibits under certain penalties the divulging of any information which may have come into this Government's hands as a result of such a code-breaking.' H.R.Rep.No.1895, 81st Cong., 2d Sess., 1 (1950). The narrow reach of the statute was explained as covering 'only a small category of classified matter, a category which is both vital and vulnerable to an almost unique degree.' Id., at 2. Existing legislation was deemed inadequate.
'At present two other acts protect this information, but only in a limited way. These are the Espionage Act of 1917 (40 Stat. 217) and the act of June 10, 1933 (48 Stat. 122). Under the first, unauthorized revelation of information of this kind can be penalized only if it can be proved that the person making the revelation did so with an intent to injure the United States. Under the second, only diplomatic codes and messages transmitted in diplomatic codes are protected. The present bill is designed to protect against knowing and willful publication or any other revelation of all important information affecting the United States communication intelligence operations and all direct information about all United States codes and ciphers.' Ibid. Section 798 obviously was intended to cover publications by non-employees of the Government and to ease the Government's burden in obtaining convictions. See H.R.Rep.No.1895, supra, at 2--5. The identical Senate Report, not cited in parallel in the text of this footnote, is S.Rep.No.111, 81st Cong., 1st Sess. (1949).

The same would be true under those sections of the Criminal Code casting a wider net to protect the national defense. Section 793(e) [FN8] makes it a criminal act for any unauthorized possessor of a document 'relating to the national defense' either (1) willfully to communicate or cause to be communicated that document to any person not entitled to receive it or (2) willfully to retain the document and fail to deliver it to an officer of the United States entitled to receive it. The subsection was added in 1950 because pre-existing law provided no penalty for the unauthorized possessor unless demand for the documents was made. [FN9] 'The dangers surrounding the unauthorized possession of such items are self-evident, and it is deemed advisable to require their surrender in such a case, regardless of demand, especially since their unauthorized possession may be unknown to the authorities who would otherwise make the demand.' S.Rep.No. 2369, pt. 1, 81st Cong., 2d Sess., 9 (1950). Of course, in the cases before us, the unpublished documents have been demanded by the United States and their import has been made known at least to counsel for the newspapers involved. In Gorin v. United States, 312 U.S. 19, 28, 61 S.Ct. 429, 434, 85 L.Ed. 488 (1941), the words 'national defense' as used in a predecessor of s 793 were held by a unanimous Court to have 'a well understood connotation'--a 'generic concept of broad connotations, referring to the military and naval establishments and the related activities of national preparedness'--and to be 'sufficiently definite to apprise the public of prohibited activities' and to be consonant with due process. 312 U.S., at 28, 61 S.Ct., at 434. Also, as construed by the Court in Gorin, information 'connected with the national defense' is obviously not limited to that threatening 'grave and irreparable' injury to the United States. [FN10]

FN8. Section 793(e) of 18 U.S.C. provides that:
'(e) Whoever having unauthorized possession of, access to, or control over any document, writing, code book, signal book, sketch, photograph, photographic negative, blueprint, plan, map, model, instrument, appliance, or note relating to the national defense, or information relating to the national defense which information the possessor has reason to believe could be used to the injury of the United States or to the advantage of any foreign nation, willfully communicates, delivers, transmits or causes to be communicated, delivered, or transmitted, or attempts to communicate, deliver, transmit or cause to be communicated, delivered, or transmitted the same to any person not entitled to receive it, or willfully retains the same and fails to deliver it to the officer or employee of the United States entitled to receive it;' is guilty of an offense punishable by 10 years in prison, a $10,000 fine, or both. It should also be noted that 18 U.S.C. s 793(g), added in 1950 (see 64 Stat. 1004; S.Rep.No.2369, pt. 1, 81st Cong., 2d Sess., 9 (1950)), provides that '(i)f two or more persons conspire to violate any of the foregoing provisions of this section, and one or more of such persons do any act to effect the object of the conspiracy, each of the parties to such conspiracy shall be subject to the punishment provided for the offense which is the object of such conspiracy.'

FN9. The amendment of s 793 that added subsection (e) was part of the Subversive Activities Control Act of 1950, which was in turn Title I of the Internal Security Act of 1950. See 64 Stat. 987. The report of the Senate Judiciary Committee best explains the purposes of the amendment:

'Section 18 of the bill amends section 793 of title 18 of the United States Code (espionage statute). The several paragraphs of section 793 of title 18 are designated as subsections (a) through (g) for purposes of convenient reference. The significant changes which would be made in section 793 of title 18 are as follows: '(1) Amends the fourth paragraph of section 793, title 18 (subsec. (d)), to cover the unlawful dissemination of 'information relating to the national defense which information the possessor has reason to believe could be used to the injury of the United States or to the advantage of any foreign nation.' The phrase 'which information the possessor has reason to believe could be used to the injury of the United States or to the advantage of any foreign nation' would modify only 'information relating to the national defense' and not the other items enumerated in the subsection. The fourth paragraph of section 793 is also amended to provide that only those with lawful possession of the items relating to national defense enumerated therein may retain them subject to demand therefor. Those who have unauthorized possession of such items are treated in a separate subsection.

'(2) Amends section 793, title 18 (subsec. (e)), to provide that unauthorized possessors of items enumerated in paragraph 4 of section 793 must surrender possession thereof to the proper authorities without demand. Existing law provides no penalty for the unauthorized possession of such items unless a demand for them is made by the person entitled to receive them. The dangers surrounding the unauthorized possession of such items are self-evident, and it is deemed advisable to require their surrender in such a case, regardless of demand, especially since their unauthorized possession may be unknown to the authorities who would otherwise make the demand. The only difference between subsection (d) and subsection (e) of section 793 is that a demand by the person entitled to receive the items would be a necessary element of an offense under subsection (d) where the possession is lawful, where as such a demand would not be a necessary element of an offense under subsection (e) where the possession is unauthorized.' S.Rep.No.2369, pt. 1, 81st Cong., 2d Sess., 8--9 (1950) (emphasis added).

It seems clear from the foregoing, contrary to the intimations of the District Court for the Southern District of New York in this case, that in prosecuting for communicating or withholding a 'document' as contrasted with similar action with respect to 'information' the Government need not prove an intent to injure the United States or to benefit a foreign nation but only willful and knowing conduct. The District Court relied on Gorin v. United States, 312 U.S. 19, 61 S.Ct. 429, 85 L.Ed. 488 (1941). But that case arose under other parts of the predecessor to s 793, see 312 U.S., at 21--22, 61 S.Ct., at 430--432--parts that imposed different intent standards not repeated in s 793(d) or s 793(e). Cf. 18 U.S.C. s 793(a), (b), and (c). Also, from the face of subsection (e) and from the context of the Act of which it was a part, it seems undeniable that a newspaper, as well as others unconnected with the Government, are vulnerable to prosecution under s 793(e) if they communicate or withhold the materials covered by that section. The District Court ruled that 'communication' did not reach publication by a newspaper of documents relating to the national defense. I intimate no views on the correctness of that conclusion. But neither communication nor publication is necessary to violate the subsection.

FN10. Also relevant is 18 U.S.C. s 794. Subsection (b) thereof forbids in time of war the collection or publication, with intent that it shall be communicated to the enemy, of any information with respect to the movements of military forces, 'or with respect to the plans or conduct * * * of any naval or military operations * * * or any other information relating to the public defense, which might be useful to the enemy * * *.'

It is thus clear that Congress has addressed itself to the problems of protecting the security of the country and the national defense from unauthorized disclosure of potentially damaging information. Cf. Youngstown Sheet & Tube Co. v. Sawyer, 343 U.S. 579, 585--586, 72 S.Ct. 863, 865--866, 96 L.Ed. 1153 (1953); see also id., at 593--628, 72 S.Ct., at 888--928 (Frankfurter, J., concurring). It has not, however, authorized the injunctive remedy against threatened publication. It has apparently been satisfied to rely on criminal sanctions and their deterrent effect on the responsible as well as the irresponsible press. I am not, of course, saying that either of these newspapers has yet committed a crime or that either would commit a crime if it published all the material now in its possession. That matter must await resolution in the context of a criminal proceeding if one is instituted by the United States. In that event, the issue of guilt or innocence would be determined by procedures and standards quite different from those that have purported to govern these injunctive proceedings.

Mr. Justice MARSHALL, concurring.

The Government contends that the only issue in these cases is whether in a suit by the United States, 'the First Amendment bars a court from prohibiting a newspaper from publishing material whose disclosure would pose a 'grave and immediate danger to the security of the United States." Brief for the United States 7. With all due respect, I believe the ultimate issue in this case is even more basic than the one posed by the Solicitor General. The issue is whether this Court or the Congress has the power to make law.

In these cases there is no problem concerning the President's power to classify information as 'secret' or 'top secret.' Congress has specifically recognized Presidential authority, which has been formally exercised in Exec. Order 10501 (1953), to classify documents and information. See, e.g., 18 U.S.C. s 798; 50 U.S.C. s 783. Nor is there any issue here regarding the President's power as Chief Executive and Commander in Chief to protect national security by disciplining employees who disclose information and by taking precautions to prevent leaks.

The problem here is whether in these particular cases the Executive Branch has authority to invoke the equity jurisdiction of the courts to protect what it believes to be the national interest. See In re Debs, 158 U.S. 564, 584, 15 S.Ct. 900, 906, 39 L.Ed. 1092 (1895). The Government argues that in addition to the inherent power of any government to protect itself, the President's power to conduct foreign affairs and his position as Commander in Chief give him authority to impose censorship on the press to protect his ability to deal effectively with foreign nations and to conduct the military affairs of the country. Of course, it is beyond cavil that the President has broad powers by virtue of his primary responsibility for the conduct of our foreign affairs and his position as Commander in Chief. Chicago & Southern Air Lines v. Waterman S.S. Corp., 333 U.S. 103, 68 S.Ct. 431, 92 L.Ed. 568 (1948); Kiyoshi Hirabayashi v. United States, 320 U.S. 81, 93, 63 S.Ct. 1375, 1382, 87 L.Ed. 1774 (1943); United States v. Curtiss-Wright Export Corp., 299 U.S. 304, 57 S.Ct. 216, 81 L.Ed. 255 (1936). And in some situations it may be that under whatever inherent powers the Government may have, as well as the implicit authority derived from the President's mandate to conduct foreign affairs and to act as Commander in Chief, there is a basis for the invocation of the equity jurisdiction of this Court as an aid to prevent the publication of material damaging to 'national security,' however that term may be defined.

It would, however, be utterly inconsistent with the concept of separation of powers for this Court to use its power of contempt to prevent behavior that Congress has specifically declined to prohibit. There would be a similar damage to the basic concept of these co-equal branches of Government if when the Executive Branch has adequate authority granted by Congress to protect 'national security' it can choose instead to invoke the contempt power of a court to enjoin the threatened conduct. The Constitution provides that Congress shall make laws, the President execute laws, and courts interpret laws. Youngstown Sheet & Tube Co. v. Sawyer, 343 U.S. 579, 72 S.Ct. 863, 96 L.Ed. 1153 (1952). It did not provide for government by injunction in which the courts and the Executive Branch can 'make law' without regard to the action of Congress. It may be more convenient for the Executive Branch if it need only convince a judge to prohibit conduct rather than ask the Congress to pass a law, and it may be more convenient to enforce a contempt order than to seek a criminal conviction in a jury trial. Moreover, it may be considered politically wise to get a court to share the responsibility for arresting those who the Executive Branch has probable cause to believe are violating the law. But convenience and political considerations of the moment do not justify a basic departure from the principles of our system of government.

In these cases we are not faced with a situation where Congress has failed to provide the Executive with broad power to protect the Nation from disclosure of damaging state secrets. Congress has on several occasions given extensive consideration to the problem of protecting the military and strategic secrets of the United States. This consideration has resulted in the enactment of statutes making it a crime to receive, disclose, communicate, withhold, and publish certain documents, photographs, instruments, appliances, and information. The bulk of these statutes is found in chapter 37 of U.S.C., Title 18, entitled Espionage and Censorship. In that chapter, Congress has provided penalties ranging from a $10,000 fine to death for violating the various statutes.

Thus it would seem that in order for this Court to issue an injunction it would require a showing that such an injunction would enhance the already existing power of the Government to act. See People ex rel. Bennett v. Laman, 277 N.Y. 368, 14 N.E.2d 439 (1938). It is a traditional axiom of equity that a court of equity will not do a useless thing just as it is a traditional axiom that equity will not enjoin the commission of a crime. See Z. Chafee & E. Re, Equity 935--954 (5th ed. 1967); 1 H. Joyce, Injunctions ss 58--60a (1909). Here there has been no attempt to make such a showing. The Solicitor General does not even mention in his brief whether the Government considers that there is probable cause to believe a crime has been committed or whether there is a conspiracy to commit future crimes.

If the Government had attempted to show that there was no effective remedy under traditional criminal law, it would have had to show that there is no arguably applicable statute. Of course, at this stage this Court could not and cannot determine whether there has been a violation of a particular statute or decide the constitutionality of any statute. Whether a good-faith prosecution could have been instituted under any statute could, however, be determined.

At least one of the many statutes in this area seems relevant to these cases. Congress has provided in 18 U.S.C. s 793(e) that whoever 'having unauthorized possession of, access to, or control over any document, writing, code book, signal book * * * or note relating to the national defense, or information relating to the national defense which information the possessor has reason to believe could be used to the injury of the United States or to the advantage of any foreign nation, willfully communicates, delivers, transmits * * * the same to any person not entitled to receive it, or willfully retains the same and fails to deliver it to the officer or employee of the United States entitled to receive it * * * (s)hall be fined not more than $10,000 or imprisoned not more than ten years, or both.' Congress has also made it a crime to conspire to commit any of the offenses listed in 18 U.S.C. s 793(e).

It is true that Judge Gurfein found that Congress had not made it a crime to publish the items and material specified in s 793(e). He found that the words 'communicates, delivers, transmits * * *' did not refer to publication of newspaper stories. And that view has some support in the legislative history and conforms with the past practice of using the statute only to prosecute those charged with ordinary espionage. But see 103 Cong.Rec. 10449 (remarks of Sen. Humphrey). Judge Gurfein's view of the Statute is not, however, the only plausible construction that could be given. See my Brother WHITE's concurring opinion.

Even if it is determined that the Government could not in good faith bring criminal prosecutions against the New York Times and the Washington Post, it is clear that Congress has specifically rejected passing legislation that would have clearly given the President the power he seeks here and made the current activity of the newspapers unlawful. When Congress specifically declines to make conduct unlawful it is not for this Court to redecide those issues--to overrule Congress. See Youngtown Sheet & Tube Co. v. Sawyer, 343 U.S. 579, 72 S.Ct. 863, 96 L.Ed. 1153 (1952).

On at least two occasions Congress has refused to enact legislation that would have made the conduct engaged in here unlawful and given the President the power that he seeks in this case. In 1917 during the debate over the original Espionage Act, still the basic provisions of s 793, Congress rejected a proposal to give the President in time of war or threat of war authority to directly prohibit by proclamation the publication of information relating to national defense that might be useful to the enemy. The proposal provided that:

> 'During any national emergency resulting from a war to which the United States is a party, or from threat of such a war, the President may, by proclamation, declare the existence of such emergency and, by proclamation, prohibit the publishing or communicating of, or the attempting to publish or communicate any information relating to the national defense which, in his judgment, is of such character that it is or might be useful to the enemy. Whoever violates any such prohibition shall be punished by a fine of not more than $10,000 or by imprisonment for not more than 10 years, or both: Provided, that nothing in this section shall be construed to limit or restrict any discussion, comment, or criticism of the acts or policies of the Government or its representatives or the publication of the same.' 55 Cong.Rec. 1763.

Congress rejected this proposal after war against Germany had been declared even though many believed that there was a grave national emergency and that the threat of security leaks and espionage was serious. The Executive Branch has not gone to Congress and requested that the decision to provide such power be reconsidered. Instead, the Executive Branch comes to this Court and asks that it be granted the power Congress refused to give.

In 1957 the United States Commission on Government Security found that '(a) irplane journals, scientific periodicals, and even the daily newspaper have featured articles containing information and other data which should have been deleted in whole or in part for security reasons.' In response to this problem the Commission proposed that 'Congress enact legislation making it a crime for any person willfully to disclose without proper authorization, for any purpose whatever, information classified 'secret' or 'top secret,' knowing, or having reasonable grounds to believe, such information to have been so classified.' Report of Commission on Government Security 619--620 (1957). After substantial floor discussion on the proposal, it was rejected. See 103 Cong.Rec. 10447--10450. If the proposal that Sen. Cotton championed on the floor had been enacted, the publication of the documents involved here would certainly have been a crime. Congress refused, however, to make it a crime. The Government is here asking this Court to remake that decision. This Court has no such power.

Either the Government has the power under statutory grant to use traditional criminal law to protect the country or, if there is no basis for arguing that Congress has made the activity a crime, it is plain that Congress has specifically refused to grant the authority the Government seeks from this Court. In either case this Court does not have authority to grant the requested relief. It is not for this Court to fling itself into every breach perceived by some Government official nor is it for this Court to take on itself the burden of enacting law, especially a law that Congress has refused to pass.

I believe that the judgment of the United States Court of Appeals for the District of Columbia Circuit should be affirmed and the judgment of the United States Court of Appeals for the Second Circuit should be reversed insofar as it remands the case for further hearings.

Mr. Chief Justice BURGER, dissenting.

So clear are the constitutional limitations on prior restraint against expression, that from the time of Near v. Minnesota ex rel. Olson, 283 U.S. 697, 51 S.Ct. 625, 75 L.Ed. 1357 (1931), until recently in Organization for a Better Austin v. Keefe, 402 U.S. 415, 91 S.Ct. 1575, 29 L.Ed.2d 1 (1971), we have had little occasion to be concerned with cases involving prior restraints against news reporting on matters of public interest. There is, therefore, little variation among the members of the Court in terms of resistance to prior restraints against publication. Adherence to this basic constitutional principle, however, does not make these cases simple ones. In these cases, the imperative of a free and unfettered press comes into collision with another imperative, the effective functioning of a complex modern government and specifically the effective exercise of certain constitutional powers of the Executive. Only those who view the First Amendment as an absolute in all circumstances--a view I respect, but reject--can find such cases as these to be simple or easy.

These cases are not simple for another and more immediate reason. We do not know the facts of the cases. No District Judge knew all the facts. No Court of Appeals Judge knew all the facts. No member of this Court knows all the facts.
Why are we in this posture, in which only those judges to whom the First Amendment is absolute and permits of no restraint in any circumstances or for any reason, are really in a position to act?

I suggest we are in this posture because these cases have been conducted in unseemly haste. Mr. Justice HARLAN covers the chronology of events demonstrating the hectic pressures under which these cases have been processed and I need not restate them. The prompt settling of these cases reflects our universal abhorrence of prior restraint. But prompt judicial action does not mean unjudicial haste.

Here, moreover, the frenetic haste is due in large part to the manner in which the Times proceeded from the date it obtained the purloined documents. It seems reasonably clear now that the haste precluded reasonable and deliberate judicial treatment of these cases and was not warranted. The precipitate action of this Court aborting trials not yet completed is not the kind of judicial conduct that ought to attend the disposition of a great issue.

The newspapers make a derivative claim under the First Amendment; they denominate this right as the public 'right to know'; by implication, the Times asserts a sole trusteenship of that right by virtue of its journalistic 'scoop.' The right is asserted as an absolute. Of course, the First Amendment right itself is not an absolute, as Justice Holmes so long ago pointed out in his aphorism concerning the right to shout 'fire' in a crowded theater if there was no fire. There are other exceptions, some of which Chief Justice Hughes mentioned by way of example in Near v. Minnesota ex rel. Olson. There are no doubt other exceptions no one has had occasion to describe or discuss. Conceivably such exceptions may be lurking in these cases and would have been flushed had they been properly considered in the trial courts, free from unwarranted deadlines and frenetic pressures. An issue of this importance should be tried and heard in a judicial atmosphere conducive to thoughtful, reflective deliberation, especially when haste, in terms of hours, is unwarranted in light of the long period the Times, by its own choice, deferred publication.

It is not disputed that the Times has had unauthorized possession of the documents for three to four months, during which it has had its expert analysts studying them, presumably digesting them and preparing the material for publication. During all of this time, the Times, presumably in its capacity as trustee of the public's 'right to know,' has held up publication for purposes it considered proper and thus public knowledge was delayed. No doubt this was for a good reason; the analysis of 7,000 pages of complex material drawn from a vastly greater volume of material would inevitably take time and the writing of good news stories takes time. But why should the United States Government, from whom this information was illegally acquired by someone, along with all the counsel, trial judges, and appellate judges be placed under needless pressure? After these months of deferral, the alleged 'right to know' has somehow and suddenly become a right that must be vindicated instanter.

Would it have been unreasonable, since the newspaper could anticipate the Government's objections to release of secret material, to give the Government an opportunity to review the entire collection and determine whether agreement could be reached on publication? Stolen or not, if security was not in fact jeopardized, much of the material could not doubt have been declassified, since it spans a period ending in 1968. With such an approach--one that great newspapers have in the past practiced and stated editorially to be the duty of an honorable press--the newspapers and Government might well have narrowed the area of disagreement as to what was and was not publishable, leaving the remainder to be resolved in orderly litigation, if necessary. To me it is hardly believable that a newspaper long regarded as a great institution in American life would fail to perform one of the basic and simple duties of every citizen with respect to the discovery or possession of stolen property or secret government documents. That duty, I had thought-- perhaps naively--was to report forthwith, to responsible public officers. This duty rests on taxi drivers, Justices, and the New York Times. The course followed by the Times, whether so calculated or not, removed any possibility of orderly litigation of the issues. If the action of the judges up to now has been correct, that result is sheer happenstance.

Our grant of the writ of certiorari before final judgment in the Times case aborted the trial in the District Court before it had made a complete record pursuant to the mandate of the Court of Appeals for the Second Circuit.

The consequence of all this melancholy series of events is that we literally do not know what we are acting on. As I see it, we have been forced to deal with litigation concerning rights of great magnitude without an adequate record, and surely without time for adequate treatment either in the prior proceedings or in this Court. It is interesting to note that counsel, on both sides, in oral argument before this Court, were frequently unable to respond to questions on factual points. Not surprisingly they pointed out that they had been working literally 'around the clock' and simply were unable to review the documents that give rise to these cases and were not familiar with them. This Court is in no better posture. I agree generally with Mr. Justice HARLAN and Mr. Justice BLACKMUN but I am not prepared to reach the merits.

I would affirm the Court of Appeals for the Second Circuit and allow the District Court to complete the trial aborted by our grant of certiorari, meanwhile preserving the status quo in the post case. I would direct that the District Court on remand give priority to the Times case to the exclusion of all other business of that court but I would not set arbitrary deadlines.

I should add that I am in general agreement with much of what Mr. Justice WHITE has expressed with respect to penal sanctions concerning communication or retention of documents or information relating to the national defense.

We all crave speedier judicial processes but when judges are pressured as in these cases the result is a parody of the judicial function.

Mr. Justice HARLAN, with whom THE CHIEF JUSTICE and Mr. Justice BLACKMUN join, dissenting.

These cases forcefully call to mind the wise admonition of Mr. Justice Holmes, dissenting in Northern Securities Co. v. United States, 193 U.S. 197, 400-- 401, 24 S.Ct. 436, 468, 48 L.Ed.

679 (1904):

> 'Great cases, like hard cases, make bad law. For great cases are called great, not by reason of their real importance in shaping the law of the futture, but because of some accident of immediate overwhelming interest which appeals to the feelings and distorts the judgment. These immediate interests exercise a kind of hydraulic pressure which makes what previously was clear seem doubtful, and before which even well settled principles of law will bend.'

With all respect, I consider that the Court has been almost irresponsibly feverish in dealing with these cases.

Both the Court of Appeals for the Second Circuit and the Court of Appeals for the District of Columbia Circuit rendered judgment on June 23. The New York Times' petition for certiorari, its motion for accelerated consideration thereof, and its application for interim relief were filed in this Court on June 24 at about 11 a.m. The application of the United States for interim relief in the Post case was also filed here on June 24 at about 7:15 p.m. This Court's order setting a hearing before us on June 26 at 11 a.m., a course which I joined only to avoid the possibility of even more peremptory action by the Court, was issued less than 24 hours before. The record in the Post case was filed with the Clerk shortly before 1 p.m. on June 25; the record in the Times case did not arrive until 7 or 8 o'clock that same night. The briefs of the parties were received less than two hours before argument on June 26.

This frenzied train of events took place in the name of the presumption against prior restraints created by the First Amendment. Due regard for the extraordinarily important and difficult questions involved in these litigations should have led the Court to shun such a precipitate timetable. In order to decide the merits of these cases properly, some or all of the following questions should have been faced:

1. Whether the Attorney General is authorized to bring these suits in the name of the United States. Compare In re Debs, 158 U.S. 564, 15 S.Ct. 900, 39 L.Ed. 1092 (1895), with Youngstown Sheet & Tube Co. v. Sawyer, 343 U.S. 579, 72 S.Ct. 863, 96 L.Ed. 1153 (1952). This question involves as well the construction and validity of a singularly opaque statute--the Espionage Act, 18 U.S.C. s 793(e).

2. Whether the First Amendment permits the federal courts to enjoin publication of stories which would present a serious threat to national security. See Near v. Minnesota, ex rel. Olson, 283 U.S. 697, 716, 51 S.Ct. 625, 631, 75 L.Ed. 1357 (1931) (dictum).

3. Whether the threat to publish highly secret documents is of itself a sufficient implication of national security to justify an injunction on the theory that regardless of the contents of the documents harm enough results simply from the demonstration of such a breach of secrecy.

4. Whether the unauthorized disclosure of any of these particular documents would seriously impair the national security.

5. What weight should be given to the opinion of high officers in the Executive Branch of the Government with respect to questions 3 and 4.

6. Whether the newspapers are entitled to retain and use the documents notwithstanding the seemingly uncontested facts that the documents, or the originals of which they are duplicates, were purloined from the Government's possession and that the newspapers received them with knowledge that they had been feloniously acquired. Cf. Liberty Lobby, Inc. v. Pearson, 129 U.S.App.D.C. 74, 390 F.2d 489 (1967, amended 1968).

7. Whether the threatened harm to the national security or the Government's possessory interest in the documents justifies the issuance of an injunction against publication in light of--

a. The strong First Amendment policy against prior restraints on publication;

b. The doctrine against enjoining conduct in violation of criminal statutes; and

c. The extent to which the materials at issue have apparently already been otherwise disseminated.

These are difficult questions of fact, of law, and of judgment; the potential consequences of erroneous decision are enormous. The time which has been available to us, to the lower courts, and to the parties has been wholly inadequate for giving these cases the kind of consideration they deserve. It is a reflection on the stability of the judicial process that these great issues--as important as any that have arisen during my time on the Court-- should have been decided under the pressures engendered by th torrent of publicity that has attended these litigations from their inception.

Forced as I am to reach the merits of these cases, I dissent from the opinion and judgments of the Court. Within the severe limitations imposed by the time constraints under which I have been required to operate, I can only state my reasons in telescoped form, even though in different circumstances I would have felt constrained to deal with the cases in the fuller sweep indicated above.

It is a sufficient basis for affirming the Court of Appeals for the Second Circuit in the Times litigation to observe that its order must rest on the conclusion that because of the time elements the Government had not been given an adequate opportunity to present its case to the District Court. At the least this conclusion was not an abuse of discretion.

In the Post litigation the Government had more time to prepare; this was apparently the basis for the refusal of the Court of Appeals for the District of Columbia Circuit on rehearing to conform its judgment to that of the Second Circuit. But I think there is another and more fundamental reason why this judgment cannot stand--a reason which also furnishes an additional ground for not reinstating the judgment of the District Court in the Times litigation, set aside by the Court of Appeals. It is plain to me that the scope of the judicial function in passing upon the activities of the Executive Branch of the Government in the field of foreign affairs is very narrowly restricted. This view is, I think, dictated by the concept of separation of powers upon which our constitutional system rests.

In a speech on the floor of the House of Representatives, Chief Justice John Marshall, then a member of that body, stated:

'The President is the sole organ of the nation in its external relations, and its sole representative with foreign nations.' 10 Annals of Cong. 613.

From that time, shortly after the founding of the Nation, to this, there has been no substantial challenge to this description of the scope of executive power. See United States v. Curtiss-Wright Export Corp., 299 U.S. 304, 319--321, 57 S.Ct. 216, 220--221, 81 L.Ed. 255 (1936), collecting authorities.

From this constitutional primacy in the field of foreign affairs, it seems to me that certain conclusions necessarily follow. Some of these were stated concisely by President Washington, declining the request of the House of Representatives for the papers leading up to the negotiation of the Jay Treaty:

'The nature of foreign negotiations requires caution, and their success must often depend on secrecy; and even when brought to a conclusion a full disclosure of all the measures, demands, or eventual concessions which may have been proposed or contemplated would be extremely impolitic; for this might have a pernicious influence on future negotiations, or produce immediate inconveniences, perhaps danger and mischief, in relation to other powers.' 1 J. Richardson, Messages and Papers of the Presidents 194--195 (1896).

The power to evaluate the 'pernicious influence' of premature disclosure is not, however, lodged in the Executive alone. I agree that, in performance of its duty to protect the values of the First Amendment against political pressures, the judiciary must review the initial Executive determination to the point of satisfying itself that the subject matter of the dispute does lie within the proper compass of the President's foreign relations power. Constitutional considerations forbid 'a complete abandonment of judicial control.' Cf. United States v. Reynolds, 345 U.S. 1, 8, 73 S.Ct. 528, 532, 97 L.Ed. 727 (1953). Moreover the judiciary may properly insist that the determination that disclosure of the subject matter would irreparably impair the national security be made by the head of the Executive Department concerned--here the Secretary of State or the Secretary of Defense--after actual personal consideration by that officer. This safeguard is required in the analogous area of executive claims of privilege for secrets of state. See id., at 8 and n. 20, 73 S.Ct., at 532; Duncan v. Cammell, Laird & Co., (1942) A.C. 624, 638 (House of Lords).

But in my judgment the judiciary may not properly go beyond these two inquiries and redetermine for itself the probable impact of disclosure on the national security.

'(T)he very nature of executive decisions as to foreign policy is political, not judicial. Such decisions are wholly confided by our Constitution to the political departments of the government, Executive and Legislative. They are delicate, complex, and involve large elements of prophecy. They are and should be undertaken only by those directly responsible to the people whose welfare they advance or imperil. They are decisions of a kind for which the Judiciary has neither aptitude, facilities nor responsibility and have long been held to belong in the domain of political power not subject to judicial intrusion or inquiry.' Chicago & Southern Air Lines, Inc. v. Waterman Steamship Corp., 333 U.S. 103, 111, 68 S.Ct. 431, 436, 92 L.Ed. 568 (1948) (Jackson J.).

Even if there is some room for the judiciary to override the executive determination, it is plain that the scope of review must be exceedingly narrow. I can see no indication in the opinions of either the District Court or the Court of Appeals in the Post litigation that the conclusions of the Executive were given even the deference owing to an administrative agency, much less that owing to a co-equal branch of the Government operating within the field of its constitutional prerogative.

Accordingly, I would vacate the judgment of the Court of Appeals for the District of Columbia Circuit on this ground and remand the case for further proceedings in the District Court. Before the commencement of such further proceedings, due opportunity should be afforded the Government for procuring from the Secretary of State or the Secretary of Defense or both an expression of their views on the issue of national security. The ensuing review by the District Court should be in accordance with the views expressed in this opinion. And for the reasons stated above I would affirm the judgment of the Court of Appeals for the Second Circuit.

Pending further hearings in each case conducted under the appropriate ground rules, I would continue the restraints on publication. I cannot believe that the doctrine prohibiting prior restraints reaches to the point of preventing courts from maintaining the status quo long enough to act responsibly in matters of such national importance as those involved here.

Mr. Justice BLACKMUN, dissenting.

I join Mr. Justice HARLAN in his dissent. I also am in substantial accord with much that Mr. Justice WHITE says, by way of admonition, in the latter part of his opinion.

At this point the focus is on only the comparatively few documents specified by the Government as critical. So far as the other material--vast in amount-- is concerned, let it be published and published forthwith if the newspapers, once the strain is gone and the sensationalism is eased, still feel the urge so to do.

But we are concerned here with the few documents specified from the 47 volumes. Almost 70 years ago Mr. Justice Holmes, dissenting in a celebrated case, observed:

'Great cases, like hard cases, make bad law. For great cases are called great, not by reason of their real importance in shaping the law of the future, but because of some accident of immediate overwhelming interest which appeals to the feelings and distorts the judgment.

These immediate interests exercise a kind of hydraulic pressure * * *.' Northern Securities Co. v. United States, 193 U.S. 197, 400--401, 24 S.Ct. 436, 468, 48 L.Ed. 679 (1904).

The present cases, if not great, are at least unusual in their posture and implications, and the Holmes observation certainly has pertinent application.

The New York Times clandestinely devoted a period of three months to examining the 47 volumes that came into its unauthorized possession. Once it had begun publication of material from those volumes, the New York case now before us emerged. It immediately assumed, and ever since has maintained, a frenetic pace and character. Seemingly once publication started, the material could not be made public fast enough. Seemingly, from then on, every deferral or delay, by restraint or otherwise, was abhorrent and was to be deemed violative of the First Amendment and of the public's 'right immediately to know.' Yet that newspaper stood before us at oral argument and professed criticism of the Government for not lodging its protest earlier than by a Monday telegram following the initial Sunday publication.

The District of Columbia case is much the same.

Two federal district courts, two United States courts of appeals, and this Court--within a period of less than three weeks from inception until today-- have been pressed into hurried decision of profound constitutional issues on inadequately developed and largely assumed facts without the careful deliberation that, one would hope, should characterize the American judicial process. There has been much writing about the law and little knowledge and less digestion of the facts. In the New York case the judges, both trial and appellate, had not yet examined the basic material when the case was brought here. In the District of Columbia case, little more was done, and what was accomplished in this respect was only on required remand, with the Washington Post, on the axcuse that it was trying to protect its source of information, initially refusing to reveal what material it actually possessed, and with the District Court forced to make assumptions as to that possession.

With such respect as may be due to the contrary view, this, in my opinion, is not the way to try a lawsuit of this magnitude and asserted importance. It is not the way for federal courts to adjudicate, and to be required to adjudicate, issues that allegedly concern the Nation's vital welfare. The country would be none the worse off were the cases tried quickly, to be sure, but in the customary and properly deliberative manner. The most recent of the material, it is said, dates no later than 1968, already about three years ago, and the Times itself took three months to formulate its plan of procedure and, thus, deprived its public for that period.

The First Amendment, after all, is only one part of an entire Constitution. Article II of the great document vests in the Executive Branch primary power over the conduct of foreign affairs and places in that branch the responsibility for the Nation's safety. Each provision of the Constitution is important, and I cannot subscribe to a doctrine of unlimited absolutism for the First Amendment at the cost of downgrading other provisions. First Amendment absolutism has never commanded a majority of this Court. See, for example, Near v. Minnesota, ex rel. Olson, 283 U.S. 697, 708, 51 S.Ct. 625, 628, 75 L.Ed. 1357 (1931), and Schenck v. United States, 249

U.S. 47, 52, 39 S.Ct. 247, 249, 63 L.Ed. 470 (1919). What is needed here is a weighing, upon properly developed standards, of the broad right of the press to print and of the very narrow right of the Government to prevent. Such standards are not yet developed. The parties here are in disagreement as to what those standards should be. But even the newspapers concede that there are situations where restraint is in order and is constitutional. Mr. Justice Holmes gave us a suggestion when he said in Schenck,

> 'It is a question of proximity and degree. When a nation is at war many things that might be said in time of peace are such a hindrance to its effort that their utterance will not be endured so long as men fight and that no Court could regard them as protected by any constitutional right.' 249 U.S., at 52, 39 S.Ct., at 249.

I therefore would remand these cases to be developed expeditiously, of course, but on a schedule permitting the orderly presentation of evidence from both sides, with the use of discovery, if necessary, as authorized by the rules, and with the preparation of briefs, oral argument, and court opinions of a quality better than has been seen to this point. In making this last statement, I criticize no lawyer or judge. I know from past personal experience the agony of time pressure in the preparation of litigation. But these cases and the issues involved and the courts, including this one, deserve better than has been produced thus far.

It may well be that if these cases were allowed to develop as they should be developed, and to be tried as lawyers should try them and as courts should hear them, free of pressure and panic and sensationalism, other light would be shed on the situation and contrary considerations, for me, might prevail. But that is not the present posture of the litigation.

The Court, however, decides the cases today the other way. I therefore add one final comment.

I strongly urge, and sincerely hope, that these two newspapers will be fully aware of their ultimate responsibilities to the United States of America. Judge Wilkey, dissenting in the District of Columbia case, after a review of only the affidavits before his court (the basic papers had not then been made available by either party), concluded that there were a number of examples of documents that, if in the possession of the Post, and if published, 'could clearly result in great harm to the nation,' and he defined 'harm' to mean 'the death of soldiers, the destruction of alliances, the greatly increased difficulty of negotiation with our enemies, the inability of our diplomats to negotiate * * *.' I, for one, have now been able to give at least some cursory study not only to the affidavits, but to the material itself. I regreat to say that from this examination I fear that Judge Wilkey's statements have possible foundation. I therefore share his concern. I hope that damage has not already been done. If, however, damage has been done, and if, with the Court's action today, these newspapers proceed to publish the critical documents and there results therefrom 'the death of soldiers, the destruction of alliances, the greatly increased difficulty of negotiation with our enemies, the inability of our diplomats to negotiate,' to which list I might add the factors of prolongation of the war and of further delay in the freeing of United States prisoners, then the Nation's people will know where the responsibility for these sad consequences rests.

UNITED STATES of America, Plaintiff,
v.
The PROGRESSIVE, INC., Erwin Knoll, Samuel Day, Jr., and Howard Morland, Defendants.

467 F.Supp. 990

United States District Court, W. D. Wisconsin.

March 26, 1979.

MEMORANDUM AND ORDER

WARREN, District Judge.

On March 9, 1979, this Court, at the request of the government, but after hearing from both parties, issued a temporary restraining order enjoining defendants, their employees, and agents from publishing or otherwise communicating or disclosing in any manner any restricted data contained in the article: "The H-Bomb Secret: How We Got It, Why We're Telling It."

In keeping with the Court's order that the temporary restraining order should be in effect for the shortest time possible, a preliminary injunction hearing was scheduled for one week later, on March 16, 1979. At the request of the parties and with the Court's acquiescence, the preliminary injunction hearing was rescheduled for 10:00 A.M. today in order that both sides might have additional time to file affidavits and arguments. The Court continued the temporary restraining order until 5:00 P.M. today.

In order to grant a preliminary injunction, the Court must find that plaintiff has a reasonable likelihood of success on the merits, and that the plaintiff will suffer irreparable harm if the injunction does not issue. In addition, the Court must consider the interest of the public and the balance of the potential harm to plaintiff and defendants.

Jurisdiction in this action is grounded on 42 U.S.C. s 2280, the Atomic Energy Act and 28 U.S.C. s 1345.

Under the facts here alleged, the question before this Court involves a clash between allegedly vital security interests of the United States and the competing constitutional doctrine against prior restraint in publication.

In its argument and briefs, plaintiff relies on national security, as enunciated by Congress in The Atomic Energy Act of 1954, as the basis for classification of certain documents. Plaintiff contends that, in certain areas, national preservation and self-interest permit the retention and classification of government secrets. The government argues that its national security interest also permits it to impress classification and censorship upon information originating in the public domain, if when drawn together, synthesized and collated, such information acquires the character of presenting immediate, direct and irreparable harm to the interests of the United States.

Defendants argue that freedom of expression as embodied in the First Amendment is so central to the heart of liberty that prior restraint in any form becomes anathema. They contend that this is particularly true when a nation is not at war and where the prior restraint is based on surmise or conjecture. While acknowledging that freedom of the press is not absolute, they maintain that the publication of the projected article does not rise to the level of immediate, direct and irreparable harm which could justify incursion into First Amendment freedoms.

Hence, although embodying deep and fundamental principles of democratic philosophy, the issue also requires a factual determination by a federal court sitting in equity. At the level of a temporary restraining order, or a preliminary injunction, such matters are customarily dealt with through affidavits.

Thus far the affidavits filed are numerous and complex. They come from individuals of learning and renown. They deal with how the information at issue was assembled, what it means, and how injurious the affiant believes it to be.

The Court notes the Amici curiae briefs filed by the American Civil Liberties Union, the Wisconsin Civil Liberties Union, the Federation of American Scientists and the Fund for Open Information and Accountability, Inc., and expresses thanks for them. The Court gave consideration to the suggestion that a panel of experts be appointed to serve as witnesses for the Court to assist it in determining whether the dangers of publication are as great as the government asserts or as inconsequential as The Progressive states. However, the Court concluded that such a procedure really would merely proliferate the opinions of experts arrayed on both sides of the issue.

Both parties have already marshalled impressive opinions covering all aspects of the case. The Court has read all this material and has now heard extensive argument. It is time for decision. From the founding days of this nation, the rights to freedom of speech and of the press have held an honored place in our constitutional scheme. The establishment and nurturing of these rights is one of the true achievements of our form of government.

Because of the importance of these rights, any prior restraint on publication comes into court under a heavy presumption against its constitutional validity. New York Times v. United States, 403 U.S. 713, 91 S.Ct. 2140, 29 L.Ed.2d 822 (1971).

However, First Amendment rights are not absolute. They are not boundless.

Justice Frankfurter dissenting in Bridges v. California, 314 U.S. 252, 282, 62 S.Ct. 190, 203, 86 L.Ed. 192 (1941), stated it in this fashion: "Free speech is not so absolute or irrational a conception as to imply paralysis of the means for effective protection of all the freedoms secured by the Bill of Rights." In the Schenck case, Justice Holmes recognized: "The character of every act depends upon the circumstances in which it is done." Schenck v. United States, 249 U.S. 47, 52, 39 S.Ct. 247, 249, 63 L.Ed. 470 (1931).

In Near v. Minnesota, 283 U.S. 697, 51 S.Ct. 625, 75 L.Ed. 1357 (1931), the Supreme Court specifically recognized an extremely narrow area, involving national security, in which interference with First Amendment rights might be tolerated and a prior restraint on publication might be appropriate. The Court stated:

> "When a nation is at war many things that might be said in time of peace are such a hindrance to its effort that their utterance will not be endured so long as men fight and that no Court could regard them as protected by any constitutional right." No one would question but that a government might prevent actual obstruction to its recruiting service or the publication of the sailing dates of transports or the number and location of troops. Id. at 716, 51 S.Ct. at 631 (citation omitted).

Thus, it is clear that few things, save grave national security concerns, are sufficient to override First Amendment interests. A court is well admonished to approach any requested prior restraint with a great deal of skepticism.

Juxtaposed against the right to freedom of expression is the government's contention that the national security of this country could be jeopardized by publication of the article.

The Court is convinced that the government has a right to classify certain sensitive documents to protect its national security. The problem is with the scope of the classification system.

Defendants contend that the projected article merely contains data already in the public domain and readily available to any diligent seeker. They say other nations already have the same information or the opportunity to obtain it. How then, they argue, can they be in violation of 42 U.S.C. ss 2274(b) and 2280 which purport to authorize injunctive relief against one who would disclose restricted data "with reason to believe such data will be utilized to injure the United States or to secure an advantage to any foreign nation . . ."?

Although the government states that some of the information is in the public domain, it contends that much of the data is not, and that the Morland article contains a core of information that has never before been published.

Furthermore, the government's position is that whether or not specific information is "in the public domain" or has been "declassified" at some point is not determinative. The government states that a court must look at the nature and context of prior disclosures and analyze what the practical impact of the prior disclosures are as contrasted to that of the present revelation.

The government feels that the mere fact that the author, Howard Morland, could prepare an article explaining the technical processes of thermonuclear weapons does not mean that those processes are available to everyone. They lay heavy emphasis on the argument that the danger lies in the exposition of certain concepts never heretofore disclosed in conjunction with one another.

In an impressive affidavit, Dr. Hans A. Bethe, whose affidavit was introduced by the government and whose article, The Hydrogen Bomb: II, was a source document for Theodore Postol's affidavit I filed by the defendants states that sizeable portions of the Morland text should be classified as restricted data because the processes outlined in the manuscript describe the essential design and operation of thermonuclear weapons. He later concludes "that the design and operational concepts described in the manuscript are not expressed or revealed in the public literature nor do I believe they are known to scientists not associated with the government weapons programs."

The Court has grappled with this difficult problem and has read and studied the affidavits and other documents on file. After all this, the Court finds concepts within the article that it does not find in the public realm concepts that are vital to the operation of the hydrogen bomb.

Even if some of the information is in the public domain, due recognition must be given to the human skills and expertise involved in writing this article. The author needed sufficient expertise to recognize relevant, as opposed to irrelevant, information and to assimilate the information obtained. The right questions had to be asked or the correct educated guesses had to be made.

The ability of G. I. Taylor to calculate the yield of the first nuclear explosion from a Life magazine photo demonstrates that certain individuals with some knowledge, ability to reason and extraordinary perseverance may acquire additional knowledge without access to classified information, even though the information thus acquired may not be obvious to others not so equipped or motivated. All of this must be considered in resolving the issues before the Court.

Does the article provide a "do-it yourself" guide for the hydrogen bomb? Probably not. A number of affidavits make quite clear that a Sine qua non to thermonuclear capability is a large, sophisticated industrial capability coupled with a coterie of imaginative, resourceful scientists and technicians. One does not build a hydrogen bomb in the basement. However, the article could possibly provide sufficient information to allow a medium size nation to move faster in developing a hydrogen weapon. It could provide a ticket to by-pass blind alleys.

The Morland piece could accelerate the membership of a candidate nation in the thermonuclear club. Pursuit of blind alleys or failure to grasp seemingly basic concepts have been the cause of many inventive failures.

For example, in one of the articles submitted to the Court, the author described how, in the late 1930's, physicists in various countries were simultaneously, but independently, working on the idea of a nuclear chain reaction. The French physicists in their equation neglected to take full account of the fact that the neutrons produced by fission could go on to provoke further fissions in a many-step process which is the essence of a chain reaction. Even though this idea seems so elementary, the concept of neutron multiplication was so novel that no nuclear physicists saw through the French team's oversight for about a year.

Thus, once basic concepts are learned, the remainder of the process may easily follow.

Although the defendants state that the information contained in the article is relatively easy to obtain, only five countries now have a hydrogen bomb. Yet the United States first successfully exploded the hydrogen bomb some twenty-six years ago.

The point has also been made that it is only a question of time before other countries will have the hydrogen bomb. That may be true. However, there are times in the course of human history when time itself may be very important. This time factor becomes critical when considering mass annihilation weaponry witness the failure of Hitler to get his V-1 and V-2 bombs operational quickly enough to materially affect the outcome of World War II.

Defendants have stated that publication of the article will alert the people of this country to the false illusion of security created by the government's futile efforts at secrecy. They believe publication will provide the people with needed information to make informed decisions on an urgent issue of public concern.

However, this Court can find no plausible reason why the public needs to know the technical details about hydrogen bomb construction to carry on an informed debate on this issue. Furthermore, the Court believes that the defendants' position in favor of nuclear non-proliferation would be harmed, not aided, by the publication of this article.

The defendants have also relied on the decision in the New York Times case. In that case, the Supreme Court refused to enjoin the New York Times and the Washington Post from publishing the contents of a classified historical study of United States decision-making in Viet Nam, the so-called "Pentagon Papers."

This case is different in several important respects. In the first place, the study involved in the New York Times case contained historical data relating to events that occurred some three to twenty years previously. Secondly, the Supreme Court agreed with the lower court that no cogent reasons were advanced by the government as to why the article affected national security except that publication might cause some embarrassment to the United States.

A final and most vital difference between these two cases is the fact that a specific statute is involved here. Section 2274 of The Atomic Energy Act prohibits anyone from communicating, transmitting or disclosing any restricted data to any person "with reason to believe such data will be utilized to injure the United States or to secure an advantage to any foreign nation."

Section 2014 of the Act defines restricted data. " 'Restricted Data' means all data concerning 1) design, manufacture, or utilization of atomic weapons; 2) the production of special nuclear material; or 3) the use of special nuclear material in the production of energy, but shall not include data declassified or removed from the Restricted Data category pursuant to section 2162 of this title."

As applied to this case, the Court finds that the statute in question is not vague or overbroad. The Court is convinced that the terms used in the statute "communicates, transmits or discloses" include publishing in a magazine.

The Court is of the opinion that the government has shown that the defendants had reason to believe that the data in the article, if published, would injure the United States or give an advantage to a foreign nation. Extensive reading and studying of the documents on file lead to the conclusion that not all the data is available in the public realm in the same fashion, if it is available at all.

What is involved here is information dealing with the most destructive weapon in the history of mankind, information of sufficient destructive potential to nullify the right to free speech and to endanger the right to life itself.

Stripped to its essence then, the question before the Court is a basic confrontation between the First Amendment right to freedom of the press and national security.

Our Founding Fathers believed, as we do, that one is born with certain inalienable rights which, as the Declaration of Independence intones, include the right to life, liberty and the pursuit of happiness. The Constitution, including the Bill of Rights, was enacted to make those rights operable in everyday life.

The Court believes that each of us is born seized of a panoply of basic rights, that we institute governments to secure these rights and that there is a hierarchy of values attached to these rights which is helpful in deciding the clash now before us.

Certain of these rights have an aspect of imperativeness or centrality that make them transcend other rights. Somehow it does not seem that the right to life and the right to not have soldiers quartered in your home can be of equal import in the grand scheme of things. While it may be true in the long-run, as Patrick Henry instructs us, that one would prefer death to life without liberty, nonetheless, in the short-run, one cannot enjoy freedom of speech, freedom to worship or freedom of the press unless one first enjoys the freedom to live.

Faced with a stark choice between upholding the right to continued life and the right to freedom of the press, most jurists would have no difficulty in opting for the chance to continue to breathe and function as they work to achieve perfect freedom of expression.

Is the choice here so stark? Only time can give us a definitive answer. But considering another aspect of this panoply of rights we all have is helpful in answering the question now before us. This aspect is the disparity of the risk involved.

The destruction of various human rights can come about in differing ways and at varying speeds. Freedom of the press can be obliterated overnight by some dictator's imposition of censorship or by the slow nibbling away at a free press through successive bits of repressive legislation enacted by a nation's lawmakers. Yet, even in the most drastic of such situations, it is always possible for a dictator to be overthrown, for a bad law to be repealed or for a judge's error to be subsequently rectified. Only when human life is at stake are such corrections impossible.

The case at bar is so difficult precisely because the consequences of error involve human life itself and on such an awesome scale.

The Secretary of State states that publication will increase thermonuclear proliferation and that this would "irreparably impair the national security of the United States." The Secretary of Defense says that dissemination of the Morland paper will mean a substantial increase in the risk of thermonuclear proliferation and lead to use or threats that would "adversely affect the national security of the United States."

Howard Morland asserts that "if the information in my article were not in the public domain, it should be put there . . . so that ordinary citizens may have informed opinions about nuclear weapons."

Erwin Knoll, the editor of The Progressive, states he is "totally convinced that publication of the article will be of substantial benefit to the United States because it will demonstrate that this country's security does not lie in an oppressive and ineffective system of secrecy and classification but in open, honest, and informed public debate about issues which the people must decide."

The Court is faced with the difficult task of weighing and resolving these divergent views.

A mistake in ruling against The Progressive will seriously infringe cherished First Amendment rights. If a preliminary injunction is issued, it will constitute the first instance of prior restraint against a publication in this fashion in the history of this country, to this Court's knowledge. Such notoriety is not to be sought. It will curtail defendants' First Amendment rights in a drastic and substantial fashion. It will infringe upon our right to know and to be informed as well.

A mistake in ruling against the United States could pave the way for thermonuclear annihilation for us all. In that event, our right to life is extinguished and the right to publish becomes moot.

In the Near case, the Supreme Court recognized that publication of troop movements in time of war would threaten national security and could therefore be restrained. Times have changed significantly since 1931 when Near was decided. Now war by foot soldiers has been replaced in large part by war by machines and bombs. No longer need there be any advance warning or any preparation time before a nuclear war could be commenced.

In light of these factors, this Court concludes that publication of the technical information on the hydrogen bomb contained in the article is analagous to publication of troop movements or locations in time of war and falls within the extremely narrow exception to the rule against prior restraint.

Because of this "disparity of risk," because the government has met its heavy burden of showing justification for the imposition of a prior restraint on publication of the objected-to technical portions of the Morland article, and because the Court is unconvinced that suppression of the objected-to technical portions of the Morland article would in any plausible fashion impede the defendants in their laudable crusade to stimulate public knowledge of nuclear armament and bring about enlightened debate on national policy questions, the Court finds that the objected-to portions of the article fall within the narrow area recognized by the Court in Near v. Minnesota in which a prior restraint on publication is appropriate.

The government has met its burden under section 2274 of The Atomic Energy Act. In the Court's opinion, it has also met the test enunciated by two Justices in the New York Times case, namely grave, direct, immediate and irreparable harm to the United States.

The Court has just determined that if necessary it will at this time assume the awesome responsibility of issuing a preliminary injunction against The Progressive's use of the Morland article in its current form.

However, the Court is acutely aware of the old legal adage that "bad cases make bad law." This case in its present posture will undoubtedly go to the Supreme Court because it does present so starkly the clash between freedom of press and national security. Does it go there with the blessing of the entire press? The Court thinks not. Many elements of the press see grave risk of permanent damage to First Amendment freedoms if this case goes forward. They feel appellate courts will find, as this Court has, that the risk is simply too great to permit publication.

Furthermore, if there is any one inescapable conclusion that one arrives at after wading through all these experts' affidavits, it is that many wise, intelligent, patriotic individuals can hold diametrically opposite opinions on the issues before us.

Recognizing that both sides at the moment may seem adamant, the Court nonetheless was greatly impressed by the arguments in the Amicus brief submitted by the Federation of American Scientists through its director, Dr. Jeremy J. Stone.

This group, with half of America's Nobel laureates in its ranks, urged The Progressive To recognize the damage the article could do to both nuclear non-proliferation policies and First Amendment rights. It sees the dangers of the present confrontation and suggests that similar cases can arise in the future involving this or other technologies. The group notes that it is possible for example, that a technology such as recombinant DNA could someday surface means of destruction that ought not be published while, at the same time, provoking crucial issues of public policy that badly need to be publicly discussed.

The group suggests that the accommodating of such conflicting interests is not best done in the glare of a judicial spotlight, but that the parties, seemingly at odds can, with effort, satisfy both their interests with a non-legal resolution.

The government seeks only the deletion of certain technical material and, in the Court's opinion, would have an interest in settling this case out of court. On the other hand, the Court believes that The Progressive Has an obligation to its colleagues in the press and does not really require the objected-to material in order to ventilate its views on government secrecy and the hydrogen bomb.

In this context, the Federation urges that the Court give the parties every last chance to try to resolve the matter out-of-court, so as to simultaneously moot the case and set a desirable precedent for the future.

NOW THEREFORE, acting on this suggestion, the Court herewith poses to the parties a final choice:

We will now adjourn until 2:00 P.M. At that time the case will be recalled. In the interim, each party is to consider whether it would be willing to meet with a panel of five mediators appointed by the Court to attempt to resolve the parties' differences.

The Court recognizes that today is the deadline for the May issue of The Progressive and that the temporary restraining order expires at 5:00 P.M. this afternoon. If everyone is willing to attempt mediation, the temporary restraining order would have to be extended by mutual agreement.

If the parties agree to mediation, each side will be asked to submit to the Court the names of two senior weapons scientists and two representatives of the media. From these names the Court will select two people from each category and will then itself approach a respected lawyer or retired jurist and ask that person to chair the group. The given individuals would compose a mediating panel. This panel would have to receive appropriate clearance.

The panel would meet with the parties and report back to the Court in 10 days on its progress or lack of it, in dealing with the specific deletions at issue.
At the time of the report, the Court will then either dismiss the case by stipulation of the parties, or in the event of inability to agree, issue a preliminary injunction.
If, at 2:00 P.M. either or both sides are unable to agree to this proposal, the Court will regretfully issue the preliminary injunction.

SO ORDERED this 26th day of March, 1979, at Milwaukee, Wisconsin . . . .

CONCLUSIONS OF LAW

1. This Court has jurisdiction over the subject matter of this action pursuant to 42 U.S.C. s 2280 and 28 U.S.C. s 1345.

2. Publication or other disclosure or communication of the Restricted Data contained in the Morland article would likely constitute a violation of the Atomic Energy Act, 42 U.S.C. s 2274(b).

3. The pertinent provisions of the Atomic Energy Act, 42 U.S.C. s 2274(b) and s 2280, apply to the defendants and are not constitutionally vague or over broad.

4. Because defendants intend imminently to publish the Restricted Data contained in the Morland article, unless restrained by order of the court, plaintiff, United States of America, is entitled to a preliminary injunction, Pendente lite, prohibiting publication or disclosure of the article pursuant to 42 U.S.C. s 2280.

5. In view of the showing of harm made by the United States, a preliminary injunction would be warranted even in the absence of statutory authorization because of the existence of the likelihood of direct, immediate and irreparable injury to our nation and its people. New York Times Co. v. United States, 403 U.S. 713, 730, 91 S.Ct. 2140, 2149, 29 L.Ed.2d 822 (Justice Stewart concurring); See also, Near v. Minnesota, 283 U.S. 697, 716, 51 S.Ct. 625, 75 L.Ed. 1357 (1931).

6. The facts and circumstances as presented here fall within the extremely narrow recognized area, involving national security, in which a prior restraint on publication is appropriate. Issuance of a preliminary injunction does not, under the circumstances presented to the Court, violate defendants' First Amendment rights.

7. Plaintiff has proven all necessary prerequisites for issuance of a preliminary injunction restraining defendants from publishing or disclosing any Restricted Data contained in the Morland article until a final determination in this action has been made by the Court.

SO ORDERED this 28th day of March, 1979, at Milwaukee, Wisconsin.